THE BEST OF

WOMEN'S CONFERENCE

THE BEST OF

WOMEN'S CONFERENCE

*Selected Talks from 25 Years
of BYU Women's Conferences*

BOOKCRAFT

SALT LAKE CITY, UTAH

Library of Congress Cataloging-in-Publication Data

Women's Conference (1974–1999)
   The best of Women's Conference: selected talks from 25 years of Women's
   Conference. p.   cm.
   Includes bibliographical references.
   ISBN 1-57345-654-3 (hardcover)
      1. Women in the Mormon Church—Congresses.   2. Mormon women—
Religious life—Congresses.   I. Title.

BX8641.W73 1999a
289.3'32'082—dc21   99-462255

Printed in the United States of America   72082-2843
Publishers Press, Salt Lake City, UT

10   9   8   7   6   5   4   3   2

CONTENTS

PUBLISHER'S PREFACE

⟨∞⟩

*E*very spring for the past quarter-century, Latter-day Saint women have gathered at Brigham Young University to share ideas, gain spiritual insights, and enjoy the emotional strength that flows between sisters united in a common purpose and faith. The BYU Women's Conference has become a worldwide event, with thousands attending in person and tens of thousands more receiving satellite broadcasts of selected talks. It touches lives in a most powerful way.

In celebration of the silver anniversary of this conference and of the step into the future symbolized by the year 2000, the Women's Conference committee and Deseret Book Company are pleased to offer this commemorative volume of more than fifty landmark addresses. These talks represent hundreds of presentations that have lifted hearts and lightened burdens over the years.

No attempt has been made to update talks that were delivered years ago. We thought it valuable to retain a sense of historical context and preserve the materials as they were given. Such an approach demonstrates both the distance we have come as women and the eternal nature of the truths that have sustained us and continue to do so. It might seem surprising to some in the world that addresses more than two decades old could still have such relevance, but those immersed in the gospel of Jesus Christ know that the Source of living water never changes or runs dry.

We acknowledge gratefully all the contributors to Women's Conference, those featured in this publication and also the many others who give so willingly of their talents to bring about the grand event each year. In their honor, and in honor of the spirit brought to the conference by every person who attends, we offer *The Best of Women's Conference*.

"BY KNOWLEDGE SHALL THE CHAMBERS BE FILLED"

 ⌒∞⌒

Marilyn Arnold

*E*very few years I find myself pulling a slender gray volume in a blue dust jacket off my shelf and reading in it. I am always better for it and always incredulous that I could have neglected it so long. The book is a collection of essays about watching birds and about contemplating life. The title is *Something about Swans*, the author a woman named Madeleine Doran, whose roots happen to be in Salt Lake City but whose life led her to become one of the world's foremost Shakespearean scholars. I had the good fortune to come to know her when I began taking courses in Shakespeare from her at the University of Wisconsin nearly twenty-five years ago. A small, graying woman in horn-rimmed glasses and suede Hush Puppies, she quietly, surely, opened the eyes of my understanding and instilled in me a love for Shakespeare that has become one of the rocks upon which I have built a quarter century of reading, writing, and teaching.

But Madeleine Doran knew more than Shakespeare. She knew the sounds and habits of birds; she knew flowers in their thousand species; she knew the pleasure and importance of discovery; she knew what fed the human spirit. She was a staple of wisdom and knowledge from which I drew sustenance through the taxing rigors of graduate school. And I never got past feeling tongue-tied in her presence.

Just a few weeks ago, I lifted the volume on swans again from its familiar place. In the collection's second essay, Miss Doran writes of the pleasure of knowledge pursued and discovered with no thought for its utility:

"Think how much of the world's knowledge is in a strict sense 'useless,' how much of it has been acquired for its own sake, by amateur and scientist alike. It matters to me not at all in any practical way that this

Marilyn Arnold, professor of English and dean of graduate studies at Brigham Young University, is a widely published scholar and lecturer in modern American fiction, most notably the work of Willa Cather and Eudora Welty. She received her Ph.D. degree from the University of Wisconsin. She has served on the Sunday School General Board and on Church writing committees for Young Women and Relief Society.

heavy, dark rock on my desk—a memento of a morning on a summit in the Rockies—is a piece of granitic gneiss, sparkling with biotite mica, dotted with orange lichen, and recording a history of the building up and the wearing down of a mountain range. Or that this piece of red scoria, idly picked up from an Oregon lava bed—a stone light in the hand and full of holes—has a very different history to tell. But how agreeable to try to read these histories! . . . Learning in this pure sense is detached from ourselves and therefore gives the pleasure and freedom that go with the absence of self-concern. . . . If knowledge were only gained to be put to uses we could foresee, we should have by now learned very little. Anyhow, for whatever reason, the accumulation of 'useless' knowledge is one of the pleasantest things in life. It commits us to nothing, it costs us nothing (except time, and sometimes money, both of which might be worse spent); it is a pursuit without danger of boredom, and without any necessary period."[1]

Then she alludes to her first sighting of the elusive prothonotary warbler that appeared quite unexpectedly and unearned in a branch above her head while her friends in the Audubon Society searched for it elsewhere. The thrill of the first sighting is good, she says, but so will the second and third sightings be good. "If one of them comes back next spring, we shall have a keener pleasure than just recognition. Its return will give us the pleasure of recurrence at the same time and place and therefore a sense of the stability of things."[2]

She had never seen the bird before, and yet she knew it on the instant because she had studied its picture, had read of its habits and habitat, and knew that one such bird had been seen in the area. She will recognize it if it returns another year, and she rejoices in the sense her knowledge gives her of "the stability of things." We are gathered here to consider many things, but most important among them, the truth spoken by Isaiah that "wisdom and knowledge shall be the stability of thy times" (Isaiah 33:6), meaning our time or any time.

Another woman of my acquaintance whom I deeply revere, now eighty years old, tells of the beginnings of her wisdom, and of her stability, in a wonderful book titled One Writer's Beginnings. The epigraph to Eudora Welty's small, personal memoir is a passage from the book itself, but it tells a good deal about an environment that opened doors to wisdom and knowledge for a small child, that led her to her loves and steadied her in her pursuit of them:

"When I was young enough to still spend a long time buttoning my shoes in the morning, I'd listen toward the hall: Daddy upstairs was shaving in the bathroom and Mother downstairs was frying the bacon. They would begin whistling back and forth to each other up and down the stairwell. My father would whistle his phrase, my mother would try to whistle, then hum hers back. It was their duet. I drew my buttonhook in and out and listened to it—I knew it was 'The Merry Widow.' The difference was, their song almost floated with laughter: how different from the record, which growled from the beginning, as if the Victrola were only slowly being wound up. They kept it running between them, up and down the stairs where I was now just about ready to run clattering down and show them my shoes."[3]

There, surely, is a child's anchor in knowledge—parents conversing through the medium of art and the child recognizing not only the music but also the nature of the song and the relationship that produced that rather wonderful, spontaneous duet.

What Eudora Welty remembers about her childhood is mainly how she learned what she would need to know her life through. (And in some sense, hers is the best book ever written on child rearing, even though—or maybe because—it offers not one word of conscious advice.) On her book's first page, Eudora Welty recalls that her "father loved all instruments that would instruct and fascinate." She remembers the drawer in the "library table" where he kept maps and a "telescope with brass extensions, to find the moon and the Big Dipper after supper in our front yard, and to keep appointments with eclipses." That drawer also contained "a magnifying glass, a kaleidoscope, and a gyroscope," along with "an assortment of puzzles composed of metal rings and intersecting links and keys chained together."[4] Christmas to her father always meant "toys that instruct" and teach a child how to build things. And there were also the "elaborate kites" he made himself. "With these gifts," she says, "he was preparing his children." Then she adds, "And so was my mother with her different gifts." Welty continues:

"I learned from the age of two or three that any room in our house, at any time of day, was there to read in, or to be read to. My mother read to me. She'd read to me in the big bedroom in the mornings, when we were in her rocker together, which ticked in rhythm as we rocked, as though we had a cricket accompanying the story. She'd read to me in the dining room on winter afternoons in front of the coal fire, with our cuckoo clock ending the story with 'Cuckoo,' and at night when I'd got in my own bed. I must have given her no peace. Sometimes she read to me in the kitchen while she sat churning, and the churning sobbed along with *any* story."[5]

Welty says further: "It had been startling and disappointing to me to find out that story books had been written by *people*, that books were not natural wonders, coming up of themselves like grass. Yet regardless of where they came from, I cannot remember a time when I was not in love with them—with the books themselves, cover and binding and the paper they were printed on, with their smell and their weight and with their possession in my arms, captured and carried off to myself. Still illiterate, I was ready for them, committed to all the reading I could give them."[6]

Welty remembers that even during the years when her father was struggling to establish himself in his profession, her parents regularly sent off for books, selecting them carefully. She recalls that in addition to the "bookcase in the living room, which was always called 'the library,' there were encyclopedia tables and dictionary stand under the windows in our dining room. Here to help us grow up arguing around the dining room table were the *Unabridged Webster*, the *Columbia Encyclopedia*, *Compton's Pictured Encyclopedia*, the *Lincoln Library of Information*, and later the *Book of Knowledge*."[7] She remembers reading all of the books in her parents' bookcase, each one in turn as it came on the shelf, top row to bottom.

Welty speaks gratefully of her parents' initiating her early into knowledge of the word, especially by way of the alphabet, which in her day, she says, "was the keystone to knowledge. You learned the alphabet as you learned to count to ten, as you learned 'Now I lay me' and the Lord's Prayer and your father's and mother's name and address and telephone number, all in case you were lost."[8] She remembers strict Mrs. Calloway at the library, who had a rule that only two books could be checked out at a time. "So two by two, I read library books as fast as I could go, rushing them home in the basket of my bicycle. From the minute I reached our house, I started to read. Every book I seized on, *Bunny Brown and His Sister Sue at Camp Rest-a-While* to *Twenty Thousand Leagues Under the Sea*, stood for the devouring wish to read being instantly granted. I knew this was bliss, knew it at the time. Taste isn't nearly so important; it comes in its own time." She remembers that her mother's insatiability matched her own: "Now, I think of her as reading so much of the time while doing something else. In my mind's eye *The Origin of Species* is lying on the shelf in the pantry under a light dusting of flour. . . . I remember her picking up *The Man in Lower Ten* while my hair got dry enough to unroll from a load of kid curlers."[9]

Surely, all of this takes you back, as it does me, to childhood and the books we treasured—for their covers, their smell, their illustrations, and the words that spoke magic to our eager eyes and ears. Even the heft of them, the comforting presence of them—like weights on the corners of a map of the universe—held things in place for us. I don't have a great many specific childhood memories, but I do have vivid memories of some early experiences with books. When I was very small, I had a treasured storybook, which I discovered one rainy day to be missing from its place on the bookcase shelf. Alarmed, I searched the house for it, then ran outside to interrogate my brothers. Sure enough, one of them had carried it to a neighbor's and left it outside, in the rain. It was, of course, ruined, and I have never recovered from the loss. I wish I could stroke its dear cover even now.

It was always my job at spring housecleaning time to dust individually every book in the glass-doored bookcases in our living room. This dusting was a ritual of June, as surely as it was a ritual to haul the bedsprings outside, lean them against the garage, and with the hose squirt a year's accumulation of dust from their wire coils. I remember turning the books over in my hands, dawdling over them, feeling their slick or rough paper, running my finger down the grooves in their covers, pondering their titles: *Illustrious Americans*, *Ethelbert Hubbard's Scrapbook*, *Tom Sawyer*, *Heart Throbs*, the complete stories of O'Henry, *Popular Mechanics*, gold-trimmed encyclopedias, *The Comprehensive History of the Church*, my father's high school grammar book, signed in a boyish hand, and my mother's college yearbooks. And each year, new Christmas and birthday books swelling the collection.

I, too, fell in love with words, and as I have grown up cherishing good books and well-turned phrases, I, too, remember a mother who read daily, no matter how late the hour or how weary the day. My mother is one given to proverbial sayings as well as to reading. How many times I heard her say, "It'll never be seen on a galloping horse" (if we children were making too much of something), or, "It's an awful lot on the end of your nose" (if we were paying too little attention to something). One of her favorites was, "Don't go to bed until you have learned something new." How well I remember her predictable quip at each fine new idea or worthwhile piece of information: "Well, I can go to bed now." She also knew many wonderful poems and stories by memory, learned from her mother. Countless times I dried dishes or rubbed her feet to "Little Orphan Annie came to our house to stay," or "Lambikin and Drumikin," or "Three little kittens one stormy night."

Forgive the personal reference, but this is a woman who loves reading so much that she refused to give it up even when she lost most of her vision several years ago. With a specially crafted eyeglass, she worked and struggled in discouraging but dogged persistence to make what peripheral vision remained in her left eye focus on a text through this glass. It took weeks and months, but now, by holding the page right against the glass she wears, she can make out a few blurry letters at a time, if the text is not too small. She puts these letters together to make words and she reads. Not rapidly, not without frustration, but she reads. And my father, too, is a reader, though he has no taste for fiction or "official" poetry. It was a history book, a biography, or a religious book that I saw always by his reading chair. Surely, it is this hunger for knowledge and this love of wisdom and words that have undergirded my life. "Wisdom and knowledge shall be the stability of thy times."

I am not a poet, except at heart, but occasionally I try to give clarity to an experience or a feeling by jotting a few words in something resembling poetic form. Last August presented one such occasion, my unexpectedly coming upon three pairs of pajamas my mother had made for me in the days when she was able to sew. It was an emotional moment for me, and only words could capture it and hold it.

> It is a perilous thing
> to clean out drawers
> in storage rooms.
> They contain not simply
> the scarves and gloves and socks
> of other seasons,
> but the apparel of other lives.
>
> In the last drawer of the old chest,
> stacked neatly in pastel checks—
> pink, aqua, beige—lie three pairs
> of short pajamas, in collarless,
> cool summer cotton. One worn old,
> one middle-aged, one young. All three unworn

since that cloudless summer morning
eight years past when my mother awoke
to find her vision gone,
dissolved permanently in dusky haze.
Those pajamas she made for me
when she saw, when she was invincible.

And I am middle-aged,
and there will be no more pajamas.
But these I will not wear and make old.
These are what I have that she
made for me when she saw,
when she was invincible.
Here they are safe. They will never fray
at the edges or grow thin with wear.

And now she is old,
and she is not safe after all.
My love is no protecting drawer
of closeted security,
and I crumble with the thought
of her fragility.

Perhaps too seldom do we properly credit the power and importance of the word. Too often we forget that wisdom is never couched in slovenly language. In his moving, powerful discourse on faith, Alma has a good deal to say about words, in particular about the word of God as it is planted like a seed in our hearts, there to swell and sprout and grow. His test for confirming the goodness of God's word can apply, I think, to other kinds of words as well: "It must needs be that . . . the word is good, for it beginneth to enlarge my soul; yea, it beginneth to enlighten my understanding, yea, it beginneth to be delicious to me" (Alma 32:28). Even the nonscriptural books we read should, I believe, enlarge the soul, enlighten the understanding, and be delicious to us. The books I read from in the beginning are not ponderous books, nor are they heavy with learning, but because of the writers' great gifts and keen insights, they are wise and delicious; they taste good.

This talk very nearly had two titles because I could not part with either of the two I had chosen. Both candidates are from Proverbs, one from chapter 25, verse 11: "A word fitly spoken is like apples of gold in pictures of silver." The passage that yields the other title, the one finally chosen, is in chapter 24, verses 3 and 4: "Through wisdom is an house builded; and by understanding it is established: and by knowledge shall the chambers be filled with all precious and pleasant riches." In this scripture the link between wisdom, knowledge, and stability is explicit, just as it is in Isaiah. Note the language. A house is "builded" through wisdom, and "established" by understanding. The poet is speaking of stability here, of a strong, enduring structure built and maintained through wisdom and understanding. But verse 4 lifts the value beyond utility: "And by knowledge shall the chambers be filled with all precious and pleasant riches." Here the poet speaks not only of the stability that comes through wisdom but also of the stabilizing richness and joy that knowledge brings to our lives. Wisdom and knowledge not only build the house of our intellect and spirit but furnish it in wonderful ways. Words fitly spoken, like "apples of gold in pictures of silver," offer spiritual nourishment, the sustenance of beauty and wonder. They give stability to the soul.

Certainly, there is scarcely more beautiful language anywhere than is found in scripture. It is obvious that the Lord cares very much about language and that many of his prophets were inspired poets. We are fortunate that the King James translators of the Bible were sensitive to aesthetic values. To illustrate the importance of the way something is said, let me compare one passage from the King James Version, 1 Corinthians 13:1, with two much later versions, which were written in an effort to make scripture more accessible to the modern reader. What the revisers forgot is that people learn things from poetry at a secret level that may be more important than explanations or familiar expressions.

The King James Version reads: "Though I speak with the tongues of men and of angels, and have not charity, I am become as sounding brass, or a tinkling cymbal."

The Revised Standard Version reads: "If I speak in the tongues of men and of angels, but have not love, I am a noisy gong or a clanging cymbal."

I could say a lot about what has been lost in meaning, power, and beauty in the revision, but your ear has already registered its disappointment.

Now listen to the verse as it is printed in the Living New Testament: "If I had the gift of being able to speak in other languages without learning them, and could speak in every language there is in all of heaven and earth, but didn't love others, I would only be making noise."

The poetry has been lost entirely, and with it the capacity of the passage to touch and inspire us. Art has its own wisdom, and we tamper with it only at some peril.

The wise books that bring joy and stability to our lives are the books that carry knowledge and truths that endure in language worthy of them. It is well to remember that all books are not created equal, that all books are not rooted in principles that lead us to understanding and stability. Bookstore shelves are lined with volumes that contain the so-called popular wisdom of the day, how-to books that guarantee everything from slender hips to mystic communication with rocks. For the most part, the theories on which these books are built do not last even as long as the cheap paper on which they are printed. Today's cure-all is tomorrow's Edsel. The most offensive, and yet sometimes inadvertently the funniest, of these hard-sell wonder books are those claiming that spiritual rewards follow material pursuits, or vice versa. You will be enraptured to know that the latest in the "Millionaires of the Bible" series is titled *The Millionaire Joshua: His Prosperity Secrets for You*. Inside, the reader is told, "Yes, the Bible is the finest prosperity textbook that has ever been written! The great people of the Bible had no psychological hang-ups on the subject of prosperity and success being a part of their spiritual heritage. They intuitively knew that true prosperity has a spiritual basis."[10] This stuff is more comical than the comics. Surely, here is proof of Proverbs 15:2: "The tongue of the wise useth knowledge aright: but the mouth of fools poureth out foolishness."

Capitalizing as it does on our desire for the quick cure, this sort of thing is surely a contributor to the instability of our time. Furthermore, it is the antithesis of the Savior's gospel. You might be interested in some of the titles I encountered in a quick browse through a small bookstore: *How to Invest $5,000 Even If You Don't Have It, Think and Grow Rich, You Can Have It All: The Art of Winning the Money Game and Living a Life of Joy, The Magic of Getting What You Want*.

And now consider: "Lay not up for yourselves treasures upon earth, where moth and rust doth corrupt, . . . but lay up for yourselves treasures in heaven" (Matthew 6:19–20); "where your treasure is, there will your heart be also" (v. 21); "take no thought for your life, what ye shall eat, or what ye shall drink; nor yet for your body, what ye shall put on. Is not the life more than meat, and the body than raiment?" (v. 25).

Consider these titles: *Inspire Yourself: One Hundred Guides to Victorious Days, The Psychology of Winning, Looking Out for #1, Celebrate Yourself, Winning through Intimidation.*

And now consider: "Blessed are the poor in spirit: for theirs is the kingdom of heaven" (Matthew 5:3); "blessed are the meek: for they shall inherit the earth" (v. 5); "he that findeth his life shall lose it: and he that loseth his life for my sake shall find it" (Matthew 10:39); "for what is a man profited, if he shall gain the whole world, and lose his own soul? or what shall a man give in exchange for his soul?" (Matthew 16:26).

Instead of racing to scores of self-help books whose principal inspiration is the dollar sign and whose object is to focus our attention solely on ourselves, why not take the Savior at his word: "Come unto me, all ye that labour and are heavy laden, and I will give you rest. Take my yoke upon you, and learn of me; for I am meek and lowly in heart: and ye shall find rest unto your souls. For my yoke is easy, and my burden is light" (Matthew 11:28–30).

Add to the books I have just mentioned, the advertisements that bury us daily and the headlines of the grocery store tabloids that insult us even as they entertain us, and you begin to understand why Isaiah made a special plea for the stability of true wisdom and knowledge. Of course, were these sensational scandal sheets to disappear, we might find waiting in checkout lines quite a drag, with only the gum and lifesavers to contemplate. What on earth would we do without this sort of edification: "Hell found in outer space: Scientists listen to screams of the damned on Satan's planet"; "Surgeons from UFO save my life, sailor claims"; "Pilgrims say they see Moses appear above old apple tree?"

As an antidote to all of this printed noise, we might remember that the word is so important that it is used in scripture to designate the Savior himself: "In the beginning was the Word, and the Word was with God, and the Word was God" (John 1:1). In the nonscriptural reading we do, how much better, surely, to read the well-crafted words of intelligent beings who have learned new things in this world and shared their discovery—or, more likely, who have shared their quest for understanding—than to suffer the assault of graceless language and extravagant claims.

With your indulgence, I want to share just a few "apples of gold in pictures of silver" with you, a few of the many things that over the years have stuck in a groove in my gray matter. Emily Dickinson has long been a favorite. Try this teasing taste of her cryptic wisdom:[11]

> It dropped so low—in my Regard—
> I heard it hit the Ground—
> And go to pieces on the Stones
> At bottom of my Mind—
>
> Yet blamed the Fate that flung it—less
> Than I denounced Myself,
> For entertaining Plated Wares
> Upon my Silver Shelf—

Just as I had difficulty selecting a title, so did I have difficulty selecting from the long list of things I would like to have shared with you. This will surely come as a great surprise, but I decided to read something from Willa Cather, a brief portrait of Antonia Shimerda, an immigrant pioneer to the plains of Nebraska, a woman of integrity who had a hard life, but a good life, a woman whose strength of character showed in every aspect of her being, in every gesture. Jim Burden, seeing her after twenty years, says of her:

"Antonia had always been one to leave images in the mind that did not fade—that grew stronger with time. . . . She lent herself to immemorial human attitudes which we recognize by instinct as universal and true. . . . She was a battered woman now, not a lovely girl; but she still had that something which fires the imagination, could still stop one's breath for a moment by a look or gesture that somehow revealed the meaning in common things. She had only to stand in the orchard, to put her hand on a little crab tree and look up at the apples, to make you feel the goodness of planting and tending and harvesting at last. All the strong things of her heart came out in her body, that had been so tireless in serving generous emotions. . . . She was a rich mine of life, like the founders of early races."[12]

We began with a Shakespearean scholar; let's end with Shakespeare, with King Lear, to me the greatest of his plays. I think nowhere else in English literature is so much said so powerfully about human values and character. You remember the story. The aging king, desiring to be done with kingly responsibilities but wishing to retain all the symbols of power, decides to divide his kingdom among his three daughters. The size of each daughter's portion is to be determined by the eloquence of her overt profession of love for him. The youngest, Cordelia, the only one who truly loves him, pridefully refuses to submit to his foolish test and is disinherited. The two older daughters, lavish in their expressions of love, inherit the kingdom but soon show their true colors. They refuse their father his retinue of knights and abuse him to the point that he is cast out on the heath in a terrible storm. Suffering and deprivation cost the once-selfish old man his wits, but they also ennoble him. We sense the change when he steps back and invites his fool to enter the protective hovel ahead of him. Moreover, he realizes for the first time what it is to be an outcast, living in unsheltered poverty. His thoughts extend to the ragged and homeless in his kingdom:

> Poor naked wretches, whereso'er you are,
> That bide the pelting of this pitiless storm,
> How shall your houseless heads and unfed sides,
> Your loop'd and window'd raggedness, defend you
> From seasons such as these? O, I have ta'en
> Too little care of this! Take physic, pomp:
> Expose thyself to feel what wretches feel,
> That thou mayst shake the superflux to them
> And show the heavens more just. (III:iv)

Here is a changed man. And the change becomes even more apparent near the end of the play when in the midst of battle he and his daughter Cordelia—whose husband's forces have waged war against those of her wicked sisters—are reunited. Here is this ragged, honorless, half-mad, deposed old man, and this is how his loving daughter addresses him. She refuses to diminish him; she accords him the respect due a mighty king:

> How does my royal lord? How fares your Majesty?

Then that chastened man, who earlier would not have bowed to anyone or anything, falls on his knees before his daughter. She begs him not to kneel, and he replies:

> Pray, do not mock me.
> I am a very foolish fond old man,
> Fourscore and upward, not an hour more nor less;
> And to deal plainly,
> I fear I am not in my perfect mind.
> Methinks I should know you, and know this man;
> Yet I am doubtful; for I am mainly ignorant
> What place this is; and all the skill I have

> *Remembers not these garments: nor I know not*
> *Where I did lodge last night. Do not laugh at me;*
> *For (as I am a man) I think this lady to be my child Cordelia.*

Greatly moved, she cries, "And so I am! I am!" He continues:

> *Be your tears wet? Yes, faith, I pray weep not.*
> *If you have poison for me, I will drink it.*
> *I know you do not love me; for your sisters*
> *Have, as I do remember, done me wrong.*
> *You have some cause, they have not.*

And she replies, "No cause, no cause." (IV:vii)

Cordelia forgives him; in fact, she had never blamed him. His joy in that realization is so full that he forgets all about the battle and the wrong done him by his other daughters. Even when the tides of war turn and he and Cordelia are taken prisoners, his only thought is to be with her:

> *Come, let's away to prison.*
> *We two alone will sing like birds i' th' cage.*
> *When thou dost ask me blessing, I'll kneel down*
> *And ask of thee forgiveness. So we'll live,*
> *And pray, and sing, and tell old tales, and laugh*
> *At gilded butterflies. (V:iii)*

Here, my dear sisters, are riches enough to fill a thousand chambers.

Notes

1. Madeleine Doran, *Something about Swans* (Madison: University of Wisconsin Press, 1973), 26–27.
2. Ibid., 27.
3. Eudora Welty, *One Writer's Beginnings* (Cambridge: Harvard University Press, 1984), [xi].
4. Ibid., 3.
5. Ibid., 5.
6. Ibid., 5–6.
7. Ibid., 6.
8. Ibid., 9.
9. Ibid., 30.
10. Catherine Ponder, *The Millionaire Joshua: His Prosperity Secrets for You* (Marina del Ray, Calif.: DeVorss, 1978), 3.
11. Emily Dickinson, "It dropped so low—in my Regard," in *The Complete Poems of Emily Dickinson*, ed. Thomas H. Johnson (Boston: Little, Brown, 1960), 366.
12. Willa Cather, *My Ántonia* (Boston: Houghton Mifflin, 1918), 352–53.

FOR SUCH A TIME AS THIS,
THE TIME IS NOW

$\sim\!\!\infty\!\!\sim$

Norma B. Ashton

I have a favorite general authority. In one of his talks he said, "Some spend so much time getting ready to live for an unknown future that they discover there is suddenly no time left to live."[1] This has been a fairly common theme in recent times. And yet the pendulum has swung far to the other extreme in many segments of today's society: ignore inhibitions; do what you feel like doing; discard any moral values that are restrictive; live for the pleasure of the moment.

In considering these pleasures of the moment, it is well to remember that the "nows" determine to a great extent the "forevers." For this reason, even though we want and must enjoy the "right nows," we should keep tomorrow and forever in perspective. Waiting for a brighter future may cause us to lose a beautiful today.

Our children smile as they remember the little sayings I used to put over a lesson as they were growing up, but now I find them using them in their own homes occasionally. One such saying is, "That which is good, you pay for before you get it. That which is bad, you pay for after you take it, and the price is usually higher than you expect."

Let me illustrate with the story of Maggie Bellows, who was an internationally known journalist. Her articles appeared in many papers. Foreign countries invited her for seminars. Her husband was associate editor of the *New York Times*. In her home in Phoenix she entertained heads of state, movie stars, and many important authors and journalists. During one June Conference she came to Salt Lake City to write an article on the activities of Mormon youth. I was asked to be her hostess.

She was so important that the First Presidency gave her a private interview. Some of the women leaders of our auxiliaries held a luncheon

---

Norma B. Ashton graduated in elementary education and English from the University of Utah. She has given extensive service to the Church and the community. She is the wife of Elder Marvin J. Ashton, a member of the Quorum of the Twelve Apostles. They are the parents of four children.

for her. She did not smoke in the Church Office Building, but always as she walked out she lit a cigarette. (Now this is not a Word of Wisdom story.) After a long, full day I took her to the Hotel Utah for a lovely dinner. To me the food was so welcome, but as I ate she stirred hers around a little and smoked. Then she excused herself with these words: "I am going to call my seventy-year-old mother in Phoenix. She is dying of lung cancer, and if she is conscious I will go to her bedside; if not, I must go on to New York." On returning to the table, she reported that her mother was still in a coma and asked if I could take her to catch her flight to New York.

About five years later we were in Phoenix. I picked up a local paper, and the headline of one of the articles read "Maggie Bellows Memorial Fund." Startled, I read on and found that this great journalist had died of lung cancer at age fifty. A memorial was being established in her honor. Then I remembered very clearly a statement she had made that evening we had dinner together. "I smoke a lot, but it is about my only vice. Don't you think the Lord will forgive me if that's all I do?" I remember saying, "I suppose he will."

This woman had everything to live for. She was productive and successful; she had a good marriage and admiration from many; but with all her warnings, she let her desires for today wipe out many good tomorrows. I think the Lord will forgive her, but I also think she paid a much bigger price than she intended—twenty years less of the good life that could have been hers. Certainly to enjoy the "nows," we must consider and pay the price.

In John 10:10 Jesus says, "I am come that they might have life, and that they might have it more abundantly." Our challenge is to learn to have the abundant life today *and* tomorrow. For our purposes today, let's think together about ways that an abundant life can be a daily experience, for inevitably, that lifestyle will spill over into the tomorrows.

The "if only" trap catches us all at times. "If only I had money or power or influence, or a slim, trim figure, or a beautiful face, or great talent, or a bigger home, or a more prestigious job, I would be happy." Yet on every hand we find people who have some or all of these things, and we are aware that there is no happiness in their daily lives.

Some time ago I read a statement made by one of the richest, most beautiful women of our time, Elizabeth Taylor. She said, "I have never known one really happy day in my life."

Avoiding the present moment is almost a disease in our culture. Many of us condition ourselves to sacrifice the present for the future. There was a girl on vacation in Hawaii who spent all her time at the pool or the beach turning and tanning, even though she was often uncomfortable. She missed the palms, the beautiful scenery, even other fun activities just so she could go back to her office and show off her tan. Many others say they will be happy when the mortgage is paid or when the children get into school, or go on missions, or find mates.

Can we analyze ourselves? Do we feel that we must sacrifice ourselves for the future? When that future does arrive, it becomes today, and we will probably go on using it to prepare for some other wonderful tomorrow. Tomorrow's happiness is so elusive. Life is what happens to you when you have other plans. Our task is to find the abundant life along the way, to pause and relish each twenty-four hours that we are given by our Father in heaven.

Erich Fromm has said that happiness is not a gift of the gods. If that is the case, what can we do to prevent our losing this beautiful today?

Three verbs come to mind that might be helpful as we plan our attack on achieving great todays: *loving, learning,* and *living.* These are rather vague words, so let's elaborate on them using more specific examples.

The eighth Psalm is a good starting place for *loving.* It gives us reason to love ourselves. "What is man, that thou art mindful of him? and the son of man, that thou visitest him? For thou hast made him a little lower than the angels, and hast crowned him with glory and honour" (Psalm 8:4–5). Wordsworth wrote, "Trailing clouds of glory do we come from God, who is our home." "A little lower than the angels." "Trailing clouds of glory." What do these truths tell you about yourself?

All of us come to earth as God's creation. Each has an innate nobility. Then worldly falsehoods disseminated by the father of lies start to clutter up our lives. "You aren't any good." "You are not worthy." "You must fit this mold." "You can't do anything right." "Try harder—think less; you can't improve." And on and on. Satan tries to jerk away those clouds of glory, and he is good at jerking.

To love ourselves, we must realize who we are and examine our feelings about ourselves. It is our obligation and opportunity to eliminate the negative and to nourish our real selves with humble pride and conduct worthy of one a little lower than the angels. Self-worth can't be verified by others. You are worthy because you say it is so. I realize this isn't an easy assignment. Even a prophet has to struggle for this realization.

Spencer W. Kimball and Harold B. Lee were close friends. They went into the Quorum of the Twelve just a few weeks apart. President Kimball said he always admired this friend so very much; in fact, he almost envied President Lee for his talents. He took every occasion to tell President Lee how he felt. Often he would say, "Harold, I wish I could play the organ as you do." "Harold, you speak so well. I wish I could do as well." "Harold, you can see the gist of a problem in such a short time. I wish my mind were so clear." Then, related President Kimball, in one of their weekly meetings in the temple President Lee made a fine presentation to the other members of the Twelve. As they walked out of the temple together, again President Kimball turned to his friend and said, "You did a magnificent job with your report this morning. I wish I could do as well as you do." "Well," said President Kimball with a twinkle in his eyes, "I guess Harold had had enough. He stopped, put his hands on his hips, and, looking me straight in the eye, said, 'Spencer, the Lord doesn't want you to be a Harold B. Lee. All he wants is for you to be the best Spencer W. Kimball you can be.'" With a smile on his face, President Kimball said, "Ever since then I have just tried to be the best Spencer W. Kimball I can be." And would you say that he has been very successful doing that? That is an answer for all of us. All the Lord asks of us is to be the best we can be with what we have.

Eliminating negative thoughts and actions about ourselves can be a difficult task. We think we have to tear ourselves down. Somehow we think a gracious "thank you" for a personal compliment is egotistical, so we deny the kind words. Have you ever told someone how nice she looked only to have her say, "Oh, I look terrible, I haven't had time to do my hair"? Or when you compliment her on her lovely dress, you hear these words: "Oh, this old thing. I bought it for almost nothing at the cut-rate store." Or if you say, "You gave a good talk," the reply is, "I was frightened to death. It was terrible."

Let me illustrate with an article entitled "Don't Sell Yourself Short":

"At a party I was much attracted to a pretty girl with a charming personality. A fellow who was doing publicity for a big diamond firm sauntered up to her, spoke of her graceful posture, and told her she was so pretty. He said he would like to use her as a model for photographs to advertise some of his jewels. She could pose with a million dollars' worth of diamonds in necklaces and bracelets. She laughed and said she would love to. 'But,' she added, 'my hands are awful.' And she spread them out to him with her fingers wide apart.

"Up to that moment I hadn't noticed her hands, which were a bit red and rather large. But after that uncalled-for remark, I almost forgot about her hair, which was so lovely, her large violet eyes, and engaging smile. I saw nothing but her hands. She seemed to have so many hands. You don't have to ring bells and wave flags in an attempt to advertise your good points, but must you throw brickbats?"[2]

We don't have to degrade ourselves in public. We don't have to point out our flaws. We do need to work on them. If there is something you don't like and can change it, work on changing. If not, accept what God has given you and work with what you have. "For all have not every gift given unto them; for there are many gifts, and to every man is given a gift by the Spirit of God. To some is given one, and to some is given another, that all may be profited thereby" (D&C 46:11–12).

As Spencer W. Kimball was taught, a copy is never as valuable as the original. Each of us is an original made by God, and we diminish ourselves and our Maker when we question our worth.

We mistakenly think that things or people make us unhappy. But really that is not so. We make ourselves unhappy by the way we let ourselves act or react to the words or deeds of others. As our love for ourselves grows, and we don't feel the need to justify and explain our actions, we can use our energy in also loving others.

My husband often says, "Never let yourself be offended by someone who is learning his job." Because we are a lay church and because we all change jobs at what seem to be brief intervals, we are all constantly learning how to fulfill new assignments. No one should ever let himself be hurt by a brother or sister in the gospel. We are each too worthy to be upset by someone else.

The second word we mentioned for happy todays is *learning.* Intellectuality itself probably can't get us to the celestial kingdom. It must be coupled with spirituality, virtue, and application. There is an old Persian proverb I like: "One pound of learning requires ten pounds of common sense to apply it."

In order to move ahead day by day, we need to be aware of the world around us. We need to use our minds and make decisions that are based on current information. Basic moral principles of the gospel of Jesus

Christ never change, but practices and implementation do—or why would we have continuous revelation? Some of us have a hard time embracing changes that are probably planned. We spend some good todays struggling with pain as we try to correlate the past with today.

President Kimball takes every opportunity to tell others that his Camilla has never stopped learning—how, in fact, she took classes each year at the University of Utah or at the Institute of Religion on that campus.

Our mind is an amazing thing. President Jeffrey R. Holland has said that what the mind can conceive and believe, it can achieve. A famous psychologist once said, "Be careful what you expect. You will probably get it."[5]

In an Education Week talk at the institute of religion at the University of Utah, Sister Leisel McBride told the following story as it was reported in a Chicago paper: One Friday afternoon a man found himself locked in a refrigerator car. He called until he was hoarse. He banged on the well-insulated walls. At last he realized that working hours were over until Monday morning. He sat huddled in a corner or scrawled his thoughts on the walls with his pencil. One sentence was weakly written and the words slanted off at an angle. It said, "I am slowly freezing to death. These words will probably be the last I write." On Monday morning his fellow workers found their associate in a corner, and he was, indeed, lifeless. The unusual circumstance was that the refrigeration in that car had been turned off on Friday, and there was only a normal, livable temperature in the car.

If a mind can snuff out a life, surely, if properly used, it can also help bring the abundant life. When we learn how to use such a powerful tool to solve our own problems and help with our progress, the effect can be exhilarating. We cheat ourselves when we rationalize or place the blame for our circumstances on someone else. Somehow we would all like excuses for our mistakes, our lack of happiness, or our slow progress.

Have you ever heard, "I'm like this because I'm the middle child," or "I came from the wrong side of the tracks," or "My boss doesn't like me," or "My husband just doesn't understand," or "I'm naturally shy"? Others may be responsible in the beginning for some of our problems, but they are not responsible for the way we act or the way we solve our problems. Learning to cope with all phases of life is an important part of the learning process.

Dr. Sterling G. Ellsworth and Dr. Richard G. Ellsworth, in their book

Getting to Know the Real You, tell the following story: Two girls were standing in the hallway at the high school. They were not attractive. They had large noses and braces on their teeth. As they stood there, along came the captain of the football team. He had an inflated ego and was aggressive and superficially confident. He looked at the two girls and said, "You girls are really ugly. You are bad news. Why don't you get lost?" He sauntered down the hall and then looked back. One girl burst into tears, and he laughed. But the other girl looked him right in the eye and said, "Buddy, *you* have the problem, not I. You must have had a fight with your mother, or something. What are you doing going around at eight-thirty in the morning telling other people that they are bad news? What is the matter with *you?*" This girl was secure. She had learned of her intrinsic worth. The other girl let someone else crush her. Her whole day was probably ruined.[3]

Our egos are fragile and easily wounded; however, our minds are tools that can teach us that as others attack us, say unkind words, ignore us, or hurt us in any way, they are the ones who are hurting and insecure. This is a hard lesson to learn, but if we can learn it we won't waste beautiful todays in tears and hurt feelings.

There is another art to be learned to make each day easier. Decisions, decisions, decisions. I really don't know how one learns to make them quickly, but I do know that I can waste a lot of time on a good day ago-nizing over a proper menu for a dinner party or what kind of gift I should give someone special.

A great banker said that the secret to his success was following this advice: "When you have a decision to make, make it and go ahead. You will make some mistakes; but you will make no more mistakes than if you took a month to decide, and you will have thirty days where you didn't have to worry about it."

The story of Zode, as told by Dr. Seuss, puts a humorous light on this problem. Zode came to a fork in the road and couldn't decide which road to take, no matter how he pondered. So he decided to take both, and he started off for both places at once. And that is how he ended up—no place at all with a split in his pants. Prompt decision-making can make a day brighter.

There are so many dimensions of learning, so much our minds can do. President J. Reuben Clark said that all domains of knowledge belong to us, for in no other way could the great law of eternal progress be satisfied.

After spending full time with her husband for the four months after his surgery, Sister Kimball finally joined the general authorities' wives at our monthly luncheon. She was asked to say a few words to us. In four months, she told us, she had been out in public only four times—having spent each day by her husband's side—yet there was never a word of complaint. Instead, she said, "I have learned that every experience in life is a learning experience. During these last few months I have learned so much. I have become aware that one is never above learning nor too old to learn."

From her we can learn that when sorrow and tragedy come into our lives, it is normal to react with tears and anguish. But if we have learned to trust in God, we won't be paralyzed by these feelings, and we can move forward and often experience "the peace . . . which passeth all understanding" (Philippians 4:7). As we learn of God's ways and grow through testing, our troubled days can be good days, learning days. Theodore Rubin said that happiness is found more frequently in times of struggle than in times of triumph. Even in trials and sorrow, learning can take place. Without the benefit of constant learning, our todays become stagnant, our lives out of date, and our progress limited.

All the loving and all the learning are then put to the test as we live day by day. What shall I do? What shall I leave undone? After whom shall I pattern my life? How shall I dress? For whom shall I vote? Where shall I go to school? How should I act? Actually, we must find our own answers. So many of us would like a Church program or policy outlined for every contingency in our lives. Then we wouldn't have to reason it out for ourselves. When we made a mistake or experienced a failure, we could shrug our shoulders and say, "It's not my fault. I only followed the manual." That would be the easy way but not the growing way. As the Lord told Oliver Cowdery, "Behold, ye have not understood; you have supposed that I would give it unto you, when you took no thought save it was to ask me" (D&C 9:7).

Sometimes two right principles do conflict. Our agency is given to us to decide what is right for us at this moment. Satisfaction comes as we solve our own problems, using gospel guidelines while we exercise our agency. All of us have stood at the crossroads and doubted our wisdom to choose the right path. It is our right and our responsibility to determine what is best for us at any given time. As we do so, may we use our power to decide and to live with our decisions, without being ridden with guilt.

At times we choose to do some things well, leave some things undone, or do some things not so well so we can hurry on to more important tasks. "Ought tos" and "shoulds" are usually not commandments. Do you ever feel as though you have broken a commandment when you haven't gotten all the " shoulds" done? (A "should" is unhealthy only when it gets in the way of healthy, effective behavior.) "Ought tos" and "shoulds" shouldn't get bigger than we are.

President Stone of the Modesto California Stake told us that his wife felt she should always serve home-baked bread to him and their eight children. He loved the bread and so did the children, but one day he banned homemade bread from their table. He helped his wife realize that there were more important things at that time in her life than homemade bread. She needed more time for him and for herself. It was one thing that helped her be less tired.

Can you give away a bushel of peaches instead of canning them if your husband wants you to go on a date with him? Can you choose to take a class instead of sewing all your children's clothes and not feel guilty when your neighbor's children march into church in their home-sewn dresses? On some days can you throw the covers up quickly on the bed so you can hurry off to play tennis because you decide you need exercise more than a perfectly made bed? Can you use your agency in these seemingly insignificant ways without feeling weighed down with guilt? If so, you are living well today.

In daily living, self-judgment and guilt can ruin a day or many days. Some around us may flaunt their spiritual blessings as they talk of children who filled missions, who had temple marriages, and who are models in every way. And as we listen, we judge ourselves as failures. I once heard my husband suggest that such a father should go to his closet and thank his Father in heaven very often but also consider how he might make some who weren't so fortunate feel when he talked of his model family.

The size of a family, conduct of children, positions held may be indicators, but they don't necessarily determine our status in the eyes of God. In fact, who is to say that the parents who go on loving and trying to help a wayward child through long years or the women with no children who teach, serve, and live with quiet dignity will not have a greater reward than those who are fortunate enough to have a model family? I somehow think they will.

Enjoyable days come from enjoying and working with what we have today instead of yearning for different circumstances. Often there is a great desire to look to tomorrow, to "jump out of season." The young person who drives before the legal time; the student who is bored with school and, wanting spending money, drops out to get a job that pays minimum wages; starry-eyed couples who mistake infatuation and physical attraction for enduring love and rush to the altar—these and so many others jump out of season.

A young mother with several children decided that it was the season for genealogy work. While her children ran around the neighborhood, rather neglected, her genealogy sheets covered the floors and tables of her home. When a friend came to call and saw the state of affairs, she asked why this woman spent all her time with her ancestors and so little time with her children. The genealogist thought for a moment and then answered, "I guess it is because I can get along with the dead better than with the living."

Another mother was so anxious to get back to school that she left several teenagers to fend for themselves. Today that woman has her doctorate, but most of her children are in serious trouble with drugs and the law. Education is wonderful, as is genealogy, but there is the right season for them. Even though out-of-season activities may beckon enticingly, they usually bring on some stressful todays. Remember, results of unwise actions are often not evident until after the fact. I hope that we won't jump forward or backward out of season and miss the season of life in which we find ourselves. I believe that happiness comes when we allow ourselves to grow according to the season in which we find ourselves planted today. Spiritual experiences usually come as we do our routine tasks following gospel guidelines.

There are many more aspects of living than we have touched on today. Examine your own life. See where stress is causing uncomfortable todays; then move to correct the situation. Seek help, if necessary. No one is perfect, even if you have a neighbor you might think is a supermom. There is no such person.

All of us hope to reach some magical goal where our job is recognized as well done and our just rewards will be bestowed upon us. But especially as Latter-day Saints, we need to remember that our goal is eternal progression and that there is no such end of the journey. Therefore, if we haven't enjoyed ourselves along the way, we have missed the only joy there really is.

As the threads of the gospel weave back and forth through our daily living, unexpected joys and sometimes miracles will enrich our lives. Testimonies can grow stronger. I like the story found in the ninth chapter of Mark, where the father brought his sick son to the disciples of Jesus to be healed, but they failed to heal him. The father lost hope. Then came Jesus, who said, "If thou canst believe, all things are possible to him that believeth." The father answered, "Lord, I believe." And the son was healed (see Mark 9:15–29).

If we can believe, our days can go from joy to joy.

General Douglas MacArthur wrote: "People grow old only by deserting their ideals. Years may wrinkle the skin, but to give up interest wrinkles the soul. . . . You are as young as your faith, as old as your doubt; as young as your self-confidence, as old as your fear; as young as your hope, as old as your despair."[4] To me he is saying we should love and learn and live each day that is ours to live. "For behold, this life is the time for men to prepare to meet God; yea, behold, the day of this life is the day for men to perform their labors" (Alma 34:32). Your own expectations are the key. If you expect to be happy and fulfilled in life, most likely that is what will happen.

In a shopping mall the other day, a tall, good-looking youth walked toward me. When he got close enough, I could read these words on the front of his T-shirt: "I'd try having a positive mental attitude." As he moved on past me, I saw these words on the back of the shirt: "But I know it won't work."

I promise you that the daily enjoyment of life does work if you work on it and want it to. Love yourself and all of God's children. Appreciate your innate nobility. Take charge of your own life by using your agency wisely and without guilt feelings. Be your own best self, not a carbon copy. Stay pliable by reaching into the great fountains of knowledge offered both in secular areas and in gospel teachings. Then joy can be yours all along the way, and the nows will be more rewarding than the dreams of tomorrow.

Notes

1. Marvin J. Ashton, "Faith in Oneself," in *Faith* (Salt Lake City: Deseret Book, 1983),
2. Gelett Burgess, "Don't Sell Yourself Short," *Reader's Digest*, August 1954, 14.
3. See Dr. Sterling G. Ellsworth and Dr. Richard G. Ellsworth, *Getting to Know the Real You* (Salt Lake City: Deseret Book, 1980), 65–66.
4. Quoted in William Manchester, *American Caesar* (New York: Dell Publishing, 1978), 836–37.

ROLLER-COASTER PARENTING

❧

Janene Wolsey Baadsgaard

Can you remember your first time on a roller-coaster ride? I remember too well, especially that first big hill. I clenched my teeth, held on so tight my knuckles went white, and wondered hysterically, "Why did I ever want to go on this ride? I must be crazy. I know I'm going to pass out, throw up, fall out, and die!"

I was terrified, and it must have shown, because my mother took one look at me and yelled, "*Scream, Janene, scream!*" I followed her advice and let out a blood-curdling scream. A strange thing happened. The ride didn't suddenly become any less scary, but I started having a good time because I quit trying to hide my fear. Family life is like that. You find yourself laughing one minute, screaming the next. Motherhood especially is one colossal, wild journey full of ups and downs, twists and turns. One of the important quests in life is to discover what frees us up to enjoy the ride.

Most of us are like my young son Joseph. One day after he had been caught punching his brother and I plastered him with a reprimand, he lowered his eyebrows and grumbled back at me, "Why did we have to come down from heaven anyway?"

"Why, Joseph," I answered, "when you were in heaven, you shouted for joy because you were so happy about the chance to come down to earth and get a body and experience everything here."

"Oh yeah?" Joseph answered. "Well, if I did, I was just teasing."

Joseph expresses well what many of us feel when we're faced with life on the uphill side. Like that first big hill on the roller-coaster ride, we find ourselves wondering, "Why did we have to come down from heaven anyway?" In 2 Nephi 2:25 we learn why: "Men are, that they might have joy." Do we really believe that? Do we really believe that the reason we

Janene Wolsey Baadsgaard, a homemaker and freelance writer, is the author of several books on family matters. She has been a columnist for the *Deseret New*, written articles for the *New Era* and the *Ensign,* and taught at Utah Valley State College. She serves as the home and family education teacher in her ward Relief Society. She and her husband, Ross, are the parents of nine children.

exist—men, women, and children—is to have joy? Then why are all of us so serious so much of the time?

Feeling joy and finding humor can be learned, practiced, reinforced, and internalized just like any other skill. Humor is not just telling jokes but a way of looking at life and responding to it positively. When we decide to respond to life this way in spite of our circumstances, it's easier to find the silly or absurd around us. Take, for example, the church bulletin board notice announcing: "There will be meetings in the north and south ends of the church. Children will be baptized on both ends." Or the sign on a hospital bulletin board: "Research shows that the first five minutes of life can be the most risky." Someone alert to absurdity had penciled underneath: "The last five minutes are pretty risky, too."

Humor's lenses allow us not only to see what's funny around us but to deflate a bit of life's very real troubles. One concentration camp survivor advised her daughter: "Take life lightly. . . . Pain is inevitable, but suffering is optional." That is a profound thought. We can't control what happens to us, but we can choose how to respond. I think of the well-known athlete being carried off the football field with a serious injury. The newspapers reported that through clenched teeth he quipped to the stretcher-bearers, "My mother was right. I'm so glad I have on clean underwear."

To keep healthy we not only have to exercise and eat right, we have to laugh regularly and think right. People who treat a stress or a threat as a challenge rather than as a negative event generally have more fun and energy to cope with everyday difficulties. With our families or on the job, humor can break a conflict cycle and foster cooperative solutions to problems. One wife tells of a time when she and her husband had started arguing and couldn't stop the cycle. Because they were both being dramatic anyway, she decided to play out the scene to the hilt. She clutched her heart and threw herself on the floor, yelling, "Oh, you're so right it's killing me!" Her sudden burst of insanity drained the steam out of the conflict. Another wife released her resentment over her husband's too-frequent hunting trips by placing a classified advertisement: "Husband for sale cheap. Comes complete with hunting and fishing equipment, one pair of jeans, two shirts, boots, black Labrador retriever, and too many pounds of venison. Pretty good guy, but not home much from October to December and from April to October. Will consider trade." After approximately sixty-six phone calls, some of them serious, the wife placed another ad: "Retraction of husband for sale cheap. Everybody wants the dog, not the husband." Being able to laugh—instead of bemoaning our fate or resenting other people—is mentally healthy.

I admit it isn't always easy to reverse a bad mood. When I'm having a bad day or dark thoughts, I can usually change the way I feel by changing the way I think. I start that mental process by mentally finishing this thought: "I am so grateful for . . ." Joy comes when I pay attention to all the things I'm grateful for instead of all my problems. While I was in bed because of premature labor a few years ago, I became telephone buddies with Blanche, a woman who was confined to bed because of a stroke. Before her stroke, Blanche had been wheelchair bound for thirty years because of a doctor's devastating error in surgery. Her husband, unable to face the trauma, left her to raise their four children alone. Now bedridden, she had every reason to focus on what she had lost. Instead, in our telephone conversations she chose to focus on what she had retained. From her bedroom window, Blanche could see a single tree. During our conversations, she would describe in detail the intricate changes the seasons brought to her tree. "It's such a miracle to be able to see," Blanche said one day. "I have so much to live for. I am so grateful I can see."

Blanche spoke with the same detail of her grandchildren. Unable to walk, often alone, Blanche could have been miserable. Instead, she chose gratitude. And her grateful heart showered her with beauty and blessings everywhere she looked, even when her entire landscape was limited to a tiny bedroom.

Over the weeks of waiting for my baby to reach end of term, I took prenatal lessons from Blanche on celebrating life: I am the only one who can give my children a mother who loves life, no matter what. I learned from watching her to see life as it really is. Life as it really is—even not at its best—is downright amazing.

I sometimes forget, however, that I don't experience true joy on a smooth celestial highway. To experience joy, I have to experience its opposite. Without sorrow and pain, like the uphill climb on the roller coaster, there is no hill to descend, no thrill or reward, no true joy.

Before I met Blanche, I had learned this lesson the hard way. One evening, soon after my husband and I moved into our first new home, we seeded our front yard with grass. The next morning my husband told me it was important to keep the dirt wet or the grass seeds wouldn't sprout. Then he kissed me on the cheek and left for work.

Since it was the middle of a hot July, this wet-dirt assignment was a full-time job. On top of that, I was pregnant and had two baby daughters to care for. I remember standing out on the front porch, feeling light-headed and nauseated, squirting the dirt for hours while my one- and two-year-old daughters tumbled down the steps, threw their shoes in the ditch, and stuffed tiny rocks up their noses. After days and days of constant watering, our front yard began growing the biggest, greenest weeds in the whole neighborhood.

"This is my life," I remember mumbling as I sprayed the dirt. "All I do is water weeds. I feed one end of the girls and clean up the other. Nothing I do really matters. All I do is water weeds."

A few days later, I started having serious complications with my pregnancy, and late one night I began hemorrhaging. My husband quickly called a neighbor to watch our children and raced me to the emergency room of the nearest hospital. After the doctor arrived at the hospital and slowed the bleeding, he told us that our baby had died.

Leaving the hospital that night with empty arms was one of the hardest things I've ever done. When we arrived home, we found our two baby daughters asleep on our bed. Now, I'd always loved my daughters but never quite as I did at that moment.

"Thank you, God," I whispered. "They are alive. It is such a miracle to have a child who is alive."

Several days later when I went out to check on our front lawn of weeds, I found something I hope I never forget. If I got down on my hands and knees and took out a magnifying glass, I could see tiny green blades of grass so fine they looked like green sewing thread. All my watering was starting to pay off. It occurred to me that perhaps all the work involved in caring for a family was like our newly seeded lawn. It seems to be all work and weeds at first. It's hard to see the tender seedlings or take joy in their growing. But in time my children, like the lawn, will not require my constant care, and our mutual growing season in my home will have passed all too quickly.

So let's not put off living and loving and laughing. The joy of life is in the ride. So stop waiting. Eat more ice cream, go barefoot, watch more sunsets, laugh more, cry less, let out a few screams, and get into the adventure of it. Let's quit viewing life as a long, hard, uphill ride to the ultimate destination of heaven. I'm sure heaven will be wonderful, but so is life right now. There is more joy and wonder right here in our own lives than we are willing or able to enjoy. Just think . . . all this and heaven, too!

BECOMING A DISCIPLE OF CHRIST

c◯◯◯∘

Marilyn S. Bateman

From the beginning of time, God has reserved choice lands and promised great blessings for his righteous followers. In the Book of Mormon, the prophet Lehi speaks of a land of promise, a land that is choice above all other lands (see 1 Nephi 2:20). Lehi's journey with his family to the promised land is symbolic of our journey through life to our promised land. Ultimately, it is our return to the land in which God and his Son, Jesus Christ, dwell.

To receive an inheritance in the heavenly city of God, we must learn how to put off the "natural man" and "[yield] to the enticings of the Holy Spirit" (Mosiah 3:19) while journeying through the wilderness of mortality. We must "search diligently in the light of Christ . . . and . . . lay hold upon every good thing" (Moroni 7:19) so the Spirit will bear a personal witness to us of the truth of all things. The Good Shepherd will call us (see Alma 5:38), and if we put aside the things of the world, we will hear his voice and follow him. We will become one of his disciples.

In our journey to this land of the heavenly city, whose builder and maker is God, we will encounter many obstacles and challenges. There will be ruts and holes of grief and despair, rivers of tears, and mountains of sorrow, and each person will travel a different road. Each must blaze her own trail. My sister-in-law Maryland Scholes writes:

"We are the solitary pioneer of our own lives.

"No one has journeyed our path before us.

"No one began the trek with our particular assets and liabilities.

"No one will endure our exact set of hardships.

"No one has challenged our meanest enemies or stilled the terror of our darkest moments.

"Only we can struggle toward our own frontier—and our own safety and our own personal promised land."

But we need not travel the road alone. President Gordon B. Hinckley

Marilyn S. Bateman, wife of Brigham Young University president Merrill J. Bateman, is a mother and grandmother. She has served in leadership and teaching positions in ward and stake auxiliaries. The Batemans are the parents of seven children.

entreats us to develop a "simple faith, an unquestioning conviction, that the God of Heaven in his power will make all things right and bring to pass his eternal purposes in the lives of his children."[1]

When we believe that we "can do all things through Christ" (Philippians 4:13), our burdens will become lighter, and we will find that "peace of God, which passeth all understanding" (v. 7) as we travel the road in the fellowship of our brothers and sisters in the gospel.

In 1843, my great-great-grandparents James Lewis Burnham and Mary Ann Huntley Burnham, along with their four little children, joined the Saints in Nauvoo, Illinois. James and Mary Ann had joined the Church earlier that year while living in Beaure County, Illinois. James had been a minister of the Christian church, but upon hearing the "good news" of the gospel he could only acknowledge that he had no authority to preach. He and his wife, Mary Ann, were baptized into The Church of Jesus Christ of Latter-day Saints. He preached and advocated its doctrine faithfully until the day he died.

James and Mary Ann's youngest child, a little girl named Maria Antoinette, died the year after their arrival in Nauvoo. At the time, James was also failing in health: he was afflicted with a lung disease. Nevertheless, he labored quarrying rock for the Nauvoo Temple. He and Mary Ann were anxiously looking forward to the temple being completed so that they could receive their endowments and be sealed together for eternity.

In the summer of 1845, James's health grew worse. In October, he passed away. His death preceded the birth of another baby daughter by four days. That daughter, Mary Ann Burnham Freeze, later wrote: "This was a trying time for my mother, being left in sorrow and destitute of all worldly goods. She had no relatives near to help her. But the Saints were very kind to her in her afflictions. Her relatives in the East would gladly have sent means to take her back but it was no temptation to her. She had cast her lot with the Saints of God and would rather remain with them in poverty than have the wealth of the whole world elsewhere."[2]

In February 1846, the famous exodus from Nauvoo began. Mary Ann had no means to move herself and her family from the city, so they remained while the mob took over Nauvoo. They were then forced to leave or lose their lives. She received a wagon in exchange for her city property, was lent a yoke of cattle, and began that memorable, toilsome journey with her four young children. She later told of the mob searching their wagon for arms, the obscene language that they used, and how terribly she suffered from fear. She arrived in Winter Quarters late in the fall of 1846 and remained there for a year and a half. Then she, along with others, was compelled by the government to move back to the east side of the river out of Indian Territory.

In the depths of poverty, she let Brother Daniel Wood take her second son, Wallace, who was ten (and who is my great-grandfather), and her third son, George, who was eight, to the Valley with him. This was a severe trial for Mary Ann. She was separated from her young sons for five years because it wasn't until 1852 that she was able to start her trek west. Through the kindness and help of some of the brethren and sisters, she was finally able to cross the plains with the rest of her children. They arrived in Salt Lake City on 8 October 1852.

As I think of Mary Ann's life, my heart confirms the truth of Elder M. Russell Ballard's observation regarding our early pioneers: "Each wagon and handcart was heavily laden with faith—faith in God, faith in the Restoration of His Church through the Prophet Joseph Smith, and faith that God knew where they were going and that He would see them through."[3] My pioneer forebears paid a heavy price for their discipleship. But they came to know their Savior.

In January 1847, while the Saints were at Winter Quarters preparing to begin their westward journey, the Lord told the prophet Brigham Young: "My people must be tried in all things, that they may be prepared to receive the glory that I have for them, even the glory of Zion" (D&C 136:31).

Much the same message has always been given to the children of God. In Isaiah 48:10 we read: "I have refined thee, but not with silver; I have chosen thee in the furnace of affliction." Elder Orson F. Whitney many years ago said: "No pain that we suffer, no trial that we experience is wasted. It ministers to our education, to the development of such qualities as patience, faith, fortitude and humility. All that we suffer and all that we endure, especially when we endure it patiently, builds up our characters, purifies our hearts, expands our souls, and makes us more tender and charitable, more worthy to be called the children of God . . . and it is through sorrow and suffering, toil and tribulation, that we gain the education that we come here to acquire and which will make us more like our Father and Mother in heaven."[4]

So often the things that teach us the most and give us the greatest insights into God's ways happen while we are struggling. If we turn to

God for strength, feelings and sure knowledge pour into our thinking through the light that quickens our understanding. Recently I was pondering how I could be a better friend to my mother. She is a great lady, very active and healthy, living an independent life. But she is alone. My father died a number of years ago, and she has become widowed again in recent years. Loneliness is her greatest challenge.

As I was thinking about my mother, I felt a great sorrow for the difficult life she has had. She was only three when her mother died and nine when her father passed away. She was sent to live with an aunt who was kind but not motherly to her. My mother has been forced to fend for herself throughout most of her life.

As I thought about this, I knew that the Lord is aware of the trials Mother has endured and that he loves her. I also became aware that my grandmother felt great sorrow that she hadn't been able to mother and nurture her daughter in her growing years. I felt my grandmother's presence, and it was made known to me that as I loved and cared for my mother (her daughter), so my grandmother would be by my side and care and watch over me throughout my life.

In this life, we can have help from both sides of the veil. The Lord tells us in the scriptures: "I will go before your face. I will be on your right hand and on your left, . . . and mine angels [will be] round about you, to bear you up" (D&C 84:88).

If we remain true and faithful to the gospel of Jesus Christ and endure to the end, the Lord tells us that the promised land will be ours. The blessings and the riches of eternity will be our inheritance (see D&C 78:18). It is through meeting the challenges of our mortal journey that we become disciples of Christ. As we put our trust in him, he will bless us according to our faith. As we go through pains, sicknesses, afflictions, and temptations of every kind, our Savior will be there to succor us. He has paid the price through his atoning sacrifice to know us and to know how to help us. He knows how to deliver us safely back home. He is our Deliverer—our all!

Notes

1. Gordon B. Hinckley, "Faith of the Pioneers," *Ensign*, July 1984, 6.
2. Burnham family records in possession of author.
3. M. Russell Ballard, *Ensign*, May 1997, 60.
4. Orson F. Whitney, as quoted in Spencer W. Kimball, *Tragedy or Destiny*, Brigham Young University Speeches of the Year (Provo, 6 December 1955), 7.

"UNTO THE LEAST
OF THESE MY BRETHREN"

Stacey Bess

About eleven years ago, I began a career that changed my life forever. At age twenty-three, I had just earned a degree in elementary education—mostly to humor my mother and my husband. I had absolutely no intention of teaching school. I had been a stay-at-home mom since I was seventeen years old, and I liked it that way. But my mother kept urging me, "Honey, you are so young, and young marriages often don't work out. Just get a degree you can fall back on if you need to." So I enrolled at the University of Utah. Two days after I graduated, in the middle of winter, my husband said, "Honey, just go to the Salt Lake City School District and turn in your resume. It's the middle of the school year. They're not going to hire you." My mom, who was visiting, nodded, "No, they won't hire you." My response was, "Mom, I really want to rock my children like you did yours." My mom had brought a rocking chair over from England and had rocked all seven of her children in that chair. Even as adults, we still go home, climb into that chair, and feel loved by her.

That was the legacy I wanted to pass on to my children. But mostly to get Mom and Greg off my case, I went to the Salt Lake City School District. In my mind I could hear Mom saying, "They won't hire you. Don't worry. It's the middle of the school year." I walked into the building and handed my resume to the secretary. She looked up at me, checked the paperwork, smiled, and said, "Honey, you are young." I said, "Yeah."

She looked down at my paperwork again. "You graduated two days ago?" Again I answered, "Yeah." She chuckled. "Well, it is the middle of the school year, and we're just about ready for Christmas break. We don't have any job opportunities, but it looks like you did your student teaching in a neat place, you have pretty good grades, and we'll consider you in

---

Stacey Bess taught at the school for homeless children in Salt Lake City for eleven years. Author of the book *Nobody Don't Love Nobody*, she speaks throughout the country on service, children, and making a difference in the community. She and her husband, Greg, have four children, who range in age from eighteen to two. She serves as advisor to the Mia Maids in her ward.

33

the summer." I shook her hand and thought with relief, "Yes! I'm going home." As I headed toward the glass double doors in the district offices, a reflection caught my eye. Right behind me a very large gentleman was walking out of his office. "Miss Bess," he called, "come here." I turned and saw the sign above his door: Personnel Director, Assistant Superintendent. I followed him into his office and sat down. He stared intently at my paperwork. "You're young," he noted.

"Yes."

"Did you really graduate two days ago?"

"Yes."

"Would you like to be a teacher?"

I lied. "Yes."

He sat for a long time and then told me about a job opening at a school with no name, but I really wasn't listening because I wanted to stay home with my children. Finally he said, "Miss Bess, it is the middle of the school year. We don't have any other opening, but I will put your paperwork right on top. And in the summer, we will call you back."

Elated, I shook his hand and grabbed the door handle. Then this gentleman changed my life forever. He said, "Miss Bess, sit down."

I turned. "Sir, did I do something wrong?"

He said, "No, but I'm about to."

I sat down again, slowly. "What?" I asked.

"Miss Bess, I am not supposed to do this, but I am going to offer you a job."

I was terrified. I looked down and noticed that my hands were shaking, so I sat on them so he wouldn't see. "Oh, Stacey," I said to myself, "don't cry in your first real job interview."

I swallowed over and over. "Sir, where do you want me to go?"

"Miss Bess, I'd like you to teach at the school for the homeless."

I lost the battle with my tears. The only thing I could get out of my mouth was, "Dr. Anderson,[1] I'm trained to be an elementary school teacher. I'm not trained to teach grown-ups." He laughed. "Miss Bess, two, three, sometimes four hundred homeless children pass through this one school in a year."

I said, "Really?"

And I lied again: I promised him I'd think about the job. I shook his hand, and then I walked down the long hall to the parking lot. There I climbed into my car, held onto the steering wheel, and sobbed. All the way home, I'm embarrassed to say, I closed my eyes at stop signs and red lights and said to my Heavenly Father, "How dare you! How dare you send me there. I have no proven skills. I've never taught anywhere. How dare you do this to me!" Then I remembered my husband and my mother were in on it. I pulled into the driveway and saw my very sweet husband watching for me from the living room window. I was mad. I swung open the screen door just as he opened the front door. He looked at my face, smeared with tears and mascara, and said, "Oh, honey, you got a job, didn't you?"

"Yes, I did," and I sat him down on the couch and told him what I knew and how I felt about the homeless. He agreed, "No, I can't send you there, Stacey. We both know what it's like as you get off the Sixth South viaduct." Prostitutes and drug dealers. Mothers pushing carts. It's awful. "No, honey, you don't have to go there," he said.

I climbed into bed that night reassured that no one would ask me to take that job. About 2:30 in the morning, I woke up, tossing and turning, and couldn't go back to sleep for almost an hour. At 4:00 A.M. I woke up again, my heart pounding. After about four days of these night terrors, I got the message. My subconscious was saying, "Pay attention!" So I got up and knelt by the living room couch. I let go of my rebellious anger. This time, instead of telling my Heavenly Father what I would or wouldn't do, I listened for a very long time. I remember saying, "Heavenly Father, why me? I'm just a kid. I don't have any skills."

After the longest time, the answer came back, "You have been prepared for a lifetime. It is not your skills I am after. It is who you are inside."

I told Greg the following morning that I was going to take the job. Then I called Dr. Anderson and accepted.

He said, "I knew you would. Be there on January 3. The school is under the Sixth South viaduct. It doesn't have an address. You'll know it when you see it."

On my first day, I drove down the wrong side of the road under the viaduct. When I got to the end, I couldn't see any evidence of a school. What I did see were twelve boxcars in a row and railroad tracks everywhere. I was lost. I started to turn back when I noticed a line of cars parked bumper to bumper under the bridge. Puzzled because there were no businesses around, I watched for a minute. Car engines turned on and then tiny fingers rubbed fog from the windows. I was stunned. Families were sleeping in those cars—in Salt Lake City, Utah. Suddenly a small boy jumped out of one of the boxcars. I started to roll the window down. As he ran in front of my parked car, our eyes met, and he looked at me with the most horrid, hate-filled eyes. I froze. As I was trying to absorb that experience, out of nowhere a man tapped on my passenger window. He had two teeth, and a big hunk of scrambled egg hung from the side of his long beard. I screamed. Realizing that he had terrified me, he ran around to my side where the window was partly down and said, "Ma'am, are you lost?"

"I think so."

His beautiful blue eyes—the most beautiful I've ever seen—came to life, and he said, "Ma'am, are you the new schoolteacher?"

I couldn't lie. "Yes," I said.

He pulled open my car door and said, "Come on. People here are dying to meet you. Let me help you."

I handed him my briefcase, my open purse with a few dollar bills kind of hanging out, and my wire basket. Like a perfect gentleman, he helped me out of my car and wrapped his arm around me. "Ma'am, could I teach you how to live on the streets?"

I said, "Sure."

He said, "First of all, ma'am, don't ever give all your belongings to a total stranger." He looked me up and down. "You are a might bit proper. I have no idea why you're here." Then he pointed to my car and said, "Never leave your windows rolled down or your car doors unlocked."

I said, "Okay."

This lovely gentleman's name was Joe. Pointing to a battered aluminum shed, he said, "Always go directly to your school. Do your teaching and go home." But then Joe walked me in the opposite direction from the shed. After about forty feet, I started to get nervous. "Joe, where are we going?"

"Shhh. Follow me," he answered.

I did what he said. That naïve twenty-three-year-old followed a homeless man. I will be honest. I was so frightened I could hardly walk. We got to the far side of the viaduct where fifteen adults huddled around a fire. Gretchen, Jim's wife, was the cook. She opened their circle, welcomed me in, and lovingly wrapped her arm around me. "Honey," she said, "you're shaking. Are you cold?"

I lied, "Yes." I was terrified, not cold.

She said, "Honey, what is your name?" I told her. Then she introduced me to each of the mothers and fathers in the circle. Each told a bit about their child. Mostly it was something naughty, but each one, in their own way, said to me, "Please, love my child." Not one of them asked if I was a good reading teacher or if I knew a lot about math.

As I readied myself to go greet my new classroom, Gretchen held me against her and said, "Honey, I've just got one question. Where did you use to teach before?"

All eyes were on me. I looked down at the fire because I was so embarrassed. "Nowhere, Gretchen. I've never taught anywhere before."

She said, "Honey, you ain't going nowhere but up. You've started at the bottom."

I was sure that the Lord had sent me there, but it took all of the courage I had that first day to walk into my classroom and see the filth and sadness and loss and the toddlers picking stuff off the floor and eating it. Thirty-five children crowded in a corner around one boy who was entertaining them. "Ladies and gentleman," I cleared my throat, "my name is Stacey, and I'm your new teacher. Take your seats." They didn't move. The boy in the corner kept talking, and they kept laughing and listening intently to him. After I had called them to order three times, that very powerful young man finally said, "She's ready. Take your seats."

I was dying to see who was in the center of that attentive circle. As everyone took their seats, I discovered a beautiful, eleven-year-old young man named Zachary, the same boy who had earlier given me that withering glare in front of my car. He sat in the back of the class. I introduced myself with a scrapbook I had assembled for that purpose. I turned the pages, showing them pictures of my family and things that I loved. Then I got to my all-time three favorites, the three C's. "The first C is chocolate cake." I smiled at them. "Not in order, of course. My second C is children." No one smiled. "The third C," I told them, "is Diet Coke and, yeah, that might have been first." Still no one smiled. Suddenly a mouse scurried out from under the cupboard, ran across the floor, and raced across my feet. I screamed, climbed up on a little stool, and leaned against the chalkboard. I think I even swore. I'm not terribly proud of that, but, after all, a mouse *did* run across my feet. No one moved except Zachary. In the back of the room, with a ruler, he tap-tap-tapped on his desk.

The next day was no different. Day after day I faced this painful world and every night I went home crying. I complained to my family, "No one should have to endure these people. No one should have to see the sadness and the loss and the emptiness."

"Just get through the month, honey," Greg comforted me. "Then you can quit."

Hardest of all, at the end of every day Zachary would catch me by the door and shove me against the wall. "Go home, Proper. You don't belong here."

I watched and cried and cried and watched, and one day I had had enough. I called Zachary into my classroom after school. "Zachary, I need to talk."

He sat in my chair, put his feet up on my desk, turned his baseball cap sideways, and said, "Whadda ya want?"

I said, "Zachary, I'm having a hard time here. Help me. Just answer one question. Why do you hate me so much?"

He said, "Miss Stacey, please don't take it personal. I'm sure you're a fine teacher, but I hate all women."

I said, "That isn't fair, Zachary. I came that way."

"Miss Stacey, look over at the wall and imagine something. You're three or four years old, and your momma lines up all her kids. If she points to you, you look enough like her, and she keeps you. If you don't, she doesn't. I didn't. I love my daddy, Stacey, but he goes to different cities every year. You know, sometimes I've been in different schools seven times in one year. I have loved a lot of people, but then I always have to leave. I've decided never to trust anyone again." He took my hand. "I bet you're a good teacher, but I will not trust you." Then he left.

When I went home that night, I told my family about Zach. Nichole said, "Mom, don't worry about teaching him any math or reading or spelling. Just teach him about love and trust. Show him that people follow through when they say they will." What Nichole didn't know was that I didn't want to teach about trust. I didn't want to follow through. I wanted to get through the month and quit. But her words haunted me all that night, and the following morning I told him, "Zachary, I will stay. I want you to know that I want to leave, but I will stay and be the one person in your life who will prove to you that there are people who do love, who do stay. I will stay for you and for all the other Zacharys who pass through my school this year."

He laughed. "Sure you will."

For three months Zachary and I built a very sweet relationship. In fact,

I was starting to fall in love with these people who filled my days. Then I received frightening news from my doctor. I had cancer in my neck, and it had to be removed right away.

I said, "Oh, Dr. Swenson, not now when I'm just falling in love with these people. I'm just catching on."

He said, "You'll go back. I don't know how far the cancer has traveled, but tell them that you will be back."

I sat on the floor in my classroom one morning with twenty-five students sitting against me, feeling my neck and rubbing their hands on my cheeks. But not Zachary. He sat in the back drumming rhythmically with his ruler. When everybody left, I grabbed his arm and pulled him towards me. "Don't touch me," he said bitterly. "You lied. I was trusting you and loving you and now you're leaving." I could have talked with this kid forever and it would not have helped.

When Greg and I went into the hospital, Dr. Swenson had said to Greg, "Please do not bring your young children. We'll be moving her from the surgery center into the recovery area, then into another recovery area, and finally to the cancer floor."

I was coming to after the surgery and had a trachea tube down my throat. My mother had told the staff that I was a fighter, so my arms were restrained. My leaden eyelids were still closed, but I could feel a drip-drip on my chest. The anesthesia kept me from thinking clearly, but my brain was shouting, *I'm bleeding, and no one's doing anything.* Then I heard giggling and talking, and I got angry. *You're all having a party, and I'm bleeding!* I thought. I listened more carefully and could hear my husband at the head of my bed and my mother near my wrists. I also heard an unfamiliar voice, a child's voice, that haunted me terribly, but I couldn't make out the words. I began shaking, and my mother held my hands very tightly. "Stacey, open your eyes and look straight up."

With effort I blinked and saw my dear friend Zach, who had bribed an orderly with five bucks and had broken onto the recovery area floor. There he stood over me, big tears splashing down onto my bandages. "Zachary," the doctor cautioned, "if you don't quit crying over her, we'll have to change the bandage."

The nurse pulled the tube out of my throat (I do not remember any of this) and I said, "Zachary, what are you doing out of school?"

"Teacher," he answered, "you told me you loved me, and I believed you. I came here today to make sure they keep you with us."

Zachary's arms were filled with wrapped and tagged presents. "Zachary, where did you get the gifts?"

"I just got them. That's all you need to worry about."

I fear that we have hosted many stolen gifts in our home. Zachary, now nineteen, is a remarkable, fascinating human being. He and I still talk on the phone quite often. Of course, he always calls collect. We have not cured him of that. He lives on the island of Kauai, in Hawaii, where he owns his own business. He has lived with us on and off for a few weeks at a time. One night just before I flew to Tennessee to address the National Association of Professor Educators (professors who train teachers), we talked. Nothing excites me more than teaching professors what teachers need to know to teach children better.

"Zach," I said, "I will tell them what you would like me to tell them. Why have you stayed so connected to me? What was it about my school that caused you never to forget us?"

"I don't know."

"Was I good teacher?"

"I don't know."

"Well, was I a good math teacher?"

"Did you teach math?"

I finally gave up on that concept. At the end of the phone call, as I do with each of my students or family members that call home, I said, "Zachary, I love you."

For about thirty long seconds, he didn't say anything. Then he answered, "That's what I want you to tell the people. You loved me. And when I was faced with life's choices of whether to be a success or not, I kept hearing your voice, 'I love you.'"

That night I kept waking up. My husband patted me and said, "That was a good thing, honey. Go to sleep. That was a good thing."

Zachary is still a very successful young man by my standards. I don't know whether he will experience homelessness again, but he has never forgotten the principle that I hold so dearly, that Christ holds so dearly: "Love one another."

My second school friend debunked every concept I ever had about homeless children. Children who have experienced loss build walls around themselves. To reach them you must creatively and tenderly chip away at their defenses, sometimes for weeks, sometimes for months. Not Alex.

I first met Alex at the bottom of the stairs as I went through the alarmed doors to meet my class. I very cautiously put out my right hand to hold his and said, "Hello, Alex. My name is Stacey. I will be your new teacher."

He yanked my hand, pulled me towards him, and said, "Wow, you're beautiful!"

His sweet brother, Anthony, standing behind him, was bashful and very embarrassed. I said to him, "It's okay."

We climbed to the first landing on the stairs. Again Alex took my hand, swung me around, and said, "I gotta tell you something else. You've got the greatest brown eyes I've ever seen."

Anthony was ready to have a nervous breakdown at that point. "It's okay. He's all right," I reassured him.

At the top of the stairs, Alex grabbed me by the hand one more time. "I'll go to class after I tell you one more thing."

"All right, one more thing."

"I have been kicked out of every school I have ever been in."

"You haven't!"

Anthony nodded his head. Alex continued, "Miss Stacey, I have a problem."

I wanted to say, "Oh, really?" But I responded evenly, "You do?"

"Yes. I have a problem with these don't-be-a-kid rules. Things like 'Shut up' and 'Sit down' and 'Don't bug your neighbor.'"

"Yeah?"

"Do you have those in your school?"

"Well, if I'm talking, I would like you to listen."

"Listen to me for a minute," he said. "Do you like to talk?"

"Yes, that's why I'm a teacher."

"So do kids. And if you listened more, you would learn more. Miss Stacey, do you like to sit still?"

"No, Alex. When I'm talking before an audience, I walk back and forth like a wild animal. I can't sit still."

"Neither can we."

I am so grateful that my homeless students don't sit at chairs or in assigned seats. I can let them move around wherever they want as long as they are learning.

Then he asked the most important question. "Miss Stacey, is there anybody in your life that you just love to bug?"

"Yeah, I'm married to him." Something told me that Alex would appreciate my latest prank. "Alex, I'm going to tell you what my two older children and I did the other night. We got a big, two-gallon pitcher of water and put it in the fridge. The next morning, when we could hear Dad singing in the shower, we tip-toed into the bathroom and poured ice-cold water all over him."

"Could I just ask you one question? Was he naked? Did he chase you?"

"Well, Alex," I said, wondering where this might lead, "he did. Wouldn't you run, if you had ice-cold water poured all over you?"

"I like you," he said.

We went into class and sat down on the floor. We were very late, and my teaching partner was just beginning "Jam Session." Jam Session is the students' time to say whatever they want, and I mean *whatever*. Alex's eyes got bigger and bigger as he listened. When we finished, he pulled me up off the floor, "Don't call this Jam Session anymore. I want you to call this Kid Power."

"Why?"

He said, "Grownups think *power* for kids is a dirty word. But if we had power, and you taught us how to use it, we wouldn't be trying to take it all the time."

He was right. I had just sat through a psychiatrist's session on teaching kids to use their power. I said, "Okay, we'll call it Kid Power now."

He went on, "My brother Joe tells me that I don't need an alarm clock. He'll be the alarm clock. To wake me up in the morning, he slugs me on the side of the head. At home I have no power. I will come to your class with no power, but I will expect it when I'm there."

I realized I was dealing with a very strong little spirit who had much to teach but who was also very damaged. Every day while I taught at the fifth-grade table, he would go over to the snack cupboard, look at me, almost daring me to watch, and take some food, which he put inside his clothing—in the cuffs of his socks, in pants pockets, up shirt sleeves. After two weeks of watching, I said, "Alex, we've got a little problem."

"Yes, we do. You've let me steal from you."

I knew why he was stealing. In our classroom we call it "creative taking" because we know why the children do it. Our job is to teach them to get past their loss so they understand why they take things. I said, "Alex, why do you steal food?"

"Miss Stacey, I don't eat what I take," he answered. "When I put the food against my body, it takes the emptiness away."

I knew that. I made a deal with him: "I will teach you how to get rid of emptiness and loss if you will keep your hands out of my cupboard." The other part of the deal was he could have the grand prize at the end of two weeks if he dealt with loss properly. You see, homeless children go through loss maybe seven times a year; you and I, seven times in a lifetime.

Alex was marvelous. For two weeks, he would come up to me and say, "I am empty," and I would hug him. Or he would come into class and say, "Joe's outside. He hit me this morning. Please go out and talk with him," and I would go out into the hall and very quietly say, "Joe, I'll beat the snot out of you if you touch him again." His brother Joe would smile and say, "I'm sorry. I know you love him," and it would stop for a little while.

At the end of two weeks, Alex said, "All right, I'm ready for the grand prize. I've been talking to my buddies, and I know that I can have just about anything, right?"

"Well, within reason."

"Good. Do you know who Karl Malone is?"

"Yeah, I know who he is."

"Well, I'm moving in two weeks, and I want to meet him."

"Oh, Alex, I only know *who* he is—but I will try."

"If anybody can do it, you can."

That night I called my friend Judy, who works with a volunteer group that had some connections to the Jazz office, and through much prayer and a beautiful letter to Mr. Malone, Alex and I were standing in the school lobby within about forty-eight hours of sending the letter. Alex was on the left, I was on the right. We were holding hands. I was shaking so violently Alex leaned over to me and said, "Knock it off."

"I'm nervous. Look at him."

"Teacher, he is a regular guy."

As I approached Karl Malone, my nose was level with his belt buckle. I offered him my hand. "Mr. Malone, my name is Stacey Bess. Thank you so much for coming to our school. Please come upstairs and give my students the talk that I've heard you give about staying in school."

After a long silence, he taught me an incredible lesson. "I have followed your career, and you should know better," he said. "Please do not hold me to a 'stay in school speech.' Don't let me hide behind my uniform, behind a podium, or behind my stardom. Let me come today and be Uncle Karl. Let me give your students what they truly need. Me."

I followed him into my classroom, leaned against the bookcases, and could not stop crying. He teased me relentlessly. Then I watched twenty-five little bodies climb all over him as he sat down on the floor. They took off his shoes and socks, measured his feet, his toes, and from his wrists to his elbows. And he loved them. He didn't care about the lice. He didn't care about the hepatitis or the tuberculosis. Like Christ would have, he sat on the floor and loved them. Only two times I got a little nervous. Little Curtis was looking at Karl's hand and I thought, "He's panicked about something." He turned it over and back, looking at one side and then the other. "Mr. Malone, one side of your hand is darker than the other." I just about swallowed my tongue.

Mr. Malone looked from me to Curtis. "Honey, when I sunbathe I just forget to flip over."

At one point Alex and Curtis were each on a leg, running their fingers through his beautiful, textured hair. Alex and Curtis have very fine, silky hair. I walked over and said, "Guys, let's give Mr. Malone just a little bit of space, shall we?"

A very large finger pointed in my direction. "You, go stand over by the bookcases and don't move."

I did what he said, which was so unlike me. Then I watched as they got to his mustache, each on one side. As they moved toward his nose I thought, "If they put their fingers in his nose, I will have a heart attack right here."

When Mr. Malone went to leave, he wrapped his arms around them, held them tight, and said, "I love you."

Alex, at age thirteen, has come back to my school. He didn't care about his cute teacher. The very first question he asked was, "Do you think Karl Malone still thinks I'm way bad?"—which is current slang for "way good." "You bet he does," I said. "You bet he still loves you."

People often ask me, "Don't you get sick when you have to walk past all those homeless grownups?" I don't because I have had the luxury of knowing them, of loving them. Every homeless adult who crosses my path has a story. Their stories tell me that their homelessness is due to being deprived of love and to devastating childhood experience. It is not a money issue. Being abused and deprived of love is a primary cause of homelessness.

My dear friend Sarah is the meanest, foulest-mouthed human being I have ever met. We were told when we moved into a new shelter, "Just steer clear of Sarah." One day I heard a loud, bellowing voice at the front desk swearing in the foulest language I had ever heard. It was early, before school was to start, so I came out of my classroom to see what was going on. It was Sarah demanding a coat. It was cold. The woman at the desk said, "No, Sarah, you live at the women's shelter. We help only *families* at the family shelter." Fuming, I walked over to the front desk and grabbed Sarah by the arm. "I have a coat, and I can give it to you."

"Who are you?" she asked

"I am the teacher."

"Is the coat good looking?" she demanded.

"I think so."

She came into my room and slammed the door shut. I was alone with Sarah! I had been warned. But I picked up the white, furry coat and draped it over her shoulders from behind. When she turned, I exclaimed, "Wow, you're beautiful!"

Tears rolled down her cheeks. "Nobody ain't never said that to me before. *You* are my friend."

I'm not sure if that was a curse or a blessing, because for the next seven or eight months she was my friend, and oh, was she my friend! I'll never forget two experiences. Once I was running down the sidewalk, late for school. She was running toward me with a vase of flowers. Two of my homeless friends came running to save me because we never know what Sarah will do. She plopped the vase down on my very pregnant tummy and said, "These are for you. I stole them."

"You didn't."

"Yes, I was walking past the nurse's station at the University Hospital, and I lifted them off the station, and no one said a word."

I wanted to say, "Honey, no one would dare say a word to you."

I could hear my male friends standing behind me, scoffing, "They're dead. Tell her they're dead."

I elbowed Kenny behind me and shot him a look: *Open your mouth one more time and you die.* Then I turned and kissed and hugged her. "Sarah, thank you."

As I walked into the shelter, Kenny said, "Why didn't you tell her those flowers were dead?"

"Kenny," I said, "Sarah has learned the most important lesson you ever learn in life: *I owe you back.* Sarah never knew that before. I gave her something as simple as a coat, and now she knows that she owes people."

Another day I was again racing in late. Sarah was sitting on the sidewalk, crying. I said, "Sarah, I'm late! But what's the matter? Do you need a hug?"

She said, "I can't bend over and get the medicine on my legs, and I need to put it on."

"I'll do it," I instantly offered. That was rash of me because I was pregnant and very prone to losing my breakfast.

When I lifted up her pant leg, I saw several ghastly, open wounds. I always keep rubber gloves in my bag because of the needles I find everywhere. As I put them on, I closed my eyes and thought, *Heavenly Father, don't let me throw up all over her. Just let me do this.* Through my mind flashed, *This is what the Savior did. He could feel just as sick as I do right now, yet he went to the poor and the suffering, and he served and he loved.* I had two minutes to put on that ointment and get out of there. I finished, hurried around the corner, and threw up all over. Once inside, I did not say a word to my teaching partner until she noticed my swollen eyes. She asked, "What's wrong? Did Sarah beat up on you?"

"No, I just had a neat experience," I said and told her about putting the ointment on Sarah's legs. I didn't tell her that I had prayed. When she looked thoughtfully at me and said, "That's what the Savior did, Stacey," it was another confirmation. I am where God wants me to be.

And what about my own children? There is nothing more painful than being away from them. But I know that the Lord knows that I am doing what is right. He has looked after us. Before I gave birth to my sweet McKenzie, I decided that I was going to quit, but I wasn't going to tell anyone. For eight years I had waited for this baby, and I was determined to rock her. As I left the shelter for the final time before my scheduled delivery day, I was greeted by Sarah and her anger. She grabbed me fiercely. Pressing up against me, she said, "I hate you."

"Why?"

"You are walking away, and you are not even saying good-bye." She was right. I was. I was going off to rock my babies. She said, "Before you leave I want you never to forget what I am going to tell you. Look into my eyes."

I looked into her irate, bloodshot eyes. She continued, "I want you to see the little girl that lives inside of me. The little girl that no one ever took the time to love, that no one ever took the time to reach, and no one ever took the time to teach. You are going to walk away from every little girl and boy that has a chance of turning out just like me. Before you have your baby, go lay your head down on the sidewalk and see if you hear the little girl that cries." As I tearfully walked away that day, she said, "You better think long and hard."

The following morning, I threw on my clothes without showering and grabbed my car keys. My husband sat up in bed, "Where are you going?"

I said, "I don't know, but I'll be back."

I drove all the way to the shelter. "What are you doing here?" my friend Jane said when I walked in. "You have a baby coming at 10:30."

I answered, "I don't know why. I couldn't sleep all night. I just needed to stand here for a few minutes."

"Well, as long as you're here, come back to the medical clinic. You can solve a problem."

I walked back to find dear Sarah. "Go ahead, Jane," Sarah demanded. "Tell her our plan." Jane is the one who picks lice out of my hair and gives me shots in the rear once a month so that I don't get hepatitis. She was the last person I would expect to say, "Stacey, we would like for you to strap your newborn baby to your chest and teach school."

I laughed. That was a ridiculous idea. But I smiled at Sarah. "I'll think about it," I promised.

On the way to the hospital, I said to my very conservative, proper husband, "I just want to pass an idea by you."

He said, "Over my dead body."

When McKenzie was four weeks old, I was sitting up in bed about 3:30 in the morning, unable to sleep. I kept saying to Heavenly Father, "Whose babies do I owe? You keep sending me these great children, and I feel like I need to be serving them; and yet I feel such a pull to the others."

I got up and grabbed a legal pad from my husband's nightstand. Maybe if I wrote down everything I had learned about these people, if I kept a family record, I would be able to let go. So, for eight hours I wrote like a fool. And for the next five or six days I kept adding to the stack of papers. When, after much prayer, I was sure I was finished, I walked to my husband, prepared to hand him the paperwork and say, "We have a family record of all the children who came to live with us while their parents were either in jail or rehab." Instead, I put the papers in his lap and out of my mouth poured, "Now you will understand why I must strap this baby to my chest and teach school."

My husband, who at the time was not very active in the Church, looked at me, with tears in his eyes, and said, "I knew the minute that crazy idea came out of your mouth that that was what you were to do. The writing process was to let you know that you weren't finished. But," he added, "I have one request. With all that I've known and all that I've seen, please don't let them hold my baby." I understood.

When I pulled up to the shelter my first day back, I strapped on my newborn with a prayer that my baby would be safe.

John, one of my very favorite people on the streets, is a beautiful black man who tells me every Valentine's Day, "I love you and please tell me that if I had done everything right, and you were single, you would marry me." I always tell him yes. He opened my car door, took a look at my sweet baby McKenzie, and said, "Wow, we did a great job, didn't we?"

Then he carried her into the shelter like a proud daddy and handed her to none other than my dear friend Sarah. Jane was standing behind Sarah mouthing, "Don't let her hold the baby." I had to, I absolutely had to. There was such a feeling inside of me that I owed this baby to these people. So, I took all the blankets off, held her sweet little body up to Sarah's neck, and I whispered, "Sarah, babies are unconditional love. They are a gift from God. Feel her. Smell her. Kiss her sweet skin."

McKenzie, being the great nurser that she was, began to suckle Sarah's skin. Sarah cried and cried as she kissed and loved and smelled. Then she began naming all of her own children who had been taken from her. She handed McKenzie back to me and said, "Your baby will do more for your students than you will ever do." I knew that was a compliment. And she was right. My sixth-grade boys, who are the coolest of the coolest, always told me, "I'll never touch your baby. I'll never have anything to do with your baby." But I caught them rocking her and singing to her. They would write lullabies at night, and as long as I wasn't watching, they would sing. Little Marie, whose job it was to walk her mommy and daddy safely back and forth to the liquor store every night, wrote this in her journal: "My teacher is funny. She really likes her baby. You can just tell by the way she kisses her all over and leaves lipstick marks all over her head. Watching her makes me happy." But at the bottom she added, "I wish somebody would have loved me like that when I was little."

In one short line, this lonely little girl summarized the longing, aching wish of every one of these homeless children—and every member of the human family—to be loved all over, to be loved completely, and to be loved unconditionally.

When we go home, I believe the Savior will ask, "Who did you love in my name?" And if we cannot name names, if we cannot look him in the eye, we will be sad.

Note

1. Except for Karl Malone, the names of people in this account have been changed to protect their privacy.

THE USES OF ADVERSITY

Carlfred Broderick

While I was a stake president, the event occurred that I want to use as the keynote to my remarks. I was sitting on the stand at a combined meeting of the stake Primary board and stake Young Women's board where they were jointly inducting from the Primary into the Young Women's organization the eleven-year-old girls who that year had made the big step. They had a lovely program. It was one of those fantastic, beautiful presentations—based on the *Wizard of Oz*, or a take-off on the *Wizard of Oz*, where Dorothy, an eleven-year-old girl, was coming down the yellow brick road together with the tin woodman, the cowardly lion, and the scarecrow. They were singing altered lyrics about the gospel. And Oz, which was one wall of the cultural hall, looked very much like the Los Angeles Temple. They really took off down that road. There were no weeds on that road; there were no Munchkins; there were no misplaced tiles; there was no Wicked Witch of the West. That was one antiseptic yellow brick road, and it was very, very clear that once they got to Oz, they had it made. It was all sewed up.

Following that beautiful presentation with all the snappy tunes and skipping and so on, came a sister who I swear was sent over from Hollywood central casting. (I do not believe she was in my stake; I never saw her before in my life.) She looked as if she had come right off the cover of a fashion magazine—every hair in place, with a photogenic returned missionary husband who looked like he came out of central casting and two or three, or heaven knows how many, photogenic children all of whom came out of central casting or Kleenex ads or whatever. She enthused over her temple marriage and how wonderful life was with her charming husband and her perfect children and that the young women too could look like her and have a husband like him and children like

Carlfred Broderick, professor of sociology and head of the marriage and family therapy program at the University of Southern California, received his B.A. from Harvard and his Ph.D. from Cornell University. He is a popular lecturer and the author of numerous books, including two textbooks. He has served in the Church as a bishop, stake president, and temple ordinance worker. He and his wife, Kathleen, are the parents of eight children.

them if they would stick to the yellow brick road and live in Oz. It was a lovely, sort of tear-jerking, event.

After the event was nearly over, the stake Primary president, who was conducting, made a grave strategic error. She turned to me and, pro forma, said, "President Broderick, is there anything you would like to add to this lovely evening?"

I said, "Yes, there is," and I don't think she has ever forgiven me. What I said was this, "Girls, this has been a beautiful program. I commend the gospel with all of its auxiliaries and the temple to you, but I do not want you to believe for one minute that if you keep all the commandments and live as close to the Lord as you can and do everything right and fight off the entire priests quorum one by one and wait chastely for your missionary to return and pay your tithing and attend your meetings, accept calls from the bishop, and have a temple marriage, I do not want you to believe that bad things will not happen to you. And when that happens, I do not want you to say that God was not true. Or, to say, 'They promised me in Primary, they promised me when I was a Mia Maid, they promised me from the pulpit that if I were very, very good, I would be blessed. But the boy I want doesn't know I exist, or the missionary I've waited for and kept chaste so we both could go to the temple turned out to be a flake,' or far worse things than any of the above. Sad things—children who are sick or developmentally handicapped, husbands who are not faithful, illnesses that can cripple, or violence, betrayals, hurts, deaths, losses—when those things happen, do not say God is not keeping his promises to me. The gospel of Jesus Christ is not insurance against pain. It is resource in event of pain, and when that pain comes (and it will come because we came here on earth to have pain among other things), when it comes, rejoice that you have a resource to deal with your pain."

Now, I do not want to suggest for a moment, nor do I believe, that God visits us with all that pain. I think that may occur in individual cases, but I think we fought a war in heaven for the privilege of coming to a place that was unjust. That was the idea of coming to earth—that it was unjust, that there would be pain and grief and sorrow. As Eve so eloquently said, it is better that we should suffer. Now, her perspective may not be shared by all. But, I am persuaded that she had rare insight, more than her husband, into the necessity of pain, although none of us welcome it.

I remember one time thinking such thoughts, such grand thoughts, and realizing that I dealt as a therapist with many people who suffered far, far more pain than I ever suffered and feeling guilty at having been spared some of the pain that my friends had experienced. Shortly after this, I developed a toothache. I'm a great chicken—I hate pain at all times. An apocryphal story was told of my mother who, as she took me to kindergarten, told the teacher I was very sensitive and, if I didn't behave, to hit the child next to me. Although that's not a true story, it truly represents my sentiments. I'll learn from others, although I don't want pain myself. So when I had this toothache, I thought here is a golden opportunity to embrace this existential experience and to join in this pain—open myself to this pain and experience it. I told myself I'm just going to sit in this pain and take it into myself and grow from it. That lasted forty-five minutes, at which time I called my dentist, "I want some pain medicine." The forty-five minutes it took between the time I took the medicine and the time the pain went away was the hardest part because I showed no moral stature, all I wanted was to get rid of that pain.

So I do not want you to think that I believe anything good about pain. I hate pain. I hate injustice. I hate loss. I hate all the things we all hate. None of us love those things. Nor, as I say, do I think God takes pleasure in the pain that comes to us. But, we came to a world where we are not protected from those things. I want to talk to you not in behalf of pain—heaven forbid—nor do I think that all pain is for the best. I'm certain that's not true. I'm certain pain destroys and embitters far more often than it ennobles. I'm sure injustice is destructive of good things in the world far more often than people rise above it. I'm certain that in this unjust awful world, there are far more victims that do not profit from their experience than those who do. So I do not want you to think I'm saying that pain is good for you. Pain is terrible.

I want to talk rather about when pain unbidden and unwanted and unjustly comes—to you or to those that you love or to these eleven-year-old girls as they get along in their lives. I want to discuss how to encounter that pain in such a way that it does not destroy you; how to find profit in that awful and unrewarding experience. I want to share with you some stories, mostly not my own, although I'm in all of them, but the pain is mainly someone else's. Some of the pain is my own. All of it is real, and all of it taught me. What I want is not to lecture to you or to sermonize you, but to share with you some lessons I have learned through pain, my own and others', that are valuable to me and, in the end, to share with you what I think I have learned from those incremental experiences.

The first two stories were extraordinarily instructive to me. They both came through opportunities I had as a stake president to give blessings. Often the Lord has taught me through blessings; as I've had my hands on someone's head, he's taught me things I did not know and sometimes didn't want to know. The first one was a case of a sister whom I'd known for years and who, in my judgment, had made some very poor life choices. She had married a handsome, charming young man who initially wasn't a member of the Church but joined the Church for her. She waited a year to marry him and then went to the temple. It was the last time he ever went to the temple. I knew he was a flake from the beginning. Out of my wisdom, it didn't surprise me that he soon returned to many of his pre-Church habits—most of the transgressions in the book that you can think of and some that I might not have.

There was great pain for this woman. A good, good woman, she kept in the Church; she kept in the kingdom; she suffered enormous pain because her husband went back to gambling and drinking and other things that were unhappy and unwholesome. But, the greater pain came when her children, having these two models before them, began to follow him. He would say things like, "Well, you can go to church with your mother and sit through three hours of you know what, or you can come to the racetrack with me, and we'll have good stuff to eat and drink and have a great time." It was a tough choice, and very often the children chose to go with him. They gradually seemed to adopt his life-style, values, and attitude toward the Church and toward sacred things. Although she never wavered from her own faith and faithfulness and her commitment to her Heavenly Father, her family was slipping away from her.

As she asked me for a blessing to sustain her in what to do with this awful situation in which she found herself, my thoughts were, *Didn't you ask for this? You married a guy who really didn't have any depth to him and raised your kids too permissively. You should have fought harder to keep them in church rather than letting them run off to racetracks.* I had all those judgments in my head. I laid my hands on her head, and the Lord told her of his love and his tender concern for her. He acknowledged that he had given her (and that she had volunteered for) a far, far harder task than he would like. (And, as he put in my mind, a harder task than I had had.

I have eight good kids, the last of whom just went to the temple. All would have been good if they had been orphans.) She, however, had signed up for hard children, for children who had rebellious spirits but who were valuable; for a hard husband who had a rebellious spirit but who was valuable. The Lord alluded to events in her life that I hadn't known about, but which she confirmed afterwards: twice Heavenly Father had given her the choice between life and death, whether to come home and be relieved of her responsibilities, which weren't going very well, or whether to stay to see if she could work them through. Twice on death's bed she had sent the messenger away and gone back to that hard task. She stayed with it.

I repented. I realized I was in the presence of one of the Lord's great noble spirits, who had chosen not a safe place behind the lines pushing out the ordinance to the people in the front lines as I was doing, but somebody who chose to live out in the trenches where the Lord's work was being done, where there was risk, where you could be hurt, where you could lose, where you could be destroyed by your love. That's the way she had chosen to labor. Then I thought, "I am unworthy to lay my hands on her head; if our sexes were reversed, she should have had her hands on mine."

Now she is doing well; one of her sons finally went on a mission. He had a bishop who took hold of him and shook him and got him to go. He went to one of those missions where people line up to be baptized when you get off the plane. He had a wonderful mission; they all but made an icon of him. He had miracles under his hands. He came back hotter than a firecracker for missions. He wouldn't leave alone his younger brother, who was planning on playing football in college instead of going on a mission, until he also went on a mission. The younger boy looked up to his brother; nobody could have turned that second kid around except his older brother. The younger went on a harder mission. He happened to have a language skill that he developed, and he turned out to be the best one at the language. He caught fire; he had spiritual experiences, and he came back red hot.

Those two boys started working with their sisters, who are harder cases; they haven't come all the way around yet. One of them looks bet-ter. One of them married a nonmember, and her husband did a terrible thing—he met the missionaries and joined the Church and started putting pressure on his wife to become active. She said, "I married you because you were out of the Church." I don't know—even Dad may repent, who knows? You know, she may yet win them all.

I know that she risked her life for service. In a blessing the Lord said to her, "When you're in my employ, the wages are from me, not from those you serve."

In the second case I had a woman who came to me who was an incest victim—the victim of a terrible family. She was abused physically. Her mother was neurotic and stayed in bed all the time to get her daughter to do all the work, including taking care of the husband's needs when he was drunk. The daughter had been abused in about every way there was to be abused—psychologically, physically, sexually.

She was not a member of the Church at that time, although this happens to members of the Church also. In high school she met a young man who was a Latter-day Saint and who started taking her to church with him. Eventually they married. He was gentle and kind and patient because she didn't come with very many positive attitudes toward men, marital intimacy, or many other things. But he was long-suffering and patient and loved her. They raised some boys.

Despite this, she had recurring bouts of depression and very negative feelings about herself because she had been taught by the people most important in her early life what a rotten person she was. It was hard for her to overcome that self-image. I worked with her to try to build her self-image. One day she said to me, "You're a stake president." She wasn't in my stake, but she said, "You're a stake president; you explain to me the justice of it." She said, "I go to church, and I can hardly stand it. When I see little girls being hugged and kissed and taken to church and appropriately loved by their fathers and mothers, I just have to get up and leave. I say, 'Heavenly Father, what was so terrible about me that, when I was that age, I didn't get any of that? What did that little girl do in the premortal existence that I didn't do so she is loved, so she is safe? Her daddy gives her priesthood blessings when she's sick. Her mother loves her and supports her and teaches her. What did I do? Can you tell me that God is just if he sends that little girl to that family and me to my family?" She said, "It's a good thing I had boys. I don't think I could have stood to raise girls and have their father love them because I'm so envious."

I would not have known how to answer her in my own capacity because that is manifestly unjust. Where, here or in eternity, is the justice in an innocent child's suffering in that way? But the Lord inspired me to tell her, and I believe with all my heart that it applies to many in the kingdom, that she was a valiant Christlike spirit who volunteered (with, I told her, perhaps too much spiritual pride) to come to earth and suffer innocently to purify a lineage. She volunteered to absorb the poisoning of sin, anger, anguish, and violence, to take it into herself and not to pass it on; to purify a lineage so that downstream from her it ran pure and clean, full of love and the Spirit of the Lord and self-worth. I believed truly that her calling was to be a savior on Mount Zion: that is, to be Savior-like, like the Savior to suffer innocently that others might not suffer. She voluntarily took such a task with the promise she would not be left alone and abandoned, but he would send one to take her by the hand and be her companion out into the light. I viewed that woman in a different way also, again realizing I was in the presence of one of the great ones and unworthy to have my hands on her head.

I think we do not understand the nature of ourselves. I think we do not understand who we are. Some people call the temple ordinances the "mysteries" of the kingdom. When I went to the temple, I thought I was going to learn which star was Kolob, where the Ten Tribes were, and other such information. But those aren't the mysteries of the kingdom; the mysteries of the kingdom are who we are, and who God is, and what our relationship to him is. Those are the mysteries of the kingdom. You can tell somebody in plain English, but they still don't know in their hearts who they really are.

I was in a foreign country giving a workshop for others in my profession. The workshop was over, and I was just exhausted. My plane left at 7:30 P.M. back to the States, and it was now 4:00 P.M. I was right across the street from the airport in a motel. I thought, "This is nap time. I am going, in the middle of the day with the sun out, to take a nap." So I called the desk and said, "I want to be awakened at 6:00, not 6:00 in the morning but 6:00 in the evening; I'm taking a nap." I put down the receiver, undressed and curled into bed and thought how deliciously wicked it was to be sleeping in the middle of the day. I had just snuggled down when the telephone rang. It was the mission president, who also was a general authority whom I had never met, but who had read in the paper that I was there. He had a problem with one of his sister missionaries. Although he'd been working with her, she had a ticket to go home on the same flight I was on. He'd labored with her and given her blessings. She'd only been out six weeks, but she was going home and nothing he was able to say changed her mind. The mission president said, "She said she had your text in college, and I told her you were here. I asked her if she would see you, and she said she would." He said, "You're it."

I protested, "It's your job; it's not my job. You're a general authority— I'm just a stake president and out of my territory at that."

He said to me, "We'll send the car for you."

This sister and I sat down together. She had her purse clutched and her ticket prominently displayed on it. She looked at me a bit defiantly, and I said, "The president tells me you're headed for home."

She answered, "Yes, and you can't talk me out of it either."

I said, "Why?"

She told me why.

It was an awful story. She did grow up in a Mormon family in Idaho— a farm family, a rural, poor family. She had been sexually abused, not just by her father, but by all her male relatives. She was terribly abused. Incidentally, I want to tell those of you who teach girls this, she had tried to tell a couple of times, and people wouldn't believe her. When she was ten years old, they had a lesson in Sunday School on honoring your father and mother. After class was over, she said to her teacher, "But, what if your father or your mother wants to do something that isn't right?"

The teacher said, "Oh, my dear, that would never happen. Your father and your mother would never want anything that wasn't right for you."

Finally, when she was fourteen, her Mia Maid teacher believed her and convinced the bishop it was so. The bishop took her out of that home and into his own home where she finished her high school years; he sent her to college, and then she went on a mission. Her father's "patriarchal blessing" when she left his home was this, "Well, aren't we fine folk now? Gonna go live with the bishop and all those holy joes over on the other side of town. Well, let me just tell you something, girl, and don't you never forget it. They can't make a silk purse out of a sow's ear." That's what she decided on her mission. She decided she didn't belong there with all those silk purses. She was having sexual feelings for the mission- aries because when you're only four or five when you first get exposed to regular sex, it isn't easy. You don't have the adult's or the teenager's sense of proportion and sense of reality and sense of the world to put it into proportion. So here were all these attractive young men, and she'd never had the opportunity to develop in her life the kinds of protections in her heart and in her mind that other people in more blessed and protected circumstances have. She was having feelings that she believed were unworthy and told herself, "My daddy was right. You can take a girl out of a family and send her to college, you can send her on a mission, but you can't change what she is—a sow's ear."

So she was going home to throw herself away because she didn't belong out here pretending to be someone she wasn't. I said to her, "Before you came on your mission, you went to the temple, didn't you? You were anointed to become a queen, weren't you, a princess in your Heavenly Father's house? That's no way to treat a princess. There may be—I can't imagine it—but there may be some justification in their backgrounds for the way those men treated you when you were young. I don't know; I can't imagine any. But, I'm confident of this, the Lord will not easily forgive you if you treat his daughter that way. You're going to throw her away, a princess of our Heavenly Father? Then what are you going to say to him when he says, 'How have you handled the stewardship that I gave you of this glorious personage who lived with me, who is my daughter, who is a royal personage of dignity and of honor? I sent her down to the earth, and how have you brought her back to me?'" She, with the eloquence of her age and circumstances, started to cry, but she stayed.

I saw her in Provo two or three years later when I was there speaking. She asked if I remembered her, and I did, which was a miracle in its own right because I forget my own children's names; I can't get them all straight. I remembered her and her name and said, "How are you doing?" She answered, "I'm growing just as fast as I can. I thought you'd want to know." She understood who she was. I told her that I felt her stewardship was to get that daughter of our Heavenly Father home, home to Heavenly Father, home where she belonged. That's the mystery of the kingdom, that's the mystery of godliness—that we are our Father's children.

Now I'm going to tell you three other stories. One of them concerns a sister I used to home teach years ago. She was something. President Benson was president of the Quorum of the Twelve and used to send out the schedules specifying when stakes had their conferences. For several years in a row we always had our stake conference on Mother's Day. It was nice because you saved money on carnations, but this lady was outraged. She couldn't see why it always had to be our stake conference on Mother's Day. She wanted the carnations and the respect for women. So she finally wrote a stern letter to President Benson calling him to repentance for not observing the importance of motherhood. She said the priesthood leaders talked a good fight, but where were they when it really counted on Mother's Day? And he changed the date of our stake conference. So you get some feel for this woman—a good woman, but not shy.

Anyway, I was her home teacher and her stake president. She was also one of those sisters who felt that if you just have a cold, it's all right to have your husband give you a blessing, but if it's anything more serious, you need at least the bishop. Stake presidents are better. If there's a general authority in the area, that's the best. She wanted real sparks—none of this home-grown stuff.

They had two or three girls, and she'd had trouble with her deliveries, which were caesarean. Her doctor told her that she had nearly died the last time. He said, "Your uterus is so thin that I could see my hand through it. It is not going to sustain another pregnancy. If you want to die, get pregnant again. Is that very clear? Will you let me take it out?" She said, "No." He said, "It's no good except to kill you." She said, "Don't take it." So he said, "All right, but I want you to know that if you have another pregnancy, you're dead."

Well, that lasted about four years. I accused her of having gone to see *Saturday's Warrior* one time too many. She decided they had a little boy waiting to come to their family. Her husband said, "Oh, no, you don't. You think you're going to get pregnant and leave me to raise those girls without you. No way; I'm not going to do that. The doctor told you, and that's sensible, and that's it."

"But I just feel there's still one up there for us."

"No way. We are not going to take any risks with your life. I'm not up to raising three daughters alone. I'm sorry; 'no' is the answer."

"Well, when President Broderick comes, let's have him give me a blessing."

He got to me first, of course, and I couldn't have agreed with him more. I didn't want that on my hands. That's what we have doctors for. So I was not very moved by this woman's ambition to have one more child and said, "Now, look, Sister so-and-so, you can't do this." But this lady is not an easy person to say no to. So her husband and I laid our hands on her head, and I heard myself telling this lady, "Sure, go right ahead and have a baby. No problem. You'll have no problem in the pregnancy; it'll be just fine. You'll have a fine big boy, nurse him, and everything will just be terrific." I could not believe I was saying it. Her husband was looking at me in horror. I left immediately.

But it happened just like the blessing said. It was just one of those stories where the Lord gives you the answer. She got pregnant. The doctor shook his head, but when the baby was delivered, it was fine. The uterus was fine; the baby was terrific. One little hitch—only it wasn't a little hitch; it was a big hitch. In the hospital somehow she had contracted a blood disease, Haverman's disease. I'd never heard of it before, and I've not heard of it since, but it's vividly etched in my memory. She broke out in spots all over. They're very irritable, like having the skin off your hand or off your back. She had at one point two hundred spots all over her body. She couldn't lie down or sit down or be comfortable anywhere, and they looked awful. It looked like she ought to wear a veil to cover these big red, size-of-a-fifty-cent-piece blotches all over her body. There was a medication she could take to relieve the symptoms. While it doesn't cure the disease, it does make the symptoms go away and allows you to live and function normally. But she couldn't nurse her baby if she took it.

"You promised in the blessing," she said, "that I could nurse this baby."

I said, "It was a throw-away line. What are you talking about?"

She said, "You promised, the Lord promised I could nurse this baby. I can't nurse him and take medication so you have to do something about this."

I said, "Look, get a bottle. Your husband can get up in the middle of the night. It'll be terrific. Take the medication; you're home free—the baby's fine. Rejoice, you've got a beautiful boy."

She would not have any of that. She wanted another blessing to take away this disease so she could nurse this baby. I wished I were not her home teacher, not her stake president. But I put my hands on her head, and I heard myself telling her that her disease would go away and she would be able to nurse this baby. Then I left for New York—not just because of that. I had a meeting in New York, but I did not want to be there hour by hour to see how this worked out.

I gave the blessing on a Sunday evening. Wednesday at 2:00 in the morning, I got a telephone call while I was in a deep sleep. I was president of this national organization and worrying about the next night when I was to give my presidential address. It was hard to sleep, but I was doing my best. The call woke me, and she said, "You promised me these spots would go away, but they're worse. I visited the doctor today, and he says they're worse. Nothing's going well. You promised. I've done every-thing I know to do. I've been on the telephone all day to people that I might have offended, even in my childhood. 'Please, please, if there's any-thing I've done to offend you, please forgive me.' I'm trying to think of anything I've ever done in my life and to set it right. But my spots haven't gone away. Why?"

"I don't have any idea why," I said.

She retorted, "Well, don't you think you ought to have an idea. You gave me that blessing."

I felt terrible. I did something I've never done before or since—I stayed up the rest of the night, what there was of it, praying. I said, "Lord, this woman's faith hangs on the blessing she received at my hands. I felt your Spirit at the time. If I was wrong, don't penalize her. Cover me." (And I started thinking of the people I should be calling.)

But she didn't call again, and I thought maybe it was all right. I got home Saturday night late, flying all day from New York, exhausted from the trip. I walked into the house, and there was a note that said, "No matter what time you arrive, call sister so-and-so." I didn't dare not do it, so I phoned her. She said, "You get on over here." Is that any way to talk to a stake president?

It was two o'clock in the morning, but I went over. She was bitter and empty. She said, "I want you to know that I have no faith left. I felt the Spirit of the Lord, the same Spirit when you gave me that blessing, that I've felt in sacrament meetings, in testimony meetings, when I read the scriptures, and in prayer. I felt that same Spirit, and here's my testimony." She raised her hands, which were covered with spots. "Well," she said, "what have you got to say?"

"Nothing."

"Don't you think you owe me an explanation?"

I said, "I have no explanation. I prayed all night. I don't have any idea why. I feel awful that I've been the instrument of your loss of faith. I can-not think of a worse thing that could have happened, that I could have spent my priesthood on, than to destroy your faith."

"Don't you think you owe me an explanation?"

"I tell you I have no explanation."

"You and the Lord—don't you think you owe me an explanation?"

"I'm not giving you any more blessings."

She said, "I think you owe me that, don't you?"

I never did anything with less grace in my life than when I laid my hands on her head. The Lord spoke to her, not of her disease and not of nursing babies, but of his love for her—that she was his daughter, that he cared for her, that he had died for her. He said that he would have died if she had been the only one. He would have suffered at Calvary for her sins, if hers had been the only ones. He didn't say one word about healing her.

The next day was fast Sunday. She came to church although she had said she never would again. With the spots she looked awful. It was not easy; she was not an overly proud woman, but it was not easy for her to appear in public looking as she did. She got up in testimony meeting, and her spots were worse than ever. She told the story and at the end she said, "I do not know why I have these spots, why my breasts have dried, but I do know this." And she bore a powerful witness of the Savior's love for her. That afternoon the spots went away and the milk came in, but not until she understood the mysteries of the kingdom, which don't have much to do with spots or milk or even with blessings, but have a lot to do with who we are and who our Father is, who our Savior is, and the relationship among the three of us.

I'm going to tell just two more stories. My mother, I trust, did not have a typical Mormon woman's life. She married three times, but she got better at it as she went along. I've been grateful to her that she didn't stop until she got a good man. He wasn't a member of the Church when she married him, but he eventually did join the Church and became a bishop—a very good man. I'm sealed to him, and I love him. I wear his ring. He wanted me to have it because in his family when somebody died, people quarreled over the teacups. He wanted me, before he died, to have the ring so no one would quarrel over it, and I could have it. I wear it with love.

He died, in some ways, in a bad way, a hard way. He was a strong man—a man who'd been a sickly youth, but he'd done some of the Charles Atlas exercises. I used to love to hear him tell about how eventually he'd turned the table on the bullies. I was one who always ran away from bullies, walked to the other side of the street and went home the other way, but I loved to hear his stories about how he'd finally gotten strong enough to take them on and beat them at their own game. I had a lot of vicarious satisfaction from his stories.

But at the end his lungs filled up with fiber so he had only five percent of his lungs to breathe with. With only five percent of the oxygen that he needed to metabolize his food, he just got weaker and weaker. His bones showed everywhere on his body. This big, beefy, all-solid-muscle man got to the point where all of his muscle had been eaten alive. I could easily carry him in my arms, although I'm not a strong man physically. He became petulant and childish because he could hardly breathe. He was constantly asphyxiated. He could hardly eat or go to the bathroom because he didn't have the oxygen to close his mouth that long. What a strain to see this strong, good man waste away.

A week before he died I asked him for a father's blessing. He could reach over only one hand because he couldn't find a position where he could breathe and get both hands together. He gave me a blessing; I'd never had one in my life before. With one hand, he gave me a father's blessing, which I treasure. Then I asked him—and it was more talking than he had done for a long time in one space—I asked, "Vic, what have you learned from this six months of wasting away?"

He said, "Patience; I was never patient. The Lord has taught me patience. I wanted to die six months ago, and he left me. I've had to wait upon him. You know those stories I used to tell?"

"Yes, the ones I liked so well."

"Son, those aren't good stories; they're full of revenge. They're not loving stories. I repent of them."

That man did not waste those six months. How many of us would have gotten bitter at God? "Why don't you take me? I've done everything; all I want to do is come home." That man spent those months being refined. I know he's presiding today over his family. We've done genealogy for his forebears and sent them up to him to work on in the spirit world. I know he presides over them today, and I know he's a better president of his familial branch in the spirit world than he was a bishop, and he was a good bishop. But, I know he was refined by his pain, by his adversity. He needed to go through that suffering. He could have been embittered; he could have been destroyed. His faith could have soured and left him, but he chose to learn from his pain. I do not want you to think that it was the pain that was good. It was the man that was good and that made the pain work for him, as indeed our Savior did.

Last Easter a friend, after having two boys (then four and two), brought a baby daughter into the world. Her husband wanted to visit her in the hospital and see the baby, but he had those little children at home.

So his home teacher was kind enough to say, "Hey, bring the kids over. We've got a bunch of kids at our house. Bring the two kids over; my wife'll watch them." (That's not quite what King Benjamin said about service, but it's one step off.) "You go and see your baby."

So he did. While he was in the hospital seeing his new baby, his two-year-old got away from that woman's care and drowned in the pool. Through CPR she was able to bring him back to his heart beating and his lungs working but never to real functioning. For two months he lay in a hospital bed, breathing, with his heart beating on machines that helped. His little knees somehow (I don't understand the mechanics of this) bent backwards. His feet bent backwards. I don't know why. In the rigidity of his coma he became deformed. He had been a perfectly whole, wonderful child, but now it was hard for me to go visit him. I would go and sit beside him, looking at his mother who was rubbing him and singing to him. It was hard.

The ward fasted every Sunday for a month for that child. They kept a twenty-four-hour vigil so that there'd be somebody he knew there when their faith made him whole. He was blessed by the stake patriarch, by the stake president, by a visiting general authority who was kind enough to add that additional duty to his busy schedule. In all those blessings the mother took hope. I will not say that she was promised flatly, but she took hope by what was said, that the child would live, that she would raise him in this life, and that he would perform many gracious acts and achievements. She would not even tolerate anyone's raising the possibility that he would not get better because she felt that everyone's faith had to be whole and focused.

I never saw so many people at the hospital—dozens of people kept vigil, fasted, and prayed for this child. After two months it became clear the child was wasting away and was not going to get better. His mother was the last to finally acknowledge what everyone else came to see—he was not going to live. It was costing, I forget how many, thousands of dollars a day. So they finally decided to do the gracious thing and let him return to his Father. It was the hardest thing they ever did. They prayed, fasted, consulted with priesthood leaders and finally, finally, decided the only thing to do was to pull the tubes. His mother said, "I can't stand it. I don't want to kill that little boy again. How many times is he going to die?"

So his grandmother went and held him in her arms when they pulled the tubes, but he didn't die. He lived another two weeks. I cannot express to you how spiritually exhausted everybody was when he finally died. The family had spent days and nights for weeks with him. Everybody had scarcely slept in two and a half months. Just a week before that baby died, the newborn got a temperature of 105 and was taken to the hospital and diagnosed with spinal meningitis. It was a misdiagnosis, but they put the baby in the room just right down from the other baby.

Her husband said, "Honey, let me go bless the baby."

She said, "You get your priesthood hands off my baby." She didn't want God to take that baby too. She said, "God's got all the babies he wants. Why does he want my baby? God doesn't need him on a mission—don't tell me that." People are not always helpful with the things they say. "God needs him worse than I need him—don't tell me that. He's got billions of babies, and I only have one; I have one two-year-old. Don't tell me he has a mission that can't wait fifty or sixty years more on the other side. There's lots of work for him here. We'll keep him busy."

At the graveside the grandmother gave the opening prayer, and the grandfather dedicated the grave. In a somewhat unusual choice, both the boy's parents spoke. Can you imagine that? What they said was this: "We trust our faith will never again be tried as it has on this occasion. The things we have faith in have come down to a short list, but that list is immovable. We do not have faith that God must do what we entreat him to do." Earlier she had cried out to God, "I asked for a fish, and I got a serpent. I asked for a loaf, and I got a rock. Is that what the scriptures promise?"

But after it was all over, at her little son's graveside, she was able to say, "I am content that God be God. I will not try to instruct him on his duties or on his obligations toward me or toward any of his children. I know he lives and loves us, that he is God. He's not unmindful of us. We do not suffer out of his view. He does not inflict pain upon us, but he sustains us in our pain. I am his daughter; my son is also his son; we belong to him, and we are safe with him. I used to think we were safe from grief and pain here because of our faith. I know now that is not true, but we are safe in his love. We are protected in the most ultimate sense of all— we have a safe home forever. That is my witness."

And that is my witness to you, that God lives, and he does not live less though you have injustice and adversity and pain and unkindness and violence and betrayal. God is in his heaven. We chose to come to an unjust world and suffer. But God is God, and he loves us. His son died for us. There is for each of us, because of who we are and who he is and who we are together, hope. There is hope. The uses of adversity are whatever use we put them to—for you and for me, for the parents of the little boy, for the lady with Haverman's disease, and for the incest victims, for my dad, for all of us—the uses of adversity are the uses we put them to. May they hone us and purify us and teach us and not destroy us, because of who we are and who God is and what our relationship to him is, is my fervent prayer.

THE UNKNOWN TREASURE

Jutta Baum Busche

One evening in late summer of 1940, the Baum family—the mother, two sons, one adopted son, two daughters, and a little baby—gathered in their dining room in the absence of the father, who was a soldier in the war. The mother had been busy all afternoon improvising a supper from such limited supplies as dandelion greens, turnips, and potatoes. As she placed the food on the table and looked around at the children, she asked, "Where is Jutta?" Startled, the three boys looked at one another, and then one by one guiltily dropped their eyes. The mother repeated her question more urgently: "Where is Jutta?" Finally, one of the boys said in a subdued voice, "She is still tied to a tree in the forest. We forgot to loosen her. We were playing a war game."

This incident was typical of my childhood. At the time I was only five and already a tomboy. I grew up mainly among boys and enjoyed participating in their war games. I served principally as their "weapons carrier," though occasionally I stood in as "the enemy." I am grateful to my Heavenly Father that I was born at that time in Germany. Wartime was full of sacrifices, fear, panic, pain, and hardships, but it was also a time of vivid memories, learning, and growth, because real learning often happens only in times of hardship.

During the war years, I remember, each evening as darkness came, I would take a small backpack containing some extra underclothing, a pair of stockings, and a pair of shoes, and walk about three kilometers (just under two miles) from home to a tunnel to spend the night alone in a compartment of a stationary train kept there to furnish shelter for civilians who were afraid of the almost nightly air raids. I also remember the first banana I ever had and how good it tasted. The war had just ended, and a merciful soldier from the occupying forces gave it to me. I

Jutta Baum Busche, born in Dortmund, Germany, married F. Enzio Busche, a publisher and printer. They were converted to the Church in the first years of their marriage. In 1977 her husband was called to the First Quorum of the Seventy. She has since served as the wife of a mission president and as a temple matron. The Busches are the parents of four children and the grandparents of nine.

remember very vividly our meager diet of water soups, nettle spinach, dandelion greens, turnips, and the molasses that people in our town were fortunate to obtain from a damaged railroad car. I remember very well the smell of sheep wool, which we sheared ourselves and spun into yarn, making sweaters and dresses for ourselves. I saw, as a consequence of our lack of food and medical assistance during those years, my sixteen-year-old sister and my nineteen-year-old brother become ill and finally die. The death of my brother, to whom I was very close, hurt me terribly and filled me with a deep awareness of how fragile life is.

In our home there was little religious education, although my parents were Protestant. My family simply did not talk about religion. But my father's brother was a Protestant minister. I remember a time when this uncle's wife came to visit. Before my aunt arrived, my father instructed us, "When she is here, we must have a prayer before we eat." I will never forget how comical and strange it was to hear my father offer a blessing on the food in words and tone of voice so unfamiliar to us that it struck me as hypocritical. Yet, as I grew up, frequently in the evening I knelt at my bedside on my own initiative to pray to my Heavenly Father because, even without religious instruction, I felt in my heart that there must be someone whom I could trust and love—someone who knew me and cared about me. What a privilege it would have been to be reared in a family that was well-grounded in the restored gospel!

When the missionaries first came to our door in Dortmund, Germany, my husband and I had not been married long. Our first son was only three months old. I was and always will be grateful each minute of my life for the message that came to us through these young missionaries. I was impressed with many things about these young men. One was the loving way they talked about their families. Another was their attitude about their message. There was no facade. I sensed such humble honesty in their expressions of testimony that I was compelled to listen. What they told me about angels and golden plates intrigued me enough that I wanted to learn why such nice young men could believe in such strange things.

I learned from them that we are all children of a loving Heavenly Father and that we are here on this earth to learn, to grow, and to love. I learned that we lived with God as his spirit children, his sons and daughters. We walked and talked with him. We knew him and he still knows us. We raised our hands in support of the plan to come to this earth.

Achieving our full potential in our journey here depends on our free choices. That message needs to penetrate every act of our daily lives.

I have since discovered that one great stumbling block to our progress in faith is rule-keeping that does not spring from an honest heart. Too many people imply in their attitude toward others that our Heavenly Father expects a perfect conformity to established rules. But Jesus Christ never condemned the honest in heart. His wrath was kindled against the hypocritically empty rule-keeping of the Pharisees. Jesus preached that through repentance we become free from sin; *however, only as we become honest, do we feel the necessity of repentance.*

When at age thirteen I was confirmed a member of a Protestant faith, the minister quoted John 8:32: "Ye shall know the truth and the truth shall make you free." This scripture had no meaning for me until I found the true gospel and learned the value of free agency—the right to make one's own decisions in one's own way. For me the truth that makes one free is twofold: the truths of the restored gospel, which provide a map of eternal realities, and the skill of being truthful with oneself and others, which leads to genuine repentance and integrity.

Self-honesty is the foundation for developing other spiritual strengths. Self-honesty will determine whether obstacles and problems we face in life are stepping stones leading to blessings or stumbling stones leading to spiritual graveyards. Marcus Aurelius, an ancient Roman philosopher, observed the connection between honesty and spiritual growth nearly two thousand years ago: "A man's true greatness lies in the consciousness of an honest purpose in life founded on a just estimate of himself and everything else, on frequent self-examinations, and a steady obedience to the rule which he knows to be right, without troubling himself about what others may think or say, or whether they do or do not do that which he thinks and says and does."[1] According to Marcus Aurelius, then, self-honesty is both a prerequisite to greatness and the core quality of integrity.

A time of great insight into the principle of self-honesty came for me when my husband accepted a full-time call in the Lord's service, making it necessary for us to say good-bye to all those whom we had grown to love in our home ward in Dortmund and everyone with whom we had been associated. The transition was not easy for us.

I remember well the adjustments we had to make when we came to live in Utah. My first calling in our ward was to serve as a Relief Society teacher. I watched the other teachers very closely and was deeply impressed with their striving for perfection in their teaching. Even their hairdos and immaculate dress showed their striving for perfection. I admired how fluent and articulate they were in the English language. How could I, with my poor English, compete with them and be their teacher? I was eager to learn and was so glad to hear that there was a stake preparation class for Relief Society teachers.

When I attended the training meeting for the first time, I was full of high hopes. I was not prepared for the question I was asked about what kind of centerpiece I would use when I gave my lesson. How incompetent I felt! I had no idea what a centerpiece was or what its purpose in the presentation of a lesson could be. Negative feelings about myself began to undermine my confidence.

Other efforts to fit in were equally discouraging. I felt very intimidated by my many wonderful neighbors with their seven, eight, or nine children. I became very shy when I had to reply that we had only four, and I could not even mention to these people the deep hurt I had experienced when I found that for health reasons my family would have to be limited to four children.

I continued to feel inferior as I watched the sisters in my ward and saw them planting gardens and canning the produce. They exercised daily by jogging. They sewed and bargain-shopped. They went on heart fund drives and served as PTA officers. They took dinners to new mothers and the sick in their neighborhoods. They took care of an aged parent, sometimes two. They climbed Mount Timpanogos. They drove their children to and from music or dancing lessons. They were faithful in doing temple work, and they worried about catching up on their journals.

Intimidated by examples of perfection all around me, I increased my efforts to be like my sisters, and I felt disappointed in myself and even guilty when I didn't run every morning, bake all my own bread, sew my own clothes, or go to the university. I felt that I needed to be like the women among whom I was living, and I felt that I was a failure because I was not able to adapt myself easily to their life-styles.

I could have benefited at this time from the story of a six-year-old who, when asked by a relative, "What do you want to be?" replied, "I think I'll just be myself. I have tried to be like someone else. I have failed each time!" Like this child, after repeated failure to be someone else, I finally learned that I should be myself. That is often not easy, however, because our desires to fit in, to compete and impress, or even simply to be approved of, lead us to imitate others and devalue our own backgrounds, our own talents, and our own burdens and challenges. I had to learn not to worry about the behavior of others and their *code* of rules. I had to learn to overcome my anxious feeling that if I didn't conform, I simply did not measure up.

Two challenging passages in the Bible remind me that I must overcome self-doubts. One is Proverbs 23:7: "For as he thinketh in his heart, so is he." The other is Romans 12:2: "Be not conformed to this world: but be ye transformed by the renewing of your mind, that ye may prove what is that good, and acceptable, and perfect, will of God." When I tried to *conform,* it blocked my being *transformed* by the Spirit's renewing of my mind. When I tried to copy my wonderful sisters as I taught my class with a special centerpiece and other teaching techniques that were unfamiliar to me, I failed because the Spirit still talks to me in German, not in English. But when I got on my knees to ask for help, I learned to depend on the Spirit to guide me, secure in the knowledge that I am a daughter of God. I had to learn and *believe* that I did not need to compete with others to be loved and accepted by my Heavenly Father.

Another insight from Marcus Aurelius is, "Look within. Within is the fountain of good, and it will ever bubble up, if thou wilt ever dig."[2] Sometimes our great potential for good is veiled from us by the negative judgments of others. For instance, one day in Germany I had a meeting with our eleven-year-old son's school teacher. I was very saddened to hear that she judged our son to be lacking in sufficient intelligence to follow the course of mathematics of that school. I knew my son better than the teacher did; I knew that, on the contrary, mathematics was his real interest and within the scope of his capabilities. I left feeling very depressed. When I got home, I saw in the eyes of my son his high expectations as he enthusiastically inquired about what his teacher had said. I knew how devastated he would be if I were to tell him his teacher's exact words. It was the Spirit that gave me the wisdom to rephrase his teacher's concerns. I told him that the teacher recognized his great talent for mathematics and that only his lack of diligence would separate him from great achievements, for his teacher held high hopes for his future. My son took this to heart, and it did not take long before he became the best student of mathematics in his class. I do not even dare to think what would have become of him had I reported exactly the teacher's negative remarks.

God works through the positive power of his love. When we truly learn to love God, we learn to love all things—others, ourselves, all creation, because God is in all, with all, and through all. We need not be afraid, and we need not hide behind a facade of performance. When we come to understand this *unknown treasure*—the knowledge of who we really are—we will know that we are entitled to the power that comes from God. It will come when we ask for it and when we trust his leadership in our lives. Our efforts should not be to *perform* nor to *conform* but to be *transformed* by the Spirit. Again, "Be not conformed to this world: but be ye transformed by the renewing of your mind, that ye may prove what is that good, and acceptable, and perfect, will of God" (Romans 12:2).

Many pressures bind us to the world. Being honest in heart frees us to discover God's will for our lives. I am always touched in our monthly ward testimony meetings where my faith is strengthened by my neighbors who tell how they have been *buoyed up* to meet the challenges and trials that have come their way. So often their testimonies reveal serious challenges they have had to face—challenges that are not evident unless one opens up one's heart to another. I know that as I walk down our street and pass all the beautifully tended homes of my neighbors, I am inclined to think that all is well with them, that they do not struggle as I do. It is through the honest testimonies they bear that I learn to see their hearts, and we become united in feelings of love.

We, the children of the covenant whose eyes have been opened, have a great responsibility to be always aware of who we are. Although we might be absorbed in meeting our daily challenges and opportunities for growth, we cannot afford to live one day or one minute without being aware of the power within us. What a privilege I had to serve as the first matron in the Frankfurt Temple! I had to depend constantly on the Spirit; otherwise, it would have been impossible to succeed. The challenge to establish a fully functioning temple seemed overwhelming, but the more overwhelming our tasks are, the more we understand that there is only One who can help, our Heavenly Father. Only when we draw unto him can we learn how real he is, how much he understands, and how much he is willing to help. He knows that we are not perfect and that we are struggling; and when we accept ourselves with our weaknesses in humility, sincerity, and complete honesty, then he is with us. As Paul told the Corinthians, "Eye hath not seen, nor ear heard, neither have entered into the heart of man, the things which God hath prepared for them that love him" (1 Corinthians 2:12).

Notes

1. Marcus Aurelius, as quoted in *TNT: The Power within You*, ed. Claude M. Bristol and Harold Sherman (New York: Prentice-Hall Press, 1987), p. 52.
2. Marcus Aurelius, as quoted in *Great Books of the Western World*, vol. 12, ed. Robert Maynard Hutchins (Chicago: University of Chicago Press, 1952), p. 283.

THE RIPPLE EFFECT:
BUILDING ZION COMMUNITIES

Julene Butler

*B*uilding Zion can be like tossing a pebble into a pond. Just as ripples work their way outward from one pebble, growing ever larger, so a Zion community can begin with one person working within a family—that first small circle, then gradually moving outward, expanding into broader groups, spreading the principles of godhood through larger circles of people and communities.

What do I mean by *communities?* A community can be a geographic cluster of people, such as a city or town or perhaps a ward or neighborhood. But it is not limited to such groups. Webster's definition specifies groups organized around a "unifying trait."[1] A community might be a local bird-watching group, a political party, the people we work with, or fans of a basketball team during the playoffs. A circle of friends might qualify as a community.

Our Church leaders often note that our homes are laboratories in which we may learn and practice gospel principles.[2] Each community in which we participate is a broader circle for practicing the principles we first experience in the family setting. Those communities offer us opportunities to observe the consequences of good and bad behaviors.

Think for a moment of examples of Zion in the scriptures. The city of Enoch was an entire city of people whose every desire was to live righteously. We are told, "Enoch and *all his people* walked with God, and he dwelt in the midst of Zion; and it came to pass that Zion was not, for God received it up into his own bosom" (Moses 7:69; italics added).

Fourth Nephi gives us another example of a Zion community. These people had seen Christ when he visited the American continent, had felt his loving influence, and were motivated to be one and to teach their

---

H. Julene Butler received her bachelor of arts degree in English and her master of library science degree from Brigham Young University. She earned a Ph.D. in communication, information, and library studies from Rutgers University. She is an assistant university librarian for public services at the Harold B. Lee Library at Brigham Young University. She serves as Relief Society president in her ward.

children and their children's children to live together in love and righteousness.

Notice that both these examples of Zion consist of large groups of people, communities of Saints; they were Zion societies. Hugh Nibley suggests that Zion, by its very definition, cannot exist in isolation. We cannot "have all things in common" or "be of one heart and one mind" in isolation from our brothers and sisters, our neighbors and friends.[3]

We need others in order to thrive. In fact, we need them simply to survive. Primitive tribes understood this truth, especially as it related to their physical survival. They came together for protection and nourishment. The same is true in a spiritual sense. If we are to thrive spiritually, or simply survive spiritually, we need each other. We can make only so much spiritual progress in isolation from one another, and then our progress stops.

Over the years, I have heard many women comment that they learned gospel principles most deeply through their roles as wife or mother. They are speaking from their hearts, and I know they are bearing witness to the truth. The sacrifice and selflessness required in those relationships require women to reach deep within their souls. Some seem to suggest, however, that it is only in the context of marriage and family that we can prepare for godhood, and the implication is that a person who lives alone somehow misses the chance to learn those same lessons. I believe very differently. Let me tell you why.

I have two sisters, whom I love dearly. Patsy is the mother of five; Paula, the mother of nine. Each has supported her husband through years of Church activity. Their daily routines over the years have been very different from mine. But on many, many occasions, as we've talked to each other about our latest struggles and discoveries, I have realized that we are on the same path. My experiences are teaching me the same lessons they are learning. Our experiences occur in different settings, but my soul is being stretched to much the same extent as theirs.

A loving Heavenly Father gives each of us the opportunities we need to reach godhood. So when I say that we cannot survive spiritually if we are alone or that we can progress only to a certain point in isolation from each other, I speak more of a condition of the heart than of the nature of our life's circumstances.

Now, back to the idea of isolation. To punish criminals, we remove them from the community, locking them behind bars. Prisoners of war describe the horrors of one especially severe type of punishment: prolonged solitary confinement. Psychologists maintain that extended periods of solitary confinement can lead to severe psychological damage.

One of Satan's strongest tools is to isolate us from each other, to turn our thoughts away from those around us and, in so doing, prevent us from reaching out to others and finding strength through unity. Satan does not want Zion to flourish, and he knows he can stop it most easily by attacking its roots, by dividing righteous people from one another.

Think back on your life for a moment. Have you ever felt alone, deeply alone? I have at times in my life. I am a single woman confined to a wheelchair, who lives alone (by choice!) some distance from immediate family. At one time I honestly felt that if I were to slip in the shower or become ill, none of my neighbors would realize it for weeks. I believed they would never miss me or wonder what had become of me. (That is certainly not true now, and I don't believe it was true then, but at that time, I felt very isolated.)

When I look back on that time of my life, I realize that I was suffering in other ways, too. My physical health was poor. I was on an emotional roller coaster. I thought mostly of myself and my own troubles, I couldn't (or wouldn't) look outward, and I had no desire to serve those around me. I wasn't even aware that people around me had needs that I might have filled. I felt alone, and self-pity and negative behavior reinforced that alone-ness. If I were to characterize myself at that period of my life, I'd say I was very immature—emotionally and spiritually.

I find it interesting that the New Testament word that is translated as "perfect" in scripture, such as "Be ye therefore perfect," may be more correctly translated as "finished" or "complete" (Matthew 5:48, note b). We are here on earth to learn and grow. The process of maturing, of becoming spiritually complete, is a lifelong process.

I had an amusing experience years ago one summer when I needed help with my yard. Yardwork is a little tough from a wheelchair! A good friend who shared my home at the time usually took care of things outdoors, but that summer she wasn't well and couldn't tackle the weeds and other details. I didn't want to ask family or friends for help because I didn't want her to think I was being critical. I fretted and stewed and decided that the only answer was for someone to offer their help, so I prayed intensely that someone would notice our situation. A few days later, my visiting teacher came. We had a pleasant visit. As she stood on our porch saying good-bye, she noticed the yard problem. "Hmmm," she said, "it looks like you're having trouble keeping up with your yard work. But that's okay; none of us mind."

I laughed to myself and silently shared the joke with Heavenly Father. After all, I had prayed that someone would notice. My prayers had been answered, very literally. I learned from that experience to pray in specifics but also to be willing to ask for help when I need it. Perhaps more importantly, I realized that if we are to be a Zion people, we must not only keep our eyes open and notice the needs of those around us but also keep our hearts open—and be one, reaching out and doing for others what they are unable to do for themselves.

In Relief Society a few weeks ago, our teacher spoke of her "kind of naughty" children who are now teens and young adults. She told us how she longs for them to change their lifestyle and how she continues to do all she can to help them get back on the path. She is a counselor in a high school, where she has many opportunities to work with young people who are also "kind of naughty." That day in Relief Society she said, "I've come to realize that as I work with these students at school, I can love them the way I hope other people will love my children." That sounds like Zion behavior to me—lifting and blessing others, reaching out to help when we see a need, praying that others will do the same when they notice our needs.

We're given specific information about a Zion society in the Book of Mormon: "And it came to pass that there was no contention in the land, because of the love of God which did dwell in the hearts of the people. And there were no envyings, nor strifes, nor tumults, nor whoredoms, nor lyings, nor murders, nor any manner of lasciviousness; and surely there could not be a happier people among all the people who had been created by the hand of God. There were no robbers, nor murderers, neither were there Lamanites, nor any manner of -ites; but they were in one, the children of Christ, and heirs to the kingdom of God" (4 Nephi 1:15–17; italics added).

I have always loved the phrase: "nor any manner of -ites." Imagine a classless society with no "haves" and "have-nots," no divisions among the people. The Savior teaches love and unity. But Satan works to divide and separate us. He introduces contention within our wards, neighborhoods, and families. He whispers things like "How can I talk to her? She doesn't speak English well enough" or "I don't like to visit teach her. Her house is always a mess!" or "Oh them! They never go to church. I can't let my kids play with their kids." I have a friend who seldom goes to church. She attends when her grandchildren are baptized, when they sing in the Primary sacrament meeting program, when they leave for their missions, and again when they return. But other Sundays she's at home or at work. She once told me that only one person in her ward treats her "like a real person." Whatever their reason for not drawing her in, whatever her reason for not reaching out to them, she and her ward are not yet "in one."

How do we improve? How do we reach the point where we truly are one? The scriptures hold the answer. "There was no contention in the land, because of the love of God which did dwell in the hearts of the people" (4 Nephi 1:15).

In a recent general conference, Elder Henry B. Eyring said that through a "unity of [our] faith in Jesus Christ" we will receive the help we need to change our natures and become one. "It is our surrender to the authority of Jesus Christ which will allow us to be bound as families, as a Church, and as the children of our Heavenly Father," he taught. "The Spirit of God never generates contention. . . . It unifies souls."[4]

With the love of God in our hearts, we are able to see the beauty and goodness within each person we meet, no matter where they stand in relation to perfection (or maturity or completeness). Often that beauty is not readily evident.

I think of the first time I went into Manhattan alone. I drove in from my New Jersey home to attend some meetings at New York University. I had carefully planned my day. I called ahead to get the number of the bus that ran from Port Authority to lower Manhattan. When I asked about the return trip, I was told to get back on the same bus, which would then go down to Battery Park, make a loop, and head back uptown. But after lunch, when I went to the bus stop, several buses with my number drove right past me. Finally one stopped and the driver said, "Lady, we're not going to load you and your wheelchair onto this bus just to unload you in two blocks where this line ends!" I asked him how to get uptown from there, and he told me I had to head west six blocks to catch the uptown bus. Then he drove away.

I had been in the city often enough with friends to know that only some streets had curb ramps. Very often my friends had to help me up a curb when we crossed a street. But I couldn't panic for long. I really had only one choice, so I headed west. Approaching the first intersection, I could see through the crowds that there was a down curb-cut I could use. But I couldn't yet see across the street to the other side. The light changed. I started across and halfway there discovered there was no ramp ahead. I glanced cautiously from side to side at the crowd walking across the street with me, trying to decide if I dared ask anyone for help. Before I could ask anyone, a man stepped up, said, "Let me help you," and then boosted me up the curb. He was the last person I would have considered asking. The same thing happened every time I needed help; and often the least likely looking individuals were the first to offer help.

I think of 1 Samuel 16:7: "The Lord seeth not as man seeth; for man looketh on the outward appearance, but the Lord looketh on the heart." The Lord looks on the heart; we need to learn to do the same. As we let the love of God into our hearts, the Spirit will teach us how.

To paraphrase Elder Eyring, we can learn to be one by using our similarities to help us understand one another and our differences to complement each other. Each of us has unique gifts and abilities that will help build up Zion, help us be one.[5]

Let me illustrate with one more personal example. My good friend Linda is blind. When I lived in New Jersey, she and I often ran errands together. We were quite a pair: a blind woman, her guide dog on the harness, and a woman in a motorized wheelchair. I had more fun than Linda did because I could see people's reactions to us. We always got a reaction. Some people smiled and said hello. Others pretended there was nothing unusual about us. Still others stared openly. When we shopped together, we became very good at using our individual abilities to benefit each other. We made a great team! Getting items from the top shelf had always been a problem for me. Linda could reach what I couldn't. (She's not very tall, but she has a higher reach than I do!) I would direct her ("a little bit to the right, now up . . . oops, too far—there!"). Linda and I learned the importance of each person sharing her unique strengths.

Though we do not currently live the united order, we are expected to live the law of consecration. We are to consecrate our time, our means, and our talents to building up Zion. We are each given different types and amounts of talent and time and material goods. And we covenant to consecrate what we have.

Hugh Nibley teaches that the express purpose of the law of consecration is to build up Zion. Contrary to what some believe, says

Nibley, "we do not wait until Zion is here to observe it; it is rather the means of bringing us nearer to Zion." In other words, we help create Zion by becoming a Zion people as we consecrate our energies and possessions and abilities.[6]

If we are to build Zion, we must move beyond ourselves and even beyond our families. We must allow our influence to ripple out into the communities that we belong to (our ward, our neighborhood, our friends) and practice Zion principles in these wider circles. We must look for each others' strengths and work in concert, one with another. We must wear off the rough edges of selfishness that form when we isolate ourselves. May we each find our unique gifts and talents, nurture them, and enlarge our desire and ability to consecrate those gifts to building up the kingdom of God. As we do, ripples of righteousness will flow outward, and Zion will begin to flourish.

Notes

1. Merriam Webster's Collegiate Dictionary, 10th ed., s.v. "community."
2. See, for a recent instance, Dale E. Miller, *Ensign*, May 1998, 29–31.
3. Hugh Nibley, *Approaching Zion*, vol. 9 of *The Collected Works of Hugh Nibley*, ed. Don E. Norton (Salt Lake City: Deseret Book and Foundation for Ancient Research and Mormon Studies, 1989), 394.
4. Henry B. Eyring, *Ensign*, May 1998, 68, 67.
5. Eyring, *Ensign*, May 1998, 68.
6. Nibley, *Approaching Zion*, 390.

FRUITS OF FAITHFULNESS: THE SAINTS OF THE CZECH REPUBLIC

⚜

Olga Kovářová Campora

Introduction by Carol Cornwall Madsen

In September 1955, after a month of performances on its first European tour, the Mormon Tabernacle Choir reached the city of West Berlin. At the end of a long, tense day of traveling through Russian-occupied East Germany, Choir members were relieved to arrive in the Allied sector of Berlin. As they descended the huge stairs of the railroad station, tired and apprehensive, they were startled to hear the strains of a familiar hymn. As Time Magazine reported, waiting for the Choir on the station steps was a large group of German people who, upon seeing the Americans, "burst into the great Mormon hymn, 'Come, Come, Ye Saints.' The Americans joined in," English merging with German, "to thunder the final phrase, 'All is well! all is well!' "[1] Tears of joy and love were their common language.

Many of those singers were refugees, fleeing from the escalating restrictions imposed by Communist rulers, which were dramatically enforced six years later by the construction of the Berlin Wall. Turning an afternoon rehearsal into a free concert, the Tabernacle Choir sang to a hall filled with refugees and Church members who had been permitted to leave East Berlin temporarily. Emotions ran high as the Choir sang well beyond the allotted rehearsal time, closing with the hymn that had welcomed them. "This was not only music," reported the Berlin Telegraf, "it was the building of a human bridge."[2]

A hundred years after it was written, William Clayton's hymn bridged those years and spoke its message of hope to another dispossessed people, not only in Germany but throughout Eastern Europe. Like their latter-day forebears, Eastern European Saints relied on their faith and the promises of the gospel to support their commitment to the Church during forty years of isolation. For those beleaguered Saints, the words rang true: "Gird up your loins; fresh courage take. Our God will never us forsake."[3]

As this simple Mormon hymn reflected the spirit and endurance of Latter-day Saints long denied religious liberty, so music would also

81

eloquently express the joy of liberation forty years later. On Christmas morning, 1989, in Berlin, culminating a three-day celebration that began with the actual and symbolic opening of the Brandenburg Gate, Leonard Bernstein conducted an international choir and orchestra in a performance of Beethoven's stirring Ninth Symphony before an audience that spilled out of the concert hall into every available space surrounding it. In this majestic musical setting, the powerful poetic expression of universal love, "Ode to Joy," penned by German poet Friedrich von Schiller, magnificently conveyed the significance of that great moment in history. Impulsively changing the word Freude *("joy") to* Freiheit *("freedom") in the chorus, Bernstein declared that "this heaven-sent moment" excused his poetic license because both words expressed the exuberance of the thousands who listened to this celebration of the irrepressible human spirit. As von Schiller had written in his "Ode":*

> *Millions, bravely sorrow bearing,*
> *Suffer for a better time!*
> *See, above the starry clime,*
> *God a great reward preparing. . . .*
> *Joy [freedom], of flame celestial fashioned,*
> *Daughter of Elysium,*
> *Every man a brother plighted,*
> *Where thy gentle wings are spread.*[4]

Can anyone forget the joyful expressions on the faces of those who crossed unchecked through the openings in the Berlin Wall or stood shoulder to shoulder in Prague's famed Wenceslas Square to celebrate their country's freedom that miraculous winter?

Dr. Olga Kovarova shared in the miracle of those events. She had experienced the debilitating bonds of political oppression and had given meaning to the phrase "a steadfastness in Christ" (2 Nephi 31:20) by transcending those bonds and advancing His work in a Communist nation. Shortly after her baptism into the Church nine years ago, while still a doctoral student of education and pedagogy in Brno, Czechoslovakia, Olga Kovarova faced a dilemma. She had been taught the gospel of Jesus Christ in secret, she had been baptized under cover of night to avoid detection, and she had met each week with the handful of Saints in her hometown at great risk. Now, she had an opportunity to continue her studies in the free society of Austria, where she had relatives, but she also felt a commitment to remain in her native country. After weeks of prayer, fasting, and counsel with Church leaders, who wisely left the decision to her, she chose to finish her schooling at home.

What an inspired choice that was! Since receiving her Ph.D. in educa-tion, Olga has been determined to fill the ethical void in Communist ideol-ogy by teaching ethics and morality in her university classes in Brno and introducing such concepts as love and joy and the meaning of life to hun-dreds of young people at the yoga camps she conducts each summer. To keep those principles alive for her students, she started a newspaper, which she called The Art of Living, *a unique and dangerous venture for this young woman so continually under the scrutiny of Communist censors. "Czechoslovakia is ethically sick and it needs to be made ethically well," she boldly wrote in an early issue and then introduced Christian principles as guides to a better life. But to write about God's love without mentioning his name and to elaborate the theme of her newspaper, "Men are, that they might have joy" (2 Nephi 2:25), within the framework of Marxist-Leninist ideology were sometimes, she admits, beyond her powers. She was success-ful enough, however, to have many readers say to her, "Olga, you must be very happy, because you write such joyful things." Since the 1989 revolu-tion, she has seen her ideas incorporated into a textbook for high school teachers,* Self-Education in Ethics and Morality, *which has been adopted by universities throughout her country.*

Her search for a higher moral purpose brought Olga into the Church. The branch she joined was small, its members mainly those faithful ones who had joined before the war. Olga was the first young woman baptized in more than forty years. She decided the branch needed revitalization. Eight years and forty-seven converts later, including her own family, the branch is vigorous, youthful, and growing. It is not difficult to see how that happened. Olga is literally a Latter-day Saint. From her deep-rooted faith to her childlike humility, she radiates the spirit of the gospel. One who knows that best is Elder Martin Pilka, one of her converts and the first missionary from Czechoslovakia in recent times. "Olga," he wrote to me in his hesi-tant English, "is a very good sister but for most members she is also author-ity, because she is clean and full of love. I know that God chose her. Through Olga and Otakar Vojk; (whom Olga calls her spiritual father) was the Church restored in a big part of our country. Through Olga came to the Church a lot of young people and through Olga and this people the Church is living today." Indeed it is—in Czechoslovakia and throughout the world.

*D*ear sisters, brothers, and friends, I open my heart in faith to share with you experiences I have had living in East Central Europe in the beautiful country of Czechoslovakia. Until the end of 1989, life in Czechoslovakia was under full Communist control that had lasted forty years. I want to explain what living in these circumstances has meant to me. I believe that among people there is only one language that helps us to understand each other fully: it is the language of our heart, which is the language of love and of the Spirit of God. I am grateful that I can open my heart to you in this love.

Let me begin with an analogy. An Austrian scientist studied the life of crayfish. They, like lobsters, have at the base of their antennae small pockets where sand is deposited. The sand helps give these creatures their sense of equilibrium. If the sand is removed, they become disoriented until it is replaced.

In our bodies, we have a similar need for equilibrium, which comes from filling our hearts with the Spirit of God. If we do not keep that Spirit, we lose our spiritual balance.

In Communist-dominated life, I saw that people lost their individuality, their personality. They became dependent—literally—upon the Communists in all aspects of their lives. Someone was always watching what they did. People came to depend so much upon the leaders of the Communist party that they were reluctant to express their feelings openly. They became incapable of being happy. Only occasionally with trusted family and trusted friends would they show feelings. The Communists taught people to be honest, to be chaste, to work hard, and to be unselfish. They even had special schools to teach Communists how to influence people to live this way. But the Communist leaders were not honest with their people. They had privileges that were denied others, they did not live moral lives, and therefore they could not be models for non-Communists. The younger generations saw that hypocrisy and became very cynical. As a result, all people learned to lead two lives: one a private life, and the other a public life. In the Book of Mormon is a description that fits very well the majority of Communist leaders:

"And it came to pass that they did have their signs, yea, their secret signs, and their secret words; and this that they might distinguish a brother who had entered into the covenant, that whatsoever wickedness his brother should do he should not be injured by his brother, nor by those who did belong to his band, who had taken this covenant.

"And thus they might murder, and plunder, and steal, and commit whoredoms and all manner of wickedness, contrary to the laws of their country and also the laws of their God" (Helaman 6:22–23).

Heavenly Father has allowed people to have experiences under rulers who not only govern without God's laws but who impose laws contrary to God's laws. Most Czechs grew up without a sense of direction. Nor could they find one. Communists do not believe that the way a person thinks about reality is important. The Marxist-Leninist philosophy places the highest value on material things. For that reason, those living under this ideology found their lives impoverished, lacking spiritual and higher cultural values. Albert Einstein said that the goal of material welfare is the same goal that a drove of pigs has. Our people longed for higher goals.

One year before our revolution, the movie depicting the life of Mahatma Gandhi was shown in Czechoslovakia. I noticed that most young people sat through this film not just once but two or three times. Although Gandhi's ideas are spiritual and most young people in my country do not believe in God, they were touched by Gandhi's idea of nonviolence. During our revolution, I saw in some Czech shop windows displays of nonviolence featuring Jesus Christ and Gandhi. Gandhi was quoted as saying, "Always, whenever I felt despair, I would realize that in the end truth and love always prevail." The Czech hunger for a spiritual and cultural life beyond Communist materialism was clear.

Among the leaders of the Czechoslovak Revolution in 1989 were university students. I find it very meaningful that it was called the Velvet Revolution. I will always remember the two students, very good friends, who came to my office. "Olga," they shouted, "we are bringing excellent news. The mills of the gods have started to grind again." We looked at each other and without another word, tears came to our eyes and we hugged. Two days later our nation came together: in Brno about one hundred thousand people gathered on the main square. We held hands and sang our national anthem. I felt the love of God among all the people so strongly: their hearts began a new beat, their souls began to live, life again had meaning for them. After forty years of an alien history, a history imposed on us by another nation, the history of the Czech people resumed. Then I recalled, in Paul's words: "Where the Spirit of the Lord is, there is liberty" (2 Corinthians 3:17).

I know that the Velvet Revolution was a miracle of God. The French author Antoine de St. Exupery in his book, *The Little Prince*, wrote: "What is essential is invisible to the [human] eye."[5] In America many have told me: "We prayed many years for freedom in your country." Brothers and sisters, I thank you for this gentle yet powerful help and influence. Our Czech youth were the embodiment of God's miracle, for as it is written in Ether 4:12, "Whatsoever thing persuadeth men to do good is of me; for good cometh of none save it be of me."

In many ways God has been persuading men and women toward good in our country. The Czechoslovak Mission was organized in 1929 by Elder John A. Widtsoe, the president of the European Mission. A young elder from the German-Austrian Mission, Arthur Gaeth, was chosen to preside over the mission. He was succeeded by Wallace Toronto, also one of the first missionaries. He and the elders had to leave when the Nazis occupied the country. After World War II, President Toronto returned with a larger number of missionaries, including our current president, Richard W. Winder, and Edwin B. Morrell, later president of the Austria Vienna East Mission. But by 1950, two years after the Communists had come to power, the mission was closed and would not be reopened until July 1990.

During the years of Communism, the Church could not exist publicly, even though a lot of other churches could. The Czech Latter-day Saints could not preach, hold meetings, baptize, or ordain members to the priesthood. The penalty for breaking that Communist law was prison for three to seven years.

Nevertheless, the LDS Church continued to exist. About fifty members were active to the extent that they were in contact one with another. These members—despite Communist repressions and the fear of imprisonment—were faithful, never betraying their innermost ideals. Mostly older members, they gathered from time to time in their own homes because it was dangerous to meet every Sunday.

I joined the Church eight years ago, during this dark period under Communism. In Brno, the second largest city in Czechoslovakia, where I attended the Masaryk University, I met the Vojkůvka, family. They had belonged to the Church for more than thirty years, yet that was a well-kept secret. I came in contact with them through my interest in yoga. A schoolmate who knew that I was interested in yoga told me one day, "Olga, I traveled last Sunday to my parents, and I met on the train a wonderful man. He is about seventy-five, and he is an expert in yoga." She had taken his address, so I visited this man. He appeared to me seventy-five in his age but in his heart nearer eighteen and full of joy. This was so unusual in Czechoslovakia at that time of cynicism. We started to speak of life, and I saw that he was not only educated but knew how to live joyfully. I became very good friends with him and with his whole family. The family consisted of the elder Mr. Otakar Vojkůvka, his son, Gad, daughter-in-law, Magda, and their two children, Gad and Miriam, ages fifteen and thirteen. We had many discussions over many months.

The spirit in the Vojkůvka family was something very different for me. When at one point I asked the elder Mr. Vojkůvka about the meaning of their lives, he answered with a single sentence: "God sent us to the earth to sow joy, life, and love into souls and flowers." With this sentence a door opened for me into a different life—a life I had never imagined. I wondered where he learned this philosophy of life. One day I told them, "I have looked for many of the things you tell me in the New Testament, but I do not find them. Where do you read these things?" "Yes, it is true," they admitted. "They are not in the New Testament. We have a different book." They then gave me *A Skeptic Discovers Mormonism*,[6] translated into Czech. Overnight I read the entire book. I returned the next day to the family. Not certain that they were Mormons, I asked them if they knew how I could contact these people, the Mormons, and if I could get a copy of the Book of Mormon. They then gave me a Book of Mormon in Czech. I noted on the binding "Church of Jesus Christ of Latter-day Saints," so later that day I checked in the encyclopedia to find out about this church. There I read about Joseph Smith and how he was a crazy man—not normal, the article said—and I read there many other bad things about this church. Full of curiosity, I began to read the book anyway, but although I felt a strong spirit in the book, I did not read far. When I met with the Vojkůvka, family again, I told them, "I could not read all this book because I read one page and I felt questions." They told me, "It's okay, Olga. It is good that you have questions." So began a time of questions and learning the gospel.

Let me share my first clearly spiritual experience. Again it concerned my search for a higher purpose than materialism. While reading the Book of Mormon, I came to 2 Nephi 2:25 and read, "Adam fell that men might be; and men are, that they might have joy." I felt as if I had discovered a lost but important understanding for which I had been searching over many years. Yes, women and men are that we might have joy! That night I suddenly awoke, sat up and saw around me a light, and felt the same light in my heart. I realized that no longer did I just believe in God; I *knew* that Heavenly Father and Jesus Christ exist. I felt their love, not only for me, not only for good people, but for all people.

After my conversion, I had to wait half a year to be baptized. It was 1983 and because we had no baptismal font, we needed to wait until summer when we could be in the woods and not be noticed. The police would not be expecting a religious activity in the dark; however, as we neared the reservoir near Brno at about ten on the evening of my baptism, we noticed many fishermen. We waited, and the time dragged on— fifteen minutes, then thirty, then forty-five. I felt very disappointed and sad, wondering if this unexpected setback meant I was not sufficiently repentant. I silently questioned Heavenly Father: "Perhaps I am not well enough prepared, perhaps my testimony is not strong enough." Yet, I felt a great desire to be baptized. Finally, a brother who had been baptized a year or so earlier suggested, "I think we must pray and ask Heavenly Father to make it possible for Olga to be baptized." This was my first miracle with a priesthood prayer. Within a few minutes of our quiet prayer, most of the fishermen left the river's edge, and the three who remained were some distance away. You can imagine my feelings of joy as I came up out of the water.

Then an older brother asked me, "Do you know why there were many fishermen by the water tonight?"

"Yes," I answered, "so that I would better realize my responsibility for my sins."

"Of course," he answered, "but also remember that Jesus, as he walked by the Sea of Galilee, said to Simon Peter and Andrew, who were casting a net into the sea, 'Follow me, and I will make you fishers of men'" (Matthew 4:19). I felt his meaning was that I should soon be an instrument in God's hands to bring young people into the Church. In the confirmation blessing the elder Vojkůvka, who had not overheard this conversation, also said that I was the first young woman convert in almost forty years and that through me many people would come to the Church.

I soon realized that I had become one new link in the chain of women who have been significant among Latter-day Saints in Czechoslovakia.

In the 1920s, after World War I, the Brodilova family—a mother and two daughters—lived the gospel and prayed for the missionaries to come to Czechoslovakia. Others also became role models for me: Miloslava Krejci, baptized in the 1930s and ever active in genealogical research, was one of the Brno Branch stalwarts. Olga Snederflerova, wife of our district president in Prague, shared her quiet, steady faith since joining the Church in the late 1940s. In the early 1980s, Norma Toronto Morrell, wife of President Edwin Morrell and sister of Wallace Toronto, shared her love with us during frequent, supportive visits from Vienna with her husband, who presided over the Czechoslovak and neighboring Latter-day Saints. Four years ago, Barbara Woodhead Winder, then general president of the Relief Society, visited our branches and helped us to feel a part of the greater Church. Now she presides as companion to President Richard W. Winder since the re-opening of the Czechoslovak Mission in July 1990. All these women who preceded me are strong examples of love and patience.

At first, however, I did not know of them, and I was surprised to find at my first Sunday meeting that our Church group consisted of seven old people. They smiled at me with kindness, but I asked myself, "How special is this Church? It is only for old people." In time I would understand the reason. Most young members had escaped Czechoslovakia because all members were persecuted. Brother Vojkůvka, for instance, was questioned many times in secret places. In government documents, it was written of him, "Be careful. This man has a great influence on young people." In these days the Church had, of course, no missionaries. Latter-day Saint families had long been persecuted, questioned by the police, and warned not to teach their children about God and not to baptize them, even out of the country. Therefore, we dared to meet only in the evenings, at first once a month, and later once a week, when it was already dark outside and the neighbors were occupied with doing something other than being interested in people gathering. The blinds were pulled down, the windows had to stay closed, and we did not sing hymns for fear of being overheard. In these meetings, however, we strongly felt the spirit of the Holy Ghost. At first we were only seven; by 1989, we were about sixty in this one room. We had only one Book of Mormon among us; it was over forty years old, from before the time of Communism. The neighbors, noticing the many visitors, wondered why their elderly neighbor Mr. Vojkůvka, had so many young friends. One neighbor asked him, "Mr. Vojkůvka, what do you celebrate each Sunday? So many young people are coming to your house." He answered simply, "We learn to be happy." After the revolution, this neighbor returned to say, "I think that I too need your school of life."

So, before the revolution, every Sabbath was for me the happiest day of the week, because I could partake of the sacrament and learn more about the gospel, which would help me during the whole coming week. A few months after my baptism, a friend of mine also joined the Church, and we started to pray and discuss with the Vojkůvka family how we might do member-missionary work. We decided to invite our many university friends to a School of Wisdom, prior to our Sunday meetings, where we would teach the youth about the gospel, about Jesus Christ, and about Heavenly Father.

During those eight years before the Velvet Revolution, there were baptized about fifty young people and a few older people, including my parents, whom I had been afraid to tell about my belief in God. My parents had been Protestants, but in our home we were not spiritually awakened. There was no LDS church in Uherske Hradiste, the town where I was born, and at the Masaryk University, atheism was required. Belief in God was not permitted. Sometime after my conversion, I began yoga lectures in my hometown. At my invitation, my parents attended. After visiting three times, as we sat together at home that day, they asked me, "Olga, what are you doing? This is so special. Where did you learn such wonderful things about life? We didn't tell you anything like this." Then I had the courage to bring out the Book of Mormon and speak to them about the gospel and the Church. My father is now a branch president in Uherske Hradiste, where we now have eighty-two members and four missionaries after only two years of missionary work.

To think this miracle began with something so simple as our School of Wisdom classes—Brother Vojkůvka and a few young members offering gospel education to Czech atheistic youth. We knew that some of those attending the seminars were from the secret police, and before the Velvet Revolution, we could not openly talk about God or Jesus Christ, or even about love. So we taught university students seven ideas: first, admiration for good things in life; second, self-respect; third, being interested in living; fourth, finding joy in living; fifth, expressing gratitude; sixth, loving others (as Jesus intended); and seventh, enthusiasm—finding the burning within. The purpose of these principles was to help the youth build meaningful relationships with others and to bring them to a more spiritual life. We taught through examples, stories, and Bible parables. I was many times questioned by the secret police, but they were kind to me. Sometimes I could tell by their special questions that they knew I was a Church member, but since we did not organize or teach against our government, I was probably safe.

The Vojkůvka family were also experts in yoga. To help youth experience these seven gospel ideas to find spirituality and joy in life, we arranged yoga summer camps where they exercised outdoors, ate well, and learned to live happily together. There were about eighty people at each one-week camp. Even during one week at a camp, a participant's behavior was often changed for the better. We didn't pray or mention Heavenly Father, but we held hands before eating our food and expressed gratitude for being together.

For eight years now, we have held six or seven weeks of camp each summer. Our young LDS members taught at the camp, as if they were full-time missionaries. I am now teaching at the Missionary Training Center in Provo, Utah, and I receive letters from newly baptized LDS youth in Czechoslovakia who tell me how these seven ideas and other associations with us led them from being atheists to becoming believers in God. Each year we taught five to six hundred youth and middle-aged people from all over Czechoslovakia. We see that these people are already partially prepared to receive the new missionaries.

I am so grateful to Heavenly Father that the Czech Mission has been opened once again. We have six branches, and others are soon to be organized. Thirty-six missionaries are at present serving in Czechoslovakia, and eight more are studying at the MTC, among them four sister missionaries and one couple.

Missionary work will help the Czechoslovak people come to a new morality, based upon the eternal principles of the gospel. There is a great need for a new moral order. The president of Czechoslovakia, Vaclav Havel, speaking on New Year's Day, 1991, said, "Freedom surprisingly opened doors upon undesirable characteristics and showed the depth of moral decay afflicting our souls." Many Czech people are looking for a life full of truth. Who can be better examples of such a life than LDS missionaries? Czechs who seek a better life see the missionaries as positive examples of spiritually minded youth. Czechs also need strong families based upon prayer. We may have freedom, but without spiritual understanding, freedom leads people astray. Austria Vienna East Mission President Dennis Neuenschwander, now a member of the Second Quorum of the Seventy, wrote in a Christmas letter to family and friends in 1990: "Through the gospel, faith in Jesus Christ springs forth where there has been emptiness. Hope abounds where once there was despair. Charity is replacing destructive cynicism. Lives are changed as the light of the gospel penetrates the darkness."

We need more young elders, more sister missionaries to provide positive examples of young women living the Gospel, and more older couples as examples for our families and to help build the branches.

Brothers and sisters, we love you and we need you. To you in America I want to say, as did the Lord, "Arise and shine forth, that thy light may be a standard for the nations" (D&C 115:5).

Notes

1. "Music from the Tabernacle," *Time Magazine*, 19 September 1955, 55.
2. Ibid.
3. *Hymns of The Church of Jesus Christ of Latter-day Saints* (Salt Lake City: The Church of Jesus Christ of Latter-day Saints, 1985), no. 30.
4. Friedrich von Schiller, *An Anthology for Our Time* (New York: Frederick Ungar Publishing, 1960), 42–45.
5. Antoine de St. Exupery, *The Little Prince* (New York: Harcourt Brace Jovanovich, 1971), 70.
6. Timberline Wales Riggs, *A Skeptic Discovers Mormonism*, 5th ed. (Salt Lake City: Deseret Book, 1961).

DAUGHTERS OF GOD

Elaine A. Cannon

At a world's fair, treasured art was featured in two pavilions sponsored by religious organizations. One exhibit included Michelangelo's haunting *Piéta*—Christ crucified, lying across the lap of grief-stricken Mary. The Mormon exhibit featured Thorvaldsen's incredibly compelling *Christus*—the risen Lord with his arms outstretched, showing his nail-pierced hands to the multitudes who would come unto him. I learned a powerful lesson about attitude when I overheard a guide explain to a tour group, "This religious group has the dead Christ, and the Mormons have the risen Savior."

One looks at the works of artists through the centuries who have dealt with the nativity—Mary, Joseph, and the baby Jesus. How different they appear when seen through a variety of artists' eyes. The artists deal with the same people and the same tender theme, but their interpretations vary from ornately robed and haloed figures to simply sketched suggestions of the Holy Happening.

We look at ourselves—Mormon women all bound together by church affiliation and similar standards—yet how different we are!

Day by day I deal with these differences in women in the way they see things and what this does to their lives as they struggle to work out personal salvation according to their own views of prophets, principles, and problems.

Oh, how we differ! Our roots and the sum of our memories mark us. Sometimes the anguish of the struggle is more painful than pain itself. Sometimes, for a while, confusion rules. Sometimes people are only convinced the gospel is true. They are not yet converted.

As I look at you, I see such a cross section. This makes our sociality here interesting as well as challenging. It is recorded in the Doctrine and

Elaine A. Cannon served as general president of Young Women from 1978 to 1984. She previously served with the Youth Correlation Committee, the YWMIA General Board, the LDS Student Association, and the Church's General Activities Committee. She has been the author or co-author of several books, associate editor of the *New Era*, and a newspaper columnist. She and her husband, the late D. James Cannon, had six children.

Covenants: "That same sociality which exists among us here will exist among us there, only it will be coupled with eternal glory, which glory we do not now enjoy" (D&C 130:2). Since this is so, should we not now love each other more and not be angry or judgmental over differences? I sense some anger.

The things that matter most must not be sacrificed for those that matter least. It seems to me that it is time, then, for the women of the Church to behave with a sense of belonging instead of a sense of separateness. We are not women of the world, after all. We are sisters. We are daughters of God. We are children of the covenant who are marching to the same drummer, though we may be singing a separate song. Matthew Arnold wrote this truth: "Such a price the Gods exact for song: To become what we sing."

As we spend this time together, may we find something that will help us as we sing our songs and live our lives, help us in our similarities as well as in our differentness, in our public and private problems, and in our copings and our contributions.

May the Spirit of the Lord, whom I love and bear witness of, fill us with love, with joy, and with understanding so that we may feel close to each other and be moved to become more like him.

Sisters, one powerful alikeness we share is the inimitable hope and promise we enjoy through affiliation with this, his church on earth. I am sure you agree. It is like the world's fair: whether we see things as Michelangelo or as Thorvaldsen, we are concerned with Christ. How we look at life will be affected by how we consider Christ.

And so I am going to talk with you about baptism today—about baptism and confirmation and the laying on of hands for the gift of the Holy Ghost, and of covenants, commitments, the sacrament, disciplines, freedoms, light, and love. I'm going to talk about taking upon us the name of Jesus Christ and what that means to us as women in The Church of Jesus Christ of Latter-day Saints.

THE ORDINANCE OF BAPTISM

Being a member of The Church of Jesus Christ of Latter-day Saints, baptized by immersion, took on a new importance to me a few years ago. Before the Washington Temple was closed to the public and dedicated for its service, I wandered through on tour.

The day was gorgeous, colors were rampant in the surrounding woods, and the building was breathtaking with pristine spires rising to the sky.

And the spirit there was surging. I was excited and grateful to be there. Everyone else was curious. Washington, D.C., is home for people from all over the world who staff the embassies based there, and hundreds of people with wide-ranging national backgrounds came, some in family groups. There were service people of high rank with their aides dusting the paths ahead and professional people in the arts hiding behind dark glasses. Each looked different, but all reacted similarly. They were thoughtful. They were touched. There were searching questions in discussions with missionaries after. They took every brochure they were offered. They bought copies of the Book of Mormon eagerly. They wanted to buy replicas of what they called the angel "Gabriel." (They hadn't heard of Moroni.) There were none for sale, of course.

One handsome young Scandinavian ski pro with sun-streaked hair and a hand-knit turtleneck sweater stood next to us as we silently toured the last section of the building. The final room housed the white baptismal font resting on twelve oxen. He looked hurriedly about as we went into the room and asked, "Where can I find out more about this church?" Swiftly to his side came several who knew just how to tell him more.

A distinguished-looking gentleman standing by me before the baptismal font said, "I feel I am being guided or swept into something beyond my control—something very deep and wonderful. I've never had a feeling like this. What do I have to do to get in there?" He pointed toward the twelve oxen silently supporting the font.

"Die," I replied.

The Mormons nearby laughed, of course, while I quickly went on to tell him about baptism for the dead and for the living. We talked about repentance and faith, about how Christ died for us and came forth so that we might not have to suffer the spiritual death that our serious mistakes—our sins—impose. We talked about not feeling clean enough to meet the Savior if that were suddenly to happen tomorrow. He shook his head sadly. "I'm not good enough," he said. "If I could just start over. I just don't feel clean enough inside."

I explained the symbolism of the ordinance of baptism—of being buried in the water and coming forth a new being, of being washed clean in the process. Being a man whose business is with people and the symbols used to motivate them, he understood at once and said, "Sprinkling just doesn't do it, does it?"

Then we took him to talk with the missionaries.

Sprinkling may not do it, but neither does perfunctory performance or casual acceptance of the vital ordinance of baptism.

Every woman of whatever age, including the precious little sisters eight and over, should thoroughly understand the sacred act of baptism. Mothers, grandmothers, aunts, babysitters, and special friends of children can teach the blessing of baptism better if they understand it. To our non-member friends we can be eternally helpful if we can properly explain the purpose and symbolism of baptism and testify of him whose name we take upon us when the ordinance is performed.

We talk of these things because they are the very basis of our lives, the basis of Christ's doctrine for us. In a climate where some barter their church membership for political expediency or for a moment's pleasure in sin, or who forfeit church-related blessings because they do not fully understand yet, it is well for us to review these things again lest we too fall. Understanding brings more appropriate behavior. We will be more valiant. We will give more willingly and serve more compassionately and effectively. We will love better.

TAKING UPON US HIS NAME

In the first few chapters of Mosiah in the Book of Mormon, the power-ful sermon of King Benjamin is recorded. Those ancient Americans were deeply moved as they listened to King Benjamin teach of Christ, who was yet to be born. And they cried out in one voice that they wanted to make a covenant with Christ and take upon themselves his name. Then King Benjamin said:

"Ye have spoken the words that I desired; and the covenant which ye have made is a righteous covenant. And now, because of the covenant which ye have made ye shall be called the children of Christ, his sons, and his daughters. . . . There is no other name given whereby salvation cometh; therefore, I would that ye should take upon you the name of Christ, all you that have entered into the covenant with God that ye should be obedient unto the end of your lives. And it shall come to pass that whosoever doeth this shall be found at the right hand of God, for he shall know the name by which he is called; for he shall be called by the name of Christ" (Mosiah 5:6–9).

When the Savior first came to the Nephite people, he spoke of bap-tism and its covenant act more than a dozen times in one chapter, as recorded in Third Nephi, chapter 11. He said: "Whoso believeth in me, and is baptized, the same shall be saved; and they are they who shall inherit the kingdom of God. . . . This is my doctrine, . . . and whoso believeth in me believeth in the Father also, and unto him will the Father bear record of me, for he will visit him with fire and with the Holy Ghost" (3 Nephi 11:33–35).

We came to earth trailing clouds of glory. We go, one day, to whatever eternal reward is ours. Our Creator has given us the principles and procedures to get through life and to guide us back into his presence. His church is the institution, the framework with which the fulness of his guiding gospel may be found and the necessary ordinances performed with valid authority that binds them in heaven as well as on earth.

His church is named after him—The Church of Jesus Christ of Latter-day Saints. We meet in the name of the Lord. We pray in his name. We covenant in his name. We take his name upon us in sacred ordinances. As sisters, what does this mean to us specifically? What difference does this make in our lives? How does this set us apart from other women in the world—this taking upon us the name of Jesus Christ?

Traveling for the Church has given me a perspective that has set me thinking about names. We meet delightful women and girls named Tammie, Maren, Carolyn, Susan, Chieko, Lani, Birgitta, Marja, Cheri, Anja. And we have met a whole new batch of little ones named Camilla—proof that the visits President and Sister Kimball have made are remembered with warmth and purpose. There are many little boys named Spencer these days too, all over the Church.

Some time ago, we had a party at our home for a special family occasion. We were honored that President and Sister Kimball came. As I was welcoming them, my sister quickly brought her little son over to meet them. "President Kimball," she said, "this is Mark Spencer Cook."

President Kimball bent his knees so that he could look eye-to-eye with this little boy. Then he took the child's hand firmly in his own and said, "Well, Mark Spencer Cook, do you know what I give to little boys named Spencer?"

"No," came a shy reply.

"I give them a dollar. Camilla, do you have a dollar?"

Obviously Sister Kimball is very important to her husband. When she took upon herself his name, Mrs. Spencer Woolley Kimball, she accepted all the delights as well as the vital duties that a wife is entitled to.

Now, though a little girl be named Camilla and a boy be called Spencer, this does not guarantee she or he will be like them—partner to a prophet or prophet of the Lord. But there is, of course, much that can be said for the power of suggestion. This is true as well for those of us who have formally taken upon us the name of Jesus Christ.

GIFTS OF THE HOLY GHOST

We take upon us his name, we share in it. In return, he endows us with the gifts of the Holy Ghost—with the power to testify of him to others, power to be effective in our service and callings, power to discern needs of our loved ones, power to discern truth from error. And we receive promptings necessary for making sound value judgments in the many facets of our lives. We need only to listen to the still, small voice and cultivate this spirit within us. Surely we daughters of our Heavenly Father, whether we are young or old, needful or momentarily fulfilled, can better meet the mighty work of womanhood if we have his Spirit with us.

I had a tender experience as a young mother that I think proves this point. I had a new baby brought to me for nursing for the first time since the delivery. As I began the motherly task of feeding the baby, I was prompted by the Spirit that this baby was not mine. I love all babies, but if I have a choice, I'd prefer to care closely for my own. I checked the identification tag, the wrist bracelet, and the name tape on the baby's back. All indicated I had the right infant, but the Spirit told me otherwise. Subsequent hospital investigation of the baby's footprints confirmed that a mistake had been made. The Spirit working through a mother righted a terrible wrong.

Now, if we take upon us the name of Jesus Christ, we take upon us the obligation of being obedient to his will for us, to his timetable for the fulfillment of our dreams, to the way he answers our prayers.

When we covenant with the Lord to take upon us his name, we also take upon us the burden of helping mankind in our special, womanly way. Oh, sisters, can't we do better to bring ourselves together in heart and purpose though our activities may vary somewhat? Can we not go forth determined to help each other draw closer to Christ, as well as endure the daily grind?

It becomes increasingly clear that the work of women in the plan of life is as critically important as is the administrative and ordinance work of the priesthood. We love, we comfort, we create, we nurture, we teach, we right wrongs, and we provide the atmosphere for heaven on earth. The responsibility of birth falls to us. But the bountiful blessings of being born *again* come only through Melchizedek Priesthood ordinances. What a magnificent method for both women and men.

As we grow in understanding of our relationship with Christ, it makes all the difference in how we feel about ourselves, how we behave, how we assess the antics of the spiritually starved, and how we embrace the principles God has given us to live by. Gradually, as we grow, and through his grace, we become more and more like him. This is a mighty work. It is his work.

I am not only comforted but also excited at what I am seeing among the young women and the older sisters across this worldwide church. Though some are disgruntled, there seems to be a new upsurge of wonderful, committed women. Sisters, the wash *is* being done. The babies *are* being loved and trained. Young women *are* standing firm against peer pressure. People *are* sensitively spreading the good word. Prayers *are* being offered more carefully and testimonies expressed more fervently. We have in the Church today women of all ages who are aware, who care. They understand what it means to take upon them the name of Christ. Their lamps are filled. They are ready. They await the bridegroom.

MAKING A DIFFERENCE

Meanwhile, they are making the difference in the quality of life of those about them. For example, I met a superb missionary who was older than the other elders. I learned that he had had a very troubled past. When I asked how the change came in him, he replied with tears in his eyes, "My mother prayed me straight. Endlessly, tirelessly, she prayed for me." His record of baptisms adds jewels to his mother's crown.

A family with three teenage children had dropped into inactivity in a Scandinavian stake. The home teachers, the visiting teachers, the priesthood leadership had not been able to reach these people. Then a young woman was called to be a class president. Her attitude was, "If I am called to serve, I will serve with success through the power of God." And she was successful. She reached that family; one of them now serves as branch leader for the young women.

A single woman joined the Church under difficult circumstances some years ago. When I talked with her recently, she told me of thirty-one members of her family and of nearly thirty others she had helped into the Church. "I told the Lord that if I came into the Church, I didn't want to be in alone. I've talked more to him than anyone else in these past years.

I tell him that if he'll open the doors, I'll walk through and get the people."

As wonderful as these and other women like them are, we can all be even better. We need more women who, having been willing to take upon them the name of Jesus Christ, are then willing to take upon them the work he has designated for the sisters.

We need more women who know Jesus Christ and who will teach and testify of him. We need women who are studying the scriptures, who know the word of God and experiment upon the word; women who will move by knowledge and also by faith, who will "be no more as children, tossed to and fro, and carried about with every wind of doctrine, by the sleight of men, and cunning craftiness, whereby they lie in wait to deceive" (Ephesians 4:14).

Dr. Charles D. McIver, in an address at the North Carolina College for Women, said, "When you educate a man, you educate an individual; when you educate a woman, you educate a whole family." Brigham Young said that if he had to educate either his sons or his daughters, he would choose his daughters because they would influence generations.

In the process of becoming educated, let us grow spiritually in our knowledge of Christ. This is the all-important knowledge. With this knowledge comes change.

We need women who are more valiant and who are not ashamed of the gospel of Jesus Christ, who can stand up and be counted, who use the Spirit within them to discern. These are the peaceful women. Frustration and depression are not part of their being.

We need women who are willing to make a wholesome difference. Robert Frost's often-quoted poem regarding two roads comes to mind. The one *not* taken made all the difference. And isn't this true with Mormon women and the path we choose to take? Someone once suggested that for evil to flourish, it simply requires that good men and women do nothing. For good Mormon women to do nothing—to simply bask in their latter-day blessings—seems to me to be a pitiful breach of promise and purpose.

We need more diligent women to love their husbands into gentility or to just love their husbands and children better. If they haven't done either yet, then we need them to open their hearts and extend the reach of their affection and effectiveness to others.

So whether we are named Maren, Margit, Susan, Helen, Brigitta, or even Camilla, the Lord needs women who will take upon themselves his ways, his will, and his work, as well as his name.

If each of us will begin to do this with the power that is in us, we will soon notice a mighty change in our lives. Trials and troubles won't get the better of us. The gates of hell will not prevail against us, and the heavens will shake for our good (see D&C 21:6). Our hearts and our homes will be filled with unspeakable love. Our wards will be stronger and our numbers will swell. Good will be done.

You see, taking upon us the name of Christ and then living as if we have can make all the difference.

OLD TESTAMENT INSIGHTS: WOMEN, WIT, WISDOM

⤨

Aileen Hales Clyde

I was drawn to the poetry of the Old Testament by my literate mother, who often chose to read to me when I was a child, from Genesis, Psalms, 1 Samuel, 1 Kings, and Isaiah. The more common Bible stories were introduced to me not at home but in Sunday School or Primary. Before I could read, I had heard many times, "In the beginning God created the heaven and the earth. . . . And God said, Let there be light: and there was light. And God saw the light, that it was good: and God divided the light from the darkness. . . . And God said, Let the waters under the heaven be gathered together unto one place, and let the dry land appear: and it was so. And God called the dry land Earth; and the gathering together of the waters called he Seas: and God saw that it was good" (Genesis 1:1, 3, 9–10). And so on through the Creation, with the assurance in each case, "And God saw that it was good." I would hear my mother's voice asserting and confirming as I sat on her lap and sometimes drifted off to sleep, "And God said, Let us make man in our image, after our likeness: and let them have dominion over the fish of the sea, and over the fowl of the air, and over the cattle, and over all the earth, and over every creeping thing that creepeth upon the earth. So God created man in his own image, in the image of God created he him; male and female created he them. . . . And God saw everything that he had made, and, behold, it was very good" (Genesis 1:26–27, 31).

That still strikes me as a good beginning. And as a child it impressed upon me that God was my creator and that he saw his work as good. What I heard from the Bible when I was very young rings in my ears still and provided a dependable buttress against the difficult paradoxes that I later discovered abounded in scriptures and also in life.

Aileen Hales Clyde has served as second counselor in the Relief Society General Presidency. She has also served as a regent of the Utah System of Higher Education and chaired the Utah task force on gender and justice. Sister Clyde received her bachelor's degree in English from Brigham Young University, where she taught part-time for ten years. She and her husband, Hal M. Clyde, are the parents of three sons.

The household where I grew up included three brothers, no sisters, and parents who encouraged wide-ranging discussions of what was, what should be, and how we each had a part in figuring things out. My identity as a person sprang from these discussions. By the time I was through adolescence and was reading scriptures seriously on my own, I had noted that in the Old Testament a woman's worth was tied to her marital status and that her father was usually the broker in that important arrangement. Women were possessions of their fathers or their husbands. The tenth commandment does not even give the wife first priority in a man's listed possessions. "Thou shalt not covet thy neighbour's house, thou shalt not covet thy neighbour's wife, nor his manservant, nor his maidservant, nor his ox, nor his ass, nor any thing that is thy neighbour's" (Exodus 20:17). I saw that fertility had very different consequences for women and for men. Childbirth was the key to a woman's worth. Stories of Rachel, Sarah, Samson's mother, and Hannah, all manifest the stigma and disgrace associated with barrenness. As a young woman, this impressed me as very sad and very unfair.

Old Testament references to women are limited, but they provide rich glimpses into female ways. In Genesis 21, for example, after Sarah has weaned her miracle baby Isaac, she tells Abraham to send Hagar and her son Ishmael away. Abraham is deeply grieved until God tells him that Ishmael, too, will lead a great nation. Thus assured that the child will survive, Abraham gives Hagar a bottle of water and some bread and sends her and the child into the wilderness of Beersheba. In the Beersheba desert, dehydration comes quickly. Poor Hagar had been expelled before, but this would be much worse because of the child. After the water is long gone, Hagar, who cannot bear to see her child die, places him under a shrub for some particle of shade and goes "a good way off, as it were a bowshot" in distance, and weeps (v. 16). An angel of God "call[s] to Hagar out of heaven" (v. 17) and tells her that God has heard the cries of her son. That detail is more important than I ever before knew. An angel heard Hagar, but God heard the child. For over a year now, I have worked on a state task force on child abuse. In this connection, I have heard harrowing reports of the ritual abuse of children. Some of those small children, who never met one another, independently report that they had help from angels and that despite their pain they had felt God's love. In the case of Ishmael, God opens Hagar's eyes and she sees a well of water. She refills the bottle, gives the lad a drink, and he lives (see

Genesis 21:14–20). In seven short verses we are caused to contemplate banishment, thirst, mother's love, miraculous water, relief, and God's love. This brief passage still evokes various responses from me. I feel the pain of empathy for Hagar, earlier proud and fulfilled, now low and desperate. Then, in a wondrous turn, God's power works in her and she can act and deliver again her son. I feel elation and relief. The wonder in such scripture is the more I look, the more I see.

Having been raised on Bible stories, I appreciate the need to forewarn as well as invite people to search the scriptures. The Old Testament, particularly the book of Genesis, is not for the faint-hearted. As the incident with Hagar suggests, these are families that are capable of harshness, deception, violence, and self-service.

The story of Jacob reveals an entire family whose members constantly deceive one another. The men do it, and the women do it. There is no gender bias in deception. Jacob, with his mother Rebekah's help, deceives his brother Esau and his father Isaac in order to secure for himself the coveted birthright and its blessing. Later, Jacob's uncle Laban deceives Jacob by substituting Laban's elder daughter Leah for the younger daughter Rachel, whom Jacob loved so much. I find Genesis 29:20 perhaps the loveliest verse in the Old Testament: "And Jacob served seven years for Rachel; and they seemed unto him but a few days, for the love he had to her." Jacob, in turn, deceives Laban over ownership of their livestock. Rachel deceives her father, Laban, over possession of his beloved family icons. Much later, Jacob's own sons deceive him about their younger brother Joseph's disappearance. Jacob's sons, Simeon and Levi, deceive the people of Shechem over the defiling of their sister Dinah, "which thing [the defiling] ought not to be done" (Genesis 34:7). But what the brothers did, after their father's peaceful negotiation with the people of Shechem, was to roar into the city, brandishing swords. They killed every man, "and all their little ones, and their wives took they captive" (Genesis 34:29). This in no way restored Dinah's honor. The violence was self-serving and ego-raising. Jacob's son Judah deceives his widowed daughter-in-law Tamar by reneging on his promise to let her marry his last son. Tamar, in turn, deceives her father-in-law Judah to expose his wrongful deception.

In reminding you of these imperfect people, I spared you Sodom and Gomorrah, also in Genesis. When I hear people bemoaning the awful state of the world, implying that things are worse than ever before, I think, "They are not readers of the Old Testament." The Old Testament writers are quite willing to expose their characters' imperfections. This is no white-washed history. And we should take comfort that while we have not eliminated all their transgressions, most of us know better and do better, much of the time.

Among the Old Testament women are some who were initiators of action and decisions that blessed Israel and bless us, their spiritual descendants. Shiphrah and Puah in Exodus are known to us by their names and also by their occupation. The Egyptian king, fearing a slave revolution, ordered the Hebrew midwives to kill all male babies at birth, "but the midwives feared God, and did not as the king of Egypt commanded them, but saved the men children alive" (Exodus 1:17). When confronted by the king, they explained that "the Hebrew women are not as the Egyptian women" (v. 19) and are so vigorous in birthing that they and the babies were gone before the midwives arrived to assist. This prevarication was a combination of civil disobedience and divine obedience. Their yes to God's command required a no to the king's command. Their own safety seemed to be of no consideration to them. They dealt with their dilemma and stood accountable before God and the king.

In Judges 11 is a gem of a story that I never heard in church. I still remember the impact that it had when I first read it privately and carefully. It is an account in forty verses of a remarkable young woman, acted upon but also capable of acting. She is known to us as Jephthah's daughter. Her father was "the son of an harlot" (v. 1), surely one of the ten ugliest and most biased labels in any language. Jephthah bore the stigma of that label. Banished not only from his father Gilead's house but from Israel, he lives in Tob, where he becomes known as a man of valor. When the Ammonites make war against Israel, the elders of Gilead seek Jephthah to lead the Israelite army, and he bargains with them to be instated as head of his father's house if he wins. Then he makes what is both an unnecessary and disastrous vow. "And Jephthah vowed a vow unto the Lord, and said, If thou shalt without fail deliver the children of Ammon into mine hands, Then it shall be, that whatsoever cometh forth of the doors of my house to meet me, when I return in peace from the children of Ammon, shall surely be the Lord's, and I will offer it up for a burnt offering" (vv. 30–31). The vow was unnecessary, because the spirit of the Lord had already come upon him, and he knew he would be aided to victory. It was clearly disastrous because anyone coming from his home to meet him would be someone whom he loved and who loved him.

After a great slaughter, the children of Ammon were "subdued before the children of Israel" (Judges 11:33). And who comes out "with timbrels and with dances" (v. 34) to meet her victorious father on his return from battle? Jephthah's daughter, his only child! Now this great warrior, full of victory and power, does not berate himself for this state of affairs. Instead he berates his daughter. "When he saw her, . . . he rent his clothes, and said, Alas, my daughter! thou hast brought me very low, and thou art one of them that trouble me: for I have opened my mouth unto the Lord, and I cannot go back" (v. 35). In contrast, with remarkable equanimity, she sees what must be and offers herself so that her father can fulfill his vow. We have no record of her fear or of any need for pity or for apology from her father. The record does tell us, though, that she asks for time—time to "bewail her virginity" (v. 37), time to grieve for the family she will not have, two month's time to go into the mountains with her friends before she yields herself as her father's sacrifice. There was no substitution this time. God had not required this act, but Jephthah's daughter submitted herself for her father's honor. That she took comfort with companions suggests strongly to me the importance of and strength in sisterhood. Much later, in Hebrews 11:32–33, the rash Jephthah is remembered for his faith, but I remember his nameless daughter for her courage and for her strength in her friends. Her friends remembered her, too. Judges 11 concludes, "And it was a custom in Israel, that the daughters of Israel went yearly to lament the daughter of Jephthah the Gileadite four days in a year" (vv. 39–40).

Tucked immediately after the book of Judges is the short but familiar book of Ruth. The story of Ruth has come to represent for me a remarkable story of conversion. The Moabitess, whose husband, father-in-law, and brother-in-law have died, chooses to follow her mother-in-law to Israel, where she would be exiled in a culture that hated Moabites and where a woman's survival depended on a husband, father, or brother. But she knows God and loves her mother-in-law. Her words in this beautiful Hebraic passage testify of her loyalty to both. "And Ruth said, Intreat me not to leave thee, or to return from following after thee: for whither thou goest, I will go; and where thou lodgest, I will lodge: thy people shall be my people, and thy God my God: where thou diest, will I die, and there will I be buried: the Lord do so to me, and more also, if ought but death part thee and me" (Ruth 1:16–17).

When Naomi herself, realistic and wise, saw Ruth's steadfastness, she "left speaking unto her" (v. 18), which does not mean she stopped talking to her but that she quit trying to convince her of the difficulties they would face in Israel. "So Naomi returned, and Ruth the Moabitess, her daughter in law with her, which returned out of the country of Moab: and they came to Beth-lehem in the beginning of barley harvest" (Ruth 1:22). But barley was not all they harvested.

Those two became a great team. The last three of the four chapters in the book are very adult reading. Boaz, a kinsman of Naomi's husband, allowed Ruth to glean in his field. He was quite quickly stricken by her. "And when she was risen up to glean, Boaz commanded his young men, saying, Let her glean even among the sheaves, and reproach her not: and let fall also some of the handfuls of purpose for her, and leave them, that she may glean them, and rebuke her not" (Ruth 2:15–16).

A careful reading indicates how greatly complicated it could be for a righteous Israelite man to marry the widow of his kinsman's son, recently from Moab. But Naomi and Ruth helped, and Boaz never quite knew what hit him. "So Boaz took Ruth, and she was his wife: and when he went in unto her, the Lord gave her conception, and she bare a son. And the women said unto Naomi, Blessed be the Lord . . . for thy daughter in law, which loveth thee, which is better to thee than seven sons, hath born [a son]. And Naomi took the child, and laid it in her bosom, and became nurse unto it. And the women her neighbours gave it a name, saying, There is a son born to Naomi; and they called his name Obed: he is the father of Jesse, the father of David" (Ruth 4:13–14).

In a culture hostile to the leadership of women, these women worked toward an end the writer carefully emphasizes. Obed is the father of Jesse, the father of David, through whose line—carefully detailed for us in the first chapter of Matthew—came Jesus, who is called Christ.

Following Ruth in the Old Testament is 1 Samuel, which actually pre-dates the book of Ruth by five hundred years. The story of Hannah, a favored wife of Elkanah, is full of detail and marvelous glimpses of human striving to reach and serve God. Elkanah had two wives: Hannah, who was barren, and Peninnah, who was fertile. Once a year Elkanah took his family to the city of Shiloh to worship and to offer "sacrifice unto the Lord of hosts." "And when the time was that Elkanah offered, he gave to

Peninnah his wife, and to all her sons and her daughters, portions: But unto Hannah he gave a worthy portion; for he loved Hannah: but the Lord had shut up her womb." And this troubled Hannah greatly, so that she wept and often did not eat. "Then said Elkanah her husband to her, Hannah, why weepest thou? and why eatest thou not? and why is thy heart grieved? am not I better to thee than ten sons?" (1 Samuel 1:2–8).

One time when they were at Shiloh to make their offering, Hannah waited until all had eaten and drunk and then returned to the temple alone. Eli the priest was seated "by a post of the temple" (v. 9), apparently unnoticed by Hannah. He had his own problems. His two sons, the priests Phinehas and Hophni, who were supposed to serve the Lord, were "vile," and he knew it (1 Samuel 3:13).

"Now Eli was very old, and heard all that his sons did unto all Israel; and how they lay with the women that assembled at the door of the tabernacle of the congregation. And he said unto them, Why do ye such things? for I hear of your evil dealings by all this people. Nay, my sons; for it is no good report that I hear: ye make the Lord's people to transgress." He expressed concern not only for their pernicious example but also for their own souls—to no avail. "If one man sin against another, the judge shall judge him: but if a man sin against the Lord, who shall intreat for him? Notwithstanding they harkened not unto the voice of their father" (1 Samuel 2:22–25). So perhaps Eli had also come to the temple at a quiet hour with a private grief and petition.

Hannah had returned to this special place of worship to beseech the Lord to hear her prayers for a child. She vowed that if the Lord would give her a son, she would in turn "give him unto the Lord all the days of his life. And it came to pass, as she continued praying before the Lord," we are told, "Eli marked her mouth. Now Hannah, she spake in her heart; only her lips moved, but her voice was not heard: therefore Eli thought she had been drunken" (1 Samuel 1:11–13).

Here is a biblical case where a priesthood leader misunderstands a woman, and she, in dignity, yet with respect, clarifies for him. "And Hannah answered and said, No, my lord, I am a woman of a sorrowful spirit: I have drunk neither wine nor strong drink, but have poured out my soul before the Lord. Count not thine handmaid for a daughter of Belial: for out of the abundance of my complaint and grief have I spoken." And in a record all too brief, but wonderful nevertheless, Eli hears and understands. Then, exercising the office he is called to, he says, "Go in peace: and the God of Israel grant thee thy petition that thou has asked of him" (1 Samuel 1:15–17).

Hannah responds with grace and full composure. No doubt Eli's words were full of bright promise, but she seemed immediately restored from sorrow by power beyond both her own hopes and the priest's words. "So the woman went her way, and did eat, and her countenance was no more sad" (1 Samuel 1:18). Eli's blessing must have been confirmed to Hannah by the Spirit's witness. Later she sings a song of faith and strength, not well enough known by the latter-day daughters of Zion. "There is none holy as the Lord: for there is none beside thee: neither is there any rock like our God. . . . He raiseth up the poor out of the dust, and lifteth up the beggar from the dunghill, to set them among princes, and to make them inherit the throne of glory: for the pillars of the earth are the Lord's, and he hath set the world upon them" (1 Samuel 2:2, 8).

Too often Hannah is remembered for bargaining with God and then giving her son Samuel to serve in the temple. Her faith and capacity for love and sacrifice deserve more of our emphasis. And surely she could represent an ideal to priesthood leaders who occasionally misread the obvious signs and would delight in clarification as evenhanded and reasonable as Hannah's.

These books are what I call religious. They teach me not only about the people but about God and faith. Other books have other emphases, and as our eighth Article of Faith suggests, we need to read the scriptures to discern such differences. The Prophet Joseph wrote the Articles of Faith in response to a request for a brief history of the Church from a Chicago newspaper editor, John Wentworth. Joseph included in his reply thirteen statements of belief that distinguished some of the similarities and differences between Latter-day Saint doctrine and that of other religions. The eighth article begins, "We believe the Bible to be the word of God as far as it is translated correctly." This qualification—"as far as it is translated correctly"—suggests to me a certain attitude toward scripture. I am not to distrust or dismiss whatever I may find hard to understand or sympathize with; rather, I am to read prayerfully, deeply, and thoughtfully, as did Joseph Smith. I am to read with all my wits about me. I am to ponder and question in order to learn.

Often in scripture we are to learn by negative examples as well as positive ones—and rarely do we encounter characters who are flawless. That is true of Esther and her cousin Mordecai in the book of Esther, as well as the more obvious villain Haman, the determined enemy of the Jewish people then scattered and under Persian rule. The author of the book of Esther unfolds the tale of Esther and Mordecai's loyalty to their people with an emphasis that is not primarily religious. The book opens with details of a lavish royal celebration lasting seven days. The men and women are separated during the festivities and on the seventh day when the king Ahasuerus is "merry with wine" (Esther 1:10), he sends his chamberlains to fetch his queen, Vashti, so all can see her beauty—and she refuses to come. The chamberlains who have to report the affront are enraged, and the king is "very wroth, and his anger burn[s] in him" (v. 12). No doubt the liquor lent significantly to the riling, for the offense quickly takes on cataclysmic proportions. A drunk chamberlain offers his own opinion that "Vashti the queen hath not done wrong to the king only, but also to all the princes, and to all the people" in all the provinces of Ahasuerus's vast kingdom (v. 16). He was sure that when the report of Vashti's refusal got abroad that all women would show disrespect for their husbands. And thus it was decided that Vashti would come before the king no more, that her royal estate would be given to another, and that a decree would be sent throughout the empire commanding that all wives should give their husbands honor. This mandate would also go to every province, translated into the various languages, proclaiming that "every man should bear rule in his own house" (v. 22).

The only verse of even minimal human tenderness in the whole book of Esther begins the next chapter. We see the king and he has sobered up. "After these things, when the wrath of king Ahasuerus was appeased, he remembered Vashti, and what she had done, and what was decreed against her." This hint of a sad morning-after memory is as close to regret as this story of vanity and court intrigue will come. In brief, Esther is rounded up at the behest of her cousin Mordecai for the beauty contest held to replace Vashti. She gains the approval of the king, and, in a tale intricately woven, she becomes the queen. There is much intrigue and much danger in the story, involving Esther, Mordecai, and Haman, an enemy of the Jews. Yet I find it significant that after Esther becomes the queen, and as soon as she gains power, she, who has so recently faced death herself, requires the death of the sons of Haman. "Let Haman's ten sons be hanged upon the gallows," she says (Esther 9:13).

Not only has the anti-Semite Haman been defeated in this tale, but no sons will be left to resume his vendetta against the Jews. We can see on close and careful reading what is seldom derived from passages selected without context: the purpose of the book of Esther is mainly to intensify the Jewish people's loyalty to their traditions and religion at a time when they are being threatened by the invasion of Hellenism and national disintegration. The author's message in this book is clearly not religious. God's name appears nowhere in it. There is no mention of prayer. Devotion to one's race takes the place of genuine religious feeling. The vividly drawn characters are all, except perhaps for Vashti, notably designing, revengeful, even cruel.

My growing affinity for life and its diversity in my time is enriched by the human variety and divine connections so memorably recorded in the Old Testament. Reading there for personal meaning is an adventure that has never disappointed me. I have discovered in those books all kinds of lives, and they have taught me much about mine.

THE SAVIOR:
AN EXAMPLE FOR EVERYONE

Karen Lynn Davidson

In talking about the Savior, perhaps the place to start is by recalling the announcement of his birth. Those unsuspecting shepherds who thought they were in for just another cold winter's night watching some sleepy sheep must have been very surprised when the angel appeared to them and announced: "Behold, I bring you good tidings of great joy, which shall be to all people" (Luke 2:10). The announcement of those good tidings is fairly straightforward—"Behold, I bring you good tidings of great joy"—but why do you suppose the angel needed to add, "which shall be to all people"? Is it possible that the angel added those words because at that moment the shepherds needed some reassurance? Perhaps they were afraid that the angel had made a mistake, that these blessings were not really meant for lowly shepherds; but the angel stipulated without any ambivalence that the tidings were for *all people*.

Think for a moment how in those times so few things would have been for all people. In those times people took for granted that different groups had different laws, privileges, and customs; in fact, virtually nothing accrued to you simply because you had been born and existed as a human being. That is quite a modern idea. Society's assumptions about you and your assumptions about yourself would have depended on your race, your sex, and the class you had been born into. Nothing, until the Savior's announcement, was really for all people. And while some may think otherwise, the Savior never added a footnote to his life or to his list of teachings that said, "By the way, everything that I have done and everything that I have said is relevant to only 48 percent of the

Karen Lynn Davidson received her B.A. and M.A. degrees in English from Brigham Young University, where she was concertmistress of the BYU Philharmonic Orchestra for five years. She earned a Ph.D. in English from the University of Southern California and was director of the honors program and an associate professor of English at Brigham Young University. She has also served as a member of the Music Committee of the Church. She is married to David A. Davidson.

population; the other 52 percent will have to look someplace else to find the way, the truth, and the light, because what I have said and what I have done are not relevant to women." Instead, he came to teach all people, both men and women, the kind of life our Father in heaven would have us lead.

Yet often, sometimes without even realizing it, we women hear certain of the Savior's teachings and we think that while it is a beautiful message, it doesn't apply to us, or at least not very forcefully. I would even guess that nearly every woman has at some time, in some way, excused herself from really responding to the admonitions of the Savior, simply because she is a woman. What a tragedy it is to think that the one perfect life that was ever lived, the one infallible example that we have, the one teacher we have as to what to do with our earth life, is somehow not fully for us.

Some may have a hard time believing that they do this. You may be saying to yourself, "Maybe I don't live a perfectly Christlike life, but I don't use the fact that I'm a woman as an excuse for my shortcomings." I am sure that our rejection of the full responsibility of a Christlike life is rarely quite this conscious or this deliberate, but some things may be happening that are difficult to recognize. Those subtle rejections are what I would like to examine—some of the ways we as women consciously or unconsciously decline the responsibility of living a fully Christlike life.

As we look at what the scriptures tell us about the Savior's life, we see a personage of many facets. One side of his behavior is the side that is most often represented in verse, in music, and in paintings—the gentle side of Christ. He could shed tears, he could bless little children, he could be kind to someone who had been rejected by every other person. He rejected the worldly notions of dominion, power, and bosshood. On the other hand, no one who has ever lived has shown more strength, more courage, more perseverance, more willingness to stand up for truth or rebuke wrong, even at tremendous cost, than has the Savior. He spoke up for unpopular causes. He was willing to speak the truth, even when it cost him his life. If his inner inspiration told him something was right, he did it. That confirmation was all he needed. He didn't need an okay from any of his friends. He had the strength to stand alone. He had absolute confidence in himself and in his Father—confidence to lead out in what was right.

It is this side of the Savior's character—the side that grows, helps others to grow, leads, speaks out, and seeks first and foremost the approval of his Father—that too many women ignore. Many women assume, without really thinking about it, that this part of the Savior's example really has nothing to do with them.

But what on earth would cause a woman to decide that half of Christ's attributes were not relevant to her? Her Creator didn't give her a second-rate mind or second-rate talents. No general authority ever told her to act weak or simple-minded or incompetent. The scriptures do not tell her that she is less than a whole person. What is the source of this dreadfully destructive message? What would cause a woman to shy away from the full responsibility of a Christlike life by saying, "These things are beyond what I'm expected to do. These teachings are not meant for me because I know I could never measure up"?

The fact is that we don't have to look too far. We are surrounded every day by influences that teach women these untruths. How happy Satan must be when he sees women, particularly Latter-day Saint women, absorbing day by day the idea that we are incompetent, unreliable, unimaginative, and unimportant. The sources of these lies are numerous, but I would like to mention briefly three sources that suggest to women that it is all right to accept the gentle side of Christ's example but not the strong side.

The first important and pervasive negative influence is one that none of us escaped. Those who are involved in elementary education or who have studied children's literature can bear me out, as can some recent scholarly studies. This first villain is many aspects of our school experience, particularly the elementary school textbooks we learned to read from. (Textbooks are gradually improving in reflecting girls and women with more dignity and in a more interesting way, but the ones we learned from are almost certain to have done us damage.) When children read these books, what do they see boys doing? The boys invent things. They go on hikes. They take care of animals. They talk about what they want to be when they grow up. What do the girls tend to do in these stories? The girls watch the boys. They admire them. They make food and serve it to the boys. They go shopping for new dresses and do other things that will make them pretty, and they help their mothers.

One study showed that in stories where one sex demeans the other, out of sixty-seven stories, the little boys demeaned the little girls in sixty-five. In two out of the sixty-seven, the little girls demeaned the little boys. Girls are pictured in children's books only one-half as often as boys and are main characters of the stories only one-fourth as often. And the thing that really hurts is that when the little girls are the main characters in the story, they don't *solve* the problems presented in the story; they *are* the problems presented in the story. Usually they have to be rescued by their fathers or their big brothers or even their little brothers.

Regarding classroom experience other than with textbooks, let me refer to a recent study on teacher-student interaction in the elementary school classrooms: "It appears that the types of behavior which elicit teacher feedback in elementary classrooms differ for boys and girls. Boys receive most of their negative feedback for nonacademic behavior—making noise—and most of their positive feedback for academic performance. Girls are most likely to receive negative feedback for their academic work and positive feedback for nonacademic behavior, namely being neat. Differences in teacher-student interaction patterns may contribute to sex differences in students' beliefs regarding the causes of their successes and failures and in their willingness to take on new challenges. Girls are likely to attribute their failures to lack of ability and their successes to hard work. Boys are likely to attribute their failures to lack of hard work and their successes to their own abilities." That is a crucial distinction. A little girl who is brought up under the influence of these messages from textbooks and these interactions in the classroom is being told that somehow she intrinsically just doesn't have what it takes to follow the Savior's pattern. She is not strong. She is not courageous. She is not resourceful or dependable. She is not important for herself, as a person. She is not active. In all these ways, she is being told that, because she is female, she lacks or had better learn to pretend to lack these qualities, because that's how girls are.

The second negative influence is advertising. Although some advertisers are becoming much more conscious of the way in which they may be demeaning the role of women, it is impossible not to sense the negative impact of the image of women in most advertisements. What is the role of women in most TV advertisements? The woman is shown in very limited roles, usually in very limited locations—mainly the kitchen and the bathroom. She is full of problems, again, just like the little girls in the elementary school readers. Often it is a rather simple problem centered on the kitchen or the laundry, but the problems have her so baffled that many times a man must enter and offer a solution.

The newspaper columnist Carrie Beauchamp recently discussed the unfortunate role representations in the media:

"Television commercials are the worst offenders, compounding the role model of subservient female with the subliminal message of the authoritative male voice. Time and again we are hit with variations of the same theme [of the] hopeless, insecure female being directed and reassured by the off-camera man who knows all. I might not be so offended by these scenes, if there was any hope that the man knew anything about the subject at hand. Just once, I would love to see one of those men get in front of the camera, bend over the tub, and scrub that ring out himself. The latest trend in commercials is the spontaneous woman-on-the-street interview, which then cuts to a similar interview with her husband. It was bad enough when wives were being embarrassed in front of God, their mothers-in-law, and the world for not knowing what they should have discussed before they were married right along with how many children they wanted—that he would prefer stuffing to potatoes—but now women are being barraged with a new level of guilt for not knowing that men notice the softness in clothes. After blushing with embarrassment, the wife is asked in the most condescending tones by that off-camera voice: 'Now, what brand of softener will you buy next time?' It is as if she were a three-year-old who will learn only by repeating the brand name aloud fifty times. . . . It is hard enough to survive as a wife, mother, and worker in this society. Credits are few and far between and self-respect hard enough to maintain without adding new burdens like buying the right clothes softener."

The women shown in advertisements often appear shallow, preoccupied with short-term goals. Most of them do not leave the impression of being concerned with eternal goals or the significant pressures of life. By implication, these more profound questions are left to men. It would be very difficult to overestimate the harm of these influences that we and our sisters and our daughters are subjected to almost every day. Instead of being pictured as someone who is concerned with deep family problems, someone who is capable of seeking the virtues and achievements of a Christlike life, the woman in the advertisement is thrown into a crisis for fear her mother-in-law will see that the dishwasher left spots on the crystal.

The third influence is that of movies and television. Although in real life many women devote themselves unselfishly to important kinds of service and to high ideals, movies and especially television almost never reflect this fact. Instead, whether it is comedy or more serious drama, women are shown as selfishly seeking their own advantage or as asking approval from others in a very shallow way. These women are either cunning and manipulative, trying to obtain their own goals, or childishly dependent.

In addition, the main female characters of movies and television are almost always young and attractive, attributes not necessarily true of the main male characters. Many older actors can play a romantic lead in a film, but almost always the main female characters are young and attractive, leaving women who do not fit this image with a lesser view of their own worth. When Brooke Shields appeared on the cover of *Time* magazine, she was fourteen years old. The cover article described her as "the female figure that women in the United States now want to look like." Can you imagine women wanting to look like a fourteen-year-old? These young and attractive women are the ones who are admired and the ones people pay money to see. No other women seem worthy of this attention.

What kind of a Christlike view of herself can a woman have when every day she is told that she is not important unless she is beautiful and charming—that women tend to be shallow and selfish and worth only what their physical appearances or their underhanded manipulations can gain for them? Again, Satan must rejoice when he sees women told again and again, "This is all you are; this is all you are worth." The confidence, the outward reach that anyone, man or woman, must have in order to make the first steps toward godhood are certainly not compatible with this very low-minded view of women conveyed by the media.

I would now like to discuss the Savior's most important teachings meant for all people, and I want to suggest that some women do not take these teachings seriously. The first of the three messages I have chosen is that any individual is of worth, that every human being is important—bond or free, Greek or barbarian, male or female. The shepherd leaves the ninety and nine to go after the one. Heaven rejoices when one single soul is saved. Do you accept this teaching that every human being is of infinite worth in terms of yourself? Let me list just a few negative ways of thinking, because I want to suggest that if any of these assumptions reflect your view of yourself, you have demeaned yourself and have accepted a less than full vision of yourself.

1. If you feel that your worth depends on being young and physically attractive, you have in a sense rejected the Savior's teachings about the

intrinsic worth of every human being. You have also set the stage, I think, for a very difficult life for yourself. One of my students recently went into the closet for her twenty-first birthday. She simply was not going to tell anyone that she was turning twenty-one. Already she was withdrawing because she was worried about her age. Doctors' offices and clinics are full of women who cannot cope with the trauma of their thirtieth or their fortieth or their fiftieth birthday. Because of external and relatively un-important reasons, they have lost their feelings of self-worth. Can you imagine the Savior withholding his love from an elderly or less attractive woman? Yet we do not make the same allowances for ourselves. I hope that Latter-day Saint women will know that their essential worth and the things important to them are not tied up with their age or attractiveness.

2. If you convey to any woman—to yourself, your mother, your room-mate, your sister, your daughter, or your girl friend—a message that just because she is a woman, certain skills and professions and achievements are beyond her capacity, you have labeled her unfairly. You have told her that she is a member of a second-class group. The Savior never told her that. You have not truly recognized her as an individual, and you have missed the point of one of the Savior's most important teachings. You have steered her away from the possibility of a fully Christlike life because you were not seeing her individual, unique worth.

3. If, because you are a woman, you hold back from accepting leader-ship positions, from speaking up in class, or from doing the best work you are capable of, you have not really accepted yourself as a person of dig-nity and importance and ability. I am sorry to report that at BYU we have thousands of women students who are dabblers as far as their school work is concerned—also a few men who fall into that category, but more women than men by far. Tithing funds are supporting them in this dabbling, and I feel that the day will come when they will be held respon-sible for the waste of these sacred tithing funds. It is a tragic human waste, and it is a tragic financial waste. If a woman has a vision of her own indi-vidual worth, she will not dabble.

4. If you find yourself having to define yourself in terms of someone else, you have not really understood what the Savior meant by dignity and individual worth. Every woman, married or single, must be able to define herself in terms of herself and not in terms of her relationship or lack of relationship with someone else. The prophets have stressed many times that marriage is an appropriate and universal goal. But it has been

my observation that the best marriages, the best engagements, are not the results of directly seeking after marriage. The best marriages seem to be a by-product of pursuing many different kinds of worthy goals. In other words, a young woman at Brigham Young University or anywhere else who devotes her full attentions and energies to finding a husband may well find one, but this perhaps will not be the best kind of match. The best marriage will be the one that comes when the young woman is not so much concerned with finding the right one as with *being* the right one.

When Harold B. Lee first saw the woman who was to become Freda Joan Lee, she was wheeling her crippled stepfather into sacrament meeting in a wheelchair. Now it would be my guess that many women would have liked to sit in ambush for that very, very eligible widower, handsome Harold B. Lee. I imagine there were women who were contriving to sit by him in church or to bring by a little bottle of jam. I imagine there were women who were buying new dresses in hopes that he would notice them, but the ambush tactics did not work. What did work was that the future Sister Lee was doing what she was supposed to. Without exception, the presidents of the Church have chosen for their wives women who have a sense of their own worth, who have made their mark before they were married, and who continued to make a mark after they were married.

If a woman devotes her total energies and time and talents to getting married, then she is not inclined to see herself in terms of her individual worth. She has defined herself only in terms of someone else. She does not understand what the Savior taught about individual worth. If you are single or if you are married, do not wait for someone else to make you happy. Do not wait for someone else to bring you forward. Do not wait for someone else to enable you to do important things during this life. The Savior taught that you are important just for yourself, not just as you are defined in terms of someone else.

Another of the Savior's crucial teachings is that of service. The way we show our love for him is through serving others, because when we serve others, he has told us, we are serving him. We all acknowledge the importance of service within the home; unfortunately, many women do not see in themselves the additional capacity for large-scale service outside the home. But the Church cannot afford to give up half of its leadership just because women might decide it is more appropriate to hang back and pretend that they won't or can't serve. We must have leaders, both men and women. We must have women who are willing to rebuke error and wrong and to speak up for moral standards that we as Latter-day Saints know are right.

The early sisters of the Church never thought of acting simple-minded and incompetent or of coasting along inconspicuously in the Church. Before they joined the Church, they were bound by the horrible limitations of supposedly proper Victorian womanhood. They were to be submissive, pure, pious, and domestic—which are all fine qualities, but that was the ceiling. Those teachings of society told them they were subservient, a piece of furniture, someone's possession, only an ornament. But after their conversion, they were free. They learned something different about themselves. When Joseph Smith organized the Relief Society, he stated specifically that the sisters were responsible for their own sins, for their own salvation, and for their own spiritual gifts. Women such as Eliza R. Snow and Emmeline B. Wells knew they were needed badly, so they served. Is the need of the Church any less now for us? Shouldn't our beliefs help to keep us from the kinds of influences we looked at earlier?

It is not just the Church that needs the leadership and influence of *all* the righteous people—there is a whole world out there badly in need of voices to speak out for right causes. In one respect the Church does not have a very good reputation in the world: we do not have a good reputation for supporting righteous community and national causes. Our excuse usually is that we are too busy with our Church assignments. I am not sure that excuse will do in all cases. Can we really ignore the millions of our nonmember brothers and sisters who need us? There are many who never join the Church in this life, but they still need us. They need what we know. Imagine what examples we could be. Imagine how many people could be drawn to the Church if we would lend our strengths and talents to the needs of our communities, such as the need to eliminate child abuse and child alcoholism, the need for righteous leadership on school boards, the need for community youth leadership, the need to assist lonely, elderly people as well as the underprivileged of the world.

As we think about helping in these causes and lending our service and talents outside our Church, we should be prepared to do more than just flutter in and say, "Here I am; what can I do to help?" It is much better to go in and say, "Here I am; let me tell you about my skills. I am a nurse (or an accountant, or a lawyer, or an artist, or a writer, or I have had administrative experience). I have very conspicuous parenting skills. I have a degree in home economics; therefore, I am especially qualified to go on a health mission." Have the skills, not just the willingness. When we see a wrong, let's be capable of more than just indignation. Let's be skilled enough to express our indignation in a way that will convince other people and then be able to suggest and carry out some solutions. As President Harold B. Lee said, "It's good to be faithful; it's better to be faithful and competent."[1]

We have been talking about service outside the home, but I do not think that being skilled and alert and competent is likely to make anyone a worse mother. I think it is likely to make someone a much better mother. I know because I am the daughter of such a mother, and I think that those who are also the daughters of such mothers will agree that we can count this as one of the greatest blessings of our lives. So in the home as well as outside the home, the ideal of service is important. Conspicuous and significant kinds of service that will serve as a beacon to many people are the results of our preparing ourselves with the skills to perform them.

Another critical teaching of the Savior is that of eternal progression. "Be ye therefore perfect, even as your Father which is in heaven is perfect" (Matthew 5:48). The doctrines of the Church do not refer to people in the hereafter as "kings and clinging vines" or as "gods and shrinking violets." Instead, we learn of "priests and priestesses, gods and goddesses." The Savior taught that both men and women must move forward in the development of spirituality, that all must seek wisdom and knowledge. President Harold B. Lee said, "The gospel has nothing to do with being. The gospel has only to do with becoming."[2] Yet how many people—and again, I think, particularly women—are content just to *be* instead of to *become*, to be passive, to wait, to react just as they have been taught through textbooks and the media instead of planning their own growth and working on it steadily. It is not enough to say, "Oh, my husband is doing wonderfully; my children are doing wonderfully." I hope the woman who speaks these words is also doing wonderfully, because no one else's growth can substitute for her own.

We have looked at three of the Savior's most important teachings—individual worth, service, and eternal progression. We have also mentioned that his life took in many facets. One side was gentle; it was the side that women find the most natural role model, at least at first glance.

One side was very strong and effective. Let me conclude just by listing four points that I think will be true of a woman who truly accepts the Savior as an example in her life.

First, if a woman truly accepts the Savior as her example, she will, when she sees in the world a need for service or expertise, train for that service and then make the finest possible contribution as a professional or volunteer within the context of her other responsibilities.

Second, if a woman truly accepts the Savior as her example, she will accept his teachings concerning individual worth and dignity. She will see herself as a unique person, not subject to someone else's idea of the role she should play. She will find what is right for her and allow other women the same flexibility. There is no one way for a woman to be. We can each be very different. Different things can be important to us, and that is all right.

Third, if a woman truly accepts the Savior as her example, she will not accept the world's false limitations, the handcuffs that printed materials or broadcast materials would place upon her. These false messages serve the purposes of Satan. The serious work of the world and the responsibility for being competent belong to women too.

Fourth, if a woman truly accepts the Savior as her example, she will seek principally for his approbation and validation. She will not let her happiness or feeling of self-worth depend on other human beings whose vision may be helpful on the one hand, but whose vision possibly may be limited, on the other hand, by some of these pervasive false influences that we have been talking about.

To know that we are daughters of our Father in heaven should give us a tremendous sense of joy but also a tremendous sense of responsibility. I hope we can say to ourselves, "I am the daughter of my Father in heaven. As his daughter, I know that I am important because I am me. I know I am capable of great growth, capable of significant service. I will not cancel myself in any way by yielding to false influences that tell me that I am a shallow being or a being of lesser worth or lesser ability. I know that the Savior's examples and teachings were to all people. I will please my Father in heaven by taking his daughters seriously."

THIS IS A TEST.
IT IS ONLY A TEST.

⌒⟨∞⟩⌒

Sheri L. Dew

𝓜y mother made me take piano lessons. And because I am her eldest and she had not yet been worn down by the thankless task of prodding five children to practice every day, my whining about hating to practice fell on deaf ears. The fact that I eventually studied piano for fifteen years is largely a tribute to Mother's resilience. I wish I had a dollar for every time she prophesied that I would thank her one day for all of the musical torture. As always, she was right. I have thanked her, again and again, for that introduction to the keyboard, because somewhere between those first bars of "Here we go, up a row, to a birthday party" and "Rhapsody in Blue," I fell in love with music, especially classical music, which in its more magnificent passages made my heart feel like it was going to leap out of my chest—in other words, it made my young spirit soar.

Here, again, Mother deserves all the credit. I couldn't have been more than ten or eleven when she gave me a stack of classical albums, introducing me to some of the great composers whose works were characterized by dramatic musical passages and what I call the Big Finish.

I would lie in front of the stereo for hours, listening to the third movement of Rachmaninoff's second piano concerto or his "Prelude in C# Minor," all the while imagining myself at a shiny black concert grand in Carnegie Hall. I pictured my debut there, standing ovation and all. I imagined that I would be humble but brilliant—brilliant enough to move an entire audience, including Mother, to tears. Somewhere in all of my daydreaming, I caught a vision of how it would feel to play so beautifully that others' hearts would soar.

At that point, Mother no longer had to encourage me to practice. Once I had a vision of the possibilities, the motivation to master the

Sheri L. Dew is the second counselor in the Relief Society General Presidency. She grew up in Ulysses, Kansas, and graduated from Brigham Young University with a degree in history. A popular speaker and writer, she is vice-president of publishing at Deseret Book Company.

piano came from inside. Am I saying that practicing suddenly was enjoyable? Absolutely not! It was often sheer drudgery. But I found a technique that helped me endure those tedious hours of practice, day in and day out. When I set out to tackle a new piece, I would master and memorize the Big Finish first, all the while visualizing myself in concert where the audience jumped to its feet at the last chord. Imagining how grand the Big Finish would be kept me going through months of rehearsal on technical passages that didn't provide nearly the same sense of drama but that had to be mastered nonetheless. In short, my progress on the piano and my motivation to practice increased dramatically when I caught a vision of my potential.

We are temporarily afflicted with the amnesia of mortality. But just as my spirit was stirred by the majesty of those dramatic musical passages and the possibility of performing them flawlessly, through the power of the Spirit we can often "catch a spark," as President Joseph F. Smith taught us, "from the awakened memories of the immortal soul, which lights up our whole being as with the glory of our former home."[1] It is the Spirit that will also shed light upon our ultimate potential—the grandest finish of all.

If, on the other hand, we are not able to catch a vision of the Big Finish, meaning a clear image of who we are and what we are becoming—how can we be willing to practice? Life, like classical music, is full of the difficult passages that are conquered as much through endurance and determination as through any particular skill.

Remember the announcements that used to interrupt your regularly scheduled television programming? "This is a test of the emergency broadcasting system. It is only a test. If this were a real emergency, you would be notified through this station." You've probably seen the poster that reads, "Life is a test. It is only a test. Had this been a real life, you would have been instructed where to go and what to do." It reminds me of a greeting card a friend gave me that shows a frazzled woman who says, "Mother told me there would be days like this . . . but she failed to mention they could go on for months at a time."

There are times when days feel like months and when life feels like the test that it is, days when the vision and hope of a Big Finish are dimmed by immediate demands, days when one might wish for a mortal exam that was a little more manageable.

For indeed, this life is a test. It is only a test—meaning, that's all it is.

Nothing more, but nothing less. It is a test of many things—of our convictions and priorities, our faith and our faithfulness, our patience and our resilience, and in the end, our ultimate desires. In the long run, as Alma taught, whatever we truly desire, we will have. "I know that [God] granteth unto men according to their desire . . . ; yea, I know that he allotteth unto men . . . according to their wills, whether they be unto salvation or unto destruction" (Alma 29:4).

Thankfully, our experience here is an open-book test. We know why we're here, and we have from prophets ancient and modern an extensive set of instructions that never become passé or grow outdated.

Yes, life *is* a test of many things. But at the risk of sounding simplistic, may I suggest that the mortal experience is largely about vision—our vision of ourselves and our ultimate Big Finish. And vision is determined by faith. The firmer our faith in Jesus Christ, the clearer our vision of ourselves and what we can ultimately achieve and become.

The adversary, of course, is intent on obstructing our vision and undermining our faith. He will do anything and everything to confuse us about who we are and where we're going because he has already forfeited his privilege of going there.

A vision of our potential is central to survival, both spiritually and physically. I've always been curious about Lehi and his family. Just imagine the family home evening when he informed his wife and children that the Lord had directed them to pack a few belongings and foray into the wilderness, leaving behind their life of comfort. I doubt any of them were enthusiastic about the news. Can't you just imagine the dialogue?

"You want us to do what? To pack a few things and leave home?"

"Yes, that is what the Lord has asked us to do."

"Where are we going?"

"I'm not entirely sure. I know only that we must leave Jerusalem. And by the way, we'll need to travel light. So leave most of your things here."

"When will we come back home?"

"That isn't entirely clear. Perhaps never."

We know how Laman and Lemuel responded initially and in perpetuity. Why didn't Nephi, their younger (and presumably less mature) brother, react the same way? He probably wasn't thrilled with his father's news, either.

The difference is a classic demonstration of the power of vision. While Laman and Lemuel rebelled, Nephi asked the Lord if he might see what his father had seen. He had the faith to seek his own vision: "I, Nephi, . . . did cry unto the Lord; and behold he did visit me, and did soften my heart that I did believe all the words which had been spoken by my father; wherefore, I did not rebel against him like unto my brothers" (1 Nephi 2:16). That vision, or sense of purpose, sustained Nephi through a life of trial and tribulation. It helped him pass the test, so to speak.

Joseph Smith was persecuted from the time he announced that he had seen the Father and the Son until he died a martyr. How did he do it? Let us never forget that his prophetic mission began with a vision. "I have actually seen a vision; and who am I that I can withstand God, or why does the world think to make me deny what I have actually seen? For I had seen a vision; I knew it, and I knew that God knew it, and I could not deny it, neither dared I do it; at least I knew that by so doing I would offend God, and come under condemnation" (Joseph Smith– History 1:25).

"Where there is no vision, the people perish," Solomon proclaimed (Proverbs 29:18).

And perhaps nothing is more vital today than having a vision, manifest by the Spirit, of who we are and what we can become, of our intrinsic value to the Lord, and of the unparalleled role we must play in these latter days. We are literally the offspring of God, his begotten sons and daughters, with the potential of exaltation (see Acts 17:29; D&C 76:24). "The Spirit itself beareth witness with our spirit, that we are the children of God: and if children, then heirs; heirs of God, and joint-heirs with Christ" (Romans 8:16–17).

But how do we get a clear vision of who we are? How do we gain an eternal perspective compelling enough to move us to action and to govern our choices and priorities? From whence cometh the vision?

I'm sensitive to the issue of vision at the moment, because I'm going through that midlife eye crisis where I can't seem to hold things far enough away for me to read them. Because of my changing eyesight, I find myself turning on lights and lamps everywhere.

Light is a key to vision! And Jesus Christ is the ultimate Light, the "light which shineth in darkness" (D&C 6:21), the light which chases "darkness from among [us]" (D&C 50:25). Faith in Jesus Christ is the key to vision, to seeing ourselves as the Lord sees us. So to improve our vision, we must increase our faith in and connection to the Savior.

It is no accident that faith—not only *believing in* Jesus Christ but *believing* him—is the first principle of the gospel. President Gordon B. Hinckley has said that "of all our needs, I think the greatest is an increase in faith."[2]

"Blessed art thou, Nephi," the son of Lehi was told, "because thou believest in the Son of the most high God" (1 Nephi 11:6). In Alma's brilliant discourse we are told, "If ye will awake and arouse your faculties, even to an experiment upon my words, and exercise a particle of faith, yea, even if ye can no more than desire to believe, let this desire work in you, even until ye believe in a manner that ye can give place for a portion of my words" (Alma 32:27).

Can't you just hear the Savior saying, "If you only *want* to believe that I will do for you what I have said I will do, will you experiment? Try me. Put me to the test."

As Lehi and his family learned, their Liahona worked according to their faith in God (see Alma 37:40). When they became slothful in their devotions and ceased to exercise faith, the marvelous works ceased. That is in keeping with divine law, for, as Elder James E. Talmage taught, "Faith is of itself a principle of power; and by its presence or absence, . . . even the Lord was and is influenced, and in great measure controlled, in the bestowal or withholding of blessings."[3] Therefore, let us not "be slothful because of the easiness of the way. . . . The way is prepared, and if we will look we may live forever" (Alma 37:46).

Looking. Seeing. Seeking our own vision.

We sometimes tend to define unbelievers as apostates or agnostics. But perhaps that definition is too narrow. What about those of us who have received a witness of the divinity of the Savior and yet deep in our hearts don't believe he will come through for us? We believe he'll do it for others—for President Hinckley, the Quorum of the Twelve, the stake Relief Society president—but not for us.

Have you ever carefully selected a gift for someone only to present the gift and have it fall flat? Perhaps a simple "Thanks" feels nonchalant and even ungrateful. Similarly, it must be disappointing to the Lord, who offered the ultimate sacrifice, when we by our unbelief essentially refuse his gift and therefore his offer of help.

Not long ago a friend who is a respected gospel scholar told me about a fireside he had given on the power of the Atonement. Two sisters came up to him afterwards and said, "What you have taught is great, but frankly it sounds too good to be true."

The Lord's gift to us *is* too good to be true—which makes a tepid reaction to that gift all the more regrettable. More than once Nephi chastened his older brothers for their unbelief: "How is it that ye have forgotten that the Lord is able to do all things according to his will, for the children of men, if it so be that they exercise faith in him?" (1 Nephi 7:12).

How indeed? It is a question we might ask ourselves. The Lord *can* do all things. But it is our faith in him, even our willingness to believe, that activates the power of the Atonement in our lives. "We are made alive in Christ because of our faith" (2 Nephi 25:25). I love Nephi's words when he tells his brothers, speaking of the Lord, "And he loveth those who will have him to be their God" (1 Nephi 17:40). Or in other words, those who accept him and his gift.

One would think it would be easy to embrace and have faith in the gift of the Atonement. But I fear that some Latter-day Saint women know just enough about the gospel to feel guilty that they are not measuring up to some undefinable standard but not enough about the Atonement to feel the peace and strength it affords us. Elder Bruce R. McConkie said that too often the best-kept secret in the Church is the gospel of Jesus Christ. Perhaps some of us don't know how to draw the power of the Atonement into our lives; others aren't willing to seek its blessings. And some don't ask because they don't feel worthy. It's quite the irony that the gospel of the great Jehovah, which contains the power to save every human being and to strengthen every soul, is sometimes interpreted in such a way that feelings of inadequacy result.

Do you remember the exchange in the animated classic *The Lion King* between the deceased King Mufasa and his lion cub, Simba, who turns to riotous living after his father's death? Simba sees his father in a vision, and when he attempts to justify his aimless lifestyle, his father teaches him a divine truth: "You have forgotten who you are because you have forgotten me." Truman Madsen has said that the cruelest thing you can do to a human being is to make him forget that he or she is the son or daughter of a king. There is a direct relationship between our personal experience with the Lord and how we see ourselves. The closer we grow to him, the more clear and complete becomes our vision of who we are and what we can become.

I have tender feelings about the connection between our faith in the Lord and the way we see ourselves because I have spent much of my life struggling to feel that I measured up. Growing up, I was painfully shy. The phrase "social reject" comes to mind. To make matters worse, I hit five-foot-ten in the sixth grade. Five-foot-ten is not a popular height for a sixth-grade girl. I was a Mormon in a very non-Mormon community. The fact that I had a great jump shot didn't translate well socially. The guys were my best friends—but not my dates. And I was a farm girl. Though our little town had all of four thousand residents, there was a clear social distinction between the town kids and the country kids. I laugh about this now. But it wasn't very funny then. There was nothing cool about being a tall, sturdy (as Grandma used to call me), Mormon farm girl. I couldn't do what my friends did or go where they went. I was different, and for a teenager, different is deadly.

The summer after my sophomore year in high school I had an experience that convinced me I was destined to a life of mediocrity. Our small MIA went to Education Week at Brigham Young University, and one of the classes I attended was on the dreaded topic of self-esteem. One day, mid-lecture, the presenter suddenly pointed at me and asked me to stand and introduce myself. I could manage nothing more than to mumble my name and slump back down in my chair. It was pathetic.

I had obviously not demonstrated what the speaker was hoping for, so she pointed to another young woman in the audience—a tall, thin girl with beautiful, long hair. Poise oozed out of her cells as she stood and introduced herself, concluding with a gracious word of thanks to the speaker for her marvelous presentation. All the while I was thinking, "Oh, sit down. She didn't ask for a eulogy." But the comparison between the two of us wasn't lost on me. The lecturer only made things worse when she said, "It seems that the young girl from Kansas doesn't feel as good about herself as the girl from Salt Lake City does."

I can still picture myself in the back seat of our car as we drove home to Kansas. Between little bursts of tears, I contemplated the future, and things didn't look promising. I didn't measure up, and I feared I never would. Now I don't want to overstate things. I had great experiences growing up, and I had disappointing experiences—just like you. But I suffered with a deep feeling of inadequacy.

My insecurities followed me to college at the Y, and as a result I suffered socially, scholastically, and spiritually. When, during graduate school, a friendship ended in a disappointing way, I hopped in my little Toyota and drove home for a few days of consolation. For a week I moped around the house feeling sorry for myself. Then one afternoon I walked down to my brother's room and noticed his journal on his nightstand. Brad was thirteen, and I thought it might be fun to see what pearls of wisdom he had written. The entries were predictable—about sports and girls and motorcycles. But then I came to the entry he had made the day I arrived home unexpectedly from BYU: "Sheri came home from BYU today. I'm so glad she's home. But she doesn't seem very happy. I wish there was something I could do to help her, because I really love her."

As you can imagine, the tears began to flow. But the sweet emotions unleashed by my brother's words triggered an even more powerful sensation, for almost instantly I had a profound feeling of divine love and acceptance wash over me and, simultaneously, a very clear impression that I ought to quit focusing on everything I didn't have, because I had enough, and start doing something with what I did have.

For me, it was a profound moment. I didn't pop up and suddenly feel confident about life, but I couldn't deny that the Spirit had spoken and that the Lord loved me and felt I had something to contribute. It was the beginning of seeing myself with new eyes.

Now let's fast-forward a decade to my early thirties when I faced a personal disappointment that broke my heart. From a point of view distorted by emotional pain, I couldn't believe that anything or anyone could take away the loneliness or that I would ever feel whole or happy again. In an effort to find peace, comfort, and strength, I turned to the Lord in a way I had not before. The scriptures became a lifeline, filled as they were with promises I had never noticed in quite the same way—that he would heal my broken heart and take away my pain, that he would succor, or run to, me and deliver me from disappointment.

Fasting and prayer took on new intensity, and the temple became a place of refuge and revelation. What I learned was not only that the Lord could help me but that he would. Me. A regular, farm-grown member of the Church with no fancy titles or spectacular callings. It was during that agonizing period that I began to discover how magnificent, penetrating, and personal the power of the Atonement is.

I pleaded with the Lord to change my circumstances, because I knew I could never be happy until he did. Instead, he changed my heart. I asked him to take away my burden, but he strengthened me so that I could bear my burdens with ease (see Mosiah 24:15). I had always been a believer, but I'm not sure I had understood what, or who, it was I believed in.

President George Q. Cannon described what I experienced: "When we went forth into the waters of baptism and covenanted with our Father in Heaven to serve Him and keep His commandments, He bound Himself also by covenant to us that He would never desert us, never leave us to ourselves, never forget us, that in the midst of trials and hardships, when everything was arrayed against us, He would be near unto us and would sustain us. That was His covenant."[4]

And it all begins with the willingness to believe. "For if there be no faith among the children of men God can do no miracle among them" (Ether 12:12).

Do you believe that the Savior will really do for *you* what he has said he will do? That he can ease the sting of loneliness and enable you to deal with that haunting sense of inadequacy? That he will help you forgive? That he can fill you with optimism and hope? That he will help you resist your greatest temptation and tame your most annoying weakness? That he will respond to your deepest longing? That he is the only source of comfort, strength, direction, and peace that will not change, will not betray you, and will never let you down?

An unwillingness to believe that the Savior stands ready to deliver us from our difficulties is tantamount to refusing the gift. It is tragic when we refuse to turn to him who paid the ultimate price and let him lift us up. *Life is a test.* But divine assistance is available to help us successfully complete this most critical examination.

Since that difficult period ten years ago, I have had many opportunities to experience the workings of the Lord in my life. He hasn't always given me what I've asked for, and the answers haven't always come easily. But he has never left me alone, and he has never let me down.

Each experience with the Savior leads to greater faith, and as our faith increases, our vision of and confidence about who we are grows clearer. The more we visualize and sense through the impressions of the Spirit our ultimate potential, the more determined we become to achieve it. It's the difference between your mother hounding you to practice the piano and your reaching the point where you want to do it yourself. You simply will not be denied the ultimate reward.

Why is it vital that we as LDS women have a clear vision of who we are and what we are about and have a bedrock faith in the Lord Jesus Christ?

Sister Patricia Holland said something that I find profound: "If I were Satan and wanted to destroy a society, I think I too would stage a full-blown blitz on women."[5]

Is that not exactly what he has done? Hasn't he tried to discourage and distract us in every conceivable way? Doesn't he try to block our understanding of how spiritually sensitive our natures are, how anxious and willing the Lord is to speak to us, and how vital we are to the plan and purposes of the Lord? Satan wants us neutralized, because he knows that the influence of a righteous woman can span generations.

His stated purposes are clear: he desires to make us miserable like unto himself (see 2 Nephi 2:27). He wants us to fail the test, to give up any hope of the Big Finish. Peter delivered a no-nonsense warning: "Be sober, be vigilant; because your adversary the devil, as a roaring lion, walketh about, seeking whom he may devour" (1 Peter 5:8). Indeed, through eons of practice the adversary has perfected the arts of deception, deceit, despair, and discouragement.

Many of his tactics are bold and brazen and played out daily on everything from the Internet to the nightly news. But despite the fact that the adversary's handiwork is outrageously displayed at every turn—pornography, abuse, addiction, dishonesty, violence, and immorality of every kind—many of his strategies are brilliant for their subtlety. "And others will he pacify, and lull them away into carnal security, that they will say: All is well in Zion; yea, Zion prospereth, all is well—and thus the devil cheateth their souls, and leadeth them away carefully down to hell" (2 Nephi 28:21). C. S. Lewis said something similar: "The safest road to Hell is the gradual one—the gentle slope, soft underfoot, without sudden turnings, without milestones, without signposts."[6]

See if any of the following techniques sound familiar:

1. As we have been discussing, Satan tries to blur our vision of why we're here and get us preoccupied with this life. He would have us distracted by and involved in anything and everything except what we came for.

2. He wants us to feel insignificant—that no matter how hard we try, we'll never make much of a difference. Oh, sure, our work is necessary but not very important. *That is a big fat lie.* It is a diversion designed to keep us so focused on any perceived injustices that we completely

overlook the opportunities and privileges that are ours, that we underestimate the vital nature of our contribution, and that we never come to understand the power we have to change lives.

Elder Henry D. Moyle said: "I have a conviction deep down in my heart that we are exactly what we should be, each one of us. . . . I have convinced myself that we all have those peculiar attributes, characteristics, and abilities which are essential for us to possess in order that we may fulfil the full purpose of our creation here upon the earth. . . .

" . . . That allotment which has come to us from God is a sacred allotment. It is something of which we should be proud, each one of us in our own right, and not wish that we had somebody else's allotment. Our greatest success comes from being ourselves."[7]

The world can make us feel that we're just another number—to the IRS, to the bank, to the guy who reads the gas meter. Every time I go to New York City on business, and though I love the pulse of that city, I feel swallowed up—by hundreds of skyscrapers that block the light from reaching the ground and by a sea of black limousines carrying important people doing important things. The sheer number of people can make you feel like a tiny blob in a mass of humanity. And yet the Great Jehovah, the creator of worlds without numbers, has extended the unparalleled invitation for us to come unto him one by one (see 3 Nephi 11:15). He who knows even when the sparrow falls also knows our names, our needs, and our desires.

The gospel, with its sanctifying and redeeming power, is available to all. "Thus we may see that the Lord is merciful unto all [I love that word] who will, in the sincerity of their hearts, call upon his holy name. Yea, thus we see that the gate of heaven is open unto all, even to those who will believe on the name of Jesus Christ" (Helaman 3:27–28). There are no qualifiers relative to age, appearance, intellect or talent, marital status, ethnicity, social standing, or Church calling. When I think of the times in my life that I have felt excluded—because I didn't have the right marital status, or the right look, or the right social connection—it comforts me to know that the Keeper of the ultimate gate, the Host whose guest list I most want to be included on, has placed no limitations on my accessibility to him. He has invited *all* of us to come unto him, to learn to hear his voice, to attach and commit ourselves to him, and to ultimately enter his presence. During the Mount Timpanogos Temple dedication, President Gordon B. Hinckley said that in the temple there is no aristocracy, "only the aristocracy of righteousness."[8] All of us are eligible to come unto Him to the extent to which we seek to take upon us the name of Christ and reflect his image in our countenances. For he has promised, "Every soul who forsaketh his sins and cometh unto me, and calleth on my name, and obeyeth my voice, and keepeth my commandments, shall see my face and know that I am" (D&C 93:1).

3. Satan tries to wear us down by creating the image that there is nothing glamorous in enduring to the end. It's the very reason I learned the Big Finish first, to keep the ultimate reward in front of me so that I would keep practicing those difficult technical passages that required as much endurance as skill. I have always hated talks on enduring to the end because the very phrase makes life seem like drudgery rather than an adventure. And yet the most haunting regret imaginable would be to pass through the veil and, with the full sweep of eternity opened before our eyes, realize that we had sold our birthright for a mess of pottage, that we had been deceived by the distractions of Satan, and that the Big Finish would never be.

4. The adversary encourages us to judge and evaluate each other—a practice that is demeaning both to the person who judges and to the one who is judged. Recently a young woman whose marriage has crumbled told me how much she loves the gospel but how weary she is of feeling that she'll never be accepted because her life hasn't unfolded as she expected it to. If there is anyplace in the world where every one of us should feel accepted, needed, valued, and loved, it is as sisters in The Church of Jesus Christ of Latter-day Saints. We ought to give up telling each other how to live our lives. It is wonderful to talk about principles, which apply equally to each of us, but it is rarely helpful to suggest how those principles should be applied.

For example, our prophet has spoken clearly about the importance of building strong families. That's the principle. How that is accomplished, however, will vary from family to family. We could do more good by encouraging each other to develop our spiritual sensitivities so that we can receive inspiration about our own lives. The need for spiritual acuity is universal, for the Lord is in the best position to give advice.

5. Lucifer whispers that life's not fair and that if the gospel were true, we would never have problems or disappointments. Bad things shouldn't happen to good members of the Church, should they? The adversary would have us believe that with baptism comes a Magic Kingdom Club

Card and that if our lives aren't like perpetual trips to Disney World, we're getting short-changed.

The gospel isn't a guarantee against tribulation. That would be like a test with no questions. Rather, the gospel is a guide for maneuvering through the challenges of life with a sense of purpose and direction. "I feel happy," President Brigham Young said. "'Mormonism' has made me all I am, and the grace, the power, and the wisdom of God will make me all that I ever will be, either in time or in eternity."[9]

6. The adversary attempts to numb us into accepting a sliding scale of morality. Sometimes rationalization overtakes even the best among us. "R-rated movies don't bother me," we sometimes hear. "I go for the story, or the music, and skip over the profanity and the sexually explicit scenes." Yet advertisers pay millions of dollars for a few seconds of airtime on the bet that during brief but repeated exposures to their products we'll be persuaded to try them. If sixty-second ads can influence us to spend money we don't have to buy things we don't need to impress people we don't even like,[10] then how will minutes, hours, months, and years of watching infidelity, violence, and promiscuity affect us? The litmus test for entertainment of any kind is simple: Can you watch or participate in it and still have the Spirit with you?

7. The adversary promotes feelings of guilt—about anything. Pick a topic. You can feel guilty for having a large family—how can any one woman possibly care for eight or nine children? Or for having no children at all—you're not doing your duty. For working outside the home— don't you know what the prophet has said about mothers who seek employment? Or for choosing to stay home—what's the matter, no ambition?

Guilt does not originate with the Savior, who invites us to step to a higher way of living and a more ennobling way of thinking, to do a little better and perhaps a little more. Promptings that come from him are hopeful and motivating rather than defeating or discouraging.

8. Lucifer works hard to undermine our innate tendency to nurture and care for others. His object is to get us so busy and caught up in the "thick of thin things" that we don't have time for each other. Voice messaging is efficient, but it doesn't replace a listening ear and a caring heart. If the adversary can cause us to focus more on our differences than on our similarities, if he can confuse us about who our sisters are and what their eternal potential is, if he can keep us so busy running from one

commitment to another that we no longer have time for each other, he has made great strides towards neutralizing the strength and influence that we have.

We need each other. We need each other's testimonies and strength, each other's confidence and support, understanding, and compassion. It is as Martin Luther said: "The kingdom of God is like a besieged city surrounded on all sides by death. Each man [and woman] has [a] place on the wall to defend and no one can stand where another stands, but nothing prevents us from calling encouragement to one another."[11]

9. The adversary would have us hung up on perfection and stymied by the commandment to become perfect. He wants this glorious potential to loom as a giant stumbling block rather than the promise of what is ultimately possible—in other words, to make the Big Finish seem little more than a dream. Every prophet in this dispensation has explained that we should expect not to achieve perfection in this lifetime. The goal instead is to become pure, so that we are increasingly receptive to the promptings of the Holy Ghost.

The Savior doesn't want us to be paralyzed by our errors but to learn and grow from them. He sees us as works in progress. The faith of the brother of Jared was so strong that he was allowed to behold the Lord (see Ether 3:13). Yet prior to that remarkable event, there was a time when the Lord chastened him for three hours (see Ether 2:14). If the scriptural account had ended there, minus the "rest of the story," our impression of this righteous man would be different. The rest of *our* stories remains to be told. It is purity, rather than perfection, that we are seeking at this stage of our eternal quest.

10. Lucifer would have us so busy—with family, friends, careers, and every soccer league in town—that there's no time to live the gospel. No time to fast and pray, to immerse ourselves in the scriptures, to worship in the temple—all the things we need to do to "study" for our mortal test. In other words, he wants us to be a little more concerned with the world than with the gospel, a little more interested in life today than in life forever.

11. He delights in portraying religion as something restrictive and austere rather than liberating and life-giving. He depicts the Father and the Son as aloof rulers rather than our deified Father and Elder Brother who love us, who have a vested interest in our future, and whose motive is to help see us through this life so that we are worthy to return to them. He paints eternal life as something out of reach, even other-worldly,

something for prophets and a few other select people, a condition you and I could never hope to achieve. And he does everything he can to block the memory of our former home.

He loves it when we seek for security in bank accounts, social status, or professional credentials when ultimate security and peace of mind come only from a connection with the Lord Jesus Christ. He claims victory when we rely on others for spiritual strength—on husbands, leaders, friends, family members. He doesn't want us to find out how intimate our connection with our Father and Elder Brother can be and how palpable and sustaining their love is.

In short, he tries to keep us at arm's length from Jesus Christ. Oh fine, if we profess him to be the Savior—talk is cheap. And if the adversary can keep us so distracted that we never really seek, embrace, and commit ourselves to the Lord, then we will also never discover the healing, strengthening, comforting power available because of the Atonement. We will never know that because of the Savior we have access to everything we need to pass this test.

The antidote to the distractions of the adversary is Jesus Christ. Light *is* stronger than darkness. Jesus Christ illuminates our vision of who we are and why we are here and gives us courage to move forward in the journey toward our heavenly home. The potential reward *is* too good to be true, a Big Finish that makes Rachmaninoff pale by comparison.

Just as Satan's motives have been clearly identified, so are the Savior's, whose express work and glory is to "bring to pass the immortality and eternal life of man" (Moses 1:39). "He doeth not anything save it be for the benefit of the world; for he loveth the world, even that he layeth down his own life that he may draw all men unto him" (2 Nephi 26:24). The contrast between the Savior and Satan is stunning. It is the quintessential difference between light and dark, arrogance and humility, self-interest and charity, power used to destroy and power used to bless. It is the battle between good and evil personified.

Eleven years ago President Ezra Taft Benson issued this charge: "There has never been more expected of the faithful in such a short period of time than there is of us. Never before on the face of this earth have the forces of evil and the forces of good been as well organized. . . . The final outcome is certain—the forces of righteousness will win. But what remains to be seen is *where* each of us . . . will stand in the battle—and *how tall* we will stand. . . . Great battles can make great heroes and heroines."[12] You have been called to live and work and raise families in the twilight of the dispensation of the fulness of times, and you are nothing less than the best the Lord has ever had. You are heroines in every sense of that word, which is why the Lord needs us to arise and be everything we can be. President Howard W. Hunter put it this way: "There is a great need to rally the women of the Church to stand with and for the Brethren in stemming the tide of evil that surrounds us and in moving forward the work of our Savior. . . . Only together can we accomplish the work he has given us to do and be prepared for the day when we shall see him."[13]

I believe him. The impact of righteous, determined, pure-hearted women today is immeasurable. It doesn't matter where you live, whether or not you have children, how much money you have, or how talented you think you are—or aren't. This is a day when the Lord and his kingdom need women who are firmly grounded in their testimony of Jesus Christ, women of vision who have their sights trained on the purpose of life. Women who can hear the voice of the Lord, expose the distractions of the adversary for what they are, and press forward with a sense of purpose and a desire to contribute. Women who are articulate as well as compassionate. Women who understand who they are. And where they are going. And are determined to not let anything keep them from getting there.

Good women all over the world are desperate for leadership, for role models, for the assurance borne out in lives well lived that families are important, that virtue is not outdated, and that it is possible to feel peace and purpose in a society spinning out of control.

We have reason to be the most reassured, the most determined, the most confident of all women. In saying this, I don't minimize our personal disappointments. But we know what we're here for. And we know that we are beloved of the Lord.

We are members of the most important and potentially influential women's organization in the world, the only such organization founded by a prophet of God and led by women who do so under the direction of, and therefore with access to, the power of the priesthood of God. Remember President Spencer W. Kimball's statement nearly twenty years ago about the vital role righteous women would play during the "winding-up scenes" of this dispensation.[14] Well, these are the winding-up scenes.

I have a friend who is an executive with a Fortune 500 company. One day we sparred verbally over a definition of the word *power*. His response interested me: "Power is influence. If you have influence, you wield power."

If my friend is right—and I am inclined to agree with him—then collectively and individually we have tremendous power. The influence of the sisters of this Church is overwhelming. We need not be shy or apologetic about who we are and what we believe. Nowhere else in the world are there 4.1 million women who, because of their beliefs and vision of the eternal possibilities, seek after and defend all that is virtuous, lovely, of good report, or praiseworthy—women who are devoted to building, lifting, helping, and loving. Talk about influence!

Who is better suited to defend the sanctity of home and family? Who better prepared to celebrate virtue and integrity? Who better to demonstrate by example that women can be strong and savvy and articulate without being shrill, angry, or manipulative?

Are we not like Captain Moroni's armies who, though vastly outnumbered, were "inspired by a better cause, for they were not fighting for monarchy nor power but they were fighting for their homes and their liberties, . . . yea, for their rites of worship and their church" (Alma 43:45).

You and I compose a pivotal battalion in the army of the Lord! Remember what happened when Captain Moroni hoisted the title of liberty? "Behold, whosoever will maintain this title upon the land, let them come forth in the strength of the Lord" (Alma 46:20).

May we arise as sisters in this, the greatest cause on earth. May we go forward together in the strength of the Lord. More than ever he needs our faith and faithfulness, our vitality and our ingenuity, our unwavering commitment and conviction. We are witnesses of the Lord Jesus Christ, the living capstone of all that has come before us and a vital link to all that lies ahead.

This life is a test. It is also a glorious privilege. May we work toward the kind of Big Finish the apostle Paul described as he anticipated his journey back home: "I have fought a good fight, I have finished my course, I have kept the faith: henceforth there is laid up for me a crown of righteousness, which the Lord . . . shall give me at that day" (2 Timothy 4:7–8).

May we build and keep the faith. May we go forward together with a clear vision of who we are, what we are about, and how vital our contribution is to the Lord's kingdom. This is The Church of Jesus Christ of Latter-day Saints. We can make the difference the Lord needs us to make. I know we can. More importantly, he knows we can. For in the strength of the Lord, we can do all things.

Notes

1. Joseph F. Smith, *Gospel Doctrine* (Salt Lake City: Deseret Book, 1939), 13–14.
2. Gordon B. Hinckley, *Ensign*, November 1987, 54.
3. James E. Talmage, *Jesus the Christ* (Salt Lake City: The Church of Jesus Christ of Latter-day Saints, 1949), 318.
4. George Q. Cannon, *Gospel Truth*, sel. Jerreld L. Newquist, 2 vols. (Salt Lake City: Deseret Book, 1974), 2:170.
5. Patricia Terry Holland, "'Many Things . . . One Thing,'" *A Heritage of Faith: Talks Selected from the BYU Women's Conferences* (Salt Lake City: Deseret Book, 1988), 17.
6. C. S. Lewis, *The Screwtape Letters* (Philadelphia: Fortress Press, 1980), 56.
7. Henry D. Moyle, *Improvement Era*, December 1952, 934.
8. Gordon B. Hinckley, Mount Timpanogos Utah Temple dedication, American Fork, Utah, 13–16 October 1996, in minutes recorded by Lowell Hardy.
9. Brigham Young, *Journal of Discourses*, 26 vols. (London: Latter-day Saints' Book Depot, 1854–86), 8:162.
10. See Mary Ellen Edmunds, *Thoughts for a Bad Hair Day* (Salt Lake City: Deseret Book, 1995), 57.
11. Martin Luther quoted in Jeffrey R. Holland and Patricia T. Holland, "Considering Covenants: Women, Men, Perspective, Promises," *To Rejoice as Women: Talks from the 1994 Women's Conference* (Salt Lake City: Deseret Book, 1995), 105.
12. Ezra Taft Benson, "In His Steps," address to Church Educational System personnel, Anaheim, California, 8 February 1987.
13. Howard W. Hunter, *Ensign*, November 1992, 96.
14. Spencer W. Kimball, *My Beloved Sisters* (Salt Lake City: Deseret Book, 1979), 15–17.

IT'S ABOUT TIME

⟨∞⟩

Mary Ellen Edmunds

*I*n the Book of Mormon, Alma teaches his son Corianton that only men measure time; God doesn't (see Alma 40:8). I'm an earthling, and so for me—at least for now—I have to measure time. That is no small thing, trying to measure time. President Ezra Taft Benson has said: "Time is numbered only to man. God has your eternal perspective in mind."[1]

We use the word *time* in so much of our conversation: leisure time, part-time, full-time, overtime, prime time, high time, daytime, spring-time, Father Time, once upon a time, time after time. Have you heard yourself say things like "I remember the time when . . . " "Where did the time go?" "Take your time," "Have you got a minute?" "I'll have it ready in no time," "Timing is everything," "What time is it?"

We all know what time is, and we speak of it constantly, but it is a little hard to define or describe. I found this definition in one dictionary: "A finite extent of continued existence."[2] So you can ask someone, "Do you have a finite extent of continued existence that you could share with me?"

Have you ever in your whole life run out of time?

Time is a gift. It's a gift from God. We can't demand more, and we can't insist on less. We can't buy more, and we can't sell any (otherwise, it wouldn't really be a gift). Everyone in the world receives the same amount of time every day. "I have told you many times," Brigham Young said, "the property which we inherit from our Heavenly Father is our time, and the power to choose in the disposition of the same."[3]

Time is our life—it's our day to prepare to be with God forever and ever. Time is given to us for that preparation, for repenting and forgiving and trying to be good and do good. Alma taught his son Corianton,

---

Mary Ellen Edmunds has served as a director of training at the Missionary Training Center in Provo, Utah, and as a member of the Relief Society General Board. A graduate of the College of Nursing at Brigham Young University, she has been a faculty member in that same school and has served full-time proselyting and welfare missions in Asia and Africa.

further, that "there was a time granted unto man . . . a probationary time, a time to repent and serve God" (Alma 42:4).

In the hymn "Improve the Shining Moments," there is this statement: "Time flies on wings of lightning."[4] Sometimes that is so true that it makes me sick. Remember when summer used to be three months long? Remember when Christmas vacation was days long instead of just a few hours? Last year we didn't have July. I don't know what happened, but we didn't have July.

In President Gordon B. Hinckley's biography is an insight into this reality of so much to do and how quickly time passes: "Apparently the tendency to shoehorn too much into any twenty-four-hour period was a Hinckley family trait. During one month when Virginia had her hands full with a heavy load of family and Church responsibilities, Marjorie outlined the list of things pressuring her second-oldest daughter and concluded matter-of-factly, 'Life gets that way every once in a while when you belong to the true church.'"[5]

Is life that way for you? Are you busy? Are you tired? Are you weary, empty, depleted, cross? Has hurrying and being too busy become a habit with you?

So much of my life is "management by crisis." I feel sometimes that I don't know how to slow down, or sit down, or get out of the fast lane—and I don't really know how I got in it. I missed an off-ramp!

We all have a long list of things to do, whether written down or rattling around in our brain: pray; study; exercise; plant a garden, eat it; raise brilliant, cheerful, reverent children; clean a basement; write in a journal; avoid fat, calories, movie theater popcorn, and evil thoughts; pray for your enemies; do visiting teaching; store a year's supply of food (but not on your body! We're not supposed to look like Welfare Square); say yes to everything anyone asks you to do and hunt for more things to do; plant trees; remember the pioneers . . .

And we want to do everything so quickly. We hunt for fast-food, shortcuts, one-hour photo developing, express elevators, condensed books, instant soups, and ten-minute oil changes. Personally, I look for labels that say "Just add water." I can do that. And I have a 72-minute kit.

But there's much in life that isn't instant and isn't fast. Mothers don't sign up for an easy plan to have a baby in a few weeks. It's almost always around nine months—longer for elephants, shorter for guinea pigs. Skills and relationships and testimony and character traits—there are a lot of things that take time. For the most part, the things in our life that matter the most will have to be attended to. We will have to budget some time—make and take some time—for them. It's a process, sometimes a lifelong process. Enoch and his city were taken up "in process of time" (Moses 7:21).

One of our challenges is to figure out which are the most important things in our life—where we should be putting our time and our energy and our other resources—right now, in this season of our lives. President Harold B. Lee taught: "Most men do not set priorities to guide them in allocating their time [maybe he meant women do?] and most men [and women] forget that the first priority should be to maintain their own spiritual and physical strength [don't forget that]; then comes their family; then the Church; and then their professions."[6]

Elder Dallin H. Oaks warns us that "the treasure of our hearts—our priorities—should not be the destructible and temporary things of this world."[7] How do we set priorities? Elder M. Russell Ballard taught: "Find some quiet time regularly to think deeply about where you are going and what you will need to do to get there. Jesus, our exemplar, often 'withdrew himself into the wilderness, and prayed' (Luke 5:16). We need to do the same thing occasionally to rejuvenate ourselves spiritually as the Savior did."[8]

As I was thinking of my life and priorities, it occurred to me that if I had spent as much time that particular day reading the scriptures as I had spent going through the newspaper, the *TV Guide*, junk mail, or catalogs, and so on, I could have built a ship and crossed an ocean or had some other adventure in the scriptures. But there are just those days when junk mail is all I can handle.

What are the things in your life to which you are intensely devoted and dedicated? What are the things you spend your time on—not just the amount of time, but your best time? Your children? The scriptures? Pondering? Exercising? Eating? A book club? Visiting? Attending the temple? Reading?

Let's say you had to drop four things from your life to free up some time. What would you drop? And how would you decide? For what would you drop everything? Your answers would reveal much about your priorities.

We don't put first things first to get them done and out of the way— we put them first because of the critical effect they have on everything that follows. It's like building a house on a rock rather than on sand. And if we're always putting third things first, perhaps our foundation is too sandy and not rocky enough.

First things first isn't only about importance. It's about order—what we do first, what we focus on and make time for and in which order. When I first read in the Doctrine and Covenants about creating "a house of order, a house of God" (D&C 88:119), I thought that meant that all the cupboards and closets and shelves in heaven were neat and orderly. Of course, it's more a matter of things happening at the right time and in the right order, first things first.

Some things are fundamental and foundational in our lives—soul builders. Doing the right things in the right order, as much as we are able, increases our capacity to use time well. That is the way we can stretch seconds and magnify minutes.

Here are some phrases from hymn 226 again:

> Improve the shining moments;
> Don't let them pass you by.
> Work while the sun is radiant;
> Work, for the night draws nigh.

We must improve the shining moments—improve our time. That means we increase the value of, take advantage of, or make good use of those moments. For the word *improve*, one dictionary even listed, "make use of for spiritual edification."

So how do we *improve* our time? Part of that has to do with how we choose to spend it—in what order and how much for which task or which project. President Ezra Taft Benson taught us that "when we put God first, all other things fall into their proper place or drop out of our lives. Our love of the Lord will govern the . . . demands on our time, the interests we pursue, and the order of our priorities."[9]

First things first, and everything else falls into place.

We have lots of chances to choose among a lot of things that are good, enjoyable, important, and exciting, not just between good and bad. If it were always a choice of doing good or bad, choosing would be easier, but mostly it is a choice between many things, all of which are good, important, valuable, and enjoyable. "The highest challenge we have in mortality," Elder Neal A. Maxwell said, "is to use our free agency well, making right choices in the interplay of time and talents."[10]

We perhaps become more like God in our choice of how to use our time and other resources than we realize. We've heard a lot about how long it took the pioneers to walk to Zion and some of the suffering they went through. I think of who they were, who they became, as a result of their experiences, and I ask myself, "Who am I becoming? Who and what am I becoming by my experiences and my choice of time as I rush through life pulling not a handcart but one of those little suitcases with two wheels. Who am I becoming?" I thought about that one Sunday as I was racing over Iowa and Nebraska in a jet at hundreds of miles an hour. I couldn't even see the trail.

I wonder how my use of time fits in to Moroni's invitation to "come unto Christ, and be perfected in him, and deny yourselves of all ungodliness" (Moroni 10:32). Are there things that are ungodly about the way I use time?

What does it mean to deny myself? As I'm thinking about how to use my time, what does it say or show about me if I can delay some less-important things and work really hard to keep first things first? It's worth thinking about, and when I have some free time I will.

"Time cannot be recycled," President Spencer W. Kimball said. "When a moment has gone, it is really gone. . . . Wise time management is really the wise management of ourselves."[11] It's true. Much of managing our time has to do with self-discipline and self-control.

Here are just a few suggestions. Maybe you can pick out one or two that might be helpful for you.

Make appointments with yourself. You look on your envelope or your seventeen-holed paper and see if you have made any appointments with you (or in my case, MEE). Make appointments with yourself just to do what you need to do, and then if someone calls, you can say, "Oh, I have an appointment that day."

Simplify. I like the idea, or the concept, of simplifying. It can be a time-saver. I spend a lot of time in my basement, where there's matter unorganized, trying to find a 1983 *Ensign* or a particular toy that I want to play with or a box of stuff. I get emotionally attached to things and it is very hard for me to give them away. I have much, much, much precious trash, but if we simplify, we could have more room in our closets—and imagine a home with an empty drawer! I get sick of hearing myself say, "I've got to get organized!" I think the last words I'll utter before I die are, "I've got to get organized!"

Have a bag to take with you. In that bag you can put some things you could work on for a few minutes if you find yourself waiting: you could read a lesson or write a note or sew on a button or paint an oil painting. (Big bag.) Think of it—if you could just capture and protect an "extra" few minutes every day . . .

Plan. It's wise to use some of our minutes to plan—to anticipate—to look ahead and think ahead and figure out what might be happening, or what we *want* to have happen, and then ask ourselves, "When can I do this?" and "How shall I accomplish that?" to bring about what we most need and want to do. Sometimes emergencies have a way of jumping right into first place. If we're not careful and aware, some of the time we had tried to guard for visiting someone, for pondering or contemplating, or for communicating with our Heavenly Father, might get eaten up with the crises that come along. If we give some thought to how and when (and if) we're going to do something, it may reduce the number of crises we have to deal with.

For me the right time to plan is in the morning. That's when I seem to be the most optimistic, the most awake. It may be exactly the opposite for you—your best planning time may be right before you go to sleep, or in the middle of the day—or twice a year. Whatever it is, figuring out your own best time will save you time. I find that when I'm tired, when my battery is running low, when I'm exhausted and weary, is not a good time to plan because I don't always make my best decisions then. Everything looks bigger and harder.

Write things down. For many of us writing things down is critical. Some people can do without pencil and paper. They know the date of everything that ever happened in the history of the world, and everything that is going to happen, and they can recall the names of all the general authorities with their middle names and their wives' maiden names, and all the temples. Some people can remember without writing things down, but for the rest of us, writing a few things down helps.

I recommend making lists as a result of prayerfully, carefully, thinking. Often we receive promptings and reminders of things that are important to us. If we don't write them down, we might forget them, and we might miss an opportunity or a good idea or some important spiritual guidance.

I don't know that having something really fancy to write in makes much difference. One day I was writing something in my planner, and my mother said, "I have a planner." "I didn't know that," I said. "Can I see it?" She said, "Sure." She handed me an envelope; on the back she'd written a few things she needed to do that day, or soon. It worked just as well for her as my seventeen-holed, neatly ruled planner worked for me!

Don't waste time. Don't get in the habit of wasting time, or "killing" time— as if you could kill time without injuring eternity![12] There are so many more ways to waste time today. "I deplore the terrible waste of the intellectual resources of so many people . . . who devote countless hours watching mindless drivel," President Gordon B. Hinckley said. "This old world needs straightening up."[13]

I'm often extremely busy, and yet I'm wasting time. How about you? Other times I can be relaxing, thinking and feeling, pondering—and I'm using time very, very well! I don't want to mistake busyness for being effective or using time well. More busyness is not evidence that I'm good at using my time. In fact, doing the right things at the right time more often than not means being quiet and listening and feeling. So whatever you do: Don't let lists run your life. Sometimes it feels so good to be listless. Just listless. Take a break! Give it a rest! Slow down! Turn off the machines. Be quiet. Be still.

My friend Peggy has a clock with hands that have sort of collapsed and a lot of numbers that are haphazardly scattered toward the bottom. You never can say, "The big hand is on the . . . and the little hand is on the . . . " because the hands are just sort of twitching. They never go anyplace. Across the clock's middle is written, "Who cares?"

Elder J. Richard Clarke said that the "proper use of leisure requires discriminating judgment. Our leisure provides opportunity for renewal of spirit, mind, and body. It is a time for worship, for family, for service, for study, for wholesome recreation. It brings harmony into our life."[14] How long has it been since you walked anywhere slowly, just thinking and feeling? Or gone outside and looked at the stars? Or watched the sun rise or set? Or played in the sandpile with a child, or laughed at the jokes from *Boys' Life*? I repeat, just being busy is not a sign that time is being used well.

One important thing in my life that troubles me, because I'm not good at it yet, is that I don't want to seem too busy for people, to help or just be with people. That's hard for me. It's hard to be interrupted when I'm "on a roll." People are a high priority, and the most important things in our lives—our highest priorities—are not interruptions: they are our air, our water, our bread, our life, our eternity! Jesus was willing to stop and help people. He didn't act too busy or too rushed to stop and be kind. I want to be more like the Savior, and I find that I don't exactly know how to do that always. I'd love to sit with some of you and find out how you handle that.

Elder Hans B. Ringger has taught us: "Money alone does not lift the burdens of our fellowmen. . . . The world is in need of time, and if we have but one hour to spare, we are wealthy. It takes time to listen and to comfort, it takes time to teach and to encourage, and it takes time to feed and to clothe."[15]

Yet, there are times when I have to say, "I wish I could, and I would if I could, but I can't." Anne Morrow Lindbergh said: "My life cannot implement in action the demands of all the people to whom my heart responds."[16] That's how I feel. I realize I can't do everything asked of me, even if I want to. So how do we kindly and sincerely say no to things we cannot do, and how do we say yes to things we need to do even if they are hard things?

And what about all the things that we don't get done? How stressed should we be about all the things we meant to do and weren't able to do? Let's suppose that you're doing your best on a day that is really busy. The phone keeps ringing, your cat eats your list, and your baby's teething (on your arm), you drop a gallon of milk, someone selling magazines comes to the door, and certain things you were supposed to do just aren't getting done. On those days it's comforting to remember what Elder Russell M. Nelson has said: "When priorities are in place, one can more patiently tolerate unfinished business."[17]

In Mosiah 4:27, King Benjamin teaches us about the use of time: "And see that all these things are done in wisdom and order; for it is not requisite that a man should run faster than he has strength. And again, it is expedient that he should be diligent, that thereby he might win the prize; therefore, all things must be done in order."

We are told to liken the scriptures to ourselves, so put your name or your circumstance in the verse. Let's see how it might read: "And see that all these things are done in wisdom and order; for it is not requisite that a [mother of young children] should run faster than [she] has strength [amen!]. All things must be done in order." You fill in that blank: wife of the bishop, caretaker of aging parents, Relief Society president, mother of a child with a disability, woman who has to search for water and fuel every single day, full-time student, single parent, and on and on. Or perhaps you are thinking, *Well, I wonder which five I should put in my blank!*

In the biography of President Gordon B. Hinckley is an insight into Sister Hinckley, which I love: "Her general outlook, however, was more practical than self-critical. 'I have a new project,' she wrote . . ., 'one chapter a day from each of the standard works. I have been on it for four days and am only 3 days behind. Better to have tried and failed than never to have tried.'"[18]

Good for her! Don't beat up on yourself. There is always, for almost everyone on the planet, so much to do and not enough time. That's why we have to choose and do our best to plan wisely. But maybe one of the things we need to do is relax a little bit more, to do the best we can every day and not get mad at ourselves if we can't do it all right now.

Let's be supportive and kind to each other because we may be in a different season than our neighbor, our sister, our mothers at our age, or whatever. We can't judge each other because we're in different seasons and situations. If we're not doing what others are doing right now, or if someone isn't doing what we're good at or doing, back off. Let's back off and not judge. Sometimes we harshly—even if we don't say it out loud— think, *Surely she could be more organized, have less dust, read every lesson ahead of time, never be late to anything, dress her children better, have them behave better, and be in better physical condition!* Oh, how we need to be understanding and kind.

I feel sure there will be enough time for all that we most need and want to do in this life, however long or short. But I'm also certain that there will never be a season where we'll just sit with nothing to do. We may enjoy a few do-nothing days, but there are no do-nothing seasons. I am convinced that our Heavenly Father is aware of the season each of us is in. He is not just *aware* of what that season is; he *understands* it. And our burdens will never be heavier than we can bear if we let him help and let others help.

Amulek, in testifying to the Zoramites, teaches us a great principle: "Now is the time and the day of your salvation. . . . For behold, *this life is the time* for men to prepare to meet God. . . . I beseech of you that ye do not procrastinate the day of your repentance until the end; for after this day of life, which is given us to prepare for eternity, behold, *if we do not improve our time* while in this life, then cometh the night of darkness wherein there can be no labor performed" (Alma 34:31–33; italics added).

If there are critical things that we fail to do today, either they'll still be waiting tomorrow, or they won't be there anymore. They might go away, and the opportunity or the moment may have passed. Procrastination is deadly. It can destroy time, energy, and other resources. And it can become a very strong habit—hard to break.

In hymn 229, "Today, While the Sun Shines," we sing:

> Today, today, work with a will;
> Today, today, your duties fulfill.
> Today, today, work while you may;
> Prepare for tomorrow by working today.[19]

Joseph Smith counseled: "Let us this very day begin anew, and now say, with all our hearts, we will forsake our sins and be righteous."[20] Eventually, the night will come and the day will be finished when we could have done our work. We will either have used our time well and done the things that mattered most, or we will not have done.

We must also remember that we who love the Lord have covenanted to give him time. Brigham Young said: "I want everything that the Lord places in my possession, my time, my talents, every ability I have, every penny that he has committed to me to be used to his glory, and for the building up of his kingdom on the earth."[21]

Perhaps we can consider advice, which has been given by many, to tithe our time. (Cherry, my friend, and I were wondering on one of our more exhausted days if that 10 percent could come, part of the time at least, when we're asleep; or does it have to be an "out-of-bed" experience?) Miraculously, nine minutes go further than ten, just as nine pennies go further than ten. You can't get out paper or use a computer to figure this out scientifically. It's one of those heavenly things that just is—nine minutes can go further than ten. Somehow, when we do what God asks us to do, the best we can, keeping first things first, our time seems to come back to us, added upon and multiplied. It's a miracle.

In Doctrine and Covenants 88 there's a wonderful verse about the end of time, the earth's last day. (My mother says it's evidence that I won't be there. See what you think.) "And there shall be silence in heaven for the space of half an hour"—they'll probably have to put me in my room— "and immediately after shall the curtain of heaven be unfolded, as a scroll is unfolded after it is rolled up, and the face of the Lord shall be unveiled" (v. 95). Oh, what a feeling! We'll know. We'll know in that space of half an hour what is about to happen, and then we'll have the chance to think back, *How did we use our day? How did we use the day that God gave us before the night came?*

I think, during that half hour, as I anticipate seeing the Savior, I will perhaps think more deeply about what he did for me in a very personal way in the Garden, such that he can understand everything—everything we feel, everything we experience, everything that makes us feel lonely and heavily burdened.

He knows. He understands. He's been there. He loved us that much then, and oh, how he loves us right now. There is nothing we can do to cause him to stop loving us. Nothing. And just because I don't understand unconditional love doesn't make it unreal. It is real. God loves us, the Savior loves us—they love us unconditionally. They love us right now.

Let him help you! Let them help you. Let the Savior encircle you in the arms of his love.

I pray that we will live as happily and positively and enthusiastically as we possibly can the great plan of happiness, the gospel of Jesus Christ; that we will do as much as we possibly can, in any season in which we find ourselves; that we will use this precious time that our Heavenly Father has given us, this day of our lives, to do all we can to be more like him, closer to him, and to build up and defend the kingdom of God.

And now I'll turn the time over to you. Use it well. Enjoy it. Appreciate it.

Notes

1. Ezra Taft Benson, *Ensign*, November 1988, 97.
2. *The New Shorter Oxford English Dictionary* (Oxford: Clarendon Press, 1993), s.v. "time."
3. Brigham Young, *Journal of Discourses*, 26 vols. (London: Latter-day Saints' Book Depot, 1854–86), 18:354.
4. *Hymns of The Church of Jesus Christ of Latter-day Saints* (Salt Lake City: The Church of Jesus Christ of Latter-day Saints, 1985), no. 226.
5. Sheri Dew, *Go Forward with Faith: The Biography of Gordon B. Hinckley* (Salt Lake City: Deseret Book, 1996), 347.
6. Harold B. Lee, quoted in James E. Faust, "Happiness Is Having a Father Who Cares," *Ensign*, January 1974, 23.
7. Dallin H. Oaks, *Pure in Heart* (Salt Lake City: Bookcraft, 1988), 74.
8. M. Russell Ballard, *Ensign*, May 1987, 14.
9. Ezra Taft Benson, *Ensign*, May 1988, 4.
10. Neal A. Maxwell, *Deposition of a Disciple* (Salt Lake City: Deseret Book, 1976), 68.
11. Spencer W. Kimball, "Jesus: The Perfect Leader," *Ensign*, August 1979, 6.

12. Henry David Thoreau, quoted in *Bartlett's Familiar Quotations*, 16th ed. (Boston: Little, Brown and Company, 1992), 477.

13. Dew, *Go Forward with Faith*, 457.

14. J. Richard Clarke, *Ensign*, May 1982, 78.

15. Hans B. Ringger, *Ensign*, May 1990, 26.

16. Anne Morrow Lindbergh, quoted by Neal A. Maxwell, *The Smallest Part* (Salt Lake City: Deseret Book, 1973), 46.

17. Russell M. Nelson, *Ensign*, November 1987, 88.

18. Dew, *Go Forward with Faith*, 346.

19. *Hymns*, 1985, 229.

20. Joseph Smith, *Teachings of the Prophet Joseph Smith*, sel. Joseph Fielding Smith (Salt Lake City: Deseret Book, 1938), 364.

21. Brigham Young, *Journal of Discourses*, 18:248.

FROM NAUVOO TO RUSSIA: THE REACH OF RELIEF SOCIETY

❦

Veronika Ekelund

When the Relief Society was organized a little more than 150 years ago in Nauvoo, one of its objectives was to help those in need and distress. To honor that objective in celebrating the Relief Society's sesquicentennial anniversary, sisters all over the world were encouraged to serve in their communities. My ward in Stockholm, Sweden, was no exception. The Handen Ward is a tightly knit unit with competent, loving leaders and much love among the members. Under the leadership of our bishop, Bertil Rydgren, we have learned how to cooperate and accomplish.

As stake Relief Society president, my job was to explain to the wards in our stake how the sesquicentennial anniversary was to be celebrated. All agreed that the idea of a service celebration was excellent, but everyone wondered: What can we do that will be meaningful, that will edify both the giver and the receiver?

In the Handen Ward, Relief Society president Ingrid Jusinski and her counselors thought long and hard about their project. In Sweden we hear a great deal about the suffering of the people in the former communist nations and their urgent need for help. With that in mind, Relief Society members contacted the Russian Orphanage Association in Stockholm, whose sole objective was to link needy orphanages with individuals or organizations willing to help. The association's needs were very great, and we were asked to sponsor an entire orphanage in Syktyvkar, the capital city of the forested Republic of Komi, a twenty-six-hour train ride north of Moscow. Ten months earlier, the director of the orphanage in Syktyvkar, having heard about the association in Stockholm, had written a letter pleading for help. At that time the association had been unable to find a sponsor, and the director's letter had gone unanswered.

Veronika Ekelund has served as stake Relief Society president in Stockholm, Sweden. She and her husband, Mats Ekelund, are the parents of four children. Sister Ekelund is a homemaker and teaches early-morning seminary.

None of us had ever heard of Syktyvkar, but we found it on the map, so we assumed it must exist. This would be our project.

To proceed, the Relief Society next needed Bishop Rydgren's approval. He and his counselors decided to present the project to the ward council; they, in turn, resolved to proceed under the following conditions: the project had to be realistic, and the entire ward must participate.

We began collecting donations. When we learned that during the previous winter the children had attended school in shifts because they did not have enough warm clothing, winter wear became a priority. The Relief Society and the Young Women presidents were assigned to sort through donated items, weed out the rubbish, and organize what was left. The elders quorum and Sunday School presidents were assigned to find out about visa and customs regulations. The Young Men president was to arrange transportation for the donated goods and for whoever might accompany our shipment to Syktyvkar. The Primary president acted as secretary for the committee, and the high priest group leader and the activities committee chairman helped announce the project and encouraged ward members to take their donations to designated members' homes.

The collection exceeded our wildest expectations. One sister and her nonmember neighbor donated five carloads of supplies, mostly clothing. Another family convinced a local firm to donate one thousand packages of liquid soap. Yet another family donated twelve twenty-five-pound sacks of powdered milk. We gathered such things as a refrigerator, three sewing machines, tools, clothes, shoes, skis, ice skates, and toys. When we learned that the orphanage had to eat each meal in four shifts because they didn't have enough tableware, members came in droves with plates, utensils, cups, and pots.

With the collection well under way, the committee began investigating every possible scheme for transporting the goods to Syktyvkar. One wild plan hatched another. "We can charter a plane," someone suggested; but that was out of the question with a price tag of at least thirty-thousand dollars. What about driving the goods there ourselves? Several ward members (including myself) have chauffeur's licenses, so this proposal did not seem unreasonable. We could drive through northern Sweden, cross Finland, and then continue across northern Russia to Syktyvkar, a distance about as great as from Salt Lake City to Mexico City. That idea died, however, when we discovered that certain military regions are off limits and no roads cross through the northern part of Russia in the direction of Syktyvkar. Perhaps we could ship the goods by boat to St. Petersburg and then drive from there. Once again the answer was no. We were told there are altogether too many bandits along that stretch of highway—bandits who would stop at nothing, including killing, to get at a shipment.

The bishop was now very grateful that the committee had decided not to contact the orphanage before everything was settled: transporting the goods might be impossible. If members would be at risk, Bishop Rydgren would not permit the project to continue. My husband, Mats, refused to give up hope and reminded us of the warm feeling we had received when praying about this project. We were committed to our project—to the children at Syktyvkar—and we believed that if we persisted, we would find a solution to our transportation problem.

One day it occurred to us that if our Muscovite friend Svetlana, a business colleague of Mats's, agreed to help, we could ship the goods to her, and then she could forward them to Syktyvkar. We contacted her, and she agreed to help us. All we needed to do was to find a shipping firm that forwarded goods to Moscow. That was simple enough. No firms shipped to Syktyvkar, but many shipped to Moscow, and soon we had reserved half the space in a big truck to Moscow.

Bishop Rydgren gave his consent for the project to continue, and we contacted the orphanage for the first time, through Svetlana. When they understood why we were calling, they were overwhelmed and cried with joy. They had given up all hope of receiving help. We decided that representatives from our committee would fly to Moscow, en route to Syktyvkar, and pick up Svetlana, who besides providing a solution to our transportation problems, would serve as an interpreter at the orphanage.

The truck arrived in Moscow as planned and unloaded the goods at a customs depot. Svetlana was to pick them up and see that they were loaded onto the train to Syktyvkar. She had arranged for a truck to transport the 258 boxes and the refrigerator to a garage where they would be safe until it was time to take them to the train the following day.

Not everything in Russia runs as smoothly as we are accustomed to in the West, however. When Svetlana arrived at the customs depot, the personnel there would not release the goods to her. Additional forms, she was told, would have to be supplied from Sweden. Many precious hours ticked away while Svetlana negotiated to solve the problem.

But Svetlana is both decisive and resolute. Ten minutes before the customs office closed (but altogether too late according to the personnel who work there), she produced the documents needed and convinced the staff to release the goods. When Svetlana had informed Jekaterina, director of the orphanage, how many boxes were coming, Jekaterina had dispatched three of the oldest children from the orphanage to Moscow to help load and guard the boxes. By the time everything was finally loaded onto the train, only two seats—those for Svetlana's husband and brother-in-law, who had volunteered to accompany the shipment—remained. The children had to spend the entire trip, which lasted twenty-six hours, sandwiched in a twenty-inch-high space between the goods and the roof.

During this time Svetlana learned from the children much more about Jekaterina, the forty-five-year-old director of the orphanage, and about the staff who help her and the children. The orphanage housed about sixty-eight children from widely different backgrounds. One six-year-old girl and her two younger brothers had been at the orphanage about two years. One day, some time after their father had died, the young girl returned home from school to find that her mother had locked her brothers in the apartment and left—for good. The girl could not get in, and her brothers could not get out. By the time news of this situation reached Jekaterina and she convinced the authorities to break into the apartment to save the children, two days had already passed.

Half of the children in the orphanage have no parents; the others have parents who are incapable of caring for them because of illness, mental disabilities, or imprisonment. The only man at the orphanage is an electrician. On each of the three occasions when ward members subsequently visited the orphanage, numerous children followed the men everywhere, pulling and tugging at them or trying to climb onto their backs. These children have practically no male role models, and they dearly love it when men show them some attention.

Before Jekaterina went to the orphanage, all the children had been separated into age groups. Often biological brothers and sisters lived apart in separate groups in different areas of the orphanage. Jekaterina wanted the children to have the most homelike, secure, and harmonious environment possible, so she immediately set about reorganizing the entire operation, creating new groups called families. In this new organization, biological brothers and sisters always stay together.

Today, each family group at the orphanage consists of approximately fifteen children with three daytime and two nighttime "mothers." Each family has two or three bedrooms and a living room of its own. The complex also has large cultural halls where all can assemble to dance, sing, watch or act in plays, or read poetry (the performing arts play a central role in the Russian culture).

Jekaterina and her staff love the children they serve and do all that they can for them, even taking some risks. In 1986 they wanted to give the apartments and the orphanage a sort of face-lift, to make them comfortable and cozy so that the children would have a home they could be proud of. Jekaterina realized, of course, that it would do no good to ask her superiors for money for such a project. So, rather than asking, she simply took the budget for the year and bought paint brushes, paint, wallpaper, and curtains. By April the orphanage was completely renovated. They now had a cheerful, renovated orphanage but no money to buy food. What could the political committee do about that? Nothing! Children have to eat, and the committee was forced to give them more money.

Meanwhile, as the train sped northward from Moscow to Syktyvkar, my husband and the Handen Ward's Relief Society president, Ingrid Jusinski, had embarked on a flight from Stockholm to Moscow. Once in the air, they discussed how blessed we were and how wonderful that our plans had at last come together. Finally—imagine it!—they were on their way to visit the orphanage. The flight to Moscow went quickly. Svetlana met them at the airport, and after many hugs and Russian kisses (that is, on the cheek), she excitedly told them about all the problems with customs, trucks, and the train. She was so relieved to have the shipment safely on its way. Together they set out for Syktyvkar, full of excitement.

When the group arrived, they were met by Jekaterina and a very happy delegation from the orphanage. Jekaterina reported that the goods had arrived, and that just minutes before the delegation left the orphanage, the last of the boxes had been unloaded and locked in her office. No one was to touch anything before Mats and Ingrid arrived to hand over the goods officially.

In the following two days as the Swedish delegation distributed their offerings, numerous bands of friendship were tied, and many tears of gratitude shed. Hearing about our visit, a local television station in Syktyvkar came to film the story.

The orphanage "mothers" were particularly thrilled with the sewing machines—now they could sew all they wanted for the children. One girl in her early teens who received a long brown coat was so elated that she completely forgot that others were watching her. She stood for a while smiling to the mirror and then began dancing pirouettes with a bliss that suggested she had been transformed into the most beautiful of princesses. Ingrid could not hold back her tears to see how this young girl could find such joy in a used coat.

On one of the evenings when Mats and Ingrid were there, the children and their mothers put together a cultural program. The children sang and danced Russian dances as well as their own special regional dances. The high point of the visit, however, was when everyone sat together on the floor and Mats taught them about our Father in Heaven—how he loves us and wants the very best for each and every one of us. The children sat completely absorbed in this message. When Mats finished, no one spoke. No one wanted to let go of the Spirit that they all felt.

Some talked about taking the children to visit Sweden, though with sixty-five children and fifteen leaders that seemed an impossible idea. Impractical or not, the idea would not go away.

Once Mats and Ingrid were home again, Bishop Rydgren called the ward together for a fireside. Mats and Ingrid related their experiences, showing pictures and a videotape. When the ward saw and heard what joy their efforts had brought, they wanted to do more. "Why not bring the children to Sweden for Christmas?!" There it was again, that same idea. But how? We already knew that chartering a plane would be too expensive. Someone suggested flying the children to St. Petersburg and meeting them there with private boats—but crossing the Baltic Sea in small boats in the middle of the winter would be too risky.

In Russia, Jekaterina and Svetlana also began to work on finding a way. They contacted an oil company in the region that had earned surplus profits during the year. According to Russian practices of the day, all surplus profits had to be paid to the national government. The president of the company liked the idea of sending the children to Sweden, saying, "I'd rather send the children to Sweden than the money to Moscow." He chartered a plane and paid the bill.

When we heard, we could hardly believe it. The children were coming! We had to organize ourselves quickly. With the bishop's approval, ward members agreed to house two or three children and/or a leader.

Jekaterina had to arrange passports and visas for everyone. Because visas are issued solely to persons who have received a personal invitation, we sent an official invitation by fax, naming all sixty-five children and fifteen of their leaders. At the same time, we contacted the Swedish embassy in Moscow, explaining our plans and asking them to prepare for the eighty persons who would soon be applying for visas. That made the job a little easier for Jekaterina.

The committee had their hands full again. The Primary and Relief Society presidents compiled a list of families the children could stay with. Other committee members put together a program for our guests during their visit. The group was to arrive on a Saturday and return the following Wednesday. On Sunday, out of consideration for the children, who were completely unfamiliar with church meetings of any kind, we decided to shorten our meeting schedule to a special sacrament meeting. On Monday evening we organized a ward family home evening Christmas party.

The paperwork was finally completed at both ends, and the children arrived as planned on Saturday, December 26. Happy and full of expectations, they were also nervous about riding the bus to the church where they would meet their host families—people they had never seen before and whose language they could neither speak nor understand. Of course, the children were not the only ones who were anxious or who had questions. We members waited nervously at the church, asking ourselves, "What have we got ourselves into? Will we be able to communicate? Will the children feel secure? Can we give them the warmth and love they need?" When we finally met, however, all doubts were soon replaced by happy feelings.

One host family noticed that their little guest, named Dima, could hardly see a thing, even with his glasses. The host family telephoned Mats and asked if they could take Dima to have his eyes examined and possibly even to buy new glasses. And what about any others in the group who have problems seeing? A quick dialogue with the Russian leaders revealed that twelve of the children wore glasses or had poor eyesight.

Would it be possible, we wondered, to get an appointment to examine twelve children in the next two days? We could always try. We contacted several doctors, but none of them could fit the children into their schedules. On our last attempt, we called the eye division in one of the larger hospitals in Stockholm. A receptionist listened as we explained our request. "Wait a moment," she said. "I'm going to talk to the chief." After what seemed like a very long wait, she returned and asked if the chief could call us back. Yes, that would be all right.

Fifteen minutes later, the chief called and asked for more information about our group. Then she explained, "The entire staff and I had scheduled a two-hour meeting tomorrow, during which time we do not have any patients booked. We have discussed the matter and have decided it is more important to examine your Russian guests, so if you can bring them here, we will look at them." All twelve children were able to have their eyes examined.

They needed it, too. Two of the children who wore glasses did not see very well with them; the exam revealed that they had perfectly good vision without their glasses. Two others, who were thought to need glasses, also had perfectly normal eyesight. But the remaining eight children needed new eyeglasses. With prescriptions in hand, we took those children to an optician to choose new frames and have new lenses made. When Dima took off his glasses, the raw sores on the bridge of his nose started bleeding. His old glasses were so thick and the frames so heavy that he had to use rubber bands to keep them in place. When his new glasses were ready and fitted, he could hardly believe he was wearing glasses at all, they were so light! And he could see clearly for the first time in his life.

That same evening everyone gathered at the stake center for the family home evening Christmas party. Since Russians do not have a Christmas tradition, we wanted to show the children and their leaders how and why we celebrate Christmas. To start with, some of our young people acted out the nativity scene, while Helena, one of our young women, read the story from the Bible. After each verse, Helena paused to let a nonmember, a Russian-speaking classmate of hers, read the same verse in Russian. We shared some of our other Christmas traditions, too, including Lucia, the queen of light, and several songs and dances that everyone could follow.

On Tuesday, a member telephoned Mats to tell him that the owner of a second-hand shop had heard about our visitors and wanted to donate some clothes. Mats, Jekaterina, Ingrid, and a few others went to visit the shop. To everyone's surprise, the owner had sixty-seven sacks and twelve boxes full of perfectly good clothes that she wanted to donate. The children returned to Russia with much besides their new eyeglasses.

Last summer, three families from the ward traveled to Syktyvkar to celebrate the orphanage's twentieth anniversary. The children were wild with joy to have their friends from Sweden with them again. During this visit, the question of continued help to the orphanage came up. Jekaterina responded, "You have given us so much already. Thanks to you, we now have all that we need. What we would like from you in the future is your love, your friendship and knowledge, and above all else, we want your smiles.

"When we have dark days here," she continued, "and I can assure you, at times it feels like we cannot go on, I gather the children around me and we talk about our friends in Sweden. We talk about all you have done for us, and in particular, the joy that radiates when you smile. We believe that joy comes from your faith. Please, give us your smiles. And your faith."

Mats took that opportunity to teach them again about the gospel of Jesus Christ. The Spirit was present; they all felt it, and there was not a dry eye when Mats finished speaking to them and then blessed their home. Afterwards, one of the children, who had just been taught to pray, offered a closing prayer.

We will always be grateful to our Relief Society leaders for encouraging us to celebrate the sesquicentennial through service in society. Serving the Swedish Orphanage Association has been a rewarding project. Mats once said, "I wonder who received the most: those in Syktyvkar or we in the ward?" This project has given us wonderful, unforgettable memories. In cooperation with and under the leadership of the priesthood and together with the other Church auxiliaries, we women *can* perform miracles. And in this day and age, miracles are truly necessary.

EQUALITY OF ESTEEM

Elder Marion D. Hanks

 remember no assignment that has seemed more important to me or has been given more sincere attention. In preparation, I have had the great blessing of reading talks given at previous BYU Women's Conferences and much of scripture and Church history relating to women.

We here have much about which to smile. I am highly conscious that behind our smiles there are deep and diverse and often complex and painful realities. Human life is like that, and we learn sooner or later that jolly greetings and a pat on the cheek will not resolve much that must be individually confronted, worked out, and, with such assistance as one may discover, either lived with or resolved in the best way we can. Yet all of us have much about which to rejoice and be glad in this free and fruitful land.

I sat with Elder Richard L. Evans once long ago and heard him repeat the story of the lad who had come home from school with a report card that was worrisome to his father. He was no longer first in the class; he was second. "Second," said the father, "who is first?" "Mary Smith," said the sad boy. "Mary Smith! You mean a mere girl is first, and you are second?" He said, "Dad, girls aren't so *mere* any more."

Women are getting a lot of media attention lately. News stories in the recent past have included something about the woman mayor of a major city in Florida and of seventy-five courageous Soviet women striking in the cause of Jewish emigration from Russia. There was also a story of a woman judge who was robbed on the streets of Philadelphia, attracting little attention from some who might have defended her but, interestingly, wide attention from those who thought it an act of appropriate

---

Elder Marion D. Hanks, a member of the First Quorum of the Seventy, has served as president of the British Mission, Church administrator in Southeast Asia/Philippines, and president of the Salt Lake Temple. He has served on the national executive board of the Boy Scouts of America, receiving all the special scouting awards, including an honorary National Eagle Scout Award. He and his wife, Maxine, are the parents of four daughters and one son.

retribution for her to suffer this affliction since she is a judge and thus, in their feeble minds, responsible for the troubles of those with whom she had had to deal as an instrument of justice. Then recently we have seen pictures and read stories about the Reagan ladies, whose squabble over a family book briefly simplified their husband's and father's life by pushing him off the front page.

Another news item may be more instructive than any mentioned thus far. A professor addressing a Women's Week meeting at the University of Utah saluted the gains made in recent years for women and minorities in equality of rights and opportunity, though, she said, the largest results have yet to be accomplished. Then she spoke of an *"equality of esteem,* which is an unwritten moral equality . . . and still beyond the grasp of most women and minorities."[1]

EQUALITY OF ESTEEM

Whatever our reaction to the events of the last few years, the testing and contesting, the shouting and pouting, the insistence to take sides on the question of equality, all of us can very likely respond with sympathy and appreciation to that interesting phrase, "equality of esteem." That is surely an appropriate way to characterize the attitude of Almighty God to all of his children. In his loving Father's heart there is truly "equality of esteem." Indeed, he specifically declared, "Behold, the Lord esteemeth all flesh in one" (1 Nephi 17:35).

There is added to that statement through the prophet Nephi the declaration, "He [or she] that is righteous is favored of God." That some are favored doesn't, of course, reflect on his love for all of us or on our value in his eyes and heart, but it does express the expanded opportunities that are the natural consequence of learning and obeying the law and thus enjoying the blessings that are predicated on that law. Through his prophet, the Lord said, "If it so be that the children of men keep the commandments of God he doth nourish them, and strengthen them, and provide means whereby they can accomplish the thing which he has commanded them" (1 Nephi 17:3).

As the youngest child in a large, one-parent family in my growing-up years, I understand perhaps as well as most what some of the problems associated with sustaining life on a low level of subsistence are. Some of the feminist furor of recent years has been understandable to me from that base of experience. Necessity and our mother's character and faith and her determination to remain independent as a family after our father died motivated all of us to work and contribute. Earlier, during a long period of financial stress, she had employed her special domestic skills to make jellies and jams, which our father had sold from door to door. She sewed and served others and provided a haven for many needy people who came to our home seeking counsel and comfort.

One of my earliest philosophical meanderings began as I pulled my little red wagon with the Relief Society president's distribution of welfare goods. That was the welfare program in those days for the Church, to deliver commodities to the home of the Relief Society president, who then distributed them. As I did that, being the delivery agent, I on occasion was caused to muse, "If we are not poor, who is?" But we never tasted the food. It was for the poor. And all of us worked almost from childhood, all of us together attempting to survive and to do it with the good cheer that constantly reflected Mother's view of life.

Not long ago I spoke at the funeral of a great lady who had known me from the day of my birth. I said at that service that it seemed strange to me that anyone should ever question whether women of Sister Anderson's quality were equal to men. She, with Sister Reynolds and Sister Neal and my mother and others like them, were a real presence in my life. Most were widowed, with families, none lacking anything on the score of knowledge and intelligence, all able and kind and gracious and good and representative of everything wholesome and holy, in my mind. Circumstances were difficult for my mother, but everything I experienced with her and my three sweet sisters strengthened my admiration for women. My own wife and four choice daughters have enhanced my capacity for respect for special daughters of God, as did my wife's mother and other choice individuals who have influenced my life and added to my gratitude for the refining and uplifting quality of wonderful women.

Of course, woman differs from woman, as man differs from man. Our experiences in living in Europe and Asia and traveling continually across the world have emphasized for us the great varieties of circumstances, cultures, language, families, education, sophistication, political situation, economics, talents, and opportunities for growth and development. There is much similarity among this great group here today, but there is also significant diversity. I assume that a large number of you are married and in traditional families. Some are divorced or widowed; some are the heads of single-parent families; others not yet married.

In recognition of that diversity, let me read a few paragraphs from something I wrote that was published some time ago, dealing particularly with single women. Some of the special problems for the single woman who is a faithful believer in the gospel of Jesus Christ are reflected in these brief extracts from choice Latter-day Saint women of various circumstances:

" 'Being 32 and not married has some aspects of pain known only to the single Mormon woman. As I begin to write this I am crying. My dreams seem so unattainable. But the dreams are not unusual or grandiose. They seem so simple in my mind. I hunger to be happily married. Where do I go with these dreams? . . .

" 'Maybe it is this need to "be lovable" that becomes the pain inside us. In the mind of society there must be a reason when one is not married. What is the flaw in me?' "

A widow writes:

" 'It is better for us, I think, than for the divorced or never married. We have loved and been loved, and though we become desperately lonely for the one who has gone, yet we feel married still, and still loved as we continue to love.' "

A divorced woman writes:

" 'Divorced Mormons often become alienated from the Church entirely. For those who cling vigorously to the source of blessings rather than cutting themselves off, there is yet the sometimes present problem of uneasy fellow members who regard divorced people as having something wrong with them, perhaps something contagious, like a disease, and who do not know how to act with such a one who may be innocent of any wrongdoing, even victimized.' "

To these sobering comments is added one from what to me was an unexpected source: a lovely, faithful Latter-day Saint who married out of the Church and who had hopes for a future she no longer feels will come to pass. She writes about a particular kind of singleness:

" 'I have always been a member of the Church and was active (did not miss a meeting, held three jobs at a time, etc.) up to the very day of my marriage. I married a Catholic. (Go ahead and wince. I am still kind of shocked at myself at such an incredible, complete flip!) With this in mind, I thought I would mention that one version of the single woman in the Church is the woman who married a nonmember. You know—the woman who really believed that all those faith-promoting stories on conversion would happen to her. They have not. They may not. She is no longer the unattached sister. Her hard-core non-believer is very real and loving, but not Golden Question material after all. She is alone. Sitting. Sensitive. Weeping (inside). Never wanting to give up hope; never seeing it either. It can be psychologically devastating to realize that you are now numbered among the inactive. You are still somebody's ward project. You are downing the percentages in all the books. Still, you have a testimony. You certainly think about the Church all the time. If you have ever practiced love, charity, humility, and studied the gospel in your home, it has been these married years—alone.'"

And two sentences from another sum up these candid statements: "'The Church is not only family-oriented, but it is also couple-oriented. One who lives the life of the gospel, being a single adult, must be content with these feelings and battle to be happy in spite of them.'" [2]

OFFSPRING OF GOD

The traditional, anticipated role of woman in the Church is as a partner in marriage, as wife, mother, homemaker, the heart of a family. This will forever be so. The Church will continue to emphasize the importance of home and family and of the role of parents in that setting. Motherhood will always be regarded as the highest blessing and privilege of the daughters of God. Emphasis will be given to the important nature of the home and the vital meaning of the family in preserving and building a constructive and worthwhile society. Temple marriage will continue to be a lofty objective for members of the Church. Preparation for that kind of marriage will be strongly counseled. Instructions and encouragement will be provided to help qualify people for that holy experience. But all of this must not and will not be done insensitively and without tender consciousness that there are many wonderful women (and men) in the society and in the Church, like those from whom we have quoted, who have not experienced or do not now enjoy the blessings of marriage and family in the traditional way. They are "fellow-citizens with the saints, and of the household of God" (Ephesians 2:19), entitled to every blessing and every opportunity in the kingdom on the same basis as everyone else—that is, individual desire, willingness, capacity, and worthiness.

From an unidentified author come these four lines relating to a bull-fight, which are perhaps applicable to the circumstances of those to whom we have referred:

The experts ranked in serried rows
Fill the enormous plaza full.
But only one is there who knows
And he's the one who fights the bull.

Every woman is special, a *somebody* of intrinsic worth who has been a somebody for a very long time, indeed, forever. Every daughter of God, born of divine heritage in the spirit before this world was formed, enters mortality already a special, eternal person. Each has proved herself in demanding periods of trial, has chosen the right course and pursued it with faith and courage, and comes here with credentials earned in action elsewhere. Every girl, every woman, is a somebody apart and aside from anyone else, husband or family or otherwise. If she is privileged to enjoy fruitful family association in this world, happy marriage, motherhood, then she is favored indeed and through obedience to the laws of God qualifies for eternal creative union and all the other choice blessings promised for every faithful child of God who desires them and is willing to receive them.

If the anticipated timetable for establishing a base for those blessings is delayed in this world, or disrupted, the promises still pertain. "All that [the] Father hath . . ." can be hers if she desires it and lives for it (D&C 84:38). On a plaque on the wall of my office is this choice statement: "To believe in God is to know that all the rules will be fair and that there will be wonderful surprises."

Eternal life—life with God, life of divine quality, creative progressive life, the life of exaltation—is a loving life shared with dear ones. The ultimate enjoyment of this life is a consequence of individual choice in accepting, through obedience to his commandments, the invitation of the Lord to be with him and other loved ones everlastingly. The path to earthly and eternal happiness always leads from the individual and the way each uses her agency. The prophet Lehi taught that God's children "are free according to the flesh; and all things are given them which are expedient. . . . And they are free to choose liberty and eternal life, through [Christ], or to choose captivity and death" (2 Nephi 2:27).

It is important to know how the Lord feels and who we are to him. Socrates said, "The ignorance which causes vice and immorality is not ignorance of moral principles or laws but an ignorance of self, an ignorance of who we really are."

God is our Father; he loves us; he desires for us everlasting joy. We may be confused when we are young, as Lucifer was—he who "knew not the mind of [his Father]" (Moses 4:6), who did not want men to follow the plan God presented for our mortal experience and ultimate maturity. Lucifer wanted to "destroy the agency of man" (Moses 3:4). He wanted to conduct us on a safe, round-trip journey, not one soul to be lost—and not one soul any better for having made the trip. Why? Because growth and maturing are processes involving opposition and free agency, contending forces between which we must choose.

Failure, futility, frustration, loss of self-respect because our conscience cannot approve what we have just done or decided, or long ago did or decided—these are elements of normalcy, but they are meant to be overcome as we mature in our capacity to understand what God really wants and how much he wants it. In our life before mortality he permitted Lucifer to tell his story and mislead a host of our Father's beloved children. In this world there is "opposition in all things" and freedom to choose (2 Nephi 2:11).

For parents who suffer through destructive decisions made by beloved children this should be comforting. God understands, and he believes enough in the importance of our eternal growth not to shield us from the experiences of mortal life which we came here to undertake. Perhaps we did not foresee every detail, but all of us understood in principle. This is what is at the heart of it all.

In the wonderful musical *Fiddler on the Roof,* Tevye explains that the strength of their beleaguered lives is possible because "everyone knows who he is and what God wants him to do."

What is mankind? Who are we? Is it so vital that we know? Ah, yes! The apostle Paul taught the Romans: "The Spirit itself beareth witness with our spirit, that we are the children of God: and if children, then heirs; heirs of God, and joint-heirs with Christ" (Romans 8:16–17). His testimony to the men of Athens on Mars Hill is that we are all the "offspring of God" (Acts 17:29).

I humbly confirm with you, then, what your nature is and who you are. You are unique in personality, in pattern, special. You belong here on God's earth and in this time. The Book of Mormon and Bible both declare in specific language that the earth was created for us and that it may be our eternal home. "Behold, the Lord hath created the earth that it should be inhabited; and he hath created his children that they should possess it" (1 Nephi 17:36). Isaiah, seven hundred years before the coming of Christ, taught that God formed the earth to be inhabited (Isaiah 45:18). And in the dispensation of the fulness of times it is written: "The poor and the meek of the earth shall inherit it. . . . That bodies who are of the celestial kingdom may possess it forever and ever" (D&C 88:17, 20).

SOMEONE TO LOVE

The very essence of our natures is perhaps best expressed when we are following the Savior's example of service. This was forcefully emphasized for me in the last several weeks of stake conference visits, during which I had two of the tender experiences of my lifetime. On a Saturday I stood on the steps of a stake center and listened to a lovely lady whose husband had been killed a few months before. She had a large family of little children. I told her about herself and who she is and what she can do. I didn't pretend it would be easy; it wasn't for my mother or any other in like condition. She said something I shall never forget: "Brother Hanks, we miss him terribly. We miss his taking care of us. We miss his love. But you know," she said reflectively, *"I think even more we miss having him to take care of; we miss having him to love."*

A week later I listened to a man speak of his wife who had suffered painfully over a long year of terrible illness before her death. He said, "I don't seem to think as much now about all those happy years with the children, of the wonderful coming together, of the passion, the union, her beauty, and all the sweetness of all our many married years, as I do about that one last year we had together. I think especially of the time when I was kneeling at her feet to put on her shoes for her when she couldn't do it for herself. I looked up," he said, "into those beautiful eyes filled with tears and filled with love and appreciation. I thank God that through all the pain and anguish she suffered during that heartbreaking year, I could take care of her and serve her and comfort her and help her know how much I truly love her. That picture is the one I wake up in the night with—my kneeling at her feet, putting on her shoes, and looking up and seeing those dear eyes brimming with gratitude and love."

WOMEN IN SCRIPTURE

In the scriptures we learn of the sacred roles of Mother Eve and of Mary. We may know less about Hannah, noble wife who was unable for a time to bear children. Through her humility and faith and prayers, ultimately she was blessed with that privilege. Bringing forth a son, she prepared him for a prophetic calling, schooled him and taught him and loved him and prayed with him, and helped him to get ready to hearken to the voice of God when he spoke. Samuel became a mighty prophet.

Abigail saved her family and friends through wise and courageous counsel to an irate David bent on violence and vengeance. The words of David to her when he had turned from his angry course are instructive: "Blessed be the Lord God of Israel, which sent thee this day to meet me: and blessed be thy advice, and blessed be thou, which hast kept me this day from coming to shed blood, and from avenging myself with mine own hand" (1 Samuel 25:32–33).

Abigail is described in the scripture as "a woman of good understanding, and of a beautiful countenance" (v. 3). She represents the civilizing, refining, gentling influence of choice daughters of God.

Esther saved a whole people. Orphaned, brought up by a cousin, she undertook a very dangerous mission to the king in behalf of her people. To them, with her life on the line, she sent this message, "Fast ye for me, and neither eat nor drink three days, night or day: I also and my maidens will fast likewise; and so will I go . . . and if I perish, I perish" (Esther 4:16).

In the Book of Mormon we meet an unnamed queen and learn the story of her love and faith, which reflects the unselfish service rendered by many noble women. Lamoni, Lamanite king, was taught by Ammon and touched by the Spirit and was overcome as if he were dead. He thus lay for two days and two nights, and his servants were about to take his body and lay it in a sepulchre. But his wife, the queen, had great faith in the power of Ammon, a servant of God. She sent for him, keeping vigil by the side of her husband. The words she spoke to Ammon were pertinent to the circumstance: "Some say that he is not dead, but others say that he is dead and that he stinketh, and that he ought to be placed in the sepulchre; but as for myself, to me he doth not stink" (Alma 19:5).

It is recorded that "she watched over the bed of her husband, from that time even until . . . the morrow" (v. 11). The king arose as Ammon declared he would, "and as he arose, he stretched forth his hand unto the woman, and said: Blessed be the name of God, and blessed art thou" (v. 12).

There are many other examples, but could there be a lovelier tribute to a woman than this from her grateful husband: "Blessed be the name of God, and blessed art thou"?

What do we learn from these scriptures? Again, the importance of women in motherhood and home, and leading children to leadership and contribution; gently bringing wisdom and refinement to rough men; influencing events through wise judgment and courageous action; expressing the intuitive intelligence and faithfulness of a pure woman; serving as an agent of God in prayer and healing and stilling contentions; comforting, inspiring, teaching, and bringing music and beauty and art into the congregations, as did Emma, who was invited to put together a hymnal of sacred songs which, said the Lord, are "prayer[s] unto me" (D&C 25:12).

OUR FATHER'S WILL

How does one live with integrity and self-esteem? Is it in frantic flailing for a perfection we won't find on this earth? Is it seeking to do anything and everything to meet all the standards everybody else seems to set for us, to give the faultless performance they seem to demand of us?

The apostle Paul prayed for an Israel who had, he said, "a zeal of God, but not according to knowledge" (Romans 10:2). They had the zeal but not the understanding. Their purposes were proper—they wanted to please God; they wanted the comforting assurance of his approval but thought they could accomplish this through a punctilious preoccupation with their own perfection. Like Lucifer, they did "not understand" the mind of the Father. "For they being ignorant of God's righteousness, and going about to establish their own righteousness, have not submitted themselves unto the righteousness of God" (Romans 10:3).

We may set up stern standards for ourselves or others—or struggle with standards set up by others for us—and then judge ourselves or others harshly for failing to meet them when they may have little reference to the true qualities of fidelity that constitute God's plan for us.

In the Doctrine and Covenants are these words concerning the "best gifts," which we are to earnestly seek: "For verily I say unto you, they are given for the benefit of those who love me and keep all my commandments, *and him that seeketh so to do*" (D&C 46:9; italics added).

How real and how comforting—as he is real and full of compassion and loving kindness!

We do not always remember that he understands, that he loves, that we are esteemed in his sight equally with all others. Our hope lies in learning to submit ourselves to the will of the Father, learning to accept his forgiveness and affection, to look to him and his unfailing love with confidence. For this purpose Christ came into the world, as he clearly explained (3 Nephi 27:13; John 4:34; 5:30).

We are here to learn the lesson, also, that we are here to do the will of the Father. And how do we discover his will? How do we find him? Pascal gave us a line: "You would not seek me had you not found me." God is closer than we know, more truly concerned for us than we understand. And the best in us is better than we know and reaches out and up, seeking him.

We worry about our faith: does he really exist? We worry about our worthiness: could he love me? We remember our sins: is he really willing to "rescue a soul so rebellious and proud as mine"?[3] We want to find him. We would like to yield to his will. But how do we do that? How do we qualify for the relationship that we so earnestly desire?

We do this through prayer, of course, and through studying the scriptures. I believe we can find him best by learning to know the Christ, who seems nearer, who was "made flesh, and dwelt among us" (John 1:14) and of whom Paul wrote that "God was in Christ, reconciling the world unto himself" (2 Corinthians 5:19). God was making himself known through his Son. "If," Paul declared to the Romans, "when we were enemies [that is, apart from God], we were reconciled to God by the death of his Son, [how] much more, being reconciled [brought back into unison with him], we shall be saved by his life" (Romans 5:10).

SAVED BY HIS LIFE

Being reconciled to God by Christ's death, we can be saved by his life. That means we have to *know* about his life, doesn't it? We are reconciled to God through the life of his Son. When we've seen him, Christ said, we have seen the Father. He came to do the Father's will, to say what he had heard his Father say, to do what he had seen his Father do. In coming to know him, we come to know the Father and the Son, and knowing them is peace in this world and life eternal in the world to come.

The scriptures constantly encourage us to—

"Seek this Jesus of whom prophets and apostles have written" (Ether 12:41)

"Be faithful in Christ" and remember him (Moroni 9:25)

"And partake of his goodness" (2 Nephi 26:33)

"And bring forth works of righteousness" (Alma 5:35)

"And lay hold upon every good gift" (Moroni 10:30)

"And partake of his salvation" (Omni 1:26)

"And be perfected in him" (Moroni 10:32).

We are taught to "remember, remember that it is upon the rock of our Redeemer, who is Christ, the Son of God, that [we] must build [our] foundation" (Helaman 5:12); "feast upon the words of Christ; for behold, the words of Christ will tell you all things what ye should do" (2 Nephi 32:3). Christ is "the right way" (2 Nephi 25:29).

Nephi, at the height of his concluding testimony, said that he had charity for his own people and great faith in Christ; he had charity also for the Jew and for the Gentile. "But," said he, "behold, for none of these can I hope except they shall be reconciled unto Christ, and enter into the narrow gate, and walk in the strait path which leads to life, and continue in the path until the end of the day of probation" (2 Nephi 33:7–9).

These scriptures are a sure source of discovery. Each of the standard works has remarkable windows of knowledge and understanding and insight to lead us to him. Nephi said that the writings of prophets "persuadeth them to do good; . . . maketh known unto them of their fathers; and . . . speaketh of Jesus, and persuadeth them to believe in him, and to endure to the end, which is life eternal" (2 Nephi 33:4).

Why are we to read the Book of Mormon, along with the other magnificent scriptures? Because the book, like all the other scriptures, has a single central aim; and that is to prepare the world for the coming of Christ, to celebrate his meridian advent, his holy atoning sacrifice, and his death and resurrection, and to prepare the earth for his coming again.

Each of these great volumes that constitute our scriptural heritage testifies in similar fashion. But they respond not to the lazy, or to the indifferent, or to the unconcerned, or to the mind diluted with too much of what one may see in books or television programs or otherwise that is inconsistent, indeed incompatible, with the Spirit of Christ. One does not need to be a scholar to learn from and rejoice in the scriptures, but they do not yield their spiritual treasures to those who do not seek, ask, knock, search.

We are promised personal revelation. As we read, as we listen more carefully than perhaps we have done, as we seek to organize our comprehension of the gospel, as we get the strength of it into our bloodstream and share it with others, personal revelation becomes the key to our understanding, to our use of agency and our accountability. Through the Spirit we may know the truth of all things.

That leads me to the major thing I want to say to you.

THE TEMPLE

There is a special place where one may learn more about the Savior than anywhere else I know. If we are praying and seeking and trying to learn, and if we are walking reasonably well on the path he laid out, there is a place to go where he has promised to "manifest himself to his people," where we can come to know him. That place is the temple.

The temple has been called by someone "the binding point of heaven and earth," but the meaning of that is not immediately comprehensible to many of us. My soul was really comforted when President David O. McKay spoke to me of the "bewildering" experience of going for the first time to the temple. That is why we must know we are involved in a long learning experience, not a single journey "through the temple."

In the temple one may learn many things, chiefly, I believe, by thinking and feeling and learning to comprehend and apply in our own lives the concepts beyond the symbols. There *are* concepts beyond the symbols. Again, one does not have to be a scholar, but a little guidance may help.

What is done in the temple is often thought of as chiefly benefiting the dead. Perhaps the greater blessing comes to the living who serve the dead in the pattern of their Lord and who pray and worship and put themselves in the path to enjoy the Spirit that is constantly accessible in the temple.

In the dedicatory prayer of the first temple of this dispensation, a prayer revealed from God, the Prophet made known the great personal blessings that can come to us from going to the temple in the right spirit and often enough in order to begin to comprehend the experience through repetition, through thought, through prayerful effort.

Listen to these four promises as indicative of what may be experienced through temple service, temple worship. They can be read in the dedicatory prayer of the Kirtland Temple.

> *That they may grow up in thee,*
> *and receive a fulness of the Holy Ghost,*
> *and be organized according to thy laws,*
> *and be prepared to obtain every needful thing.*
> (D&C 109:15)

What a magnificent picture of what can be—to "grow up" in the Lord, to enjoy a fulness of the Spirit, to organize our lives according to his laws, and to be prepared to obtain every needful thing. In the temple we may "grow up," *mature*, in the Lord. *Maturity* is a key word to me. God is perfectly mature in every eternally important quality. There is no immaturity in his response to one who makes a mistake, no quick judgment, no condemnation. There is love and a way provided for us to recover from the consequences of our mistakes. There is no immaturity in Christ, no lack of love.

Peter—who knew him well, who himself failed him and denied him, and who wrote, I have no doubt, through tears and a broken heart—said: "[Jesus], when he was reviled, reviled not again; when he suffered, he threatened not; but committed himself to him that judgeth righteously" (1 Peter 2:23).

Christ was perfectly mature. We are not. We are learning.

When God made these promises, there was an historical preparation. When he first instructed Moses and his people to build the little tabernacle in the wilderness, their prototype temple, he said, "Make me a sanctuary; that I may dwell among them." He revealed the pattern of that building and all that pertained to it and said, "There I will meet with thee, and I will commune with thee" (Exodus 25:8, 22).

In that remarkable dedicatory prayer at Kirtland in 1836 are these opening words, after the salutation: "For thou knowest that we have done this work through great tribulation [the people have sacrificed for this temple]; and out of our poverty we have given of our substance to build a house to thy name, *that the Son of Man might have a place to manifest himself to his people*" (D&C 109:5; italics added).

A temple is built that the Son of Man might manifest himself to his people! A few days later in that same temple, the Lord declared: "Let the hearts of your brethren rejoice, and let . . . all my people rejoice, who have, with their might, built this house to my name. For behold, I have accepted this house, and my name shall be here; and *I will manifest myself to my people in mercy in this house*" (D&C 110:6–7; italics added).

What does that mean? Does that mean that occasionally God will come to his house and occasionally the pure in heart may see him? Hear the words of Elder John A. Widtsoe, that pure and saintly man with the great mind and the humble heart. I wish your generation could have known him better, or at all. He said of this promise of God that he will "meet" and "commune" with his people there—does it mean the occasional visit or the occasional personal manifestation or "does it mean the larger thing, that the pure in heart who go into the temples, may, there, by the Spirit of God, always have a wonderfully rich communion" with the Lord?[4]

In the temple we can, as the scriptures attest and as I personally attest, feel the presence of the Lord in the warmth, the love, and the kindness of those who serve there, in the sense of spiritual presence one may feel. This, to me, is the glorious blessing of the temple, that in temples the Son of Man *does* manifest himself to us through the Spirit in the principles and ordinances and covenants. A temple truly is a place of revelation to those who go with minds freed from ordinary earthly cares and there learn to walk with him on the path he has walked and prescribes for us.

Has it occurred to you in going to a temple or thinking about it that the principles around which the sacred covenants of the temple are formed, which are often thought to be the heart of the experience, are those principles that were absolutely fundamental in the mortal life of the Lord Jesus Christ? It is his pattern we are following, through his blood we are symbolically cleansed and blessed, through his life, "saved by his life," that we are learning.

We do not discuss in detail or in the exact vernacular what happens in the temple, but we are learning the gospel there, and we are learning it out of the scriptures and through revelation and in a way understandable to those who prepare themselves. We learn, for instance, that we make a covenant with reference to the principle of doing the will of God. We have spoken of that. *Christ* came to do the will of the Father. *We* came to do the will of the Father. That is our mission. In the temple that principle is strongly taught. Does it not become manifest to us as we sit and ponder that the highest and holiest exemplar of this great quality, the capacity to do the will of the Father, in all history is the One who in Gethsemane said, "Not my will, but thine, be done"? (Luke 22:42). Do we not walk in his paths, even though they lead us through our own Gethsemanes, when we seek to do the will of our Father?

In service, in sharing, in giving, are we not representing in its highest and holiest form the path of the Savior? When we make a commitment to give what we have to give, to serve usefully, are we not following in his path and pattern?

What is the basic principle by which God governs and which was central in the life of our Lord? Was it not that love which Christ declared, the love of the individual for God, of person for person, of each of us for our neighbor? Was it not the love of God and love of our fellowmen that he said are those commandments upon which all others depend for meaning and for substance? Was it not that love that caused him to give everything? "Therefore doth my Father love me, because I lay down my life, that I might take it again. No man taketh it from me, but I lay it down of myself" (John 10:17–18). *"No man taketh it from me, but I lay it down of myself"* (italics added).

And what of our commitment to purity and honor and integrity and self-discipline, of loyalty to holy commitments? In his great encounter with the devil at the beginning of his mission and throughout his ministry, Christ was "in all points tempted like as we are, yet without sin" (Hebrews 4:15). He met the tests we are meeting right now, and he positively and absolutely rejected the enticements and blandishments of the tempter. Is not this the path we are here to learn to follow?

And finally, what of priorities? We are taught priorities in the temple: "Seek ye first the kingdom of God, and his righteousness" (Matthew 6:33), and then whatever else you need that is important to your joyful life will be added.

But a respected writer has said: "We are half-hearted creatures, fooling about with drink and sex and ambition when infinite joy is offered us, like an ignorant child who wants to go on making mud pies in a slum because [she] cannot imagine what is meant by the offer of a holiday at the sea."[5]

In the temple we walk for a time with One who bought us with a price. We cannot fully understand the price, but we can seek to understand this: "Know ye not that your body is the temple of the Holy Ghost which is in you, which ye have of God, and ye are not your own? For ye are bought with a price: therefore glorify God in your body, and in your spirit, which are God's" (1 Corinthians 6:19–20). "Daily in the temple," it is written, "and in every house, they ceased not to teach and preach Jesus Christ" (Acts 5:42).

You may be interested to consider one last matter. There are some women who come from the temple (thoughtful, very bright women, sensitive, sweet women) uneasily thinking that somehow they have less value than men in the eyes of God. I have the sure conviction that that is not true, not what we are meant to learn. Repeated exposure to the remarkable institution of the temple leaves me believing the opposite to be so.

The scriptures teach us that Adam and Eve are placed in the garden in a beautiful union. Lucifer finds Adam alone and tries to convince him and fails. He then finds Eve alone and holds out the importance of knowing good and evil to her. She with spiritual perception and intuitive wisdom sees, beyond the blandishments of the tempter, the importance of the commandment that they multiply and replenish the earth. Somehow she understands the mighty importance of that instruction. She partakes of the fruit and then finds Adam and tells him about this special commandment, which they cannot in their present condition fulfill. He eats, they become mortal, and, when God calls him to account for that decision, notes that he was led to do so by the woman whom God had given him with the commandment that she should *remain* with him.

Alma explained: "Now we see that Adam did fall by the partaking of the forbidden fruit, according to the word of God; and thus we see, that by his fall . . . [they became] as Gods, knowing good from evil, placing themselves in a state to act, or being placed in a state to act according to their wills and pleasures, whether to do evil or to do good" (Alma 12:22, 31).

In short, they became free—free to have a family, free to learn to truly love, free to act according to their wills, whether to yield to the plan of God or subject themselves to the devil, free to enjoy the fruits of the plan of redemption, the plan of mercy, the plan of happiness, free to choose and to be accountable.

Eve did the right thing, made the right choice, had the intuitive comprehension to see the end from the beginning. What if they had made a different choice and stayed in the garden? That seemed so plausible; it seemed so good there. Somehow she knew better.

"And in that day Adam blessed God and was filled, and began to prophesy concerning all the families of the earth, saying: Blessed be the name of God, for because of my transgression my eyes are opened, and in this life I shall have joy, and again in the flesh I shall see God. And Eve, his wife, heard all these things and was glad, saying: Were it not for our transgression we never should have had seed, and never should have known good and evil, and the joy of our redemption, and the eternal life which God giveth unto all the obedient" (Moses 5:10–11).

Most of us know Lehi's declaration that concludes "men are, that they might have joy." Preceding it are these words: "Adam fell that men might be" (2 Nephi 2:25).

Eve made a choice. We honor her. *We honor her.*

And so we must choose, and sometimes the choices are between options that are or seem good, or may seem against counsel—whether to remain in the garden in unchallenged comfort, or to become vulnerable, subject to death, and candidates for eternal life.

I come from the temple believing that Eve understood, that through a woman's intuitive faith she knew what must be done, that Lucifer intensified the difficulty but illuminated the vital importance of her choice. I have always believed since I began to think at all seriously that that dramatic event is meant to emphasize the absolute importance of the principle of agency and accountability, the magnificent miracle of motherhood—that incredible, dangerous journey into the deep valley to bring forth life; the responsibility of fatherhood—the lifelong love and labor of a priesthood leader in a family.

Hear these words from the scripture: "Ye [who] have . . . received Christ Jesus the Lord . . . walk ye in him: Rooted and built up in him" (Colossians 2:6–7).

Oh, there is so much we have yet to learn, and I think many of you here are way ahead of the rest of us, you pure and sweet women.

I said there were several writings on the wall in my office. I have already quoted one, and I end with another. A young lady came to my office years ago declaring her confusion because the father whom she loved was not the father she felt she could respect. I talked with her a long time about him. There were things she didn't know, dear things, unselfish, lovely things to balance, or at least to be taken account of in her criticism, in her anguish. I talked to her of the Savior. I wanted to help her know and love her father and her Savior, and I was praying a simple, familiar prayer: Lord, help me now.

She went away, and things changed at home and have remained changed. A year later she came back just before Christmas, with a shadow box for me. She had dried beautiful flowers and hand lettered and put in the box these words:

> Though Christ a thousand times in Bethlehem be born,
> If he is not born in thee, thy soul is still forlorn.
> She was and is no longer forlorn.

I think we will not be forlorn if we come unto Christ, if we learn patiently that we cannot accommodate everybody's estimate of what we ought to be or do, if we walk in the way our own conscience will approve, if we seek to measure as God measures, and if we esteem ourselves and others as he esteems us. I testify that he is good and loves us and wants us to "make it," that he is pulling for us, that his anxiety, his whole plan, his great sacrifice in sending his Son and the sacrifice of that Son in giving his life, all were meant to help us meet the dramatic or drastic or difficult test life lays upon us.

Notes

1. Joan Hoff-Wilson, *Salt Lake Tribune,* 7 March 1987; italics added.
2. Marion D. Hanks, "'Magic Aplenty,'" in *Woman* (Salt Lake City: Deseret Book, 1979), 99–101.
3. *Hymns of The Church of Jesus Christ of Latter-day Saints* (Salt Lake City: The Church of Jesus Christ of Latter-day Saints, 1985), no. 193.
4. John A. Widtsoe, "Temple Worship," *Utah Genealogical and Historical Magazine,* April 1921, 56.
5. C. S. Lewis, *The Weight of Glory and Other Addresses* (Grand Rapids, Mich.: William B. Eerdmans Publishing, 1965), 2.

BUILDING THE KINGDOM FROM A FIRM FOUNDATION

c∞っ

Marjorie P. Hinckley

We are in a time when the winds of adversity and sophisticated criticism and bitter attack have become the order of the day. It therefore becomes the exciting responsibility of those of us who have inherited a firm foundation from the faithful ones who preceded us to build the kingdom, while others may wear out their lives trying to destroy it.

Like many of you, I grew up in a family where there was a firm foundation of faith. And so my love for my Savior began at an early age. Hanging on our bedroom wall when I was a child was a very large print of a famous painting of the boy Jesus teaching the wise men in the temple. Mother had positioned the picture so that the first thing our eyes saw when we awakened each morning was the beautiful face of Jesus. I was grown and long gone from the home before I realized what a profound effect this had had on my life.

My love and appreciation for the Savior took on a new dimension when we visited the Holy Land. We arrived in Nazareth at noon. The main street was narrow and uphill, crowded with merchants selling their wares, everything from fish from the Sea of Galilee to nylons. The noise was deafening. Schoolchildren were on their way home for lunch. At the bottom of the street was a very large camel. A group of children were gathered around it, chattering with excitement. Two boys about nine years of age were making their way up the street, one walking backwards as they threw a ball back and forth. "Was this the way it was when Jesus was a boy?" I asked myself. "Did he go home for lunch and stop to look at the camel and throw a ball with his friends?" I began to understand more fully that even though he was divine, omnipotent, the Prince of

---

Marjorie Pay Hinckley, homemaker, civic leader, and long-time Church worker, has traveled extensively throughout the world with her husband, President Gordon B. Hinckley. In her travels she has spoken at conferences and mission seminars and in the dedicatory services of twenty temples. An ardent genealogist and temple patron, she has taught and presided in all the Church auxiliaries. She and her husband are the parents of five children.

Peace, the King of Glory, he also was mortal. He lived on the same earth we live on. He had to overcome even as you and I. He had to discipline himself to get up in the morning and do his chores. He had to study and learn to get along with his peers and learn obedience. My love for him knows no bounds.

But even though my love for the Savior and my faith in him are deep and satisfying, I believe what President Harold B. Lee once said in addressing a large group of Young Adults at a fireside in the Salt Lake Tabernacle. He talked of testimony, and what he said applies also to faith:

"The testimony we have today will not be our testimony of tomorrow. Our testimony is either going to grow and grow until it becomes as the brightness of the sun, or it is going to diminish to nothing, depending on what we do about it."[1]

While traveling with President and Sister Lee, I heard him say many times to the missionaries that a testimony must be reborn every day. This can happen in many, many ways. Sometimes it is as miraculous as the dedication of a beautiful temple in Freiburg, Germany, or in Korea, or as small as a sunset, or a verse of scripture that touches a tender spot. But mostly it comes from living the gospel. Jesus said in John 7:17: "If any man will do his will, he shall know of the doctrine."

Now when we develop this firm foundation of faith, what do we do with it? The following answer from President Spencer W. Kimball has become a well-known favorite: "We had full equality as [our Father's] spirit children. . . . Within those great assurances, however, our roles and assignments differ."[2] So your way of strengthening your faith and building the kingdom is different from my way because our roles and assignments are different. Some of us are married; some are not. Some of us have children and grandchildren and even great-grandchildren. Some have none. Some are widowed, some divorced. Some are affluent. Some live on the edge of poverty. Some are students; others have full-time careers. Some are full-time homemakers.

It is the mothers of young children I would like to address first. These are golden years for you. These are years when you will probably do the most important work of your lives. Don't wish away your years of caring for small children. Life is what happens to you while you are making other plans. This is a time of great opportunity for you to build the kingdom. When you teach children to love their Heavenly Father, you have done one of the greatest things you will ever do. If you can be a full-time homemaker, be grateful. If not, you must do what is best for you. I for one have never felt a need to apologize for my role as a full-time homemaker.

These are busy, busy days for you. I have seen women in all kinds of circumstances—Chinese women working on road repairs, European women working in the fields, Asian women sweeping streets—but it is my opinion that American women, especially Mormon women, are among the hardest working women in the world. They plant gardens and bottle the produce; they sew and bargain shop. They go on the heart fund drive. They take dinners to new mothers and the sick in their neighborhoods. They take care of aged parents. They climb Mount Timpanogos with Cub Scouts, go to Little League games, sit on the piano bench while Jennie practices, do temple work, and worry about getting their journals up-to-date. My heart bursts with pride when I see them come into church on Sunday, some as early as 8:30 in the morning, their children all clean and shiny, their arms loaded with supplies, as they head for classes where they teach other women's children. They scrub their houses with little or no domestic help and then try to be the glamour girl in their husband's life when he arrives home at night. But remember, my dear young friends, that you are now doing the work that God intended you to do. Be grateful for the opportunity.

My concern for you is that you are trying to cover all the bases at one time. You cannot be everything to everyone all the time. Sister Belle S. Spafford, in her parting words to the Relief Society sisters in the Tabernacle some years ago, said:

"The average woman today, I believe, would do well to appraise her interests, evaluate the activities in which she is engaged, and then take steps to simplify her life, putting things of first importance first, placing emphasis where the rewards will be greatest and most enduring, and ridding herself of the less rewarding activities.

"The endless enticements and demands of life today require that we determine priorities in allocating our time and energies if we are to live happy, poised, productive lives."[3]

This does not mean, however, that you should have nothing in your hands but a broom and a dustpan and nothing in your head but laundry procedures and economical casseroles. Be creative. Reach out and embrace the things this wonderful world has to offer. I met a mother in Florida who was taking a class in, of all things, bird watching. It was exciting to walk through Cypress Gardens with her and share her enthusiasm for the birds that abound there. To her children a sparrow will never again be just a sparrow.

The danger and challenge is that much of what we do does not have eternal consequences. Much of the time we are running to and fro and spinning our wheels. And much of what we do is for the wrong reasons. When my neighbor had a son in grade school, the PTA was raising money by having a cookie sale once a week during the noon hour. The students paid a nickel for a cookie. Each class had a turn to furnish the cookies. It came my neighbor's turn to send a dozen cookies to school with her Ronald. The day preceding was a hectic day. No time for baking cookies. But how could she not send homemade cookies? What kind of mother would they think she was? It was after midnight when she took the cookies out of the oven. The next morning she proudly sent Ronald to school with a dozen homemade, beautifully decorated cookies. When Ronald came home from school that day she asked, "Well, did you buy a cookie at noon?" "Yeah," he responded, "but by the time I got to the table all the store-bought cookies were gone. I had to buy a homemade one."

I love the scripture from Doctrine and Covenants 10:4: "Do not run faster or labor more than you have strength." Choose carefully each day that which you will do and that which you will not do, and the Lord will bless you to accomplish the important things that have eternal consequences. Let me tell you of two women who have done this under some difficult circumstances.

Ann is a single parent, a divorcée. While some divorcées feel that there is no place for them in this society, and especially in the Church environment, Ann has kept her eye on the big picture and moved steadily forward. It has not been easy, especially when her children were young. It was a challenge to provide both physically and spiritually for her two sons and one daughter, but she taught them well. Now both her sons and her daughter have filled missions. Ann went back to the University of Utah to increase her education and her earning power. While she was in school she took care of an unfortunate woman who was practically housebound. This job gave her some much needed money, while she also performed a loving service. And, believe it or not, during this time she was the Relief Society president in a large, family-oriented ward. She ran that organization as if she had nothing else in the world to do.

At the end of her next to last quarter in school, the grant that made it possible for her to attend school ran out. Her recently returned missionary son said, "Don't worry, Mom; we'll get you through." The dean called her in. He had gone over her record and had concluded that her work had been so outstanding that the university would waive the student teaching requirement and the rest of her class work and make her eligible for graduation with the upcoming June graduating class. The Lord blessed her because she learned early to eliminate the unnecessary and do the things that had eternal consequences. She operated from a firm foundation of faith. In so doing she blessed her children and helped to build the kingdom.

Another women who looked toward the eternal consequences of her actions was Francie. As a child Francie suffered embarrassment when she walked out of a lighted area into the dark because she often walked into a light pole or stepped into a hole or ran into objects that she could not see because she suffered from night blindness.

She loved the outdoors and spent the summers of her early childhood in Rico, Colorado, a mining town in the beautiful Colorado Rockies. The summer after the fourth grade she was walking around the small town one evening with some friends. The girls were looking up and talking about the stars. Francie wondered why she could not see them.

By age sixteen or seventeen she found that she could not see many things at night. The doctors were puzzled, and though she felt some frustration, she compensated for her problem in various ways. One was to simply avoid going places she didn't know well at night, even some places in the house, or she would find a friend to use as a guide. Her frustrations were mounting, but perhaps it was fortunate that she did not know what was ahead of her.

At the end of high school she began to set her goals with incredible drive and faith for one so young. In three years she graduated from BYU with honors, the first young woman to graduate in youth leadership with an outdoor emphasis. She had more than once completed the BYU survival trips in the rugged desert and had proved to herself that if she capitalized on what she had and did not give in to her limitations, she could do anything.

Upon graduation she served a mission to Italy and was known as the "sergeant" because she worked so hard and encouraged others to do the same. While on her mission she found that she could no longer read the small print in the scripture footnotes. Immediately upon her return home she was diagnosed by the family ophthalmologist as having retinitis pigmentosa, an irreversible disease of the retina, which would eventually lead to total blindness.

This upsetting news did not stop her. Once again she packed her bags and left home, this time for Michigan State University in Lansing where she completed her master's degree in educational curriculum and then continued to do all the course work for her Ph.D.

While in Michigan, she met her husband, and now they have four lovely children. At this writing, she is legally blind. She is employed part-time at the University of Michigan as an academic adviser.

She pursues her Church work with vigor, is a Cub Scout leader, and serves in the Primary presidency, and always she is a missionary. She has taught in the women's organizations by having a friend record the lessons from the manual on tape to which she listens and stores up the information in her mind. She works as a volunteer in the school her children attend. They go as a family to community activities, lectures, and museums. By necessity she has chosen carefully that which she will do and has concentrated on those things that have eternal consequences.

"The scriptures give me comfort and direction in the things that are most important to do," she says. "I have learned to work with what I have rather than what I don't have. I have strong feelings about my good heritage with noble ancestors who worked hard to do the things they felt were right. Their good qualities are something I can capitalize on. I have a spiritual heritage from my Heavenly Father. I have felt his divine guidance and have received blessings that are beyond measure and sometimes beyond what I deserve."

We are talking here about faith and building the kingdom from a firm foundation. May I say to Francie, "You, Francie, *are doing it* and sweeping us all onto a higher plane in the process. We are learning from you about courage and faith and building the kingdom."

And now a word to women who, for various reasons, are part-time or full-time career women. Today is your day, sisters. Never have there been so many doors open to women. It was not too long ago when, according to a report made by the University of Utah, more than half the women graduated in six majors: elementary education, English, home economics, sociology, history, and nursing.

These are very worthy pursuits. But the opportunities are widening, and more and more we see women getting law degrees, medical degrees, MBAs, degrees in computer science, and even degrees in electrical engineering. What a tremendous contribution they are making in the business world. Our women bring to the corporate world a firm but soft touch. Hardly realizing it, they bring a special quality of friendship, flexibility, love, and understanding to the professional environment. They are making this a better place for all of us, as their faith and integrity and their understanding of right and wrong flavor everything they do.

And now to my peers. On my seventieth birthday I repeated to myself all day long something I heard Stephen L Richards's wife say when she was in her nineties. She said, "Oh, to be seventy again! You can do anything when you are seventy." Now a few more seasons have slipped away and it is even better, for now I can brag about being the same age as President Ronald Reagan. One woman who turned seventy-five on President Reagan's seventy-fifth birthday said, "If President Reagan is anything like me, he must go into the Oval Office on occasion and say, 'Now what did I come in here for?'"

Contrary to rumor, these *are* golden years, if you have a measure of good health. At this age, my dear contemporaries, we no longer have to compete with anyone. We don't have to prove anything—we just have to enjoy it all. How many of you have told your children how wonderful it is to be this age?

In 1985 Sister Camilla Kimball addressed the Women's Conference at BYU. She was ninety years old at the time and still going strong, perhaps not physically, but certainly spiritually and mentally. She inspired us all with her continuing drive to learn and her ability to make us all reach beyond our inclinations. And later, at age ninety-two, she took up oil painting.

There is so much we can do to be an influence, perhaps not in ways we have once known, but in many other ways. Last year in the Upland Terrace School in the Granite School District, which three of my grandchildren attend, grandparents gave the equivalent of two hundred hours of volunteer service. Who can measure the worth of a grandmotherly or grandfatherly influence in the classroom!

You will appreciate a letter written to Ann Landers that appeared in the newspaper some time ago. "Dear Ann Landers," it began. "I am a twenty-two-year-old graduate student who would like to express my admiration for some people who have taught me more than all the books I ever read." If you are over seventy, you can take this personally:

"Dear Older American, I want you to know how much you have improved the quality of my life. Today I was driving down the street. You were sauntering uptown, your white hair shining in the sun, a smile on your face. You waved when I went by, though you had no idea who I was.

"On my first job as a cashier, I was nervous and scared. The line was long and everyone was impatient. You let the others go first because you didn't mind waiting. When your turn came you said: 'Take your time. My, but you have pretty eyes.' I could have kissed you.

"You say, 'Have a nice day,' in the elevator and talk about the weather. I can tell by your gnarled hands that you've done a lot of hard work and I admire that.

"You have an aura of calmness that so many of my generation will never know in their mad rush for money and status. Thanks, Older American, for being there."

So if we are too tired to go mountain climbing with the grandchildren, it's all right. We can still reach out and lift someone.

Sisters, we are all in this together. We need each other. Oh, how we need each other. Those of us who are old need you who are young. And, hopefully, you who are young need some of us who are old. It is a sociological fact that women need women. We need deep and satisfying and loyal friendships with each other. These friendships are a necessary source of sustenance. We need to renew our faith every day. We need to lock arms and help build the kingdom so that it will roll forth and fill the whole earth.

May I close with these words attributed to Lucy Mack Smith: Let us "watch over one another . . . that we may all sit down in heaven together."[4]

Notes

1. Harold B. Lee, *Stand Ye in Holy Places: Selected Sermons and Writings of President Harold B. Lee* (Salt Lake City: Deseret Book, 1984), 91.
2. Spencer W. Kimball, *Ensign*, November 1979, 102.
3. Belle S. Spafford, "The Wonderful World of Women," *A Woman's Reach* (Salt Lake City: Deseret Book, 1974), 23.
4. Minutes of the Female Relief Society of Nauvoo, 24 March 1842, Archives of The Church of Jesus Christ of Latter-day Saints, Salt Lake City, Utah.

"MANY THINGS . . . ONE THING"

୧୦୦୧

Patricia Terry Holland

*F*rom my varied experience of listening to and speaking with many of our sisters, both younger and older, I know something of the struggles and the pain and the anxiety that concern women of our time. Every era has its problems. My limitations surely won't allow me to address every problem, anticipate every question, or meet every need, but I promise you two things. First, I promise you my love. You are my sisters and my friends. And second, I promise you my honesty. It's important to me that you know I speak from the honesty of my heart.

Our theme this year is unity of faith and diversity of works. That obviously suggests the unity and diversity among many women, but it also has an application within each individual woman—*her* unity and *her* diversity. For a moment may I speak of *woman* and see what significance it might have for *women*.

To do so, I must begin by being just a little autobiographical. Just after my release from the general presidency of the Young Women in April 1986, I had the opportunity of spending a week in Israel. It had been a very difficult and demanding two years for me. Being a good mother, with the ample amount of time needed to succeed at that task, had always been my first priority; so I had tried to be a full-time mother to a grade-schooler, a high-schooler beginning to date, and a son preparing for his mission. I had also tried to be a full-time wife to a staggeringly busy university president with all of the twenty-four-hours-a-day campus responsibility that can be required of both of us at a place like Brigham Young University. And I had tried to be as much of a full-time counselor in that general presidency as one living fifty miles from the office could be. Sister Ardeth Kapp and the others were wonderfully patient with me. I will never be able to thank Ardeth enough. But in an important period of

Patricia Terry Holland, educator, musician, and homemaker, served as first counselor in the Young Women General Presidency. She studied music and voice with a member of the faculty of the Juilliard School of Music in New York and also attended Dixie College and Brigham Young University. She and her husband, Jeffrey R. Holland, president of BYU, have three children.

forming principles and starting programs for the Young Women, I worried that I wasn't doing enough—and I tried to run a little faster.

Toward the end of my two-year term, my health was going downhill. I was losing weight steadily and couldn't seem to do anything to halt that. Furthermore, I wasn't sleeping well. My husband and children were trying to bandage me together even as I was trying to do the same for them. We were exhausted. And yet, I kept wondering what I might have done to manage it all better. The Brethren, always compassionate, were watching and at the end of the two-year term extended a loving release. As grateful as my family and I were for the conclusion of my term of service, I nevertheless felt a loss of association—and, I confess, some loss of identity—with these women whom I had come to love so much. Who was I and where was I in this welter of demands? Should life be as hard as all this? How successful had I been in my several and competing assignments? Or had I muffed them all? The days after my release were about as difficult as the weeks before it. I didn't have any reserve to call on. My tank was on empty, and I wasn't sure there was a filling station anywhere in sight.

It was just a few weeks later that my husband had the assignment in Jerusalem to which I have referred, and the Brethren traveling on the assignment requested that I accompany him. "Come on," he said. "You can recuperate in the Savior's land of living water and bread of life." As weary as I was, I packed my bags, believing—or, at the very least, hoping—that the time there would be a healing respite.

On a pristinely clear and beautifully bright day, I sat overlooking the Sea of Galilee and reread Luke 10:38. But instead of the words there on the page, I thought I saw with my mind and heard with my heart these words: "Pat, Pat, thou art careful and troubled about many things." Then the power of pure and personal revelation seized me as I read, "But one thing [only one thing] is truly needful."

In Israel in May the sun is so bright that you feel as if you are sitting on top of the world. I had just visited the spot in Bethoron where the "sun stood still" for Joshua, and indeed on that day it seemed so for me as well. (Joshua 10:13). As I sat pondering my problems, I felt that same sun's healing rays like warm liquid pouring into my heart—relaxing, calming, and comforting my troubled soul. I found myself lifted to a higher view of my life.

Spirit to spirit, our loving Father in Heaven seemed to be whispering to me, "You don't have to worry over so many things. The one thing that is needful—the only thing that is truly needful—is to keep your eyes toward the sun—my Son." "Learn of me," he seemed to say, "and listen to my words; walk in the meekness of my Spirit, and you shall have peace in me" (D&C 19:23). Suddenly I did have peace. I knew, as surely as I know you sit before me, that my life had always been in his hands—from the very beginning! And so are the lives of all of you, of every woman who wants to do right and grows in capacity and tries to give all she can. The sea lying peacefully before my very eyes had been tempest tossed and dangerous many, many times. All I needed to do was to renew my faith, get a firm grasp of his hand, and together we could walk on the water.

I had, for a few months, been pushed to my extremity, but that is always God's opportunity. I had learned so much, and yet now I was learning even more. The Son was enlightening my world. We all at one time or another find ourselves in the midst of a turbulent sea. There are times when we, too, would like to cry out, "Master, carest thou not that we perish?" (Mark 4:38). I suppose it is for this very purpose that so many of us are drawn together today as women of faith, seeking solace and sisterly strength to carry us safely to drier and firmer ground.

I would like to pose a question for each of us to ponder. How do we as women make that quantum leap from being troubled and worried, including worries about legitimate concerns, to being women of even greater faith? One frame of mind surely seems to negate the other. Faith and fear cannot long coexist. While you think of faith and walking hand in hand with God, I would like to examine why I believe there are so many worries—"troubles," Luke 10 calls them—and to note some of the things we are legitimately worried about.

I have served as a Relief Society president in four different wards. Two of these wards were for single women, and two were traditional wards with many young mothers. As I sat in counsel with my single sisters, my heart often ached as they described to me their feelings of loneliness and disappointment. They felt that their lives had no meaning or purpose in a church that rightly puts so much emphasis on marriage and family life. Most painful of all was the occasional suggestion that their singleness was their own fault—or worse yet, a selfish desire. They were anxiously seeking for peace and purpose, something of real value to which they could give their lives.

Yet at the very same time, it seemed to me that the young mothers had easily as many concerns as they described to me the struggles of trying to raise children in an increasingly difficult world, of never having enough time or means or freedom to feel like a person of value because they were always stretched to the ragged edge of survival. And there were so few tangible evidences that what they were doing was really going to be successful. There was no one to give them a raise in pay, and beyond their husbands (who may or may not have remembered to do it), no one to compliment them on a job well done. And they were always tired! The one thing I remember so vividly with these young mothers was that they were always so tired.

Then there were those women who through no fault of their own found themselves the sole provider for their families financially, spiritually, emotionally, and in every other way. I could not even comprehend the challenges they faced. Obviously, in some ways theirs was the most demanding circumstance of all.

The perspective I have gained over these many years of listening to the worries of women is that no one woman or group of women—single, married, divorced, or widowed, homemakers or professionals—has cornered the full market on concerns. There seems to be plenty of challenges to go around. And, I hasten to add, marvelous blessings as well. In this, too, we are united in our diversity. Every one of us does have privileges and blessings, and we do have fears and trials. Some of these fears, anxieties, and worries have been pointed out to me from those of you who met with us at this conference last year. A partial list taken from the evaluation sheets you filled out one year ago notes concerns ranging from loneliness to raising children to inactive husbands to physical health and self-esteem.

The complete, longer list is staggering! It seems bold to say, but common sense suggests, that never before in the history of the world have women, including Latter-day Saint women, been faced with greater complexity in their concerns.

In addressing these concerns I am very appreciative of the added awareness that the women's movement has given to a gospel principle we have had since Mother Eve and before—that of free agency, the right to choose.

But one of the most unfortunate side effects we have faced in this matter of agency is, because of the increasing diversity of life-styles for women of today, we seem even more uncertain and less secure with each other. We are getting not closer but further away from that sense of community and sisterhood that has sustained us and given us unique strength for generations. There seems to be an increase in our competitiveness and a decrease in our generosity with one another.

Those who have the time and energy to can their fruits and vegetables develop a great skill that will serve them well in time of need—and in our uncertain economic times, that could be almost any day of the week. But they shouldn't look down their noses at those who buy their peaches, or who don't like zucchini in any of the thirty-five ways there are to disguise it, or who have simply made a conscious choice to use their time and energy in some other purposeful way.

And where am I in all of this? For three-fourths of my life I was threatened to the core because I hated to sew. Now I *can* sew; if absolutely forced to, I *will* sew—but I hate it. Imagine my burden over the last twenty-five or thirty years, faking it in Relief Society sessions and trying to smile when six little girls walk into church all pinafored and laced and ribboned and petticoated—identical, hand sewn—all trooping ahead of their mother, who has the same immaculate outfit. Competitive? I wanted to tear their pleats out.

I don't necessarily consider it virtuous, lovely, or of good report, or praiseworthy—but I'm honest in my antipathy toward sewing. If even one sister out there is weeping tears of relief, then I consider my public shame at least a partial blow against stereotyping. I have grown up a little since those days in at least two ways—I now genuinely admire a mother who can do that for her children, and I have ceased feeling guilty that sewing is not particularly rewarding to me.

We simply cannot call ourselves Christian and continue to judge one another—or ourselves—so harshly. No Mason jar of Bing cherries is worth a confrontation that robs us of our compassion and our sisterhood.

Obviously the Lord has created us with different personalities, as well as differing degrees of energy, interest, health, talent, and opportunity. So long as we are committed to righteousness and living a life of faithful devotion, we should celebrate these divine differences, knowing they are a gift from God. We must not feel so frightened; we must not be so threatened and insecure; we must not need to find exact replicas of ourselves in order to feel validated as women of worth. There are many things over which we can be divided, but one thing is needful for our unity—the empathy and compassion of the living Son of God.

I was married in 1963, the very year Betty Friedan published her society-shaking book, *The Feminine Mystique,* so as an adult woman I can look back with only childhood memories of the gentler forties and fifties. But it must have been much more comfortable to have a pattern already prepared for you and neighbors on either side whose lives gave you role models for your own; however, it must have been even that much more painful for those who, through no fault of their own, were single then, or who had to work, or who struggled with a broken family. Now, with our increasingly complex world, even that earlier model is torn, and we seem to be even less sure of who we are and where we are going.

Surely, there has not been another time in history in which women have questioned their self-worth as harshly and critically as in the second half of the twentieth century. Many women are searching, almost frantically, as never before, for a sense of personal purpose and meaning—and many Latter-day Saint women are searching, too, for eternal insight and meaning—in their femaleness.

If I were Satan and wanted to destroy a society, I think I too would stage a full-blown blitz on its women. I would keep them so distraught and distracted that they would never find the calming strength and serenity for which their sex has always been known. He has effectively done that, catching us in the crunch of trying to be superhuman instead of realistically striving to reach our individual purpose and unique God-given potential within such diversity. He tauntingly teases us that if we don't have it all—fame, fortune, families, and fun, and have it every minute all the time—we have been short-changed; we are second-class citizens in the race of life. You'd have to be deaf, dumb, and blind not to get these messages in today's world, and as a sex we are struggling, our families are struggling, and our society struggles. Drugs, teenage pregnancies, divorce, family violence, and suicide are some of the ever-increasing side effects of our collective life in the express lane.

As a result, we are experiencing new and undiagnosed stress-related illnesses. The Epstein-Barr syndrome, for one, has come into our popular medical jargon as the malady of the eighties. Its symptoms are low-grade fevers, aching joints, and other flulike symptoms—but it isn't the flu. It carries with it overwhelming exhaustion, muscular weakness, and physical debilitations—but it isn't the dreaded AIDS. Its victims are often confused and forgetful; but, no, it isn't Alzheimer's. Many feel suicidal, but this disease lacks the traditional characteristics of clinical depression.

And yes, it can strike men, but three times out of four it doesn't. This illness is primarily a woman's disease, and those most vulnerable are the so-called "fast-track" women in high-stress, conflicting roles.[1]

When I recently mentioned this to the young women in our BYU student body, I was flooded with telephone calls and letters saying, "I have it! I have it! I must have Epstein-Barr!" Well, whether they do or do not, I can't say. But the body and its immune system are affected by stress. Those calls and letters tell me that too many are struggling and suffering; too many are running faster than they have strength, expecting too much of themselves. We must have the courage to be imperfect while striving for perfection. We must not allow our own guilt or the feminist books, the talk-show hosts or the whole media culture to sell us a bill of goods—or rather, a bill of no goods.

I believe we can become so sidetracked in our compulsive search for identity and self-esteem and self-awareness that we really believe it can be found in having perfect figures or academic degrees or professional status or even absolute motherly success. Yet in so searching externally, we can be torn from our true internal, eternal selves. We often worry so much about pleasing and performing for others that we lose our own uniqueness—that full and relaxed acceptance of ourselves as persons of worth and individuality. We become so frightened and insecure that we cannot be generous toward the diversity and the individuality and, yes, the problems, of our neighbors. Too many women with these anxieties watch helplessly as their lives unravel from the very core that centers and sustains them. Too many are like a ship at sea without sail or rudder, tossed to and fro (as the apostle Paul said) until more and more are genuinely, rail-grabbingly seasick.

Where is the sureness that allows us to sail our ship whatever winds may blow—with the master seaman's triumphant cry, "Steady as she goes"? Where is the inner stillness we so cherish and for which our sex traditionally has been known?

I believe we can find it—the steady footing and the stilling of the soul—by turning away from the fragmentation of physical preoccupations, or superwoman accomplishments, or endless popularity contests and returning instead to the wholeness of our soul, that unity in our very being that balances the demanding and inevitable diversity of life.

One woman who is not of our faith but whose writings I love is Anne Morrow Lindbergh. In commenting on the female despair and general torment of our times, she writes: "The Feminists did not look . . . far [enough] ahead; they laid down no rules of conduct. For them it was enough to demand the privileges. . . . And [so] woman today is still searching. We are aware of our hunger and needs, but still ignorant of what will satisfy them. With our garnered free time, we are more apt to drain our creative springs than to refill them. With our pitchers, we attempt . . . to water a field, [instead of] a garden. We throw ourselves indiscriminately into committees and causes. Not knowing how to free the spirit, we try to muffle its demands in distractions. Instead of stilling the center, the axis of the wheel, we add more centrifugal activities to our lives—which tend to throw us [yet more] off balance.

"Mechanically we have gained, in the last generation, but spiritually we have . . . lost."

She emphasizes, "[For women] the problem is [still] how to feed the soul."[3]

I have pondered long and hard about the feeding of our inner self, of the "one thing needful" amidst too many troublesome things. It is no coincidence that we speak of "feeding the spirit" just as we would speak of feeding the body. We need constant nourishment for both. The root word *hale* (as in "hale and hearty") is the common root to words like *whole, health, heal,* and *holy.* President Ezra Taft Benson recently said on this campus: "There is no question that the health of the body affects the spirit, or the Lord would never have revealed the Word of Wisdom. God has never given any temporal commandments—that which affects our stature affects our soul."[3] We need so much for body, mind, and spirit to come together, to unite in one healthy, stable soul.

Surely God is well balanced, so perhaps we are just that much closer to him when we are. In any case, I like the link between *hale, whole, health, heal,* and *holy.* Our unity of soul within diversity of circumstance—our "stilling of the center"—is worth the effort of this conference and anything else that may encourage it.

As I noted previously, I believe we make too many external quests seeking peace or fulfillment. Only rarely do we consider the glorious possibility within us, within our own souls. We seem never to remember that divine promise, "The kingdom of God is within you" (Luke 17:21). Perhaps we forget that the Kingdom of God is within us because too much attention is given to the Kingdom of Women outside us, this outer shell, this human body of ours, and the frail, too-flimsy world in which it moves. So, as women of faith, we should make an inward quest.

In my contribution to this effort, may I share with you an expanded version of an analogy that I shared with the students at the beginning of their winter semester. It is my own analogy of something I read years ago, a process that helped me then and helps me still—in my examination of inner strength and spiritual growth.

The analogy is of a soul—a human soul, with all of its splendor—being placed in a beautifully carved but very tightly locked box. Reigning in majesty and illuminating our soul in this innermost box is our Lord and our Redeemer, Jesus Christ, the living Son of the living God. This box is then placed—and locked—inside another larger one, and so on until five beautifully carved but very securely locked boxes await the woman who is skillful and wise enough to open them. In order for her to have free communication with the Lord she must find the key to these boxes and unlock their contents. Success will then reveal to her the beauty and divinity of her own soul, her gifts and her grace as a daughter of God.

For me, prayer is the key to the first box. We kneel to ask help for the tasks and then arise to find that the first lock is now open. But this ought not to seem just a convenient and contrived miracle. No, if we are to search for real light and eternal certainties, we have to pray as the ancients prayed. We are women now, not children, and are expected to pray with maturity. The words most often used to describe urgent, prayerful labor are *wrestle, plead, cry,* and *hunger.* In some sense, prayer may be the hardest work we will ever be engaged in, and perhaps it should be. We sing, "Prayer is the soul's sincere desire," our most basic declaration that we have no other God before us.[5] It is our most pivotal protection against overinvolvement in worldly things and becoming so absorbed with possessions and privilege and honors and status that we no longer desire to undertake the search for our soul.

For those who, like Enos, pray in faith and gain entrance to a new dimension of their divinity, they are led to box number two. Here our prayers alone do not seem to be sufficient. We must turn to the scriptures for God's long-recorded teachings about our soul. We must learn. Surely every woman in this Church is under divine obligation to learn and grow and develop. We are God's diverse array of unburnished talents, and we must not bury these gifts nor hide our light. If the glory of God is intelligence, then learning stretches us toward him, especially learning from the scriptures. There he uses many metaphors for divine influence, such as "living water" (John 4:10) and "the bread of life." (John 6:35). I have discovered that if my own progress stalls, it stalls from malnutrition, born of not eating and drinking daily from his holy writ. There have been challenges in my life that would have completely destroyed me, would have precluded any spiritual progression at all, had I not had a copy of the scriptures by my bed and a small set in my purse so that I could partake of them day and night at a moment's notice. Meeting God in scripture has been like a divine intravenous feeding for me—a celestial I.V. that my son once described as an "angelical" cord. So box two is opened spirit to spirit through the scriptures. I have discovered that by opening them I have opened it. There I can have, again and again, an exhilarating encounter with God.

At the beginning of such success in emancipating the soul, however, Lucifer becomes more anxious, especially as we approach box number three. He knows something is coming, one very important and fundamental principle. He knows that we are about to learn that to truly find ourselves we must lose ourselves, so he begins to block our increased efforts to love—love God, love our neighbor, and love ourselves. Remember, the Lord has asked above all else that we love. Everything else we do is secondary, and in fulfilling the two great commandments, we can often measure how much we love the Lord by how well we truly love our neighbor. I firmly believe that if we did nothing else but faithfully practice love for our neighbor, we would have found our ability and success in accomplishing all else. Yet Satan's skillful deception has been to obscure this chance for near success. He has, especially in the last decade, enticed the world to engage so much of their energies in the pursuit of romantic love or thing-love or excessive self-love. In so doing we can forget that appropriate self-love and self-esteem are the promised reward for putting other things first. "Whosoever shall seek to save his life shall lose it; and whosoever shall lose his life shall preserve it" (Luke 17:33). Box three opens only with the key of charity.

Real growth and genuine insight are coming now. But the lid to box four seems nearly impossible to penetrate, for we are climbing, too, in this story, and the way inward is also the way upward. Unfortunately the faint-hearted and fearful often turn back here—the going seems too difficult, the lock too secure. This is a time for self-evaluation. To see ourselves as we really are often brings pain, but it is only through true humility that we will come to know God. "Learn of me; for I am meek and lowly of heart" (Matthew 11:29). We must be patient with ourselves as we overcome weaknesses, and we must remember to rejoice over all that is good in us. This will strengthen the inner woman and leave her less dependent on outward acclaim. When the soul reaches the stage where it pays less attention to praise, it then also cares very little when the public disapproves. Comparing and competition and jealousy and envy begin to have no meaning now. Just imagine the powerful spirit that would exist in our female society if we finally arrived at the point where, like our Savior, our real desire was to be counted as the least among our sisters. The rewards here are of such profound strength and quiet triumph of faith that we are carried into an even brighter sphere. So the fourth box, unlike the others, is broken open, as a heart and contrite spirit are broken. Or better yet, it bursts open as a flower blooms and the earth is reborn. We are reborn, too, in humility and repentance and renewal. We are born of water and of fire. We are born of the Spirit of God.

To share with you my feelings of opening the fifth box, I must compare the beauty of our souls with the holiness of our temples. There, in a setting not of this world, in a place where fashions and position and professions go unrecognized, we have our chance to meet God face to face. For those who, like the brother of Jared, have the courage and faith to break through the veil into that sacred center of existence, we will find the brightness of the final box brighter than the noonday sun. There we will find peace and serenity and stillness that will anchor our soul forever, for there we will find God. Wholeness. Holiness. That is what it says over the entrance to the fifth box: "Holiness to the Lord." "Know ye not that ye are the temple of God?" (1 Corinthians 3:16). I testify that you are holy—that divinity is abiding within you waiting to be uncovered—to be unleashed and magnified and demonstrated.

I believe that if any woman is to find her own personal identity and value for herself, her family, her society, and her God, she will have to uncover her own soul and set it free. Then it can and should range throughout all eternity, having great influence and doing much good.

As I conclude, I pray for a special spirit to be with me so that I might articulate what I have recently been feeling about this whole matter of identity—the eternal identity of our womanhood. These thoughts are my own, and I take full responsibility for them. Above all, I do not want them to be misunderstood nor to give offense.

I have heard it said by some that the reason women in the Church struggle somewhat to know themselves is that they don't have a divine female role model. But we do believe we have a Mother in Heaven. May I quote from President Spencer W. Kimball in a general conference address: "When we sing that doctrinal hymn . . . 'O My Father,' we get a sense of the ultimate in maternal modesty, of the restrained, queenly elegance of our Heavenly Mother, and, knowing how profoundly our mortal mothers have shaped us here, do we suppose her influence on us as individuals to be less?"[6]

I have never questioned why our Mother in Heaven seems veiled to us, for I believe the Lord has his reasons for revealing as little as he has on that subject. Furthermore, I believe we know much more about our eternal nature than we think we do; and it is our sacred obligation to identify it and to teach it to our young sisters and daughters, and in so doing, strengthen their faith and help them through the counterfeit confusions of these difficult latter days. Let me point out some examples.

The Lord has not placed us in this lone and dreary world without a blueprint for living. In Doctrine and Covenants 52:14 we read, "And again, I will give unto you a pattern in *all things, that ye may not be deceived*" (italics added). He certainly includes us as women in that promise. He has given us patterns in the Bible, the Book of Mormon, the Doctrine and Covenants, the Pearl of Great Price; and he has given us patterns in the temple ceremony. As we study these patterns we must continually ask, "Why does the Lord choose to say these particular words and present it in just this way?" We know he uses metaphors and symbols and parables and allegories to teach us of his eternal ways. For example, we all have recognized the relationship between Abraham and Isaac that so parallels God's anguish over the sacrifice of his son, Jesus Christ. But, as women, do we stretch ourselves and also ask about Sarah's travail in this experience as well? We could, and if we did, I believe we would learn. We need to search, and we need always to look for deeper meaning. We should look for parallels and symbols. We should look for themes and motifs just as we would in a Bach or a Mozart composition, and we should look for patterns—repeated patterns—in the gospel. One obvious pattern is that both the Bible and the Book of Mormon start off with family, including family conflict. I have always believed that symbolized something eternal about all of us as "family" far more than the story of just those particular parents or those particular children. Surely all of us—married or single, with children and without—see something of Adam and Eve and something of Cain and Abel every day of our lives. With or without marriage or with or without children, surely we have some of the feelings of Lehi, Sariah, Laman, Nephi, Ruth, Naomi, Esther, the sons of Helaman, and the daughters of Ishmael.

Those are types and shadows for us, prefigurations of our own mortal joys and sorrows, just as Joseph and Mary are, in a sense, types and shadows of parental devotion as they nurtured the Son of God himself, with Mary playing the principal mortal role. These all seem to me to be symbols of higher principles and truths, symbols carefully chosen to show us the way, whether we are married or single, young or old, with family or without.

And obviously the temple is highly symbolic. May I share an experience I had there a few months ago? It has to do with the careful choice of words and symbols. I have chosen my own words carefully so that nothing I say will be improperly shared outside the temple. My only quotations are taken from published scripture.

Maybe it was coincidence, but as someone has said, "Coincidence is a small miracle in which God chooses to remain anonymous." In any case, as I waited in the temple chapel, I sat next to a very elderly man who unexpectedly but sweetly turned to me and said, "If you want a clear picture of the Creation, read Abraham, chapter 4." As I started to turn to Abraham, I just happened to brush past Moses 3:5: "For I, the Lord God, created all things, of which I have spoken, spiritually, before they were naturally upon the face of the earth." Another message of prefiguration again—a spiritual pattern giving meaning to mortal creations. I then read Abraham 4 carefully and took the opportunity of going to an initiatory session. I left there with greater revelatory light on something I'd always known in my heart to be so—that men and women are joint heirs of the blessings of the priesthood and, even though men bear the greater burden of administering it, women are not without their priesthood-related responsibilities also.

Then as I attended the endowment session, I asked myself if I were the Lord and could give my children on earth only a simplified but powerfully symbolic example of their roles and missions, how much would I give and where would I start? I listened to every word. I watched for patterns and prototypes.

I quote to you from Abraham 4:27: "So the Gods went down to

organize man in their own image, in the image of the Gods to form they him, male *and* female to form they *them*" (italics added). They formed male, and they formed female—in the image of the Gods, in their own image.

Then in a poignant exchange with God, Adam states that he will call the woman "Eve." And why does he call her Eve? "Because she was the mother of all living" (Genesis 3:20; Moses 4:26).

As I tenderly acknowledge the very real pain that many single women, or married women who have not borne children, feel about any discussion of motherhood, could we consider this one possibility about our eternal female identity—our unity in our diversity. Eve was given the identity of the mother of all living—years, decades, perhaps centuries before she had ever borne a child. It would appear that her motherhood preceded her maternity just as surely as the perfection of the Garden preceded the struggles of mortality. I believe mother is one of those very carefully chosen words, one of those words rich with meaning after meaning after meaning. We must not, at all costs, let that word divide us. I believe with all my heart that it is first and foremost a statement about our nature, not a head count of our children. I have only three children and have wept that I could not have eight. (Some of you may have eight and weep that you can't have three.) And I know that some of you without any have wept, too. And sometimes, too many have simply been angry over the very subject itself. For the sake of our eternal motherhood I plead that this not be so. Some women give birth and raise children but never "mother" them. Others, whom I love with all my heart, "mother" all their lives but have never given birth. Therefore, we must understand that however we accomplish it, parenthood is the highest of callings, the holiest of assignments. And all of us are Eve's daughters, married or single, maternal or barren, every one of us. We are created in the image of the Gods to become Gods and Goddesses. And we can provide something of that divine pattern, that maternal prototype, for each other and for those who come after us. Whatever our circumstance, we can reach out, touch, hold, lift, and nurture—but we cannot do it in isolation. We need a community of sisters stilling the soul and binding the wounds of fragmentation.

I know that God loves us individually and collectively—as women— and that he has a personal mission, an individual purpose for every one of us. As I learned on my Galilean hillside, I testify that if our desires are righteous, God overrules for our good, and Heavenly Parents will tenderly attend to our needs. In our diversity and individuality, my prayer is that we will be united—united in seeking our specific, foreordained mission, united in asking, not "What can the Kingdom do for me?" but "What can I do for the Kingdom? How do I fulfill the measure of *my* creation? In my circumstances and my challenges and with my faith, where is my *full* realization of the godly image in which I was created?"

With faith in God, his prophets, his Church, and ourselves—faith in our own divine creation—may we be peaceful and let go of our cares and troubles over so many things. May we believe—nothing doubting—in the light that shines, even in a dark place.

Your presence here today (in all your diversity) is evidence that you are women of faith. We have gathered today in the warmth and beauty of the renewing sun (Son) of spring, just as the multitudes gathered at his feet in Galilee. We are his disciples. He accepts us as we are, even as we are growing toward what we must become. Rest in that love. Bathe and luxuriate in it. Let it relax, calm, and comfort you. Let us keep our face to the Son and come unto him. "Listen to my words," he counseled us. "Walk in the meekness of my Spirit, and you shall have peace in me" (D&C 19:23).

Notes

1. "Malaise of the '80s," *Newsweek*, 27 October 1986, 105.
2. Anne Morrow Lindbergh, *Gift from the Sea*, 20th anniversary edition, with an afterword by the author (New York: Vintage Books, 1978), 52.
3. Ibid., 51.
4. Ezra Taft Benson, "In His Steps," in *BYU Fireside and Devotional Addresses* (Provo, Utah: Brigham Young University Press, 1979), 62; also in Ezra Taft Benson, *Come unto Christ* (Salt Lake City: Deseret Book, 1983), 33.
5. *Hymns of The Church of Jesus Christ of Latter-day Saints* (Salt Lake City: The Church of Jesus Christ of Latter-day Saints, 1985), no. 145.
6. Spencer W. Kimball, *Ensign*, May 1978, 6.

COVENANTS, COME WHAT MAY

⟡

Elaine L. Jack

As the Lord's covenant people in the last days, we have much to celebrate: the restored gospel, opportunities to serve and be served, blessings of the priesthood, the Spirit that speaks to us individually, and a Father in Heaven who loves us all. Covenants bring down all those blessings from heaven. To rejoice in our covenants is to understand their importance in our eternal progression. Covenants are the essence of our mortal experience, the measure of our devotion and diligence. Kept, honored, renewed, and held sacred, covenants bind us to God.

"Wherefore, lift up thy heart and rejoice, and cleave unto the covenants which thou hast made" (D&C 25:13). The Lord covenants with us: "I, the Lord, am bound when ye do what I say; but when ye do not what I say, ye have no promise" (D&C 82:10). He is bound to bless us and reward us. No earthly promise compares with his assurance of love and blessing.

The very word *covenant* may seem exacting and hard. It may seem removed from pressing tasks at hand, if we think of our covenants primarily as historical events, such as our baptism, or as the title of our latterday scriptures, the Doctrine and Covenants. What does it mean to be a covenant people with the Lord? Why is it important in our individual lives? Is honoring our covenants just one more item in a long list of things we should be doing? And how can we give our covenants priority when we are having trouble some mornings just putting on our shoes?

Our covenants embrace the full experience of righteous living. They speak of keeping the commandments, having the Spirit with us, remembering the Savior, valuing a temple marriage, putting our families first, and serving one another. No one else can fulfill our covenants for us, and no one else can experience the joy that lights our souls when we do our part. Covenants are active, two-way commitments that bring the Savior

---

Elaine L. Jack grew up in Cardston, Alberta, Canada. She attended the University of Utah as an English major and is an avid reader. She and her husband, Joseph E. Jack, are the parents of four sons. Sister Jack serves as general president of the Relief Society of The Church of Jesus Christ of Latter-day Saints.

into our very lives and change us. We treat each other with charity. We create homes centered on gospel teachings. We work hard at being good parents, the greatest calling in the kingdom of God. And we pray. During my four years as general president of the Relief Society, nothing has meant more to me than when someone says, "Sister Jack, we are praying for you."

Imagine for just a minute that Jesus Christ is right next door, that you can walk in and talk with him at will. My little grandson David has spent some time with me lately because there is a new baby at his home. He comes into the kitchen and asks me a thousand questions, needs help with something, shows me things, or wants to make plans for our next activity. So it is with us and the Savior. Picture yourself sitting near him and going over the things he has asked you to do. The two of you shape a covenant, and then you are off to do what you have promised.

Covenant making is that simple, and Christ can be that close. He establishes the ground rules and the great rewards that follow. No earthly organization or institution can take away our opportunity to be one with God.

Others, letting God's Spirit work in them, help us keep our covenants. I was once fretting about my fourteen-year-old son, who was being consistently disagreeable. "What am I going to do with that boy?" I asked. From my wise friend Doral came this counsel, "Just love him." That's what I needed to hear. And it's what I vowed to do. It was the only thing I did all year that he didn't disagree with. I know that the Lord prompted Doral to lead me that day.

That experience reminds me of the words of a dear song, "Lead me, guide me, walk beside me / Help me find the way."[1] The Lord works miracles in our lives but not by fixing things. He didn't change my son, but he helped me to have a new attitude. The change wasn't worthy of a write-up in the *Church News*—though can't you see the headline: "Mother of Four Boys Shows Love to Teenage Son"? That might *be* worthy of a big story. Being there for our families is the daily living of our covenants. As I loved this precious son, I loved the Lord and drew near to him.

Our covenants are beautifully detailed in the Book of Mormon account of the baptisms at the waters of Mormon. Alma teaches us that when we go into the waters of baptism, we covenant to come into the fold of Christ and be numbered with his people. We covenant to take upon ourselves the name of Christ and be Saints in very deed; to bear one another's burdens, that they may be light; to mourn with those who mourn; to comfort those who need comfort. We covenant to stand as witnesses of God at all times and in all things and in all places, even until death. Then, in summary, Alma says, "If this be the desire of your hearts, . . . ye have entered into a covenant with him, that ye will serve him and keep his commandments, that he may pour out his Spirit more abundantly upon you" (Mosiah 18:8–10). Now, that is cause to rejoice!

Our joy increases when we attend the temple, covenant to follow the Savior, and focus on our eternal progression. Living our temple covenants increases our strength and effectiveness. The dedicatory prayer for the Kirtland Temple says: "And that all people who shall enter upon the threshold of the Lord's house may feel thy power. . . . And we ask thee, Holy Father, that thy servants may go forth from this house armed with thy power" (D&C 109:13, 22).

The temple is indeed a source of strength. I grew up watching my mother press her cotton temple dress before attending the Alberta Temple nearby. Our remote Canadian enclave of Mormons had no paved streets, but the temple made our whole community seem noble and grand. As a child I spent many hours on the temple grounds. My mother's parents, who lived just next door to us, had joined the Church in Scotland when they were courting; my grandmother's family immediately disowned her. She and my grandfather were alone and in love, yet they waited to be married until they could get to "Zion" and be sealed in the Endowment House in Salt Lake City. They knew, better than I knew when I was married in the temple in Cardston, that those covenants would change the course of their lives. Grandfather Anderson worked as a stone mason on the temple construction and later as the custodian, a devoted temple worker, and a patriarch. His life bore testimony of a clear spiritual understanding: "I came into the world to do the will of my Father" (3 Nephi 27:13). His spiritual strength came from the sacrifices he and Grandmother had made to live their covenants.

There is power in those eternal commitments. As we honor our commitments, the ways of the world grow less and less appealing. Each week we renew our covenants by partaking of the sacrament. That reminder gives us the opportunity to recommit, to reflect, and to look forward.

Sisters have told me of their desire to strengthen their understanding of the Lord's sacrifice. A woman in England related a spiritual experience that made Christ's atonement real to her. "I was feeling sorry for myself," she said. "I'd been struggling for nine years on my own, with children. I looked at a picture of the Savior and felt his eyes come to life. They seemed to look into my very soul, and at the same time these words came to my mind: 'I am here. I've always been by your side, taking the pain you feel as well. I drank the bitter cup for you. I'll always be here with you, every step of the way.'"

Christ's suffering in his final hours and on the cross are difficult to comprehend. He could have withdrawn, but he was able to look ahead with commitment. His love for his disciples contrasts sharply with the behavior of his detractors: his forgiveness, kindness, humility, and quiet majesty stand against a background of jeers, hollow triumphs, and cold-hearted hatred. Those final hours culminated a ministry marked by exceptional experiences: feeding the five thousand, raising Lazarus, quiet moments with close family and friends, a bitter march dragging his cross through the streets of Jerusalem. I think of those hours when my commitment lags; he was asked to do more than I will ever understand.

To "always remember him" (Moroni 4:3; 5:2) means to think not only of his crucifixion but of his life. As I take the sacrament, I like to ponder the scriptures that reveal a gentle but forceful leader healing the sick, a dear friend rescuing his faltering disciple from the sea, a listener and teacher to the woman at the well, a compassionate leader who blessed children one by one, and a Savior who gently spoke "Mary" to the woman in the garden and heard her answer, "Rabboni." These scriptural accounts help me to remember Jesus. To always remember him is to remember his example and his love. Our sacramental worship can be a renewal of covenants with our Savior in a sacred setting designed to draw us to him.

Keeping our covenants is a process. We start where we are—imperfect but trying to do better, converted but needing to learn and apply principles. The process, however, is not easy. Children falter; friends move or fall away. We mend our marriages like we used to mend socks. Sickness, death, and other experiences can devastate us if we do not trust the Lord and remember his encouragement: "Press forward with a steadfastness in Christ, having a perfect brightness of hope" (2 Nephi 31:20).

Though the way is hard, the journey is worthwhile. After the struggle come promised blessings—not always manna from heaven but covenant blessings. Always they are what we need, though sometimes they are not what we want. I've learned a lesson about that, too. When what I want is what the Savior bestows, then I know I am making progress.

A stake Relief Society president told me of an experience she had visiting a ward. During the lesson, a sister commented that her life hadn't turned out as she had expected. Several other sisters expressed the same feeling. After some discussion, they agreed that they had learned to follow the commandments—"come what may." We all will have times of "come what may." But following the commandments can turn "come what may" into "come unto Christ."

Our covenant relationship sets us apart from the world. Eliza R. Snow, general president of the Relief Society more than one hundred years ago, knew the power of covenants when she said, "We stand in a different position . . . ; we have made covenants with God; we understand his order."[2] To be a woman of covenant in these latter days is a sacred and holy responsibility. I rejoice, sisters, that we can discern what really matters in this life. Covenants matter.

Our covenants go two ways: we do our part, and the Lord does his. I have told sisters all over the Church to turn to the Lord when they need help; if we remember him, he will be there. Women tell me of their struggles and speak of the enormous challenges they face. One divorced mother of three said, "I work forty-five to fifty hours a week, and then I pray like the dickens my child support check will be in the mail." When you do all that you can, the Lord will make up the difference.

With a deep feeling of responsibility, last spring I prepared to speak at general conference. Speaking in that setting is both a great blessing and a tremendous challenge. I prayerfully considered what to say and then worked through my ideas and phrasing, draft after draft. I remembered once seeing a ninth draft for a conference talk from one of the general authorities and thought I might pass his mark. I prayed for guidance, and my husband, Joe, gave me a blessing.

Waiting for my turn to speak that Saturday morning, I wondered: "I have done all that I can. . . . Do I really believe the counsel I have given to Relief Society leaders? Do I believe that he will make up the difference?"

Then I started to worry not only about the content of my talk but the time as well. The meeting was running behind. Suddenly a calm assurance from the Lord came over me, and I knew he was with me. I climbed the stairs to the podium, rejoicing inside with a testimony of his promise: "I will go before your face. I will be on your right hand and on your left, and my Spirit shall be in your hearts, and mine angels round about you, to bear you up" (D&C 84:88).

I marvel at how the Lord made a meager number of fishes and loaves sufficient to feed five thousand. But then, aren't we all latter-day fishes and loaves? The Lord works with each of us and makes our contributions and sacrifices sufficient. He is mindful of what we are doing. He assures us: "I know thy works, and charity, and service, and faith, and thy patience, and thy works; and the last to be more than the first" (Revelation 2:19).

The sustaining power of our covenants makes a huge difference in a world that is skipping beats in all directions. The Lord's work supports us, but we must be prayerful and careful to distinguish between the Lord's work and busy work. That is not a new challenge for women. When Emmeline B. Wells was called as general president of the Relief Society in 1910, she faced sweeping national movements for change. She felt outside pressure to step up Relief Society involvement in many social issues, to redefine and reshape the organization, to refocus the attention of the Relief Society on community causes. Emmeline stood firm, advocating that sisters in the Church hold fast to their sacred covenants. Recognizing that many organizations do good in the world, Emmeline also understood that Relief Society had a much broader responsibility— to save souls, not just for now, but for all eternity. Through Emmeline's leadership, Relief Society maintained a sense of separate identity, uniqueness, and sacred mission to be understood only within the context of the restoration of all things.[3]

We see similar pressures today. Sometimes Relief Society sisters try to do it all—the world's way. That is not what the Lord has in mind. Our Relief Society today is the Lord's organization for women, prepared for the next century and the one that will follow as well. The Lord gives direction, and we follow. As President Spencer W. Kimball said, the work of the Church will progress as "the women of the Church are seen as distinct and different—in happy ways—from the women of the world."[4]

The Relief Society is working hard to expand literacy. Stories pour in from all over the world describing how lives have changed as Relief Society sisters have increased personal and family scripture study, set up summer book groups for children, helped Scouts gather books for homeless shelters, and volunteered in community literacy efforts. Some of our efforts are close to home. A friend of mine had a Native American student living with her family for six years. She grew close to this young man and loved him as if he were her own. As she has done with her children, she taught him to keep a journal so that he could see the Lord's hand in his life. Even though, years later, this young man no longer keeps his covenants, when he visits my friend he asks to see his journal. Together the two remember some of his spiritual experiences. She is grateful for that resource, those feelings on the page that he recorded and perhaps will feel again.

Each soul is valuable to our Father in Heaven. The Church has no borders, no restrictions by culture, race, or language. But illiteracy is a barrier. Members must be able to read to understand the scriptures as well as the messages of latter-day prophets.

A patriarch told of his stake president's challenge to read the Book of Mormon in a month. His wife bought a missionary copy to carry around with her and immediately began making notes in the margin as she read. His experience, however, was different. He had graduated from high school reading on only a fourth grade level. He could read the words, but his progress was painfully slow. Years earlier he had taken the challenge to read the Book of Mormon within a year and after four months was only to Alma. Reading the whole book in thirty-one days seemed impossible. Nevertheless, he sat down on March first and opened the book to 1 Nephi. He thought of Nephi returning for the plates and building a boat in the wilderness. Both had seemed impossible tasks. But, like Nephi, he began, remembering his covenant with the Lord to do all he was asked. The first day he read thirty-one pages and the next day just as many, and so it went. He finished the Book of Mormon in less than three weeks. He was blessed by the Lord to read quickly, and the skill has stayed with him, long after the challenge was fulfilled.

Our literacy efforts also help unlock the wonders of good books. In Doctrine and Covenants 88:118 we are told, "Seek ye out of the best books words of wisdom; seek learning, even by study and also by faith." The thirteenth article of faith is a good reminder for us, "If there is anything virtuous, lovely, or of good report or praiseworthy, we seek after these things."

The beauty of the world, the majesty of good literature, fine art, and music can soften the jangle of daily living. I often think of the hymn "Where Can I Turn for Peace?" when I feel in turmoil. This hymn, written by Emma Lou Thayne and put to music by Joleen Meredith, expresses a rich understanding of the Lord's covenants.

> *Where can I turn for peace?*
> *Where is my solace*
> *When other sources cease to make me whole?*
> *When with a wounded heart, anger, or malice,*
> *I draw myself apart,*
> *Searching my soul?*
>
> . . . .
>
> *He answers privately,*
> *Reaches my reaching*
> *In my Gethsemane, Savior and Friend.*
> *Gentle the peace he finds for my beseeching.*
> *Constant he is and kind,*
> *Love without end.*[5]

Living the commandments and standing as witnesses of God has been the challenge of the Lord's covenant people through the ages. When they are righteous, they have his Spirit with them; when they turn from their covenants, they stumble. The book of Numbers tells of Moses leading the Israelites in the wilderness. "I am not able to bear all this people alone," he cries to the Lord, for they did not keep their covenants (11:14). Their belief faltered, their strength left them, and they were easy prey to the ways of the world. Hence the first time they stood at the borders of the promised land, they were afraid of what they might encounter. "The people be strong . . . and the cities are walled, and very great," they said (13:28). "We saw . . . giants," said the scouts (13:33). And the people believed and cried, "Would God that we had died in the land of Egypt" (14:2). A few of them stood stalwart. Caleb said, "Let us go up at once, and possess it; for we are well able to overcome it" (13:30). Joshua, who eventually led the people to the promised land in Moses' stead, declared: "The Lord is with us: fear them not" (14:9). But the Israelites had distanced themselves from their covenants, and they wandered in the wilderness another thirty-eight years.

How many of us are up against giants? A mother I know of described the trials of her life. She had stopped attending church, stopped praying, and had given up on religion. One night she dreamt that she stood before Jesus on the Day of Judgment. She was resigned to accept a lesser kingdom for herself until she was told to say farewell for eternity to her children. "I begged, I pleaded, I promised to change," she said. "But Jesus was not going to be swayed by my rantings and pleadings. I knew in my heart he was right. I was bound by my baptism the same as he was bound by covenants. I awoke with the most physical, heartbreaking pain. . . . I was at church the next week and have never missed since." Standing as a witness of God against the powerful adversary is hard, but worth it. To see someone come back is cause for rejoicing!

Covenants are not invisible. They reach out from what we say, do, and create to touch others. Keeping our covenants, come what may, brings blessings from the Lord. These blessings may come as a gentleness of spirit, a light in our eyes, and a peace in our souls that speaks dramatically of the goodness of God. As women of covenant, we are trying to be Saints. May we rejoice in the covenants we have made with the Lord and in the promises he has made to us.

Notes

1. Naomi Ward Randall, "I Am a Child of God," *Children's Songbook of The Church of Jesus Christ of Latter-day Saints* (Salt Lake City: The Church of Jesus Christ of Latter-day Saints, 1989), 3; or *Hymns of The Church of Jesus Christ of Latter-day Saints* (Salt Lake City: The Church of Jesus Christ of Latter-day Saints, 1985), no. 301.
2. Eliza R. Snow, *Millennial Star* 33 (12 September 1871): 578.
3. See Jill Mulvay Derr, Janath Russell Cannon, and Maureen Ursenbach Beecher, *Women of Covenant: The Story of Relief Society* (Salt Lake City: Deseret Book, 1992), 180–223.
4. Spencer W. Kimball, *Ensign*, Nov. 1979, 104.
5. *Hymns*, no. 129.

MUST WE ALWAYS RUN FASTER THAN WE HAVE STRENGTH?

⟨✄⟩

Kathleen Bushnell Jensen

One night last spring I remember sitting at my kitchen table thinking in frustration. "I have not accomplished a thing this whole week." My windows still needed washing, and there were a dozen other things that I had not gotten to. I wondered why I felt so tired for not having accomplished much. I got out a pencil and paper, but, on impulse, instead of writing a to-do list, I began jotting down some of the things that had gone on that week. I was surprised. I had been to two soccer games, two soccer practices, two piano lessons, one gymnastics lesson, and one doctor's appointment. I had made a fairy costume for the Shakespeare festival for our fifth grader, gone on five one-hour exercise walks with my husband, made a poster for the first-grade teacher for teacher appreciation week, attended the ground breaking for the Bountiful temple, spent one-half day helping the fifth grade with the rain forest unit, attended two tennis matches for our senior son, prepared and served Sunday dinner for fourteen people, gone on a picnic, and hiked around Causey Dam for family home evening. I was exhausted even remembering! I had called people to serve and bring food for the grade school Shakespeare festival feast, washed and dried at least twelve batches of laundry, sobbed with my husband and our children when our dog got run over, attended a college football game, given my Primary in-service lesson, completed the cancer drive for my daughter who couldn't get it finished, lived through numerous teenager ups and downs, wrote to our missionary daughter in Germany, took our baby bunnies for first grade show and tell, planted pansies, watched a Jazz game. The list went on and on. I looked at it and thought, "Well, maybe I did accomplish something!"

I concluded that often we sell ourselves short. Maybe we're not so

---

Kathleen Bushnell Jensen has taught first grade and served as PTA president. She and her husband, Marlin K. Jensen, a member of the First Quorum of the Seventy, are the parents of eight children. She teaches the marriage and family relations class in Sunday School.

different from those hard-working pioneer women who were busy from sunup to sundown. Our days are every bit as challenging. We may not card wool, hoe beets, or slop hogs, but we need to give ourselves credit for what we do.

In fact, perhaps a more pressing question for us is, "Are we running faster than we have strength?" The role of women has changed dramatically in my lifetime. When I was a child, my mom was always home, and that was wonderfully gratifying for me, good for my self-esteem. My mother let me know somehow that when I came home, I lighted up her day. Many times I'm not home when my children come home, though I try to be. I try to do a lot of the worthwhile things for my children that my mother did for me, but it's difficult with our smorgasbord of options. When I attended college some twenty years ago, most women trained as either teachers or nurses. Any other career seemed almost eccentric. In contrast, my daughters and their friends have the world open to them. They can go into any of the professions, a wonderful change for women. But one thing hasn't changed: a day is still twenty-four hours. We still have our agency to choose what we want to do in those twenty-four hours. Therein lies the dilemma. I don't struggle so much with good and bad choices; rather, I have ten *good* choices, all worthwhile pursuits, vying for my time. It's often difficult to prioritize, to judge which things are really important and which to put on hold.

Anne Morrow Lindbergh wrote of this dilemma almost forty years ago in *Gift from the Sea*. Her words still ring true. She observes that in the modern world the women's movement has gained for women more privileges and opportunities. But "the exploration of their use, as in all pioneer movements, was left open to the women who would follow. And woman today is still searching. We are aware of our hunger and needs, but still ignorant of what will satisfy them. With our garnered free time, we are more apt to drain our creative springs than to refill them. With our pitchers, we attempt sometimes to water a field, not a garden. We throw ourselves indiscriminately into committees and causes. Not knowing how to feed the spirit, we try to muffle its demands in distractions. Instead of stilling the center, the axis of the wheel, we add more centrifugal activities to our lives—which tend to throw us off balance."[1]

How true! A few years ago I served in my ward Relief Society presidency. I was surprised to find that the problems women were having were not so much economic as spiritual and emotional. I had not known that so many women are unhappy and frustrated. This experience prompted me to think about why that is, and I have identified several possible reasons and solutions.

For one thing, we demand so much of ourselves. Most of us have a hard time saying no in this day and age. For another, it is too easy to forget to be grateful. The other day I went out to my garage, pushed the garage door opener, and was dismayed when the door wouldn't go up. I was full of exasperation and in a hurry. As I unplugged the opener and lifted the door manually, I was thinking, "I have got to get that fixed tomorrow, because I cannot manage without that garage door opener." And then I thought to myself, How odd. We've lived in our home for eighteen years, but before that we lived in a home with no garage at all. I had four small children, and I'd come home from grocery shopping and park in front. If it was raining, I'd be drenched by the time I carried in the baby, then the two-year-old, then the four-year-old, then the stroller, and finally the groceries. I'd think, "If I had a garage, life would be wonderful!" I used to envision life with a garage. I'd see garages, and I'd think, "Those people have got it made!" That day, after fuming about the defective garage door opener, I remembered what it used to be like with no garage at all and wondered, What's happened to me in eighteen years of living in this house? I never thank the Lord for my garage. I just go out and use it.

Apparently, I'm not the only one who forgets to be grateful for our many blessings. At a regional conference this year, Bonnie Pinegar spoke on this topic. She confessed that one of her self-assigned tasks is to be the worrier of the family. While her husband, Rex, is across the bed from her sleeping soundly, she is fretting about everything—all the problems of her married children, illnesses, money, anything. Finally, one morning after another restless night, she asked him, "How can you sleep with all the problems we have?" He answered, "One way, Bonnie. I count my blessings."

I don't know why that story brings tears to my eyes. I guess because I'm so lousy at counting mine. I'm the one who wants the garage door opener to be working all the time, and I forget that I'm awfully lucky to have a garage. I think we get spoiled; we want it all, and we want it now. Many times we're just not willing to wait. All that wanting makes us really unhappy.

Envy can also cause pointless frustrations. A friend of mine had needlepoint seats on all her dining room chairs. I love needlepoint. One day I looked at those chairs and thought, I'll never have that. I'll always have the kind you have to wash off real fast. I'll just never have pretty needlepoint chairs. And it's true. Maybe I won't ever have them. Needlepoint is a hobby my friend loves doing. Someday I may take up needlepoint, but perhaps I'll be too busy with grandchildren to make it a priority.

Still another reason we are needlessly unhappy is that we lose our spiritual perspective. Sometimes we forget that the Lord is aware of our presence, that he knows and cares about what we're doing. We can draw great strength from that knowledge. A notable example is early Church pioneer Joseph Millet, who recorded in his journal his experiences of homesteading in Nevada:

"One of my children came in, said that Brother Newton Hall's folks were out of bread. Had none that day. I put . . . our flour in sack to send up to Brother Hall's. Just then Brother Hall came in. Says I, 'Brother Hall, how are you out for flour.' 'Brother Millett, we have none.' 'Well, Brother Hall, there is some in that sack. I have divided and was going to send it to you. Your children told mine that you were out.' Brother Hall began to cry. Said he had tried others. Could not get any. Went to the cedars and prayed to the Lord and the Lord told him to go to Joseph Millett. 'Well, Brother Hall, you needn't bring this back if the Lord sent you for it. You don't owe me for it.' You can't tell how good it made me feel to know that the Lord knew that there was such a person as Joseph Millett."[2]

Sometimes we think we are all alone in our day-to-day struggles. We feel no one is really aware of our lives as they unfold. But the Lord is aware. He knows all; he has experienced all. The Lord knew that there was such a person as Joseph Millet. He knows there is such a person as Kathy Jensen. And he knows of you and your life.

Also, we mustn't forget "it must needs be, that there is an opposition in all things" (2 Nephi 2:11). Note that the scripture doesn't say that there's opposition in some things, but in all things, in everything. I don't know why it has to be that way. Opposition makes life a lot more difficult, but then it also makes us appreciate what we have. People who lived through the Depression appreciate money differently from the rest of us. It is often difficult for them to spend money. Some die with huge savings accounts, certain the next economic catastrophe looms on the horizon. They never give anything to Deseret Industries. They recycle, mend, patch, redesign, and reuse. My husband's father always said to him, "You need to live through a depression. You'd be a lot more careful." And maybe it's true. Experiencing opposition does give one a perspective.

When our last baby was born, I was a basket case. I was forty-two years old. No one was telling me how smart I was for having a baby at that age. After her birth, I continued to worry. At about six weeks old, she still wasn't smiling. Was she all right? Would she be autistic? This fear ballooned into a real trauma to me. Every day I'd tell the other children to interact with her, smile at her, get her to look at them, get her to smile. But she didn't smile. I'd had enough children to know that by that age babies are ready to respond, and she just wasn't responding. I became distraught and sank into worse than usual postpartum blues. I felt overwhelmed as I worried that I might have to raise a child with imperfections. I know that many others have been asked to do so, but as I asked myself if I could do what they do, or handle it, I was in turmoil for a while. I prayed and pleaded with the Lord, promising that I would appreciate everything about her—every normal annoying little thing would be a gift to me. She did finally smile and is a very normal, active little girl. A year later, when I was out in the hall during sacrament meeting trying to settle her down, I tried to remember my promise. I've tried to keep my perspective. I watch her with gratitude for her active mind and energetic body. Maybe I wouldn't have been so grateful if I hadn't experienced fear that she might not be normal.

Another way to keep perspective is to remember that "to every thing there is a season" (Ecclesiastes 3:1). When I had several small children, I tended to look at women who were out doing things—taking institute classes, tole painting, skiing—and I would think, "How do they do it? I'm so unorganized." As I look back, my advice is be content where you are. If you have young children, enjoy them! I'm old enough to know that you don't have young children very long. Those moments are fleeting. Don't wish away your toddlers and bright-eyed preschoolers. They will never be yours at that age again. Don't rush your seasons. I feet the most off balance when I'm trying to run faster than I have strength, when I'm trying to keep up with people who are single or who maybe don't have as many children at home. Our needs are different. When you have small children, you don't need to have a totally spotless home. When I go into a home that is full of young children and yet is totally spotless, I think, "What do the kids do all day? Live outdoors?" Be realistic; let your kids have some fun. Let them make messes. Don't worry about what everyone might be thinking. And don't compare your home to anyone else's.

One day several years ago, I had been harping at my children to clean their rooms and get the house looking nice. I assigned them several jobs and then left, telling them I expected to return to find everything perfect. When I got back, I found a sign on the refrigerator that our junior-high-aged daughter Julie had made. She had written, "Better to be happy and messy than clean and mean. If you agree, please sign here so we can show Mom." The missionaries had dropped by that day, and they'd signed it, all the kids' friends had signed it, everybody who had come by had signed it. It made me stop and think, What message am I sending my children? Is it more important to have a clean house or a happy house?

Sometimes we simply fail to communicate clearly by words or actions our real priorities. Many of us say, "My family is the most important thing." But do our lives show that? Every so often, we need to rethink our activities. Are the things we spend our time with really the things that are important to us? It's easy to get sidetracked when we have so many interests and opportunities.

Sometimes our seasons don't always include what we thought they would. We expect to have children and find we can't. We expect to be married and are single. We expect to raise our children a certain way and find we can't afford to be at home. We expect our children will always choose the right in the important things and they don't. And we feel guilty or ashamed that our lives don't match our ideal expectations and perhaps confused about what we should be doing now. Often we forget that we're entitled to inspiration in our lives, if we just ask for it. If we are being led by the Spirit, we don't have to feel guilty or ashamed of our choices and circumstances. We can feel secure in our own decisions. Many, many women, for example, have to work outside the home. If you and your husband have prayerfully decided that's what you need to do in your family, then do it. Feel good about your decision, and don't apologize for it. Church members often apologize for how few children they have. They'll say, "Oh, we just have two." And I want to say, "Well, that's great! What a joy to have those two!" We should never equate righteousness with numbers of children or judge what is appropriate for anyone else. A woman in our ward has eleven children. She's a wonderful mother. She comes to church with a smile on her face and even looks sane. I suspect that I am at least two children beyond my max, but clearly she is not. She's thrilled to have her eleven children. That was the right choice for her. Our place is to support and enjoy one another, not judge or compare.

I also feel that we really need to take care of ourselves. So many women give their all to their children or husband and have nothing left for themselves. We can become "depleted women," as Jo Ann Larson says in her book *I'm a Day Late and a Dollar Short . . . and It's Okay!*[3] We're always the ones who get the burnt toast or the spoon that's been caught in the disposal. It is important for our families that we value and spend some time caring for ourselves. President Marion G. Romney said: "How can we give if there is nothing there? Food for the hungry cannot come from empty shelves. Money to assist the needy cannot come from an empty purse. Support and understanding cannot come from the emotionally starved. Teaching cannot come from the unlearned. And most important of all, spiritual guidance cannot come from the spiritually weak."[4]

Neither can we afford to ignore our physical health. We owe it to ourselves and to our families to keep physically strong. Last year my husband and I agreed to start walking together in the mornings. It's been very good for both of us. It's fun, and I can tell him everything I want and he doesn't fall asleep. I have a captive audience for one hour, and so does he. Our walks have been good for our marriage, for our health, and for our mental outlook.

I recommend spending some time alone each day to think and be who you are. If you have small children, a moment alone is precious. It's easy to forget who you really are. Too often we become what we are needed for— the Cub Scout den mother, the soccer carpool driver, the PTA commissioner, the team mother—instead of who we are. Solitude is one way to not get lost in doing. Making sure you are having fun doing what you are doing is another way. Sometimes that is difficult in your own family. You may prepare a new recipe, knock yourself out working all afternoon, and then you can sit down to the meal and the kids pick out all the green things and say they'd rather have macaroni and cheese. When we're feeling that kind of discouragement, the world outside our homes seems pretty enticing. It's more gratifying to cook for a Relief Society luncheon. The other sisters rave and ask for the recipe. We get a lot of strokes that way. It's easy to be nice to people you see at a PTA meeting or in the church foyer or even at an office. It's much harder to work out a relationship with a teenaged son who's giving you a hard time. It becomes very enticing to spend your time away from home. But ultimately that is a counterfeit source of satisfaction. We need to build our family relationships, and that is all the more reason to build in fun times with the family.

Last Mother's Day I read an article about a woman who had been selected as Utah's Mother of the Year a few years ago. Her husband died when she had eight very young children, including an infant, and she raised an outstanding family in near poverty. Her son Monroe McKay said: "I tell people that she was not perfect; she simply did the best she could in that day. She didn't do the best that you wanted her to do or that she wanted to do, but she did the best she could; and that was good enough. She didn't raise perfect children either; we had our share of problems."[5]

Many times we think we have to be perfect instantly and perfect in everything: that's what causes us to run faster than we have strength. But God knew that we were all human and imperfect. He knew that we needed a Savior. If we had been capable of perfection on our own, we wouldn't need a Savior. Jesus came to help us make up the difference between what we can do at our best and what we aspire to become.

That is the comforting, good news of the gospel. If we're doing all we can do, and we keep trying, then our inevitable shortcomings and mistakes are not going to bar us from being Christ's. "See that all these things are done in wisdom and order; for it is not requisite that a [woman] should run faster than [she] has strength."

Notes

1. Anne Morrow Lindbergh, *Gift from the Sea* (New York: Random House, 1955), 52.
2. Joseph Millett Journal, as quoted in Eugene England, "Without Purse or Scrip: A 19-Year-Old Missionary in 1853," *New Era*, July 1975, 28; reprinted as " 'The Lord Knew That There Was Such a Person': Joseph Millett's Journal, 1853," in Eugene England, *Why the Church Is As True As the Gospel* (Salt Lake City: Bookcraft, 1986), 17–30.
3. Jo Ann Larson, *I'm a Day Late and a Dollar Short . . . and It's Okay!* (Salt Lake City: Deseret Book, 1991), 150–76.
4. Marion G. Romney, *Ensign*, November 1982, 93.
5. Carri P. Jenkins, "Judge Monroe McKay: Creating a Commotion," *BYU Today*, May 1992, 28.

"I CAN DO ALL THINGS THROUGH CHRIST"

Virginia U. Jensen

A few years ago a young boy was lost in a cave for several days. Searchers spent frantic hours trying to find him in the total blackness of the cave. Finally, he was found and brought to safety. It was learned that he had gotten separated from those with lights and had wedged himself into a crevice—not seeing anything or knowing which way to go. I tried to imagine what it would be like to be in total darkness. How terrifying and disorienting it would be!

This life experience we are all having can get pretty dark at times. I have been by the side of my elderly mother as she laid her husband of fifty years (my father) to rest and wondered how she could go on without him. I have been with my sister as she suffered the sudden, unexpected death of her eight-year-old son—her firstborn—and wondered, *How could this happen to such a lovely, lively boy?* I have listened to the pain of a woman who wanted desperately to be a mother and yet did not get the wish of her heart. I know single women who want to be married and have a family, and year after year find no realization of this desire. As I have visited with women all over the world, I have learned that no one is immune to sorrow and suffering of all kinds. In fact, I have come to realize that challenges and adversity, as Joseph Smith taught, are "at the core of saintliness" and are an integral part of God's plan for us.[1] When Joseph Smith was in Liberty Jail, he cried to the Lord for comfort, and the Lord gave it to him, saying, "If the very jaws of hell shall gape open the mouth wide after thee, know thou, my son, that all these things shall give thee experience, and shall be for thy good" (D&C 122:7).

There is a lot of the "natural man" attitude in me, and there are times when I have thought, *This certainly does not feel like it's for my good.* Then

Virginia U. Jensen serves as first counselor in the Relief Society General Presidency. A homemaker, she and her husband, J. Rees Jensen, are the parents of four children and the grandparents of six. She has served in numerous volunteer and Church service missionary assignments and enjoys gardening, grandchildren, and family activities.

I think of other women and what they have done. I think of Eve, for example. Her calling was to be the "mother of all living" (Genesis 3:20). A rather daunting task, don't you think? I have only four children, and yet there have been times when I have felt like "the mother of all living." And it's not as if she had a handbook to rely on! Yet she was steadfast and true, pushing on despite hardship and heartbreak. And in the end she "blessed the name of God" and "was glad, saying: Were it not for our transgression we never should have had seed, and never should have known good and evil, and the joy of our redemption, and the eternal life which God giveth unto all the obedient" (Moses 5:11–12).

I think also of Noah's wife, whose name is not recorded for us. Sometimes we forget that she must have stood by him during all the years of preaching and building, and I cannot even begin to imagine what housekeeping was like on the ark. And then, when they were once again on dry ground, she and her family began all over again. She, too, was a faithful daughter of God who endured and overcame by faith.

Surely all of us are moved by the fortitude and faithfulness of the women of the Restoration, whose calling it was to lay the foundations of the Church in the latter days. Many of them repeatedly sacrificed their homes in Kirtland, in Missouri, in Nauvoo, and elsewhere. They packed up their households and began again and again, with more than mortal courage.

Faithful women in every age have learned, "I can do all things through Christ which strengtheneth me" (Philippians 4:13).

In my backyard is an extensive rock garden with huge rocks. My grandchildren love to climb those rocks. For them, it is like mountain climbing because the rocks are so big and they are so small. One day five-year-old Will was scrambling up and down with relative ease, but his younger brother, James Patrick, who was only two at the time, was having a great deal of difficulty. The rocks were very large compared to his little two-year-old body. Now, James Patrick is a determined young man and was not about to give up, but he was making no progress, and his hands were getting scratched and beginning to bleed from his attempts. His knees got banged every time he slid back down a rock.

His wise and watchful mother was surveying the scene from the kitchen window. As she saw his frustration about to overtake him, she stepped outside and said, "You can do it, James Patrick. Keep trying. You can do it. I know you can." Spurred on by her words of encouragement, he gritted his teeth, made one more attempt, and got himself to the top.

His mother went back into the house, and James Patrick played at the top of the yard for a while, where I was pulling weeds. When he decided he'd had enough and started to climb down, I heard him quietly whisper to himself as his foot started to slip, "I can do it. I can do it."

We live in a world filled with rocks of all sizes. It was created that way by divine design, as a proving ground for our faith and a vital step in our eternal progression. One of the great tasks of our mortal life is to learn that, through the grace and mercy of Jesus Christ, we can climb every rock, or overcome every challenge, that we encounter.

Some of the rocks in our lives are self-chosen. For example, most mothers would admit that their children can be both their greatest blessing and their greatest trial. Many of the things mothers slog through daily—fixing meals, doing laundry, running the perpetual carpool, helping with homework, sitting up late at night with sick babies or heartsick teenagers—are natural outgrowths of the choice to have children. It's not always convenient to be a mom, and it's certainly not always easy. Yet we would make that choice again if we were starting from scratch, rocky though it may be at times. Sometimes it helps to remind ourselves that we really wanted those children.

I remember when I was wheeled out of the delivery room after giving birth to my first child. I had two thoughts. The first was *Did anyone get the license number of the truck that just hit me?* The second was *Wow, my mother did this for me.* Suddenly I had an incredible increase in appreciation and love for my mother, and I realized I had a tremendous debt to repay her in love, respect, devotion, and service.

The same idea of self-chosen challenges applies to single women. I know many who have chosen professions that are rewarding, but I don't know one whose job is problem free. Climbing over rocks is part of the mortal experience.

Another mortal reality is that we will encounter in our earthly sojourn some climbs that we would not have chosen for ourselves, over rocks that leave our hands and knees scraped and bleeding. That will happen even to faithful, tithe-paying, temple-attending, scripture-reading, Homemaking-meeting-supporting, 100-percent-visiting-teaching Latter-day Saint women. In the words of Carlfred Broderick, "The gospel of Jesus Christ is not insurance against pain. It is [a] resource in [the] event of pain."[2]

My friend Chris Stevens, a beautiful young mother of six who lost her beloved husband to cancer two years ago, knows something of the resources available to those who trust in the Lord. "Never forget that the Lord sees the big picture," she writes. "Never, ever doubt how intricately the Lord can be involved in your life if you allow him. He knows exactly when and where to place the next piece in the puzzle of life to best complete the picture." Chris goes on to bear testimony of the Lord's loving, guiding hand in putting together puzzle pieces that made it possible for her young children to go on without their father. Here is one of the many faith-promoting incidents she relates:

"In the fall, just three weeks before his death, one of Robert's colleagues at work called to tell me of his concern and love for him. They all wanted to do something for Robert to help relieve his mind of concerns for his family. They had learned that we were in a new home that did not have any landscaping, and they wanted to put in our front yard. A couple of days later this same man called back to report that the response had been so good they would also be doing the side yard. The next day he called to say, 'Be ready for a lot of people to show up Saturday. We have enough sod coming to do your whole yard.' On Saturday, about seventy-five of Robert's coworkers and family members showed up ready to work. When they left three hours later our whole yard was sodded, tulip bulbs had been planted, a new lawn mower and weed eater had been put together, and there was money left over for trees."

Chris continues: "On Sunday, October 29, our oldest child, Ryan, had his missionary farewell. Two days later, as Robert lay dying, his boss came to our home to hand deliver a letter from the president of the company. He hand delivered the letter so that it would arrive before Robert passed on. The company had voted to forgo a Christmas party and had placed the money that would have been spent on that party in an account for us. The balance in the account was $10,000. The tremendous burden of the cost of the funeral was lifted off my shoulders with this unbelievably generous gift."

Chris closes her letter: "No, I don't doubt the love of my Father in Heaven. I don't doubt what part he can play in our lives. He may bless us through other people, but he is the director. Bitterness and doubt have no place in trials when we know that all experiences are for our good in the eternal perspective."[3]

It's safe to say that none of us would choose to scale the rock that Chris faced, that of losing a husband or other loved ones. Yet sometimes such rocks surface in our paths, and we have no choice but to find a way over. Chris's letter displays a great deal of faith and hope.

Elder Neal A. Maxwell has said: "Daily hope is vital, since the 'winter quarters' of our lives are not immediately adjacent to our promised land. An arduous trek still awaits, but hope spurs weary disciples on. Jesus waits with open arms to receive those who finally overcome by faith and hope. His welcome will consist not of a brief, loving pat, but, instead, being clasped in the arms of Jesus."[4]

I love to work in my garden and plant things and then watch them blossom into something wonderful. I have learned that one must get to know one's garden in order to have success in cultivating it. There is a spot where for years I planted one thing after another without much success. When, over time, I came to understand the subtleties of that spot—how long the sun shone on it each day, when it fell into shade, how much water could be expected there, and the characteristics of the soil—then I was able to select plants that could flourish there.

There is another Garden we must come to understand in order to experience the fullness of its import in our lives. We must all come to realize in a profound way what Jesus did for us in the Garden of Gethsemane and on Calvary's hill.

Consider the account preserved for us of Christ's last hours on earth. In Matthew 26 we read of how he approached Gethsemane with his disciples, "and he took with him Peter and the two sons of Zebedee, and began to be sorrowful and very heavy. Then saith he unto them, My soul is exceeding sorrowful, even unto death: tarry ye here, and watch with me" (Matthew 26:37–38). What do you suppose it means to be "sorrowful . . . unto death?" Perhaps there are those listening today who have felt that same kind of soul-crushing sorrow. Try to imagine the weight of that sorrow, and notice that even Christ, who obviously had a strong and loving relationship with his Father in Heaven, sought additional strength from his earthly friends. Jesus pleads, "Tarry ye here, and watch with me." Has there ever been a time in your life when you have said to someone, "Don't leave me; stay with me"? We crave a loved one's presence when a spiritual night falls.

The scripture continues, "And he went a little further, and fell on his face, and prayed." Now, this is not the peaceful, contemplative prayer we often see in the paintings: Christ "fell on his face." "And [then Jesus] prayed, saying, O my Father, if it be possible, let this cup pass from me:

nevertheless not as I will, but as thou wilt" (Matthew 26:39). The Savior clearly knows what it is like to come up against a rock that seems too hard to climb. And, as in all things, his response is the perfect example for our own response to trials: "Not as I will, but as thou wilt." Almost two thousand years later, the Lord described the pain of that experience: "Behold, I, God, have suffered these things for all, that they might not suffer if they would repent; but if they would not repent they must suffer even as I; which suffering caused myself . . . to tremble because of pain, and to bleed at every pore, and to suffer both body and spirit" (D&C 19:16–18).

Sometimes when we come up against adversity, it helps us just to know someone else understands what we are going through.

In the book of Alma in the Book of Mormon, chapter 7, we read of Christ and his mission on earth. Verse 11 tells us, "And he shall go forth, suffering pains and afflictions and temptations of every kind; and this that the word might be fulfilled which saith he will take upon him the pains and the sicknesses of his people."

Verse 12: "And he will take upon him death, that he may loose the bands of death which bind his people; and he will take upon him their infirmities, that his bowels may be filled with mercy, according to the flesh, that he may know according to the flesh how to succor his people according to their infirmities."

When we tremble, when we bleed, when we suffer, either in body or in spirit, he understands. None is better qualified to see us through our mortal trials than he who "descended below all things" (D&C 88:6). If we truly understand what happened in the Garden of Gethsemane, we will have confidence in his sure promise found in Hebrews 13:5: "I will never leave thee, nor forsake thee."

Just as my little grandson's mother did not immediately rush out and lift him up over the rocks, so our Savior does not remove our trials from us, though he clearly could. We are promised our trials will not be more than we can handle, but they cannot be less if we are to fulfill the measure of our creation.

President Spencer W. Kimball, who experienced so many severe trials in his life, said: "I am positive in my mind that the Lord has planned our destiny. Sometime we will fully understand. And when we see back from the vantage point of the future, we shall be satisfied with many of the happenings of this life that are so difficult for us to comprehend."[5]

The landscape of Southern Utah is filled with spectacular reminders of the refining nature of trials. In Arches National Park, harsh elements—wind, ice, and rain—have penetrated cracks in stone and dissolved the weaker materials, leaving the stronger materials to create structures so magnificent that people travel from all over the world to see them.

Similarly, the hardships we encounter in our life are the very tools the Lord uses, like a master sculptor, to shape us into the divine creations we are destined to become.

C. S. Lewis said, "God who foresaw your tribulation has specially armed you to get through it, not without pain, but without stain."[6]

President Howard W. Hunter said: "Every generation since time began has had things to overcome and problems to work out. Furthermore, every individual person has a set of challenges which sometimes seem to be earmarked for him individually. We understood that in our premortal existence.

"When these experiences humble, refine, and teach us, they make us better people, more grateful, loving, and considerate of other people in their own times of difficulty.

"Even in the most severe of times, problems and prophecies were never intended to do anything but bless the righteous and help those who are less righteous move toward repentance."[7]

In Romans 5:8 we read, "God commendeth his love toward us, in that, while we were yet sinners, Christ died for us." Think of the tremendous trust he shows in us. He trusted us that his anguish in the Garden of Gethsemane and his sacrifice on Calvary's hill would not have been in vain.

Sometimes our earthly vision is limited. It is difficult for us to understand fully Christ's promise. In 1 Corinthians 13:12 we read, "For now we see through a glass, darkly; but then face to face: now I know in part; but then shall I know even as also I am known." When we come face to face with our Savior, we will understand every rock in our mortal path, why they were placed there, and how they helped sculpt us. Then we will more fully understand the Atonement and we will thank him—oh, how we will thank him—for his sacrifice on our behalf. We will also gain perspective and realize that the actual size of our rocks was much smaller than it appeared to be when we faced them.

My grandson Peter once held a small pebble in front of his eye as he looked into the evening sky and said to his father, "Look, Dad, this rock is as big as the moon!" Like Peter's pebble, trials often block our vision and seem "as big as the moon." With eternal perspective, we see each trial only as a tiny piece of a beautiful mosaic made up of a variety of earthly experiences.

When Moses complained to the Lord that he was slow of speech and therefore ill-equipped to lead the children of Israel, God replied, "Who hath made man's mouth? . . . have not I the Lord?" (Exodus 4:11). In similar tone, the Lord comforted Moroni's fear of inadequacy in writing the record of his people by reminding him that "I give unto men weakness that they may be humble; and my grace is sufficient for all men that humble themselves before me; for if they humble themselves before me, and have faith in me, then will I make weak things become strong unto them" (Ether 12:27). The Savior trod the rockiest ground of all, the path of Calvary. Having experienced mortality, he is "acquainted with grief" (Isaiah 53:3) and asks only our meek petition for his rescuing arm.

When it seems we cannot climb any further, and we slide to the bottom of the rocks with banged and bloodied knees, he whispers, "You can do it!" And he knows that we can, because his grace is the enabling power that makes all things possible.

As Bruce Hafen explains in his book *The Broken Heart:* "The Savior's victory can compensate not only for our sins but also for our inadequacies; not only for our deliberate mistakes but also for our sins committed in ignorance, our errors of judgment, and our unavoidable imperfections. Our ultimate aspiration is more than being forgiven of sin—we seek to become holy, endowed affirmatively with *Christlike* attributes, at one with him, like him. Divine grace is the only source that can finally fulfill that aspiration, after all we can do."[8] His words echo Nephi's testimony, "We know that it is by grace that we are saved, after all we can do" (2 Nephi 25:23). These words give us the proper perspective on the interweaving of grace and agency: we must do what we can, knowing that the Lord will make up what must surely be a huge deficit.

When Jesus lived on the earth he taught using uncomplicated words and stories that all could understand, knowing that open hearts would receive the full impact of his message (see Matthew 13:3–16). His sermons and parables provide elegantly simple instructions that we might compare to a mountain climber's tools: They are compact, multipurpose, and applicable to any number of possible situations. We can distill from the New Testament a selection of these tools to carry in our spiritual backpack as we hike the steep and rocky, as well as the smooth, trails of our earthly excursion. Here are a few I have chosen, though Christ's teachings afford a wealth of others.

The first tool I recommend: *Seek God's peace.* The world teaches us to seek peace in possessions, wealth, and physical comforts and pleasures. As Paul wrote to the Corinthians, "The wisdom of this world is foolishness with God" (1 Corinthians 3:19). God's peace transcends worldly peace, for it is not based on conditions that are subject to change unexpectedly. As Christ consoled his disciples prior to his crucifixion, "Peace I leave with you, my peace I give unto you: not as the world giveth, give I unto you. Let not your heart be troubled, neither let it be afraid" (John 14:27).

President Joseph F. Smith describes the difference between the Lord's peace and that of the world: "There is no such thing as physical rest in the Church of Jesus Christ. Reference is made to the spiritual rest and peace which are born from a settled conviction of the truth in the minds of men. We may thus enter into the rest of the Lord today, by coming to an understanding of the truths of the gospel." He further writes that those who seek peace "will not find satisfaction in the doctrines of Men. Let them seek for it in the written word of God; let them pray to him in their secret chambers, where no human ear can hear, and in their closets petition for light; let them obey the doctrines of Jesus . . . . This course will bring peace to their souls, joy to their hearts, and a settled conviction which no change can disturb."[9]

Another tool: *Trust in the Lord.* Christ has traversed the route we are now climbing and knows where the obstacles lie. Brigham Young taught departing missionaries "that he who goes forth in the name of the Lord, trusting in him with all his heart, will never want for wisdom."[10]

How completely our unnamed sister in the New Testament exhibited her trust when more than wisdom was wanting. Having suffered illness for twelve years, depleted in her physical strength and worldly goods, she said, "If I may touch but his clothes, I shall be whole" (Mark 5:28). Jesus, not seeing her but feeling her use of his power, sought her in the throng: "Daughter, thy faith hath made thee whole; go in peace" (Mark 5:34). By remembering and trusting the Divine One who wishes to shape us in his image, we gain courage to overcome the obstacles we encounter in life and receive the promise of exaltation described in Alma 36:3: "Whosoever shall put their trust in God shall be supported in their trials, and their troubles, and their afflictions, and shall be lifted up at the last day."

The next tool: *Forgive an enemy*. Forgiveness is a cleansing act that softens our heart and frees us from the past, allowing us to focus on the present—the only time in which we can take action. Grudges we carry are additional weight that slows us as we climb, an unnecessary burden we must shed if we are to progress. Knowing this, Christ instructed that if someone should "trespass against thee seven times in a day, and seven times in a day turn again to thee, saying, I repent; thou shalt forgive him" (Luke 17:4). The apostles were as challenged by the difficulty of this simple admonition as we are. "Lord," they responded, "increase our faith" (Luke 17:5). Joseph Smith taught us to "ever keep in exercise the principle of mercy, and be ready to forgive our brother on first intimations of repentance . . . ; and should we even forgive our brother, or even our enemy, before he repent or ask forgiveness, our Heavenly Father would be equally as merciful unto us."[11]

Another tool: *Give thanks*. Give thanks for God's gifts to you. Do you recall the story of the ten lepers who called to Jesus as he passed through their village, pleading, "Master, have mercy on us"? (Luke 17:13). Jesus did have mercy upon them, and he caused them to be healed. "And one of them, when he saw that he was healed, turned back . . . and fell down on his face at his feet, giving him thanks . . . . And Jesus answering said, Were there not ten cleansed? but where are the nine?" (Luke 17:15–17). No matter how bleak the landscape of our lives may periodically appear, grateful eyes can find a spot of beauty somewhere. Searching for the beauty in our lives, finding it, and giving sincere thanks are an invigorating and refreshing exercise for the soul.

The last tool I recommend: *Feed his lambs*. When the risen Christ sat with his disciples on the shore of the Sea of Tiberias, he asked Peter if he loved him. The response was quick and heartfelt: "Yea, Lord; thou knowest that I love thee." Jesus responded, "Feed my lambs" (John 21:15).

He gave that injunction to Peter three times: "Feed my lambs . . . . Feed my sheep . . . . Feed my sheep" (John 21:15–17). We may sometimes feel burdened and overwhelmed by the multitude of duties jostling for our attention. We feel pressure to keep up with standards real and imagined, external and self-imposed. But remember that the gospel in its purest form consists of the simple teachings of one wearing tattered clothes and having bare feet, speaking without pretense and in gentle tones the loving message of his Father: Trust in me. Love one another. Forgive him. Go in peace. Feed my lambs. These are simple tools he has provided us to help us find our way back to him.

Toward the close of his ministry, the apostle Paul said, "I have fought a good fight, I have finished my course, I have kept the faith: henceforth there is laid up for me a crown of righteousness, which the Lord, the righteous judge, shall give me at that day: and not to me only, but unto all them also that love his appearing" (2 Timothy 4:7–8). Notice that he says nothing about winning the fight or the race, only about completing it honorably. In fact, he implies that all the contestants can be winners, that a crown is laid up "not to [him] only" but to all who look forward to the coming of Christ. Indeed, "the race is not to the swift, nor the battle to the strong" (Ecclesiastes 9:11), but "unto him that endureth to the end will [the Lord] give eternal life" (3 Nephi 15:9). We don't have to be fast, we don't have to show great prowess, but we do have to keep climbing. You can do it!

In his book *Believing Christ*, Stephen E. Robinson tells us: "In making the gospel covenant, we become part of a team whose captain and quarterback is Jesus Christ, a cosmic Heisman Trophy winner who throws nothing but touchdowns. If we are on his team, we will go undefeated." But we have "to be on his team, not [our] own and not somebody else's." Brother Robinson says further, "When we become one with Jesus Christ, spiritually we form a partnership with a joint account, and his assets and our liabilities flow into each other."[12]

In her book *The Story of My Life*, Helen Keller relates snatches of memories of the illness that took her sight and hearing when she was nineteen months old and dim recollections of how the world looked and sounded. She writes: "Gradually I got used to the silence and darkness that surrounded me and forgot that it had ever been different, until she came—my teacher—who was to set my spirit free. But during the first nineteen months of my life I had caught glimpses of broad, green fields, a luminous sky, trees and flowers which the darkness that followed could not wholly blot out. If we have once seen, 'the day is ours, and what the day has shown.'"[13]

"We have once seen. Every now and then the Spirit whispers to us of remembered light. We are not lost in a black cave. We know the source of all light! If we could truly recall for a few moments some dim memory of our premortal existence, we would do anything to assure our return to

the Father who sent us here. If we could thrust aside the veil and get an
inkling of who we were before we came to earth, we would be that much
closer to knowing ourselves as Christ knows us."

Remember little James Patrick and his mother? Just as he repeated to
himself over and over, "I can do it," we need to trust the Lord when he
promises that we can overcome our mortal trials. "God is faithful," Paul
reminds us, "who will not suffer you to be tempted above that ye are able;
but will with the temptation also make a way to escape, that ye may be
able to bear it" (1 Corinthians 10:13). Like the child's mother who recognized his ability to climb the rocks if he would just keep trying, the
Lord knows each one of us individually and personally. He knows what
we can bear. He knows what strengths we have; and, even though many
of us foolishly try to hide them, he knows our weaknesses as well. He
would not ask us to climb any rock without preparing a way for us to
accomplish it (see 1 Nephi 3:7). He knows that we can succeed, because
he has already paid the price that covers all the conditions of mortality,
including the rocks.

I love this year's conference theme: "May Christ lift thee up, and may
his sufferings and death, and the showing his body unto our fathers, and
his mercy and long-suffering, and the hope of his glory and of eternal life,
rest in your mind forever" (Moroni 9:25). We've talked about Christ's
"sufferings and death." We need to remember that none of the rest of
what has been said here has any meaning in the absence of that infinite
and eternal atonement.

Bruce Hafen writes: "The Atonement . . . makes possible the infusion
of spiritual endowments that actually change and purify our nature, moving us toward that state of holiness or completeness we call eternal life or
Godlike life. At that ultimate stage we will exhibit divine characteristics
not just because we think we should but because that is the way we are."[14]
Hence we have hope of his glory and of eternal life, not because we have
finally climbed high enough all by ourselves but because we have "come
unto Christ, and [become] perfected in him" (Moroni 10:32).

The next phrase of the conference theme is a more obscure one. What
does Christ's "showing his body unto our fathers" have to do with our
hope of eternal life? To fully understand the import of this passage, we
can turn to 3 Nephi 11, which details the Savior's appearance to the
Nephites following his resurrection. After he had introduced himself as
"Jesus Christ, whom the prophets testified shall come into the world," he

invited the people to "arise and come forth unto me, that ye may thrust your hands into my side, and also that ye may feel the prints of the nails in my hands and in my feet, that ye may know that I am the God of Israel, and the God of the whole earth, and have been slain for the sins of the world.

"And it came to pass that the multitude went forth, and thrust their hands into his side, and did feel the prints of the nails in his hands and in his feet; and this they did do, going forth one by one until they had all gone forth, and did see with their eyes and did feel with their hands, and did know of a surety and did bear record, that it was he, of whom it was written by the prophets, that should come" (3 Nephi 11:10, 14–15).

Then he called for one of those faithful prophets, Nephi, who was among the multitude, to come forward, and in one of the tenderest scenes imaginable, "Nephi arose and went forth, and bowed himself before the Lord and did kiss his feet" (3 Nephi 11:19).

There are many lessons in those few verses of scripture. First, we learn from Christ's own testimony that he is the God not just of the Israelites but of every one of the children of earth. We understand that he was slain as a sacrifice for our sins and that the body he took up out of the grave was the same one that had been laid down, with the prints of the nails and the sword still evident as a witness of his identity. This is one chief element of our hope of eternity: the indisputable reality of his own resurrection.

Picture the multitude—a "great multitude," we read in verse 1 of the chapter—going forth to feel the nail prints and to thrust their hands into his side. They didn't just send a representative up to the front to do that for them. Every one of them, one by one, filed past and experienced this solemn ritual. It would have taken many hours. Can you imagine the patience and love of our Savior to submit to such a thing? I can envision him looking lovingly into the eyes of each person who came forth, saying a few kind words to heal each soul and ignite the flame of testimony in every heart. Can there be any question of his concern for us as individuals? Can we suppose that "borrowed light" would ever be enough for us, when he took such great pains to be sure that every single person there could bear a personal witness?

Finally, think about Nephi for a minute. This was the faithful prophet whose ministry had begun more than thirty years earlier, when the lives of the faithful were threatened unless the signs of Christ's birth were given. He had been with them through that crisis, through the terrible and frightening era of the Gadiantons, and through the subsequent deterioration of the Church due to pride. He had borne powerful testimony and cried repentance to a generation steeped in abomination, raising his brother from the dead and performing many other mighty miracles, which only made the wicked people angrier. For more than thirty years he had remained faithful to the cause to which he had been called.

Picture him now among the multitude. The Lord whom he had served all these long, persecution-filled years had finally come, as he had promised. Can you imagine the feelings of Nephi's heart when the Savior called him by name and invited him to come forward? Was there any question in his mind that Jesus Christ knew him personally and recognized the work he had done?

I testify that our Savior's knowledge of you is no less personal. He knows the sacrifices you have made and are making. He recognizes the efforts you make to keep a Primary class in order, to teach a two-year-old to pray, to help out at the cannery so that his children will be fed, to get a concept through to a Sunday School class full of teenagers. He knows how you've worked and the discipline required to be worthy to attend his temple. Won't all those efforts seem worth it when one day he calls you to come before him?

His knowledge of you goes beyond a catalog of your deeds. He knows you individually and completely. He understands your darkest hours when things seem as black as a cave with no light. He understands when you are feeling unworthy or forgotten or depressed or desperate or alone. He constantly and gently invites you to open up those dark recesses of your heart to him that he may fill them with his light. You can't shock him. You can't surprise him. He won't turn away from you in disgust, shaking his head and saying, "Oh, this is worse than I thought. There's nothing I can do here." When he healed the sick, he often forgave their sins as well. His healing extends to the crippled heart just as surely as to the crippled leg.

All this we learn because of "the showing his body unto our fathers." How grateful I am for the Book of Mormon, which preserves for us this miraculous account. May "his mercy and long-suffering, and the hope of his glory and of eternal life, rest in [our minds] forever" (Moroni 9:25). May we feel the peace, his peace, that comes from a true knowledge of our Lord and his atoning sacrifice. May we be lifted up in him, that we may lift each other over all the rocks we encounter in the paths of our mortality. May we never forget that we "can do all things through Christ which strengtheneth" us.

Notes

1. Truman G. Madsen, *Joseph Smith the Prophet* (Salt Lake City: Bookcraft, 1989), 76.
2. Carlfred Broderick, *My Parents Married on a Dare* (Salt Lake City: Deseret Book, 1996), 123.
3. Chris Stevens to Virginia U. Jensen; used by permission.
4. Neal A. Maxwell, *Ensign*, November 1994, 36.
5. Spencer W. Kimball, *Faith Precedes the Miracle* (Salt Lake City: Deseret Book, 1969), 105.
6. C. S. Lewis, *Letters of C. S. Lewis*, ed. W. H. Lewis (New York: Harcourt Brace Jovanovich, 1966), 219.
7. Howard W. Hunter, "Why Try?" *New Era*, January 1994, 6.
8. Bruce C. Hafen, *The Broken Heart: Applying the Atonement to Life's Experiences* (Salt Lake City: Deseret Book, 1989), 20.
9. Joseph F. Smith, *Gospel Doctrine* (Salt Lake City: Deseret Book, 1939), 126.
10. Brigham Young, *Discourses of Brigham Young*, sel. John A. Widtsoe (Salt Lake City: Deseret Book, 1954), 323.
11. Joseph Smith, *Teachings of the Prophet Joseph Smith*, sel. Joseph Fielding Smith (Salt Lake City: Deseret Book, 1938), 155.
12. Stephen E. Robinson, *Believing Christ* (Salt Lake City: Deseret Book, 1992), 29, 25.
13. Helen Keller, *The Story of My Life* (New York: Bantam Books, 1990), 5.
14. Hafen, *Broken Heart*, 18.

DRIFTING, DREAMING, DIRECTING

Ardeth Greene Kapp

Of our day, Elder Bruce R. McConkie said, "Great trials lie ahead. All of the sorrows and perils of the past are but a foretaste of what is yet to be. And we must prepare ourselves temporally and spiritually."[1] And even with the reality of that kind of a backdrop, President Spencer W. Kimball admonishes us, "Make no small plans, for they hold no magic to stir men's souls."[2] This reminds me of Dickens's *A Tale of Two Cities*. The story begins with the contrasts of that day:

"It was the best of times, it was the worst of times, it was the age of wisdom, it was the age of foolishness, it was the epoch of belief, it was the epoch of incredulity, it was the season of Light, it was the season of Darkness, it was the spring of hope, it was the winter of despair, we had everything before us, we had nothing before us, we were all going direct to Heaven, we were all going direct the other way—in short, the period was so far like the present period, that some of its noisiest authorities insisted on it being received, for good or for evil, in a superlative degree of comparison only. . . .

"It was the year of Our Lord one thousand seven hundred and seventy-five."

We are living in the times spoken of in the scriptures when peace shall be taken from the earth. Of our time our prophet has said: "To be a righteous woman is a glorious thing in any age. To be a righteous woman during the winding-up scenes on this earth, before the second coming of our Savior, is an especially noble calling. The righteous woman's strength and influence today can be tenfold what it might be in more tranquil times."[3] Each of us will determine whether this day spoken of as the great and dreadful day will be recorded in our journal of life as a truly great and glorious day in which we are privileged to take part, or if, in fact, it is recorded only as a day of turmoil, conflict, and confusion.

Ardeth Greene Kapp has a master's degree in curriculum development from Brigham Young University and has been a popular teacher, writer, and speaker. In April 1984 she was called to serve as general president of Young Women. She is married to Heber B. Kapp.

236

President Harold B. Lee was referring to our day, I believe, when he said: "We have some tight places to go before the Lord is through with this church and the world in this dispensation, which is the last dispensation, which shall usher in the coming of the Lord. The gospel was restored to prepare a people ready to receive him. The power of Satan will increase; we see it in evidence on every hand. There will be inroads within the Church. There will be, as President Tanner has said, 'Hypocrites, those professing, but secretly are full of dead men's bones.' We will see those who profess membership but secretly are plotting and trying to lead people not to follow the leadership that the Lord has set up to preside in this church." Knowing the nature of man, the prophet continues, speaking as a seer: "You may not like what comes from the authority of the Church. It may contradict your political views. It may contradict your social views. It may interfere with some of your social life. But if you listen to these things, as if from the mouth of the Lord himself, with patience and faith, the promise is that 'the gates of hell shall not prevail against you; yea, and the Lord God will disperse the powers of darkness from before you, and cause the heavens to shake for your good, and his name's glory' (D&C 21:6)."[4]

It is while a person stands undecided, uncommitted, and uncovenanted, with choices waiting to be made, that the vulnerability to every wind that blows becomes life-threatening.

Uncertainty, the thief of time and commitment, breeds vacillation and confusion. It is in taking a stand and making a choice to follow our leaders that we become free to move forward. We are then released from the crippling position of doubtful indecision and confusion. We then have access to power and influence, so much so that we can hardly keep pace with our opportunities. It is in or by using our agency and making firm decisions that we turn the key.

Let me share with you a few lines from *The Agony and the Ecstasy* by Irving Stone. On the very brink of creating what for many has become his greatest masterpiece, Michelangelo is faced with a decision that once made, must be lived with. He had completed a multitude of drawings suggesting hundreds of ways he might carve the *David*. He had been vacillating, contemplating, considering all the alternatives, the many options, weighing and waiting. Now he must make a choice.

"He burned his earlier drawings, settled down to the simplest beginning, probing within himself. . . . What could he find in David triumphant, he asked himself, worthy of sculpturing. Tradition portrayed him after the fact. Yet David after the battle was an anticlimax, his great moment already gone. Which, then, was the important David? When did David become a giant? After killing Goliath, or at the moment he decided that he must try. David, as he was releasing with brilliant and deadly accuracy the shot from the sling; or David before he entered the battle when he decided that the Israelites must be freed from their vassalage to the Philistines? Was not the decision more important than the act itself, since character was more critical than action? For him, then, it was David's decision that made him a giant, not his killing of Goliath. This was the David he had been seeking, caught at the exultant height of resolution. . . . The man who killed Goliath would be committed all his life to warfare and its consequence: power. . . . To act was to join. David would not be sure he wanted to join. He had been a man alone. Once he tackled Goliath, there would be no turning back. . . . It was what he sensed that he would do to himself, as well as what the world would do to him, that made him doubtful and averse in changing the pattern of his days. His had been a hard choice indeed."[5]

It was in realizing the importance of David's hard choice and his faith to act that the door was unlocked, allowing Michelangelo to decide about his own mission in marble. Recognizing David as the giant at the moment of his decision allowed Michelangelo to make his decision; and the choice having been made, his tempo changed and with it came strength, power, and hidden energies:

He soared, he drew with authority and power, he molded in clay . . . his fingers unable to keep pace with his thoughts and emotions, and with astonishing facility he knew where the David lay. The limitations of the block began to appear as assets, forcing his mind into a simplicity of design that might never have occurred to him had it been whole and perfect. The marble came alive now."[6]

Each of us must release her own *David* from the imperfect marble that holds it captive, and each of us will greatly hasten that process as we follow the counsel of the prophet. President Kimball has said, "Be wise in the choices you make. . . . Sharpen the skills you have been given and use the talents with which God has blessed you."[7] As we make right choices, we are driven by an exhilaration that causes us to hunger and thirst and feel new energies that lift us, like Michelangelo, toward our goal. "When his right hand tired of driving the hammer, he shifted it to the left, the chisel in his right moving with the same precision and prob-ing sensitivity. He carved at night by candlelight."[8]

I view this conference as an experience that has brought each of us in closer touch with the marble, though imperfect, with which we must work. It is in continuing to make right choices, decisions, and commit-ments that we are released to move forward at a hastened pace and lengthen our stride. If we remain motionless on the brink of indecision, we allow our voice, our example, our potential for good to be held impris-oned, as it were, in a slab of marble. Our testimonies, our commitments, and our covenants may lie deep inside, but until we can cut away all the debris that obscures this treasure, it cannot be recognized by others or even trusted by ourselves. On the consequences of a vacillating position, President J. Reuben Clark said, "The spiritual and psychological effect of a weak and vacillating testimony may well be actually harmful instead of helpful."[9]

Of this I am sure, and feel impressed to promise: as we seek divine direction, we will find our own block of marble to be more magnificent, with greater potential, than any of us have yet realized. The prophet has called each of us to be known as women of God, and when the history of this era is reviewed, it might be said of us, as it was of Queen Esther, "Who knoweth whether thou art come to the kingdom for such a time as this?" (Esther 4:14).

Even with these truths and inspiring examples before us, I feel concern for some who may feel discouraged and that we get our moralities mixed up with our realities, that the gulf between morality and reality is too big, the stakes too high, the requirements too rigid, and the rewards too uncer-tain. In response to this earnest concern, I have prepared some thoughts that might be considered as we each examine and reexamine our own choices and decisions and opinions. In an attempt to give order to these ponderings, I have labeled them "Drifting, Dreaming, and Directing."

It has been my observation, and it is my confession as a former partic-ipant, that many people drift along with the crowd in the Church. Many good people drift to sacrament meeting and Sunday School, even family home evening, and they drift through a casual study of the scriptures. The drifters fall into at least one of two groups. In the first are those who step into the mainstream, getting deeply involved with Church activity and floating with the current, comfortable with a sense of false security that they are in the right place. Others, who form the second group, accepting a few selected principles, resist being part of the flow, the mainstream, and choose to get out into the eddies at the edge, freed from the demands of full participation. It is difficult to decide which of these two groups is better—or worse. Those of us who are, on the basis of activity alone, very much in the Church may not necessarily have the Church very much in us; and if we left, the Church might hardly recognize the difference. Following the practices, doing the right thing but without coming to know, understand, accept, and apply the saving principles and doctrines, we may be compared to one who spends his entire life stringing the instrument—never once hearing the music for which the instrument was created or incapable of recognizing it if he did.

In matters of principle, let us stand as solid as a rock. In matters of practice, may all that we do be based upon these saving principles, and may we understand the intrinsic relationship of principles and practices. It is in making the decision to follow the admonition of the prophet and to become scholars of the scriptures that we gradually learn the doctrine that prepares us to stand on the rock of revelation and to experience less and less the restless sense of drifting, wandering, questioning, and searching.

Many good people are very faithful in following the traditions and practices. I'm reminded of a song we used to sing in Sunday School: "Never be late for the Sunday School class/Come with your bright smiling faces." The chorus ended with: "Try to be there, always be there/Promptly at ten in the morning." Ten in the morning became a practice, a tradition, for a long time. It was not a principle. Yet there were those among the faithful who felt uncomfortable about change, not unlike the feelings expressed by some today as practices and traditions are modified. When changes come, and they always will, for some it may be a test to survive because their foundation is based on practices alone, without an understanding of the eternal, unchanging principles.

Being faithful does not necessarily develop faith. The first principle of the gospel is faith in the Lord, Jesus Christ. To have faith in him is to know him, to know his doctrine, and to know that the course of our life is in harmony with and acceptable to him. It is relatively easy to be faithful, but faith is born out of study, fasting, prayer, meditation, sacrifice, service, and, finally, personal revelation. Glimpses of understanding come line upon line, precept upon precept. Our Father is anxious to feed us just as fast as we can handle it, but we regulate the richness and the volume of our spiritual diet. And we do this by the same method used by the sons of Mosiah: "They had waxed strong in the knowledge of the truth; . . . they had searched the scriptures diligently, that they might know the word of God. But this is not all; they had given themselves to much prayer, and fasting; therefore they had the spirit of prophecy, and the spirit of revelation, and when they taught, they taught with power and authority of God" (Alma 17:2–3).

Faithfulness without faith, practices without principles, will leave us and our families seriously wanting as we move closer to that time spoken of by Heber C. Kimball when he said, "The time is coming when no man or woman will be able to endure on borrowed light. Each will have to be guided by the light within himself. If you do not have it, you will not stand."[10]

May we find ourselves doing less and less drifting as we make right choices based on personal revelation that give direction to us and our families each day of our lives. And with that direction, let us develop "a program for personal improvement" that will cause us to "reach for new levels of achievement," as the prophet has admonished us.[11] He has also promised us that the Lord "will help us as we decide from day to day on the allocation of our time and talent. We will move faster if we hurry less. We will make more real progress if we focus on the fundamentals."[12] Certain principles are essential in our struggle to avoid the wasteful experience of drifting.

Now what of dreamers? Many of us are dreamers at times, wanting in some way to escape ourselves, to be free of our own limitations. I often ponder the words: "With voluntary dreams they cheat their minds." It has been said that if fate would destroy a man, it would first separate his forces and drive him to think one way and act another. It would rob him of the contentment that comes only from unity within. Choices must be decisive so that dreams and actions can be in harmony with each other. When we do something different than we know we should, it is like going into a final examination and putting down the wrong answer, even though we know the right one.

Dreaming, however, can also serve a very positive function when it fits Webster's definition of having "a goal or purpose ardently desired."

In the popular musical *South Pacific* is the delightful little song that goes, "If you don't have a dream, how ya gonna make a dream come true?" I am concerned for some of our sisters who have a magnificent dream but who will never fully realize its fulfillment because they feel that their righteous husband will take care of it, and they fail to prepare for their part in this eternal partnership.

There are some sisters who ponder the administrative structure of the Church and trouble themselves with what they think they don't have without ever coming to a full understanding of their own special and unique mission and the great blessings reserved specifically for them. We hear it expressed in terms that suggest that because women don't have the priesthood, they are shortchanged.

There are still others of our sisters who have the misunderstanding that priesthood is synonymous with men, and so they excuse themselves and have no concern for studying its importance in their own lives. The term *priesthood* is used without qualification, whether it refers to a bearer of the priesthood, priesthood blessings, or priesthood ordinances. Our hearts should cry out in either case, and we should raise our voices and shout warnings to sisters whose dreams are built on such faulty foundations.

Our greatest dreams will be fulfilled only as we come to understand fully and experience the blessings of the priesthood, the power of the priesthood, and the ordinances of the priesthood in our own lives. If we were to begin with the time a child is given a name and a blessing and then continue on through baptism, confirmation, the sacrament, callings and being set apart, patriarchal blessings, administrations, the endowment, and finally celestial marriage, we would quickly realize that all of the saving blessings of the priesthood are for boys and girls, men and women. And while that divine mission of motherhood is paramount, it is not all-inclusive. To help another gain eternal life is a companion privilege. This privilege, indeed this sacred responsibility, this noblest of callings, is denied to no worthy person. To assist in bringing to pass the eternal life of man, and to do it in dignity and honor, is the very pinnacle of my own personal dream. And for us to close our eyes to these eternal truths and not recognize them as priesthood blessings and ordinances is to keep us on the fringe area of the very saving principles—the only principles—that can make our eternal dreams come true.

It is true that as sisters we do not experience a priesthood ordination that carries an administrative function, nor do we have the tremendous, weighty burden of having that sacred responsibility heaped upon us in addition to the mission of creating and nurturing in partnership with God, first in giving birth to the Lord's spirit children and then in raising those children to serve the Lord and keep his commandments.

I have come to know that we can all, both men and women, rejoice in the sacred calling of motherhood. To give birth is but one part of this sacred calling.

After drifting and dreaming, now may we consider the directing of one's life. At my high school graduation, Oscar A. Kirkham stood at the pulpit, looking into the eyes of idealistic, enthusiastic graduates, and in his husky voice he offered this challenge: "Build a seaworthy ship. Be a loyal shipmate, and sail a true course." I don't remember anything else that he said, or what anyone else said, for that matter. But I've pondered that challenge many times over the years. In directing our lives, we want to be sure of the true course and its ultimate destination. We cannot risk being caught in the disillusionment of the fellow who was committed to going north and was in fact traveling north—but on an iceberg that was floating south.

"True points," like stars in the heavens to guide us, are readily available for anyone earnestly seeking direction. These true points of doctrine are found in the true church (see D&C 11:16). Conversion to the truth comes by accepting true doctrine, and the truth of doctrine can be known only by revelation gained as a result of obedience. The Savior taught: "My doctrine is not mine, but his that sent me. If any man will do his will, he shall know of the doctrine, whether it be of God, or whether I speak of myself" (John 7:16–17).

The skeptic of two thousand years ago might have said, "Look, if I knew for sure that the star (the sign of the Savior's birth) would appear in the heavens tonight, I would be obedient." That's like standing in front of a stove and saying, "Give me some heat, and then I'll put in the wood." We must put in the wood first, and then we feel the warmth and the heat; then we can bear testimony of its reality. In Ether we read: "Dispute not because ye see not, for ye receive no witness until after the trial of your faith" (Ether 12:6). As our faith is tried and we are found standing firm even in times of storm, we will rejoice with increased confidence and discover within ourselves the loyal shipmate that we really have as we sail a true course.

Apostles and prophets have been provided in the Church for the purpose of identifying and teaching true doctrine, lest men be "tossed to and fro, and carried about with every wind of doctrine" (Ephesians 4:14). Now, we can follow the Brethren blindly, as one of my non-Mormon friends claims that we do—and I might add that it is far safer and better to follow them blindly than not at all—but that could be an abdication of our responsibility to direct our own lives and become spiritually independent. Again, following the practices alone is not enough. We must come to know the reason, indeed the doctrinal basis, for that practice; otherwise, when the practice or tradition is questioned or changed, those who do not understand the principle are prone to waver. They may even abandon or reject the very practice intended as a schoolmaster to carry them to an understanding of a saving and eternal principle.

There were those in King Benjamin's time who were caught up in exacting the law of Moses. With blinders they followed the practices—an eye for an eye and a tooth for a tooth—until King Benjamin taught them that their practices availed them nothing unless they accepted the mission of the Savior and his atonement. Without that commitment, their practices were for naught.

While Adam was offering the firstlings of the flock, an angel appeared and asked him why he was doing it, why this practice. You will remember Adam's response. He said, "I know not, save the Lord commanded me." The practice was offering sacrifice, but the principle, in this instance, was obedience. And then Adam received a witness, after the trial of his faith. The angel explained: "This thing is a similitude of the sacrifice of the Only Begotten of the Father" (Moses 5:6–7).

As we direct our lives, it is important to understand practices and principles, their relationship as well as the differences between them. In my mind's eye, I visualize the practices as a horizontal line, a foundation, a schooling, a testing, a preparation; and the saving and exalting eternal principles or doctrine as a vertical line that links our souls to heaven and builds the relationship with God and faith in the Lord, Jesus Christ, and his mission.

There will continue to be much opposition to true doctrine; but by and by the storm subsides, the clouds disperse, the sun breaks forth, and the rock of truth is seen again, firm and lasting. There never was a true principle that was not met by storm after storm of opposition and abuse, until that principle had obtained such influence that it no longer paid to oppose it. But until that time, the opposition and the abuse have ebbed and flowed like the tide. It was a strong doctrine that rid Jesus of his weak disciples, and the same testing process continues today in determining those worthy of his kingdom.

The Prophet Joseph Smith stated: "God has in reserve a time . . . when

He will bring all His subjects, who have obeyed His voice and kept His commandments, into His celestial rest. This rest is of such perfection and glory, that man has need of a preparation before he can, according to the laws of that kingdom, enter it and enjoy its blessings. This being the fact, God has given certain laws to the human family, which, if observed are sufficient to prepare them to inherit this rest. This, then, we conclude, was the purpose of God in giving His laws to us."[13]

In our goal to apply principles and proceed with direction, it isn't intended that we arrive before we experience that witness of the Spirit. The witness sustains us in our journey. In a few lines, given so eloquently, President Kimball tells how the gospel came into the life of an unlearned Bolivian woman. In hearing of the mission of the Savior and the doctrine of the Atonement, the Spirit bore witness to her soul. With her golden-brown face turned upward, her dark eyes wide and trusting, with tears rising to overflowing, she whispered her emotions: "You mean, he did that for me?" With the confirmation of her question received, she again whispered, this time not in question but in reverent awe, "You mean, he did that for me!"

To this eternal and saving principle, I bear my fervent testimony that he did that for you and for me. With that conviction, I think with soberness of the penetrating observation by Truman Madsen: "The greatest tragedy of life is that having paid that awful price of suffering 'according to the flesh that his bowels might be filled with compassion' and now prepared to reach down and help us, he is forbidden because we won't let him. We look down instead of up."[14] We choose to remain enclosed in marble. But if we would free ourselves and come to know this truth through personal revelation, the time might come when even our routine practices could become lifegiving and done in the Lord's name with his spirit so that the whole of our lives becomes a sacred experience as we labor for him continuously.

Not long ago I witnessed what until then had been something of a routine for me, the blessing on the food. Picture with me my aged father, his body deteriorated by the devastation of stomach cancer, while his spirit was magnified and refined through suffering. He sat at the kitchen table; he then weighed less than a hundred pounds. Bowing his head, resting it in his frail, trembling hands over a spoonful of baby food—all that he could eat—he pronounced a blessing on the food, as though it were a sacred sacrament, and gave thanks with acceptance and submission, with truth and faith, because he knew to whom he was speaking.

It is in coming to know our Savior and the saving principles that he taught through the gospel of Jesus Christ that we become different. And we need to be recognized as being different. The majority of the world doesn't see the options. It is our responsibility to be obviously good and obviously right—and able to articulate our values and be advocates for truth. We may have a temple recommend and attend our meetings and practice the principles, but how we look and act, what we say and do, may be the only message some people will receive. Our acts should show that there is a power and an influence with us that the inhabitants of the world do not understand. What is it that distinguishes us from others? The distinction is that we profess to be guided by revelation. It is because of this principle that we are peculiar, since all of our actions can be under divine guidance. Having made the choice, we must stand and be visibly different. Until we make that choice, we remain anonymous, subject to the current of the meandering multitudes.

President Kimball has said: "Much of the major growth that is coming to the Church in the last days will come because many of the good women of the world (in whom there is often such an inner sense of spirituality) will be drawn to the Church in large numbers. This will happen to the degree that the women of the Church reflect righteousness and articulateness in their lives and to the degree that they are seen as distinct and different—in happy ways—from the women of the world."[15] That is our direction. That is our challenge.

All individuals are what they are and where they are by a composite of choices that direct their lives each day. The responsibility of directing is not only for our own lives, but also for others who may be looking for the light. As we build a seaworthy ship and then sail a true course, many sails will navigate safely through troubled waters into the peaceful harbor because of the unflickering light radiating from the bow of our craft. As I consider our responsibility to others, I am inspired by the words of the song:

> *Brightly beams our Father's mercy*
> *From his lighthouse evermore,*
> *But to us he gives the keeping*
> *Of the lights along the shore.*

Chorus:
Let the lower lights be burning;
Send a gleam across the wave.
Some poor fainting, struggling seaman
You may rescue, you may save.

Dark the night of sin has settled;
Loud the angry billows roar.
Eager eyes are watching, longing,
For the lights along the shore.

Trim your feeble lamp, my brother;
Some poor sailor, tempest tossed,
Trying now to make the harbor,
In the darkness may be lost.[16]

Elder Neal A. Maxwell has written, "As other lights flicker and fade, the light of the gospel will burn ever more brightly in a darkening world, guiding the humble but irritating the guilty and those who prefer the dusk of decadence."[17]

May our lights be bright without a flicker, as we tend the lights along the shore. Let us each one reach out and touch another. Let us help carry one another's burdens. In cooperation we can overcome great odds. Let us rejoice with one another. It may be just a smile, a note, a call, an encouraging word that says, "I care; I understand; I will stand by you and help you." These are life-saving measures in times of storms.

Recently I was privileged to read part of a blessing received by one of our sisters that stated that her life would continue over a period when she would see great devastation and that she would be called to go into homes of the sorrowing, the suffering, the sick and afflicted, to minister unto them, to bind up their wounds, and to cheer them. I believe that we have all been called to minister unto those in need, to bind up not just their physical wounds but also their spiritual wounds, social wounds, and wounds that are kept hidden, sometimes festering until someone cares enough to tend the lights along the shore.

These are matters of eternal consequence, and we can, if we desire, reach far enough to experience an awakening of things we have known before. Remember, President Kimball said: "In the world before we came here, faithful women were given certain assignments while faithful men were foreordained to certain priesthood tasks. While we do not remember the particulars, this does not alter the glorious reality of what we once agreed to. We are accountable for those things which long ago were expected of us just as are those whom we sustain as prophets and apostles."[18]

It is my fervent and humble testimony that the heavens are very much open to women today. They are not closed unless we ourselves, by our choices, close them. And this reality can be just as evident as in any time past. As I read of the great spirituality of women of the past and realize how the Lord communicated with them, I thrill with the spiritual manifestations that have accompanied their missions in life, literally a power evidencing the will of God made known through their instrumentality. I think of Eliza R. Snow, of whom Joseph F. Smith said, "She walked not in the borrowed light of others, but faced the morning unafraid and invincible."

The Spirit whispers to me that there are Eliza R. Snows among us even today, and there can be many, many more. We can pull down the blessings of heaven through obedience to law. These divine and sacred blessings are not reserved for others alone. Visions and revelations come by the power of the Holy Ghost. The Lord has said, "On my servants and on my hand-maidens I will pour out in those days of my Spirit; and they shall prophesy" (Acts 2:18).

Let us go forth with the faith, the vision, the direction, and the decision to abide the laws that ensure these blessings not only for ourselves and our families—but for all of God's children everywhere. Let us each feel deeply the power and strength and influence for good of our collective and united resolves. With renewed determination and confidence and commitment to the covenants we have made, let us become truly and in every way "women of God." Let us go forth in faith and confidence and prepare for the noble calling spoken of by the prophet—to be righteous women during the winding-up scenes on this earth before the second coming of our Savior.

Notes

1. Bruce R. McConkie, *Ensign*, May 1979, 92.
2. Spencer W. Kimball, Regional Representatives' Seminar, 1979.
3. Spencer W. Kimball, *My Beloved Sisters* (Salt Lake City: Deseret Book, 1979), 17.
4. Harold B. Lee, *Improvement Era*, December 1970, 126.
5. Irving Stone, *The Agony and the Ecstasy* (New York: Doubleday, 1961), 388, 390–91.
6. Ibid., 391.

7. Kimball, *My Beloved Sisters*, 43.

8. Stone, *Agony and the Ecstasy*, 394.

9. David H. Yarn Jr., ed., *J. Reuben Clark: Selected Papers* (Provo: Brigham Young University Press, 1984), 250.

10. Quoted by Harold B. Lee, Conference Report, October 1955, 56.

11. Kimball, *My Beloved Sisters*, 20.

12. Spencer W. Kimball, *Ensign*, May 1979, 83.

13. Joseph Smith, *Teachings of the Prophet Joseph Smith*, sel. Joseph Fielding Smith (Salt Lake City: Deseret Book, 1976), 54.

14. Truman G. Madsen, "Prayer and the Prophet Joseph," *Ensign*, January 1976, 23.

15. Kimball, *My Beloved Sisters*, 44.

16. *Hymns of The Church of Jesus Christ of Latter-day Saints* (Salt Lake City: The Church of Jesus Christ of Latter-day Saints, 1985), no. 335.

17. Neal A. Maxwell, *Church News*, 5 January 1970, 28.

18. Kimball, *My Beloved Sisters*, 37.

TO CHEER AND TO BLESS IN HUMANITY'S NAME

c✧◦

Ardeth G. Kapp and Carolyn J. Rasmus

ARDETH G. KAPP: Our beloved President Spencer W. Kimball taught that the influence of righteous women would be critical during the winding-up scenes on this earth before the second coming of our Savior.[1] Carolyn and I want to share with you our understanding of *influence*: service, ministering to one another. This is our time to be a righteous influence. There are righteous women throughout the world with whom we need to unite. We need not wait for a calling but can be anxiously engaged of our own free will.

We wish not to make anyone feel encumbered or burdened but to point out that little things can mean so very much. Let me draw attention to Doctrine and Covenants 64:33, which says simply, "Wherefore, be not weary in well-doing, for ye are laying the foundation of a great work. And out of small things proceedeth that which is great." Keep that in mind. Our intent is not to overwhelm but to suggest how much can happen with even small things.

In the April 1990 general conference, President Thomas S. Monson, quoting our prophet, President Ezra Taft Benson, said, "Your words, President, echo loud and clear: We must dedicate our strength to serving the needs, rather than the fears, of the world."[2] President Monson added, "Perhaps never in history has the need for cooperation, understanding, and goodwill among all people—nations and individuals alike—been so urgent as today."[3] Others who spoke in the same session reminded us of

---

Ardeth G. Kapp serves as general president of Young Women. She received her bachelor's degree from the University of Utah and her master's degree in education from Brigham Young University. She has served on the BYU faculty in the College of Education and is the author of six books. She is married to Heber B. Kapp.

Carolyn J. Rasmus serves as administrative assistant to the Young Women General Presidency. She joined the Church while in graduate school at Brigham Young University. After earning her doctoral degree, she became a professor of physical education at BYU. Later she served as executive assistant to BYU presidents Dallin H. Oaks and Jeffrey R. Holland.

the importance of caring for one another. "Service helps us overcome selfishness and sin. . . . [It] helps us cleanse ourselves and become purified and sanctified."[4] We must "live the example of the good Samaritan, who was free of prejudice and excuses and therefore truly loved his neighbor."[5] "When, for the moment, we ourselves are not being stretched on a particular cross, we ought to be at the foot of someone else's—full of empathy and proffering spiritual refreshment."[6]

The hymn "As Sisters in Zion" includes the line, "How vast is our purpose, how broad is our mission." What is our responsibility to bring relief within our own homes, our neighborhood, our community, our country, our world? To bring relief from illiteracy and poverty, to extend relief not only to the homeless but to those in spiritual darkness, depression, despair? Do we confine ourselves to our own comfort zones? Can we offer relief from rejection and abuse, relief from loneliness and isolation? Do we see service when it is close to home, across the street, down the aisle in the marketplace? Can we unite to bring relief from the devastation of drugs and alcohol and the addicting power of pornography? Our opportunity and our responsibility "to cheer and to bless in humanity's name" beckon us to service.[7]

Elder John A. Widtsoe wrote: "In our preexistent state in the day of the great council, we made a certain agreement with the Almighty. The Lord posed a plan conceived by him. We accepted it. Since the plan is intended for all men [and women], we became parties to the salvation of every person under the plan. We agreed right then and there to not only be Saviors for ourselves but measurably Saviors for the whole human family. We went into a partnership with the Lord. The working out of the plan became not merely the Father's work and the Savior's work but also our work. The least of us, the humblest, is in partnership with the Almighty in achieving the purpose of the eternal plan of salvation. This places us in a very responsible attitude toward the whole human race."[8]

To cheer and to bless in humanity's name takes us beyond our immediate neighborhood. We must tear down fences and walls and build bridges. Recently I was invited to participate in a meeting of the National Women's Leadership Task Force, a coalition of women working to stamp out pornography. As you read the following from my notes of that meeting, will you ask yourself whether you would be willing to participate with these women in that cause.

"We must have a theological and ethical base: the New Testament refers to the beloved community where each one has dignity, value, and worth."

Another woman commented, "This is a calling. Yes, because we are Christian women, but also because we are citizens. This problem erodes that covenant base which is the fiber of our republic. This problem unleashes and distorts human passion."

One woman admitted to having misjudged another, "I saw her as being different. I had an ally, and I mistook her."

Another urged, "Broaden the base. One woman can be helpful, ten women influential, one hundred women powerful, one thousand women invincible. Train women to interact in the process, to work with excellence and respect, integrity and balance."

Then another woman, quiet in nature, said, "I've been praying to get out of it. God is keeping us in it to do something about it."

The person leading the group said, "I feel the Lord put this all together. If you let in the light, he will bring in what else is needed."

Alexis de Tocqueville was quoted, "Righteous women in their circle of influence beginning in the home can turn the world around."

"When committed women are singing off the same song sheet," one woman said, "we can make a difference. We need to promote virtue. That is the bottom line. The Lord impressed upon my spirit that God will give voice to women who are standing for righteousness. I believe we are here, placed at a point in human history by God's design. My heart longs for the day when all women everywhere will stand up and speak out for righteousness that affects our homes, our communities, our nation, but most of all our families." She emphasized, "Before we do anything, however, we must have prayer support. This evil is out of the pits of hell. When the women of this nation become mobilized in righteous causes and converted into votes, when we put our heads together, pray together, put our shoulders to the wheel, we can turn this thing around. We have been called to be righteous women. Think of all you have accomplished and then ask yourself, what does God want me to do now?"

The chairman closed the meeting with this thought, "The Lord bless you and keep you and use you all for his glory, Amen."

It is not enough to strive only to promote what is good. Must we not also accept responsibility to unite our efforts and extend our influence to eradicate the bad? I would like to tell you of a Relief Society in Las Vegas that determined to break with tradition. Rather than the usual Relief

Society birthday social, nine wards united to research their community. They identified twenty major projects that could affect, protect, and guard the homes in their community. Each of the nine wards chose one activity. The sisters from one ward participated in projects leading to the dedication of the temple in that area; others focused their concern on the telephone directory, which contained twenty-five pages advertising escort services (that is, women for hire). The pornographic language and pictures in the telephone directory ads defiled the homes they were placed in. While some sisters blessed their community by participating in the completion of a temple in their midst, others blessed their community by uniting their forces to remove pornographic material from their homes.

Our labors are needed on both fronts, to promote the good and to eradicate the bad. Often we hesitate, concerned that if we take a stand we will be criticized. But we need to take that risk; we need to articulate our values. There is a proper framework for voicing our opinion. When I went to Washington, D.C., to present a paper to the Meese Commission Against Pornography, I confess it was not comfortable. I was there with representatives from *Playboy* and other magazines. Sometimes taking a stand simply is not comfortable. But I think we can be a righteous influence with dignity, with propriety, with clarity, and in support of constitutional procedures, but not with tolerance for things we know to be wrong. Sometimes Mormon women fear that it may not be appropriate for them to enter a political arena even in issues that endanger the home; however, the assignments that I have received from our priesthood leaders—our general authorities—tell me that we may not have the luxury to sit on the sidelines and hope that someone else will stand up and speak out for what we believe.

"Out of small things proceedeth that which is great" (D&C 64:33). In another stake in Draper, Utah, the stake Relief Society president gathered women together and with quilting frames border to border in the entire cultural hall, they made two hundred quilts to cover the beds in the Primary Children's Hospital. Each sister may have felt that her small contribution would not make much difference, but I think of the words of Mother Teresa, "I always say I am a little pencil in the hands of God. He does the thinking. He does the writing. He does everything—and it's really hard—sometimes it's a broken pencil. He has to sharpen it a little more. But be a little instrument in His hands so that He can use you anytime, anywhere. . . . We have only to say Yes to Him."[9]

When are the seeds for that kind of ministering planted and in what settings are they nourished? Among the Young Women Values is Good Works, which states, "We will nurture others and build the kingdom through righteous service." A letter from one young woman provides a prescription for all of us: it describes the steps and displays the fruits of service, which blesses both the server and the one being served. She writes: "Last year in my junior high school year I set a goal in Good Works, to try to help someone in some little way every day, whether it was something that I did or just said or an example that I set. I decided to do this prayerfully, so every day before I went to school I prayed and I asked Heavenly Father, let me have the influence of the Spirit to know what I should do or say." She reports that these small acts of service changed not only her attitude about herself but her attitude toward others. "I began to see how everything we do affects others. . . . I began to feel better about myself and at the same time more humble. . . . Through my actions I began to have a different outlook on all my brothers and my sisters. Everyone should be treated with respect. Through my daily efforts I feel as though I am beginning to understand what love can really be."

A feeling of wanting to reach out beyond ourselves falls like gentle rain on parched soil on those days when we may feel useless or worthless or unfulfilled or maybe even bored or lonely. It answers our deeper spiritual needs. With charity in our hearts, we can go out beyond the borders of our own comfort zone; we can let our influence be felt for righteousness in circles where we may not initially be familiar or at ease. Charity is the key. A prayerful heart gives the direction.

When we learn to listen to the Spirit in answer to our prayers, our service becomes customized by the Spirit and we'll do things that we might not otherwise have known to do. At Christmastime one year I talked to a widow on her doorstep. "My freezer is full of goodies," she said. "And obviously I don't need them," she added with a laugh as she looked down at her expanding waistline. Then she commented wistfully, "But you don't really see the lights on Temple Square unless you go there with a family." She would have traded all of the cakes and cookies for such an invitation. When we seek direction of the Spirit, our labors will be more meaningful—and maybe even require less effort.

The value and far-reaching effect of our service, however small, has nothing to do with our age or material wealth. It has to do with our willingness to give of our time and be led by the Spirit. Many lives will be healed and blessed when we reach out in a spirit of love and concern. I think of a little girl who visited a neighbor's house where her little friend had died. "Why did you go?" questioned her father. "To comfort her mother," she said. "What could you do to comfort her?" "I climbed into her lap and cried with her," she said.

Our "Jericho Roads" may be just across the street, but they're there for each of us as we travel toward home.

CAROLYN J. RASMUS: In Nauvoo the Prophet Joseph Smith taught that life is like a huge wagon wheel. Like the wheel, all of us at some time will find ourselves on the bottom, needing someone to pull us up. But as life evolves, like the revolving wheel, there will be times when we're on top of the wheel and can reach down and help lift others up. These are times when we can cheer and bless in humanity's name.

I want to share the process that has caused me to look at the whole idea of welfare in a different way. When Elaine Jack was sustained as Relief Society General President in April conference 1990, she paid tribute to Ardeth Kapp as "a great woman of vision, called by the Lord to lead the Young Women around the world at a most critical time."[10] I too believe that Ardeth is a woman of vision. Every August, after our July break, Sister Kapp shares her vision of our work for the coming year. Last year she spoke of developing attitudes of welfare among our youth, of caring for one another, serving one another and reaching out to one another. "We must," she said, "instill an attitude of welfare among our youth. Youth are an incredible resource. They are a mighty force for righteousness. It is as if we have them in waiting—on hold. I see youth as a great reserve unit, a unit ready and trained in attitudes and ready for opportunities for service."

Then she talked about the enemies of our youth: feelings of isolation and loneliness, feelings of not being valued, feelings of worthlessness. Welfare activities answer that need. "Welfare activities," Sister Kapp explained, "can provide groupings that are not just social groupings. Activities which focus on helping people provide an ideal laboratory in which young men and young women may become better acquainted with each other." Welfare activities will also "instill feelings of provident living and caring for each other among our youth. Our youth won't come to a marriage relationship with an awareness of individuals and family welfare unless teachings begin at an early age."

Finally, she mentioned that we frequently speak of "service projects" and stressed the importance of focusing instead on an attitude of ministering instead of on just the "project." A service project is an activity: we do the activity, it is over, and nothing has changed—especially our hearts.

What Sister Kapp did on that day was to expand our vision of service. Often when we speak to youth or adults and say the word *service*, they respond, "Oooh no, not another service project." Part of that is the way we as leaders look at service: do we view it as a project, or do we promote ministering to others as an attitude—one which pervades our everyday relations with others? Can you imagine what would happen if everyone determined right now to do something that could bless and cheer in humanity's name?

You may ask, "How can I get a sixteen-year-old to want to be involved in any kind of service for anyone else when a sixteen-year-old's world typically revolves only around self?" That can be a challenge, but it is usually done when the sixteen-year-olds are in groups where caring relationships can be built. Recently we received an outline of community service projects performed by Brazil area youth. We saw videos of young people: 250 young women and young men cleaned and planted trees at the police district; eighty cleaned the grounds of an avenue; 150 spent hours at the orphanage; 260 spent the day at a hospital playing with the sick children, some of whom had AIDS; 160 cleaned a public school, including the walls. We saw them working, and the change in the school was wonderful. Serving becomes fun when youth have opportunities to work together and to build caring relationships. Fun is an attitude, not an activity.

After our board meeting last August, I began to look at scriptures in a new way. I saw a pattern I had never seen before. In Mosiah 18 we read of Alma's preaching to a group gathered at the waters of Mormon. He preaches faith in the Lord, repentance, and redemption and asks if they are willing "to bear one another's burdens . . . to mourn with those that mourn . . . comfort those that stand in need of comfort, and to stand as witnesses of God at all times and in all things, and in all places" (Mosiah 18:7–9).

Usually I stop there, but one day I continued reading, "Now I [Alma] say unto you, if this be the desire of your hearts, what have you against being baptized in the name of the Lord, as a witness before him that ye have entered into a covenant with him, that ye will serve him and will keep his commandments, that he may pour out his Spirit more abundantly upon you?" (Mosiah 18:10). In other words, when we are baptized, we make a covenant with the Lord. We covenant to "serve him and keep his commandments." We—those of us who are members of his church—have already made a covenant to serve.

In a recent conference address, Elder Derek A. Cuthbert responded to the question, "How may I become more spiritual?" by explaining that we experience the Spirit when we serve. He then described ten specific ways in which service changes people, making them more spiritual.[11] As Alma promised, "Serve him and keep his commandments, that he may pour out his Spirit more abundantly upon you" (Mosiah 18:10).

Moroni teaches this same principle. Referring to requirements for baptism, Moroni says, "And none were received unto baptism save they took upon them the name of Christ, *having a determination to serve him to the end*" (Moroni 6:3; italics added). That is what each of us covenanted to do when we were baptized.

The pattern is repeated again in the Doctrine and Covenants. *"And again, by way of commandment to the church concerning the manner of baptism*—All those who humble themselves before God, and desire to be baptized, and come forth with broken hearts and contrite spirits, and witness before the church that they have truly repented of all their sins, and are willing to take upon them the name of Jesus Christ, *having a determination to serve him to the end* . . . shall be received by baptism into his church" (D&C 20:37; italics added). The principle is repeated over and over: When we are baptized, we covenant to serve him, and he covenants with us that he will pour out his Spirit upon us.

I began also to reread old articles in new ways. One of my very favorites is an article by President Spencer W. Kimball entitled "Small Acts of Service." Remember what Mother Teresa said about being a little pencil in God's hand? Listen to President Kimball's words: "God does notice us, and he watches over us. But it is usually through another person that he meets our needs."[12] Could you be that other person? Could you be used as an instrument in the hands of God to serve someone else?

Another article I read in a new light was a general conference address by William R. Bradford called "Selfless Service." The subheading summarized the message: "Many things are only interesting and enticing, while other things are important."[13]

"What *does* matter? What *is* important?" I asked myself.

My friend Kathryn and I live together. We had planned to see *Driving Miss Daisy* on the last day of our vacations. Everyone was talking about that movie and wondering if it was going to win an Academy Award. We wanted to see it. Besides going to movies, one of the things I love to do when I have time off work is to bake bread. I got carried away; that afternoon I baked eight loaves instead of four. (There is something therapeutic about having my hands in dough. I think it replaces the mud we played in as children.) We had about thirty minutes before we were to leave for the movie. I said to Kathy, "It's going to take us a long time to eat eight loaves of bread. Why don't we take one over to the Campbells?" This was during the heated debate in the state legislature about teachers' salaries. Our across-the-street neighbor, Jim Campbell, was president of the Utah Education Association and the focus of a lot of controversy. We decided the Campbells could use a loaf of bread. We rang the doorbell; Jim's wife, Barbara, came to the door. As we handed her the bread, she started to cry. She was home alone and had been for several days and nights. She said to us, "*Please* come in." I wondered what we would talk about, but I needn't have—all we had to do was listen.

When we left we felt so good we said, "Let's give away another loaf of bread. We have time now before the *second* showing of the movie." We debated about going to our next-door neighbors because only two days before their son had been convicted of sexually molesting children and was in the state prison. What would we say to his parents? We didn't know, and, I suppose, to be honest, we took the bread as an excuse because we didn't know how to start a conversation. We rang the doorbell. The father came to the door and said, "Please, *please* come in. Nobody has talked to us. We've got to talk to somebody." We listened for more than an hour to a mother and father, whose hearts were breaking, tell us about their son. When we got ready to leave, they hugged us. As we returned home Kathy said, "We missed the second showing, but who cares!"

Listen to what Elder Bradford says about selfless service. "They are not one-time special events based on entertainment and fun and games. . . . Selfless service projects are people-to-people projects. They are face-to-face, eye-to-eye, voice-to-ear, heart-to-heart, spirit-to-spirit, and hand-in-hand, people-to-people projects."[14] I began thinking how I might change an attitude of "projects" to one of ministering.

My mother is a member of the Lutheran Church. In an effort to cheer and bolster her, I send her things I think will be uplifting. I try and put something in the mail every week—something from the *Ensign* or the

New Era along with a few other thoughts to ponder. A year ago I gave her a calendar book published by *Guideposts Magazine* simply titled *Guideposts*. Every day features a thought. I bought the same book for myself so I could read what I knew she would be reading. When I called her she would frequently say, "Did you read the thought on Tuesday?" Often she would ask for my thoughts about it; sometimes I would ask her. About midyear there were three pages in the middle of the book labeled, "Thank You Notes to God." On these pages were blank lines numbered one through thirty. I wondered if she would fill in these pages. I thought she might just skip over them, but about a week later she mailed to me those three pages torn from her book. My mother is eighty-five; my father is in a nursing home. Listen to what my mother wrote as her "Thank You Notes to God." Think about the "small acts of service" that made a difference in my mother's life:

A telephone call from Mildred
A visit from Anita
A magazine from Kay
A visit with a friendly person in the mall
My family
Carolyn's concern
Lunch at Kay's
A call from Mark
A call from Evelyn
A call from Vera
A visit from our cousins in Detroit
A day of rest
A telephone call from Anita
A card from Carolyn
Meals on wheels
A telephone call from Kay
I called a friend of a friend
I'm able to get around
I had a telephone visit with Mark
I'm thankful my sister can drive
Carolyn's call was what I needed
And the last note said simply, "Thank you for your love."

Each of the things my mother was thankful for cost little if any money and took practically no time. Mother called me this past Tuesday and said, "Mark [my brother] came and took the garbage out." Do you know what it is like to take garbage out when you are eighty-five and need to hold a cane in one hand? It may not seem like a big thing, but it was enough of an event for her to call me and tell me how grateful she was.

Where do we begin? Ardeth referred to Doctrine and Covenants 64:33: "Be not weary in well-doing, for ye are laying the foundation of a great work. And out of small things proceedeth that which is great." I want to focus on the next verse, which tells us, "Behold, the Lord requireth the heart and a willing mind." How do we begin? By simply being willing. Would you be *willing* to write a note? Would you be *willing* to make a phone call? In the next five seconds, would you jot down the name of one person whose life you could bless or cheer today?

If you wrote down a name, you're willing. That's all that is asked of us, to be willing. The scriptures admonish us to be "anxiously engaged in a good cause, . . . [that we might] bring to pass much righteousness" (D&C 58:27). Look around. If each of us listened, or smiled, or wrote a note, or made a phone call to just one person, we will have blessed and cheered in humanity's name.

The following experiences reflect the attitude of ministering we are hoping to encourage.

SISTER KAPP: Last fall I was away from my home during the period of time when it would have been nice to plant tulip bulbs and daffodils. I felt a bit sad as I looked at the dark earth and realized that no bulbs would burst forth and announce spring. But on my birthday, in the middle of March, I walked out into my front yard and saw three daffodils. I wondered how that happened. I didn't remember planting daffodils. When did they come up? The next day I found more daffodils and before long discovered tulips! They sprang up every day in different places, and every morning I ran out to see what was coming up out of my ground, which to my knowledge was void of bulbs or seeds. Those seeds of love had been planted in the fall by a friend. Different plants continued coming up to delight and surprise me for about two weeks, and then a little card arrived that said, "Happy Birthday! I thought the flowers would be an announcement for spring and wanted to share spring with you this year." What a surprise. What a gift of love and service.

SISTER RASMUS: Not long ago I participated in a Young Women event in Hooper, Utah, where a sixteen-year-old girl spoke. I was so impressed with what she said that I asked her to write it down and send it to me. I share with you what Kristy McCarther learned about serving others:

"Sometimes we think that the only recognition is either a certificate or book or a necklace. But the experience and knowledge you gain from serving others is far better than any award you could receive. This last summer I set a goal to help both my grandmas keep their lawns mowed and watered. Even though they would not accept at first that I only wanted to do it to help them, they were always waiting and expected me to come. At times it wasn't my favorite thing to do, but I knew they wanted me there and that helped me know that it was right. . . . I learned the value of giving good works and service to others. I'm thankful for the Young Women program."

SISTER KAPP: I have a friend in San Francisco who has had a kidney transplant. She has been on a dialysis machine for a number of years. She keeps track of everyone from the confines of her home. Two or three weeks ago I received a letter from Irene. Inside the letter was a greeting card that was addressed to Freda Harms. Irene enclosed a note to me:

"Dear Ardie,

"I know you're busy, so you may not be aware that our dear Sister Harms in her older years is suffering from a severe illness. I know she would love to have a card from you. I have addressed and stamped it. Would you just sign your name and send it on?"

SISTER RASMUS: There are people with needs and there are people with resources; the challenge is getting them together. I had a need. I was going to be away on an assignment in Australia for three weeks and my mother, with whom I talk on the phone several times a week, couldn't imagine how she was going to survive without hearing from me. I prayed to know how we could stay close while we didn't have telephone contact.

For years I have been asking her to write her family history. I had given her a journal, I had given her blank books, and I had given her loose-leaf pages. She kept saying, "I don't know what to write. Who cares about my life?" Before I left for Australia I sat at the computer and typed about fifty questions. They were simple things like, "What was it like when you went to school?" "What do you remember about your grandmother?" "Do you remember your first Christmas tree?" and on and on. With the questions I sent her about fifty stamped postcards that were addressed to me but blank on the other side. Can you imagine what it meant to me when I got home from Australia to find twenty-four postcards in my mail box?

They were all in my mother's handwriting. Last year she wrote on each postcard a precious memory, a bit of important history.

Somehow I wanted to share this heritage with my brother and my niece and nephew. I typed the information, had the pages bound, and titled the resulting book *Post Card Jottings*, by Ella P. Rasmus. I added "Volume I" because I did not want Mother to think she was finished with this project. It has made a difference to me, and I find it has made a difference to her as she thinks back on wonderful things that have happened in her life. She sent me another postcard just a couple of weeks ago. She is working on Volume II—what she remembers about my brother and me when we were children.

"When Carolyn was about one year old, two ladies came to our door selling a set of children's books. They said, 'You should have been reading to your baby the day you came home from the hospital.' I was really worried. Was it too late? So I ordered the set and really read to her, making up for lost time. I guess that is why you came to be such an avid reader. Much love, your mother."

SISTER KAPP: Two years ago at Christmastime, when the calendar was full and the schedules were tight and the streets were full of people rushing here and there, I was invited to go to the rest home to visit some elderly people. I looked at my busy calendar and thought, "If I can just rush over and give a quick message, I can get back and hardly lose a minute." I rushed to the rest home, turned my car off, ran in, caught my breath just as I got to the door, and walked into a place where time was moving at a different pace—if it was moving at all. I was ushered into a room where tired shoulders were covered with shawls and tired feet were enclosed in slippers and heads drooped. I gave my short message and wondered what I could have said that might have made any difference at all.

I was ready to rush back into the busy world when a woman who was there visiting her grandmother asked apologetically, "Would you have a minute to talk to my grandmother? She thinks she knows you." Her look told me that she felt her grandmother's mind was perhaps even more tired than her body. I said, "Certainly I would." I followed them as they shuffled down the hall together. I hadn't noticed this woman in the audience. When we got to her room she plopped her tired body down onto the bed and raised her eyes to meet mine. I said, "Sister Dudley! Sister Dudley, you were my Primary teacher." She tugged on her granddaughter's jacket. "See, I told you she would know me." And then more memories came tumbling back and I said, "I remember when you made carrot juice for my mother. I remember when you wore that maroon dress with the big sleeves that waved back and forth when you taught us songs in Primary." She tugged on her granddaughter's jacket again. "I told you she would know me." Then she opened her arms and drew me close to her, and I felt like a child in the arms of my Primary teacher again. She asked, "Did you come all the way from Canada to see me?" "Oh, Sister Dudley," I said, "it has been forty years, but I'm here." "I knew you would know me," she whispered as she held me close.

I lingered. I left more slowly. I had a new insight, and as I walked out and sat in my car for a moment, I thought of Sister Dudley. Sister Dudley knew me because she had served me. And I knew Sister Dudley because she had served me. I began to ponder another time in the future when we will give an accounting. I think our Father will know us because we have served him. And equally important, we will know our Father because we have served him—each of us in our own way, appropriate to our own circumstance. One day we might all say, "I told you he would know me."

SISTER RASMUS: I share a note from Elder and Sister Humphreys, a missionary couple serving in eastern Nigeria: "Shortly after our arrival in Etinan, I was practicing on a portable organ when Otobong came to our apartment door to visit a former missionary couple. Otobong showed a real interest in the organ and I seized the opportunity when she indicated a desire to play. My invitation to Otobong was, 'Let us learn together.' Otobong came every Tuesday for a lesson and at least four times each week to practice. This wonderful sixteen-year-old sister learned very quickly and soon could read the notes and play the melody line. Within three weeks Otobong could play the tune as I sang along to help keep the correct time. The chords were learned quickly and in eight weeks Otobong was playing approximately ten hymns without any hesitation."

Because a young woman showed an interest and a woman took time, this young sister now plays the piano and serves her branch as organist. "Sister Otobong continues to play and teach others not only in her branch but throughout her own and other districts."

SISTER KAPP: Sometimes we feel that we need to do it all—and all at once. But that is not the case. When we give what we have according to our time, according to our energy, according to where we are at this moment in our development, then the Lord will take what we have to offer and he will make up the difference. That is the grace of God.

The dictionary in the LDS edition of the King James Version of the Bible defines *grace* as "an enabling power that allows women and men to lay hold of eternal life and exaltation after they have expended their own best efforts." So whenever you read in your scriptures the word *grace*, replace it with the words *enabling power*. We know that it is by grace that we are saved after all that we can do, and the Lord knows how far, how much, and what is appropriate for us to do. He will guide us, bring peace to our heart, and remove the guilt, because there will be other seasons to do other things.

On one occasion I remember feeling overwhelmed by my sister who had ten children. I wondered, what am I doing that matters? And my father's voice came into my mind, as though he were sitting with me, though he had been dead for years (maybe it was his mission to be a ministering angel to me that day), "My dear, don't worry about the little things; just do the big things you agreed to before you came." God bless us to keep our eye on the big things that we agreed to and not be distracted by the little things that will not strengthen us spiritually. May God bless us to experience the joy of service in this great sisterhood and find the peace "that passeth all understanding" in the gospel of Jesus Christ (Philippians 4:7).

SISTER RASMUS: As you read your scriptures, be mindful of a phrase that is repeated again and again, usually at times of battle when the people of the Lord were so outnumbered that there appeared to be no way they could ever win the battle. The phrase is simply, "And they went forth in the strength of the Lord" (see Mosiah 10:10; Psalm 71:16). That is how we will win our battles today, be they personal or societal. Of this I have a strong witness and a testimony. We are empowered and enabled and strengthened beyond all we can do because of our faith in our Lord, Jesus Christ. In his strength we can do all things.

Notes

1. Spencer W. Kimball, *Ensign*, November 1978, 103.
2. Ezra Taft Benson, *Teachings of Ezra Taft Benson* (Salt Lake City: Bookcraft, 1988), 261.
3. Thomas S. Monson, *Ensign*, May 1990, 5.
4. Derek A. Cuthbert, *Ensign*, May 1990, 12–13.
5. Hans B. Ringger, *Ensign*, May 1990, 26.
6. Neal A. Maxwell, *Ensign*, May 1990, 34.

7. *Hymns of The Church of Jesus Christ of Latter-day Saints* (Salt Lake City: The Church of Jesus Christ of Latter-day Saints, 1985), no. 309.
8. John A. Widtsoe, "The Worth of Souls," *Utah Genealogical and Historical Magazine*, October 1934, 189.
9. Mother Teresa, "Love: A Fruit Always in Season," *Daily Meditations by Mother Teresa*, ed, Dorothy S. Hunt (San Francisco: Ignatius Press, 1987), 243.
10. Elaine L. Jack, *Ensign*, May 1990, 78.
11. Cuthbert, *Ensign*, May 1990, 12–13.
12. Spencer W. Kimball, "Small Acts of Service," *Ensign*, December 1974, 5.
13. William R. Bradford, *Ensign*, November 1987, 75.
14. Ibid., 75.

SEEKING THE WILL OF GOD, BIT BY BIT

Pam Kazmaier

*W*hen I was asked to discuss seeking God's will in decision making, I was sure I should say no. I had just been watching the news on CNN, and interest rates and the stock market were falling. My husband and I had prayerfully invested five thousand dollars in the stock that was plummeting. *Obviously, I'm not a good decision maker,* I thought. I was waiting for an opening in the conversation so I could say no. Then my knees started shaking just as they do before I bear my testimony on fast Sunday at church. I felt I was supposed to say yes—that I was supposed to tell of my recent experience in making the hardest decision of my life: I quit my career as a nurse to stay at home with my two small children.

Please understand, I'm not advocating that all women should quit their jobs to stay home with their children—especially after having done it for two years. I thought I worked hard as a nurse, but being a mother is the hardest thing I've ever done.

Let me explain why this decision was so difficult. I grew up in Illinois. I was completely ignorant about Latter-day Saints. I thought they all wore black and lived in the Rocky Mountains. I was reared by a mother who was a feminist back in the fifties before that term was coined. She reared my two sisters and me not to marry or have children but to get an education and have a career. My father did not disagree.

At the age of eighteen, I entered a convent, largely because I didn't want to worry about being married and having children. I valued my mother's teachings and was afraid that if I went to college, I'd fall in love, get married, and have children. A convent seemed a good place to avoid all that.

The scriptures are another strong reason I entered the convent; they are also the reason I left. The longer I was in the convent, the more I read

---

Pam Kazmaier enjoyed hospital nursing for twenty years. Now she and her husband, Kevin Craig Kazmaier, are the parents of two active boys. Pam teaches an even more active Sunbeam class in her ward.

the scriptures and prayed, the more I felt the Holy Spirit tell me that I was in the wrong place. I didn't understand that then. I do now. I *was* in the wrong place there; I was supposed to be here.

So even though being a nun was a wonderful part of my life, after four years, I left the convent. Making that decision was very tough. I had never taken my commitment lightly. While I was a nun, I began nurse's training in earnest. I loved nursing—and I am not talking about breast-feeding. To tell the truth, I do not do nursing babies well, but I was a great nurse. I loved the nursing profession and thought I would never leave it. I started at fourteen as a candy striper and completed my training in 1977 after I had left the convent.

I was not like young Latter-day Saint women who are taught eternal values early and are groomed to marry in the temple and be wives and mothers. Those were all foreign ideas to me. But at twenty-eight I did marry. My husband Kevin supported the idea of women working and believed they should be independent. At the time of our marriage, Kevin and I decided not to have children because they'd get in the way of our work. His career came first; my career came first. It was a great match. To you, career first, family second sounds very foreign, but to us in the world, that attitude was very common.

I loved everything about the hospital—the smell, the excitement. It was just a great place; it felt like home. I joined the Church because of people I met there. I found myself taking care of patients who were different from anybody I had ever met. They were amazing; I wanted to be like them. These patients had something I didn't have—peace. I was attracted to their strength in crisis, their family unity. They were mannerly and polite, well-groomed and refined. To me, my conversion experience was a miracle. I joined the Church in Mesa, Arizona, and my life changed.

My patriarchal blessing said, "There are spirits reserved in the heavens so that you and your husband can have children." I thought, *Yeah, right. These Mormons have all these children. Not me.* Then, a year and a half later, my husband joined the Church, and his patriarchal blessing said, "There are *still* spirits reserved in heaven so that you and your wife can have children." "Oh, Kevin," I said, "I think we've got to have these children. Oh no." And so we did. We sold our Corvette and bought a family car. And here we are. At thirty-five I had my first little boy, and then at thirty-seven I had another.

I still never considered quitting work, though. I thought having the children was going to be enough. Then I had a run-in with a little pink pamphlet—*Mothers in Zion*. I hear it made quite a stir in the Church when it came out, but it didn't faze me because I didn't have any children then. When I first saw it, I thought, *Oh yeah, right, uh-huh, very good*, and I shelved it. It wasn't about me. But then one day my husband said, seeing me wrestle with motherhood and work, "Maybe you ought to think about quitting work." Ha! Quit work? He could just as well have said, "Maybe you ought to cut off your legs." I loved my job—and I was very good at it. I couldn't cook. I couldn't sew. I can't sing. I can't do anything. But give me a chest pain, and I know what to do.

I told my husband I would pray about quitting work, fully thinking the Lord would say, "Of course you can't quit your job. It's a vocation; it's a calling. You and I have done this for twenty years. You can't quit. People are waiting for you in the hospital." So I just prayed, "Okay, Lord, this is what Kevin thinks, but you and I both know . . . " and then on like that. I got up from my knees and never thought another thing about it. Here's the lesson: When you wrestle with questions like, Should I marry him? Should I not marry him? Should I move? Should I go back to school? remember this. When I have been about to go down the wrong path and take others with me, the Lord has intervened if I have stayed close to him.

The next day, this pink pamphlet that had been shelved for four years was hanging out of my bookshelves. My husband doesn't get up in my bookshelves. My kids were too little. And I hadn't been in that section— that was the dusty section. But the pink pamphlet was hanging out. That's the miracle. How did that happen? I had ten minutes before I left for work—I was never late for work—so I thought, *Okay, I've got ten minutes to read this thing. There is something in here about mothers working.* (That's how much attention I had paid to it when I first got it.) I thought, *I'm going to read something in here that will prove to Kevin that I should keep on working.* So I started reading the pamphlet, and before I knew it I was crying. I read, "No more sacred word exists in secular or holy writ than that of *mother*. There is no more noble work than that of a good and God-fearing mother." It went on and on—"a mother's role is God-ordained."[1] *Oh, brother!* I thought. *I'm sunk.* I cried all the way to work.

I had great baby-sitters. My kids were in better hands with them than they were with me. The sitters had play-dough and children's tapes and other kids running around, and everybody was happy. I left our children with the baby-sitter on the way to work and said, "Yes! I'm out of here. I'm going someplace where I know what I'm doing." But this day I drove to work sobbing.

I'm not like Abraham, who could immediately sacrifice Isaac the very next morning. I couldn't tell my head nurse, "I read this article and . . . " It took weeks and weeks, months and months. It was a very gradual change for me. I got home that night and thought, *Sure, women are supposed to leave working at McDonald's and the dry cleaners, but I have this important calling of the Lord to be a nurse.* So I checked in with the pamphlet again, only to read, "Finally President Kimball counsels, 'I beg of you, you who could and should be bearing and rearing a family: wives, come home from the typewriter, the laundry, *the nursing.*'"[2] I was devastated, shattered.

I began to pray with real intent this time. For months I prayed about it. I was on my knees to the Lord saying, "Lord, how can you expect me to give up something I am so good at to do something I am so bad at?" It didn't make any sense to me. And I heard the voice of the Lord: "I am just asking you to do something *else* now." I was speechless. I knew it was the voice of the Lord. It was that still, small voice I had read about in the scriptures. I thought, *Oh, he wants me to do something else now. It isn't like he didn't appreciate all those years of service. He's asking me to do something else now.*

I pondered that. That month I taught a Relief Society lesson in my ward and found a quotation from Harold B. Lee in the lesson materials that really helped. It began, "You may not like what comes from the authority of the Church." *Well, thank you for giving me at least that permission,* I thought. Yes, I don't like what has come from the authority of the Church. "It may contradict your political views." I'm a member of NOW, the National Organization of Women, and yes, this contradicts my political views. "It may contradict your social views. It may interfere with some of your social life." No kidding. Stuck home with two little kids, my husband's gone half the time, all my friends are at work. The hospital *is* my social life. Then President Lee goes on to say, "But if you listen to these things, as if from the mouth of the Lord himself, with patience and faith . . . "[3] In other words, I didn't have to do it right away. I was so glad he let me wean myself from full time, to part time, to on call. That is how my testimony has grown—bit by bit by bit.

The final step came for me one night when I came home after only four hours at the hospital. I drove into my driveway and saw my husband, my dear husband whom I love, outside speaking to our next-door neighbor. It was dark and cold. It gets that way in Arizona in the evenings even though it's hot during the days. There were my two little boys, barefoot and dirty. In wet T-shirts with their hair all caked, they looked like orphans. *I just left four hours ago*, I thought. *How can they look this bad already?* When I'm home I line those kids up just like my I.V. fluids. I organize them, and they are in bed and asleep by eight o'clock. They would have had their little jammies on and their baths and their prayers and their stories and their teethies brushed and everything.

It was not the moment to discuss with Kevin the differences in our parenting styles. So I went into the house, put down my stethoscope, rolled up my sleeves, and tore into the disaster area that used to be the kitchen. And I once again heard the calm voice, not my own, say in my mind, "There are others who can take your place at work, but there is no one who can take your place here." And I said, "No kidding!" Just like that. Out loud. I wasn't feeling at all spiritual at the time, so when I heard the voice of the Lord, I just said, "No kidding! No kidding."

As I said, I am no Abraham. Months had gone by since I had begun praying about work. It wasn't until the next week that I woke up one morning with the thought, I'm going to quit my job today. I need to tell Kevin. One day each week Kevin takes the kids to the sitter, and we spend the whole day together—we have lunch, go to a movie, even have an uninterrupted conversation. "Kevin," I said on this particular morning, "when you come back from taking the kids, I've got something to tell you." He didn't know that I'd been brooding about work for months and months.

Kevin was my last hurdle. He really liked my salary, really liked the fact that I was working. If there was some way I could convince him . . . I was on my knees in prayer right there by the bathtub after he left, praying, "Heavenly Father, I've got to quit today, and I don't know how to do it. I don't know how I'm going to tell Kevin, and you've got to help me."

When Kevin came home, I was sobbing. I felt like somebody had died. Kevin came in and said, "The Holy Spirit told me on the way home in the truck. You're going to quit your job today." I was so grateful to Heavenly Father for hearing my prayer so I didn't have to tell Kevin. I nodded and cried some more, and Kevin said, "It's okay. Let 'em go pound sand." I don't know what that means, but those were his words.

"How do I do this?" I asked. "I've never quit a job. I've been there at this hospital for eleven years. I love nursing. Over twenty years I've been a nurse. I don't know how to do this."

"Well, you need to go tell your head nurse."

"Yeah. Go tell the head nurse. Okay." So we got in the car and drove to the hospital. I sobbed all the way up the stairs to the sixth floor. I didn't even care who saw me. I couldn't stop crying. Doctors and patients wondered what in the world was wrong. Thank goodness my head nurse was in her office. I blurted out, "Sally, I've got to quit my job." And then she was crying and I was crying, and it was awful, just awful. But I did it. That was two years ago this week, and I am still alive.

I wish I could stand before you and say, "I just love the little ones— they're five and three now. I just love their laundry and the peanut butter and the spilled popsicles. I'm just having so much fun with my children." I really am not having fun.

What I miss most are the angels singing for me at the end of my shift. Many times when something critical happened during my shift, like a patient hemorrhaging or a difficult delivery, when I walked out to the car after work about one o'clock in the morning, I could hear the angels sing for me. I felt they were grateful. They applauded for how I had helped. These past two years I haven't heard them sing for me one time. But I know that twenty years from now they're going to sing for me again. I know they will.

And I know I am doing the right thing now, too. At times, even with very little children, you can actually get a conversation of some sort going or experience some kind of spiritual feeling with them. When that happens, I'll look at my watch and realize, I would have been counting narcotics. I would have missed this. It's not just my body that's at home now; my mind is there, too. Even when I was working part time or on call, my mind was at the hospital. I'd call the hospital, "You want me to come in? How's it going?" Because I am home day in and day out now, answering questions and being there for them, I know my children have a peace in their lives that wasn't there before.

In Matthew 6:33, the Savior instructs: "Seek ye first the kingdom of God, and his righteousness; and all these things shall be added unto you." If he had not said "first," wouldn't that be easier? Wouldn't it be great if he'd said, "Seek ye *third* the kingdom of God"? Wouldn't that be a lot more convenient? But he says, "Seek ye *first* the kingdom of God."

Seeking the kingdom of God first is *hard*. Usually I find I have to sacrifice something of the world to do it. Right now, that means putting my ambitions aside for my children.

Notes

1. Ezra Taft Benson, *Come, Listen to a Prophet's Voice* (Salt Lake City: Deseret Book, 1990), 25.
2. Ibid., 31, italics added.
3. Harold B. Lee, in "Be Not of the World," *Learn of Me: Relief Society Personal Study Guide 2* (Salt Lake City: The Church of Jesus Christ of Latter-day Saints, 1990), 23.

WOMEN OF FAITH

⌖

Camilla Eyring Kimball

*W*hen I was young I anticipated birthdays, seeing them as a mark of advancement and as opening the door to new opportunities. Then in middle age I dreaded birthdays, because they represented the closing of some doors and the approach of debilitating old age. But as I got older still—to the "My, you're looking wonderful!" stage—I started to look forward to birthdays again. There is even a temptation to exaggerate a little, because each birthday shows something of an achievement—showing that I have managed to hang on through one more cycle of the seasons. I celebrated my ninetieth birthday just a few months ago. That was quite a surprise to me, because for a whole year I had been saying I was already ninety.

Except for a little pride in surviving, I can say from experience that old age is not a status to envy, because there's not much future in it. Unfortunately, old age is a time of aches and pains and a time of unwanted dependency on others after a lifetime of being self-sufficient. It is a time of gradually slowing down. And there is a frustrating sense that there are a thousand things still undone and not enough time remaining. But on the other hand, old age does allow one time for reflecting with some satisfaction on the joys and accomplishments of a lifetime.

There are some advantages to old age, though. Now that my memory has faded a bit, I find I can enjoy reading a book the second time. I enjoyed rereading the biography of my husband and, as I read along, I kept wondering how it would all turn out!

But more seriously, there is a measure of satisfaction that as we get older we keep coming closer and closer to "enduring to the end" by being faithful to the important values in life.

Camilla Eyring Kimball, wife of President Spencer W. Kimball and beloved former "first lady" of the Church, was a strong advocate of education. The Camilla Eyring Kimball Chair of Home and Family Life was established at Brigham Young University in her honor. She served in numerous stake and ward callings in the auxiliaries, including more than sixty years as a visiting teacher. An avid gardener, she turned to oil painting in her nineties.

What are those values which are so important to hold onto until the very end? Christ told us what is most fundamental:

"Behold, a certain lawyer stood up, and tempted him, saying, Master, what shall I do to inherit eternal life?

"He said unto him, What is written in the law? how readest thou?

"And he answering said, Thou shalt love the Lord thy God with all thy heart, and with all thy soul, and with all thy strength, and with all thy mind; and thy neighbor as thyself.

"And he said unto him, Thou has answered right: this do, and thou shalt live" (Luke 10:25–28).

A woman of faith, then, is one whose heart and soul, mind and strength are committed to the pursuit of true values. First, in her heart and soul, a faithful woman acknowledges God's role in all things. Then, with her mind she seeks to understand the divine plan for this world. And finally, with the strength of her hands, she undertakes to carry out the fundamental tasks of mankind, which are to keep God's commandments and give unselfish service to his children.

First, faith. "Without faith it is impossible to please [God]: for he that cometh to God must believe that he is, and that he is a rewarder of them that diligently seek him" (Hebrews 11:6).

I am not able to get around as much as I once did, and as a result I have looked at more television than I ever did in my younger years. In watching television I like best of all the programs that tell me about nature. Television is my substitute for travel. Through the marvel of the magic box I can be transported in an instant anywhere. I can travel through a telescope to outer space or through a microscope to the recesses of the human brain.

Whether it is bees or polar bears, whales or forests, I am fascinated by the fantastic variety and intricate interdependency of the various forms of life. I marvel at God's creation in its infinite complexity. I am much too unlettered to begin understanding the grand design of God, but like one who stands before a great tapestry, I can drink in its beauty and stand admiring its intricacy without knowing exactly how the artist achieved the effect. I know God's hand is in nature. I do not know just *how* God created the world, but I am persuaded that *he did* it, and I stand in awe and wonder at the majesty of his creation. My heart is full of gratitude toward a loving Father.

Second, when we have obtained faith in the Great Creator, we are inclined to want to know what it is that would please God. He has said that he wants us to love him with all our mind.

I believe that to love God with our *mind* means to pursue understanding of his world. We are to develop the talents God has given us. There are many kinds of talents, many gifts—faith and healing, music and art, leadership and followership, and intellect, the capacity for learning. Though they are all valuable gifts, it is the last that I would emphasize here partly because of the university setting and partly because of my personal inclinations. Though we may have *other* gifts as well, all of us gathered here share the marvelous ability to acquire knowledge. We are taught that we should "seek learning, even by study and also by faith" (D&C 88:118).

I love to study; I love to learn. At one time I learned for the sheer pleasure of learning. Now I do it more for the purpose of understanding God's great creation and my role in it. As a result, I don't read much fiction any more. In the past few months I have read a book of essays that gave me new insights into gospel principles. I finished the Book of Mormon again, which ends on a stirring challenge to be "perfect in Christ" (Moroni 10:33). A *Marvelous Work and a Wonder*, by LeGrand Richards, got me thinking about the urgent preparations we need to make against the troubles of the last days. And I have read several biographies. When I read biographies, I am looking to see how God's plan works itself out in the lives of men and women. And as I read the scriptures, I stand amazed at how I can fall so far short of living all the commandments and yet know that God loves me anyway.

If "the glory of God is intelligence, or in other words light and truth" (D&C 93:36), then it is our responsibility to gather truth of all sorts, not just truths of theology, but of everything. So long as we do not become vain in our learning, it is all to the good.

There are various ways of learning—reading, discussing, and experiencing. I wish I could be in the classroom again. Books are good, but there is something special about the interchange of ideas in the classroom. I look forward each week to Sunday School and Relief Society for the stimulation I get there. And I have found that participation in community affairs gives me new and important insights.

I have always wanted desperately to increase my education. In 1912, at age seventeen, I came to Provo as a refugee from the Mexican Revolution, to finish high school and earn a teaching certificate. One day

I received a telegram from my father asking why I had not written a letter. The reason was that I did not have two cents for a stamp. But I could not give up school. Being a student and becoming a teacher were both my pleasure and my need.

Many of the people who came to BYU in those days were here at considerable sacrifice. Education was hard to come by and recognized as a precious commodity. But that is still true. Many students here today have chosen a hard road, but they are coming into possession of a fund of knowledge beyond the dreams of most people in the world. It carries with it great power for good or ill.

As a young teacher, I planned to alternate working and going to school until I had completed a graduate degree in dietetics. As it turned out, I met Spencer Kimball and married instead. That kept me from finishing my specific educational goal, but it did not stop me from being curious, nor did it stop my learning, because regular schooling is just one of the ways of becoming educated.

Reading books has opened a thousand doors for me. I worked through the Women's Club in Arizona to help establish a public library in the little farming town where we lived in order to open those same doors for others. We also benefited from having a college nearby, which provided some community education classes. And I was always active in Church teaching. As a Japanese proverb says, "To teach is to learn." I enjoyed the challenge to understanding that is a prerequisite to effective teaching.

I always did my best to encourage my brothers and sisters and my children to take advantage of educational opportunities. If there was a price to be paid, in money or effort, I considered it well worth the price.

I have found from my own experience in taking courses at the institute of religion and at the University of Utah after we moved to Salt Lake City that there is joy in learning, that it helps keep us young in spirit, and that, whatever the subject—religion or Spanish or typing or literature—it enlarges our capacity for service.

Learning is not just for one set of people or for one time of life. It is a basic activity for all mankind. We are on earth to learn—first of all the principles of salvation, and then the secrets of the world, to subdue it and make it fruitful, and to delight the mind. The Lord fosters beauty, and there is beauty in all knowledge, not just in music and painting, but in biology and geology and mathematics, too.

I know well the limits of my understanding. I make no pretension to great knowledge in any field, but I offer no apology. In comparison to our Heavenly Father, even the most learned person knows nothing. The process of education, aside from its pleasure, disciplines the mind and makes it our useful servant.

There is some risk in education, of course. It can in a sense become our master rather than our servant. If I may paraphrase another scripture: we have learned by experience that it is the nature and disposition of almost all men, as soon as they get a little *knowledge*, as they suppose, to begin to lord it over others. Learning is one of the great sources of pride. Nephi cried out, "O the wise, and the *learned*, and the rich, that are puffed up in the pride of their hearts . . . wo be unto them, saith the Lord God Almighty, for they shall be thrust down to hell!" (2 Nephi 28:15; italics added). And he wrote also:

"O that cunning plan of the evil one! O the vainness, and the frailties, and the foolishness of men! When they are learned they think they are wise, and they hearken not unto the counsel of God, for they set it aside, supposing they know of themselves, wherefore, their wisdom is foolishness and it profiteth them not. And they shall perish.

"But to be learned is good *if* they hearken unto the counsels of God" (2 Nephi 9:28–29; italics added).

Nephi is not criticizing learning. On the contrary, he exalts learning as a good thing. He points out that learning has its risks. But on the other hand, ignorance has its risks, too—just a different set.

Though at the time I did not often think of my learning as a religious activity, it clearly was, in the sense that I came to value the inherent goodness in people, to appreciate the world around me, to see the fruits of unselfish cooperation, to increase my sense of self-worth, and to feel I had a capacity to be of service to others.

The third thing a woman of faith will do is to give service to others. Once we have faith in God and have developed the talents and gifts God has given us, and then ask what to do with those abilities, we are told, "Seek ye earnestly the best gifts, always remembering for what they are given. . . . All these gifts come from God, for the benefit of the children of God" (D&C 46:8, 26).

Recent First Presidency messages in the *Ensign* have reminded me of my responsibility to strengthen others by my expression of love and confidence and have reminded me of my responsibility to help bring about Zion. Zion will come about only through sacrifice and consecration of our best efforts. If we bring our best gifts, cultivated and polished by faithful effort, together we can build a society where harmony prevails because we have put aside selfishness. I hope that over the years I may have grown a bit less selfish. At least I have tried. And I am reminded to keep on trying by the words of the prophets.

If we examine others' lives, we learn how they have coped with problems and we can take courage in our own difficulties. Whether it is in some great way or in a seemingly insignificant way, each can make a contribution to the whole community.

But we do not know in advance just what part we may be called on to play. Esther was queen of Persia. Her husband, the king, did not know she was a Jew. And when a decree had gone out that all the Jews should be killed, her uncle, Mordecai, appealed to her to step forward and plead with the king for her people. She pointed out to Mordecai that to do so would endanger her own life. He replied, "Who knoweth whether thou art come to the kingdom for such a time as this?" (Esther 4:14). The question for us is what part we have to play in the great cause. Every bit player is important to the outcome. Let us be ready for our stage entrance.

When I recently reread my husband's life story, I had fun reliving some of the great experiences we have had and laughing at our foibles, but I also relived the sorrows. I asked myself how that man ever kept on, through all he suffered, until I was reminded that what has motivated him all these years is a fierce loyalty to the Lord and to whatever calling the Lord has given him. He has done his best to bring about Zion. Perhaps he was come for such a time as this.

I would like to express my gratitude for the love and support I have received from my husband. Today is his ninetieth birthday [28 March 1985]. He has served a long and honorable probation. Many people can say by faith that he is a great and good man. I say on the basis of the longest and closest personal experience that there is no finer person in the world. He is the soul of kindness and the embodiment of commitment to do right. He comes wonderfully close to perfection in my opinion.

It is the greatest sorrow of his life, and therefore the greatest sorrow of mine, that he cannot be out among the Saints testifying of Christ and teaching the right path. There is an aching frustration after a long and active life at being so limited in what he can do. He said the other day, with a spark of the old sense of humor, "Resurrection will feel so good after all this."

With all our heart, with all our soul, with all our mind, with all our strength we will love and serve the Lord.

Women of faith will know that the Lord lives and will follow that knowledge, whatever the cost. My great-grandmother Catherine Smith, an English servant girl, was baptized to express her faith in Christ, knowing full well that it might mean the loss of her employment.

Women of faith will learn so that they might be of service. Ellis Shipp went to school to become a doctor, to help meet the needs of her community. In turn, other women cared for her children, so that she could improve her talents.

Women of faith will serve in many ways. While her husband was serving a mission, Caroline Romney Eyring took in boarders, rented her own bed, and slept on the floor rather than let her husband know her financial troubles. And she kept the secret from him that their baby, born after he left, was deaf.

The great women of the scriptures and of our own day give us innumerable examples of spiritual commitment, of the development of talents, and of willing service in a great cause. By learning we fit ourselves to contribute to the kingdom. Together we can build what no one can build alone.

I sincerely pray that the Lord will help us all to grow older gracefully, still vital and contributing and growing. I pray that he will help us develop that faith in him that serves as the drive spring to good works. I pray that he will help us improve our talents, to equip ourselves for work in his cause. And I pray that we can fulfill our destiny as children of God, striving to be like him, loving and serving his other children, and building Zion.

FINDING HOLINESS IN EVERYDAY LIFE

Mary B. Kirk

I am a visual learner. If I can see something, I can remember it, and it's real to me. Christ always said, "Come unto me." But if I want to understand and know the Savior, I have to say to him, "Come unto me. Visit me in my house, in my space on earth." And if he would come and be right there close to me, I could say, "Lord, what wouldst thou have me do?" I have a good imagination, so I can see the Savior coming up the steps with the faulty rail, standing on my porch, and gently knocking on my door, wanting to come in and bring some peace and joy to my whirlwind. And I can see myself flinging that door open and saying, "Please, Savior, come in."

That is how I remember Christ and his atonement in my everyday life. I visualize him being here with me. Maybe you are a visual learner, too, so you can see this. "Jesus, see this clutter? It's evidence of something wonderful—it's proof of Thy blessings. See all these boxes in my workroom? I know, they take up a lot of space, but they are full of scraps of fabric my friends have given to me and old clothes and blue jeans and blankets and drapes. I weave them into rugs. Then I sell them to help pay the bills, and I give them away sometimes. And best of all, I love to make them. I can be creative and use these castoffs to make something of beauty. I really have a sense of satisfaction when I do that. Thank Thee for letting me have this gift.

"See this spilled dirt? My three-year-old, Logan, and I were planting some seeds the other day, trying to get a head start on the garden. We really enjoy the earth that Thou hast given to us, and we think dirt is fascinating. When we come home, wilt Thou teach us how this works—this dirt, these seeds, and this water? How does it work? How do they all

---

Mary B. Kirk is a homemaker and a nutritional consultant. She and her husband, James S. Kirk, are the proud parents of five children. She has served as a missionary in Canada and serves now as an early-morning seminary teacher and Gospel Doctrine teacher in Sunday School. She also directs the ward and Primary choirs.

become flowers and trees and vegetables and grass? We can't comprehend it!

"Now, come in the kitchen and see the dirty dishes. My firstborn son, with us fourteen years now, is on dishes this week. He's not at all sure that he should have to take a turn doing the dishes, but we're trying to teach him responsibility and self-sufficiency. We need him to be a contributing member of our family and of the community and the world around him. So he just gets to take part in it the same as the rest of us. I know, I could have done the work for him—that would be easier in a way—but how would he learn?

"Come see my laundry room. See all these dirty clothes? I know that many people need these worse than we do, but we have them. In fact, most of them were given to us. And we use them all, but the laundry pile can be discouraging at times. I'm so grateful for . . . besides the Atonement. I know a lot of my brothers and sisters on earth don't have hot, running water—or even water. And see, the laundry is up here, not in the basement. I appreciate that! And today there are more clothes clean and folded than dirty and unsorted. When I work in here, I can see work clothes and school clothes and play clothes and church clothes. Looking at these clothes I can see Jim hard at work to provide for us. I can see one of my sons sitting on the deacon's bench, getting ready to serve the sacrament. I see my other son running track in the rain and the mud. It's right there in the laundry room. I can see them. And I can see my girls playing dress-ups, pretending to be mommies and dancers and doctors and teachers and all those wonderful things. Imagining and dreaming . . . and who cares if they got lipstick on this shawl. I don't. And then I shake the sand out of one of these little socks, and I wonder how many trucks and tractors are buried in the sandbox.

"Listen. Canst Thou hear Logan sing 'I Am a Child of God' out there by the toy box? I can, even with the washer running. And he has clean socks on now, and I am so thankful to Thee who gave him to us.

"Remember when Matt was three years old and learning to dress himself? One day he came downstairs, and he had on his shirt and a pair of underwear—with the underwear on backwards. His father, after patting him on the back and praising him for his accomplishment, gently pointed out the problem. And do you remember that Matt said, 'It's not my fault, Dad. That's the way they were in the drawer'?"

I can find holiness in that. Can you? Children come here with a lot to learn, and that's one of the things we have to teach them. We may have to try lots of times to get them to put on their underwear the right way around. We need to try even harder to get them to study the scriptures and to feel like the Savior tours their life with them and cares about *all* that they do.

So then I ask the Savior to come sit on the porch for a minute, and we continue our conversation. "Remember when we were rewiring the house here before we moved in? Of course, Thou knowest. We never really thought it was necessary to put that extra kitchen light switch on the far end by the pantry. It's not handy there at all. But now that we've decided to build the garage on the west side instead of the east side, the door will come in *right there* and it's *exactly* in the right spot. I suppose it's no surprise to Thee, but we've wondered in awe at Thy power to care for little details—unbeknownst to us—that prove Thine unending love."

Now you may think this is an odd way to feel the presence of the Savior and find holiness in your everyday life. But for me, any plan, any course, that can let me think of him more often, help me to acknowledge his hand in everything around me, feel gratitude for every aspect of my life, and serve him more readily is an okay road to take. And he teaches me as we go. I'm finally seeing that what I thought was mundane and bothersome is really meaningful and beautiful. And you can, too.

Your circumstances and work may be very different from mine, but you can find holiness in them. In Mosiah 18:12 Alma says, "O Lord, pour out thy Spirit upon thy servant, that he may do this work with holiness of heart." Put your own name in Alma's prayer, and if your desire is pure, God will grant you holiness of heart—every day.

You know, it took my husband's great insight and a personal revelation to me to finally fix in my mind the fact that eternal life doesn't start at the Savior's second coming, that it's right now. Our relationship with God and Christ goes back all the way and it goes forward all the way and today is part of it. We need to think about each day as being an integral part of the great picture. In other words, the mere fact that we are *alive today* is holy in itself. We chose to participate in mortality. So let's rejoice and be glad in it, and acknowledge our stewardship over each day, and *feel* each day's potential for holiness.

In one Bill Keane "Family Circus" comic strip, Dolly and Jeffy are sitting high on a hill looking out over things. Dolly has her arm around Jeffy's shoulders, and he is looking teachable and very intent upon what she is saying. The wisdom of her words has helped me find holiness many times since I first read it. She explains, "Yesterday is the *past*, tomorrow is the *future*, and today is a *gift*. That's why they call it the *present*." God is the author of the past and the future, and he's the giver of the present gift. He'll sprinkle holiness into today, and we will find it. He will pour out his holiness upon us at the rate that we open our eyes and perceive, open our ears and understand, and open our hearts and invite him in. And then we'll become like him.

Note

I appreciate the insight of Joan B. MacDonald in her book, *The Holiness of Everyday Life*, which helped me focus my presentation (Salt Lake City: Deseret Book, 1995).

PIECES OF PEACE

⌒⊗⌒

Janet Lee

I love the Smith Field House at Brigham Young University. I know it is just a gymnasium with a track and a few classrooms and offices, but to me it is much more. Despite its rambunctious purpose, this place brings me a peace you cannot imagine. It is a sanctuary, a haven, for me. My memories of experiences in this building provide a piece of peace as I look back through the years shared with my husband, Rex, and as I wonder about the years we will be apart.

As students, Rex and I attended devotionals and forums, basketball and volleyball games, and track meets in the field house. At lunchtime, we could buy hamburgers and brownies at the side of the track. At registration time, the entire building was filled with confused and frustrated students struggling to register for required classes before they filled up. With a little decoration and a big imagination, the field house was even turned into a dance hall. The first picture Rex and I ever had taken together was in this very building. I once wore my wedding dress here. No, we didn't have our reception in the field house, but Janie Thompson, who was in charge of BYU's annual Field House Frolics the year Rex and I were married, wanted a theatrical atmosphere. We sang "Love and Marriage" as we stepped down a tall, winding staircase. A decade later, President Dallin Oaks introduced Rex here as the founding dean of the yet-to-be-organized J. Reuben Clark Law School. Shortly thereafter, when we moved back to Provo, we came here often for family home evenings with our children. Here on this track I ran my first mile, then three, then five. I ran with Rex at my side, giving me encouragement, cheering me on. Sometimes I came in the daytime and settled my young children in the bleachers with paper and crayons or storybooks and the promise of a brownie if they were good while Mommy ran.

Janet Lee, an educator and speaker, earned her bachelor of science degree in education from Brigham Young University. She is the wife of the late Rex E. Lee, former president of Brigham Young University, and they are the parents of seven children. She has served as a member of the Young Women General Board of The Church of Jesus Christ of Latter-day Saints.

Years later, we returned to the same track after Rex's chemotherapy treatments. He walked slowly, holding my hand and gaining strength after a six-month hospital stay. For years we had been running long distances outside and thought we had graduated from a track, but that winter he needed the stability of temperature, and we enjoyed the comradery of friends. He loved greeting people as we walked the track. His voice boomed all through the field house. "Hi, Pete. How are you, Glen? I'll race you," he joked to runner friends as they passed him by. I thought he wouldn't want to draw attention to himself, with his chemically induced baldness and ponderous pace, but he loved their smiles as they passed. Some would stop and walk with him awhile to chat and then be on their way.

By spring, Rex was running two laps and walking one, and by early summer we were running outside together and all over Provo. The following summer, he became president of BYU, and once again, we returned to the field house for sporting events and winter runs when it was snowy outside.

How could I not love this building? My memories are one way I find peace. They have carried me, they brighten my life, and they are a wonderful blessing—a piece of my peace.

I have contemplated peace a great deal over this past year. I have thought a lot more about peace when I haven't had it than when I have. I have told myself, "As soon as I get the hospital bills paid, then I will feel peace . . . as soon as I figure out our finances and feel secure . . . as soon as I answer all the kind letters people have written . . . as soon as I get used to kneeling by our bed each night alone to pray . . . " The list goes on and on. I foolishly put a condition on my peace.

Gradually I have learned not to postpone peace but to accept it as a gift when it comes piece by piece. If I look, I can find pieces of peace in each day—even in a bad day. Life does not have to be perfect to have moments of perfect happiness. They come with the smile of a child, the kindness of a co-worker, the satisfaction of a job well done, or the appreciation of a sunset, a blossom, a familiar melody, or even a well-scrubbed sink.

The Savior has promised us peace: "Peace I leave with you, my peace I give unto you: not as the world giveth, give I unto you" (John 14:27). The promise of peace is unconditional. He didn't say, "My peace I leave with you if nothing difficult ever happens in your life" or "My peace I give unto you unless you don't find the right person to marry, unless you have financial reverses, unless you experience poor health, or unless your children struggle."

The Savior didn't qualify his promise. He simply said, "My peace I give unto you," but note that he added "not as the world giveth, give I unto you." We must accept our Savior's gift of peace and recognize it as his peace, not the superficial peace of the world.

We can be relaxing on a beautiful beach, feeling the rhythm of the ocean, the sun in the sky, and a refreshing breeze and still not be at peace. By contrast, we can be anywhere in the workplace, the laundry room, or even in the car and feel a piece of his peace when we are in tune with the Spirit because, as we are told in Doctrine and Covenants 6:23, the Lord speaks peace to the mind. Some of my most inspirational moments have come while folding socks at midnight, making orange juice early in the morning, or praying alone in my car. Other pieces of peace come after action—we make a decision, accomplish a task, or work toward a goal.

We cannot remain in that state of peace forever. Daily concerns, mundane responsibilities, duties, and tasks creep into our sanctified moments of still assurance. Usually peace does not come without effort, and most of the time, our pieces of peace do not last very long. In my search for peace over the past year, I continue to return to John 14:27. That scripture has three parts that speak to me of peace: past, present, and future.

PAST PEACE

Of past peace, the Savior tells us: "Peace I leave with you" (John 14:27). That was his gift to us as he left this earth—remembering him and all he has done for us will bring us peace. In my quiet moments of mourning, sometimes I succumb to questioning. Rex's death was untimely. Couldn't someone have done something to keep him here? I think of his pain during those last few years. I remember the agony of his last two weeks, and I wonder if even I completely understood his suffering. I wonder if anyone did. Then I remember the words of Elder Neal A. Maxwell: "Can we, even in the depths of disease, tell [our Savior] anything at all about suffering? In ways we cannot comprehend, our sicknesses and infirmities were borne by Him even before they were borne by us."[1] It is wonderful to know that no matter what happens to us on this earth, there is someone who understands everything. Thoughts of the Savior's love and compassion for Rex's suffering and my sorrow bring peace. I know that he understands all of our sorrow.

We can also find peace as we reflect on our own good memories. But what about memories that are uncomfortable or even painful? If we need ecclesiastical or professional help, we must seek it immediately so we can begin to move forward. Even then, our brief, daily pieces of peace can be part of the healing process. If our uncomfortable memories simply consist of things we wish we had or hadn't said or done, we must apologize or rectify our error. If we cannot improve the situation, then we need to let the memory go. That is hard to do sometimes. For those of us who lie awake nights rewriting the script of our past actions, peace can be elusive.

When Jesus came forth from the tomb and appeared to his disciples, his first greeting was: "Peace be unto you" (Luke 24:36). He did not ask, "Did you see how unfairly I was judged, how cruelly I was treated, or how brutally I was crucified?" He did not ask to be pitied or to have his enemies attacked. Christ knows that resentment and recrimination do not bring peace. They cause us to stagnate, leaving us unable to move ahead vigorously because we stumble when we constantly look back at what has been. "All crosses are easier to carry when we keep moving," Elder Maxwell counsels us.[2] During this past year, as my heart has yearned to cease grieving, I have prayed for peace, and I receive that blessing as I keep moving.

PRESENT PEACE

When the Savior tells us, "My peace I give unto you" (John 14:27), he promises the continuation of his gift of peace while we struggle with all that is temporal. Sometimes we miss this gift. Recently, I found a letter I wrote to Rex in the fall of 1991. We often wrote letters or notes to each other, expressing feelings that were difficult to share in person during his nine-year struggle with cancer. Sometimes we delivered these letters in person, with a smile and a hug. Other times they were tucked into a pocket or purse to be discussed later. I must admit I wrote more than he did. I had a need to pour out my feelings.

I knew he read my notes; we often talked about them. But I never knew he saved them. During the past year, as I have gone through his things, I have found letters and notes in pockets, briefcases, drawers, and files. In this particular letter to Rex, I told of an experience with our daughter. I wrote: "This afternoon . . . I took Wendy home, and as we were driving she talked to me a little about how excited she was about the baby, but our talk ended with an account of all the aches and pains and discomforts of pregnancy. She had an understanding ear as she recounted to me such things as a misshapen figure, swollen hands and feet, and a total off-balance, awkward feeling. 'Will I ever be the same again?' she asked as she got out of our car. I smiled and answered that she would, but as I was driving away, I thought, 'No! She will never be quite the same again.' Life is never the same after a big change of any kind in our lives.

"For a few seconds, as I drove along University Avenue, I began to feel sorry for myself and for you for the changes that have happened in our lives over the past four years. I was longing to be relieved of the constant worry, wishing you could be completely well again, wanting our lives to be like they were before you got sick. I took Wendy's question and applied it to you and to me. Will we ever be the same again? I startled myself when I answered 'No!' out loud at a stoplight.

"But as I drove up the hill toward the administration building, the most peaceful feeling came over me. I had been crying, but I stopped and listened as soothing thoughts poured into my mind. The thoughts were neither new nor profound, but what made them pierce my soul was that I felt the power of their source. 'Life's experiences are to be enjoyed and appreciated as they come,' I seemed to be hearing. Life is like a book, a play, or a puzzle. It is difficult to see it in its entirety until it is completed, but to look back or ahead too much takes away from the enjoyment close at hand, and besides that, we miss something important. . . . We must look for the good things about now and enjoy them with all of our hearts. 'No, we will never be the same again,' I thought to myself. And life will continue to change. But life will always be good."

My letter to Rex had been found to remind me of what I had momentarily forgotten. Love and peace overflowed in my heart that day, that moment, as I read.

FUTURE PEACE

But what of our tendency to worry about the future? Our Savior's words assure us: "Let not your heart be troubled, neither let it be afraid" (John 14:27). This is my hardest challenge now. If I spend too much time thinking about the past or the future, I will miss the peace that comes from the present. But I cannot enjoy the present to its fullest unless I feel at peace with the past and the future, trusting that like the apostle Paul, I will have strength to face all conditions by the power that Christ gives me (see 2 Corinthians 4:14–16; 12:9).

My niece Mollie is a young missionary. Her ups and downs are perhaps intensified by her missionary experience and her youthful exuberance, but in a miniseries sort of way her letters represent all of us in our struggle for peace. She writes to her family: "It's so funny, a missionary's life. I feel so happy with just me, my ability to talk and pray to God. . . . Last night as I packed my three huge suitcases filled with a ridiculous overabundance of things, I almost felt SICK at how much happiness I had placed on *things*. Razors, lotion, soap, clothes, shoes. I mean, yes, they are essentials, but why did I have to bring SO MUCH? I hope you don't mind, but I have given SO much away. The people here just don't have anything."

Is this the same Mollie who made an emergency call the day before she left the MTC requesting four extra bottles of Victoria's Secret pear-scented lotion?

She continues: "I'm glancing out my window on the bus—yellow sun, green trees, fields, huge sky. Oh, how beautiful life is. I take joy in loving the Savior. I want to praise him in everything I do. I want my life to glorify him. I love the simplicity of happiness." She was in a really peaceful mood right then.

But four days later, Mollie was transferred, received a new companion, and suddenly faced the challenges inherent in change. She writes: "I'm struggling. . . . It's hot, about 115 degrees. I hope we can be in tune enough to find the souls that are ready." She adds: "I can feel the boards of the wooden bed on my bum through the two-inch mattress. I remember my fluffy feather bed, folded over double, and white satin, down comforter at home. It's wonderful, though, and I appreciate my life here and at home so much more."

Two weeks later she writes: "Do you know what? I'm being refined. Do you know what else? It hurts."

In Mollie's next letter the opening line is: "I got lice, and I cried! I told my companion I just couldn't do this anymore. I hit a wall. I was crying and sitting there, wet hair, bugs all over my scalp, wondering how I was going to live through the day. As I was crying, I looked at the wall. The picture of Christ in his red robe looked back at me. . . . I just cried, 'What can I do? What more can I give?'"

Later in the same letter she writes of finding resolution and peace: "Last night I read in the B of M a line, 'Thy will and not mine be done.' I have been trying to squeeze the Lord's will into mine. And yes, it fit, but like a puzzle piece in the wrong place. There were gaps and places where it was overlapping or too tight. I realized that I need to do the Lord's will and let my will go."

Like Mollie, I too have had to learn about the error of trying to squeeze the Lord's will into mine. When Rex was diagnosed with cancer in 1987, for days I begged and almost demanded of the Lord that Rex be made well. But my heart ached, and I could find no peace. I then began to reason and bargain, but still I felt no peace. Finally, one day my prayer began, "Thy will be done," and the peace I was searching for filled my heart. I thought I would never forget that lesson.

Yet, two weeks before Rex's death, I had to learn it once more. Again I had been trying to squeeze the Lord's will into mine. Again I had to let go of my will to find peace. The Lord didn't need my permission, but in allowing me to submit my will, a gift of peace was given to me by a loving Father in Heaven. He knew it would be easier for me to let Rex go if I could be allowed to do it willingly. Like children who resist being pulled away from play without warning, we struggle, but we can go willingly when allowed our agency. By putting my trust in the Lord, I gained a peace that would have been impossible had I continued to struggle against his will. At times like these, we arrive at a new understanding, and peace accompanies us for a time. Yet, we so often need reminders, guidance, and strength. We so often have to learn and relearn life's lessons.

Some days we think we would have greater peace if we were granted our heart's desire. On other days, we think peace would come if we could simply escape our current burdens. In one of my favorite fantasies, I have returned to the Garden of Eden. The way is so easy. My needs melt away. I bask in the beauty of God's finest creations and walk in the constant, calming presence of the Father and his Son. I feel unprecedented peace.

Yet, I realize that every act of God is purposeful, including the fall of Adam and Eve. They and their posterity had to fall away from permanent peace. We, as the children of Adam and Eve, also face challenges inherent in a fallen world. We spend sleepless nights surrounded by confusion, worry, fear, and discouragement. We struggle, and we ache for others who struggle. We encounter mistreatment and prejudice, injustice and unforgiveness. Sometimes we feel we are either failing or falling short of what is expected of us. Often we long for an easier way. In essence, we are longing for a Garden of Eden. We are asking to live as Adam and Eve once lived, surrounded simply by peaceful circumstances. At a glance, such conditions would seem to provide permanent peace; however, "Adam fell that men might be; and men are, that they might have joy" (2 Nephi 2:25). I find a connection between the Fall and finding joy, or eternal peace.

With all my heart, if I could change the course of these past ten years as our whole family has experienced the pain of Rex's cancer, I would do so. And yet, I would never want to give up the growth: the understanding, the insights, the compassion, or the increased love for each other and for our Savior. Without the Fall, we would remain as children, without spiritual maturity, without knowledge, without realizing our ultimate potential of becoming exalted sons and daughters of God. My occasional desire to return to the Garden of Eden or escape to a life of ease is a misdirection, not the way to everlasting peace.

Christ healed bodies, minds, and souls. But after he healed the lepers, were they free from other struggles? After he restored sight to the blind, were they free from fear? Were the five thousand Christ fed ever hungry again? Was the sea calmed by Christ's hands stirred by future storms? Yes. As Helaman warned his children, the winds will continue to blow (see Helaman 5:12).

I often think of the tender last moments Christ shared with his apostles. Concerned, Christ tells his disciples that the time has come for him to leave. Full of heartache, the apostles turn to their Lord, who senses their sorrow. He replies, "Nevertheless I tell you the truth; It is expedient for you that I go away; for if I go not away, the Comforter will not come unto you; but if I depart, I will send him unto you" (John 16:7). If we expect mountains to move, seas to part, thunder to cease, and blinding light to point the way, we will miss the Savior's offering, his gift of comfort and peace. Peace comes as we truly rely on the Holy Ghost.

Like the fall of Adam and the crucifixion of Christ, there is something very significant, even essential, in being surrounded by conflict and finding peace in the midst of, or even because of, tribulation. "It is expedient for *you* that I go away," the Savior said (John 16:7; italics added).

The Lord promises safety and protection. He offers to all the gift of peace. Sometimes peace comes dramatically, like the calming of a raging sea (see Mark 4:39). Most of the time, however, peace comes quietly, as a subtle feeling of wellness, a renewed sense of God's omnipotent power, and the still, small voice whispering God's messages: words of comfort, thoughts of hope, feelings of strength, and a reassurance of love—the language of peace.

In the last days of Rex's life, he was given medication to ease his pain. As a result, he was sedated and could not talk, and I was not sure how much he could hear. I began to feel an almost desperate need to speak with him, to hear and be heard. I felt a sense of panic and insecurity. I felt out of control, as if I were falling away from all that was familiar to me. Desperate with heartbreak and weariness, I fell to my knees and prayed. As I expressed my urgent concerns to my Father in Heaven, I began to understand that the words I needed to speak to Rex and hear from him had already been given to me. I began to recall past conversations with Rex—conversations we had shared over many years. I sensed the comfort of the Holy Ghost as feelings and thoughts lifted me to a higher sphere, where souls could communicate without conventional conversation. Peace was being spoken to my mind. I was on sure ground again. Words unspoken now seemed insignificant and unnecessary. A lifetime of sharing each other's triumphs and sorrows had been stored in our hearts.

Now, in his hospital room, I thought about the many things he had been asked to do, and I was aware that what we were about to do was the most difficult of all. Memories flooded over me, and I concentrated on tender moments as well as milestones in our lives. Each time we had faced a turning point, I asked Rex what I could do to help him. His answer was always the same and always unequivocal: "Just be happy, Janet." Now, in the midst of our final challenge together, his words came back to me, and I knew what he would tell me if he could. I had never considered peace as part of the process of letting go. Yet when his final moment came, and I knew he was free from his pain, I felt his joy. Unexpectedly, my personal sadness was subdued as we shared his final triumph. I whispered: "I am so happy for you, Sweetheart." As I walked out of the hospital that afternoon, his words filled my heart: "Just be happy, Janet," and I felt a moment of peace in my mighty whirlwind.

The Lord can speak peace to our minds wherever we are. We don't have to be in the temple or on a beautiful beach. Sometimes we are in the midst of trials and strife. It is the gift of peace that brings joy, surety, and solace—the kind of peace that can never be taken away. Piece by piece throughout a lifetime, we will long to return to the presence of the Prince of Peace. Our pieces of peace will fit together like a puzzle as our life takes shape after the pattern of our Savior. Because we are mortal, at times we will be unable to find the peace that is our gift, but our Savior's love can lift us soaring to new heights. In three short lines, Victor Hugo sings my theme song of this past year:

> *Be like the bird who, halting in [her] flight on a limb too slight*
> *Feels it give way beneath [her],*
> *Yet sings knowing [she] hath wings.*[3]

The boughs beneath us break sometimes. We will not fall. We have wings of truth, wings of faith, wings of glory—gifts of peace from our Savior, Master, and King.

Notes

1. Neal A. Maxwell, *Even As I Am* (Salt Lake City: Deseret Book, 1982), 116–17.
2. Neal A. Maxwell, *Deposition of a Disciple* (Salt Lake City: Deseret Book, 1976), 30.
3. Victor Hugo, quoted in Marilyn Arnold, *Pure Love: Readings on Sixteen Enduring Virtues* (Salt Lake City: Deseret Book, 1997), 389.

THE POWER WITHIN: TO SEE LIFE STEADILY AND SEE IT WHOLE

Rex E. Lee

The 1990 BYU Women's Conference continues a tradition begun in 1976. I want to compliment this year's chair, Carol Lee Hawkins, and the dedicated, perceptive women who have worked with her in putting together more than forty lectures, workshops, panel discussions, and performances. Their job has not been easy nor free from controversy, but few things that are really worthwhile enjoy either of those luxuries. We are grateful to them for their efforts.

As participants we differ widely in age, and even among those who are the same age, there is a sizable range to the challenges and circumstances that each of us faces. The conference committee has deliberately and conscientiously chosen session topics to cover a broad spectrum of individual needs and interests. I would be surprised, even a bit disappointed, if you agreed with everything said during the conference. I invite you, in the finest tradition of the gospel and the free and open society guaranteed by our Constitution, to approach each experience not only as an evaluator, an assessor, of the worth of what is said but also as one who is trying to learn from new ideas and new points of view—some of which you may disagree with. You may well conclude that although all the issues presented are important to you or to others, in some cases you will not be sure what the right attitudes or answers are. In other words, you may come away from this experience with new questions as well as new insights and answers.

Many of the sessions have been designed for men as well as for women. A justified complaint being voiced today by women—and some men— is that society has both erroneously and presumptuously assumed that social concerns are and should be the domain of woman. That is one of

Rex E. Lee, tenth president of Brigham Young University, was the founding dean of the J. Reuben Clark School of Law at BYU, served as the solicitor general of the United States, and maintains a private appellate law practice before the United States Supreme Court. His juris doctor degree is from the University of Chicago Law School, and he holds five honorary doctor of law degrees. He and his wife, Janet Griffin Lee, have seven children.

many gender-based generalizations with which I do not agree. Unfortunately, because women are not only discussing these issues but also acting upon them as well, most of the responsibility has fallen in their laps.

As I look over the topics for this conference—relationships with aging parents, self-esteem for children, providing aid for abuse victims, and dimensions of service—I see very clearly why Carol Lee and her committee would like more men to attend. These are not women's issues. They are people's issues. Women are making gigantic efforts to find solutions to these concerns, but they should not be expected to do it alone.

The theme of this year's conference is adapted from a poem Matthew Arnold wrote describing those authors who gave him solace and strength amidst the uncertainties and problems of his own day:

> ### BE HIS
> My special thanks, whose even-balanced soul,
> From first youth tested up to extreme old age,
> Business could not make dull, nor passion wild;
> Who saw life steadily and saw it whole.[1]

The theme also derives in part from 2 Timothy 1:7: "For God hath not given us the spirit of fear; but of power, and of love, and of a sound mind."

In order to grow in wisdom and knowledge and to become like God, who is omnipotent, all-powerful, we are told that each of us—man and woman—must grow in power.

But what kind of power is godlike?

Karen Lynn Davidson helped answer that question for me in a talk she gave at a BYU Women's Conference several years ago. In her description of the Savior, she clarified how power can be a godlike attribute: "[The Savior] rejected the worldly notions of dominion, power, and bosshood. On the other hand, no one who has ever lived has shown more strength, more courage, more perseverance, more willingness to stand up for truth or rebuke wrong, even at tremendous cost, than has the Savior. He spoke up for unpopular causes. He was willing to speak the truth, even when it cost him his life. If his inner inspiration told him something was right, he did it. That confirmation was all he needed. He didn't need an okay from any of his friends. He had the strength to stand alone. He had absolute confidence in himself and in his Father—confidence to lead out in what was right."[2]

We are told that the power God shared with his Son, Jesus Christ, he shares willingly with all his children, as they develop increased faith in him. "Downright solid faith," said Elder A. Theodore Tuttle, "is the one thing that gives vitality and power to otherwise rather weak individuals."[3]

It is this power—the kind described by Karen, not by the world—that will help us meet and deal courageously with the uncertainties of life. It is power that will lift us up over our stumbling blocks, so that we may see life steadily and see it whole.

It is my testimony to you that each one of us has within us this power. The purpose of this conference is to explore and examine that gift.

Notes

1. Matthew Arnold, "To a Friend," *The Poems of Matthew Arnold,* 2d rev. ed., ed. Miriam Allott (New York: Longman Group Ltd., 1979), 111.

2. Karen Lynn Davidson, "The Savior: An Example for Everyone," in *Woman to Woman* (Salt Lake City: Deseret Book, 1986), 102–3; see also this volume, 112–22.

3. A. Theodore Tuttle, Ensign, November 1986, 73.

THE FIRE OF THE COVENANT

⟨∞⟩

Gerald N. Lund

𝒯he time was fall 1838. The place was Caldwell County, Missouri.
Tensions were running high. In the previous two years, more than five
thousand Latter-day Saints had moved into what had been a sparsely
populated county. The old settlers were getting nervous. Too many
Yankee Mormons were moving in. Missouri had entered the Union as a
slave state, and it wanted to stay that way. The militia and mobs began
to prowl. On the night of 24 October, a mob broke into an isolated settlement, burned the haystacks, torched the barns, and then kidnapped
three Latter-day Saint men and threatened to take them back to Jackson
County to execute them.

When word reached Joseph Smith in Far West, he called out the
Mormon militia under the direction of David Patten, who was second
senior member of the Quorum of the Twelve. He gathered a group of men
to ride out and intercept that group.[1] On the way, they stopped at James
Hendricks' home and asked him to join them. While he prepared, his
wife, Drusilla, filled with great fear but also faith, got his gun down from
the fireplace and handed it to him. As he left she said, "Don't get shot in
the back."[2]

They rode all that night. Just at morning they came upon a little place
called Crooked River. They didn't realize at first that the mob was
camped right across the river. The little band of Mormons was coming
from the west, and the rising sun was in their eyes. The Saints couldn't
see the mob as they began to cross the river. One of the Missouri picket
guards first saw the brethren coming and opened fire. Patrick O'Bannion
was hit immediately and died before noon. A fierce battle erupted.
Another man, Gideon Carter, was shot in the face and killed instantly.
As David Patten tried to fall back across the river, he was shot in the

Gerald N. Lund, author of several books, is a zone administrator in the Church
Educational System, with which he has been associated for more than thirty years. He
has led tours to Europe, the Holy Land, Central America, and LDS Church history sites.
He and his wife, Lynn Stanard Lund, have seven children. He serves as the teacher
development leader in his ward in Bountiful, Utah.

stomach. He died before nightfall, the first apostle martyred in this dispensation.[3] And James Hendricks? As the furious fire erupted, he turned, ran for shelter, and caught a ball in the back of the neck. He fell to the ground paralyzed from the neck down.[4]

On October 27, two days later, in Jefferson City, Missouri, Governor Lilburn W. Boggs received a wildly exaggerated account of what had happened at Crooked River. He was told that the whole Missouri militia had been massacred when actually they had lost only one man. The Mormons had lost three dead and seven wounded. In great anger, Governor Boggs issued an executive order that, among other things, read, "The Mormons must be treated as enemies and must be exterminated or driven from the state."[5]

About twelve miles west of Far West was a small settlement named Haun's Mill for its founder, Jacob Haun, who had built a grist mill there on Shoal Creek. October 30 was a beautiful Indian summer day.[6] About four o'clock in the afternoon, the women were sitting on their porches shucking corn or doing other things to prepare for the winter. The men were out doing the last of the work in the fields, and the children were playing close by. Suddenly they heard a low rumble and looked up. Across the meadow and the trees, they saw about 240 men riding toward them. The captain of the Haun's Mill militia ran out, waving his hat and crying, "Peace! Peace!" Instead, the riders opened fire. The scene of tranquillity erupted in terror. Children screamed. Women ran to rescue their children. The invaders fired at everyone in sight. Fathers grabbed their sons and ran for the blacksmith's shop, the strongest building in the settlement. The mob showed no discrimination whatsoever. One woman, Mary Stedwell, darted across the road, headed for the millpond. Bullets pinged all around her as she ran across the millrace. Finally one bullet found its target: Mary was shot through the palm of her hand, and, fainting, fell behind a log. Later, the Saints dug out between fifteen and twenty bullets from the log that sheltered her.[7]

Far more serious, the men and boys who had run into the blacksmith shop had made a terrible mistake. The heavy logs making up the walls had never been chinked, leaving great cracks all the way around the building. As the Saints barricaded the door, the mob dismounted, stepped up to the walls, put the muzzles through the cracks, and opened fire. In the deadly hail of bullets, most of the men were killed outright, and others were wounded. Finally the mob broke through the door and walked around, systematically shooting the survivors. Warren Smith had taken his two sons in with him for protection: Sardius was ten, and Alma was seven. In terror the boys dived beneath the blacksmith's bellows. They watched as a man put a gun to their father's head and pulled the trigger. A member of the mob heard them cry and looked underneath the bellows where he could see Sardius. He tried to pull the boy out, but when he couldn't, he simply put his rifle under the bellows, against Sardius' head, and pulled the trigger. Alma, whimpering in terror, burrowed deeper beneath the bellows. Another man reached in with his muzzle, couldn't quite reach Alma, but fired anyway, blowing away Alma's hip joint. Twenty minutes later, when the mob rode away with clothing and treasures they had looted from the cabins, they left seventeen dead and thirteen wounded. The Haun's Mill massacre became a tragic event in our history.

The day after the Crooked River killings in Far West, knowing the great tension and danger, Joseph Smith had sent word to all those in outlying settlements and villages to come into Far West for protection.[8] On October 26, Jacob Haun had driven into Far West and looked up Joseph Smith. John D. Lee, who happened to be standing there, wrote the following: "The morning after the battle of Crooked River, Haun came to Far West to consult with the Prophet concerning the policy of the removal of the settlers . . . to the fortified camp. Col. [Lyman] Wight and myself were standing by when the prophet said to [Mr. Haun], 'Move in, by all means, if you wish to save your lives.' Haun replied that if the settlers left their homes, all of their property would be lost . . . and burn[ed]. 'You had better lose your property than your lives; one can be replaced, the other cannot be restored; but there is no need of you losing either if you will only do as you are commanded.' Haun said that he considered the best plan was for all the settlers to move into and around the mill, and use the blacksmith's shop and other buildings as a fort in case of attack. . . . [Finally the Prophet said], 'You are at liberty to do so if you think best.' Haun then departed, well satisfied that he had carried his point. The Prophet turned to Col. Wight and said: 'That man did not come for counsel, but to induce me to tell him to do as he pleased; which I did. Had I commanded them to move in here and leave their property, they would have called me a tyrant. . . . ' [And then sadly the Prophet said], 'I am confident that we will soon learn that they have been butchered in a fearful manner.'"[9] The irony is that Jacob Haun went back to Haun's Mill and didn't tell the settlers the whole truth of what had taken place between him and Joseph Smith.[10] Jacob Haun was not one of the seventeen who were killed. He was one of the thirteen wounded and thus had to live out his life knowing the dreadful consequences of his refusing to follow counsel.

Let's go back a few years to the fall of 1830. Four missionaries were called by direct revelation to go to the western border of the United States in Independence, Missouri, on what is now known as the mission to the Lamanites. Parley P. Pratt, Oliver Cowdery, Peter Whitmer Jr., and Ziba Peterson all left New York and, at Parley P. Pratt's recommendation, stopped at a place where Parley had once lived called Kirtland, Ohio. There they received a warm and wonderful reception. Many accepted their message, including names well known in Church history: Frederick G. Williams, Sidney Rigdon, Isaac Morley, John Murdock, and so on.[11] In Kirtland, an eleven-year-old girl named Mary Elizabeth Rollins lived with her uncle. She heard that these missionaries had left what they called the Golden Bible with Brother Isaac Morley. She records: "I went to his house just before the meeting was to commence, and asked to see the Book. Brother Morley put it in my hand; as I looked at it, I felt such a desire to read it, that I could not refrain from asking him to let me take it home and read it, while he attended meeting. . . . He finally said, 'Child if you will bring this book home before breakfast tomorrow morning, you may take it.' . . . when I got into the house, I exclaimed, 'Oh, Uncle, I have gotten the "Golden Bible."' . . . We all took turns reading it until very late in the night—as soon as it was light enough to see, I was up and learned [by heart] the first verse in the book. When I reached Brother Morley's . . . , he remarked, 'I guess you did not read much in it.' I showed him how far we had read. He was surprised, and said, 'I don't believe you could tell me one word of it.'" She then quoted him the first verse she had memorized and told him the story in detail of everything they had read up to that point. "He gazed at me in surprise, and said, 'Child, take this book home and finish it. I think I can wait.'"[12]

This eleven-year-old is the same Mary Elizabeth Rollins who was living with her family in Independence three and a half years later. In July 1833 a mob of some five hundred men, angry at the influence of the growing community of Mormons, attacked the printing office of The Evening and the Morning Star, run by W. W. Phelps. Living close by with her uncle, Mary Elizabeth and her sister Caroline saw the mob coming in and turned and ran for shelter. They ducked behind a split rail fence some distance away and watched as the mob demolished not only the press and the type but the very building. They tore the roof off and then tore the walls down. As the two girls, ages fifteen and twelve, huddled there in terror, Mary Elizabeth saw huge stacks of paper being thrown from one of the upper windows. Because she knew W. W. Phelps well, she knew the papers were the Book of Commandments, a collection of revelations sent from Kirtland to be printed. "Caroline," she said, "we must save those." Her twelve-year-old sister replied, "If we do, they will kill us." Mary Elizabeth said, "Nevertheless we must do it." They jumped up, ran to the building, and picked up as many of those sheaves of paper as they could carry. Two men took after them. The girls darted through the fence, ran deep into a cornfield, threw down the papers and themselves on top of them, and began to pray mightily when they heard the men tromping through the cornfield. Eventually the men gave up and left. Thanks to Mary Elizabeth and Caroline Rollins, we now have a few copies of the original Book of Commandments.[13]

Mary Elizabeth is one of my favorite people in Church history. One night, Mary Elizabeth awakened to see a figure standing in the air at the foot of her bed. She did what any wise girl would have done: she pulled the covers over her head. When she finally got the courage to look out, the person was gone. The next day, on the street, she passed Joseph Smith. The Prophet said, "Mary Elizabeth, I understand you had a visitation last night." She said, "How did you know that?" And he said, "Because the angel came to me. He said he had come to you and could not deliver the message because you had hid under the covers. He also said that he was greatly offended."[14] I guess angels aren't used to that kind of treatment.

Let me relate another story. Vilate and Heber C. Kimball were driven out of Far West to a swampy bend on the Mississippi River. They lived in terrible conditions. For a time, they lived in a log lean-to built onto the back of someone else's house. After a year or so of that, Heber was finally able to build Vilate their own one-room log cabin. Then Heber spent years in missionary work, often in England. Finally after all the years of sacrifice, they reached a point in 1845 when Heber was prosperous enough to be able to build a beautiful two-story, brick home. Vilate and Heber moved into that home in November 1845. They locked the door and walked away without receiving a dime for it in February 1846.

They were not the only ones who left painfully. In the middle of April 1846, Bathsheba and George Albert Smith faced a similar situation. On her last day in Nauvoo, Bathsheba tidied up her home, swept the floor, put the broom in its accustomed place behind the door, and then stepped outside to a waiting wagon, leaving behind rooms full of beloved items and a house ready for occupancy by strangers.[15] I have wondered what kind of woman would walk away from her home, leaving it to her ene-mies and be sure it is swept clean before she does so.

Ten years later, in October 1856, the Willie Handcart Company had been caught in the first of some furious storms on the high plains of Wyoming. They suffered terribly. Finally in the last week of October, the first relief wagon from Salt Lake appeared. The handcart pioneers were given a limited amount of flour and food but were told the rescuers could do little more until they found the Martin company. Help was ahead, however: waiting at Rock Creek, only sixteen miles away, were other wagons filled with blankets, medicine, food, and beef. But that sixteen miles was through a howling blizzard. The Willie company was camped at the base of Rocky Ridge, which is a three-mile pull, some of it very steep and the last part extremely rough. In the midst of a howling bliz-zard, they set out to cover that sixteen miles to the supply wagons. It took them almost twenty-four hours from the time they left camp till the last one of the company finally arrived at Rock Creek.

Two people in the Willie Handcart Company were Jens and Elsie Nielsen, well-to-do converts from Denmark who had sold their farm to travel to Zion. When they reached Iowa City, Jens had enough money to buy wagons and teams and outfit his family very comfortably, but the Church agents there asked if anyone had anything extra to help those who did not have enough. Jens Nielsen took enough money to buy one handcart, supplies for himself and his wife, his son, and Bodil Mortensen, a young girl they were responsible for, and gave the rest to the Church agents.[16]

The Nielsens started up Rocky Ridge. The children, Jens's own son and the girl accompanying them, were so weak and sick that they were riding in the handcart. Jens Nielsen pulled for fourteen or fifteen hours in snow until his feet were so badly frostbitten that he barely hobbled along. Somewhere between Rocky Ridge and Rock Creek, Jens collapsed. "Elsie, I can go no farther. You go on without me."

"I will not leave you, Jens," Elsie said, and she helped him into the cart with the two children. Jens Nielsen was six foot two and weighed two hundred and thirty pounds. Elsie Nielsen was four foot eleven and weighed one hundred pounds.[17] She pulled them all the rest of the way to Rock Creek. Jens lived, but both children died before morning.

As I read those stories and journals and diaries, I have many questions. Why was the cost in human lives so high? If these were the Lord's people, why weren't the storms tempered? Why were the innocent people in Haun's Mill, who didn't know what had taken place between Jacob Haun and the Prophet, allowed to become part of what happened in that tragedy? What happened to a Sardius Smith, who was killed at age twelve and, because of wicked men, never had the opportunity to grow to adulthood, marry, and have children in this life?

What about the calendar of the exile? When the Church moved from New York to Ohio, it was January. The Saints were forced to flee from Kirtland in December and January. They were driven out of Jackson County in November and December. They were driven out of Far West in January and February, and they left Nauvoo in February. Is that accidental? If the Lord really loves his people, why is no one driven out in May or June occasionally?

Some of the hardest questions for me are these: Why didn't they give up? What was it about this people that drove them on? And, I suppose most sobering, What would I have done in those circumstances? That question comes up over and over again. Would I have been strong enough? Would I have remained a believer?

These stories are the *whats* of the Restoration story; and they are astonishing, remarkable, incredible, and inspirational. But of far more value to us than knowing what happened is knowing the *why*. Why did this happen? Why were these people so remarkable? Why did they go on? To answer these questions we have to go back further even than Joseph Smith. These people had a tremendous love for and loyalty to Joseph Smith, but that's not what drove them. That's not what made them what they were. One thing I've learned in all my research is that they didn't think they were remarkable at all. I really believe that if we had a chance to ask them, "Why did you do such great things?" they'd say, "What things?" or "Who, me? You can't be talking about me." They didn't view themselves as unusual in any way.

Why was the way so hard? Why was the cost so high? Part of the answer is in Moses 1:39: "For behold, this is my work and my glory—to bring to pass the immortality and eternal life of man." That is what these stories are all about: God's work. They are God's story, and it is an incredible one. He says in his own words that his purposes are twofold: to bring to pass our immortality and our eternal life.

President Boyd K. Packer described our existence as a three-act play: the premortal life is act one; mortality, where we are now, is act two; and the postmortal life will be act three.[18] If a person comes into a play during act two, it is not surprising for him to be puzzled. Unless he knows what has happened in act one, and unless he has a sense of what will happen in act three, a lot of act two will not make sense. So let's talk briefly about God's plan for us. Some time in the distant past, we were born spiritually. Before that we were intelligences. As spirit children, male and female, we lived with our heavenly parents in the celestial kingdom. If we were with God and our heavenly mother in the celestial kingdom, what ever would have possessed us to leave? Isn't that what we are after—to be back in the celestial kingdom with God? So why did we have to leave? This is a very important point. Most of the Christian world's idea of heaven is to return to live with God, but we believe there is something far more significant. Not only do we want to live *with* God, we want to be *like* God. That is what eternal life, God's life, means. What was God like when we were there living with him in the celestial kingdom? Three things are significant. First, he had a glorified, immortal, physical body. We did not; we were only spirits. Second, he had a divine nature, every attribute in absolute perfection. We did not. Third, he had an eternal wife, and they were able to have eternal children. Thus we were living with God in heaven, but we certainly were not like him.

To move forward, to become like God, we had to have a body. Having a body is not just an incidental by-product of mortality. It is one of its central purposes. Until we can be connected with a physical, elemental body, we cannot have a fulness of joy (see D&C 93:33–34). In addition, to be like God, we have to acquire divine attributes. Those two objectives brought us to earth. As I understand it, to prove ourselves, we needed four things: first, an imperfect world; second, a mortal body that could endure sickness, irritation, tiredness, and other ills so that we could gain experience; third, agency, for without choice there is no morality; and fourth, opposition, as Lehi explained (see 2 Nephi 2:11), because we can't exercise agency with nothing to choose between and no conflicting enticements toward good or evil. The Fall was necessary to gain a battlefield, and thus began the plan of God. In scriptural terms, life comes down to one word: *warfare*. Metaphors of war—from "put on the armor of righteousness" (2 Nephi 1:23) to "rejoice not against me, O mine enemy: when I fall, I shall arise" (Micah 7:8)—are found everywhere in scripture. The Spirit helps us in many ways—instructing, comforting, and strengthening us—but the ultimate battle is absolutely individual. It is not a team event. It is not a spectator sport.

That is what those early Saints knew. This vision in their hearts drove them to do what they did. Joseph Smith was the means. He was the one chosen to open the Restoration so that we could have the priesthood and the Church, the ordinances and the covenants. But what those people saw was the *why* behind it all.

So what drove these people? Why did an eleven-year-old girl want to read the Book of Mormon? Why did she and a twelve-year-old risk their lives to save a batch of papers? Why did fathers and husbands leave their desperately ill and poor families to serve missions? Why did a cultured and refined woman walk away from a beautiful two-story brick home and never look back? Because these people had a clear vision of God's plan for them, and it never wavered in their hearts.

Let me explain. By September 1846, most of the Saints had crossed Iowa at a terrible price and were preparing to winter at Winter Quarters. (Before that winter was over, about six hundred died at Winter Quarters.) On September 25, Brigham Young received word of the Battle of Nauvoo from a group who had just come from Nauvoo. The last ones still in the city were the poor, the widowed, and the orphans who had not been able to find a way to leave. Mobs finally came in and drove them out, picking up the men and throwing them in the river, driving the women and children with bayonets, threatening to kill them if they crossed back over the river. When Brigham Young received word of that, even though the rest of the Saints were in the most destitute and terrible of conditions themselves, he gathered the brethren and said: "The poor brethren and sisters, widows and orphans, sick and destitute, are now lying on the west bank of the Mississippi, waiting for teams and wagons and means to remove them. Now is the time for labor. Let *the fire of the covenant*, which you made in the house of the Lord burn in your hearts like flame unquenchable."[19]

Brigham Young didn't talk to them about the suffering of those poor people. He called to their minds the covenants they had made with God in the house of the Lord. He went on: "[I want every man who is able to] rise up with his teams and go straightway. . . . This is a day of action and not of argument." Before too many days had passed, almost a hundred wagons were moving east to go and rescue the poor.[20] I love that phrase, "the fire of the covenant," because that is what drove these people. That is why they did what they did.

Why was the way so hard then? Why is it still so hard today? We have to remember what God is about. Remember, his work and his glory is to bring to pass our immortality and our eternal life. To make us like him is not something that is done by waving a wand. At a time when the Saints were driven barefoot across sleet-filled prairies, when it was reported that women and children were marched thirty miles and left bloody footprints in the snow from their lacerated feet[21]—at that very time in our history, the Lord said in revelation: "Whoso layeth down his life in my cause, for my name's sake, shall find it again, even life eternal. Therefore, be not afraid of your enemies, for I have decreed in my heart, saith the Lord, that I will prove you in all things" (D&C 98:13–14). Why? Because a god doesn't buckle under pressure. When things get really rough a god doesn't say, "Hey, I'm outta here. I don't want to do this." Who "will abide in my covenant, even unto death, . . . may be found worthy," he says (v. 14). Worthy of what? Worthy to be with God. Worthy of godhood.

The early Saints had the fire of the covenant in their hearts. That fire helped them demonstrate faith, and out of faith came great power. Mary Elizabeth Rollins, after she read the Book of Mormon, after she saved those papers, wrote of yet another experience in her journal. When she and her group of Saints were driven out of Jackson County, they camped in the low bottomlands of the Missouri River. Mobbers threatened the Mormons with death if they didn't leave the county. One or two families, when it was all finished, were left on the south side at the mercy of the mobs because there was not money enough to ferry everyone across the river. Greatly fearing, those who were left decided to fish during the night, hoping to sell their catch, if any, to get enough money to ferry over. The next day, they brought in three small fish and a catfish that weighed fourteen pounds. In her journal Mary Elizabeth says, "On opening it, what was their astonishment to find three bright silver half dollars [in its stomach], just the amount needed to carry the rest" of them across the ferry to join their brothers and sisters.[22] Coincidence? No, the power of faith.

Amanda Smith was the wife of Warren Smith and the mother of Sardius and Alma, who was so brutally wounded in Haun's Mill. When her little son was carried out of the blacksmith shop, she said, "I looked at the wound. It was the size of a small melon. There was no hip joint, there was just shattered bone and a huge gap." She laid him down and asked her son, "Alma, do you believe the Lord made your hip?"

"I do, Momma."

"Alma, do you believe he can make you another one?"

"I do, Momma."

She then bowed her head and prayed. She asked the Lord, "If it's your will that my son be taken, then take him now in his innocence, but if it is not your will, then help me." No sooner had she finished that prayer than words began to flow into her mind. She directed her son Willard to go to a firepit, get some ashes and pour water over them, and bring that water to her. She directed another child to go down to the millstream and find the roots of some slippery elm. She bathed the wound, the ash making a lye that bleached the flesh until, she said, it looked as white as chicken flesh. And then she packed the wound with a slippery elm poultice, following the directions of the Spirit.[23] Nine years later, in the spring of 1847, Alma Smith, his mother, and other family members left for Utah. Alma Smith walked every step of the way, without a cane, without a crutch. He was preserved for a long life of service. I can imagine him telling his story and walking back and forth without a limp to show his listeners what God can do for those who keep their covenants.[24]

So, if God can work miracles, what of those who died or whose limbs were not restored in the exodus to Zion? In a Sunday School class in southern Utah some thirty years after the Willie and Martin Handcart Companies reached Salt Lake, a Sunday School teacher was being critical. What a foolish decision it had been to leave so late in the season and to be caught in the winter storms, he noted. How easily the tragedy could have been avoided. An old man in the back of the class stood up and said, in substance, the following: "I ask you to stop this criticism. You are discussing a matter you know nothing about. Cold historic facts mean nothing here for they give no proper interpretation of the questions involved. Was it a mistake to send the handcart company out so late in the season? Yes! But I was in that company and my wife," and he named some others. "We suffered beyond anything you can imagine and many died of exposure and starvation, but did you ever hear a survivor of that company utter a word of criticism? No one of that company has ever apostatized or left the church. . . . I have pulled my handcart when I was so weak and weary from illness and lack of food that I could hardly put one foot ahead of the other. I have looked ahead and seen a patch of sand or a hill slope and I have said, 'I can only go that far and there I must give up, for I cannot pull the load through it.' I have gone on to that sand and when I reached it the cart began pushing me! I have looked back many times to see who was pushing my cart, but my eyes saw no one." And then he said, "I knew then that the Angels of God were there. Was I sorry that I chose to come by handcart? No! Neither then nor any minute of my life since. The price we paid to become acquainted with God was a privilege to pay, and I am thankful that I was privileged to come in the Martin Handcart Company."[25] This brother had not lost the vision, the fire of the covenant. Doctrine and Covenants 84:88 reads, "Whoso receiveth you, there I will be also, for I will go before your face. I will be on your right hand and on your left, and my Spirit shall be in your hearts, and mine angels round about you, to bear you up."

In 1842, a few weeks after organizing the Relief Society, Joseph Smith made a most remarkable statement. He said to the sisters: "If you live up to these principles, how great and glorious will be your reward in the celestial kingdom! If you live up to your privileges, the angels cannot be restrained from being your associates."[26] That is the promise to all. That is why we too—the inheritors of the fire of the covenant—will continue in carrying out God's work and his glory. That is the legacy left to us by these remarkable people who were driven by a vision of what they could become and did not falter from it.

Notes

1. Ivan J. Barrett, *Joseph Smith and the Restoration: A History of the Church to 1846* (Provo: Brigham Young University Press, 1973), 391–92.
2. Leonard J. Arrington and Susan Arrington Madsen, "Drusilla Dorris Hendricks: 'Mother's Little Christian'" in *Sunbonnet Sisters* (Salt Lake City: Bookcraft, 1984), 29–30.
3. Barrett, *Joseph Smith and the Restoration*, 392.
4. Arrington and Madsen, *Sunbonnet Sisters*, 30. See Carol Cornwall Madsen, *In Their Own Words: Women and the Story of Nauvoo* (Salt Lake City: Deseret Book, 1994), 161–68, for the rest of Drusilla Dorris Hendricks' story.
5. Joseph Smith, *History of The Church of Jesus Christ of Latter-day Saints*, ed. B. H. Roberts, 2d ed. rev., 7 vols. (Salt Lake City: The Church of Jesus Christ of Latter-day Saints, 1932–51), 3:175.

6. Much of the description that follows is drawn from Barrett, *Joseph Smith and the Restoration*, 399–401. See also B. H. Roberts, *The Missouri Persecutions* (Salt Lake City: Bookcraft, 1965), 232–37.

7. Smith, *History of the Church*, 3:186.

8. Leland H. Gentry, "History of the Latter-day Saints in Northern Missouri from 1836 to 1839," Ph.D. dissertation (Brigham Young University, 1965), 432.

9. Gentry, "Latter-day Saints in Northern Missouri," 432–33; spelling standardized.

10. Gentry, "Latter-day Saints in Northern Missouri," 432.

11. *Church History in the Fulness of Times* (Salt Lake City: The Church of Jesus Christ of Latter-day Saints, 1993), 79–82.

12. Adapted from "Mary Elizabeth Rollins Lightner," *Utah Genealogical and Historical Magazine* 17 (July 1926): 194. For more details, see "Mary Elizabeth Rollins Lightner: A Mormon Girl with Courage," in Arrington and Madsen, *Sunbonnet Sisters*, 13–20.

13. Adapted from "Mary Elizabeth Rollins Lightner," 196. See also Barrett, *Joseph Smith and the Restoration*, 250–51.

14. Adapted from Mary Lightner, "Testimony of Mary Elizabeth Lightner," address to Brigham Young University, 14 April 1905, Provo, Utah, BYU Archives and Manuscripts, typescript, 3.

15. Susan Easton Black and William G. Hartley, ed., *The Iowa Mormon Trail: Legacy of Faith and Courage* (Orem: Helix, 1997), 112.

16. Adapted from "Bishop Jens Neilsen: A Brief Biography Prepared by Albert R. Lyman," unpublished manuscript in possession of the author, 2–3.

17. As reported to the author in an interview with two grandchildren of Jens and Elsie Nielsen, 17 October 1996.

18. Boyd K. Packer, "The Play and the Plan," Church Educational System Fireside for College-age Young Adults, 7 May 1995.

19. Black and Hartley, *Iowa Mormon Trail*, 163; italics added.

20. Black and Hartley, *Iowa Mormon Trail*, 163.

21. Barrett, *Joseph Smith and the Restoration*, 264.

22. Adapted from "Mary Elizabeth Rollins Lightner," 197.

23. Adapted from Jean Brown Fonnesbeck, "From an Old Diary," *Young Woman's Journal* 29 (July 1918): 386–87.

24. Fonnesbeck, "From an Old Diary," 388–89.

25. Maurine Jensen Proctor and Scot Facer Proctor, *The Gathering: Mormon Pioneers on the Trail to Zion* (Salt Lake City: Deseret Book, 1996), 196.

26. Joseph Smith, *Teachings of the Prophet Joseph Smith*, sel. Joseph Fielding Smith (Salt Lake City: Deseret Book, 1938), 226–27.

"A VOICE DEMANDS THAT WE ASCEND": DARE THE ENCOUNTER

Ann N. Madsen

A little over three thousand years ago the children of Israel camped before Mount Sinai (Exodus 19:2). The Lord invited the people to become a "kingdom of priests, and a holy nation" (Exodus 19:6) and commanded Moses to prepare the people for a personal encounter with their God. "Sanctify them to day and to morrow, and let them wash their clothes and be ready against the third day: for the third day the Lord will come down in the sight of all the people upon mount Sinai" (Exodus 19:10–11).

But the people were not ready. Moses alone climbed to the peak of that mountain. "And all the people saw the thunderings, and the lightnings, and the noise of the trumpet, and the mountain smoking: and when the people saw it, they removed, and stood afar off. And they said unto Moses, Speak thou with us, and we will hear: but let not God speak with us, lest we die" (Exodus 20:18–19).

So they would not go up.

The ideas I share with you here are about "going up," about daring the encounter which our forefathers feared. In Abraham Joshua Heschel's words: "Daily a voice demands that we ascend. . . . There are no easy roads, there is no simple advice. . . . The way of [man] is a way of rising to the peak of the mountain. . . . The vision of reaching the peak gives meaning to our touching its border."[1]

How I love the people who have helped me catch a vision of the peak and a glimpse of the Lord there.

Our relationship with the Lord is the prototype for all our other relationships. We had a closeness with the Lord before we came here. We are

Ann Nicholls Madsen received her master's degree in ancient studies at Brigham Young University. She has taught the Old Testament at BYU and has also taught at the BYU Center in Jerusalem. She served with her husband in the New England States Mission, where he presided, and has lectured with him in Scandinavia, the United States, and Austria. She has contributed articles to the *Ensign* and the *New Era* and numerous compilations on gospel topics.

not establishing, but reestablishing, that relationship. He is no stranger to us. Over and over again, he invites us to come to him: "Draw nigh to God, and he will draw nigh to you" (James 4:8; see also D&C 88). "Return unto me, and I will return unto you" (Malachi 3:7). In Jeremiah, the Lord explains, "For I know the thoughts that I think toward you . . . thoughts of peace, and not of evil, to give you a future of peace."[2]

"Then shall ye call upon me [probably in that future], and ye shall pray unto me, and I will hear you.

"And ye shall seek me, and find me, when ye shall seek me with all your heart.

"And I *will be found of you*, saith the Lord" (Jeremiah 29:11–14; italics added).

This is no idle pursuit. How do we find him? Where do we find him? I will focus on six areas that have proven fruitful to me in my search.

The companionship of the Spirit is our goal. He it is who bears witness of our Father and his Son and carries their messages to our hearts and minds. Where can we hope to find that companionship, to feel that spirit? In the temple? At sacrament meeting? Is this enough? No, surely not. We all can prepare a home or an apartment where he will feel welcome.

FURNISH THE HOME WITH VIRTUE SO THAT THE LORD WILL FEEL AT HOME THERE

Bruce Hafen, the dean of the BYU Law School, speaks of the world today as a polluted river. We are like fish swimming in the pollution, often carried by a current of which we are only vaguely aware, until someone swims against the current, and we see the contrast. The Lord has commanded us to stand in holy places. But how do we do that in such a world? Where are the holy places? I suggest that we should make our homes holy places. And I have five suggestions under that heading:

Furnish the Home with Great Books

I'm the kind of person who finds it very difficult, after I have purchased a volume or have checked it out from the library, not to finish the book. I am a book finisher, or I *was* a book finisher, but I have discovered that is not always the wisest course. Someone has said, "Don't reach your white-gloved hand into mud and expect the mud to come out 'glovey.'" I read reviews of the movie I want to see so I know what to expect. But if I discover, after I arrive at the theatre, that it's not what I had been led to believe, then even though I hate to waste the money, I leave.

Art That Lifts Can Furnish a Home

We should fill our homes with precious objects for remembering, things that bring back memories of uplifting moments in our lives—a delicate, painted Japanese fan stands open on my bedside table. There are all kinds of objects that may be beautiful because of what they mean to us and because of what we identify with them. There are all kinds of art reproductions that can be purchased relatively inexpensively. Simple, beautiful art changes the whole character of a room.

Orderliness, Another Chance at Design

Orderliness in the home really is a chance at design. Occasionally I try to see my home with new eyes. I get so accustomed to the stack of papers that gets higher and higher on my desk; then my mother comes to visit, and I think, "That really looks terrible there." When we had the BYU religion faculty in our home for a social some time ago, I saw cobwebs and dirt I didn't realize had been there. We need to look with new eyes once in a while. We would invite the Lord into a clean and orderly place. I've used the word orderly for a purpose. Clean is for Saturday nights. Orderly can be for most of the time.

Television Sparingly, So Sparingly

It is the polluted water in which we swim. I think the remote control is an essential part of television today. There are things that we can't turn off fast enough to avoid leaving an indelible image in our minds. We need to be able to "click" it away immediately.

The problem with us is, unlike computers, we can't dump trash. My computer has a sign that appears periodically with the message, "The memory is nearly full; store to disk." And then if I want to save what I have, I need to store it someplace else. It also has the commands: "erase" or "erase whole disk." My Macintosh has an outline on the screen of a garbage can labeled "trash." One command I can give is "empty trash." I can put whatever I want to dispose of into the trash file. Then I press the button marked "empty trash," and it's gone forever. But, unfortunately, our minds are not like that. We see an image, and it's recorded indelibly.

I read once about doctors who did a study of patients under full anesthetic who could later remember, under hypnosis, the conversation in the operating room while they were undergoing surgery. That frightens me. The things we see, the things we experience, the things we allow into our minds are there. To remove them requires conscientious effort.

Furnish the Home with Glorious Music

Our spirits respond to certain chords, melodies, and modulations in spite of ourselves. We are lifted or beaten down by music. In 1878 Joseph Young said:

"Man of himself is an instrument of music; and when the chords of which he is composed are touched, and salute the ear, the sounds appeal to his spirit and the sentiment to his understanding. If the strains are harmonious, he endorses and enjoys them with supreme delight; whether the tones are from a human voice or from an instrument, they arrest his attention and absorb his whole being."[3]

We've all seen young people with their whole being absorbed by music. Lex de Azevedo, an LDS musician, gave a talk some time ago called "Put 'No Trespassing' Signs on Your Mind," in which he said:

"Music can also affect your emotions. Music speaks in a language more powerful than words, for it is the language of emotion. Words communicate ideas. Music communicates feelings. While words get stuck in the thinking part of our brain, music sails through to reach the innermost corners of our emotional being. It is our emotions and feelings that really govern our lives and actions. This is precisely why music is such a wonderful, dangerous, exciting power. . . .

"Music is an instant recall mechanism to past memories. We can relive spiritually uplifting moments as well as times we would best forget. Images—good and evil—parade before our minds when we hear the music associated with them. Music is an effective means of indoctrination for good or evil, for we will not soon forget that which we learn with music."[4]

Ads on television teach us that so quickly. How many times have all of us driven in our cars and started humming a tune, the last tune we heard? Often, the music was an accompaniment to an advertisement, whose words were designed to induce us to buy a product. We carry many musical memories with us.

De Azevedo ends by saying our minds are sacred: "Let us put up 'No Trespassing' signs on our minds. Do not allow anyone to pollute your mind. Each thought is important. Do you realize that with each thought we inch our way toward heaven or hell? The key to overcoming the world is in controlling our minds. . . . If we program our minds properly[,] our bodies will follow.

"I submit to you the unclean things of our society are largely the culture that is produced by a telestial world. Let us not ask what evil we can tolerate, but let us find ways of filling our minds with celestial stimuli.

"For only to the extent that we feed our minds celestial food will we have the strength, spirituality, [and] motivation to reach our divine potential."[5]

There are songs that I sometimes find myself singing. I realize that when I'm the most uplifted, when I've felt the Spirit, there are certain songs from "The Messiah," and from other beautiful compositions that give words and music to the feelings of my heart. Good music has the power to put us in tune with Heaven.

Constructing a positive environment that incorporates all these elements helps us furnish a virtuous home, in which we can practice godliness. We can learn eventually to respond in a godly manner. We can learn godly attributes and incorporate them into our lives. In the Old Testament, the high priest wore on his head a hammered gold crown on which was engraved, "Holiness to the Lord." On each of our temples there also is a sign proclaiming, "Holiness to the Lord." It is a promise to put that on a building. I wonder if we could, at least in our minds, have that kind of promise on our homes. "Holiness to the Lord"—in this place there will be only those things conducive to the presence of the Lord's Spirit. While this is a lofty ideal, we can work to make our homes holy places.

We can be aided in this process by becoming close to people who are close to the Lord. We should invite them into our homes. A beautiful woman in Hawaii shared a line from her patriarchal blessing with me, "Seek women companions who live beautiful and clean lives, lives that our Heavenly Father meant for women to live." After I heard that, I realized I'd done that all my life. I've been drawn like a moth to a flame to women who were spiritual and uplifting. I have looked for and found every year of my life a new friend, full of righteousness, someone who I knew was better than I was, and I knew if I spent time with her, I could become better as well. My friends are such queenly women. As I look back on the thirty or forty years I have known some of them, I wonder how I had the ability as a young woman, wife, and mother to choose such friends, who contribute a continuing righteousness to me. Every day I feel as if I'm bathed in righteousness. Our circle of encouraging, faithful friends will help us to make wise choices. They will be there in our times of struggle, pain, and grief to lift and bless us. Find friends; look for friends. Don't try to go it alone.

We also benefit from those men and women whose full-time preoccupation is to listen to and serve the Lord. In our wards, we must listen to the bishop and our home teachers, who have been called to serve and bless our lives. They are not paid for that service; they do it voluntarily. Sometimes they do it well, sometimes not so well, but they do it. Our home teachers' coming shows they love us. We may not need any message they might bring; their message is inherent in their coming. What we need is to know they care about us.

There is a right way to influence others. It is called righteousness. And righteousness does influence others. As we are righteous, people are drawn to that, as I am drawn to women of righteousness as friends. It is my personal feeling that there is a spirit that accumulates in a home as righteous people come and go there. I had the privilege of living in the New England mission home for three years. I can remember sitting in that living room, sometimes all alone, being so tired. I've never been so tired in my life as I was on my mission. Sitting there very tired and just absorbing the surrounding spirit, I thought, "President McKay was here. Levi Edgar Young was here. Spencer W. Kimball was here. Just a few weeks ago, Hugh B. Brown was here." All the things they said, the prayers they offered, the feelings they experienced in that room seemed to be reflected. We could feel it; it was there; it is still there.

I feel the same way about my own home. When we first moved into our home three years ago, it had been empty for quite a while and had been left by two older people who had passed away. But, I had the feeling that they still lived there. I didn't feel as if it were my house. I kept thinking, "Have I made a terrible mistake? What am I doing in this house?" The house I had lived in for fifteen years had been crowded with the pronouncements of blessings and the settings apart for missions. I remember where the chair sat, facing the fireplace, when our children were set apart for their missions. Now I was in this home where no children of mine had lived. Was it ever going to be the kind of home I wanted it to be? Then I realized, after the first Thanksgiving dinner with our children and grandchildren, it was different. Things were broken; there was dirt on the walls, and the carpet was dirty. But in addition, there was a different feeling. We have family prayer there daily. Now the place in the kitchen where we kneel to have our family prayers in the

morning with the sun streaming in the window is a sacred spot. There
have been a few blessings given in that home. The members of the BYU
Religion Department came a few weeks ago. When I look around, I see
them there. I see other people whom I love and admire. That's how I feel
about homes. There is a spirit in the home. People used to walk into the
New England mission home and say, "What is it about this house?" I
wanted to say, "Well, there's Levi Edgar Young, and there's S. Dilworth
Young, and there's Hugh B. Brown, and Spencer W. Kimball; that's what's
about this house."

YOU WILL FIND THE LORD IN THE SCRIPTURES

The scriptures are his books; he is there. "Immerse yourself in the
scriptures, and the distance narrows between yourself and Deity." I think
it was President Kimball who said that. When I lived in the mission field,
we used to study for two hours in the morning with the missionaries. We
couldn't send them down to study and then not study ourselves, so for
three years, I studied for two hours almost daily. When we returned to
Provo from our mission, however, I was really tired and started sleeping in
each morning. I did that day after day and, finally, after six months, I felt
rested. But I didn't read the scriptures. I didn't have study class with
myself for two hours every morning. After six months had passed, I felt
as if I were never going to adjust as a returned missionary. I thought,
"There's something wrong with me. All the spirituality I've ever known
in my life has now leaked out; I used it all on that mission, and I'm never
going to have those good feelings again." One day, I thought, "Maybe I
should study the scriptures again; that might help me." So I got up every
morning, and from then until now, I have studied the scriptures daily. My
husband chides me and thinks I'm a "scriptureholic." I teach the scriptures at BYU, so I'm required to study to teach. I'm so glad I need to. It's
such a privilege.

Now I study on the telephone with a friend every morning but
Saturday and Sunday. I'm so appreciative that we have this appointment,
that we call each other every day and read. We don't discuss theology.
We have long conversations sometimes, but we just *read* the scriptures.
We psychoanalyze each other and do a few things before or after, but
when we're ready to read the scriptures, we say a short prayer, asking the
Lord to bless us and then we read. Recently, she said to me, "This is so
great." We finish, and she'll say, "I'm not going to say this again, Ann.
You'll just laugh at me if I say it, I know." And I'll say, "What?" and she'll

say, "This is so great." And I'll say, "Yes, you did say that yesterday, you know." That was even after reading Leviticus.

Cathy Thomas, who also teaches part-time in the BYU Religion Department, and I have studied Greek together. I do the same thing to her. We get finished with studying, reading the New Testament, I haltingly, she really reading in Greek, helping me, teaching me as we go. I say, "I feel wonderful, but I was so tired when we started. What happens that, although we've studied so hard for this last hour or two hours, I feel great? What's happened to me?" I don't know what it is; I don't know how to explain it exactly, but I feel better afterwards. I feel as rested as if I'd had a long nap.

I'd suggest occasionally reading other English translations besides the King James Version. If we sometimes read another translation, we may see things we completely missed before. We all have a tendency to avoid seeing the familiar. We come to familiar scriptures, and they run off us like water off a duck. We read, "Choose you this day whom ye will serve; . . . but as for me and my house, we will serve the Lord" (Joshua 24:15). We say, "Oh yes, I know that," and go across it. But if we read it in another translation, it's just different enough that we *think* when we come to it, and we hear it and see it in a way that we may not have seen it before. I'd suggest as another English translation the New International Version. I've found that particular translation is very close to the Hebrew and Greek translations, but it's also different enough to shake us a bit, so that we have to think about what we're reading.

We should also read the words of those who have seen the Lord or who have established a secure relationship with him. There is such power in their words. Their words have been preserved for this very purpose so that we can feel that power. They are his witnesses. Courageous Abinadi declared just before he was to die, "He is the light and the life of the world; yea, a light that is endless, that can never be darkened; yea, and also a life which is endless, that there can be no more death" (Mosiah 16:9). And Joseph Smith, who like so many other prophets first saw the heavens opened as a young and innocent lad, reported:

"I saw a pillar of light exactly over my head, above the brightness of the sun, which descended gradually until it fell upon me.

" . . . When the light rested upon me I saw two Personages, whose brightness and glory defy all description, standing above me in the air. One of them spake unto me, calling me by name and said, pointing to the other—'This is My Beloved Son. Hear Him!'" (Joseph Smith—History 1:16–17).

I love those words because they carry with them the power of the experience of the man, a chosen servant of the Lord, fourteen years of age, to whom God and his Son appeared. When I read that, the Lord has the opportunity, the Spirit has the opportunity, to testify of its truth. That's why I loved to quote it to people when I was a missionary. In Isaiah 43:10–11 we read, "Ye are my witnesses, saith the Lord. . . . I, even I, am the Lord; and beside me there is no saviour." We also can become the witnesses of whom he speaks.

WE MUST TRULY REPENT, TRULY FORGIVE

We will find the Lord if we prepare ourselves to feel comfortable in his presence. No unclean thing can enter the Lord's presence. We must truly repent, truly forgive: two sides of the same coin. We must purify our own lives without procrastinating or finding excuses to avoid this mighty change. Hugh Nibley has said, "The wicked can always find someone wickeder than they. It is a shabby substitute for repentance to point to someone wickeder than you are. It will give you a virtuous feeling. It will surely block up the way to your own repentance."⁶ We often say, "Well, I'm not as bad as so and so," and that somehow makes us feel better. We do block the way to our own repentance by finding people wickeder than ourselves. In J. Richard Clarke's classic devotional on repentance delivered at BYU in 1984, he quoted Elder Orson F. Whitney, who said:

"Repentance is not that superficial sorrow felt by the wrongdoer when 'caught in the act'—a sorrow not for the sin, but for sin's detection. Chagrin is not repentance. Mortification and shame alone bring no change of heart toward right feeling and right living. Even remorse is not all there is to repentance. In highest meaning and fullest measure, repentance is equivalent to reformation; the beginning of the reformatory process being a resolve to 'sin no more.'"⁷

I love what we learn from the scriptures: "Resist the devil, and he will flee from you" (James 4:7). Sin no more, leave your sins. Bishop Clarke continued by quoting Elder Nephi Jensen:

"Faith unto repentance is the great eternal saving principle. Faith unto repentance cleanses the mind, purifies the heart, chastens the affections, nerves the will with resolute strength to conquer evil, and ennobles and perfects character."⁸

Bishop Clarke warned us that repentance is no trifling thing. He called it "an arduous journey from darkness to light"[9]; of course, God is in the light. Our journey is toward him. President Kimball taught us, "Repentance is the Lord's law of growth, his principle of development, and his plan for happiness."[10] It is the normal daily process we should be going through in order to be happy.

Tshuv is the Hebrew word for repentance, which means "to return, to turn back." Remember when the Lord said, "Return unto me, and I will return unto you" (Malachi 3:7). "Draw nigh to God, and he will draw nigh to you" (James 4:8). Those are not just tautologies saying, "Well, if I'm close, you'll be close." The Lord meant that we should leave our sins in favor of his presence, so that we could come into his presence. We must *forsake* our sins. It was Lamoni's father, the king in the Book of Mormon who understood and exclaimed in his first prayer, "I will give away all my sins to know thee" (Alma 22:18). I wonder if that won't be true for each one of us? If we want to know the Lord, ultimately we will have to give away all our sins. I'm not saying we can't know him until we've given them all away, but we need to be in that process if we want to meet him.

We must trust in the Atonement. Our only real affirmation of the Atonement is our own repentance. Otherwise, we mock God. President Kimball also said, "God is good. He is eager to forgive. He wants us to perfect ourselves and maintain control of ourselves. He does not want Satan and others to control our lives."[11] We don't want other people to control our lives. God doesn't want Satan and other wicked people to lead us into doing things that are not good. "We must learn that keeping our Heavenly Father's commandments represents the *only* path to total control of ourselves, the only way to find joy, truth, and fulfillment in this life and in eternity."[12] In the video *The Faith of an Observer*, a documentary about Hugh Nibley, that splendid man said with the accumulated wisdom of his seventy-five years, "There are only two things we can do with distinction in this life: repent and forgive." I would suggest that we cannot understand the one without experiencing the other.

Dennis Rasmussen in his wonderful little book *The Lord's Question*, taught me this: "To hallow my life, [God] taught me to endure sorrow rather than cause it, to restrain anger rather than heed it, to bear injustice rather than inflict it. 'Resist not evil,' [Jesus] said in the Sermon on the Mount (Matthew 5:39). Evil multiplies by the response it seeks to provoke, and when I return evil for evil, I engender corruption myself. The chain of evil is broken for good when a pure and loving heart absorbs a hurt and forbears to hurt in return. The forgiveness of Christ bears no grudge. The love of Christ allows no offense to endure. The compassion of Christ embraces all things and draws them toward himself. Deep within every child of God the light of Christ resides, guiding, comforting, purifying the heart that turns to him."[13]

What a privilege we have to forgive those who offend us or even sin against us. I love Carol Lynn Pearson's poem "The Forgiving":[14]

> Forgive?
> Will I forgive,
> You cry.
> But
> What is the gift,
> The favor?
> You would lift
> Me from
> My poor place
> To stand beside
> The Savior.
> You would have
> Me see with
> His eyes,
> Smile,
> And with Him
> Reach out to
> Salve
> A sorrowing heart—
> For one small
> Moment
> To share in
> Christ's great art.
> Will I forgive,
> You cry.
> Oh,
> May I—
> May I?

Sometimes I say out loud to myself, "Oh, may I, may I?" What an attitude about forgiveness. God tells us that he will forgive whom he will forgive (D&C 64:10). I think he meant that he is ready to forgive all of us when we repent; however, he reminds us that we must "forgive all men." I would add, if we want to be like him. He is willing to forgive all of us. A dear friend taught me that we learn to forgive by changing ourselves. Joseph Smith instructed, "The nearer we get to our Heavenly Father, the more we are disposed to look with compassion on perishing souls; we feel that we want to take them upon our shoulders, and cast their sins behind our backs."[15] I think that's a great barometer to test ourselves to see how close we are getting to God. The closer we are to our Heavenly Father, the more we have these feelings of compassion and desire to forgive and forget.

HE WILL FIND US IF WE WILL BE WHO WE ARE

We are each unique; we are each different from everyone else. We should respect that uniqueness and be ourselves. Socrates said, "The ignorance which causes vice and immorality is not ignorance of moral principles or laws, but ignorance of self." Carl Rogers commented on a curious paradox: "When I accept myself as I am, then I change."[16] We must first be honest with ourselves; we can fool many people much of the time, but in this one relationship, God knows us better than we know ourselves. We can't trick him.

We try to hide, though. A short time ago in my afternoon Old Testament class a strapping ex-football player walked into the class with a big soft drink in his hand (this is 3:00 in the afternoon), sat down behind a young woman and positioned his head right behind her head. Thinking that then he wasn't seen, he began to drink, the big cup coming up behind her head and going back down, coming up behind her head and going back down. I think sometimes we behave the same way—like children who hide their heads and think they are invisible to others. That's how Mike acted with his drink. He was in full view to me. I knew what he was doing. And sometimes it was all I could do not to laugh—it struck me so funny that he was hiding behind her head with that big cup. What a waste of time it is to make excuses, to rationalize, to defend ourselves to God. Remember, as he was sending Samuel the prophet to find David among his family, the Lord said to him, "The Lord looketh on the heart" (1 Samuel 16:7). The Hebrew says *le lev*, which means "to the heart." God looks *to* the heart. He looks to it and into it, not just on it.

Our cousin Jack Adamson once wrote some lines in a prayer of dedication that have continued to mean much to me: "We ask for a greater freedom, that inner freedom that comes from an honest searching of ourselves. Let us be the first to know our own corruptions and evasions and surrenders. . . . Be to us, God of our Fathers, the fire and the rain; stretch and shrink us. Send us sweetness and pain. And give us the courage to be vulnerable. What we are not, let us not pretend to be. What we are, let us discover and express."[17] We each have acquired layers of mortality made up of earthly habits, but beneath these, our spirits are sons and daughters of God. As my friend in Hawaii put it so well:

"We must understand that each of us has a pedigree of divinity. We are daughters of a perfect God. That realization alone gives worth to each of us. We must continue to build ourselves and love ourselves enough that when challenges face us, we will use these opportunities to grow rather than to fall. Every woman carries within herself the makings of a successful social being. Joy, strength, and our own future are all within us, and not out there someplace. We make the difference."

James Allen wrote: "Man is made or unmade by himself; in the armoury of thought he forges the weapons by which he destroys himself; he also fashions the tools with which he builds for himself heavenly mansions of joy and strength and peace. . . .

"Of all the beautiful truths pertaining to the soul which have been restored and brought to life in this age, none is more gladdening or fruitful of divine promise and confidence than this—that man is the master of thought, the moulder of character, and the maker and shaper of condition, environment, and destiny."[18]

We need to catch the vision of ourselves, of the powers within us. Sometimes we delude ourselves into thinking someone else is responsible for our sins. We see ourselves as a victim. The message of free agency is that "I am not a victim." We are responsible for our choices. We can change.

I love this scripture hidden away in the little book of Micah. Micah was lonely in a very wicked generation and in the midst of his proclaiming what was going to happen to that generation, he said: "Therefore I will look unto the Lord: I will wait for the God of my salvation: my God will hear me. Rejoice not against me, O mine enemy: when I fall, I shall arise; when I sit in darkness, the Lord shall be a light unto me" (Micah 7:7–8).

In *our* darkest moments, is the Lord a light unto us? We all have darkest moments, but if, in those moments, there is still that light—it may not be a very big light—but if there's a light, and it's the Lord, and we feel that, we can see it. "When I sit in darkness, the Lord shall be a light unto me."

Eliza R. Snow saw the vision, which she states so powerfully: "[We are] women of God,—women fulfilling high and responsible positions."[19] We walk the earth among wondrous princes and princesses whose potential, like our own, is beyond our comprehension. But God knows who I am and who you really are. Sometimes it may seem as if he is the only one who knows who we really are. Often, we ourselves forget who we are. We must find out from him about ourselves. In 1 Samuel 16:7, we read, " . . . the Lord seeth not as man seeth; for man looketh on the outward appearance, but the Lord looketh on the heart." By deliberately using our agency to heighten our awareness of God, we become more conscious of him. We can try to maintain eternal perspective to see, more nearly, through his eyes, hear through his ears. When I'm having a struggle, I often pray, "Heavenly Father, help me see this one thing the way you see it. I know I can't take in everything, but please just help me see it the way you're seeing it. Help me see this person the way you see him or her."

WE WILL FIND HIM IF WE CALL OUT TO HIM

Pray; talk to the Lord; reach upward; bare your soul to him. Pray for those you love, and for those you hate. Pray for your enemies. Pray for forgiveness. Tell him what you dare not speak aloud to anyone else. Pray for yourself. One morning on the deck of our cabin in the mountains we knelt in morning prayer with a wonderful couple who are our dear friends. One of them led us in prayer, and as he did, my soul was enlarged and my understanding enlightened when he said, "If we have offended thee, in any way, we ask thy pardon. Help us to live consistent with the covenants we have made." He prayed other things, but these two ideas were burned into my heart. In what ways do I offend the Lord? Do I live each day consistent with the covenants I have made with my Heavenly Father? Am I truly grateful? My daughter Mindy told me recently of a prayer she had offered: "Thank you for all the things we forget to thank you for all the time." Then she enumerated them: "I have clothes that fit me now that I'm pregnant. People used to have to wear whatever they had."

It is so easy to *speak* the truth. I often plead with the Lord to help me to *live* the truths that I so easily speak. After the pleading, we must learn to listen. Sometimes, before the "Amen" is said, the answer comes. We start praying, and we pray and pray, and in some of the spaces between, we receive the answer. Sometimes the answer is disguised in the words of the four-year-old who repeats a memorized line in the Primary program, or in a quiet conversation with a friend, or in the words of a faintly remembered patriarch whose blessing has yellowed. Or sometimes it may even come as I drive alone in the car, heading for the paint store, intruding upon my remodeling plans with such power that I cannot deny its source. Sometimes answers may come even before the questions or the pleading. I must learn to store the truth for future reference.

I love the iconography in ancient paintings of a man representing God with his right hand outstretched through the clouds. Later, after Nicea, people forgot that we are truly made in God's image and substituted in their paintings only an outstretched hand which appears to be parting a veil of clouds. I love this image because it represents to me the many times in scripture when the Lord pleads, "My hand is stretched out still" (Isaiah 9:12). I also identify it with the temple. After all we can do, there is grace. How monumentally important it is that Moses saw God and even more for us that Joseph Smith saw the Father and the Son. Joseph found out for himself and for all of us that our prayers are directed and answered by exalted Persons. They are real—they are not the abstractions men impose on us in our day. Can I ever be grateful enough to Joseph Smith for putting me in touch with the true God, creator of this earth, whose plan included a Savior who has borne my griefs and has carried my sorrows and healed me with his wounds—the promised Messiah, my personal Redeemer?

WE WILL FIND HIM IF WE TRUST HIM

God can be trusted. He lives. I am a teacher, and it is my pleasure to teach the Old Testament. It is pure joy to show my students that threading its way through that marvelous work is the absolute certainty of a living God who loves and pleads with his children to trust him. There is indeed a cloud of witnesses.

The Lord chooses many metaphors to teach his children this trust. He compares himself to a shepherd, responsible for all his sheep; to a father, whose son is Israel whom he rescues from slavery with an offer of freedom; to a potter who cannot change the substance of the clay, but who wishes to shape it masterfully; to a refiner of silver who after the dross has been burned away looks for his own reflection in the finished work.

Dare the encounter with God. It is up to each of us. We must choose. God does indeed stand with his arms outstretched, waiting, and a voice within us demands that we ascend. Such an encounter has its risks and its costs because, once we know, we become responsible. But, once we know, all his options are open to us. That is one of the unique teachings of the Restoration. His course is not easy, even now. He weeps or rejoices over us just as we do over our children. Our constant questioning, "Where art thou, Lord?" is mirrored in his final question to us, just as he called for this earth's first children in the garden. "Adam, Eve, where art thou?" (Genesis 3:9). The day will come when I myself, the me whose heart he can read, will be the only answer that will be given.

My daughter Emily has written: "Obedience to the commandments teaches us who we really are and what we really want and, at the same time, obedience enables us to know God and Jesus Christ whom he has sent, to understand their will for us and to choose once again with both body and spirit this time to sustain their plan. It is a choice that we make over and over, all day, every day; and each right choice adds to our knowledge of the truth. If we are faithful, the time will come when we will stand before our God in his glory and see ourselves as we truly are. Then at last, we will comprehend all truth as we exclaim, 'Oh, I see, I'm just like you.'"

In 1 John 3:1–3, we read: "Behold, what manner of love the Father hath bestowed upon us, that we should be called the [children] of God: therefore the world knoweth us not, because it knew him not. Beloved, now are we the [children] of God, and it doth not yet appear what we shall be: but we know that, when he shall appear, we shall be like him; for we shall see him as he is. And every [one] that hath this hope in him purifieth himself, even as he is pure."

This is my witness. I know that God lives. I know that Jesus Christ atoned for my sins. It makes it much easier to repent when I know that the Atonement is real. I know that Joseph Smith was a man of integrity and when he said he saw God, he did. I love the Book of Mormon. I don't know how it could happen. I've tried to translate, and in six months nobody could translate a book like the Book of Mormon alone. I know that it is true and that God intends us to have it in our hands to guide and teach us. I love the living prophets. I know that Ezra Taft Benson has been called of God to lead us. I will do what he tells me to do to the very best of my ability. Then the Lord will see that I really want to know him. I pray that we each will be blessed in our quests to find the Lord. I hope

I've been able to paint a picture for you or open a window for you, that you can see him more clearly.

Notes

1. Abraham Joshua Heschel, *Israel: An Echo of Eternity* (New York: Farrar, Straus and Giroux, 1969), 225–26.
2. I have translated some of the biblical quotations directly from the Greek or from the Hebrew, so the wording may differ somewhat from the King James Version.
3. Joseph Young, "Appendix," *History of the Organization of the Seventies* (Salt Lake City: Deseret News Steam Printing Establishment, 1878), 14–15.
4. Lex de Azevedo, "Put 'No Trespassing' Signs on Your Mind," *Church News*, 11 September 1982, 10.
5. Ibid.
6. Hugh Nibley, "Great Are the Words of Isaiah," Sidney B. Sperry Symposium, 28 January 1978; transcribed by author from tape in her possession.
7. Roy W. Doxey, *Latter-day Prophets and the Doctrine and Covenants*, 2 vols. (Salt Lake City: Deseret Book, 1964), 2:257; quoted in J. Richard Clarke, "The Healing Power of Christ," in *Brigham Young University 1983–84 Fireside and Devotional Speeches*, ed. Cynthia M. Gardner and Karen Seely (Provo: University Publications, 1984), 101.
8. Nephi Jensen, *The World's Greatest Need* (Salt Lake City: Deseret News Press, 1950), 63; quoted in Clarke, "Healing Power of Christ," 101.
9. Clarke, "Healing Power of Christ," 101.
10. Spencer W. Kimball, "The Gospel of Repentance," *Ensign*, October 1982, 2.
11. Ibid.
12. Ibid.
13. Dennis Rasmussen, *The Lord's Question* (Provo, Utah: Keter Foundation, 1985), 63–64.
14. Carol Lynn Pearson, "The Forgiving," in *Picture Windows* (Salt Lake City: Gold Leaf Press, 1996), 59; used by permission.
15. Joseph Smith, *Teachings of the Prophet Joseph Smith*, Joseph Fielding Smith, ed. (Salt Lake City: Deseret Book, 1976), 241.
16. Carl R. Rogers, *On Becoming a Person* (Boston: Houghton Mifflin, 1961), 17.
17. Jack Adamson, prayer of dedication for the University of Utah Art and Architecture Center, 29 September 1971.
18. James Allen, *As a Man Thinketh* (Salt Lake City: Bookcraft, 1964), 13.
19. Eliza R. Snow, "Great Indignation Meeting," *Deseret News Weekly*, 19 January 1870.

IN THE COVENANT OF GRACE

⌒∞⌒

Carol Cornwall Madsen

An old Hebrew legend relates a conversation that Moses had with the Lord. In the story, Moses asked God to grant him three wishes, one of which was to explain by what law He governed the world. Why, Moses wondered, did He allow the just to suffer and the unjust to enjoy happiness or, at other times, permit both to be happy or both to suffer? In answer, God showed Moses His great treasure troves and explained the destination of each, including the various rewards for the good and the just—those people, He said, who give alms to the poor and care for widows and orphans. "But for whom is this treasure?" Moses asked when they came upon one of immense size, and God answered: "Out of the treasures that I have shown thee I give rewards to those who have deserved them by their deeds; but out of this treasure do I give to those who are not deserving, for I am gracious to those also who may lay no claim to My graciousness, and I am bountiful to those also who are not deserving of My bounty." Then he said to Moses, "Thou canst not grasp all the principles which I apply to the government of the world, but some of them I shall impart to thee. When I see human beings who have no claim to expectations from Me . . . but who pray to Me and implore Me, then do I grant their prayers and give them what they require for subsistence."[1]

Moses expected an answer expressed in terms of logic and law, but the Lord answered him with spiritual truths that defied logic and transcended law. "I will meet the demands of justice and reward the good for their deeds," the Lord was saying to Moses, "but I will also serve the claims of mercy. My love extends to all, deserving of it or not." We can recognize the truth of this legend as we begin to understand the place of grace in our lives.

We have probably at times asked the same questions Moses asked. Like

Carol Cornwall Madsen is an associate professor of history and a research historian with the Joseph Fielding Smith Institute for Church History at Brigham Young University. She and her husband, Gordon A. Madsen, are the parents of six children. She serves in her ward Relief Society.

him, we tend to be justice oriented, programmed to expect rewards for good behavior and punishment for bad. But the equation begins to break down, and with it our sense of certitude, when our good efforts seem to go unrewarded and the undeserving seem to prosper. Only when we recognize that we ourselves are often undeserving of God's goodness do we begin to see the blessing it is that life is not wholly governed by our concept of justice, that there is, thankfully, a superior law by which God governs his world.

Paul explained to the Romans the transcendent power of this higher principle. "As by the offence of one judgment came upon all men to condemnation; even so by the righteousness of one the free gift came upon all. . . . For as by one man's disobedience many were made sinners, so by the obedience of one shall many be made righteous. . . . Where sin abounded," Paul concluded, "grace did much more abound" (Romans 5:18–20). Christ's sacrifice, he explained, allows grace to rule our destiny.

I believe we can learn something about this free gift from the parable of the prodigal son (see Luke 15:11–32). Our attention and empathy frequently focus on the faithful older brother, who stayed at his father's side, tending his own inheritance but receiving no celebration and feeling that his erring brother was unjustly rewarded. Perhaps we even tend to identify with him as we seek to live good lives ourselves. But who of us can claim to be the older son? Who of us has not left the Father's presence to tarry awhile in a sin-filled world, succumbing to our own weaknesses but yearning to return one day to our Father's house, even as a servant? The operative power in this story is grace, not justice. The parable is a reminder to us of the limitless reach of God's grace, and God's grace is our hope.

We are rightly taught that most blessings are earned, but as a result we sometimes come to see them as our "right." Such a concept, Lowell Bennion has cautioned, blurs our "vision of God's grace," so freely given.[2] We learn in Ephesians 2:8–9 that "by grace are [we] saved through faith," but "not of [our]selves: it is the gift of God: not of works, lest any man should boast." "What we do by our own effort," Brother Bennion has suggested, "is to prepare ourselves to receive the gifts of Deity. . . . Grace," he says, "precedes, accompanies, and completes individual effort and merit."[3] Our faith is manifest in our works, in both our acceptance of the saving ordinances of the gospel and our Christian service. Our efforts show our willingness to follow God's plan for our salvation and to heed his word to "be not weary in well-doing" (D&C 64:33). They are expressions of gratitude for his blessings, for that unmerited gift of life itself, which he has so graciously given us. They are opportunities to return good for good.

Remember the story of Jean Valjean, the major character in Victor Hugo's *Les Misérables*, the novel that has become such a moving musical production in recent years? At the beginning of the story, Jean Valjean has been released from prison after serving nineteen years for stealing a loaf of bread. As a former prisoner, he is unable to find a place to stay but is finally given refuge in the home of the bishop of Digne, who kindly offers him food and rest. During the night, however, Jean in desperation steals the bishop's silverware and flees. He is immediately captured and returned to the good bishop. Without any censure, the bishop not only gives Jean what he has stolen but also adds his silver candlesticks to the gift, asking only that he use the silver as a means of living an honest life. After nineteen years of undeserved punishment, Jean is given a new life through undeserved mercy. He commits his life thereafter to proving worthy of that merciful act. Grace begets grace.

There is a beautiful symmetry in the doctrines of grace and works. Balancing the Lord's counsel to be engaged in good works are comparable scriptural reminders that "it is by grace that we are saved, after all we can do" (2 Nephi 25:23). The two are complementary. God's grace unlocks the door to salvation, and our faith and works lead us through it and take us closer to him. Both grace and works are freewill offerings—doing for others what they cannot do for themselves: God for us through his grace, and we for others through our works.

Sometimes, in our zeal to do well, we upset the symmetry. We tend to magnify works and forget grace. By defining well-doing as something beyond our daily commitments to family, work, and Church, as many of us do, we diminish the meaning and value of our good works on behalf of those nearest to us, our first responsibilities. In a recent reading of Proverbs 31, which describes the virtuous woman, I found that out of sixteen verses that enumerate her qualities, fifteen praised her good works in behalf of her husband, her children, her servants, and the household for which she was responsible (Proverbs 31:10–31). Whether our primary duties are in or out of the home, or whatever the makeup of our families or households, each of them makes its own claims on us, often leaving us little time and energy for additional well-doing. But life continually changes, and opportunities to serve beyond the needs of our immediate circle really do knock more than once. Were we to look in on our lady of Proverbs some years later, with her children grown and her household cares lessened, perhaps the ratio would be reversed and most of the verses would praise her good works beyond her household.

What I am suggesting, sisters, is that we remember that in our cycle of life there is a season for everything, and whatever we do that produces good, at home or abroad, can be counted as good works and well-doing. Even Eliza R. Snow, who continually urged the sisters to attend to their "social duties," also cautioned them to "let [their] first business be to perform [their] duties at home." "But," she promised, "inasmuch as you are wise stewards, . . . you will find that your capacity will increase, and you will be astonished at what you accomplish."[4]

I would hope that when our need to be engaged in well-doing outpaces our physical capacity, the feelings of guilt that often beset us at those times would surrender to feelings of peace and gratitude for the place of grace in our lives. How often has God told us, My grace is sufficient for you? (see Ether 12:27). Do we ever really ponder what that means? I think he wants us to give grace its due in our lives, to yield ourselves to that unearned blessing more often so that it might lighten our spiritual load and diminish our sense of inadequacy. I think it means to depend more than we do on the enabling power of God's grace to accept and meet our daily commitments, to realize, in short, as the popular hymn tells us, "Grace shall be as your day."[5]

I also think that the Lord would have us remove the emotional and spiritual impediments we create for ourselves that hedge up our souls and deprive us of his Spirit. Perhaps you recall the dream of Martha Cragun Cox that was included in a Relief Society lesson some years ago. Martha was a plural wife and a schoolteacher in St. George in the 1880s, forced to support her children herself because of the federal prosecution of polygamists during that period. In her dream, Martha was bowed down by a heavy chain about her neck from which hung bundles containing the sorrows, disappointments, and resentments that she had allowed to grow and weigh so heavily upon her. Martha was told to place the heavy chain on a rod above the fireplace; then she removed the bundles and examined them one by one. She began to see how embittered she had become and how her resentments had grown far out of proportion to the wrongs she had sustained. She began to realize that the federal marshals, whom she had so bitterly resented, had not done nearly as much harm as they had the power to do; that the mail delivery service that had been imposed on her family to provide, though hard on her young sons, brought them needed income; that those who owed her money were just as poor as she was; and that the 10 percent of her students' tuition kept by the attorney who collected it for her was a small price to pay for relieving her of that burden.

One by one, as she examined them, the bundles began to disappear until she came to the last one, which held her unrelieved sorrow at the loss of her infant. The bundle reminded her of how she often spread out the little baby clothes "on [her] bed on lonely stormy nights when there was no one there to see or hear [her] weep over them." But that bundle also disappeared as she took it from the chain. At last she felt free. When she awoke, she resolved to be truly free. "I made it a rule [from that day on]," she wrote, "to sing a song to the little children on my lap. To the little Indian boy who shared a scolding with [my son] Edward one night and went supperless to his camp, I gave a handsome new shirt to make amends. One day," she noted, "when an Indian woman came to my door with an almost naked child held under her fur robe, I got out the box [of baby clothes] and a feeling of shame came upon me as I gave the little flannel dress and other things to put upon the child, a shame for the tears I had shed over it. I told her to tell the others who had babes to come and get the rest of the things—all but the little shoes—I felt I must keep them. But when I saw the blue feet and legs of one of the little babes I said, 'That bundle must come, all of it, from my chain.'"[6]

When Martha no longer demanded justice from life, she reached a pivotal point in her spiritual understanding. Often forgiving is as difficult as repenting, but Martha experienced a spiritual rebirth when she let go of her catalogue of injustices and allowed herself to forgive. She had made room in her soul for grace when she exchanged bitterness and resentment for kindness and understanding. Through her change of heart, she experienced the transforming power of grace. As she extended it to others, she invited it into her own life. As the Lord said, "You shall receive grace *for* grace" (D&C 93:20; italics added).

May I mention an experience of my own. Some years ago, a series of unfortunate circumstances came my way. I could have coped with any one of them by itself, but collectively they overwhelmed me. I had known discouragement and despondency before and thought that time would be the healing power once again, but as days turned into weeks and weeks into months and more without a change, I knew I had begun to slip into a depression I could not wholly manage. My mind could not let go of the "what ifs" and "if onlys," and the regrets immobilized me. Though my mind told me I had to adjust to what I could not change, I nonetheless felt undeserving of these misfortunes and entitled to some resolution, some compensation, and certainly, at the very least, some comfort or peace of mind. But my demands brought no relief, and I became bitter and resentful.

Through it all I mechanically met the requirements of each day, thinking I could hide my growing sense of helplessness behind a veneer of everyday busyness. But one day my astute daughter asked, "Mother, how long do you intend to go on this way?" I was stunned. My secret, I discovered, was not as secret as I had so foolishly assumed. But more than that, her piercing question let me see, through her eyes, what I had become. I had been broken in mind and spirit by circumstances I could not control, but I had responded with self-pity and, worse, self-righteousness. I was yet to learn that in the Savior's lexicon, self-pity is not the same as a broken heart nor is a bruised ego the same as a contrite spirit. Her question began a long, hard journey in which I learned much about the Savior's patience, love, and efforts to keep us close to him.

Like Martha, I had let bitterness and pride create a barrier between me and the Lord. There was no way that his Spirit could break through that barricade and bring the comfort and strength I so longed for. Only with my daughter's question did I really begin to understand myself, my dependence on God, and especially on his mercy—his forgiveness of my pride and self-righteousness and his willingness to help me find the way back. Each step became an act of faith, of reliance on his guidance and help. I made no more demands, no defiant indictments of the Spirit, no self-righteous outbursts. I had, in a miraculous way for me, experienced a change of heart and, like Martha, felt the transforming power of God's grace. I came to know that in the end, whatever our store of good works and pile of accomplishments, or whatever our weaknesses, mistakes, and unfulfilled intentions, God looks on the heart and knows us by what he sees there (see 1 Samuel 16:7).

When we feel inadequate to meet the challenges life throws our way, we ought to consider this passage from Ether: "I give unto [you] weakness that [you] may be humble; and my grace is sufficient for all [who] humble themselves before me . . . and have faith in me" (Ether 12:27). God knows we are weak. He gave us our weaknesses. And he knows that most of us will demonstrate our weaknesses many times over before we leave this life. This is the risk of agency. But as he so wisely knew, it is through our weakness that we discover humility, and it is through humility that we find God.

We are probably never more humble than when we reach the point of acknowledging our weaknesses in that process we call repentance. Repentance means swallowing our pride, acknowledging our failures, admitting our mistakes, and recognizing our dependence on the Lord. This is not a very easy task, especially at a time when society extols independence, self-reliance, and individual rights. True humility, the scriptures tell us, is a broken heart and a contrite spirit, the elements of repentance, and repentance opens our hearts to receive God's grace. The power of God's grace, in turn, enables us to overcome our weaknesses. Christ's atonement broke the tyranny of justice and opened the way for God's mercy to claim "all those who have a broken heart and a contrite spirit; and unto none else can the ends of the law be answered" (2 Nephi 2:7).

Let me tell you about the transforming power of humility and grace in the life of Waltrout Jeromin of Hamburg, Germany. A child of the war, displaced from her home and left without material resources, and worse, without faith, she eventually married, only to lose her husband several years later in an accident. Her sons helped her as they grew older, but life was never easy for the Jeromins. One day Waltrout reached a point where she saw no solution, felt no hope. For the first time in her life, she turned to prayer. In one of those missionary miracles, two elders just happened to be on her street that day. Within the hour of her prayer, they rang her doorbell. When she looked out the window of her apartment, she saw two young men, their figures clearly visible in a glow that set them apart from the gathering darkness of the evening, even though the porch light was not on. When the missionaries told her they had come to bring a message of hope and peace, Sister Jeromin brought them into her small apartment and with unabating tears listened as they taught her of God's love for her and the atoning sacrifice of his Son. As the missionaries later explained, "We were not sure she heard anything we said; she just cried through the whole lesson. But she accepted the gospel right from the beginning, and her life changed completely."[7] A broken heart, a contrite spirit, and a life touched by grace.

We are living in a time of dramatic social change, much of it directly related to women. It has raised unanswered questions and unresolved issues for many of us, leaving us at times angry, confused, frustrated, and even discouraged. Each of us, I believe, must seek our own answers to the troubling questions and find our own peace. Mine came as my son and daughter went into the mission field. As I saw through them the gospel's power to transform lives, like Sister Jeromin's, I began to rediscover the central place of the gospel in my life. I began to reassess my hierarchy of spiritual needs and to let go of those issues that seemed to me to be secondary to that basic truth. I felt a few of the bundles begin to slip off my chain.

We may not fully understand the theology of the Atonement nor completely comprehend the depth of God's love and mercy for us in giving us the free gift of life by the sacrifice of his Son. But I think we all yearn to feel the touch of grace in our lives, moments that capture the soul and hold it, a willing hostage, away from the assaults and demands of the unjust world in which we live.

My missionary daughter discovered that the moments may be fleeting and unexpected but powerfully moving and life changing. New to the town of Newport, Wales, she and her companion were asked to accompany the elders in their district to visit a man named Brian. Brian was sixty-five years old, a former army surgeon who had served in the Persian Gulf War. He told the missionaries that his only child, a daughter, had been brutally raped and murdered by a man the family knew. A few weeks later, he had been diagnosed with acute leukemia. His wife, unable to cope with such overwhelming tragedies, took her own life. In the year since then, Brian had given up their home, distributed his belongings among relatives, and moved into a housing development for the poor. He spent most of his time in the hospital undergoing painful treatments for his disease. In the evenings he read the Bible, often taking it with him as he walked along the road, standing under a streetlight to read, mainly to help keep his mind from the constant pain. That was where he met the missionaries.

"So much happened that day in his room," my daughter Marianne wrote, "but basically he just opened his heart up to us. He was finally able to be honest with someone about his pain because the Spirit so strongly touched him. He said that he felt as though we had brought Jesus into the room with us. He is such a humble man, and I just cried as he told us about his life. He has such a strong belief in God and Jesus, and he is so forgiving. He is praying for an opportunity before he dies to see the man who murdered his daughter and to be able to forgive him face to face. As we sat there listening to him, he said to us, 'You are truly disciples of Christ, and I know you are an answer to my prayers. Each night I pray to God to ease my pain, and today you have done that. My body still aches, but my heart has been lifted, and my burdens are gone.'" My daughter concluded, "I saw the Spirit change a suffering man's life . . . for a few hours he had peace, and I was able to be a part of that." Brian had eased his emotional pain through his tremendous act of forgiving, and God had lifted his spirit through the power of His grace.

I believe that our need to feel those moments of grace is like Susan Greene's, who, after a long, hard winter in Cache Valley in 1874, wrote: "I begin to feel almost impatient for the snow and frost to quit the earth, and let the sun warm and prepare it for the labors of the husbandman and the reception of seeds and plants. You know I must have my little flower-garden if there is the least chance for such a thing, wherever I am."[8]

Moments of spiritual connection are like Susan's garden. They comfort, inspire, and refresh the spirit, and we must have them wherever we are. They are the power that lifts us from the bench to bear testimony, the feeling of wholeness that follows honest prayer, the sudden illumination when we recognize spiritual truth in words we hear or read, and they are the healing of our souls when we can truly forgive those who have wronged us. But, like the garden, they are not always self-generating, and they have need of constant nurturing. We can be catalysts for such moments in each other's lives if we follow the counsel of Peter to the Ephesians: "As every [one] hath received the gift," he said, "even so minister the same one to another, as good stewards of the manifold grace of God" (1 Peter 4:10).

If I have learned anything from my study of our Latter-day Saint fore-mothers, it is that they were good stewards of that gift. They exhibited through the most ordinary acts of their daily lives an abiding conscious-ness of the blessings of the gospel. It was their defense against adversity and their impetus to serve. Such simple things as a Sunday sermon, a neighbor's testimony, a friend's visit, a gathering of sisters, their diaries attest, were moments of reaffirmation of God's goodness in bringing the gospel to them. As good stewards, they ministered to one another in a myriad of ways because they needed each other, drawing together in a community of faith, love, and support. As Emmeline Wells said of the women with whom she had worshipped and worked throughout her long life, "I loved [them] as much as if bound by kindred ties, closer, perhaps, because our faith and works were so much in tune with our everyday life."[9] Their problems are our problems. They worried about their children, struggled as single parents or working mothers, battled crises of faith, and often felt lonely and overwhelmed with work and responsibility. But they were linked together as sisters in the gospel, willing to share one another's burdens as well as joys in whatever way their circumstances permitted.

I think of the women who donated their Sunday egg money to send their sister Saints to medical schools, or to pay the publishing costs of a friend's book of poetry, or to send their beloved leader, Eliza R. Snow, as their proxy on a pilgrimage to the Holy Land.

I think of those women who ministered to one another through their Church callings. One of the most memorable times in Mary Ellen Kimball's life was the day she received the temple ordinances from her sister-wife Vilate in the Nauvoo Temple. "I was overwhelmed by love and admiration for her," Mary Ellen wrote. "I knew her to be a Saint. No one could fill that position so well without the Spirit of our Saviour to assist them to do it."[10] The Logan Temple was the setting for another spiritual exchange. On Mary Ann Maughan's birthday in 1894, seventy of the Logan Temple and Relief Society sisters commemorated the day with her by acting as proxies for her kindred dead.[11] What an act of love that was, not only for Mary Ann but for the seventy deceased women who were given a gift of eternal value that day.

I think of Elizabeth Ann Whitney, who opened her home to Emma and Joseph Smith, total strangers to her, when they arrived in Kirtland, Ohio, in the harsh winter of 1831, a home that would become the setting of some of Joseph Smith's most significant revelations. It was the beginning of a relationship of loyalty and love between Emma and Elizabeth Ann. And I think of Sarah Cleveland, whose home in Quincy, Illinois, provided a place of rest and refuge for Emma, a stranger to Sarah, when she fled Missouri with her young children, leaving her husband behind in Liberty Jail. Is it any wonder that Emma Smith chose these good women to be her counselors in the Nauvoo Relief Society, the organization devoted to compassion and caring?

Ministering one to another as good stewards, even in such modest ways, became a binding act for both giver and receiver. Martha Needham was only one of many who relished these intimate and spiritual experiences with the women she served and declared that she "wanted to spend the rest of her life in doing good to others and blessing and confirming them."[12]

These were not extraordinary women, and their lives, like ours, unfolded against all the exigencies of daily living. But their faith in the reality of eternal life and their understanding of God's mercy as the operative power in this life gave transcendent meaning to each day's experience. Indeed, like the Savior, in whom their lives were centered, they lived from grace to grace, growing in knowledge and faith through their daily struggles and depending on the enabling power of grace to meet the challenges that always lay before them. Each said in her own way, "I have done the best I can and leave the rest to the Lord."

The words of Zina Young, taken from her testimony at a women's meeting in Salt Lake City in 1874, are for me the consummate metaphor for Peter's admonition. "It is a blessing to meet together," she said to the sisters assembled. "The Spirit of God is here, and when we speak to one another, it is like oil going from vessel to vessel."[13] All of the comforting, healing, and empowering qualities of consecrated oil are invoked in that image of woman ministering to woman.

Now, let me return to the Hebrew legend. In his dialogue with the Lord, Moses had hoped to penetrate God's inscrutable ways. The Lord's answer, however, was just as inscrutable to Moses. But the answer revealed the nature of God, and if Moses was listening with spiritual ears, he heard a clear and indisputable message in the unspoken words of God's answer. The Lord said to Moses in words he could hear: "I am gracious to the deserving and also to those who make no claim to my graciousness. I extend my love, my forgiveness, and my compassion to all, and give them what they need for their sustenance."[14] His unspoken words were "Now go, and do thou likewise" (see Luke 10:37). That is the covenant of grace.

Notes

1. Louis Ginzberg, *The Legends of the Jews*, trans. Paul Radin, 6 vols. (Philadelphia: The Jewish Publication Society of America, 1987), 3:134–36.
2. Lowell L. Bennion, "For by Grace Are Ye Saved," *Dialogue*: 1 (Winter 1966): 102.

3. Ibid., 102, 101.

4. Eliza R. Snow, "An Address," *Woman's Exponent* 2 (15 September 1873): 68.

5. *Hymns of The Church of Jesus Christ of Latter-day Saints* (Salt Lake City: The Church of Jesus Christ of Latter-day Saints, 1985), no. 30.

6. Martha Cragun Cox, "My Dream of a Chain," Journal, typescript, Archives of The Church of Jesus Christ of Latter-day Saints, Salt Lake City, Utah.

7. My son, Grant, shared this account with me from his missionary experiences.

8. "Letter to the Woman's Exponent," *Woman's Exponent* 2 (1 April 1874): 166.

9. *Relief Society Magazine* 3 (February 1916): 68.

10. Mary Ellen Able Kimball, Autobiography, holograph, LDS Church Archives.

11. "Journal of Mary Ann Weston Maughan," in *Our Pioneer Heritage*, comp. Kate B. Carter, 20 vols. (Salt Lake City: Daughters of Utah Pioneers, 1959), 2:413.

12. Cache Valley Relief Society Minutes, Book B, 1881–1914, 5 March 1910, p. 438, LDS Church Archives.

13. Minutes of the Senior and Junior Co-operative Retrenchment Society, 3 October 1874, LDS Church Archives.

14. See Ginzberg, *Legends of the Jews*, 3:134–36.

HOUSE OF GLORY,
HOUSE OF LIGHT,
HOUSE OF LOVE

CX

Truman G. Madsen and Ann N. Madsen

TRUMAN: Like you, we are keenly aware that the subject of the temple is both intimate and sacred. In 1893, at the time of the dedication of the Salt Lake temple, Elder Franklin D. Richards said: "The temples are full of telegrams from the heavenly world for you. . . . The blessings of heaven are treasured up there, and these temples are the great repositories of eternal life, glory, honor and immortality, waiting for the children of God to come up and bring their offerings of broken hearts and contrite spirits, and draw upon those treasures."[1]

ANN: When Elder Richards wrote that in 1893, there were three operating temples in the world. Today there are about fifty operating temples and as many more under construction or announced. This seems to be just the beginning. Our access to temples will dramatically increase with these many new temples. In this amazing multiplication, temple dedications will no longer be rare. They may still be once in a lifetime, but now that glorious experience will happen to Latter-day Saints all over the world.

How can we prepare ourselves for the wonderful experience of temple worship? Let me answer that question by describing how my love for the temple began and how Truman helped me prepare for my first visit to the house of the Lord. He gave me a copy of the Doctrine and Covenants to study two hundred underlined verses that referred to the temple. There were hours of tutoring in front of the University of Utah institute building between classes. And there was a fireside series on temples at the old

Truman G. Madsen and Ann N. Madsen are the parents of three children and a Navajo foster son and the grandparents of sixteen. Brother Madsen, an author and lecturer, is a professor emeritus of philosophy at Brigham Young University. He serves as president of the BYU Fifth Stake. Sister Madsen, an Isaiah scholar and poetess, has taught ancient scripture at Brigham Young University for more than twenty years. She serves as a visiting teacher and teaches the sixteen-year-olds in Sunday School.

Eighteenth Ward in Salt Lake City, where two of the lectures were given by a young Truman G. Madsen.

Did I have a hunger for the treasures of the temple? Oh yes! And was it satisfied? With a feast!

TRUMAN: In the final lecture of that fireside series, entitled "Personally Vital Temple Purposes," I was astonished to hear myself say in public, "In the temple I was inspired to go to Ann Nicholls and ask her to marry me." That was news to everyone—including Ann. It was even news to me. I gasped. She gasped. We have since said to our children that we had a temple courtship as well as a temple marriage.

ANN: On a beautiful June day in 1953 Truman led me to an altar in the Salt Lake Temple so that we could kneel across from each other and look into each other's eyes and into the clear blue eyes of President David O. McKay as he officiated at the ceremony that would bind us to one another from that day to this moment and then forever, according to our faithfulness.

TRUMAN: Our long experience in temple worship together began on that day forty-five years ago. We'd like to share with you some of what we have learned in that time.

As a framework, we'll consider the following questions:

How does the temple help us see ourselves as we really are?

How does the temple help us better understand the role of women in the plan of salvation?

How do we find Christ in the temple and how do we approach him there?

What level of purity is necessary before we enter the temple and how will the temple further purify us?

How do we access the light and truth that is in the temple?

What can we learn in the temple about praying?

How does our love for our families and those we serve expand through temple worship?

How do we take the temple home with us and how can the teachings of the temple transform our homes?

HOW DOES THE TEMPLE HELP US SEE OURSELVES AS WE REALLY ARE?

ANN: In the temple we are taught the beauty of holiness, the grandeur of virtuous lives. We sometimes live far beneath our spiritual potential,[2] and when we fall short, Satan reminds us of our inadequacies and seeks to pull us down to even lower levels. Yet "daily a voice [in each of us] demands that we ascend, that we rise to the peak of the mountain."[3] Isaiah invites us powerfully, "Come ye, and let us go up to the mountain of the Lord, to the house of the God of Jacob; and he will teach us of his ways, and we will walk in his paths. . . . Come ye, and let us walk in the light of the Lord" (Isaiah 2:3–5).

TRUMAN: Jesus the Christ spoke of himself as a temple. Likewise he chooses that highest of names for us: "Know ye not that ye are the temple of God, and that the Spirit of God dwelleth in you?" (1 Corinthians 3:16). "The elements are the tabernacle of God; yea, man is the tabernacle of God, even temples" (D&C 93:35). That is the vision he offers us of the radiant beings we can become.

Everything that we can say of Christ he promises us in potential. In his dedicated temples the power of his life and atonement and spirit enters our lives, and his endowment of power gradually transforms us into his likeness. Two powerful words, "as if," are part of our temple experience. It is "as if" Christ himself personally ministers and administers every promise and every covenant to us.

ANN: We *can* learn to be like Christ. He has "called us to glory and virtue," as Peter explained, and has "given unto us exceeding great and precious promises: that by these [we] might be partakers of the divine nature" (2 Peter 1:3–4). His temple ordinances act as a compass, to point the way. It is not a crooked path. It is straight and narrow, and it requires our hearts, total commitment, and faith.

Elder Henry B. Eyring says it so well: "It is uncomplicated. We simply submit to the authority of the Savior and promise to be obedient to whatever He commands."[4]

When Thomas asked Jesus, "How can we know the way [or the path]?" He replied simply, "I am the way" (John 14:5–6).

TRUMAN: The temple helps us see ourselves as we really are, divine children of our Heavenly Father with the potential to become like him. It teaches us that this is how God sees us.

Two little girls were sitting together in Sunday School. One whispered to the other, "My grandfather is the prophet." After thinking that over the other replied, "My grandfather is God."

In the eyes of our heavenly parents we are noble children, children of destiny. Just as we see great promise and good in our children and perfection in our grandchildren, he says to you: "You're wonderful just as you are! You're beautiful now! You can become a queen!"

ANN: One afternoon in the New England Mission home, Truman invited me to join him at the close of a missionary zone leaders' meeting. He found me upstairs in our room, exhausted.

As Truman left, I sank to my knees and said simply, "If you have something you want me to say, Lord, just tell me and I'll say it. But I'm running on empty." I had learned such prayers are answered. I started to go down, and I remember right where I was on the stairs when I had an unmistakable impression, "Tell them they are my sons." And in a flash I knew as never before what it meant that I was his daughter. The power of that experience still resonates in me.

TRUMAN: As spirits, we are born of heavenly parentage. In the quickening processes of the temple we become Christ's—in mind, spirit, and body. Thus, when Joseph Smith first sent the Twelve to England he instructed them to teach: "Being born again comes by the Spirit of God through ordinances."[5]

The highest ordinances of rebirth are given to us in the temple. Jesus submitted to all these ordinances, received the powers of godliness, and after the Mount of Transfiguration said, "All power is given unto me both in heaven and in earth" (Matthew 28:18). He said to his disciples at the climax of his life, "Be of good cheer; I have overcome the world" (John 16:33).

If we submit in that same pattern, we, through him, can overcome the world. How is it done? Modern revelation tells us. "For whoso is faithful unto the obtaining these two priesthoods of which I have spoken, and the magnifying their calling, are sanctified by the Spirit unto the renewing of their bodies" (D&C 84:33).

Joseph Smith taught that through this process we become a new creation by the Holy Ghost and that the fulness of the Holy Ghost is given in the temple (see D&C 109:15). We are purged of sin and sinfulness and we are prepared for his presence. We are enlightened by his Spirit. And we are transformed by it. He even taught that this process has, as he put it, "visible effects."[6]

I have seen beautiful, white-haired sisters in the temple and have thought to myself, *Who can believe that there is anything but exalting truth in our temples when they see a face like yours?* Their faces are the mirror of consecrated lives. My grandfather once remarked that a photo gallery of such women would convert the world to Christ.

HOW DOES THE TEMPLE HELP US BETTER UNDERSTAND THE ROLE OF WOMEN IN THE PLAN OF SALVATION?

TRUMAN: Hugh Nibley has studied world ritual for more than fifty years (one of his illuminating articles on the temple appears in the *Encyclopedia of Mormonism*). He has spoken of the temple as "Eve's show." This insight not only is emblazoned in the temple ordinances from first to last but is presupposed by them.

Our understanding of Eve is a radical inversion of many other religious traditions. The Pearl of Great Price describes God breathing into Adam the breath of life, or *ruach* in Hebrew. Joseph Smith taught, however, that when *ruach* is applied to Eve, it should be translated as *lives*.[7]

Patricia Holland adds an important insight about the nature of Eve's motherhood: "Could we consider this one possibility about our eternal female identity? . . . Eve was given the identity of the mother of all living years, decades, perhaps centuries before she ever bore a child. It would appear that her motherhood preceded her maternity, just as surely as the perfection of the Garden preceded the struggles of mortality. I believe *mother* is one of those very carefully chosen words, one of those rich words, with meaning after meaning. We must not, at all costs, let that word divide us. I believe with all my heart that it is first and foremost a statement about our nature, not a head count of our children."[8]

So Eve is a magnificent mother, but she is more. She is the life of those around her, her husband most of all. She feeds him, clothes him, loves him. But men are alive in at least three ways other than physically: intellectually, spiritually, and creatively. Woman innately has power to enliven, quicken, nourish, and magnify all these lives. In the temple we learn from Eve many essential roles of womanhood.

Some will argue, Was not Eve the terrible cause of the fall of the human race? Is she not justly maligned? Is not woman intrinsically evil?

On the contrary. The temple teaches there is something intrinsically good, even divine, in woman. She is the heroine who led the way into this obstacle course of mortality. Eve and then Adam would partake of the fruit, with drastic, yet ultimately glorifying, consequences. In the book of Moses, Eve sees unerringly and comforts Adam: "Were it not for our transgression we never should have had seed, and never should have known good and evil, and the joy of our redemption" (Moses 5:11). Eve in truth is inspired. What could be more Christlike than her sacrificial decision to seek the redemption of our Father's family rather than avoid the bitter cup? A woman was the first to taste death and the first to witness resurrected life. That is no coincidence. It is a lasting testimony of God's trust in woman.

Hence the temple doctrine is unequivocal. Eve receives and gives. She is an equal partner. She did not leave the garden for trivial, selfish gratification but to open the way for the birth and rebirth of the whole human family.

A woman's blessings in the temple are transcendent. The ultimate relationship for a man and a woman can be found in temple marriage. Many traditions tend toward a negative view of marriage as an embarrassment, a necessary evil. But in a temple perspective, God commands the grandeur, the celebration, and the perpetuation of marriage and family. Women and men are equal partners: a king only with a queen, a priest only with a priestess, a patriarch only with a matriarch. This is the eternal truth: God glories in the sanctity and beauty of woman.

If only you could have this wave of divine recognition and approval and trust fill you to the brim! It is one of the treasures of the temple. The more you look for it there, the more you will find it.

HOW DO WE FIND CHRIST IN THE TEMPLE?

ANN: Anciently the children of Israel, led by Moses, built a sanctuary. We often refer to it as a "tabernacle," but in Hebrew it is called *ohel moade*, or the "tent of meeting"; it was the place where Moses met the Lord and spoke with him "face to face" (Exodus 33:11). Our temples are also places where we can come into his presence.

In the Doctrine and Covenants we read, "My glory shall rest upon it; . . . my presence shall be there, for I will come into it, and all the pure in heart that shall come into it shall see God" (D&C 97:15–16).

TRUMAN: Elder John A. Widtsoe taught that it is a glorious promise that those who enter the temple shall see the face of God. But, he wrote, what that means to most of us for now is that "the pure in heart who go into the temples, may, there, by the Spirit of God, always have a wonderfully rich communion with God."[9]

How do we prepare ourselves to one day enter God's presence? One essential way is attending the temple. Modern revelation teaches: "Therefore, sanctify yourselves that your minds become single to God, and the days will come that you shall see him; for he will unveil his face unto you, and it shall be in his own time, and in his own way, and according to his own will" (D&C 88:68).

ANN: We are to come to the temple in reverence, open-souled, able to cultivate silence. President James E. Faust taught us at the General Young Women's Meeting in 1998: "Hold your soul very still and listen to the whisperings of the Holy Spirit. Follow the noble, intuitive feelings planted deep within your souls by Deity in the previous world. In this way you will be responding to the Holy Spirit of God and will be sanctified by truth."[10]

We are asked to be quiet and speak only in whispers in the temple. It is easy to sense why. It is so that we can learn to be comfortable communing. It is to help us find Christ in the temple.

Some years ago I wrote these lines:

> Would God have us know silence?
> In this time of brazen bells
> Does He invite us
> To a place apart
> To bend in some secluded spot
> To listen?
> Is snow descending
> Soundlessly
> His lesson?
> When He calls to us
> In the still, small voice
> Elijah heard,
> Will we not have to wait,
> With Elijah,
> For surcease
> From the wind, fire and quake
> Of our daily din
> That our Lord's
> Own mild, yet piercing voice
> Might shimmer
> In our souls?
> God
> Whispers into enraptured silence,
> "Be still
> And know that I am God."

TRUMAN: We must all learn when to speak and when to keep silent. Once when I gave Ann a blessing, these words came to me: "You will know when to speak and when to keep silent." We are counseled, "Remember that that which cometh from above is sacred, and must be spoken with care, and by constraint of the Spirit . . . ; wherefore, without this there remaineth condemnation" (D&C 63:64).

We must show the Lord how far he can trust us. He surrounds our temple covenants with sobering requirements that we keep in our hearts what is sacred.

WHAT LEVEL OF PURITY IS NECESSARY BEFORE WE ENTER THE TEMPLE?

ANN: When you think of purity, you might think of a newborn baby. Can we as adults somehow learn to approach the purity of a child? We must strive for purity of heart, purity of mind, purity of language, and purity of behavior. How can we attain conscious innocence?

The Lord has said, "Prepare yourselves, and sanctify yourselves; yea, purify your hearts, and cleanse your hands and your feet before me, that I may make you clean; that I may testify unto your Father, and your God, and my God, that you are clean from the blood of this wicked generation" (D&C 88:74–75).

We need to know what clean feels like in order to get our bearings in this sometimes muddy world. We dress in white in the temple to represent purity. We offer broken hearts and contrite spirits, as pure as we can be, and that is acceptable to a loving Father.

Isaiah says it so well: "Wash you, make you clean; put away the evil of your doings from before mine eyes; cease to do evil; . . . relieve the oppressed, . . . plead for the widow. Come now, and let us reason together, saith the Lord [Jehovah]: though your sins be as scarlet, they shall be as white as snow" (Isaiah 1:16–18). That is pure.

TRUMAN: Our weekly opportunity to cleanse ourselves is at the sacrament table. How does the sacrament help us in the purifying process? It reminds us regularly of our commitment to be cleansed by Jesus' blood, shed for us in the Atonement. We all know that blood stains, but the blood of Christ purges us and purifies us.

After the birth of our daughter Mindy's third child, her doctor said to me, "Your daughter is hemorrhaging. We can't stop the bleeding. A hysterectomy could save her, but she might not survive that surgery."

"What are you telling me?" I asked. "I'm telling you to pray," he answered. We prayed and administered to her. Mindy, frightened, anxious, and weak was trying to calm herself. She began whispering the sacrament prayers. As she lay there bleeding, she reached the phrase, "that they may do it in remembrance of the blood of thy Son, which was shed for them" (D&C 20:79). Revelations come in hospitals. Mindy was given a new understanding of the life-giving power of Christ's atoning sacrifice. She was healed, and she returned to the sacrament and the temple with added insight and gratitude.

ANN: By partaking of the symbols of Christ's body and blood, when attended by the Spirit, we are washed clean, rinsed from the grime and filth of the world in completion of the changing process we call repentance. We give away all our sins that we may know the Lord. The tiny cup of water offered us in the sacrament is enough to gradually cleanse the inner vessel—that part of us that only the Lord sees (see Alma 60:23).

TRUMAN: As Joseph Smith and Oliver Cowdery bowed their heads in the Kirtland Temple they heard the sweetest words of acceptance we can pray to hear: "Behold, your sins are forgiven you; you are clean before me; therefore, lift up your heads and rejoice" (D&C 110:5).

Throughout our lives we can continue the refreshing and regenerating process of becoming pure. We're promised that the time can come when we will have "lost every desire for sin" and will even "look upon sin with abhorrence."[11]

ANN: "What are these which are arrayed in white robes?" we are asked in the book of Revelation (7:13). We think of those made pure through temple worship.

President Boyd K. Packer has written: "Our labors in the temple cover us with a shield and a protection, both individually and as a people."[12]

President Carlos E. Asay of the Salt Lake Temple wrote in a recent *Ensign* article: "I like to think of the garment as the Lord's way of letting us take part of the temple with us when we leave. It is true that we carry from the Lord's house inspired teachings and sacred covenants written in our minds and hearts. However, the one tangible remembrance we carry with us back into the world is the garment. And though we cannot always be in the temple, a part of it can always be with us to bless our lives."[13]

From the pristine white clothing worn inside the temple we take this precious part to be with us night and day. It is a daily reminder of what we have seen, heard, and felt. It shields us from the fallout of evil in the world. It helps maintain the radiance we have glimpsed in the house of the Lord.

HOW DO WE ACCESS AND UNDERSTAND THE LIGHT AND TRUTH THAT IS IN THE TEMPLE?

TRUMAN: The temple is called by the Lord "a house of learning" in which we will be "*perfected* in [our] understanding" (D&C 88:119; 97:14; italics added).

Elder John A. Widtsoe was given a patriarchal blessing when he was a little boy in Norway. "Thou shalt have great faith in the ordinances of the Lord's house," he was told.[14] Later in life he became an able soil chemist. He had tried in vain to find a formula that would pull together many years of research. He suggested to his wife, Leah, that they go to the temple and "forget the failure." In the temple the formula came to him as pure intelligence. Out of such experiences, he said, "I would rather take my practical problems to the House of the Lord than anywhere else."[15]

He testified: "The endowment is . . . so packed full of revelations to those who exercise their strength to seek and to see, that no human words can explain or make clear the possibilities that reside in the temple service. The endowment which was given by revelation can best be understood by revelation; and to those who seek more vigorously, with pure hearts, will the revelation be greatest."[16]

It is common knowledge that keeping the Word of Wisdom is a prerequisite for entering the temple. Our emphasis on the health benefits, the "run and not be weary" (D&C 89:20) promise at the end of the revelation, sometimes obscures a related promise: "And shall find wisdom and great treasures of knowledge, even hidden treasures" (D&C 89:19).

Joseph Fielding Smith, as president of the Salt Lake Temple, often spoke of his favorite scripture: "That which is of God is light; and he that receiveth light, and continueth in God, receiveth more light; and that light groweth brighter and brighter until the perfect day" (D&C 50:24).

One night Elder Harold B. Lee sat with the president of the Manti Temple looking up toward the floodlighted spires. A dark storm raged around them. The temple president said, "You know, Brother Lee, that temple is never more beautiful than during a storm."[17]

Jesus said that he is "the light [that] shineth in darkness and the darkness comprehendeth it not" (John 1:5; D&C 45:7). In the Greek, this reads "the darkness did not overtake the light." In other words, no engulfing darkness can totally obliterate the divine light that is deep in us. And in his temple our light cleaves unto his light, our truth embraces his truth, and our virtue loves his virtue (see D&C 88:40).

Anticipating the first temple in our dispensation the Lord said: "If thou shalt ask, thou shalt receive revelation upon revelation, knowledge upon knowledge, that thou mayest know the mysteries and peaceable things—that which bringeth joy, that which bringeth life eternal" (D&C 42:61).

The mysteries of godliness are locked in the ordinances of godliness.

ANN: Robert L. Millet helps us understand one way we access and understand the truths that are presented to us in the temple. He writes: "We do not see things as *they* really are; we see things as *we* really are."[18]

Taking our covenants seriously transforms *us*. I heard anthropologist Professor Merlin Myers explain this once. Simply put, he said: "Scientists use mathematical symbols, a symbol system to let themselves into reality [truth]."[19] But the most powerful symbols transcend mathematics.

1. Ordinances are a symbol system (baptism, sacrament, temple ordinances, etc.).

2. Ordinances contain patterns of action or modes of behavior.

3. We act and are conditioned, and only then do we see into reality or truth.

4. Then a transformation occurs in us so we can see as God sees.

That means finally the "temple goes through us" after many times of our "going through the temple."

Our five-year-old grandson was taught in a recent Primary Sharing Time that each of us has two bodies and that they are alike. Later, as he left the house to go to church, he said excitedly, "Mom, I'm going to feed my spiritual body!" That sums it up.

The temple is the Lord's university. For entrance you do not need to have a 3.8 grade-point average. To qualify, the Lord asks only that you bring a broken heart and a contrite spirit to his altar. You must be willing to consecrate yourself, with the integrity to keep sacred things in your heart and with a tremendous desire to serve the Lord Jesus Christ.

"Therefore," says the Doctrine and Covenants, "in the ordinances thereof, the power of godliness is manifest. And without the ordinances thereof, and the authority of the priesthood, the power of godliness is not manifest unto men in the flesh; for without this no man can see the face of God, even the Father, and live" (D&C 84:20–22).

Sister Wendy L. Watson taught us a related truth at a recent BYU devotional. "When you interact with someone repeatedly over time, it changes you. That's why what you watch on TV or read or see in magazines is so critical. So watch what you watch. Be careful with whom or what you are interacting. These recurrent interactions change your cells. They change your soul. They change your countenance."

She continues with a question: "So, who would you most want to be like? Whose image would you like engraven on your countenance? . . . The Savior entreats us to come unto him. . . . He wants us to have increasingly repeated interactions with him, and to really get to know him. And because he never changes, the changes that would occur through our interaction with the Savior would all be in us. . . . As we really come unto him, we can become like him."

She goes on to say that the Savior is the ultimate and only true and living agent for change. He is the source of all change for good. "His desire is for you to change, to have a change of heart, a change of nature . . . in fact, he did all that he did so that you could change."[20]

Thus we are taught "that through the power and manifestation of the Spirit, while in the flesh, [we] may be able to bear his presence in the world of glory" (D&C 76:118).

Isaiah asks us who can dwell with God in everlasting burnings and answers the question powerfully: "He that walketh righteously, and speaketh uprightly; . . . that shaketh his hands from holding of bribes, that stoppeth his ears from hearing of blood, and shutteth his eyes from seeing evil; he shall dwell on high" (Isaiah 33:15–16).

I love Truman's account of his first encounter with this brightness in the temple. I cannot tell it as well as he, but I can feel it.

TRUMAN: I was sitting alone in the celestial room of the Salt Lake Temple after receiving my own endowment. I had only begun to grasp the meaning of the experience, but gradually, I felt a burning of light and peace—more penetratingly than ever in my life. I felt as if I hardly wanted to breathe or move, and I sat there like a statue lest I somehow break or diminish the flow of brightness.

ANN: I had a similar feeling at the dedication of the Washington Temple in November 1974 when President Spencer W. Kimball prophesied there would be thousands of temples. I wanted to linger in the room at the close of the dedicatory services, a room so full of light. It was almost impossible to go away from the glory I felt.

WHAT CAN WE LEARN IN THE TEMPLE ABOUT PRAYING?

TRUMAN: The Lord calls his temple a "house of prayer" and teaches us to come there for "the offering up of your most holy desires unto me" (D&C 88:119; 95:16).

We can take our deepest concerns to the temple and spread them before the Lord and expect to come away lightened in both senses of the word: no longer carrying burdens of care and with an understanding of the course we should take. Have you felt such reassurance and solace?

Elder Franklin D. Richards said: "If occasion should require, if sorrow, affliction or distress overtake, we may go to the House of the Lord and find a panacea that can be found nowhere else for the ills of mortal life."[21] Seek this solace.

One day a sister in our ward commented on how beautiful our seventeen-year-old Emily was and how happy she was to see her each day at the temple open house. I didn't know what she meant. We had been there as a family on the first day of the temple open house, but I had no idea that every day from then until the dedication Emily had walked from high school up to the temple, just to be there. When I asked her, "What did you do there? Why did you go each day?" She answered simply, "I went through the regular tour and then I would sit in the celestial room as long as they would let me—just to feel the presence of the Lord, to pray, to commune."

Have you ever felt like that? Have you been drawn to the temple like our Emily? Each day she would start for home but end up in the temple. It was like a magnet to her. It was wonderfully habit-forming.

ANN: Feeling this closeness to the temple is not automatic, but it can be sought after, if we seek with all our hearts. "And ye shall seek me, and find me, when ye shall search for me with all your heart. And I will be found of you" (Jeremiah 29:13–14).

Little by little the Lord reveals himself to us and in turn, we present ourselves to him, revealing as much as we dare until we are able to lay it all before him.

Let me tell you about a wonderful word in Hebrew which embodies our finally being able to open ourselves to the Lord. It is *hinunee*. It is the common answer of prophets when the Lord calls them to be his messengers.

Abraham said it. Samuel said it. Isaiah said it. It means, "Behold, here am I," with the implicit intent "I am at your service, what will you have me do?" It is another way of saying, "Thy will be done." Christ said it first when he offered himself in the heavenly council to do for us what we could not do for ourselves.

To open ourselves to the Lord entails risks and costs, because once we offer, we will be sent and we become responsible. But once we go, we are on his errand and he promises to bless us. He wants us to succeed—to return to him. He weeps or rejoices over us just as we do over our children (see Moses 7:28–40).

So in the days ahead, when there is no other way to approach the Lord to tell him what you are willing to give, just whisper, *hinunee*. It is another way of saying, "Behold the handmaid of the Lord; be it unto me according to thy word" (Luke 1:38).

TRUMAN: Joseph Smith once said, speaking of our not asking enough or being thankful enough in our prayers: "We have not desired as much from the hand of the Lord through faith and obedience, as we ought to have done, yet we have enjoyed great blessings, and we are not so sensible of this as we should be."[22]

Sometimes in the temple we feel like we are praying in the Garden of Eden and life is all beauty and goodness. And sometimes, it is as if we are praying in the Garden of Gethsemane, and it is too hard to bear. Either way, the temple is a retreat and a place of Christ's intensive care, where his rays come together in focus and peace. When we taste consolation in the temple, we will recognize it later as we kneel at home and seek to commune with him there.

ANN: There is a window where I routinely pray. I have been watching spring come as I kneel there each day. The trees begin with a pale green fuzz and there are red and yellow tulips peaking up, sometimes through snow. One day I watched two deer nibbling on our flowers. One morning recently, as I prayed in this sacred place, all at once I realized that I was feeling precisely as I do in the temple. It was such an electric moment. It was almost as if I *was* in the temple. I had begun praying just before dawn. As I continued in prayer the sun suddenly came over the mountain. First its brightness dazzled me, even with my eyes closed and then I felt its warmth. It took my breath away. It was such a ready symbol of God's presence.

I have been pondering lately about what *glory* means. "And the glory of the Lord shone round about . . . " (D&C 76:19) or "I was clothed upon with glory."[23] Maybe we miss tiny bits of glory when we fail to notice sunrises and sunsets. I think I had a tiny glimpse of glory in that moment at my window. And the silence of the morning at first light was a necessary preparation. My mind was like a clean slate.

What about praying for each other? Joseph Smith taught the sisters in Nauvoo, "It grieves me that there is no fuller fellowship—if one member suffers all feel it. By union of feeling we obtain power with God."[24] Jesus said, "Be agreed as touching all things whatsoever ye ask of me" (D&C 27:18).

Recently I wrote to a friend who is seriously ill: "This morning we were in the Mount Timpanogos Temple, and stood in that unique sacred circumstance to pray for you. How blessed we are to live in a time when we walk out of the world into such holy precincts and feel the glorious difference. And then reenter the world with the determination to keep the holiness with us."

My friend Shirley says she often prays for something while she is in the temple and receives her answer later, outside. So the temple becomes the channel through which our prayers ascend, and later we can access the answers somewhere else. I love that concept.

HOW DOES OUR LOVE FOR OUR FAMILIES AND THOSE WE SERVE EXPAND THROUGH TEMPLE WORSHIP?

TRUMAN: President Howard W. Hunter said that "the purpose of the temple is to reunite the family of God." He also said, "In the ordinances of the temple the foundations of the eternal family are sealed in place."[25]

A dear friend of ours, Mary Finlayson, was asked to write on the Spirit of Elijah. She wrote: "I have spent the last four years in an effort to knit together my grandfather's unravelling family, and I have loved every minute of it. . . . I will never forget the feelings of family I had when they arrived at the Lion House [for our first family reunion]—feelings of love without conditions, complete belonging, and an overwhelming desire to serve each one in any way possible. . . . I don't know how it works but I suddenly saw why we are led by our prophets to do these things. I now believe that those feelings that surge up in us as we gather our earthly families, [now living or gone ahead] are a type. At some point, if we continue to grow toward it, we will feel those same automatic feelings of sacrificial love toward everyone we encounter. In short, I think we're just practicing on our blood relations for the real thing. At some point, we will gaze at any face and recognize instantly our kinship, sprung from the same Father."[26]

ANN: What do you think about as you sit waiting for a temple session to begin? Once, as I sat bathed in the silence, I looked again at the name of the person for whom I had come. I felt a sudden kinship, though two hundred years separated us in time. I whispered in my heart to her through the thin veil, "Welcome to this beautiful temple, Sarah. I hope that you will love it as I do." Since that singular day when I sensed her reality, I try to reach out to the person for whom I am officiating. I tell her how I pray that she will accept the covenants and love them. I tell her how grateful I am that I can do this for her because it is such a blessed opportunity for me to ponder anew the wondrous truths that I have treasured for many years. There are many quiet moments throughout the endowment ceremony when no words are being spoken. In these times she will see the endowment with spirit eyes enlightened by her time in the spirit world. And I will search again, using all the capacity a body provides. I will inquire, "Lord, what do you have for me here today?" We will both have a unique opportunity through this sacred pattern to better understand godliness.

Even the arithmetic of our temple service teaches us. Only once do we receive our own endowment. From that moment, each time we enter the temple—hopefully hundreds of times—we enter to serve others. This is the pattern of Jesus, who reaches out to all of us as our Savior. In our small reaching, beyond ourselves to our families and those we serve, we can learn to become saviors on Mount Zion.

I heard a wonderful story of Ghandi which illustrates this transcendent giving principle, a more complete consecration. Ghandi was traveling on a slow-moving train in India when one of his sandals slipped off and tumbled down the embankment. One of his followers started to jump down to retrieve it as the train lumbered along, but Ghandi restrained him. He quickly unfastened the other sandal, tossing it beside the first so that whoever found it would have a pair. I want to learn to feel like that.

TRUMAN: The world assumes that our relatives are dead, gone, and indifferent to us. It is just the other way around. They are alive—perhaps more alive than we. They are close at hand and concerned about us.

Joseph Smith taught: "Enveloped in flaming fire they are not far from us. They know and understand our thoughts, feelings, and motions and are often pained therewith."[27]

Yes, and surely they rejoice with us as well. I can testify that as the air is thinner on high mountains so the veil is thin in the temples of the Lord.

Our loved ones in the spirit world know what this life is like. They are not, the Prophet teaches, "idle spectators."[28] They yearn over us. My good counselor, James Harper, tells the story of a woman who was baptized as proxy for her mother, a mother who had been handicapped and terribly difficult to live with. Her daughter felt both healing and forgiveness in that process.

ANN: Our family shared a tender experience as we went to the temple to perform baptisms, endowments, and sealings for the family of my grandfather's uncle John Pearson. Before we took our grandchildren up to the temple to be baptized for the Pearson family, I read to them from my grandfather's missionary journal, which he kept while serving his mission in England. In his journal, he wrote of each member of that family and how he loved them and longed to bring them into the Church. We assigned each grandchild a name from these entries; they saw the people for whom they would be baptized through my grandfather's eyes.

The sunny morning when we went to the temple in behalf of my grandfather's family was almost exactly one hundred years since my grandfather had written these things in his journal. I told our grandchildren that Grandfather Nicholls was a fine missionary who died shortly after his return home. Surely he had plenty of time in the spirit world to complete the teaching begun in 1894. As we went into the font area some missionaries were just finishing but lingered to watch our family. Later they approached me and said, "We could feel the presence of the Pearson family as you did those baptisms. Thank you."

TRUMAN: As I stood waist deep in the font, inviting my grand-daughters and then grandsons to join me there, one by one, it all seemed like closing a circuit—like coming home. Perhaps I sensed a little of what Wilford Woodruff describes in the St. George Temple; it was as if the baptismal room itself was charged. Swept up in the feeling, I wept, and made a mistake in the wording, but was grateful to be kindly corrected. Later, with my hands on still-moist heads I felt the blessing of conferring the gift of the Holy Ghost. It was not perfunctory. It was reality.

ANN: As we were leaving the temple I pointed out the bas-relief of the Samaritan woman at the well with Jesus. It is on the far wall in the waiting room of the Provo Temple so our grandchildren had to peek inside to sec it. I asked them, not having any idea what they would answer, "Why do you think they have that story in the temple?" I had nothing particular in mind. Instantly, one of those guileless, intrepid souls spoke right up. "Because Jesus is telling her who he is and that's what happens in the temple. He tells us who he really is."

TRUMAN: God unites us by love. Satan's whole work is to separate and isolate us by discord, anger, hate, and the clamor for rights. All of us know what isolation feels like. We need to know what the unity of love feels like. I believe that it is impossible to feel the Spirit of the Lord and not feel love. And perhaps vice versa. When we know what love feels like we cannot help loving others. Love is contagious.

ANN: We all have moments when we feel like no one loves us. "Nobody loves me, nobody understands, nobody cares." But in the temple it is different. God's gentle, unfailing love fills his house. We can access it there: we can open ourselves to God's love as his children. Christ cares for us precisely because he participated in what we are going through. He yearns to gather us under his wings and nourish us, to "encircle [us] in the arms of [his] love" (D&C 6:20; 3 Nephi 10:4).

Temple workers themselves contribute to this feeling of love and caring. I remember entering the Frankfurt, Germany Temple. The man at the recommend desk, whose gray hair and lined face showed he had survived World War II, extended his hand to shake mine as he said, "Velcome to the house of the Lord." I wept as I sensed the reality of entering God's own house.

TRUMAN: Do you think those who are in the temple every day feel that love in a special way? Do they feel it constantly? We heard a fine temple president, Elder Carlos E. Asay, and his wife explain their view. President Asay spoke of the endowment as an "exchange of love." God loves us enough to give us commandments and make covenants with us that will inspire and can ultimately exalt us. Keeping covenants keeps us from sinning. We should be willing to honor the trust extended in eternal covenants by keeping them. Is this not "an exchange of love?" he asked.

ANN: What a touching moment it was for me when a dear friend confided about a year after her husband's death: "He adored me." Then weeping, she continued, "Now nobody feels that way about me any more." I could feel some of her devastation. All I knew to say was, "The Lord loves you deeply. Pray to feel *that* love in his house."

President Asay also taught us, "The temple is the bridge between heaven and earth—the seen and the unseen—and the bridge is love." We feel such love for the Lord Jesus Christ, who pleads our cause before our Father. I know he truly loves me. He truly loves you. The Spirit helps communicate that love.

TRUMAN: Such love is a taste of immortality. As Elder Parley P. Pratt wrote, the Spirit "develops beauty of person, form and features."[29] A sensitive temple worker once shared with me a glimpse of this ultimate blessing. He had officiated in the presence of many aged and infirm and arthritic couples as they performed sealings. He felt admiration but also sympathy for their slow-moving, patient labor. Then he suddenly saw them as they would be in the resurrection. He could hardly find words: "They were exquisite . . . splendid . . . youthful . . . lovely."

Elder Henry B. Eyring tells of a mother who was driving down a freeway hardly able to see through her tears. She had just visited her son, a convicted murderer, in prison. "Why, why?" she cried out. "Why am I the mother of such a son?" And a voice from on high replied, "Because you are the only one on this planet who will go on loving him."[30]

There are ways, too deep and poignant to describe, that the Lord's temple service can reach the hardest of cases, bring faith to the faithless, and hope to the hopeless. Christ teaches in holy places that he never gives up. Neither should we.

ANN: Covenants bind us by love. Elder Henry B. Eyring once said that he had been taught that covenants were like a business contract, in which one person agrees to do something and the other agrees to do something else in return. But after serious reflection, he felt something new, something more powerful about our covenants with God. Covenant keeping is not a cold business deal but a warm relationship, bound by love.

Elder Eyring explained, "The Lord, with whom I am blessed to have made covenants, loves me and you with a steadfastness about which I continually marvel and which I want with all my heart to emulate." He goes on to say, "We are blessed by the Abrahamic covenant, and we are bound by it. But we are not bound by compulsion. We are bound by his love for us and by the love He evokes in us."[31]

All other virtues spring from this Christlike love. We forgive, we have mercy, we have empathy, we are willing to lift and bless and help when we are filled with that love. How can we give in to anger or impatience when our hearts are brimming with love? No wonder the scripture cries out, "Pray . . . with all the energy of heart, that ye may be filled with this love" (Moroni 7:48). We can pray daily for that sweet selflessness. Charity never stops, never fails. It even reaches back to us from beyond the veil.

HOW CAN WE TAKE THE TEMPLE HOME WITH US? CAN OUR HOMES BE HOLY?

TRUMAN: We've had the privilege of attending three temple dedications, two with our family. The latest was the Mount Timpanogos Temple dedication, which we attended with a whole row of our children and their children. As the services progressed, we looked across that row and saw their upturned faces as they sang, "The Spirit of God Like a Fire Is Burning." At the conclusion we overheard Max, then age ten, whisper to his mother, "Thanks for bringing me here!" We were knit closely that day. We were one. We remembered that President Lorenzo Snow instructed little children to give the Hosannah Shout at the top of their lungs because that would be the way they would greet Jesus Christ at his second coming.[32]

ANN: Our homes can, like the temple, be holy sanctuaries in this far-from-holy world. Bruce Hafen, when he was provost at BYU, described the world today as a polluted river. We are like fish swimming in the pollution, often carried by a current of which we are only vaguely aware, until someone swims against the current. Then we see the contrast.[33]

The Lord has commanded us: "Behold, it is my will, that all they who call on my name, and worship me according to mine everlasting gospel, should gather together, and stand in holy places" (D&C 101:22).

How is a Zion built? By producing and gathering the "pure in heart." Eliza R. Snow learned from the Prophet that the curse on the earth would not be lifted all at once, but that each time we dedicate a temple we lift the curse a little. Our homes can be the minitemples, the points of light that will recreate a little bit of heaven on earth leading to the Millennium. All of us are "home-makers." We make a home wherever we eat and sleep. There are several things we can do to help make our homes holy.

TRUMAN: We can help make our homes holy by dedicating them. Ann and I have painted, fixed up, shined, and then dedicated each of our homes. We were really dedicating ourselves to the purposes of the Lord in our family. We even dedicated our temporary apartment in Jerusalem.

All the things we say, the prayers we offer, the blessings that are given, the feelings we experience—both good and bad—accumulate in our homes and are felt by those who come there. We add something to the sum each day. That's a sobering thought.

ANN: We can help make our homes holy by setting priorities. Family is first. Someone must be primarily responsible for dividing the tasks that keep a home going—no matter how many machines we have to cut down our work. We can't all abdicate everything. Orderliness, cleanliness, music, social life, decor—the abundant life is far different from merely existing in a space together. Someone or ones *must* have that as a priority or it will never happen.

Is home a place of beauty? Is home just a place to eat and sleep? Is there no lovely corner to curl up in to read a book? If spring is lagging outdoors, can we bring it inside with a pot of daisies or daffodils on the table for dinner—not for company, just because it's spring? If family is first then shouldn't there be flowers for family? You will notice the temple grounds are alive with beauty. So can our homes be.

TRUMAN: We can help make our homes holy by creating order and fixed points to count on.

In the temple we learn a planned sequence. Do we have such fixed points in our home regimen? When do we sit together and share? Everyone in the family can count on family home evening as a fixed point in their week for planning family events and simply to celebrate being together.

ANN: What about dinner time? Let's dine together! What a novel idea! Before you say, "Our family just can't," think about it. There is such an emphasis on good nutrition these days. We fill our freezers with well-balanced meals in individual, dated packets and then run in all directions, leaving each person to heat a nutritious meal in the microwave and eat it on the run all alone. Isn't nursing our babies a type that should teach us something? We have to do that together. From infancy to adulthood, we communicate through food. Dinner is a time to share. It's a time for bonding. It's an informal temple preparation class.

TRUMAN: We had a fixed point at our house that worked for us—5:30 P.M. was inviolate. Everyone worked around it. That was our family's daily appointment to eat dinner together; that was when we had family prayer; that was when we read the scriptures and were spiritually fed. But I think what we all remember best was that we talked. We did not let the urgent rob us of this important time together.

We can help make our homes holy by living what we've learned in the temple. When we keep our temple covenants, they help us to cheerfully, patiently reverence one another at home. We become sanctifying influences to each other and all who come there. We quietly learn to live celestially, like Christ, creating a little bit of heaven on earth. Patience and prayer are part of the process.

ANN: When the Provo Temple was to be dedicated, we made plans to prepare our family for what we anticipated as a once-in-a-lifetime experience. We had a series of family home evenings focusing on the temple: one honoring our ancestors; one celebrating our wedding day, complete with photo album, ring, the story of our courtship, and so on; one explaining what we could of the activities that would go on in the temple. The culmination was a family visit to the temple open house—the first time our children would actually be able to enter the Lord's House with us. In preparation we each bathed carefully, washed our hair, put on all clean Sunday clothes, and drove to the temple. We explained to our children that this kind of cleanliness was part of the symbolism of purity which is essential for entering the presence of the Lord in his house.

TRUMAN: We learned an unexpected lesson from this experience. We arrived to an empty parking lot. There we were, all scrubbed, clean, excited, and expectant. But the door was locked; it was a Monday. What a let down. But the lights were all on so I went to look inside, pressing my nose against the glass. There was the temple president, showing his own family through the temple. Seeing us, and having compassion, he invited us to join them. We knew for a moment how it felt to be denied entrance to the temple. And just as suddenly, we experienced more joy than we had prayed and planned for.

ANN: Our homes can become holy places and still be lived in. They can be clean, orderly, and reverent—within the parameters of keeping happy, growing children in them.

As a grandmother I remember the first time the whole family came for Thanksgiving dinner to our newly remodeled house. The paint was fresh, and there was not a mark on any wall. I had foolishly hoped to preserve its pristine appearance for a week or two. As they all left, I gasped at little muddy footprints that ran the length of the new silver gray carpet and handprints on the walls and windows and mirrors. My newly clean home! But then I caught myself. I've learned to cherish fingerprints.

TRUMAN: Orson Pratt gives us a wonderful vision of glorified homes in the future: "In the latter days there will be a people so pure in Mount Zion, with a house established upon the tops of the mountains, that God will manifest himself, not only in their temple . . . but when they retire to their [homes], behold each [home] will be lighted up by the glory of God, a pillar of flaming fire by night."[34]

CONCLUSION

TRUMAN: We have spoken of the ideal, the vision. It may seem remote, distant, even utterly beyond us. But we can have a foretaste in this world. As Joseph Smith admonished: "Let these truths sink down in our hearts, that we may, even here, begin to enjoy that which shall be in full hereafter."[35]

Ponder these confirming words in a letter to a remarkable woman, Eliza R. Snow, from apostle Wilford Woodruff. The letter was written fifteen years after she became a widow and thirty years before her death. Note the sense of fulfilled promises and the allusions to the temple.

"Thy soul has been inspired by the spirit of God and eternal light and truth. Thy lamp hath been lit at God's holy altar where the oil was pure and the spirit free so thou couldst weigh eternal truth . . .

"Thy words and testimony will live and speak in flames of holy fire. Ere long thou wilt be clothed with immortality and clothed with light. Thy garments are clear of the blood of fallen man. Thy soul is as pure as the crystal stream that flows from its snowy bed. Thou hast been true and faithful and are sealed unto eternal life and secured unto thyself a crown of glory. No power shall take it. It awaits thy coming. Soon this blessing will be thine. Ah, what joy!"[36]

ANN: No wonder Eliza could say to the women of her day and to us: "We are women of God, women fulfilling high and responsible positions, performing sacred duties."[37]

We finish with the invitation with which we began: Come, let us go up to the temple where the Lord will teach us of his ways, and we will walk in his paths until we have learned them (see Isaiah 2:3).

Jesus moved from grace to grace to become more and more. And when a sick sinner asked, "Lord, if thou wilt, thou canst make me whole," He replied, "I will. Be thou whole" (see John 5:6). We, too, can be made whole. The temple is absolutely necessary for that to happen in our lives. It is the finishing of our faith. It is the crowning of our lives on earth. It is the only place on earth where our families can be knit together, bound by a love which Jesus has demonstrated once and for all in the Atonement.

In that holy house we can see ourselves as we really are; we can find Jesus Christ and understand who he really is; we can understand a new level of purity and learn to pray with power. As we search the teachings we receive, we will know how to overcome the devil and, ultimately, how to part the veil.[38] The temple is the bridge of love between this world and the next.

May we invite you with the words of Isaiah: "O house of Jacob, come ye, and let us walk in the light of the Lord"—the sunshine of his love (Isaiah 2:5).

I have tried to describe my feelings about the temple in the following lines:

> In the temple
> The quiet closes round me
> like fog.
> God's house reverberates
> with silence,
> filled with echoes
> from the faithful
> who have followed the light
> to here, like a star.
> White, we come clothed in white
> to this place,
> of radiant light.
> Dear Host
> of this Heavenly House,
> if I come,
> clothed in the pure white
> of a new lamb,
> with my heart as new,
> may I, too,
> be lighted?

Notes

1. Franklin D. Richards, *Collected Discourses*, ed. Brian H. Stuy, 5 vols. (Burbank, Calif.: BHS Publishing, 1987–92), vol. 3, 12 February 1893.

2. See Brigham Young, *Journal of Discourses*, 26 vols. (London: Latter-day Saints' Book Depot, 1854–86), 9:33.

3. A. J. Heschel, *Israel: An Echo of Eternity* (New York: Farrar, Straus & Giroux), 225.

4. Henry B. Eyring, *Ensign*, May 1998, 68; see also Mosiah 3:19.

5. Joseph Smith, *Teachings of the Prophet Joseph Smith*, sel. Joseph Fielding Smith (Salt Lake City: Deseret Book, 1938), 162.

6. Joseph Smith, *The Words of Joseph Smith*, ed. Andrew F. Ehat and Lyndon W. Cook (Orem, Utah: Grandin Book, 1991), 4.

7. Smith, *Words of Joseph Smith*, 203.

8. Jeffrey R. Holland and Patricia T. Holland, *On Earth As It Is in Heaven* (Salt Lake City: Deseret Book, 1989), 94.

9. John A. Widtsoe, "Temple Worship," *Utah Genealogical and Historical Magazine* 12 (April 1921): 56.

10. James E. Faust, *Ensign*, May 1998, 89.

11. Smith, *Teachings of the Prophet Joseph Smith*, 51; Alma 13:12; 27:28.

12. Boyd K. Packer, *The Holy Temple* (Salt Lake City: Bookcraft, 1980, 265.

13. Carlos E. Asay, "The Temple Garment," *Ensign*, August 1997, 22.

14. Quoted in Leon R. Hartshorn, *Exceptional Stories from the Lives of Our Apostles* (Salt Lake City: Deseret Book, 1972), 277.

15. John A. Widtsoe, *In a Sunlit Land: The Autobiography of John A. Widtsoe* (Salt Lake City: Milton R. Hunter and G. Homer Durham, 1952), 177.

16. Widtsoe, "Temple Worship," 63.

17. Personal conversation with Truman G. Madsen.

18. Robert L. Millet, *Alive in Christ: The Miracle of Spiritual Rebirth* (Salt Lake City: Deseret Book, 1997), 28.

19. Merlin Myers, devotional address, Brigham Young University, Provo, Utah; notes in possession of author.

20. Wendy L. Watson, "Change: It's Always a Possibility," devotional address, Brigham Young University, Provo, Utah, 7 April 1998; notes in possession of author.

21. Richards, *Collected Discourses*, vol. 3, 12 February 1893.

22. Smith, *Teachings of the Prophet Joseph Smith*, 90.

23. Joseph Smith, *History of The Church of Jesus Christ of Latter-day Saints*, ed. B. H. Roberts, 2d ed. rev., 7 vols. (Salt Lake City: The Church of Jesus Christ of Latter-day Saints, 1932–51), 1:133.

24. Smith, *Words of Joseph Smith*, 123.

25. Howard W. Hunter, *Ensign*, February 1995, 2.

26. Mary Finlayson to Ann N. Madsen, 17 April 1995.

27. Smith, *Teachings of the Prophet Joseph Smith*, 324.

28. Smith, *Teachings of the Prophet Joseph Smith*, 231.

29. Parley P. Pratt, *Key to the Science of Theology* (Salt Lake City: Deseret Book, 1948), 101.

30. Personal conversation; used by permission.

31. Personal conversation; used by permission.

32. Lorenzo Snow, in Journal of B. H. Roberts (uncataloged), April 1893, 193.

33. See Bruce C. Hafen, devotional address, Brigham Young University, Provo, Utah; notes in possession of author.

34. Orson Pratt, *Journal of Discourses*, 16:36.

35. Smith, *Teachings of the Prophet Joseph Smith*, 296.

36. Wilford Woodruff, *Wilford Woodruff's Journal, 1833–1898*, ed. Scott G. Kenney, 9 vols. (Midvale: Signature Books, 1983–85), vol. 5, July 1857.

37. Minutes of Relief Society Organization, Salt Lake City, Archives of The Church of Jesus Christ of Latter-day Saints, 1842; notes in possession of author.

38. Sheri L. Dew, address in Logan, Utah, March 1998; notes by Mindy Davis.

STRESS AND COPING: THE HASSLE HAYSTACK

Elaine Sorensen Marshall

$\mathscr{S}$tress is one of the most overworked words in modern life. Yet, more than in any previous generation, our lives at home, work, and church are complicated—by contact with more people, increasing complexity of choices, and by a growing number of important but unrelated tasks and demands. Popular magazines promote "tests" to measure stress, with endless lists of "Ten Happy Habits" to reduce stress. Stress reduction is becoming a common prescription in clinical health-promotion and risk-reduction programs. Is all of this just a trendy sign of our time? No. Research in health and social sciences indicates that stress really can make you sick. Stress has been associated with stomach troubles, headaches, and many other health problems. It can make life miserable or even lead to early death from heart disease and stroke.

What is stress? I found twenty-nine different definitions lurking among library volumes in the social sciences. I am sure that there are more, but I stopped upon finding the following statement: "I would advocate that the word 'stress' be stricken from our vocabulary as soon as possible."[1]

Some have attempted to define stress according to an index of particular, difficult life events. Self-administered "stress tests" in checkstand magazines instruct the reader to check the number of stressful events in her or his life. The list includes everything from death, divorce, and jail terms to pregnancy, retirement, sexual difficulties, and Christmas—on the same list. Supposedly, enough of such events in one year threatens your health. One year, my score was so high I should have been in the coronary unit. Ironically, that was the year I seemed to cope best.

Actually, recent research indicates that daily hassles, more than major life events, most threaten quality of life and health. Some social scientists

---

Elaine S. Marshall serves as associate dean of the College of Nursing at Brigham Young University. She has been a missionary to Colombia and has served on a general Church writing committee. Her recent book on children's stress won an award from the National Council on Family Relations. She is married to Dr. John Marshall and is the mother of four children.

have noted that though major life changes, such as divorce and bereavement, are more dramatic, daily hassles may have greater influences on our actual health.[2] Somehow, we seem to marshal our resources and come through the "big" things in life. Certainly we suffer, but people bring casseroles; we seek help; we pray; and we grow stronger. It is the last-straw, flat-tire stuff that raises our blood pressure, increases muscle tension, and initiates all the physiological stress responses that scientists know make us sick and threaten our health and lives.

The hassle pile-up is what gets to us. A few years ago, I had endured separation and divorce, the loss of a son, reduction of income, selling my home, moving to a new town, getting a job, going back to graduate school, putting my children into a new school, staying up at night through four successive cases of chicken pox—all on the official "Life Stress Events" list (okay, maybe not the chicken pox). Then one day, when I arrived too late for my haircut appointment, after frantically running to children's lessons, my school, and my job, I became hysterical, thrashing and sobbing. The hairdresser stood stunned, but I couldn't stop. That last-straw hassle had toppled me over the edge. (Since that traumatic event, I cut my own hair.)

Psychologist Richard Lazarus defines stress as a "relationship between the person and the environment that is appraised by the person as taxing or exceeding his or her resources and endangering his or her well-being."[3] That subtle phrase "appraised by the person" means that whatever I *think* is stressful *is* stressful. Events that exhilarate one person may devastate another. We may each decide whether something challenges us to grow or threatens our very sense of survival. Women, men, and children all experience stress and hassles uniquely. Life is stress! The goal is not to eliminate stress but to cultivate effective ways of coping with it, growing from it, and perhaps even thriving on it. Researchers are thus turning away from studying the sources of stress to observing how people respond, cope, and grow. Many of their findings are well-known. Let me focus on three that may be less familiar to you.

VIEWING LIFE AS A JOURNEY

One basic strategy for effectively coping with stress is to see that life is the journey rather than a way to a final rewarding end or even to a continual series of better-than-now destinations. I am just discovering this, after living nearly half a century saying, "Life will be better after the final exam . . . after I graduate . . . when I go on a mission . . . when I get home from my mission . . . when I am married . . . after the baby is born . . . after the bills are paid . . . " I have a friend who says, "Life is what happens while you are making other plans." I know today that my stress *is* my life.

We hear the generic "life is a journey" metaphor everywhere from billboards to popular self-help books. If that metaphor has lost its power for you, try a different word: Your life may be an expedition, an adventure, an assembly line, a book in progress, a pilgrimage, an excursion, a parade—whatever image best conveys the process for you. But it *is* a process, moving through time, offering interesting insights, challenges, and pleasures along the way. It is not a quick, straight shot to heaven and perfection.

FAITH AND LOVE

Latter-day Saints know that health is enhanced, healing happens, and hassles are put in perspective when we vigorously exercise faith in God. Current scientific studies are also reporting that prayer correlates with higher numbers of positive outcomes to physical illnesses. Treatment programs for addicts encourage faith in a higher power. Popular authors and television talk-show hosts are promoting daily gratitude journals. They have proven effective: list five things for which you are grateful every day, and by the end of the year you will feel more energy and less stress. Life is better when we are responsive to our daily blessings, sensitive to spiritual moments, and honor the sacred things waiting to be noticed in our daily life.

Another intangible but documented stress reducer is love. In study after study, people with a variety of physical, psychological, and emotional illnesses fared better than expected if they had meaningful supportive relationships. Loving relationships improve health and reduce stress.

In the health sciences, we call this "social support"—that is, nurturant people who are important to you, who love and need you, and who help you when you need it. There are some people who nourish our souls, whose very presence makes life better. My friend Martha is like that to everyone who knows her. I see her only occasionally and seldom talk for long, but I need only be near her, and life is easier. On the other hand, some people swallow the energy out of a room, drain us, or make us feel less competent, more tense. When our hassle level is high, we need to be far from these people for a time.

Soon after my grandmother died, my grandfather had a stroke that left him unable to speak. Already predisposed to perfectionism and solitude, human interaction became uncomfortable and tense as he struggled to be understood. His simplest request to move a chair became an irritation to him and the person trying to help. By a lovely miracle of sensitivity, a friend gave him a long-haired, white cat. Soon the cat responded to his strokes, seemed to love him as he gave love, and made him feel competent and needed once more. Tension lessened as we all learned to communicate again. This was a miracle of the power of giving and receiving love at the simplest level.

We need love from others, and we need to give love. Giving love and service promotes mental and emotional health. To give freely does not mean being a martyr, however, or giving from an empty reservoir. Some people give beyond their strength, beyond wisdom, and tax their health. Listen to Anne Morrow Lindbergh's words on the danger to women of giving in ways that do not replenish the spirit: "Is this then what happens to woman? She wants perpetually to spill herself away. All her instinct as a woman—the eternal nourisher of children, of men, of society—demands that she give. Her time, her energy, her creativeness drain out into these channels. . . . Woman spills herself away in driblets to the thirsty, seldom being allowed the time, the quiet, the peace, to let the pitcher fill up to the brim." Lindbergh does not argue for a stance of selfishness, however, but for "purposeful giving": "Purposeful giving is not as apt to deplete one's resources; it belongs to that natural order of giving that seems to renew itself even in the act of depletion. The more one gives the more one has to give—like milk in the breast."[4]

Another way we combat stress is by loving in a special way that developmental theorists call "generativity"—giving to and guiding the next generation. Those who feel a sense of "parenting," though they may not be parents, have a larger perspective and purpose beyond today's hassles. Teaching and mentoring the next generation in any part of our life lends purpose and reduces competitive stress in our own lives. A recent popular magazine listed the four hundred "best" physicians for women, according to peer nomination. My husband, who has spent a career teaching physicians, was not on the list, but he delighted in counting a dozen names who were "his residents" with the same joy as if they were his own children. I realized at that moment that drawing energy from such generative giving promotes health and wisdom.

WORK

Among the most common effective antidotes for stress is work. That may be hard to believe because for many of us work is a primary source of stress. To be a stress reducer, work must be loved, and not everyone can find that in the work of their employment. To find a vocation that you love would surely add years of health to your life. But if you are not fortunate in your employment, you must find some activities, both physical and mental, over which you have a sense of control and achievement. You may find you need to balance the satisfying mental exertion of your workplace with a physical interest or vice versa.

Though I love my work, I spend hours in a building, at a desk, among students, in meetings, or near a computer. Eventually such work, though intellectually stimulating, adds to my stress. I need some physical work or play. Though I claim to be allergic to formal exercise, I know activity could reduce my sense of stress and help me be healthier. I love gardening and even housecleaning, and I usually take the stairs at work, but I fall far short of a healthy, stress-reducing lifestyle. My father, who drives cattle, lifts bales of hay, and literally sweats for fourteen hours a day, never complains of stress.

IMAGINATION

The strategies I've mentioned so far may be familiar to you, but the last remedy may be new: imagination. To use imagination to cope does not mean to fantasize and escape into a more comfortable alternative reality. Facing truth, speaking truth, and respecting truth are the foundations of physical and emotional health. Among cancer patients, for example, guided imagery and positive affirmation have both been shown to enhance health, but not until the individual has first faced the truth of his or her medical diagnosis, treatment, and prognosis.

Once we are able to confront and integrate the truth of our lives, however, imagination can be the soul's medicine. Imagination, that uniquely human attribute, allows us to find meaning in the challenges of our lives, whether traumatic events or daily hassles.

While my mother was dying, her body was terribly swollen, and for a time she moaned as if, I perceived, in childbirth. As I washed her and combed her hair, I imagined myself midwife to the one who bore me. I was attending to her as she labored for another passage. I treasure that image. It helps me tolerate the grief of her loss. I have since become aware that this is a common metaphor in poetry, literature, and personal stories. A daughter's care of a dying mother is a return to the essential maternal story of passage.

Two other words, *imagery* and *magic*, are found in the word *imagination*. Imagery can expand our reality and positively reframe stressors almost too harsh for endurance. Coping images are everywhere, if we search among the ordinary, expecting magic and miracles.

In a startling, often-told psychology project, three groups of subjects were assigned a different activity. One group was asked to spend one-half hour a day practicing free throws on a basketball court; the second, to spend one-half hour a day off the court, without a ball, imagining successful free throws in the mind; and the third group was to do nothing. At the end of two weeks, the three groups were brought to a basketball court and asked to make ten free throws. The scores of those who did nothing remained the same. The scores of the group who practiced and the group who imagined the practice both improved and performed equally. Imagery became magic.

Faith, love, work, and imagination are powerful tools, important gear, for coping with life stress on life's journey. So are moderation in life habits of diet, exercise, sleep, and personal maintenance. No matter how well equipped we are, there will be times we simply cannot forge ahead, and we must slow down a while to rest and reflect. We may even choose to reroute our course. I have found life to be a journey forward, and sometimes backward, or even sideways, toward perfection. Striving, progress, stumbling, repentance, and growth have been important milestones on my eternal path. But if I accept life as a journey, then I can expect and accept the rocks and the slippery spots as well as the smooth pavement.

Notes

1. Joseph T. Mullan, "The (Mis)meaning of Life Events in Family Stress Theory and Research," paper presented at the Preconference Theory Construction and Research Methodology Workshop, National Council on Family Relations Annual Meeting, October 1983, St. Paul, Minnesota, 11.
2. See Richard S. Lazarus and Susan Folkman, *Stress, Appraisal, and Coping* (New York: Springer, 1984); Anita DeLongis, James C. Coyne, Gayle Dakof, Susan Folkman, and Richard S. Lazarus, "Relationship of Daily Hassles, Uplifts, and Major Life Events to Health Status," *Health Psychology* 1 (1982): 119–36.
3. Lazarus and Folkman, *Stress, Appraisal, and Coping*, 21.
4. Anne Morrow Lindbergh, *Gift from the Sea* (New York: Random House, 1955), 45, 47.

I SPEAK FROM MY HEART: THE STORY OF A BLACK SOUTH AFRICAN WOMAN

◦⧜◦

Julia Mavimbela

Introduction by Carol Cornwall Madsen:

Several years after the death of her husband, this extraordinary South African woman moved with her five children to a small home on a rocky parcel of land in Soweto, a township outside Johannesburg. There she reclaimed the rocky soil and planted a garden, continuing her lifetime dedication to organic gardening for food and remedial use. The garden attracted the children nearby, who began, under her tutelage, to plant their own gardens. In reclaiming these often tiny plots of land, making them beautiful as well as useful, the children learned nature's law, the law of return. I believe the law of return has been the guiding principle of Julia Mavimbela's life, for through initiative, determination, and remarkable vision, she has reclaimed not only unused land but scarred and impoverished lives, making them fruitful and productive.

With the help of her sister's earnings and her own, Julia acquired the education necessary to qualify her to be a teacher. She later became one of the first women principals in the Transvaal. In addition to her duties as principal and unbeknown to her superiors, she also taught a class of forty children who were too poor to attend the school. She conducted auctions and improvised other methods to raise money for her teachers when a severe depression cut off their paychecks. She organized the Homemakers Club, where mothers taught homemaking skills to one another, and in the wake of World War II started community Waste Not, Want Not clubs in which she instructed women how to recycle their clothes and use every scrap of food. She instigated a successful campaign to raise the literacy level of black women, organizing a group that now has 783 branches throughout the republic, teaching women to read and write. Julia is proud to say that because of these skills, "All the mothers today are becoming very special women in their way of life."

Her concern extended to the restless young boys she saw about her who

371

lacked leadership and purposeful activities. She organized a club for them and, being a former physical education teacher, taught them sports. Through her leadership and coaching, the boys won numerous awards in youth competitions.

The 1976 riots in Soweto, which devastated the township and brought about harsh government restrictions, catalyzed Julia to further community action. At great risk she expanded her gardening project throughout Soweto, mobilizing her growing army of youthful gardeners to help repair the damage done by the riots, clearing rubble and planting trees, and helping others to provide scarce food by planting their own gardens. Again, through these acts of reclamation, came a healing lesson. "Where there is a bloodstain," Julia taught, "a beautiful flower must grow."

The riots impressed on Julia even more emphatically the need for women to unite to protect their common interest, the survival and future of their families. Thus she became a founding member and eventually copresident of Women for Peace, a multiracial organization that now numbers more than fifteen thousand women. With the strength of the organization behind her, she personally petitioned government ministers to intervene when young people were illegally detained or unnecessarily harassed by officials and deprived of their schooling. The peace this organization is working for is not just the absence of war and rioting but the peace that comes from living together as neighbors, bonded by a common land and a share in the bounties it affords. Through Women for Peace as well as the National Council of Women of South Africa, which she also headed for several years, Julia has worked in behalf of women and families throughout the republic. Her own words tell of her commitment:

"I give thanks to God that he has made me a woman. I give thanks to my Creator that he has made me black; that he has fashioned me as I am, with hands, heart, head to serve my people. It can, it should be a glorious thing to be a woman. It is important for women to be aware of their common lot. It is important for women to stand together and rise together to meet our common enemies—illiteracy, poverty, crime, disease, and stupid unjust laws that have made women feel so helpless as to be hopeless."

In 1981 Julia encountered two Mormon missionaries and joined the Church within two months. From that time on she has been an unofficial assistant to the missionaries assigned to Soweto, many of whom assisted in bringing her and her companion, Sister Dolly Ndhlovu, to America. Fluent *in several languages, she has translated for them and helped them gain entry into many homes. She is also Relief Society president in the Soweto Branch.*

Ever the missionary, on one occasion, when the mission president brought some television equipment to her branch to show some Church videos, at least fifty curious children poured into the yard to see what was happening. Immediately Julia began teaching them "I Am a Child of God." They were eager to sing and learned it quickly. Then Julia asked them, "How many of you will go to your homes right now and teach this song to your families?" Every hand went up. She quickly added, "When you teach this song to your parents, tell them that we meet in church in this very room every Sunday morning at 9:00, and they are all invited to come and sing the song with us."

Despite urgent pleas to remain and a substantial increase in pay, Julia has recently resigned a teaching post to serve as a self-appointed full-time missionary. "I feel my greatest work is yet to come," explained this youthful seventy-one-year-old woman to President R. J. Snow, the mission president.

Whatever is yet ahead for Julia Mavimbela to do, she has already created a legacy of Christlike love, forgiveness, and service that invests the term Latter-day Saint with genuine meaning. A hundred years ago another Mormon pioneer woman also brought imagination and courage to the challenges of her spiritually and physically impoverished frontier community: "As far as I am able," this pioneer woman wrote, "I will spread light into darkened chambers."

Throughout Julia's long life, and with the aid of the additional light of the gospel for the last eight years, Julia, like her spiritual sister before her, has spread lifegiving light wherever she has found darkened chambers in the minds, the hearts, and the spirit of her people.

I come from a country of many, many languages—South Africa—especially my little area, which is called Soweto. As I greet you, I also bring you the greetings of all my brothers and sisters in South Africa and especially in Soweto. We love you. We learned the greatest love from you when your good sons and daughters came and won our hearts to the gospel, for which blessing we thank you.

I will tell you just how I came in touch with the Church. Because of the work I had been doing in Soweto, many people seemed to feel that if anything went wrong, I was the one to see about correcting it. I think that's what happened on the last day of September in 1981 when a group of Anglican women came to my home and asked me to help clean up the Dube Boys' Club, which was in terrible shape and which they were trying to bring back.

I was very reserved with these women, very stiff. I saw in their eyes that they had come to exploit me, to use me to promote their own causes. I refused them flat, but when they had left, something touched my heart. I had never snubbed anyone before, and I asked myself, out of all the women in Soweto, could they have just thought of my name? I felt I should humble myself and go to the boys' club.

So the following morning, without telling the Anglican women that I had changed my mind, I went to the club. As I came near I noticed two white boys (as I called them), greeted them, and asked them what they were doing. They said they were helping, and I asked, "Why? Where do you come from?"

"From America," they said, and that blew me down, for there is really no connection between America and my Soweto.

"Well," I said and walked into the office of the club. I had hardly entered when they were there on my heels.

"Will you please shake our hands?" they asked. "You have been so friendly. For the past three weeks, yours is the only hello that has uplifted us."

I was shy about talking with them. I said, "Come along, now, that is just how I greet people."

Next they proposed, "Can we come to your home?" This question was very challenging to me, because at that time in Soweto whoever admitted a white into his home was considered a traitor.

I took a breath and, just to appease them, said, "All right, but you must give me three days to go and clean my little house. I'm a woman who is always on the street, and cobwebs are hanging." I thought they might forget, but indeed, after those three days had passed, on the dot they were there at my door.

I let them in and had another shock when I read *Elder* on their name tags. Elder? I started to shiver. In my church, an elder was an untouchable, and I had just let two elders into my house. They gave a prayer and started with the lesson. I listened, but I want to tell you, my brothers and sisters, what they said carried no weight with me whatsoever. I said to myself, oh, they are just from another one of those groups that come to preach to us, and I dismissed them. Then they asked, "Can we come again next week, same day, same time?"

Something hit hard on my heart. I said, "Okay," and they were there again.

This time they came with two sisters, a group of four. And still, nothing they said touched me. The third week they looked on the wall at the wedding photo of my husband and me. They wanted to know where he was, and I told them that he had died. This time they kindled a spark of interest in me. They asked, "Did you know that you can have someone be baptized for him?" I want to tell you, my eyes opened wide because I had been taught that it was improper even to speak of someone who had died. The religions I knew totally rejected the dead, and to talk about them was heathenism and would lead to excommunication. Therefore, the missionaries were teaching me enlivening news. This time, they kindled a spark in me.

I answered, "It is strange for me to hear you whites talk about the dead as if they were alive. Will you come and explain this to me?" The next week, when they visited me, I was a settled woman, very attentive, most absorbing, willing to learn and understand. I could feel something turning in me, and from then on, I wished I could be with the missionaries almost every day.

As the lessons went on, more opened in my mind, in my heart. Soon I decided, "Come along, I'm ready for baptism." I chose a date, with no previous knowledge of what that date meant in my life or in the life of my family. I just said to myself, the 28th of November I'm getting baptized. When the missionaries came, they said, "No, Sister Julia, we are going to baptize you on the 23rd." But I said, "Please, the 28th." And later, that date became something of a testimony to me that genealogy is living because the date I chose was the date my father had died. As I was four years old at the time, I had not known much about it. I still knew nothing on the day of my baptism, but when I began to do genealogy, the two dates came together.

That was how I joined the Church. I feel that I became involved with the Church by being involved with the people.

My country is a country of many problems, some known to you. As one of South Africa's kings, King Goodwill Zwelithini of Zululand, has said, "When two widely divergent cultures meet at the tip of the African continent, it leads to a startling chapter in the history of the world, and attention is focused on the outcome." This same king, when asked about how he saw the future, said, "No problem at all if we can come together." That is the most important message I bring you: only when we come together can we understand one another.

At times some of the problems in my country make people think they can hardly open their doors or walk out in the streets and come back whole. There have been quite a few unpleasant times—1976, for example, which found Soweto most unhappy as a result of riots against changes in the educational system.[1] That was one of the most challenging times of my life—to see what we called schools going up in flames, what we called libraries being battered down, and, worse still, the waste of all that young talent when the educational programs ceased. All of what I would call our treasure was being destroyed. Later, strikes saw parents out of work, which made things worse for many families. I am grateful to the Lord that something was touched in me at that time. I developed a plan to try to help the young people, and my plan was to try to engage the hand to engage the mind.

With nothing to start with, I asked for the use of an abandoned church-yard that belonged to the Salvation Army. It was infested with rodents; it was covered with waste. I was allowed to use it, perhaps because it saved the owners from the endless summonses they would have received for failing to keep the property clean. I collected the little children, from four to ten years old, to go into that churchyard and start gardens.

I have always found pleasure in a garden. At times as a mother it isn't possible to get away from the family when some annoyance comes up. But if you can go into the garden, I can assure you, brothers and sisters, it's such a beautiful place. When you break up the soil, you feel your own heart melting, and by the time you have done a little work, often you forget what had disturbed you.

So I taught my little ones at that time, as we were dealing with the lumps of dirt, that these lumps could be overcome if we worked them with the knowledge that we were preparing to get something out of the soil. And when we began putting in the little plants, I would say to the children, "You see? Now the trouble you perhaps see at home, cover it with the soil, like we're doing with the plants. See what good things you can grow if you nurse this little patch." I could see us all begin to feel more peaceful, more at ease, though I, too, had been tense and frightened to speak of anything positive during the days of unrest when we were starting those gardens.

At times there was no water. We absolutely couldn't use water from the taps because of the high bills, so we had to use kitchen waste water. I took sand from the river and put it in tins, and then I would take the kitchen waste water and filter it through the sand into our little gardens. Even despite these efforts, sometimes we couldn't get enough water to cover the whole patch. And then I would say, "Come. Let's go home. Let's all pray. There is someone above us who sees what we are doing. We'll surely see something happen." At times, brothers and sisters, it was as if a telegram or telephone call went directly to the Lord. The next morning I would come to the patch, and there had been a good rain overnight. I can't tell you of the excitement I saw in those beautiful little faces, all convinced that surely there was someone interested in and caring for the work they were doing.

Then it came to me that I could use the gardens not only for cultivation but also for schools. When I bought a package of seeds, perhaps carrots, I would say, "Fine. Now you can see how to spell the word. From the picture you will get the answer of what word it is." Soon we brought little exercise books and pens and all sat down to write the word c-a-r-r-o-t, and then the children could learn the word *car*. There had been several scrap cars in the yard before we cleaned it, and I had insisted that one be left as a shelter for our seedbeds. I wrote the word *car* on it, so the children would see it whenever they worked. The word *rot* we associated with our compost heap. In this way, the children also learned the elements of the larger word *carrot*. Our school became very interesting, and at the end of the week we would dramatize what we had learned. This play carried many through their examinations.

Finally, as time went on, we found that the gardens were also attracting not only the younger children but also the youth who were hunted down like rabbits during the rioting or whenever things got out of control. So my little gardens became a sort of refuge home. If the police would pass and find the children busy with me, they would just walk on.

And, joy! As people watched us struggle with long stubborn weeds, they offered to help, and that was a beginning of family gardens. With almost no tools, we worked like ants. Where there had been dumping, we cleared, and we filled potholes and planted trees. I moved from corner to corner of Soweto. I was in demand almost around the republic, replacing the negative with the positive and with beneficial skills. With no school and no work for many, something had to be done. As Salvation Army yards were opened near Mofolo Park, we asked, "Can you allow us to clean and plant?" My great challenge of 1976 was referred to in *Soil Sense*, published the following year:

"Mrs. Mavimbela dreams and schemes to get the youth involved in making Soweto greener . . . to make them feel that their surroundings belong to them, that they are responsible for them and therefore will not destroy them. She wishes not only to repair the physical damage of the recent riots, but also the mental and moral damage, and her message to youth is, 'Where there was a blood stain, a beautiful flower must grow.'"

As you have heard, I am also involved in several organizations. Because of the unrest in 1976, Women for Peace was founded, which ultimately had fifteen thousand members of all races. The women in my country believe that we can come together to bring about change. Our men don't come together—I don't know why—but mostly women's organizations are the ones that work to bring about the understanding that is so desperately needed. We have made provisions to translate for the black sisters in these organizations who do not speak English or read it easily, so that they get the matter in their own mother tongue. These are some of the issues we are concerned about, to see that all women, educated or not, be taught to make the right choices for their families:

In the shops several types of powdered milk have been sold, some for whiteners or creamers. Many of these are dangerous to feed babies as replacements for mother's milk because they lack nutrition. We stood up to the shopkeepers, notifying them we felt they must make it clear in their stores what products are not good for babies. Their answer: they cooperated. We sent our members to investigate some areas and supervise others to be sure that this matter was carried out.

We have also worked for the passage of the Matrimonial Property Act. In my country a woman who is widowed may not operate her property unless her eldest son takes over. The son becomes responsible for the mother. We feel it is so silly that a son should stand in for his father. It makes the oldest son feel that all he has to do is sit and wait until daddy dies and then take over. He is encouraged not to be a working child but to wait to get whatever his mother and father have acquired. We have fought this situation and seen a matrimonial act pass, but it solves the problems only for our white sisters. Nevertheless, the law commission is at present investigating possible changes in the law relating to black marriages.

I bring up this example to show that not until you present your case will officials know what you need and where to start making changes. By making the problems known to the right people, you may get answers.

Many black women in South Africa live in "customary marriages," what you call common-law marriages. These marriages occur when two parents agree that they want to stay together, but their union has not been recognized by a formal ceremony. Customary unions can be registered in Natal, but not in the other provinces. Chief Mongosuthu (Gatsha) Buthelezi in Zululand, Natal, has taken the lead in liberating the black women to administer their estates when they are widows and also to sign their own travel documents. Nevertheless, we are still fighting for the women in the other provinces because we feel that all women should be the same before the law. Outside Natal, if the husband in a customary marriage dies, it is very difficult for the wife because she has no claim whatsoever on the estate. We confronted the minister of justice with this issue, and he agrees that the situation for these women is very unjust. He said he is distressed and will do something as soon as possible.

We looked into the pay of our teachers. To discuss this issue, I must again bring in that word that is the tale of South Africa—*apartheid*. Representing teachers of all colors—white, black, and brown—we went to the minister of education to request that the pay scale for teachers be improved. Soon white teachers were paid much better, and the pay for colored teachers was not so bad. It was the blacks, overburdened with work, who received just a small and unsatisfactory increase. And blacks are still struggling. But that partial defeat doesn't keep us from knocking on the door of the minister. When we make him uncomfortable, that's when we feel very happy as women.

Then I come to the question of black children who have been detained. That issue we have also attacked as women. We have spoken with leading officials, and they have given us hearing. And some have seen the injustice that has been dealt. We see improvement as the leaders have arranged the release of some of the children. But now these children are overaged; they may no longer be accepted into the schools. Women for Peace has found volunteer, unpaid teachers to help these children who are unable to return to the classroom because of their age.

A few who have continued their studies have taken their examinations, I think with success.

We go together, women of all races, to our leaders. We have broken the law by mixing races in our organizations, by making them above color lines, and we let the leaders know that. Despite the laws, they have accepted us. They know that what we stand for and what we bring them makes sense.

Our men, particularly our young men, don't have the patience we black women have. We believe in following the Bible when it says, "Let us reason together." If we cannot reason with our leaders, we might lose what we shouldn't lose.

I do feel, brothers and sisters, that little change will be accomplished until the women of the nation rise together and put their case to the leaders in one strong voice, not challenging with fists but making the men remember that they too have children, they too live with problems that affect their families. Mothers are the key to solving most problems. We must make the men remember when they are in their seats of office that they are not immune from the issues their families face. Life is the same for all. Economic sanctions from other countries may or may not contribute to the solution of my country's problems, but the power of change lies with us, the people within the country. We women will talk to our leaders, talk to them even if they close their doors on us.

We are not where we can say all is well. But we say all can be done, and we feel it will be done.

Note

1. On 16 June 1976, a group of fifteen thousand Soweto high school students marched to the stadium of the Orlando West Junior Secondary School to protest a recent edict by school authorities that their arithmetic and social studies courses be taught in Afrikaans. (Although this was the immediate cause of the demonstration, other changes and limitations in the education system had led to student dissatisfaction and frustration.) The students were confronted by a police detachment that, failing to disperse them with tear gas, fired on them, killing two students and injuring several others. This action resulted in riots throughout Soweto and soon throughout South Africa. In the next few months protest marches, strikes, and demonstrations were met with harsh repression. The schools in Soweto were closed, and many schools and other public buildings were burned. Except for brief periods, schooling did not resume until 1978, so the students were left with neither educational opportunities nor any productive projects for a year and a half. Furthermore, many students were arrested for their part in the demonstrations and riots and held in jail for long periods of time.

AFTER ALL WE CAN DO: THE MEANING OF GRACE IN OUR LIVES

∽✴∾

Robert L. Millet

*T*he matter of the grace of God, as mediated through Jesus the Christ, has for the last fifteen years seemed to "occupy my mind, and press itself upon my feelings" (D&C 128:1). I have not desired to become a crusader or to be a part of some new theological craze in the Church but have sought with real intent to better understand what it means to trust in and rely "upon the merits, and mercy, and grace of the Holy Messiah" (2 Nephi 2:8).

IN CONTEXT

I have felt for some time that the concept of the grace of Jesus Christ deserves more of our attention as Latter-day Saints, especially as it is such a central doctrine in the Book of Mormon and the New Testament. Perhaps some of us have been hesitant to perceive the truthfulness and eternal relevance of this doctrine because it brings us face to face with our own limitations. Perhaps we shy away from it because we sense that we may have to alter our present way of viewing things. Whatever the cause, it just may be that we have not enjoyed the quiet, pervasive power that comes to those who acknowledge their weakness and turn to him who has all power. I believe, however, that there is wisdom in presenting this doctrinal message in context, in the way it is presented in scripture—the context of the Atonement. That is to say, grace is not a doctrine that stands alone; it is inextricably tied to several others and therefore makes sense and brings peace only when seen in that context.

Latter-day Saints have often criticized those who stress salvation by grace alone, and we have often been criticized for a type of works-righteousness. The gospel is, in fact, a covenant—a two-way promise.

Robert L. Millet is dean of Religious Education and professor of ancient scripture at Brigham Young University. He serves as president of the BYU Fourteenth Stake. He and his wife, Shauna Sizemore Millet, are the parents of six children and the grandparents of one.

The Lord agrees to do for us what we could never do for ourselves— forgive our sins, lift our burdens, renew our souls and re-create our nature, raise us from the dead and qualify us for glory hereafter. At the same time, we promise to do what we *can* do: receive the ordinances of salvation, love and serve one another (see Mosiah 18:8–10), and do all in our power to put off the "natural man" and deny ourselves of ungodliness (Mosiah 3:19; see Moroni 10:32). We must do more than offer a verbal expression of faith in the Lord, more than confess with the lips that we have received Christ into our hearts. The scriptures of the Restoration add perspective and balance to the majestic teachings of the apostle Paul on the matter of salvation by grace. We know without question that the power to save us, to change us, to renew our souls is in Christ. True faith, however, always manifests itself in faithfulness. Good works evidence our faith, our desire to remain in covenant with Christ. But these good works, though necessary, are not sufficient.

Too often we view grace as that increment of goodness, that final gift of God that will make up the difference and thereby boost us into the celestial kingdom, "after all we can do" (2 Nephi 25:23). To be sure, we will need a full measure of divine assistance to become celestial material. But the grace of God, through Jesus Christ our Lord, is available to us every hour of every day of our lives. "True grace," as one non–Latter-day Saint writer has suggested, "is more than just a giant freebie, opening the door to heaven in the sweet by and by, but leaving us to wallow in sin in the bitter here and now. Grace is God presently at work in our lives."[1] The grace of God is a precious gift, a power enabling us to face life with quiet courage, to do things we could never do on our own. The Great Physician does more than forgive sins. He ministers relief to the disconsolate, comfort to the bereaved, confidence to those who wrestle with infirmities and feelings of inadequacy, strength and peace to those who have been battered and scarred by the ironies of this life (Isaiah 61:1–2; Alma 7:11–13).

Few things would be more sinister than encouraging lip service to God but discouraging obedience and faithful discipleship. On the other hand, surely nothing could be more offensive to God than a smug self-assurance that comes from trusting in one's own works or relying upon one's own strength. Understanding this sacred principle—the relationship between the grace of an infinite being and the works of finite man—is not easy, but it is immensely rewarding.

WHO'S IN CONTROL?

I cannot speak for the Church. I am, however, an expert on my own feelings. I have come to know firsthand some of the despondency and guilt associated with falling short of my goals, of trying to do it all, of striving to make myself perfect. The apostle Paul seems to have been addressing a similar problem in his day. He wrote: "Brethren, my heart's desire and prayer to God for Israel is, that they might be saved. For I bear them record that they have a zeal of God, but not according to knowledge. For they being ignorant of God's righteousness, and going about to establish their own righteousness, have not submitted themselves unto the righteousness of God. For Christ is the end of the law for righteousness to every one that believeth" (Romans 10:1–4).

I have been associated with many wonderful, caring people who struggle often with feelings of inadequacy, who hope against hope that one day—in some distant age in the future—in spite of their frailty in this sphere, they might qualify to feel comfortable where gods and angels are. Since it is true that the gospel of Jesus Christ is intended to liberate us, to ease and lighten our burdens, to bring that comfort and rest found in no other way, why do some of us struggle at times? Why do we find ourselves simply going through the motions, doing our duty in the Church but finding little fulfillment and enjoyment in it? Why do we carry our religion as a burden rather than a joy?

I suspect that many Latter-day Saints will agree to the same faulty orientation I find occasionally in myself. My greatest frustrations seem to come as a result of my efforts to "handle it" myself or, in other words, my failure to trust in and rely on the Lord. Maybe our culture contributes to our dilemma; maybe it's the constant chant of "You can do anything you put your mind to" or "You have unlimited possibilities and potential" that tends to focus our attention away from the powers of the divine toward our abilities, our merits, and our contributions. Our problems cannot be solved by humanity alone, no matter how impressive our accomplishments. The programs of society will not fill the soul's yearning for solace. In fact, we almost need to work at cross purposes to social trends, to attune our ears to a quiet voice that beckons us amidst the loud babble of competing voices. That quiet voice pleads with us simply to come unto Christ. The answer to individual hurt and personal pain cannot be found in congressional decisions, in personnel management, or in louder cries of victimization. Solace comes in and through Jesus Christ. The most pertinent crusade in which the Christian is involved is the quest for personal peace, for purity of heart, all of which come from Christ through the ordinances of the priesthood and by the power of the Holy Ghost. The scriptures teach plainly and persuasively that coming unto Christ entails a moment of decision, a poignant point in our progression wherein we realize that man-made solutions are in reality "broken cisterns, that can hold no water" (Jeremiah 2:13) and that only through yoking ourselves to the Master may we rid ourselves of the burdens of Babylon.

Few things in this life are exactly as they seem. We live in a time, for example, when we hear constantly the importance of being in control, in charge, in power. We must have access to and management over all variables. We operate by plans and formulae and procedures, surrounded by lists and tables and charts. A harsh reality facing those acclimated to and successful in this fallen world is that spiritual things cannot be programmed. We cannot require or demand or shape spiritual experience. The Spirit is in control, not us. The Lord through his Spirit works his marvelous wonders in his own time, in his own way, and according to his own will and purposes. To enter the realm of divine experience, therefore, is to enter a realm where we are not in complete control. We can seek to be worthy, strive to be in a position to be blessed, plead and pray for divine intervention, but we do not force the hand of the Almighty.

Though such matters as self-reliance and self-confidence may prove valuable in some of life's dealings, the reciprocal principles of submission, surrender, and having an eye single to the glory of God are essential if we are to acquire that enabling power described in scripture as the saving grace of Jesus Christ. It is as if the Lord inquires of us: "Do you want to possess all things such that all things are subject unto you?" We, of course, respond in the affirmative. He then says: "Good. Then submit to me. Yield your heart unto me." The Lord asks further: "Do you want to have victory over all things?" We nod. He follows up: "Then surrender to me. Unconditionally." Odd, isn't it? We incorporate the powers of divinity only through acknowledging our own inabilities, accepting our limitations, and realizing our weaknesses. We open ourselves to infinite strength only through accepting our finite condition. We, in time, gain control through being willing to relinquish control.

I am haunted by the words of Paul in his second epistle to the Corinthians. Paul was required to spend a significant amount of time defending his apostolic calling. Having been a zealous Pharisee and even a persecutor of the Christians before his conversion and not having been one of the original witnesses of the resurrection of Christ, he felt the need to testify to his detractors that his call had indeed come from God. In doing so with the Corinthian Saints, he described some marvelous spiritual experiences the Lord had given to him. "And lest I should be exalted above measure," Paul hastened to add, "through the abundance of the revelations, there was given to me a thorn in the flesh, the messenger of Satan to buffet me, lest I should be exalted above measure. For this thing I besought the Lord thrice, that it might depart from me. And [the Lord] said unto me, My grace is sufficient for thee: for my strength is made perfect in weakness." Paul then remarked: "Most gladly therefore will I rather glory in my infirmities, . . . in reproaches, in necessities, in persecutions, in distresses for Christ's sake: for when I am weak, then am I strong" (2 Corinthians 12:7–10).

No one really knows what his "thorn in the flesh" was. Was it a lingering sickness, perhaps malaria, so common in Galatia? Was it a memory of his past, a hellish reminder of who he had once been? Was it an evil spirit that dogged his steps and wearied him in his ministry? Perhaps one day we'll know. Whatever it was, however, it forced Paul to his knees in humility. His impotence in the face of this particular challenge was ever before him. I rather think that when Paul states that he "besought the Lord thrice" for the removal of the thorn that he is not describing merely three prayers but instead three seasons of prayer, extended periods of wrestling and laboring in the Spirit for a specific blessing that never came. Indeed, as he suggests, another kind of blessing came—a closeness, a sensitivity, an acquaintance with Deity, a sanctified strength that came through pain and suffering. Up against the wall of faith, shorn of self-assurance and naked in his extremity and his frightening finitude, a mere mortal received that enabling power we know as the grace of Christ. As the Savior explained to Moroni, when we acknowledge and confess our weakness—not just our specific weaknesses, our individual sins, but our weakness, our mortal limitations—and submit ourselves unto him, we transform weakness into strength (see Ether 12:27).

As Jacob, son of Lehi, affirmed: "Wherefore, we search the prophets, and we have many revelations and the spirit of prophecy; and having all these witnesses we obtain a hope, and our faith becometh unshaken, insomuch that we truly can command in the name of Jesus and the very trees obey us, or the mountains, or the waves of the sea." Now note these words: "Nevertheless, the Lord God showeth us our weakness that we may know that it is by his grace, and his great condescensions unto the children of men, that we have power to do these things" (Jacob 4:6–7).

Too much of my own frustration over the years has come as a result of my refusal to let go and thus let God. Something—I suppose it is the natural man, the prideful self that automatically asserts its own agenda—drives me to want to do it myself. Oh, I believe in God, to be sure—that he loves me, that he sent his Son to earth to help me. All too often, however, my actions have betrayed my limited orientation, my vision of Christ as a type of spiritual advisor, a sort of celestial cheerleader who stands on the sidelines and whispers encouragement but not the Lord God Omnipotent who came to earth to make men and women into new creatures by empowering them to do what they could never do for themselves.

In an eagerness to draw closer to Christ, some Church members seem to have begun to cross a sacred line and go beyond that reverential barrier that must be observed by true followers of the Christ. They speak of Jesus as though he were their next-door neighbor, their buddy or chum, their pal. This is not the way to intimacy with the Savior. Oddly enough, strangely enough, it is not through humanizing Jesus, through trying to make him one of the boys, that we draw closer to him and incorporate his saving powers. It is, rather, through recognizing his godhood, his divinity, his unspeakable power. In short, the more I sense his greatness, his infinity, his capacity to transform the human soul, and my utter helplessness without him, the more I come unto him. Remember, it is through recognizing our own nothingness and weakness that we derive strength (see Mosiah 2:20–21; 4:11–12; Moses 1:10).

Sometimes we speak of Jesus as our Elder Brother. He is, of course, our elder brother in that he was the firstborn spirit child of God in the premortal existence. But it interests me that the Book of Mormon prophets never speak of Jehovah as our Elder Brother. Rather, he is the Almighty God, the Eternal Judge, the Holy One of Israel, the Holy Messiah, the Everlasting Father, the Father of heaven and of earth, the God of nature, the Supreme Being, the Keeper of the gate, the King of heaven, and the Lord God Omnipotent. Elder M. Russell Ballard recently explained: "We occasionally hear some members refer to Jesus as our Elder Brother, which is a true concept based on our understanding of the premortal life with our Father in Heaven. But like many points of gospel doctrine, that simple truth doesn't go far enough in terms of describing the Savior's role in our present lives and His great position as a member of the Godhead. Thus, some non-LDS Christians are uncomfortable with what they perceive as a secondary role for Christ in our theology. They feel that we view Jesus as a spiritual peer. They believe that we view Christ as an implementor, if you will, for God but that we don't view Him as God to us and to all mankind, which, of course, is counter to biblical testimony about Christ's divinity. Let me help us understand, with clarity and testimony, our belief about Jesus Christ. We declare He is the King of Kings, Lord of Lords, the Creator, the Savior, the Captain of our Salvation, the Bright and Morning Star. He has taught us that He is in all things, above all things, through all things and round about all things, that He is Alpha and Omega, the Lord of the Universe, the first and the last relative to our salvation, and that His name is above every name and is in fact the only name under heaven by which we can be saved.

" . . . [W]e can understand why some Latter-day Saints have tended to focus on Christ's Sonship as opposed to His Godhood. As members of earthly families, we can relate to Him as a child, as a Son, and as a Brother because we know how that feels. We can personalize that relationship because we ourselves are children, sons and daughters, brothers and sisters. For some it may be more difficult to relate to Him as a God. And so in an attempt to draw closer to Christ and to cultivate warm and personal feelings toward Him, some tend to humanize Him, sometimes at the expense of acknowledging His Divinity. So let us be very clear on this point: it is true that Jesus was our Elder Brother in the premortal life, but we believe that in this life it is crucial that we become 'born again' as His sons and daughters in the gospel covenant."[2]

Too many of my efforts and, unfortunately, too many of my prayers have been bent on succeeding—according to my own predetermined plan. Instead of opening myself to divine direction and incorporating the powers of heaven, I wanted to be able to look back on life and sing with gusto, "I did it my way!" Too little time was spent in sacred submission; on too few occasions did I say the words (and mean it!), "Thy will be done, O Lord, and not mine." Instead of praying to know my limits, to know when my offering was acceptable, I prayed for more drive and more willpower. I have since come to believe that "fallen man is not simply an imperfect creature who needs improvement: he is a rebel who must lay down his arms."[3] The saving and ironic truth is this: as we submit, we come to know his will. As we surrender, we come to gain his power. As

we yield our hearts unto God, our affections and our feelings are sanctified by his grace. As President Ezra Taft Benson has taught, once we turn
our lives over to the Lord, we discover that he can do far more with us
than we could ever do with ourselves.[4]

It is one thing to say to God, "Thy will be done," and another thing to
entirely mean it. It takes moral courage and spiritual foresight to mean it. It
takes divine aid. As a part of the dedicatory prayer of the Kirtland Temple,
the Prophet Joseph Smith implored: "Help thy servants to say, *with thy grace
assisting them:* Thy will be done, O Lord, and not ours" (D&C 109:44;
italics added). It is true that praying "Thy will be done" may entail
submitting to difficult or challenging circumstances ahead. C. S. Lewis
provides a slightly different approach to this scripture: "'Thy will *be done.*'
But a great deal of it is to be done by God's creatures; including me. The
petition, then, is not merely that I may patiently suffer God's will but also
that I may vigorously do it. I must be an agent as well as a patient. I am
asking that I may be enabled to do it. . . .

"Taken this way, I find the words have a more regular daily application. For there isn't always—or we don't always have reason to suspect
that there is—some great affliction looming in the near future, but there
are always duties to be done; usually, for me, neglected duties to be caught
up with. 'Thy will be *done*—by me—now' brings one back to brass tacks."
Further, Lewis explains that "Thy will be done" may also imply a readi-
ness on our part to receive and experience new and unanticipated blessings. "I know it sounds fantastic," he adds, "but think it over. It seems to
me that we often, almost sulkily, reject the good that God offers us
because, at that moment, we expected some other good."[5] "Thy will be
done" thus represents our petition that the Almighty work his wonders
through us, that he soften our hearts to new ideas, new avenues of understanding, and open us to new paths and new doors of opportunity when it
is best for us to move in another direction.

IN WHOM DO I TRUST?

There is a passage in the Book of Mormon that can be rather frightening. Jacob explained: "And [Christ] commandeth all men that they
must repent, and be baptized in his name, having perfect faith in the
Holy One of Israel, or they cannot be saved in the kingdom of God" (2
Nephi 9:23). Perfect faith. *Perfect* faith! Who do you know that has
perfect faith, at least as we gauge perfection? I suggest that Jacob is here
driving at a point that we are prone to miss—those who have perfect

faith in the Holy One of Israel are those who have learned to trust in him completely, to trust in his purposes, as well as his timetable. To come out of the world is to realize that we cannot place our trust in the world. "To come out of the world," President Stephen L Richards observed, "one must forsake the philosophy of the world, and to come into Zion one must adopt the philosophy of Zion. In my own thinking," he continued, "I have reduced the process to a simple formula: Forsake the philosophy of self-sufficiency, which is the philosophy of the world, and adopt the philosophy of faith, which is the philosophy of Christ. Substitute faith for self-assurance."[6]

If I trust completely (or perfectly) in Christ, then how much do I trust in myself? Answer: None. My works are necessary. My reception of the ordinances, the performance of my duties in the Church, acts of service and kindness—these are a part of my Christian covenantal obligation. They are the things I strive to do. But let us come face to face with the reality that there are not enough loaves of bread, enough home or visiting teaching appointments, enough meetings—believe it or not!—or enough encouraging notes to assure my exaltation. My good works are necessary, but they are not sufficient. I cannot work myself into celestial glory, and I cannot guarantee myself a place among the sanctified through my own unaided efforts. Therefore, even though my own merits are essential to salvation, they alone will not take me where I need to go. Rather, it is by and through the merits of Christ. This transcendent truth should create, not feelings of futility, but feelings of deep humility.

"Suppose we have the scriptures," Elder Bruce R. McConkie explained, "the gospel, the priesthood, the Church, the ordinances, the organization, even the keys of the kingdom—everything that now is, down to the last jot and tittle—and yet there is no atonement of Christ. What then? Can we be saved? Will all our good works save us? Will we be rewarded for all our righteousness?

"Most assuredly we will not. We are not saved by works alone, no matter how good; we are saved because God sent his Son to shed his blood in Gethsemane and on Calvary that all through him might ransomed be. We are saved by the blood of Christ (Acts 20:28; 1 Cor. 6:20).

"To paraphrase Abinadi [see Mosiah 13:28], 'Salvation doth not come by the Church alone; and were it not for the atonement, given by the grace of God as a free gift, all men must unavoidably perish, and this notwithstanding the Church and all that appertains to it.'"[7] Or, as Elder

Dallin H. Oaks observed: "Man unquestionably has impressive powers and can bring to pass great things by tireless efforts and indomitable will. But after all our obedience and good works, we cannot be saved from the effect of our sins without the grace extended by the atonement of Jesus Christ."[8]

Lehi addressed his son Jacob with these words: "Wherefore, I know that thou art redeemed." Why was he redeemed? Because he was such an obedient son? Because he had followed the direction of his elder brother? Because he was sensitive and submissive and faithful? We know that he was all of those. But note Lehi's words: "Wherefore, I know that thou art redeemed, because of the righteousness of thy Redeemer" (2 Nephi 2:3). Jacob was bound for glory because of the goodness of Jesus! But didn't Jacob's goodness matter? Of course it did. Jacob's carefulness to live according to the commandments evidenced his commitment to the Lord and his desire to keep his part of the covenant. But as noble a son as Jacob was, he could never save himself. As a modern revelation attests, Christ pleads our cause before the Father on the basis of his own suffering and death and perfection (see D&C 45:3–5). Imperfect people can be redeemed only by a perfect Being.

Nephi encouraged his readers to rely "wholly upon the merits of him who is mighty to save" (2 Nephi 31:19). Aaron explained that "since man had fallen he could not merit anything of himself; but the suffering and death of Christ atone for their sins, through faith and repentance" (Alma 22:14). Moroni added that the Saints of God rely "alone upon the merits of Christ, who [is] the author and the finisher of [our] faith" (Moroni 6:4). We are indeed saved by merits—the merits of our Redeemer. The debate has raged for far too long over whether we are saved by grace or by works, a squabble originating in early Christianity into which too many of the Latter-day Saints have been drawn. It is a silly argument, an unnecessary struggle, one that has generated much more heat than light. It is, in fact, the wrong question. The real questions—the ones that get to the heart of the matter—are these: In whom do I trust? On whom do I rely? Truly, as someone has suggested, the word *grace* is an acronym for a glorious concept: "God's Riches At Christ's Expense."[9]

My confidence in God is essential. My confidence in myself is incidental, inextricably tied to my trust in God. As Bruce Hafen has observed: "When we place our confidence in God rather than in ourselves, our need for self-esteem takes care of itself—not because of our

manipulation of successful experiences but because our fundamental attitude allows us access to the only trustworthy source for knowing that the
course of life we pursue is known to and accepted by God. It is not just
the mistake-free, no-fault life that pleases God. He has deliberately
placed us in a sphere where the most sharply focused purpose is to learn
from our experience and to grow in both our desires and our understanding to be like him. Obviously that includes the greatest effort and
integrity we can muster as we seek to do his will. But the heart of it all is
not *self*-confidence. It is confidence in *him*, and in his power to make us
into creatures far beyond the reach of what our goal-setting and goal-
achieving can ultimately accomplish in the process of becoming as he
is."[10]

There is, then, a life in Christ, a new life in Christ that we cannot
know or experience unless we yield to and appropriate his transforming
powers and stop trying to do everything ourselves. In the spiritual realm,
there is nothing weak about trusting, nothing passive about reliance. In
one sense, as C. S. Lewis observed, "The road back to God is a road of
moral effort, of trying harder and harder. But in another sense it is not
trying that is ever going to bring us home. All this trying leads up to the
vital moment at which you turn to God and say, 'You must do this; I
can't.'" Such submission, Lewis adds, represents a significant change in
our nature, "the change from being confident about our own efforts to
the state in which we despair of doing anything for ourselves and leave
it to God. "I know the words 'leave it to God' can be misunderstood,"
Lewis continues. "The sense in which a Christian leaves it to God is that
he puts all his trust in Christ: trusts that Christ will somehow share with
him the perfect human obedience which He carried out from His birth
to His crucifixion: that Christ will make the man [or woman] more like
Himself and, in a sense, make good his [or her] deficiencies."[11] In a word,
I am incomplete or partial, whereas Christ is whole or complete. As I
come unto Christ by covenant, we (Christ and I) are complete. I am
unfinished, whereas Christ is finished. Through "relying alone" upon the
merits of the Author and Finisher of my faith (Moroni 6:4; compare
Hebrews 12:2), I become finished or fully formed. I am so very imperfect,
while Christ is perfect. Together we are perfect. Truly, as the apostle Paul
taught, we "are complete in him, [who] is the head of all principality and
power" (Colossians 2:10). Those who come unto Christ become perfect
in him (see Moroni 10:32). Those who inherit the celestial kingdom are

just men and just women who have been "made perfect through Jesus the mediator of the new covenant, who wrought out this perfect atonement through the shedding of his own blood" (D&C 76:69).

GRACEFUL LIVING

Knowing as we do that we are saved by grace, after all we can do (see 2 Nephi 25:23), how shall we then live? What does it mean to live by grace? Consider the following simple points:

It is unhealthy, inappropriate, and spiritually counterproductive to compare ourselves with others, whether in terms of perks or crosses. None of us knows what goes on in the hidden parts of another's life, either the successes or the failures. We are told by the Savior to judge righteous judgment (see JST Matthew 7:1); that includes a warning against judging ourselves too harshly as a result of what we think we know about others. Always remember that the Lord can do extraordinary things with very ordinary people, if they will let him. President Joseph F. Smith explained that "to do well those things which God ordained to be the common lot of all mankind, is the truest greatness."[12]

Jesus warned about being unduly anxious or concerned about having enough food or clothing for the future (see 3 Nephi 13:25). That is good counsel about life in general; the disciples would do well to stop worrying and fretting so much about making the cut. The more we learn to trust the Lord and rely upon his merits and mercy, the less anxious we become about life here and hereafter. "Thus if you have really handed yourself over to Him," C. S. Lewis wisely remarked, "it must follow that you are trying to obey Him. But trying in a new way, a less worried way."[13]

The work of spiritual transformation is only partly our work. We will become holy people as we do our best to keep our covenants and then, as Moses said, "Stand still, and see the salvation of the Lord" (Exodus 14:13). C. S. Lewis taught that God "will make the feeblest and filthiest of us into a god or goddess, a dazzling, radiant, immortal creature, pulsating all through with such energy and joy and wisdom and love as we cannot now imagine, a bright stainless mirror which reflects back to God perfectly (though, of course, on a smaller scale) His own boundless power and delight and goodness. The process will be long and in parts very painful; but that is what we are in for. Nothing less. He meant what He said."[14]

The Lord God loves us and desires to save us with an everlasting salvation. There is no quota on the number of saved beings, no bell curve to determine our final standing in the royal gradebooks. We can make it. God knows that and desires for each one of us to know it as well. Lucifer would prefer, of course, that we think otherwise. Whereas the ultimate blessings of salvation do not come until the next life, there is a sense in which people in this life may enjoy the assurance of salvation and the peace that accompanies that knowledge (see D&C 59:23).

True faith in Christ produces hope in Christ—not worldly wishing but expectation, anticipation, assurance. As the apostle Paul wrote, the Holy Spirit provides the "earnest of our inheritance," the promise or evidence that we are on course, in covenant, and thus in line for full salvation in the world to come (Ephesians 1:13–14; see also 2 Corinthians 1:21–22; 5:5). That is, the Spirit of God operating in our lives is like the Lord's "earnest money" on us—his sweet certification that he seriously intends to save us with an everlasting salvation. Thus if we are striving to cultivate the gift of the Holy Ghost, we are living in what might be called a "saved" condition.

Too many of us wrestle with feelings of inadequacy, struggle with hopelessness, and, in general, are much too anxious about our standing before God. It is important to keep the ultimate goal of exaltation ever before us, but it seems so much more profitable to focus on fundamentals and on the here and now—staying in covenant, being dependable and true to our promises, cultivating the gift of the Holy Ghost. President Brigham Young taught that "our work is a work of the present. The salvation we are seeking is for the present, and, sought correctly, it can be obtained, and be continually enjoyed. If it continues to-day, it is upon the same principle that it will continue to-morrow, the next day, the next week, or the next year, and, we might say, the next eternity."[15]

BALANCE

The principle of grace has been a part of the restored gospel since the beginning. It has been an integral part of the lives of those Latter-day Saints whose trust in the Lord is greater than their trust in other things. Living by grace is a way of life, an understanding, a perspective that comes to us as we come unto Him who embodies peace and rest. Perhaps it is the complexity of life in a modern world that drives many of us to our knees more frequently and causes us to search the scriptures with an earnestness born of pressing need. We sense more than ever the need to do our duty, to attend to our family and Church responsibilities, all as a part of keeping our covenant with Christ. That is, we come to know the value and necessity of good works. Those works, motivated by his Spirit, are evidence of our covenant. But we also seek for that balance, that critical and elusive balance in life that allows us to do our best without browbeating ourselves because of all we cannot do at the moment.

I know the Lord wants us to succeed. Discouragement and despondency are not of the Lord. They are of Lucifer. The arch-deceiver would have us lose our balance, lose track of what matters most in life, and labor to exhaustion in secondary causes. We cannot do everything we are asked to do, at least not in a few weeks or months. There is great virtue in praying that the Lord will reveal to us our limits, let us know when enough is enough, when doubling or tripling our efforts will in reality be spiritually counterproductive.

Because we are human—because we are weak and mortal and tired—we will probably never reach the point in this life when we have done "all we can do." Too many of us misread 2 Nephi 25:23 and conclude that the Lord can assist us only *after,* meaning following the time that we have done "all we can do." That is incorrect; he can and does help us all along the way. I think Nephi is trying to emphasize that no matter how much we do, it simply will not be enough to guarantee salvation without Christ's intervention. Restating Nephi, "Above and beyond all we can do, it is by the grace of Christ that we are saved." And what is true of our ultimate salvation is true of our daily salvation, the redemption of our personality and our passions, our walk and talk. Above and beyond all efforts at self-control, behavior modification, or reducing our sins to manageable categories, "everything which really needs to be done in our souls can be done only by God."[16]

There is yet another way to look at 2 Nephi 25:23. After the conversion of thousands of Lamanites by the sons of Mosiah, the brother of Lamoni, named Anti-Nephi-Lehi, counseled with his people, those who had covenanted not to take up weapons against their brethren in war. He first expressed to his people his gratitude for the goodness of God—for sending the Spirit, softening the hearts of the Lamanites, opening doors of communication between the Nephites and the Lamanites, and convincing the people of their sins. He continued: "And I also thank my God, yea, my great God, that he hath granted unto us that we might repent of these things, and also that he hath forgiven us of those our many sins and murders which we have committed, and taken away the guilt from our hearts, through the merits of his Son.

"And now behold, my brethren, since it has been all that we could do, (as we were the most lost of all mankind) to repent of all our sins and the many murders which we have committed, and to get God to take them away from our hearts, for it was all we could do to repent sufficiently before God that he would take away our stain—

"Now, my best beloved brethren, since God hath taken away our stains, and our swords have become bright, then let us stain our swords no more with the blood of our brethren" (Alma 24:10–12).

There is a very real sense in which "all we can do" is come before the Lord in reverent humility, confess our weakness, and plead for his forgiveness, for his mercy and grace. It occurred to me recently that life is repentance, that progression and improvement and growth and maturity and refinement are all forms of repentance, and that the God-fearing live in a constant state of repentance. This truth means not that we should live in a constant state of fear or frustration or anxiety but rather that we have desires for holiness and purity, longings to feel quiet confidence before God. Indeed, King Benjamin taught that those who regularly and consistently acknowledge the greatness of God and their own nothingness without Him retain a remission of sins from day to day (see Mosiah 4:11–12).

Pushing ourselves beyond what is appropriate is, in a strange sort of way, acknowledging a fear that we must do the job ourselves if we expect it to get done. Of course, we must do our duty in the Church; the works of righteousness are also necessary. What seems so very unnecessary is the type of pharisaical extremism and the subsequent negative feelings that too often characterize the efforts of some Church members. I have a conviction that God is unquestionably aware of us. He loves you, and he loves me. This I know. He certainly wants us to improve, but he definitely does not want us to spend our days languishing in guilt. I reaffirm that the gospel of Jesus Christ is intended to liberate us, to lift and lighten our burdens. If it is not doing that in our personal lives, then perhaps our approach and understanding, our orientation—not necessarily the quantity of work to be done—may need some adjustment. Balance. Balance. That is the key. I have come to sense the need to balance a type of "divine discontent"—a healthy longing to improve—with what Nephi called a "perfect brightness of hope" (2 Nephi 31:20)—the Spirit-given assurance that in and through Jesus Christ we are going to make it.

CONCLUSION

I am very much aware that many have been subjected to much pain and distress, to abuse, to neglect, to the agonies of wanting more than anything to live a normal life and to feel normal feelings but who seem unable to do so. I would say, first of all, that each of us, no matter who we are, wrestles with something. It may be our weight or height or complexion or baldness or I.Q. Perhaps it's a trial that passes in time, like a phase. Perhaps it's the torture of watching helplessly as loved ones choose unwisely and thereby close doors of opportunity for themselves and foreclose future privileges. Or we may suffer a terrible trauma when someone we love deals a blow that strikes at the center of all we hold dear and value about ourselves.

I bear my witness that the day is coming when all the wrongs, the awful wrongs of this life, will be righted. I bear witness that the God of justice will attend to all evil. And I certify that those things that are beyond our power to control will be corrected, either here or hereafter. Many of us may come to experience the lifting, liberating powers of the Atonement in this life; all our losses will be made up before we pass from this sphere of existence. Some of us may wrestle all our days with our traumas, but He will surely fix the time of our release. When a person passes through the veil of death, all those impediments and challenges and crosses that were beyond his or her power to control—abuse, neglect, immoral environment, weighty traditions—will be torn away like a film, and perfect peace will prevail in our hearts. "Some frustrations," Elder Boyd K. Packer taught, "we must endure without really solving the problem. Some things that ought to be put in order are not put in order because we cannot control them. Things we cannot solve, we must survive."[17]

Our Lord and Master seems to ask of us the impossible—to forgive those who have hurt us so dreadfully. As Bruce and Marie Hafen have observed, "It seems fair to ask why the victims of abuse should be required to do *anything* to deserve the Lord's vast healing powers in such a case. Because abuse victims suffer so many of the same symptoms of guilt and estrangement from God as do willful transgressors, the irony that they should need to forgive those who have wronged them is almost overpowering.

"Still, there lurks between the lines of the scriptures on forgiveness a message of transcendent meaning—not only about abuse victims but about all of us, and about all of the Atonement."

The Hafens continue, "What are we doing when we are willing to absorb a terrible trauma of the spirit, caused not by our own doing but by one who claimed to love us—and we absorb the trauma even to help the sinner? That picture somehow has a familiar look—we've seen all this before. Of course, because this picture depicts the sacrifice of Jesus Christ: he took upon himself undeserved and unbearable burdens, heaped upon him by people who often said, and often believed, that they loved him. And he assumed that load not for any need of his, but only to help them.

"So to forgive—not just for abuse victims, but for each of us—is to be a Christ figure, a transitional point in the war between good and evil, stopping the current of evil by absorbing it in every pore, thereby protecting the innocent next generation and helping to enable the repentance and healing of those whose failures sent the jolts into our own systems."[18]

I know of the power that is in Christ, power not only to create the worlds and divide the seas but also to still the storms of the human heart, to right life's wrongs, to ease and eventually even remove the pain of scarred and beaten souls. There is no bitterness, no anger, no fear, no jealousy, no feelings of inadequacy that cannot be healed by the Great Physician. He is the Balm of Gilead. He is the One sent by the Father to "bind up the brokenhearted, to proclaim liberty to the captives, and the opening of the prison to them that are bound" (Isaiah 61:1). True followers of Christ learn to trust in him more, in the arm of flesh less. They learn to rely on him more, on human solutions less. They learn to surrender their burdens to him more. They learn to work to their limits and then be willing to seek that grace of enabling power that will make up the difference, that sacred power that makes all the difference!

As Moroni has instructed us on the last page of the Book of Mormon, when we come unto Christ and seek, all through our lives, to deny ourselves of ungodliness and give ourselves without let or hindrance to God, "then is his grace sufficient for you, that by his grace ye may be perfect in Christ"—whole, complete, fully formed: "and if by the grace of God ye are perfect in Christ, ye can in nowise deny the power of God" (Moroni 10:32). In other words, those who completely surrender and submit to the Almighty cannot deny—block, stop, or prevent—the power of God from coming into their lives. In short, to come unto the Savior is to come to life, to awaken to an entirely new realm. Because of who Christ our Lord is and what he has done, there is no obstacle to peace and joy here or hereafter too great to face or overcome. Because of him, our minds can be at peace. Our souls may rest.

Notes

1. John F. MacArthur Jr., *Faith Works: The Gospel according to the Apostles* (Dallas: Word Publishing, 1993), 32.
2. M. Russell Ballard, "Building Bridges of Understanding," address delivered to the Logan, Utah, Institute of Religion, 17 February 1998, typescript, 6–7.
3. C. S. Lewis, *Mere Christianity* (New York: Simon & Schuster, 1996), 59.
4. See *Teachings of Ezra Taft Benson* (Salt Lake City: Bookcraft, 1988), 361.
5. C. S. Lewis, *Letters to Malcolm: Chiefly on Prayer* (New York: Harcourt Brace & Company, 1992), 25–26; italics in original.
6. Stephen L Richards, *Where Is Wisdom?* (Salt Lake City: Deseret Book, 1955), 419.
7. Bruce R. McConkie, "What Think Ye of Salvation by Grace?" devotional address, Brigham Young University, Provo, Utah, 10 January 1984; in *Doctrines of the Restoration*, ed. Mark L. McConkie (Salt Lake City: Bookcraft, 1989), 76.
8. Dallin H. Oaks, Conference Report, October 1988, 78.
9. MacArthur, *Faith Works*, 57.
10. Bruce C. Hafen, *The Broken Heart: Applying the Atonement to Life's Experiences* (Salt Lake City: Deseret Book, 1989), 120; italics in original.
11. Lewis, *Mere Christianity*, 129–30.
12. Joseph F. Smith, *Gospel Doctrine* (Salt Lake City: Deseret Book, 1971), 285.
13. Lewis, *Mere Christianity*, 131.
14. Lewis, *Mere Christianity*, 176.
15. Brigham Young, *Journal of Discourses*, 26 vols. (London: Latter-day Saints' Book Depot, 1854–86), 1:131; see also 8:124–25.
16. Lewis, *Mere Christianity*, 166.
17. Boyd K. Packer, Conference Report, October 1987, 20.
18. Bruce C. Hafen and Marie K. Hafen, *The Belonging Heart: The Atonement and Relationships with God and Family* (Salt Lake City: Deseret Book, 1994), 122–23.

WOMEN'S LIVES, WOMEN'S STORIES: THE EXTRAORDINARY IN THE ORDINARY

⸎

Julie J. Nichols

*T*he personal essay, unlike personal journals, letters, and oral histories, is not an artless form. It transforms the raw material of personal experience in the double crucible of carefully chosen language and the light of mature retrospection. A finished personal essay requires revision, a literal re-seeing; not only does the product enlighten and engage its reader but the process of writing and revising itself generates changes in the writer as she re-views her self, her place in her community, and the meaning of her experiences.

We live by stories; every person has a story that matters. Phyllis Rose in *Parallel Lives: Five Victorian Marriages* suggests that we are constantly in the process of "imposing a narrative form onto our lives" in order to make sense of experience. "Questions we have all asked ourselves such as Why am I doing this? or even the more basic What am I doing? suggest the way in which living forces us to look for and forces us to find a design within the primal stew of data which is our daily experience."[2]

Stories affect us differently than do mere assertions of principle, more profoundly than mere dogma; stories influence our actions, help us make sense of the world, and enable us to share our experience and understanding. Carol Bly, author of a fine collection of essays, *Letters from the Country*, points out that in our time, women are socialized to write their stories—"Women must write our history . . . , so that we have it—the way an athlete must have muscle."[3] At the same time, Bly notes, men are *discouraged* from writing theirs, precisely because writing one's story requires a certain amount of evaluation and self-judgment. Bly's conclusion is that, in writing their stories, women learn to evaluate and judge and are

---

Julie J. Nichols, a doctoral candidate in creative writing at the University of Utah, has taught creative writing and literature at the Waterford School, the University of Utah, and Brigham Young University. She and her husband, Jeff W. Nichols III, are the parents of four children. She serves as a Relief Society teacher and Primary pianist.

thus in many ways better prepared to recognize and help counter the ills of a male-dominated world.

But certain aspects of our culture can bar even women from enlightening themselves through personal narrative. Since 1984 I have taught English 218R—Introduction to Creative Writing, with an emphasis in literary nonfiction—at Brigham Young University. In these classes, I have watched both women and men resist coming to terms with the contradictions of their lives. For Latter-day Saint women, in particular, such resistance comes from three general sources: lack of time, because setting aside large blocks of quiet, self-reflective time is difficult when you're busy rearing children, caring for a home, and, more often than not, working outside the home; lack of knowledge about women's stories, which are infrequently mentioned in the scriptures and only recently began making their way into Church lesson manuals;[4] and fear of recrimination, from family or from official sources for expressing negative emotions, disagreement, or nontraditional thought processes.

In my classes, I try to help would-be memoirists overcome these barriers by providing structured time, abundant reading material, and plenty of theory and practice. Working together, we establish that personal narrative is the prototypical discourse.[5] We learn that telling a story we deem important forms the basis for *all* discourse. We read the works of women writers whose lives constitute their material, from Julian of Norwich and Margery Kempe in the Middle Ages to Annie Dillard and Alice Walker in twentieth-century America, as well as such Latter-day Saint women writers as Emma Lou Thayne, Mary Bradford, and Helen Candland Stark. We perform writing exercises that allow memory and feeling to rise to the surface and find form in words.[6] Though these exercises are not always successful, when my women students finally push through their resistance and produce fine essays such as the ones quoted from below, we all reap remarkable rewards.

The first reward that lies in producing a polished personal essay is pleasure—on many levels. Lorinne Taylor Morris took English 218R twice because the first time she took it, she struggled with an essay about her mother's death for months, saying to me several times, "I don't even know what I'm trying to say here." I encouraged her to continue to work with it, praising the understated tone and the importance of the story itself. When she finally came to a satisfactory ending, she said, "Now I know what I meant. I thought I was writing about how I always felt left out and how I tried to let my dad's efforts be enough. But I needed my mother to help me know who I was. I know that now. This is an essay about me as a woman."

REGENERATION

Lorinne Taylor Morris

"I was five years old when my mother died. Her death didn't seem to change my world much then. I just received more attention from relatives and neighbors, was all. In the two years since she had been diagnosed, she had evolved from my caregiver to a sick person whose bedroom I had to stay out of while the cancer ate at her body. I learned over those two years she could not care for me, so by the time of her death, I thought I had become used to living without her.

"My father had begun taking over for Mother by making the family meals. He also woke us up and got us ready in the morning. I insisted on having my hair in ponytails like my two older sisters, and though he tried to part my hair into even halves and get the ponytails straight, they always came out crooked. After he left the bathroom I'd climb onto the counter and tug up on one ponytail and down on the other. It just wasn't the way it was supposed to be.

"As the years passed my needs changed, and so did my father's role in my life. In junior high one day, I received a wink from a boy who sat a row in front of me. My friends told me this was because he liked me and wanted "to go" with me, but I didn't know what "to go" with someone meant. I found Dad that evening outside doing chores just as the sun was setting and leaving just enough light to see his faint shadow. I guess he sensed the seriousness in my voice, because he put down the bucket of feed and sat on the upper rail of the fence while I unfolded the dilemma of my day. I can't remember now what he said, but it was dark before we came in.

"When I became a quiet, emotional teenager, I realized my mother's death meant her absence from my life. During my high school years when I wanted some comfort, I often imagined what it would be like to have a mother. I would sit at night on the front steps and imagine my mother coming outside to sit by me. She would quietly open the front door, sit down next to me, and put her soft, middle-aged arm around me. I wasn't really sure what she would do next, maybe tell me not to cry or listen to me for awhile. I would eventually stop my dreaming and go to find my dad.

"But last summer the absence was relieved for a moment when I learned to bottle tomatoes. I used the old empty jars from my grandma's fruit room that had been on the shelves for years. They were covered with dust and spider webs. Some even had tiny dead bugs in the bottom. It took me hours to wash them all. Then I took them to a neighbor's house where she taught me how to blanch the tomatoes to remove the skins, then to quarter them and press them into the bottles. She showed me how to take a knife to remove the air bubbles before steaming them to seal their lids. Together we bottled more than a hundred jars.

"I took my bottled tomatoes back to my grandma's fruit room, and one by one I placed them on the dusty shelves. As I bent over, picked one of the bottles up, and placed it on the shelf, I saw my mother. Like me, she bent to pick up a bottle, placed it carefully, and stood back to admire the work she had done. At that moment she was there with me, doing the things she had done that I was now beginning to do. I understood that we are connected in ways that go far beyond death, and I whispered, 'Welcome home, Mom,' and she whispered, 'Welcome home, Lorinne.'"

Pleasure, the first reward of a story well told, is often not only cerebral but also physical—leaving both writer and reader feeling peaceful and relaxed. Lorinne experienced further pleasure; as she wrote, she discovered a new sense of herself, a sense that she belongs, even though her mother died long ago, to the community of mothers and daughters participating in the rituals that many Utah Latter-day Saint mothers and daughters share. For the first time, she recognized her rightful place in that community.

Anthropologist Barbara Meyerhoff has formulated the notion of "the great story," the set of stories by which we live our lives.[7] LDS women may be centered by stories such as: "women should be in the home," "church attendance is a measure of spirituality," "families are forever," or "repentance and change are always possible." Lorinne's essay partakes of the "great story" that says, "Everyone needs a mother; no one can take a mother's place." Meyerhoff goes on to say that personal narrative is a "little story," a story that is true for one person instead of for an entire culture. People's "little stories" can affirm or challenge the "great story." The following untitled essay by Kathy Haun Orr corroborates the "great story" that mothers are perfect. Like Lorinne's essay, it also provides pleasure—in this case the pleasure of humor:

Kathy Haun Orr

"My mother can do everything. Every year my sisters and I got Easter dresses made especially for us and dresses at Christmas for family pictures.

She made the bridesmaid dresses for my oldest sister's wedding because they couldn't find any they liked in the stores. The dresses were lavender with white lace trim, tea length, with a long, full ruffle and a v-waistline to match my sister's wedding gown. Then there's me: I've never even touched a sewing machine except to turn my mom's off when she forgot. The first time I sewed a button on was last semester when it came off my coat and my roommate wouldn't do it for me.

"My birthday cakes were always decorated with whatever I requested, from Mickey Mouse when I was three to a two-tiered cake with frosting floral arrangements when I turned sweet sixteen. I did take a cake decorating class with my best friend our senior year of high school. I loved the class, and the teacher, but my roses looked like big lumps of lard, and my clowns always fell over like they were too tired to sit up.

"My mother is the very definition of domestic goddess in the kitchen. Leftovers taste great, everything's nutritious and yummy, and she can make desserts that make your mouth water just looking at them. Until I left home for college, the only things I could cook were toast, grilled cheese sandwiches, and chocolate chip cookies. When I got up to school, my roommates mocked me in the kitchen and gave me quizzes on all the different utensils and their true use.

"My mother is into all sorts of crafts, like grapevine wreaths and quilts and the artwork for her silkscreening business. I know how to use a glue gun—I used one once to hem some pants."

Kathy concludes the essay by saying that despite the gaps between her mother's achievements and her own, her mother's love and encouragement are qualities she fully intends to pass on. The essay is fun to read and allowed Kathy to safely express her marginal position within a pervasive "great story" that LDS mothers are domestic goddesses.

Both these essays focus on a key role in a woman's life: the mother role. Being a mother is a pinnacle of accomplishment for a Latter-day Saint woman. Unconsciously or consciously, many LDS women examine their own propensities for this role with varying degrees of satisfaction or trepidation, seeking first (like Lorinne and Kathy) to connect with their own mothers and then to come to terms with the differences among their own mothers, their own individual leanings, and the "great story" about motherhood. Writing personal narrative encourages and facilitates this process.

It is especially liberating for my women students to realize that

personal narrative needn't always affirm the "great story." According to
Meyerhoff, the "little story" can also radically question the "great story."
Often its power lies in its ability to interrogate the inadequacies in the
larger cultural narrative. Several of my students who have been emotionally and physically battered have written essays probing the differences between their experiences and the LDS "great story" of the family
as the source of protection and nurturance. In all of their efforts, they
have sought to name the origins of their wounds and find balm for them.
It was the process of their writing that finally helped these women find
the power to initiate real healing.

Personal narrative can also teach. Kristin Langellier, professor of
speech communication, notes that family stories may inspire or warn family members about the consequences of certain actions and also keep stories alive that are important to the family's solidarity.[8] Often, of course,
my students write about their role as mother. The following story, which
teaches and inspires, explores the spiritual strength that can come as we
seek answers to problems in that particular role:

THE COMMITTEE

Marsha Bennion Giese

"Hannah's screams echoed in my ears long after I hung up the phone,
strident newborn cries that demanded help. A moan rolled out from
someplace deep inside me, surprising the hard silence of my hospital
room. I'd been checking on her condition with her nurse in an intensive
care unit many miles away. "We're having trouble with her I.V. sites," she
told me. "We're just running out of good places to stick her and her sites
don't last long. We've been trying to restart her for about an hour." I
knew that meant strapped down flat under bright lights, her perfect new
skin repeatedly pierced with no success. Tears ran down my cheeks and
nose onto the receiver as I listened to her report and the background
anguish.

"'How many times have you tried?' my voice choked to a whisper.

"'Well, three times, actually,' she answered regretfully. 'I've called for
some help and we're trying for a place on her head now.'

"Baby torture. My good-bye was barely audible. 'Tell her Mom loves
her and is sorry . . .' Grief curled my freshly stitched body and squeezed
at my chest. I bit into my fists through stretched sheets spreading damp-
ness out in rings like oil on water. We'd endured so much to get this baby

here, and now there was more. A new series of hurdles seemed to extend out beyond my view.

"The I.V.s were crucial as they bore her only source of nourishment during recovery from post-birth surgery on an incomplete esophagus. She clearly wanted to eat. She'd been born by emergency C-section ten days early due to placental failure, delivered weak and thin and hardly able to move from nearly starving to death in my womb. I'd been alerted to her danger when she'd quit moving within me, and from a building sense of urgency that got me to the doctor just in time. Now she searched desperately for comfort at Children's Hospital, sucking fiercely on her fists, bedding, the side of her incubator, trying to fill her still empty stomach, covered with surgical drains, I.V.s, monitor leads, alone and hungry and in pain. I needed to be there. I wanted to hold her, feed her, ease the harshness of mortality. I'd been waiting so long.

"It took us a long time to conceive her older sister, Megan, but once she came we thought we were home free—no more baby trouble. Not so. The years passed. I felt I wasn't finished [having children] and that there was a sibling for Megan possible, but month after month my hopes rose and fell—little cycles of death that took their emotional toll. We had tests. I had blessings. Stacks of temperature charts, drugs, and surgeries. Frightening bills. Hi-tech fertility care and finally, an in-vitro procedure. Nothing.

"Five years into all of this, my Aunt Mary fell profoundly and terminally ill with pancreatic cancer. Beloved by all her family, talented and politically active, she was a matriarchal figure to me, unhesitant to raise her powerful voice in song or strong opinion. I was able to care for her during her last days. She hated the waiting and terrible loss of strength. Five days before her death she whispered her thanks for my care and sighing a laugh, asked if there was anything she could do for me in return. I assured her she had already done, just by living her life and being who she was—but I added, 'Well yes, there is one thing. When you get where you're going, would you see if you can do anything about getting us our baby? I mean, whatever it takes—if it's a bureaucratic problem, get a committee together. Find out who's in charge of this and shake things up. Start a petition. Let's just get on with getting our baby here. We're ready. I don't know how it works, but see what you can do, okay?' Aunt Mary's lips sketched a smile, and she rolled her eyes. 'I'll see,' she breathed. It was our last real conversation.

"That was June. In August I was once again on a gurney wheeling to surgery for another in-vitro procedure. My husband stood at my side gripping the hand that was untaped as the embryologist rolled his big stainless steel box up past us, gave us a thumbs-up sign, and flashed four fingers. We had four of our fertilized eggs in his incubator ready to implant in my tubes. One of them was Hannah.

"It had been a roller-coaster pregnancy. The euphoria of finding out we'd been successful. We saw heartbeats on two of the embryos before nearly losing both in early miscarriage. Bed rest and weekly ultrasounds, phlebitis and childbirth refresher classes. Painting the nursery, unpacking a carefully stored layette. Months of great anticipation and anxiety—looking toward the time of completion when I could study a new little face, watch Megan bond, and rejoice with our extended families. Expectations stopped two days ago. Now we lay in separate hospitals, kept from each other by our respective tenuous health. My only physical ties to her were phone lines, my only communication her compelling screams. I'd lost awareness of my own surgery to the pain of her distance.

"Prayers formed as the cries persisted in my head. 'Help her, help me, ease her pain, send comfort please.'

"Then as I repeated these petitions, my focus turned inward from my barren room. It seemed to me that suddenly I could see Hannah in the I.C.U. from just a few feet away. Tiny and bare in her isolette, tubes and wires snaked out from her fragile body mooring her to the sophisticated equipment clustered above and to one side. But she was sleeping. Calm and relaxed on her tummy with her knees tucked slightly under her. And she was not alone. Around her with their backs to me stood a trio of women in long white gowns, their heads bending toward each other occasionally in consultation. I recognized them: my late grandmothers Nana and Mimi, and to the right, Aunt Mary. They hovered protectively at her side, shoulder-to-shoulder with each other and with the two nurses tending her equipment. As I watched, they reached to touch her, crooning her name, singing lullabies and reassuring her that life would not always be as painful. This would pass. I knew that this was the committee come to guard her and comfort both of us. My tears subsided; my muscles relaxed. I turned my gaze outward to the night-black windows and pondered the mystery of time and distance and mortal limitations.

"Over a year later I hear Hannah's approach down the hall. Her newly acquired lumbering resembles Frankenstein's gait. Her curly head pops around the corner, face alight with mischief. 'Boo!' she declares and falls backward on her bottom. 'Boo! yourself. I'm happy to see you,' is my reply as I bend to swing her up over my head. Quick and joyful and round with breast milk, we bear no trace of the awful struggle it took to get here. I bring her laughing face close to mine and look into perfect blue eyes and see eternal love and the mercy of God."

Such stories validate the teller's life, and move the hearers to wonder and reverence that we *aren't* alone on this planet; our needs are met, often, in ways we don't expect.

Stories which teach and inspire might begin also with a question: why are things the way they are in this family or community? Telling personal stories that pursue answers may clarify complex questions. Beth Ahlborn Merrell's essay does just that.

NO-NAME MARIA

Beth Ahlborn Merrell

"Ten years after my own baptism I buried myself in the waters again . . . and again . . . and again. It was a great opportunity for me to recall the importance of baptism. I did my best to prepare myself, that the spirits waiting on the other side would not be mocked.

"I was baptized thirty-seven times for Maria. She had no last name. No birth date or place. No family information. Only the location of her grave.

"I inquired of these Marias. A temple worker told me that these Latin American women had been buried in graves without proper markings. Because there was no information, they were baptized with the symbolic name Maria. I couldn't help but wonder if I had done any good in being baptized as proxy for thirty-seven women who had no names.

"Before leaving the temple, I received a printout with the information on the thirty-seven women I had served. No need looking over the names. All Marias. But I did look at the locations. Panama, Guatemala, Nicaragua—almost all Central American countries. At the bottom of the list were five women from Tegucigalpa, Honduras. My heart jumped and burned.

"August 29, 1924. Tegucigalpa, Honduras. Julia Eva Valasquez, seven years old, stood on the banks of the mountain river that ran through her family's estate. Her older brother, Roberto, fished while Julia twirled on the banks, watching the ruffled layers of her silk dress floating like magic in a rippling circle. Confident that she would dance with the best one day, she moved to the Latin rhythm that played inside her head. Bending close to the water, Julia smiled at the face she saw mirrored on the glassy surface of the pond: dark hair curled daintily around a heart-shaped face the color of creamy coffee. She flirted with her reflection, placing a lotus blossom behind her ear.

"Julia never heard the revolutionist behind her. Perhaps the music inside her head played so loudly that it drowned out any snapping twigs that might have warned her of the silent murderer. One moment she was looking into the reflection of a smiling girl, the next she was seeing the reflection of a revolutionist raising a machete over her body. His double-edged knife whistled as it fell toward her head.

"Instinctively she rolled, blocking the blows with her right arm. Roberto flew to protect himself and his sister, but his struggle was brief against the attacks made by men who came to proclaim their right against the suppression by Honduras's upper class. I've never heard anything about how my great-grandmother and Uncle Roberto found help. Roberto carried deep scars in his skull for life. Julia's dreams of dancing were shattered; she lost her right arm from the elbow. Their white mansion burned to the ground; their parents and siblings died in the flames.

"I often wonder how my great-grandmother managed without two good arms and without the extended family support upon which Latins depend. But the details of my heritage are scarce. She died before I learned to speak Spanish. She died before my first-generation LDS mother taught her the gospel. She died without telling us the names of her parents and siblings. She died, and this is all I know of her life.

"Records in Central American countries are incomplete at best. Government documents are burned periodically in the chaos of political revolutions. And when the fires die, the dead who leave no families are often buried in common, unmarked graves.

"I looked back at my printout. I asked to be baptized for a relative, but my mother told me it was impossible given our dead-end genealogy. I did not receive a heavenly visitation from a member of Julia's family; I have no physical proof that I served a relative in the temple. But in my heart I am grateful that gospel blessings are not limited to those who have proper burials or grave sites. I look forward to the day when I can perform temple ordinances for another no-name Maria."

In this essay, Beth comes to the conclusion that the ordinances performed in the temple are not in vain. In doing so, she establishes connections with the community of her family, as do Lorinne and Kathy, as well as with the community of Latter-day Saints who work in the temple. Beth also negotiates with a puzzling aspect of the "great story," and she asserts herself as someone who can respond to her circumstances and make a story that provides answers as it holds and moves its readers.

Further, by making that story a woman's story, she refutes the "great story" that canonized writings (scripture or official Church histories or manuals) are the only authoritative ones. To write ordinary women's lives thoughtfully and imaginatively makes them extraordinary, gifts not only for posterity (the *raison d'etre* for most injunctions to write personal narrative) but also for interested contemporaries.

Stories like these need to be heard. Great pleasure, great strength comes from writing and sharing these stories. We need to give ourselves and each other time and encouragement for writing the stories of the women of our communities. We can form writing groups; we can let our families and friends read our work; we can send it off to the *Ensign* and other forums. We can request that more of these stories of ordinary modern women be included in Relief Society manuals and supplements. By doing so we reap great rewards, for ourselves and all women. We validate ourselves and add to the truth of the "great stories" that make up our lives as Latter-day Saints, as women, and as extraordinary individuals.

Notes

1. Bettina Aptheker, "Imagining Our Lives," *Woman of Power* 16 (Spring 1990): 32.
2. Phyllis Rose, *Parallel Lives: Five Victorian Marriages* (New York: Vintage Books, 1984), 6.
3. Carol Bly, *The Passionate, Accurate Story* (Minneapolis, Minn.: Milkweed Editions, 1990), 47.
4. One of the five 1992 Relief Society sesquicentennial goals has been to gather stories from LDS women, including humorous anecdotes, spiritual events, and special challenges unique to local Relief Society units. Copies were to be sent to Relief Society headquarters.
5. Kristin M. Langellier, "Personal Narratives: Perspectives on Theory and Research," *Text and Performance Quarterly* 9 (October 1989): 243.
6. The suggestions in Natalie Goldberg's *Writing Down the Bones: Freeing the Writer Within* and *Wild Mind: Living the Writer's Life,* and in Gabrielle Rico's *Writing the Natural Way* are my personal favorites.
7. Barbara Meyerhoff, as quoted in Riv-Ellen Prell, "The Double Frame of Life History in the Work of Barbara Myerhoff," in *Interpreting Women's Lives: Feminist Theory and Personal Narratives,* ed. Personal Narratives Group (Bloomington: Indiana University Press, 1989), 241–58.
8. Langellier, "Personal Narratives," 264.

FINDING LIGHTNESS IN OUR BURDENS

❦

Chieko N. Okazaki

In Matthew 11:29 is one of the loveliest promises in the New Testament, the promise that those who take upon them the yoke of Christ "shall find rest unto [their] souls." This promise is embedded in a chapter of questions, warnings, and chastisements; and I think that context is important. Some of John the Baptist's disciples had come to Jesus, questioning whether he could be, in fact, the promised Messiah. Jesus did not answer them directly but instead told them to observe his works.

After they departed satisfied, Jesus spoke to the multitude through indirection and paradox. Once he warned, significantly, "He that hath ears to hear, let him hear." Once he prayed, thanking the Father "because thou hast hid these things from the wise and prudent, and hast revealed them unto babes" (Matthew 11:15, 25). He "upbraid[ed]" the cities that had not believed his "mighty works" and "repented" (vv. 20, 21). In other words, Jesus dealt with three or four different kinds of disbelief or lack of understanding, teaching with chastisement, paradox, and riddles. Then he gave this promise:

"Come unto me, all ye that labour and are heavy laden, and I will give you rest. Take my yoke upon you, and learn of me; for I am meek and lowly in heart: and ye shall find rest unto your souls. For my yoke is easy, and my burden is light" (Matthew 11:28–30).

This promise also appears paradoxical. If we are already burdened, how will taking yet another burden—a heavy yoke upon us—give us rest? And how can his burden be "light"?

These are important questions. Sometimes we feel that we should not have burdens—that there is something wrong with us if we have problems in our lives. That is not the case. Burdens are a part of life, and we

---

Chieko N. Okazaki was born in Hawaii, where she joined the Church at age fifteen. She has served as a member of the Young Women and the Primary General Boards and as first counselor in the Relief Society General Presidency. She taught for twenty-three years in the public schools of Hawaii, Utah, and Colorado and served for ten years as a school principal. Sister Okazaki and her husband, Edward Y. Okazaki, are the parents of two sons.

all struggle with burdens that are grievous to be borne. There is nothing reproachful about having burdens, and there is nothing wicked in the struggle.

In fact, I am so sure burdens are part of life that just before this meeting started, I asked the ushers to hand a note to four sisters asking them to share with us a burden they are struggling with and tell us what, if anything, seems to lighten that burden and give them moments of rest. Each of the four agreed, and I am very grateful to these sisters for their willingness to speak to us.

SISTER 1: "One burden that has been troubling me lately is loneliness. I was married a year ago, and my husband is still going to school plus working full time. We moved into a new ward and new neighborhood, and I am at home in a very lonely house a lot of the time. I don't like being alone. Being alone is especially hard for me because I get very depressed. Sometimes at night when I am starting to feel lonely and depressed, prayer helps. If I can get on my knees and talk to Heavenly Father, he assures me that I am not alone but that he is there with me. I also like to read, but unless I have a prayer I remain lonely."

SISTER 2: "My husband and I have been married for about fifteen years, but we have no children. About two years ago we started the process of adoption from Mexico, but we are still waiting. My burden is not knowing if all these delays mean that what we are attempting to do is not what Heavenly Father wants us to do or if recurring bureaucratic problems are typical. We have spent many hours in prayer and can't seem to get a definitive answer to this question. The doors keep closing, leading us over and over again to wonder, 'If the doors keep closing, then maybe that is our answer.' Yet we really want children, so we persevere. I feel that Heavenly Father loves me and wants me to be happy and I feel that being a parent will make me happy. So we persevere, even though we don't seem to get answers to our prayers—at least not the answers we are looking for. Ward members and family comfort me, but the greatest comfort is from my husband, because he shares and understands the whole situation."

SISTER 3: "I am ashamed to confess I have sometimes wished I didn't have any children. I have been blessed with four daughters. Through them I have learned that my burdens are in fact painful blessings. I have three daughters who please me and make me happy. I have one daughter who keeps me humble. She has chosen on her own to scorn Church values, leave us, and leave the Church. It is painful to raise four daughters, teaching them all the same principles, sharing together all the same family and Church traditions—and have one choose a different road. But because of her I have learned humility. I have learned to love my Father in Heaven and daily to ask on my knees for his help. How can I consistently ask him for help and protection of this girl who has removed herself from us if I don't do all he has asked of me?

"What am I doing to relieve my burden? Temple attendance, tithing, church service: I am trying to live the commandments because I am asking for a blessing in hope. And I am able to 'press forward with a steadfastness in Christ, having a perfect brightness of hope' (2 Nephi 31:20) because of something I have learned through this hard lesson. One day, weighted with the heavy burden of care and worry over this child, I was bending down picking up clothes, and the Spirit—it must have been the Holy Spirit because it spoke from my heart—said to me, 'She is your daughter, but she is my daughter, too, and you are to love her regardless of what she does.' Thereafter my heart took hope and my burden was lighter."

SISTER 4: "In January of 1990, I was diagnosed with a seven-centimeter tumor in the center of my brain. A human brain is only about fourteen centimeters by fourteen, so this tumor took up almost half of my brain. Last January—even before I knew of the tumor—I was so depressed and discouraged about other trials and marital problems I was facing in my life that I actually prayed either to die or to have my life miraculously healed in some way. The Lord answers our prayers not always as we expect: I did not find myself dead; instead I found myself with a brain tumor, no husband, and four little children to continue rearing. I was in despair until I received a blessing from a very spiritual man who told me it was the Lord's will for me to live. That was confusing because only hours before the doctors had insisted my tumor was probably inoperable because of its location in the center of my brain. Yet in the blessing I was assured that I would learn many things that would help me carry out my purpose on earth.

"The first thing I learned was that I need the *will* to live. No matter what storms we face, we need to have the will to live. The tumor is now in remission. I have had radiation therapy, and we are waiting to see what will happen. The second essential lesson I learned through this ordeal came to me while I was on my knees in prayer looking at a picture of the

Savior. In anguish I asked, 'How can you let me go through this? I am a good daughter. I am faithful. I strive to be righteous. I take care of my children. I attend church. Why is this happening to me?' Then I suddenly remembered a day a few years ago, when I had prepared a lunch for my children who were playing outside in the sprinklers. I had made a very healthful lunch: carrot and celery sticks and tuna on whole wheat bread. I called the children in from playing, putting my all into being a wonderful mother. But they looked at this lunch in disgust and said, 'Mom, you are the worst mother in the world. This is gross. I can't believe you make us eat this junk. Aunt Becky up the street gives her kids Oreo cookies and Kool-aid for lunch every day. In fact, they have Oreo cookies and Kool-aid picnics every Sunday.' I wanted to boot them outside, and say, 'All right, go hungry. Go over to Aunt Becky's and play. I'll eat it.' But instead I crouched down before them on my knees and tried to explain, 'I give you this kind of food and these vegetables because I love you. These are the foods you need to grow big and strong, and you will need strong bodies to get you through this life.' With this memory, a peace and a calmness came over me as I realized that the storms and burdens that come to us are burdens that make us healthy and strong. They will prepare us for the steps that still remain as we become what we want to become."

Thank you, sisters, for your courage in sharing your burdens with us.

These sisters' situations remind us that all of us have burdens and that what might be easy for one person is an ultimate test for another. We cannot judge the heaviness of another's burden until we have borne it ourselves, nor can we easily prescribe what will work to ease another's burdens. Yet our challenges and burdens are not meant to crush us but to strengthen us. Note the double promise: "I will give you rest" (Matthew 11:28), says the Savior, and also "ye shall find rest unto your souls" (Matthew 11:29). In some cases, the promised rest will be his gift; in others, it will be something he helps us find ourselves.

I would like to explore now three ideas drawn from my own experience about how we can receive the promised rest: first, the resources of survivorship in each of us; second, the ability to identify blessings in disguise; and third, the power to choose our response to adversity.

BEING A SURVIVOR

I am convinced that we are all survivors. In all of us, there is a toughness that we can capitalize on. Our hope in Christ and our faith in his gospel provide us with an enormous resource of resilience and courage to call upon. Think of the Apostle Paul, cheering the Roman Saints by acknowledging the genuine afflictions and persecutions they were suffering and then triumphantly asserting, "We are more than conquerors through him that loved us" (Romans 8:37).

I am a survivor of cancer. On Tuesday morning, 3 March 1973, when I was a teacher in a school near Denver, I woke up with a pain in my side and found a lump in my breast. I called my doctor. He had a specialist waiting, and we made the surgical appointment for Friday. My husband and I signed the consent forms for the biopsy to be performed and analyzed on the spot; if it proved malignant, a mastectomy would be performed as part of the same operation. After Ed's priesthood blessing and with him beside me, I lay quietly and let the anesthetic take effect, falling asleep, as it were, with a question. When I woke up, with Ed still beside me, I knew what the answer had been.

Counseling was available at the hospital plus a support group in the community for women who had had similar operations. My doctor was also very helpful and encouraging as I went through the prescribed course of radiation, which seems to have been successful. I am in remission. But I also know that this cancer could recur at any time or that another cancer could develop. The operation was an event to be dealt with and to be put behind me. The cause of the operation—cancer—is something that I have to live with every day as a possibility; and, of course, I live with the effects of the operation as well.

I do not feel frightened or discouraged. Ed and I are both cheerful, optimistic people; and he was a great strength to me while I was recuperating from the operation and the radiation therapy. Since the exact cause of breast cancer is unknown, I cannot take specific steps to avoid a recurrence. I can take general precautions—such as eating a healthy diet, exercising, getting enough sleep, and watching for the danger signals of cancer. But the rest of it is simply out of my hands.

Making that clear—what I could and could not do—was an important step. It was as if a great weight rolled away. I have never mistaken worry for action, and I did not fool myself now that worrying about this condition was the same as doing something about it. So I just laughed and said, "I have survived cancer! What's next?" You see, I'm sure there will be something else, but my best prevention and also my best preparation is to lead a life that, besides being physically healthy, is spiritually and emotionally healthy as well.

I remember seeing a television special about women who had been sexually abused as children. The therapists and others who worked with them referred to them as "incest survivors" or "abuse survivors" rather than "incest victims" or "victims of sexual abuse." To me, there is a world of difference between these terms. One leaves you passive, helpless, dependent. The other communicates toughness, resilience, and self-reliance. We are all here today, and we have arrived by many paths. Not one of those paths has been free from chuckholes, washouts, and even avalanches—but we have survived the journey up till now. Let's give ourselves credit for that. We can call ourselves not victims but survivors. And Paul gives us the right to call ourselves not just survivors but conquerors. That should lift our hearts!

I love Mother Lucy Mack Smith for this very quality. What a great lady she was! She had a tender and loving heart—and a tough backbone. She suffered under repeated blows of fate, but she did not give up despite losing their farm, Alvin's unnecessary death, their repeated financial reverses, the scorn and contempt of neighbors who mocked Joseph's vision, relentless persecution, and the Church's moves from one community to another. All of these adversities could have broken a woman of less resilient spirit, but she did not give up. When her cherished companion, Joseph Smith Sr., died soon after the Saints were driven out of Missouri, she wrote: "I returned to my desolate home; and I then thought that the greatest grief which it was possible for me to feel had fallen upon me in the death of my beloved husband. Although that portion of my life which lay before me, seemed to be a lonesome, trackless waste, yet I did not think that I could possibly find, in traveling over it, a sorrow more searching, or a calamity more dreadful, than the present."[1]

What awaited her still, of course, were the deaths of four of her sons: the fatal illness of Don Carlos in Nauvoo, the assassinations of her two noble sons Joseph and Hyrum in Carthage, and the almost immediate death of Samuel as a result of being pursued by a mob. When Joseph's and Hyrum's bodies were brought home, washed, and dressed, she wrote this moving account:

"I had for a long time braced every nerve, roused every energy of my soul and called upon God to strengthen me, but when I entered the room and saw my murdered sons extended both at once before my eyes . . . it was too much; I sank back, crying to the Lord in the agony of my soul, 'My God, my God, why hast thou forsaken this family!' A voice replied, 'I have taken them to myself, that they might have rest.'"[2]

This promise of rest is the promise that the Savior made, as we have seen, coupled with warnings that we would have to have eyes to see and ears to hear before we could understand his meaning and also that these things were hidden from the wise.

Surely Mother Smith must have wondered if there were no other way and whether this "rest" could not have been purchased in a less grievously burdensome way. She continues: "I was swallowed up in the depths of my afflictions. . . . As I looked upon their peaceful, smiling countenances, I seemed almost to hear them say, 'Mother, weep not for us, we have overcome the world by love; we carried to them the gospel, that their souls might be saved; they slew us for our testimony, and thus placed us beyond their power; their ascendancy is for a moment, ours is an eternal triumph.'"[3]

After Samuel's death, William, her sole surviving son, brought his dying wife to Nauvoo early in 1845. Her fatal condition was a result of the persecutions in Missouri, "which makes the sum of martyrs in our family no less than six in number," wrote Mother Smith in great sorrow. But she ends her narrative, not with grief but with gratitude and with her ringing testimony: "The testimony which I have given is true, and will stand forever; and the same will be my testimony in the day of God Almighty, when I shall meet them, concerning whom I have testified, before angels, and the spirits of the just made perfect."[4]

Mother Smith lived for many more years. In those years, she did not find it necessary to revise a syllable of the testimony she had uttered with such firmness and conviction. Old age bowed her down, but not bitterness. Death finally conquered her, but not despair. She was a survivor, and we can all manifest the same kind of courage through our pains and losses.

I also think of a wonderful Hawaiian woman I know, Winifred Watanabe Chinen. Her husband is not a member of the Church and has poor health. He allows her to attend her meetings but insists that she not accept any callings. Knowing his feelings, the bishop does not ask Sister Chinen to accept any callings. Sister Chinen might well feel downcast and discouraged by her situation, but instead, she says: "I've decided that I do not need any calling. I volunteer for whatever I can do, in whatever capacity I can be of use in our Relief Society to relieve the president of any mundane responsibilities." Happily she cares for the sacrament cloths, brings flowers for the chapel, does visiting teaching, and renders compassionate service. "Being there and helping" at any Relief Society function is her calling. Her very countenance radiates a "brightness of hope" (2 Nephi 31:20). Instead of dwelling on the things she cannot do, she focuses on what she can do, attends her meetings with real gratitude, and constantly seeks out others in her neighborhood to help them. I would wager that she does as much good as any so-called fully active Latter-day Saint in Hawaii.

RECOGNIZING BLESSINGS IN DISGUISE

The second gospel principle that helps us lighten our burdens and find the rest promised by Christ is the ability to recognize blessings in disguise. I have always loved the scripture in Hebrews that tells us to "entertain strangers: for thereby some have entertained angels unawares" (Hebrews 13:2). Many times, experiences that we would not seek voluntarily and that come to us in bitter guises turn out to be blessings in disguise.

Ed was called to preside over the Japan Okinawa Mission in 1968, and one of the first things we did when we reached Japan was to visit all of the cities in our mission. We had never been there before, and we knew that it was important for us to understand as much about Japan, the Japanese people, and their culture as we could. When we went to a city for the first time, we would try to take a quick tour so that we would understand its physical layout and some of its important public areas, and we did that also in Hiroshima. We went to the Memorial Shrine, built at ground zero, and then visited the Atomic Age Museum, which documented the damage and preserved relics from that strange and destructive energy. The photographs helped us understand what the statistics meant. The bomb, which exploded about 1800 feet in the air, destroyed 4.7 square miles of the city. More than 92,000 people were dead or missing. We were filled with the sorrow of that event—the enormous destruction, the tragic loss of lives, the terrifying vision of what could happen to our planet if nuclear weapons were used again. It was very sobering for Ed and me, for we stood on both sides of that long-ago deed. It was our country, the United States of America, that had made the decision to use that bomb against Japan, the homeland of our ancestors. We grieved equally for those who had done the deed and for those who had suffered from it.

Our burden was lifted by the Saints in Hiroshima when we falteringly tried to express our confused and sorrowful feelings. "Yes, it was a terrible thing," they said, "but it was a blessing in disguise. You must not dwell on anything but the blessing." Brother and Sister Nishihara, whose son is now president of the Japan Osaka Mission in which they serve as a couple, said, "How could we have accepted the gospel if we had still been trying to believe in the divinity of the emperor? Or how could our country have moved forward economically if all of our energies and ambitions were being channeled into military purposes? It took this terrible blow to free us from the paths of the past and let us choose a new direction."

Thanks to them and to the other Saints of Hiroshima, we gained a new perspective on what had happened. We came out of the museum with our minds filled with images of devastation and destruction; but the reality of Hiroshima is that it is a thriving, lively city. There are no ruins, no shattered buildings. The city has been rebuilt. The many survivors of the bomb have gone on with their lives, just as Ed, who was wounded in Italy fighting with the 442nd Infantry in the U.S. Army, went on with his life. No one would have chosen such a devastating thing—and whether the decision to drop the bomb was right or not is something that lies beyond my wisdom—but I do know that in choosing to interpret it as a blessing, the Saints and the other residents of Hiroshima made the right decision.

I feel very strongly that we must never allow ourselves to linger in "what if's" or "if only's." Possibilities that seem more desirable to us but that are not possible sap the strength from our hands and the courage from our hearts. They become a snare to our feet so that we stumble and lose our way. All we can do is our best. We cannot control how things turn out. We cannot control the circumstances that life hands us.

In 1987, I retired from my job as principal, and Ed and I decided to move to Salt Lake City. In August 1988, Ed and I were invited to an interview with the Missionary Committee, and we suspected that it might be a mission call. Ed had an appointment for a physical already scheduled with his doctor, so at the end of the examination, he mentioned that we might like to think about going on another mission.

The doctor shook his head firmly. "You should be very careful about any strenuous activity, and you absolutely must not leave the country. Any other questions?" It turned out that Ed had a rare heart condition in which the muscle in one part of his heart had atrophied and was not working. The doctor told us later that he had not expected Ed to live out the year.

The Missionary Committee asked us if we would accept a calling to head the Missionary Training Center in Tokyo, and Ed had to tell them what the doctor had said. We were both bitterly disappointed that the calling could not be extended to us; but now, two years later, we see that it also was a blessing in disguise. I know my husband. He would not have spared himself, even if he had felt ill. He would have pushed himself beyond his strength in working with the missionaries and staff, interviewing missionaries until late at night, and working with the members. I think it is literally true that he would not have survived the year.

Instead, by following his medical plan consistently and working with the doctors, he has experienced a remarkable regeneration and renewed strength. Furthermore, I was here to accept a calling to the Primary general board and then, in March 1990, my current calling to the Relief Society general presidency. It has been a great blessing to both of us. I rely on Ed's constant support, his cheerfulness, his lively interest, and his intelligent analysis of my assignments. He truly companions me and is my partner as I have been his companion and partner in his callings. How foolish we would have been to think of the calling that could not be extended to us with disappointment or to feel that we had somehow been inadequate!

CHOOSING TO CHOOSE

In choosing to call ourselves survivors, not victims, and seeing the blessing behind the disguise, we exercise our precious gift of moral agency. Choosing to choose lightens our burdens and helps us find rest. One of the most powerful promises in the scriptures is in 2 Nephi 10:23: "Therefore, cheer up your hearts, and remember that ye are free to act for yourselves—to choose the way of everlasting death or the way of eternal life." That *is* a message of cheer and bright hope!

While I was going to high school, I had to live away from home and put myself through school by working as a maid. I was only fourteen, and I spent many nights feeling weepy, anxious, and frightened. What I had to do seemed so hard, and three years seemed so long. Then I discovered a wonderful fact. If I concentrated on how I was feeling, I only felt worse. But if I chose to behave cheerfully, resourcefully, and calmly, my mood changed. In other words, if I concentrated on how I wanted to behave, my feelings changed to match my behavior. The wonderful thing about choosing, for me, was that I didn't have to believe it would work. I just had to choose.

For example, when I would get up at 5:30 in the morning with a long list of household tasks to be accomplished before leaving for school and a long list afterwards, it was easy to feel overwhelmed, alone, and discouraged. Where could I find time to be happy? Where was there time to cheer myself up? But I was making it too hard. If I simply came into the school with a smile on my face and said, "Oh, good morning, Mr. Chuck," to my vice principal, he would look up, smile warmly back, and say, "Oh, Chieko, it's good to see you. How are things going? Are you doing all right with your schoolwork? Have you heard from your family?" In the ten minutes before the bell rang, my spirits would lift as if by a miracle. I felt consoled by Harry Chuck's concern and bolstered by his obvious confidence in my ability to handle both schoolwork and a demanding job. My teachers were equally supportive and kind. If I had decided instead that I felt too sad to talk to Mr. Chuck and had skulked past with my head down, I would have paralyzed myself with my own bad mood.

The important point is that I did not wait until I felt like smiling and saying hello. I *chose* to smile and say hello, and *then* my mood changed. I'm not saying that we should cover up serious emotional problems or try to deal with severe depression by pretending that everything is all right. Mental and physical problems need professional help and appropriate medical care. But where we can choose, I think it is incumbent upon us to exercise our agency.

What motivated me all through high school and college was an overwhelming desire to be a teacher. I was greatly inspired by my sixth-grade teacher, Mrs. Yuriko Nishimoto, who truly loved children and was the kind of person I wanted to be. I chose not only to get an education, which was what my parents also wanted for me, but to be an educator as my life's work. I carried that vision in my heart and in my mind. I measured my daily decisions against that vision. Was this what a teacher did? How she spoke? What she knew? How she behaved? What did I need to do to reach my goal? Would this activity help me reach that goal? If not, then what should I do instead?

I had not realized how powerful those cumulative choices had become; but when I was a senior in high school, Benjamin Wist, the dean of the Teachers College at the University of Hawaii came to visit our school. In the afternoon, the teachers held a tea for him, and I was invited to attend and help serve. In mingling and conversing with the teachers in the room, he at one point noticed me. "And what grade do you teach?" he asked, inviting conversation.

I stared back at him in astonished delight. "Do I look like a teacher?" I remember exclaiming.

"Yes, you do," he responded.

I felt as if I had just been crowned queen. "Thank you very much," I said proudly. "I want to be a teacher, and next year I hope to be entering your college."

He looked at me keenly and smiled kindly. "I will remember you," he said.

And he did. How I cherished that compliment! I realize now that he was seeing, manifested on the outside, the inner vision of myself that I had nurtured and labored for. It was the sum total of my choices up to that point, and those cumulative choices carried me through my college education and through the many challenges and opportunities that came to me later.

Another story from later in my life illustrates the power of our choices to alter adverse circumstances. When we moved to Utah, I was the first exchange teacher from Hawaii to teach at Uintah Elementary School in Salt Lake City. Ed was going to the University of Utah, working on his master's degree in social work. I had taught elementary school for three years in Hawaii and loved it thoroughly. I knew I could be a successful teacher. But still, I felt twinges of apprehension. Utah was a new place, new people, new customs. It had not been all that long since the end of World War II, and we were braced for some racism.

So I was not really surprised when Edith Ryberg, my principal, called me into the office a few days before school started. I could tell instantly that something was wrong. Hesitantly, she said, "I'm very sorry to say that three of the mothers of students assigned to your second grade have requested transfers to a different room. They don't want their children to have a Japanese teacher."

Her face was so sad; I hastened to lift her burden. "Oh, no problem!" I said cheerfully. "Don't worry about it. It's fine with me to make the switch. I came here to serve the children; and if the parents feel that way, I wouldn't be able to teach their children very successfully, even if they stayed in the classroom. I will love whoever comes into my class, so assign whoever will feel comfortable."

She looked at me in amazement, then breathed "Ooof!" in great relief. "This was so hard for me to do." When I told Ed about the incident that night, I still was not tempted to feel hurt and rejected. I threw back my shoulders, laughed, and said, "Well, three out of thirty-five isn't bad! I have thirty-two students who want me, and three more who are going to have that chance. And they're going to be *lucky* students to get me for their teacher! In fact, I feel sorry for those three whose parents want them in a different class."

Then I poured all my efforts into making that first day a great success. In those days of limited and expensive travel, Hawaii was pretty exotic; and I was Japanese-American from Hawaii. That made *me* pretty exotic, too, so I resolved to be exotic! I sewed a fuschia-colored dress that showed off my skin and black hair and tucked a fuschia flower behind my ear. I was the most vivid thing in the whole school that first day!

The custom at that time was for each teacher to meet her children on the playground, call the roll so that each child would know where to line up, and then lead her children into their new classroom. The other two second-grade teachers, as a courtesy to me, the new teacher, said, "Would you like to assemble your class first?" I was absolutely delighted. It was exactly what I had hoped for.

I knew there was a lot of curiosity about me because many second-grade mothers were there with their children. In a neighborhood school, mothers would bring a kindergarten child for the first day, and maybe even a first-grader, but not a second-grader unless there was some special situation. Well, I was that special situation, and there they all were—including mothers of second-graders assigned to the other rooms. It could have been a threatening situation. I could have chosen to feel frightened and let the children and parents register that fear. Or I could have chosen to be ultra stern and rigidly professional to cover my anxiety. But what I wanted the children to feel was my own joy and excitement.

I still remember opening the roll book, calling each child's name clearly, looking directly at each child as he or she came into line, smiling, and making some comment. "James Backman—what a nice name!" (He came and stood before me and said, "My dad is the president of the Salt Lake Board of Education.") "Beth Benson—how carefully you've tied your hair ribbons!" (And she said, "My dad is an apostle in the Church!") I could have felt just a *little* intimidated. But when I led them off, I could feel their anticipation.

That very afternoon, the principal took me aside, smiling a little. "Chieko," she said, "I just wanted you to know that those three mothers—you know, the ones who wanted their children in the other classrooms?—have come and asked if their children can be transferred back to you. I told them opportunity knocks only once." She laughed, "Can you imagine how furious the other mothers would be if I tried to talk them into transferring their children *out* of your room?"

I was smiling a little myself. That was one of many experiences I had in choosing my attitude and my mood, choosing how I would respond instead of letting circumstances respond for me.

These three principles of the gospel have been great resources to me in dealing with adversity: first, seeing myself as a survivor, as one of those who are "more than conquerors through him that loved us" (Romans 8:37); second, recognizing blessings, even when they come in disguise, so that we can entertain "angels unawares" (Hebrews 13:2); and third, deliberately exercising the power to choose and consistently choosing "the way of eternal life" rather than "the way of everlasting death" (2 Nephi 10:23).

When our burdens are grievous to be borne, when we face a world in which it seems that there is only struggle and no rest, I hope we can remember the immense strength of our sisterhood, the reservoirs that we have within us, and the unfailing wellspring of the Savior's love for us, even in the midst of adversity.

For me, choosing to view burdens "lightly," so to speak, and exercising the divine gift of our free agency in this way is what brings us from hope to faith. I love Nephi's words, "Wherefore, ye must press forward with a steadfastness in Christ, having a *perfect brightness of hope,* and a love of God and of all [people]. Wherefore, if ye shall press forward, feasting upon the word of Christ, and endure to the end, behold, thus saith the Father: Ye shall have eternal life" (2 Nephi 31:20; italics added). What I love about this scripture is that nearly every element in it lies within our choice: whether we feel like it or not, we can choose to "press forward"; we can choose to be "steadfast in Christ"; we can choose to "feast upon the word of Christ"; and we can choose to "endure to the end." It is my testimony, proved through many experiences, that when we make choices like these, we are choosing to act in hope, and when we do, I believe that the Lord supplies the "brightness" for us.

We have, as well, a remarkable degree of choice about "having . . . a love of God and of all [people]," also a part of this scripture. Yet we also know that the pure love of God, or charity, is the gift of the Father, for Moroni urges us: "Wherefore, my beloved brethren [and sisters], pray unto the Father with all the energy of heart, that ye may be filled with this love, which he hath bestowed upon all who are true followers of his Son, Jesus Christ" (Moroni 7:48). So again the reciprocal dynamic holds: if we *choose* to act in love, the gift of pure love will be given us.

There are many scriptures of comfort and consolation. This one from the Old Testament possibly refers to the Millennium, but it can also be seen as true for us in this life whenever we turn to the Savior with our burdens: "Do not fear, O Zion. . . . The Lord your God is with you, he is mighty to save. He will take great delight in you, he will quiet you with his love, he will rejoice over you with singing" (New International Version Zephaniah 3:16–17; see also KJV). May we feel the stillness of that love and hear the rejoicing in that song and remember his promise: "Come unto me, all ye that labour and are heavy laden, and I will give you rest" (Matthew 11:28).

Notes

1. Lucy Mack Smith, *History of Joseph Smith by His Mother,* ed. Preston Nibley (Salt Lake City: Bookcraft, 1979), 314.
2. Ibid., 324.
3. Ibid., 325.
4. Ibid., 327.

"MAY CHRIST LIFT THEE UP"

❦

Virginia H. Pearce

𝓜y son, be faithful in Christ; and may not the things which I have written grieve thee, to weigh thee down unto death; but may Christ lift thee up, and may his sufferings and death, and the showing his body unto our fathers, and his mercy and long-suffering, and the hope of his glory and of eternal life, rest in your mind forever" (Moroni 9:25).

I hope you won't mind if we delay talking about that verse for a while. I'd like to take you around the neighborhood, through some friendly streets and alleys, and then finally in the back door, where we'll meet up once again with Mormon and Moroni.

For our first detour, let me take you back three or four years to a spring morning. I was driving to work down South Temple Street in Salt Lake City. The sun was shining; the world seemed fresh and alive; there were daffodils everywhere and lots of that vibrant new green that we see only in the early spring. I was feeling good. It was one of those days when everything seemed to be right in my world. You know the kind of day. I was overwhelmed with love for my husband—he seemed particularly handsome and good; my children seemed like they were going to make it in the world. And they were nice people, too. We were all in good health; in fact, at that moment I felt extraordinarily healthy and strong. I thought about all of the wonderful people—friends, neighbors, associates at work—who made my world so good. My thoughts went to the day ahead. Yes, it was going to be a good one. There was work ahead that I felt I could do—work that was satisfying and interesting and that might even make a difference. I'm telling you, the cheerfulness in my car was almost edible!

Yet even as I was reviewing how great my life was, part of me was looking on saying, *What's going on here? None of the hard data in your life has changed that much, and yet everything seems wonderfully better this morning*

Virginia H. Pearce, former first counselor in the Young Women General Presidency, received a master's degree in social work from the University of Utah. She and her husband, Dr. James R. Pearce, are the parents of six and the grandparents of seven.

than it was last week! My analytical nature surfaced: *Maybe the biorhythms are peaking; perhaps there has been a sudden change in serotonin levels; maybe I created extra endorphins on my morning walk.* Anyway, even as I looked for ways to explain it (I didn't really care how it happened), the daffodils were catching the sun, and I was happy. Arriving at the office a little early that morning—isn't that what you would do on a practically perfect day?—I even had time to leaf through my scriptures.

Now, let me interrupt this happy picture and take you to a different scene. This is one a friend described to me. On this particular morning she lay in a psychiatric hospital at the bottom point of a terrible battle with an emotional illness. The war had exhausted her. She lay there thinking that she no longer knew herself. All of the talents, characteristics, and abilities she had developed over her life seemed to have fled. The things she had done in the past no longer brought meaning. Her husband, children, parents, and friends were in tatters. Prayer, scriptures, blessings—nothing seemed to help. She said the image that came to her so forcefully that morning was of a tree stump, cut off at ground level, all of the living branches gone, a maimed and broken thing.

I have been thinking of my daffodil day—and also of that tree stump. Is there a symbol, or a sign, or an idea that is so fundamental to life that it would speak to both of those days?

The ankh is a symbol common in Egyptian art. It is simple and beautiful. The ankh is called the sign of life, the symbol of life, or sometimes the key of life. We know little about its meaning anciently until the period of the Coptic Christians, when we begin to see it take more of the form and meaning of the cross.

I have told you that on that spring morning I reached for my scriptures, still thinking of my incredible sense of well-being, and started paging through the Topical Guide, stopping on the word *cheer.* As I read through the sentence stubs, I was surprised by a pattern:

"Be of good cheer: it is I" (Mark 6:50).

"Be of good cheer, little children" (D&C 61:36).

"Be of good cheer, for I will lead you along" (D&C 78:18).

"Be of good cheer; I have overcome the world" (John 16:33).

That touched a chord. Everything about my morning became an expression of gratitude to the Savior: the spring morning spoke of him, eternal ties and family relationships spoke of him, my health, strength, work—all found meaning because of him.

Now to my friend in the hospital. She said, "My mind wasn't working right, and so I was unable to get the daily reassurance that you depend on to feel good. But even without that normal reassurance, as I saw the image of the stump, I was aware of the roots. Somehow, I knew that I still had roots and that there would be growth again someday. I knew that the time would come when I would look back and see this impaired time almost like Rip Van Winkle. I knew my mind wasn't working right. But even as I knew that, I could feel those roots alive—somewhere very, very deep underground."

"Lift up your head and be of good cheer" (3 Nephi 1:13).

"Be of good cheer, and do not fear, for I the Lord am with you" (D&C 68:6).

Jesus Christ. Our sign of life, our key to life in all of its majestic and meaningful simplicity, is Jesus Christ. He fits every door, every life experience, every death experience that any mortal can possibly encounter. He is the undergirding of the daffodil days, the root which teams with the hope of life, even when it has been pruned to the ground. He stands as the fountain in ancient times as well as today. He is our key to life. He is the light and the life.

If he is the key, how can we most simply express that key in terms of us, in terms of what we feel and think and do? Again, the simplicity of his life showed us the way. He said, "This is the gospel which I have given unto you—that I came into the world *to do the will of my Father*" (3 Nephi 27:13; italics added).

If I could borrow a simple phrase—not even a complete sentence, but just the heart of a sentence—to express the key of life in practical everyday language for us, I would use this phrase, written by Alice T. Clark in her article on humility in the *Encyclopedia of Mormonism*: to "joyfully, voluntarily, and quietly submit one's whole life to the Lord's will."[1]

This phrase seems to me so basic. Like the ankh, it is beautiful in its clean and simple design. It cannot be spoken without a deep and complete faith in Christ and his doctrine. And the speaking of it weds that faith to its partner, agency. When we gathered in that council in heaven, before the foundation of this world, and heard the plan in all of its simple beauty, we understood about our need for faith as well as the importance of our Father's gift to us: agency. And we understood about the central and saving role of our Elder Brother. I'm sure it seemed wonderful in its simplicity to us then, just as it does now.

Everything since that premortal experience persuades and calls for us to exercise faith in Christ, using our agency to choose him and his ways.

Scriptural synonyms give rich and deep meaning to this phrase: "spiritually . . . born of God" (Alma 5:14).

"To take upon them [his] name . . . , and always remember him" (D&C 20:77).

To "love God with all your might, mind and strength" (Moroni 10:32).

"An eye single to the glory of God" (D&C 4:5).

"That . . . we shall be like him" (Moroni 7:48).

To offer "a broken heart and a contrite spirit" (2 Nephi 2:7).

I love the picture of the charming little girl on the Mary Engelbreit greeting card, her heart in outstretched hands and the caption reading "Here!"[2]

If, in fact, we do choose to submit our whole lives joyfully, voluntarily, and quietly to the Lord's will, what are some things that will follow? What will some of the immediate and natural outcomes be?

We will live our covenants, because living them is a happy choice. Covenants are not restrictive burdens; they are offerings joyfully made. We will strive to live covenants within that glorious cycle of repentance and growth. "I delight to do thy will, O my God: yea, thy law is within my heart" (Psalm 40:8).

Let me tell you about my friend Pat Pinegar, Primary General President. One day we were in a meeting together. There was a long and belabored discussion about sexual morality, particularly concerning young people. We were discussing their vulnerability and the tragic results of sin, but most of all we were talking about how to convince them to obey the law of chastity. Why would they want to remain chaste, against the flow of the world and their natural desires? There were many voices, lots of ideas, and then Sister Pinegar said, "I don't understand all of this. It seems so simple. Why don't we teach them to obey just because they love Heavenly Father?"

Stops you short, doesn't it?

There was an extended silence in the meeting. Sister Pinegar is one who constantly strives to submit her whole life to God's will. Certainly a life lived with that motivation would be a covenant-keeping life—and a much simpler life.

Another implication: *Our accountability to God will be clearer, and our scrambling to meet the expectations of everyone else will be muted.* That seems to bring sweet relief, doesn't it? One of the difficult things about life can be all of the conflicting expectations of others. Everyone needs help; everyone has an idea of who we should be and what we should do. What if we have submitted our life to God's will? Then we receive direction from him and answer to him. Not that we won't accommodate and help others. Of course we will be doing that constantly. He has told us that we are to help and serve one another, but how, where, when, and so on, will be answered in the peaceful corners of our hearts—between him and us.

Sister Marjorie Hinckley recently said: "We each do the best we can. My best may not be as good as your best, but it's my best. The fact is that we know when we are doing our best and when we are not. If we are not . . . it leaves us with a gnawing hunger and frustration. But when we do our level best, we experience peace."[3]

Yes, when we have joyfully, voluntarily, and quietly submitted our whole lives to the Lord's will, we will not have the burden of judging ourselves or others by an outward checklist. We can never judge the inward righteousness of another. What if someone looking at my friend in the psychiatric ward condemned her for failing to do her Church work, for failing to adequately care for her family, for contributing so little to her neighborhood? What if we condemned her, not knowing that in a very real and heart-wrenching way, she was doing her best by waiting upon the Lord's will and that her holding onto the image of a root that will send forth shoots again—that simple thought—was a heroic expression of faith and agency?

Think about the Relief Society sister who seems energetically and consistently to stretch the hours of the day to serve family, church, and community. Loaves of bread, enthusiasm, and perfect visiting teaching records pour out of her front door. But we can't judge her, either. Are these things expressions of her faith and choice to align her will with the Lord's? They may be—or they may not be. Elder Dallin H. Oaks taught us about the different motivations for service. He said there are "selfish and self-centered . . . reasons for service" that are "unworthy of Saints." There are "those who serve out of fear of punishment or out of a sense of duty." "Although [these] undoubtedly qualify for the blessings of heaven, there are still higher reasons for service."[4] Elder Oaks then taught us that the highest reason for service is out of a pure love of Christ.

Paul taught the same lesson about service: "Not with eyeservice, as menpleasers; but as the servants of Christ, doing the will of God from the heart; with good will doing service, as to the Lord, and not to men" (Ephesians 6:6–7).

What a relief! We don't have to judge ourselves or another against an incredibly long list. We are plainly and simply accountable to the Lord and to ourselves. President Gordon B. Hinckley expressed this accountability in a recent general conference address: "The work in which we are engaged is their work [meaning the Father and the Son], and we are their servants, who are answerable to them." In another talk he reminded us that it doesn't matter what others think of us: "How we regard ourselves is what is important."[5]

This accountability frees us each night, using the words of President Brigham Young, to "review the acts of the day, repent of our sins, . . . and say our prayers; then we can lie down and sleep in peace until the morning, arise with gratitude to God, commence the labors of another day, and strive to live the whole day to God and nobody else."[6]

Which brings us to the next implication: *We will view our daily, temporal tasks and duties differently—as offerings, not as repetitive or meaningless drudgery.* It seems that every task I do—be it visiting teaching, carpooling, solving problems in the workplace, changing diapers, writing memos, making arrangements on the telephone—becomes ennobled if I do it in the spirit of an offering to God. Throughout the ages, humankind has been confused about what giving one's life to God really means—what it looks like. Some have thought it means renouncing physical comfort—wearing scratchy clothes and sleeping on hard floors. Others have thought it means drawing away from earning a living or handling the things of the world, retreating from people and entangling relationships—particularly intimate family ones that require so much thought and care.

One of the startling and happy truths of the Restoration is the truth about the relationship between the temporal and the spiritual. President Brigham Young said: "If I am in the line of my duty, I am doing the will of God, whether I am preaching; praying, laboring with my hands for an honorable support; whether I am in the field, mechanic's shop, or following mercantile business, or wherever duty calls, I am serving God as much in one place as another. . . . In the mind of God there is no such a thing as dividing spiritual from temporal . . . , for they are one in the Lord."[7]

Something about our mortal life says that we cannot just give our lives to God in our hearts and then withdraw from daily living. Our temporal tasks become an expression of and a builder of our commitment to him.

Elder Henry B. Eyring illustrates this point with a story about his father, also named Henry Eyring. I will use Elder Eyring's words, because they carry the heart and meaning so beautifully:

"[My father] once told [this story] to me with the intention of chuckling at himself. . . . To appreciate this story, you have to realize that it occurred when he was nearly eighty and had bone cancer. He had bone cancer so badly in his hips that he could hardly move. The pain was great. . . .

"An assignment was given to weed a field of onions, so Dad [as the high councilor in charge of the stake farm] assigned himself [as well as others] to go work on the farm."[8]

When others who were with Brother Eyring that day told his son about it, they said that his father's pain was terrible. Brother Eyring couldn't kneel because of his hips and went painstakingly up and down the rows, pulling himself along on his stomach—smiling, laughing, and talking as they all worked together in the field of onions.

Quoting Elder Eyring again: "Now, this is the joke Dad told me on himself afterward. He said . . . after all the work was finished and the onions were all weeded, someone said to him, 'Henry, good heavens! You didn't pull those weeds, did you? Those weeds were sprayed two days ago, and they were going to die anyway. . . .

"Dad just roared. He thought that was the funniest thing. . . . He had worked through the day in the wrong weeds. They had been sprayed and would have died anyway. . . .

"I asked him, 'Dad, how could you make a joke out of that? How could you take it so pleasantly?' He said something to me that I will never forget. . . . He said, 'Hal, I wasn't there for the weeds.'"

And then Elder Eyring turns to us and speaks: "Now, you'll be in an onion patch much of your life. So will I. It will be hard to see the powers of heaven magnifying us or our efforts. It may even be hard to see our work being of any value at all. And sometimes our work won't go well.

"But you didn't come for the weeds. You came for the Savior."[9]

Do you hear our simple key? "Joyfully, voluntarily, quietly . . . "

The next implication of our simple key is this: *We will live nobly, on a higher plane, because we will constantly think above our own individual needs.*

Sometimes it is easier to recognize a lack of nobility than it is to recognize nobility. For that reason I will tell you of my less-than-noble conduct one afternoon. I was in a neighborhood store, waiting for my turn and chatting with a neighbor in line next to me. Somehow the name of a mutual acquaintance came up—actually someone we both like very much but who is quite eccentric. My neighbor told a funny story about her; that reminded me of another funny story; she topped that one . . . . Pretty soon we were laughing uproariously. Out of the corner of my eye I saw the clerk listening to us. It startled me into a recognition of what I was doing. I should have stopped. I didn't. But as I finished my transaction and walked to the car, I was overwhelmed with my smallness. They weren't mean or slandering stories, but I would have been ashamed if the subject of our stories had overheard us. I was so uncomfortable that I had to return later and apologize to the clerk as well as express my shame to my neighbor. Most of all, I had to let the Lord know that I knew that kind of behavior was wrong and I needed forgiveness. Nobility is a correlate of devotion to the Lord.

Justice Potter Stewart is an associate justice of the Supreme Court. He defined *ethics* in the following way: "Knowing the difference between what you have a right to do, and what is the right thing to do."[10]

That's a good one to think about, even memorize. "Knowing the difference between what you have a right to do, and what is the right thing to do." Quite often we have a right to lash out, to retaliate and to punish. But is it the right thing to do?

Nobility suggests that even when we receive injury, we refuse to seek petty revenge. We may seek to right a wrong, but revenge is another story. We desire to rise above our side of the story, to absorb pain and choose not to pass it on. Isn't that what the Savior did?

Next point: *We will never be truly victimized by our failures, adverse circumstances, or the bad choices of other people. Equally important, we will not be victimized by success.* Now, how could that be?

Even though our performance is uneven and awkward, there is something that we can count on as we come to Him in humility and submissiveness. It is that every event, every task that we are a party to, can be made to benefit our souls. That is a stunning thought, isn't it? Given the natural way, there are so many things that we do or that we are victims of that could hurt our souls. Only God, through the intervention of his Son, can change, in a miraculous way we don't understand, how things will affect us.

"Pray always, and not faint; that ye must not perform any thing unto the Lord save in the first place ye shall pray unto the Father in the name of Christ, that he will consecrate thy performance unto thee, that thy performance may be for the welfare of thy soul" (2 Nephi 32:9).

The Savior can turn negative things to our good. Rather than bitterness, when we turn to him, we can forgive. Then, our own suffering can help us develop the capacity to withhold judgment and to reach out compassionately to others who suffer.

Turning to the Savior can also protect us against our successes. We see every day evidence of how success can result in destroying a person's soul. The media holds up lives ruined by success. What if, on a daffodil day, we really, really think that all of the good things in our lives are there because we are simply so smart, so talented, so effective that everything we enjoy comes as a direct result of our work and brains?

Do you see my point? Pride and egotism injure a soul as surely as do the bitterness and pain of affliction and failure. Success is an affliction to the soul unless it is recognized for what it is—God's working in our lives. With success, as well as adversity, we pray that our performance will be consecrated for the welfare of our souls. And he will do that, because each prayer we offer will somehow be an expression that we are joyfully, voluntarily, and quietly desiring to give our lives to him. Then desperate days refine us rather than destroy us. And daffodil days become days of worship and gratitude rather than days of pride and boasting.

Another dimension: *We will live with the security that our real needs will be met and that we will be fully able to do our part in meeting the real needs of others.*

Not long ago our youngest child and only son—in a suit, missionary nametag on his lapel—waved as he disappeared into the plane that would drop him off in the Chile Santiago North Mission—only another hemisphere away! You know this story. I went home with that big hole in my stomach and went about my life, trying not to think of him every single minute. Well, about nine days had passed, and I was beginning to check on the mailbox more than once a day. On Thursday morning came a telephone call. A gentle man with a Spanish accent introduced himself. He said that his wife had been in sacrament meeting in Santiago the Sunday before, and our son, who had been assigned to their ward, was asked to introduce himself and bear his testimony. After the meeting she had offered to deliver a letter from him to his family, because she was leaving for general conference in Salt Lake City the following week.

You can imagine that I wasted no time in driving to the hotel to meet these good people. How do I describe that little exchange? I have just told you that you can't always judge who the people are who have joyfully, voluntarily, and quietly given their lives to the Lord. Well, I could tell with these two. The conversation between Sister Jaramillo and me was in two different languages—her husband translated as we spoke a few words. She told me that her youngest son was in the Missionary Training Center on his way to Phoenix. She told me that she had met my son and that he was a very humble missionary. And then she reached out to me and spoke gentle Spanish words. Her husband followed: "My wife is telling you that she will take good care of your son." That took two Kleenexes to wipe up. Actually, it took all I had to prevent myself from making gasping noises as she handed me the letter. I told her that I wouldn't be in Phoenix to take care of her son but that I would pray for him.

I walked out of that hotel lobby with such a feeling of peace and comfort.

What do I really expect she could or should do for James? Stop by his apartment once a week, write him notes, cheer him up with periodic pep talks, bake cookies? No. Not at all. In fact, I doubt that she will need to do anything. Then why should I feel so good? The security I feel is rooted in her devotion to the Lord's will, because that means that if my son does have some real need, the Lord will know of it and Sister Jaramillo is at least one person in that city who would unhesitatingly respond when prompted by the Lord.

I cannot tell you the security and gratitude I feel for each of you who kneels and offers herself to the Lord. You are the ones whom he will direct to teach my grandchildren, who answer the needs of my married children, who invite my missionary daughter to dinner, who carry letters home to an anxious mother, who work respectfully beside my husband. You don't need to do everything all of the time for every member of my family. But I know that if you have given yourself to do the Lord's will, you will do the right thing at the right time.

I love you.

Another implication as we use this simple key: *We will be assured success.*

This is a personal metaphor, but it helps me understand the power of guaranteed success. I hate to shop. Did I say that strongly enough? I *hate* to shop. I have very little skill and so have very limited success. And besides, I don't have good feet. Anyway, one day one of my daughters and I were shopping. She needed a particular piece of clothing for a particular occasion that would make her look close to spectacular. All this for a reasonable amount of money. Is that the worst formula? We started out in the morning full of energy and hope. But by early afternoon, we were dragging in and out of the dressing rooms. Her hair was full of static, my feet hurt, we were hungry, and we were getting grouchy. And then we had a startling idea. If we knew, absolutely guaranteed *knew*, that at the end of the afternoon we would have found the perfect dress, would it make any difference to how we felt now? We inventoried—the hair, the feet, the hunger, the discouragement—and we said unhesitatingly yes! We could easily go another three hours, *if* we knew there was unequivocal success ahead. And so we simply told ourselves that we were going to find the outfit—and, I am amazed to tell you, it worked! We were laughing and talking again instead of whining and dragging.

Could it be the same with life? Do we get exhausted because we quit believing that success is assured? You know, it is! In the sooner and later context, it might not be sooner, but it will *for sure* be later.

"Thy God shall stand by thee forever and ever" (D&C 122:4). "And the world passeth away and the lust thereof: but he that doeth the will of God abideth forever" (1 John 2:17). "He that endureth in faith and doeth my will, the same shall overcome, and shall receive an inheritance upon the earth when the day of transfiguration shall come" (D&C 63:20).

There must be dozens more implications, but I will only mention one more: *We will expect to have to make this choice many, many times.* Our ongoing responsibility is to keep offering ourselves and everything that we have and are to Him—to work actively but to cease judging each task with our mortal measurements. This is the great paradox of the gospel: In the total giving away, we receive total abundance, the only total security available. When we submit voluntarily and joyfully, far from being passive victims, we become victors, because we have accepted a partnership with an all-powerful and all-loving Being.

We aren't in the onion patch for the weeds. We are here for him. We are here with him.

Now I've worn you out. Surely we must be at the back door. Let's walk through it and sit in the living room for a last moment with Moroni 9:25.

Mormon writes his final letter (at least the last one we have) to his son Moroni. He describes the "horrible scene" (v. 20), the "depravity of my people" (v. 18), who are "without order and without mercy" (v. 18), "strong in their perversion" (v. 19), "brutal, sparing none" (v. 19). "But behold, my son, I recommend thee unto God, and I trust in Christ that thou wilt be saved" (v. 22); and then our verse:

"My son, be faithful in Christ; and may not the things which I have written grieve thee, to weigh thee down unto death; but may Christ lift thee up, and may his sufferings and death, and the showing his body unto our fathers, and his mercy and long-suffering, and the hope of his glory and of eternal life, rest in your mind forever" (v. 25).

It doesn't matter what time we live in: the time of Mormon (A.D. 421), the 1950s (doesn't everyone talk about what a good time that was?), or this very day. It doesn't matter whether we are talking about a difficult individual environment or a sin-filled culture. The only thing that provides real lifting—lifting beyond mortality and all of its chaos and troubles, beyond our own weaknesses and sins and changing fortunes, beyond our own pain and suffering and success—the only real lifting comes through our Savior and Redeemer, Jesus Christ.

Daffodils do bring gladness. Healthy, happy children cause our hearts to sing. Balanced brain chemistry and physical health maximize our enjoyment of this world. Rides in convertibles, picnics in a pine-scented forest, shelter during the cold storms of winter—these are delights I wouldn't want to have missed. Economic security lightens our load of worry. Attentive husbands and the warmth of good friends bring contentment. Accomplishment, a job well done, music, art, an exquisitely written piece of literature—yes, there are so many things that lift in happy ways, but if some of these, if all of these, were to evaporate, to be snatched away from us, cut off at ground level, we could still count on Christ: the one who did only the will of his Father, the co-creator of all that is good, the one who knows every soul—the sick, the oppressed, the gifted, the gorgeous, the abused, the charismatic, the brilliant, as well as the bumbling and stumbling soul who can't seem to make anything work. Yes, you and me. He knows us. He not only knows us but loves us so much that the focus of his mortal and heavenly life is us. His simple key is a statement about us: "This is my work and my glory—to bring to pass the immortality and eternal life of man" (Moses 1:39). He suffered himself to be lifted up upon the cross that we might be lifted up, back to our Father, clothed with immortality and eternal life. And our part is easy, as simple in design as the Egyptian ankh. In faith, each of us takes the only thing we really have—our agency—and offers it back to him joyfully, voluntarily, and quietly.

Notes

1. *Encyclopedia of Mormonism*, ed. Daniel H. Ludlow, 4 vols. (New York: Macmillan, 1992), 2:663; verb tense changed.
2. Used by permission.
3. As quoted in *Church News*, 18 April 1998.
4. Dallin H. Oaks, *Ensign*, November 1984, 14.
5. Gordon B. Hinckley, *Ensign*, May 1998, 71, 4.
6. *Brigham Young*, Teachings of Presidents of the Church Series (Salt Lake City: The Church of Jesus Christ of Latter-day Saints, 1997), 25.
7. *Young Teachings*, 22.
8. Henry B. Eyring, *To Draw Closer to God* (Salt Lake City: Deseret Book, 1997), 101.
9. Eyring, *To Draw Closer to God*, 101–2.
10. As quoted in Rex E. Lee, "Honesty and Integrity," address delivered at Brigham Young University, Provo, Utah, 5 September 1995.

LOVE IN ABUNDANCE:
THE DISADVANTAGED CHILDREN
OF INDIA AND NEPAL

‿⌾⌾‿

Cécile Pelous

Introduction by Michael J. Call

Cécile Pelous first learned about the Latter-day Saint faith when, as a student recently graduated from high school in France, she toured America and visited several large cities, among which was Salt Lake City. There her tour group attended the play Promised Valley, and by the end, Cécile found herself standing and singing with audience and cast, tears streaming down her face. When asked at the end of the tour which city had been the highlight of her trip, Cécile shocked her French friends by naming Salt Lake City. She told them she had felt something there unlike anything she had felt in other places they had visited.

Three years later, two missionaries doing their daily tracting knocked on the door of her family's home in Paris. Cécile, noticing their American accent, asked if they were from Salt Lake City in Utah. When Elder Ed Borrell from Price, Utah, claimed to be from somewhere close by, Cécile consented to talk to them. (She has since learned just how far Elder Borrell was stretching the truth.) Cécile listened to the discussions, believed, and was baptized some time later by Elder Borrell. Since joining the Church, Cécile has served in all the auxiliaries, at both ward and stake levels. She is a member of the Cergy-Pontoise Ward in the Paris Stake and has been called to serve as stake Relief Society president.

Professionally, Cécile has worked as a modelist for the best fashion houses in Paris, such as Christian Dior and Pierre Cardin, and is employed with Nina Ricci. Her job as a modelist is to take the dress designs created on paper by the designers and translate them into the full-sized prototypes from which the seamstresses will then produce the dress in the fabrics chosen by the designers. Her work is so valued by her employers at Nina Ricci that they are willing to give her three months' paid vacation every year to allow her to pursue her projects in India and Nepal. It is this very important part of her life, thousands of miles away from the fashion houses of Paris and the Cergy-Pontoise Ward, that she will describe to us.

I am not a heroine. My experience serving the children in India is a story of love and friendship.

A few years ago, I took stock of my blessings: I had been reared by loving parents, in a land of abundance; I was educated, had learned and was practicing a profession which I love; I was healthy, thanks to an abundance of nourishing food; and I knew the gospel. I also knew that many people in the world could only dream about such a life. I felt an intense need to share some of these same possibilities with those most deprived of them.

In July 1986, I boarded a plane for Calcutta, India, for my annual vacation. Armed with a first-aid certificate, suitcases full of medicine and my good will, I got off the plane determined to help my neighbor. I had read Dominique Lapierre's best-seller, *The City of Joy,*[1] and had attended one of his lectures describing the situation in India; I knew there was plenty to do.

I worked first with Mother Teresa's missionaries and then with other groups, especially with old people, babies, and handicapped children. There was dirty laundry to boil and wash, meals to prepare and serve. In the hospitals, there were the sick to feed and to give medical care to; there were the dying to bathe and to help leave this world surrounded by warmth and tenderness; there were babies to change and feed, babies so weak I wished I could somehow give them my own strength.

During this trip, I discovered a home for about a hundred aged people, most of them bedridden. The home was run by only two Catholic missionaries, one of whom had been sick for three days. With the help of another volunteer worker, I set to work. Sister Theresina, one of the missionaries, who had single-handedly been taking care of all the needs, kissed me and said, "The Lord has sent you to us." And I believed it.

That same summer in Pilkana, a slum in the outskirts of Calcutta, I was confronted by scorching heat, flooding that lasts the entire monsoon season, and people living in extreme deprivation. I also found much hope, for the children still know how to laugh and have fun with nothing, like all children in the world. That helps their parents endure their misery. I also met a European couple, the Jallais family, who had lived in India for twenty years, helping the most disadvantaged Indians become self-reliant. I also witnessed the creation of a soup kitchen and a dispensary where medical treatment was given without charge. There, those who have little give to those who have nothing. I also came across a school where young women from ages fourteen to seventeen learn to do batik paintings on cloth, a skill that one day will help them meet the needs of their families. In that school I taught the girls to make patterns, to cut out and to sew their own clothing. These girls now make clothing for other orphan children.

Finally, I discovered the *ashrams*, orphanages run by religious organizations. Each ashram houses about one hundred children, ranging from five to twelve years old. Malnutrition and poor living conditions have claimed many of their parents; wild animals have killed others. The children arriving at the ashram are near starvation; it takes them three months to get used to the idea that there will be rice for them to eat each day. Many suffer from skin diseases, fever, intestinal disorders, and rickets. Presently, the Indian welfare system has created eight such orphanages in Bengal, one of which is the Dayal Ashram, or "House of Happiness," in Banipur.

That particular orphanage is very dear to me; it was there that I discovered the "heart" of the people of India. I felt at home there; I taught the children to play, to sing, and to laugh. They taught me to sleep on the floor, to eat with my fingers, to remove my shoes before entering houses or sacred places, and to appreciate the main thing in life—love.

The children and I bonded very quickly. They call me Cécile Didi (Big Sister Cécile). During my first trip there in 1986, when I became very ill from paratyphoid, my little friends took care of me and watched over me like true little mothers. They massaged my arms and legs to relieve the cramps caused by the sickness. They watched over me as I slept, and when I awakened, I would find little flower bracelets around my wrists.

Before my first visit to Banipur in 1986, the local welfare agency had built a chicken coop to provide one egg per week to each of the eight hundred children in the city's orphanages, a precious addition of protein to a diet consisting otherwise exclusively of rice and lentils. Unfortunately, a disease had wiped out the chickens in August of that year.

When I returned to France, I said to myself, If I return to India, it will be to rebuild a chicken coop in Banipur. I went back to work at Nina Ricci and started to save my money. It did not take me long to realize that my money would not be enough. I prayed, and then I told my friends and the Paris Stake president of my plans. Three days later, I received a check from the stake, the result of a project named "Drop of Water," which the stake had organized several months previously to help relieve hunger in the world. The stake leaders had decided to donate the money raised to build the chicken coop in Banipur. Friends also contributed to the cause.

Because I knew absolutely nothing about running a chicken coop, I talked to chicken farmers in France to educate myself. I was so naive, I thought you had to have one rooster per hen to make things work!

Donations in hand, in September 1987, I returned to Banipur. I bought 120 laying hens and 120 chicks (which began to lay eggs five months later), thirty laying ducks, and enough grain to feed the birds for a whole year. I also bought materials to build a chicken coop (which the villagers built) and six months' worth of powdered milk for the children.

All the while I was giving this emergency food assistance, I insisted on reinforcing the goal of self-reliance for the ashrams; even the littlest child had certain duties in the running of the coop. In this way they learned to feel responsible for one another's well-being. As a matter of fact, each orphanage has only two adult leaders and three handicapped cooks to supervise the one hundred children.

Since 1987, I have been going to Bengal twice a year. During the first years, I had to quit my job each time I left, without any guarantee of getting it back again. But the Lord has blessed me: my current employers (who are not LDS) have granted me two paid vacations a year of six weeks each to allow me to pursue my projects. I am convinced that when we undertake to do our share on the first mile, as proposed by the Lord, the second mile is given to us.

I notice progress from one visit to the next. In Banipur, uncultivated land has been transformed into a vegetable garden for the orphanage. At first, the children, who had no tools, worked in the garden with wooden sticks. Now they have shovels and picks. Fish have been planted in the orphanage's little pond. Almost six hundred pounds of fish are regularly harvested each year from the pond. Each child can eat vegetables and eggs regularly and fish now and again.

Gaston Grandjean, a Catholic priest who has chosen to live among the poor of India, talked to me about another project, the dispensary in the village of Belari. The dispensary had been constructed through the efforts of Sorit Kumar Da, a local civic leader who gave up a life of ease to help the "untouchables," the lowest social caste in India, and the villagers after a road had been opened to the village in September 1986. Formerly serving three thousand patients per month, the dispensary now serves nine thousand, who are coming from farther and farther away for treatment. We have established a nursery, which cares for twenty-five babies suffering from malnutrition. Mothers receive 250 grams of powdered milk each week for their babies and a free checkup by a nurse. Young lives are being saved.

Also at Belari, villagers have constructed a school for forty-five children. Men, women, and children each brought bricks made in the rice fields and baked in the sun. I too made and donated my bricks. Contributions help pay the costs of construction, the teaching personnel, and the cooks at the school. As a result, while helping their neighbors, some villagers are also earning a salary.

A well has been sunk by the villagers and equipped with a pump purchased with money donated by the youth of a ward in the Paris Stake. A second well with potable water is now in operation. Infectious diseases have been reduced.

After the typhoon of November 1988, which caused widespread destruction, we established family chicken coops, selecting thirty-five families in Belari to learn how to run a coop. We gave each of them two hens and a rooster. At the end of six months, the families who hadn't eaten their capital immediately had more than thirty chickens each. These chickens became for them a means of exchange to buy rice, medicine, books, and clothing. It was a start towards autonomy.

At the beginning of 1988, the Paris Stake ordered one thousand batik greeting cards from the girls in the school at Pilkana. The girls benefitted from this opportunity to work for pay. The stake repeated the order in 1990. The Primary children of the Paris Stake donated toys, and the youth of the stake exchanged letters with the children of the orphanage. This interaction allowed the French young people to better appreciate their own blessings and to see that one can accomplish much with little.

In 1989, a friend of mine, Father François Laborde, contacted me, telling me that he felt inspired to ask me to help a teacher in Nepalgang, Nepal, named Parijat Gosh. Gosh was supporting fifty homeless children on his teacher's salary and wanted to establish a home for them. He hoped also to build a dispensary and eventually a small farm, which would permit him to feed them. I traveled to Nepalgang and evaluated the needs. When I returned to Paris, I tried unsuccessfully to raise the necessary money. Fortunately, some real estate investors gave me a great offer on my home. I accepted, feeling that the Lord was offering me a solution. I purchased a less expensive home, and with the money left over, I financed the construction of the home in Nepalgang, which was completed in 1991. The children now have a place to sleep, but they also need to be fed, clothed, and educated. Thus, my next project will be the dispensary and the farm. Once everything is built, the daily cost for food, health care, and schooling will be seventy-five cents per child—the cost of two doughnuts.

I know that when people have food to eat and clothes to wear, they can then become interested in the gospel. I try to follow Church welfare principles. I obey Indian law, and I work through Indian organizations. I am learning Bengali and Nepali. I hope to represent the Church in a good light. I give copies of excerpts of the Book of Mormon in Bengali to those who ask me questions about the Church. Each time I travel to India or Nepal, I ask for a priesthood blessing, which guides me during my entire stay. The Lord opens doors for me. Once, customs officials in Calcutta allowed me to bring in twice the amount of medicine usually allowed other volunteers who have been working in India for more than twenty years. Once, at the very last minute, I secured a seat on an already full plane headed for Nepal because I absolutely needed to go. Often, I am granted authorization from officials who are not known for their helpfulness. When the Lord wishes something, I need only to do my part for him to do his.

Of course, I realize that the needs are immense. Hundreds of schools, pumps, nurseries, chicken coops, dispensaries, and health instructors are needed to relieve the current level of deprivation in India and to prepare a better, more humane future. What I have seen accomplished is little and yet a lot. Hope has been reborn. My friends in Banipur and Belari now know that the vicious cycle of hunger and sickness can be overcome. They have found new courage and are beginning to take charge of their lives.

What prompts my actions? I cannot forget the look on the face of a grandmother, bringing her dehydrated and anemic granddaughter to the Belari dispensary, and pleading: "Save my grandchild." I also remember the image of groups of young Hindu children in the ashram of Banipur, saying their prayers, alone, without adults, with the utmost reverence. What spiritual treasures in these impoverished children! But for me, it is, above all, people, faces, smiles: those of the children—Milli, Ranu, Tulu, Sima, Boula, Aouti, and many others—and the adult leaders—Sukeshi, Shonda, Lucy, Minoti. This work has a soul.

The first time I went to India, I wanted to give a little of what I had to disadvantaged children. And I realize that in giving a little, it is I who have received much. I have cared for sick children, and they have cared for me. I wanted to be a mother for them, and I have found a family in them. I want to bring them the spirituality the gospel offers us, and I see them already living the gospel daily in their spontaneous way of helping one another and of being responsible for one another, in their disregard of material things, in their family relationships formed out of respect and love. When I think of the children of Banipur, I see them playing with little or nothing at all. They carefully place in their little treasure boxes the toys they receive from their French friends. They keep the candy wrappers which I give them and from which they will make flower garlands to welcome me back next time I visit. I see them proud of their harvests from the vegetable garden and the chicken coop. I see them, reverent in worshipping God.

For them, I discover in myself talents and energy that I never would have sought for myself. Without previous training but with the sincere desire to serve, I have been able to do much more than I thought possible. I see that what I accomplish is a part of the work of the Lord and that I am his instrument. He guides me and opens doors for me, sometimes in unforeseen ways.

Each of us has work to do on this earth and responsibilities for our neighbor, far or near. We cannot and must not remain indifferent. We are blessed because we have knowledge and a marvelous personal relationship with our Heavenly Father. For me, that is my greatest capital. The surest way to make it bear fruit is to place it in the service of others. This is a chain of unending love. Let's not wait for the Church to instruct us how to do good. If we forget ourselves in helping others, we will be blessed above and beyond what we can imagine. That has been true for me. We read in Mosiah 4:26: "I would that ye should impart of your substance to the poor, every man according to that which he hath, such as feeding the hungry, clothing the naked, visiting the sick and administering to their relief, both spiritually and temporally, according to their wants."

Doctrine and Covenants 35:14 says: "Their arm shall be my arm." This is one of the most sacred and most personal responsibilities I read in the scriptures. The Lord says that this arm that belongs to me is his arm. This mind, this tongue, these hands, these feet, this heart, this wallet—all these are the only tools he has to work with, at least as far as I am concerned. And I feel good, because I am where I should be, and the children know it. They love me, and I love them. Through love we learn to create together the conditions of their self-reliance. There is so much to do for them. Let us love them.

My friends in Nepal laughingly tell me: "You are a V. I. P., not for the world but for God." And I believe them. And that gives me the desire to move mountains for our Lord, Jesus Christ.

Note

1. Dominique Lapierre, *La Cité de la Joie* (Paris: Editions Robert Laffont, 1985); *The City of Joy*, trans. Kathryn Spink (New York: Warner Books, 1986).

MY STRENGTH AND MY SONG

୧✕୨

Janice Kapp Perry

I never sang solos until a few years ago when I was in Hawaii. A wonderful Hawaiian woman at church there said, "Will you sing a solo on our program today?" I replied, "Well, I've never really had any singing lessons. Singing solos is just not something I've done." "You know," she answered me, "that's a form of pride that President Benson talked about."

I didn't understand what she meant, but she went on. "He doesn't want us to have a fear of men or women. You're afraid there will be a better singer in the audience."

I thought, *For sure there will be.*

"President Benson said we should stand up, do our best, and look to the Lord for our approval and not to the world," she added.

I took that lesson to heart, and I have just been singing my best ever since, in the spirit of these words I heard at a Church music workshop years ago: "I'm not in rebellion against fine musicians. But as we admire orchids and roses, we also love sunflowers, asters, and wayside offerings."[1]

Did you know that both our Savior and our Prophet Joseph Smith wanted music in the last hours of their lives to bolster their strength? The Savior asked his disciples to sing a hymn with him before he went to the Mount of Olives (see Matthew 26:30), and Joseph Smith asked his companions to sing with him and for him before his martyrdom. That puts those of us who love and find comfort in music in very good company. If the Savior wanting a hymn sung is important enough to be recorded in the Gospels, that convinces me that God gave us music to help us through this life.

An idea set to music stays with us in a different way than just the words. I was in a car accident a couple of years ago. Someone crashed right into my driver's side door and shattered every bit of the glass. At the very moment my life was in danger, here's what went through my mind: "When you hear the crash, think of Jones' Paint and Glass." It was useless

---

Janice Kapp Perry received her musical training at Brigham Young University. She and her husband, Douglas C. Perry, are the parents of five children. She has served as a ward Relief Society president and sings with the Mormon Tabernacle Choir.

information then, of course, but somebody had set it to music, and it came floating up at a very unusual time. If that type of music stays with us so long, it's really important to set the gospel to music so that gospel messages come to mind in times of need.

Music enhances every situation of our lives. During difficult times, music makes the burden easier. In happy times, music enhances our happiness. And as Elder Boyd K. Packer notes, "We are able to feel and learn very quickly through music, through art, through poetry some spiritual things that we would otherwise learn very slowly."[2] As we allow it, the Spirit of the Lord does soften and tune our hearts through worthy music.

Music can touch us and make things a little easier. My daughter, Lynne, tells the following story about music:

"I was probably about halfway through my mission when I was put with a new companion. After about a week together I began to realize that my companion had some serious problems. I found out later that chemical imbalances made her very unpredictable. She would fly off the handle and shriek in rage at me over simple things or even nothing that I could detect. Having been raised in a peaceful home, I was distressed by that kind of contention. I felt like I couldn't function as a missionary under those conditions. She always apologized for these outbursts afterwards. She'd say, 'I'm sorry. I couldn't help it,' and we'd work through it. But occasionally she would have an outburst when we were driving to teach a discussion. There was no way that we could have the Spirit with us after one of those outbursts.

"One morning I was in the shower, crying. It was the only place that I could be alone. I was just kind of sobbing and praying that somehow I could find a way to deal with this for the next few months. I knew my mission president wouldn't just transfer one of us, because that would just give the problem to someone else. I received the impression that music was going to be the key to my relationship with this companion. *Music?* I thought, because I had had no indication that she was musical. But the impression was very strong. That day as we left in the car to go quite a distance to a discussion, I thought, *Okay, that was a definite impression, so I ought to act on it.* I began to hum a song of Mom's called 'Song of Testimony.' My companion recognized it and joined in humming with me. Then I started singing, and she sang with me. Though she had no musical training, she loved to sing. We finished a few other songs by the time we arrived at our appointment. As we offered a prayer before going up to the house, we both felt a sweetness and calm that we sorely needed. Many times in the three months that we were together, we had to resort to humming—and sometimes the humming would start kind of loud and frustrated, but it never ceased to make a difference in our relationship. We ended up as very good friends. She died just a few months after we returned from our missions. Her father asked me to sing 'Song of Testimony' at her funeral. I felt honored to sing at her funeral and very grateful to the Lord for turning a very stressful, contentious situation into a good friendship."

Sometimes the songs I have written come back to haunt me. I may learn something from them as I write them, or learn it later when I return to a song and feel like a hypocrite because I'm not living what I wrote. This happened to me when I was a new Relief Society president trying as hard as I could. I went to a training session with President Barbara Winder, and for three hours she told us how to improve our Relief Societies. I felt overwhelmed. I thought, *How can we do more than we're doing?* At the end of her session, she said something that made it all right: "Just choose one or two things from what we've said. And above all, 'Do not run faster . . . than you have strength'" (D&C 10:4). I went straight home and looked up that scripture. It made me feel so good I decided to write a song about it. And I tried to live that principle.

One day, however, I was at Relief Society all day for a homemaking meeting. My daughter's little girl had burned her hands badly, and I was wishing I was with her so I could see how she was. My mother was also ill, and I felt I should have been with her that day. But my nephew was here from Alaska to enter the Missionary Training Center, and I had promised to help him do his shopping all that afternoon and give an open house for him that evening for all the Utah relatives. I rushed from thing to thing, not doing anything well. Just before the open house, I remembered an item I had forgotten to buy. So I jumped into the car. The radio was tuned to an LDS music station, and when I turned the ignition key, there was my song "Do Not Run Faster Than You Have Strength." It was the strangest feeling. I looked at my radio and said, "Easy for you to say."

A few days ago I talked to Lynne about how her day was going. (Sometimes she calls up and says, "Mom, is this the complaint department?" "Yes, it is," I answer. "Go for it.") She'd had a day that rivaled one of mine. She was trying to phone people in a stake choir, write out a piece of music for their stake conference on Sunday, and prepare dinner for the missionaries. She needed to go grocery shopping, but she had also committed to do two hours of visiting teaching, and she was helping her husband get ready for a mule-packing trip. I said to Lynne, "Each generation improves on the last one," meaning busy to busier to busiest. We all do too much and get stressed. That's when music can help us gain perspective.

> I thought that I could do it all, complete each task,
>   accept each call.
> I never felt my work was done, until I had pleased
>   everyone.
> I told myself I must be strong, be there for all to
>   lean upon,
> But in the end I came to see, that's more than God
>   requires of me.
> He has said:

Chorus:
> Do not run faster than you have strength.
> If you grow weary, what have you gained?
> You will have wisdom and strength enough,
> If first you remember to fill your own cup.

Music has helped me the most at the toughest times of my life—the deaths of my father, my mother, and one of our newborn babies. In each case, music helped me gain peace in specific ways. My husband and I had a serious Rh factor problem, and our last baby was two months premature and extremely ill with Rh complications. He was given a name and a blessing, and unsure that he would live, we watched through the night. He passed away by the next morning. At that point I remembered that I had four little children at home who needed reassurance, who needed to see that I was okay so that they would be okay. Even though I felt peace of mind, I didn't really grieve the way I needed to. I didn't fully acknowledge that loss or that I might never have another baby. Twenty years later, I was remembering that experience one night and decided that because it was still somewhat unresolved in my mind, I needed to write about it. Every day for a week or two, I relived the experience, writing lyrics and composing a song that I hoped would put it to rest for me. I cried then in a way I had not cried when it happened. Since then it has been a very happy memory. I look forward to rearing that baby, as Joseph Smith said we would.[3] My feelings are only happy ones. Here is the song I wrote then:

MY HEART SANG A LULLABY

Richie was born on a day in December,
I know it was Sunday—some things you remember,
Richie's first cries were like music to me,
But no one could promise how long he would stay.
And the night seemed so long as we watched him and prayed.

Richie was gone by the light of the morning,
Before his first sunrise, before the day's dawning.
So still in our arms, it was our turn to cry,
A memorized moment as we said good-bye.
And he looked like an angel in his blanket of white.

Richie, my son, only here for a moment,
He came and he went and the world didn't notice.
But nothing's the same, especially for me,
Eternity's promise is clearer to see.
He has just gone ahead to where we'll someday be.

Chorus:
And my heart sang a lullaby
To celebrate birth,
As he crossed the veil
Between heaven and earth.
My heart sang a lullaby
For this tiny one.
A song of forever,
Of things yet to come.
Just a lullaby to carry him home.
Yes, a lullaby to carry him home.

My father died when he was fifty-seven, one year younger than I am now. I thought that was awfully young to lose my father. I'd seen him go through a lot during his last few years, so by the time he died, I felt some relief. Even the day he died, I felt exhilarated, happy for him to be free of pain. I went through his funeral with that same feeling. I didn't cry but just felt peace. A couple of days after his funeral, I was driving alone from Provo to Logan, where we were moving. I turned on the radio, early on a Sunday morning, and the Tabernacle Choir was singing: "In my Father's house are many mansions. In my Father's house are many mansions. If it were not so I would have told you. I go to prepare a place for you." At that moment I felt the impact of losing my father. But I felt a sweet peace that he had gone to prepare for us to follow. I cried all the way to Logan. It was a great, therapeutic cry. Many years later, my mother died at age eighty-one. A song we had written together, "The Woman You'll Be Some Day," comforted me then and many times since when I've wished to be with her.

I started writing music when I was about forty. I also lost the use of my hand then and could no longer play the piano with it. I've been to forty different specialists, and they have no diagnosis, no cure. One of the last people I went to was Dr. Iliff C. Jeffery, a blind osteopath. He worked hard to help me regain the use of my hand. I sometimes complained to him as he worked about how inconvenient this was and how hard it was to write music when I couldn't play the piano. One day I realized the irony of my complaining to a blind man. It was a significant moment in my life. I said, "Well, Doctor, I don't think you can fix my hand, but thank you for trying."

"I may not be able to fix it," he said, "but I may be able to help you accept a handicap a little more gracefully." I met with him two more times, and he taught me what we can learn from disabilities. We have more purpose and more humility in our prayers. We learn to trust the Lord's timing. He said, "There is a healing for every problem we have on earth, whether it be now or in the next life."

"Well, I hope for you there will be a blessing in this life," I said, "so that you can see again." He chuckled and then explained that because of pain in his eyes, he had had them removed some years before. "But," he assured me, "there will come a time when you wouldn't trade having the use of your hand for what you have learned from not having it." I couldn't see that at the time, but through the years I have come to that point and have gained peace of mind about it. I wanted to write something to honor him, and it turned into a song called "The Test." One verse is for him, this blind man that I love so much, but the song is for me and for all of us who have prayed in faith for healing or relief and the answer hasn't come in quite the way we'd hoped.

Tell me, friend, why are you blind?
Why doesn't he who worked the miracles
Send light into your eyes?

Tell me, friend, if you understand,
Why doesn't he with power to raise the dead
Just make you whole again?

It would be so easy for him.
I watch you and in sorrow question why.
Then you, my friend, in perfect faith reply:Didn't he say he sent us
*   to be tested?*
Didn't he say the way would not be sure?
But didn't he say we could live with him forevermore,
Well and whole, if we but patiently endure?
After the trial, we will be blessed,
But this life is the test.

Music can sometimes help in unusual situations. Years ago when our children were young, I had a family home evening lesson to prepare. I had a slight grudge against each person in my family that day, including my husband. I thought, *I've got to find a way to get my points across and maybe music will make them more palatable.* During the day, I wrote a verse for each of our four children and one for my husband. My irritations with them were little things, such as Steve spending an hour in the shower. So I sang his verse, and then at the end of each verse I had the family join in to sing the chorus,

Steve, Steve,
We all love Steve,
More than we can say.
We love the bad,
We love the good,
We love him any old way.

I sang a verse for each family member, and then everyone joined in the chorus with the appropriate name inserted. I figured that the chorus made up for the verse. I mentioned it to Steve years later, and he said, "Oh yeah, I remember that. Our favorite verse was the one you wrote for yourself." And I said, "Well, I wouldn't have had a grudge against myself." He said, "No, quite the contrary." And he reminded me of the words I had written for myself:

There's a sweet and gentle woman
And her age is thirty-eight.
She's more wonderful
And kind than any other.
You might even say she's perfect
And so very humble too.

We are blessed to have
Saint Janice as our mother.
And then they all sang,
Mom, Mom,
We all love Mom,
More than we can say.
We love the bad,
We love the good,
We love her any old way.

Have fun with your talents. Don't let everything be too serious.

One of the most complicated adversities many of us face is marriage. We work at this relationship our whole life. It never is perfect. My husband keeps asking me to write him a beautiful love song, and I never have gotten to it. I've tried, but I can't get it right. I thought that he deserved *a* song after thirty-six years, though. This is what I wrote:

After thirty-six years I have learned quite a lot
About what things will please him
And what things will not.
So our marriage is blissfully calm and serene
Except for a few insignificant things:

In raising our children we certainly clicked
Except I'm too easy and he's much too strict.
But a little of his way, a little of mine,
And it seems that the kids have all grown up just fine.

We both enjoy movies, but know in advance
That he'll choose adventure and I'll choose romance.
Yes, we do have a few problems like these—
Like he says half his time is spent finding my keys.

He loves his computers, he bought one for me.
He wants me to learn it, but I won't agree.
He'll talk about floppies and hardware and ROMS
When I don't even know how to turn the thing on!

When it comes to music, we're solid, it seems
Except he loves classics, and country suits me.
But in this decision we've compromised fairly—
No high-brow, no low-brow, just Janice Kapp Perry!

When it comes to TV, we're exactly the same.
We love basketball, football, all BYU games.
But I prefer watching one game at a time
While he flips the channels to watch eight or nine.
If I had the chance I would willingly choke
The guy who invented remote!
But we found a solution that works usually
His TV is upstairs, mine downstairs, you see.
And we are united each time our team scores—
I whistle and clap, and he stomps on the floor.

I'm sure he's observed I'm a little too round,
But he says he just loves me more by the pound.
Then I can't resist pointing out lovingly
That while I've gained thirty, he's gained forty-three.

Just lately he's noticed my hair's turning gray
Then quickly pretends that he likes it that way.
So I pat his bald spot and say with a flare:
"At least I am blessed with a full head of hair!"

Except for these few little things I have mentioned,
Our marriage is really quite nearly perfection.
We've had disagreements, but as I recall,
We just did things his way—no problem at all!
He may see things differently, I could be wrong,
But I get the last word 'cause I wrote the song!

Music helps us ease everyday tensions and can also strengthen us to face very serious challenges. Yesterday I received a letter from a man about the song "I Am of Infinite Worth." He wrote: "I've had a very hard life of abuse and ill health. The first time I heard this song, I broke down in tears and the Spirit of God shot through me like an arrow. I realized for the first time just who I really was—that I am a son of the most High God and am of infinite worth. . . . I was so abused through my life. I can overcome. I do not have the song, but it is impressed in my soul. And in times of tribulation and temptation, I sing that song as I put on the armor of God. Your song is my shield." Music can help us in thousands of ways. Our hymnbook is as scripture to us, and our beautiful hymns can shield us.

A few years ago, I was going through the most difficult challenge of my life. At times, alone in my room, I pleaded with Heavenly Father for some help, some comfort. I kept saying, "Just let my mom come and talk to me. Just let me see her a minute." I pleaded in many different ways. Through my prayers, I finally gained peace. But while I struggled, I kept finding myself singing the first part of a little Primary song that I had written much earlier. I wrote it, but now I was living it. I needed it.

A CHILD'S PRAYER

Heavenly Father, are you really there?
And do you hear and answer every child's prayer?
Some say that heaven is far away,
But I feel it close around me as I pray.
Heavenly Father, I remember now
Something that Jesus told disciples long ago:
"Suffer the children to come to me."
Father, in prayer I'm coming now to thee.

I have never sung those words without having a witness that he is really there, that he was hearing my prayer, and that in his own way and in his own time my prayers would be answered. And they have been answered. The things I was going through then have been resolved. I know that as you look through your hymnbook, your Primary songbook, or other music that you love, you will find comfort there to meet your challenges.

Notes

1. Attributed to Minnie Hodapp; notes in possession of author.
2. Boyd K. Packer, *That All May Be Edified* (Salt Lake City: Bookcraft, 1982), 275–76.
3. "You will have the joy, the pleasure, and satisfaction of nurturing this child, after its resurrection, until it reaches the full stature of its spirit." Joseph Smith, quoted by Joseph F. Smith, *Gospel Doctrine: Selections from the Sermons and Writings of Joseph F. Smith*, 5th ed. (Salt Lake City: Deseret Book, 1939), 455–56.

THOUGHTS OF A GRASSHOPPER

Louise Plummer

I first became acquainted with the story of the grasshopper and the ant as a young girl—not by reading Aesop's fable, but by seeing a Walt Disney cartoon. In the cartoon the grasshopper fiddles and sings and eats the leaves off trees while the ants are gathering food to store for the winter. The queen of ants warns him that he'd better prepare for winter too, but the grasshopper continues fiddling and singing. When winter comes, the grasshopper, blue from cold, can no longer play his fiddle. In desperation, he knocks on the tree where the ants live and begs them to let him in. The queen of ants gives her "I-told-you-so" speech and ends with, "So take your fiddle and"—there is a long pause—"and play." So the grasshopper earns the warmth and food of the ants by playing his fiddle.

Aesop, in contrast, is not as kind to the grasshopper. When he comes begging for food, the ant merely tells him, "You sang through the summer; now you can dance through the winter."

I remind you of this story so that I can tell you that even as a child, it made me uncomfortable. It still makes me uncomfortable. The story of the grasshopper and the ant makes me uncomfortable because *I am a grasshopper.* I dance in elevators. The second the door closes, I begin tap dancing and flinging my arms wildly about. I make faces and stick my tongue out at the hidden cameras I believe exist in every elevator. When the doors open, I stop short and stare with what I hope is a bored elevator look into the open hallway ahead.

I am a grasshopper. It takes me a full day to dismantle my Christmas tree because I dress up in the decorations. I wrap the gold tinsel around my head like a turban. I make a shawl for my neck from glass beads and paper chains. I have a special pair of vampy red high heels that I wear

---

Louise Plummer is a wife and the mother of four boys. She has a master's degree in English from the University of Minnesota and is the author of a young adult novel, The Romantic Obsessions and Humiliations of Annie Sehlmeier *(Delacorte Press). She teaches writing at Brigham Young University and has served as a Primary teacher in the Oak Hills Fifth Ward in Provo, Utah.*

only on the day I undecorate the tree. Red glass balls hang from my ears. I sing in front of the hall mirror. I sing "New York, New York—if you can make it there, you'll make it anywhere." I don't know who wrote it, but it's the kind of song that can make you a star.

I am a grasshopper. I have never prepared for winter or the Apocalypse. I do have two thousand pounds of wheat that I hope never to eat and a box of chocolate chips that won't last through next week. Last summer I tried to bottle some peaches—the cold pack method—just to see if I could do it. I bottled three jars full. They sit in my freezer like museum pieces.

I am a grasshopper. I live in a metaphorical world. I read and write fiction. I draw pictures. I dance in elevators. I sing dressed in Christmas tree decorations.

But I was raised by ants. My mother and father emigrated from the Netherlands to America in 1948 with four children. Five more children were born in Salt Lake City. My father was an electrician. My mother kept the house and us immaculately. She knitted us sweaters and baked our bread. Dinner was ready each night at 5:30 on the nose. She taught me the correct principles of work. She forced me to wash woodwork, wax floors, and clean behind the toilet, but my priorities were not the same as hers. My distress is recorded in my journal of 1959 when I was sixteen years old. The first entry reads:

"Mother has just blown her top. I am a lazy bum with no sense of responsibility, and all I do is write stories and draw and visit my friends. According to her I am no good. Which is not altogether true, but not altogether false either. I already knew everything she told me, so she really didn't have to get all fired up."

Another entry:

"I hate to get up in the morning. This morning, Mother started yelling for me to get up at the unearthly hour of 11:00. Then every five minutes, she'd come in and say, 'Are you getting up now or not?' Then I would say, 'Do I have a choice?' As soon as she leaves the room I lie back down and daydream. I like to stay in bed so that I can daydream."

And finally: "Mother is mad because she can't find the little top thing to the pressure cooker and since I was the last one to use the pressure cooker, I lost it. Well, I didn't!"

Even from these excerpts you can tell that I considered my work to be different from my mother's. I was already writing, drawing, and daydreaming. And I never outgrew it. I never intended to. If growing up meant leaving behind the imagination I loved, I didn't want to be grown up, at least, not in the same way as most of the adults I knew.

As much as I love my mother, I have not grown up in her image. But I admire her work. I love to open her linen closet and see the neatly folded sheets and pillow cases, color-coordinated, meticulously stacked. I like to stand in front of the year's supply in her dust-free basement and admire the rows of preserves, of laundry soap, of peanut butter, and of polyunsaturated oils. I like to see her white—really white laundry—blowing on the clothesline. I like to ask her for the kinds of things that I can never find in my own house, like the negative of a picture taken twenty years ago or a darning needle. She always knows where such things are located.

I clean too. I'm not always on top of it like my mother, but I do something my mother doesn't do—I write lists of things I clean up. Here's a list from my journal, dated March 3, 1984, Saturday:

"What we found when we cleaned under our bed:

"Books: one triple combination; *A Mormon Mother*, by Annie Tanner; *The Clown*, by Heinrich Böll; *The Tin Drum*, by Gunter Grass; *An Essay on Criticism*, by Graham Hough; *The Labyrinthe of Solitude*, by Octavio Paz; the December '83 *National Geographic*; the Roseville phone directory; *Be My Guest*, by Conrad Hilton; the April '83 *Popular Photography*; *Time* magazine, February 27, 1984; Louise's journal—March 1977; *The Power of Positive Thinking*, by Norman Vincent Peale; one *Reader's Digest* (February '84) including the titles 'My Angry Son' and 'Advice from Sexually Happy Wives'

"One set of Tom's office keys

"A photograph of Sam and Louise

"Photograph of Tom and completed jigsaw puzzle

"A letter from Roseville schools about Jonathan's registration

"Dishes: one red mixing bowl; two saucers; two mugs; one kitchen knife; one empty cherry cola can; one empty Haagen-Daz chocolate chip carton with lid; one Melmac cup

"One Rotex labeler

"One broken toothbrush holder

"One photograph of Dave and Sue Salmon and girls

"One empty raisin carton

"Four black lead pencils

"One red lead pencil

"Five felt tip pens

"One ball point pen

"One roll of packing tape

"One cloth handkerchief

"One pair of pantyhose

"One black high heel shoe

"Two plastic clown heads

"One plastic race car

"One page from the church directory

"Two pen caps

"One broken dart

"One hanger

"One bank deposit slip

"One seminary work sheet (Exodus 24, 25, and 27)

"One white shoe lace

"One yellow wrapping ribbon

"One Roseville bank envelope

"One disposable razor

"Three yellow legal pads, one is filled with notes on how to get rich, including the title 'You Can Negotiate Anything'

"One stake directory

"One plastic action figure

"One pair of scissors

"One metal whistle

"One roll of toilet paper

"Notes by Tom on developing a seasonal recreational facility for ultra-lites, golf, fishing, horseback riding, cross-country skiing, and key words from Norman Vincent Peale: *visualize, prayerize, actualize*

"One empty Kleenex box

"One score sheet from Yahtzee

"One belt

"One piece of chalk

"One orange peel AND

"One popsicle stick."

I'm not completely comfortable with this list, just as I haven't always been comfortable with being a grasshopper. I always wondered if there was room in a family of ants for a grasshopper, room in a community of ants for a grasshopper, or room in a church of ants for a grasshopper. My discomfort, I believe, comes from my fear of disapproval, my fear that ants will not accept me unless I am just like them.

I take comfort in Flannery O'Connor's short story, "Revelation," in which Mrs. Turpin, a middle-aged Christian Southern woman, views mankind as a hierarchy: "On the bottom of the heap were most colored people; . . . then next to them—not above, just away from—were the white trash; then above them were the home-owners, and above them the home-and-land owners, to which she and Claud belonged. Above she and Claud were people with a lot of money and much bigger houses and much more land."[1]

At the end of the story, Mrs. Turpin receives a vision that destroys her delusion of a hierarchy. She sees a "vast swinging bridge extending upward from the earth through a field of living fire. Upon it a vast horde of souls were rumbling toward heaven. There were whole companies of white trash, clean for the first time in their lives, and bands of [blacks] in white robes, and battalions of freaks and lunatics shouting and clapping and leaping like frogs. And bringing up the end of the procession was a tribe of people . . . marching behind the others with great dignity, accountable as they had always been for good order and common sense and respectable behavior. They alone were on key. Yet she could see by their shocked and altered faces that even their virtues were being burned away."[2]

I like this story because it is about redemption. Without the atonement of Jesus Christ, our virtues, whatever they are, are meaningless. We are all equally human.

King Benjamin asks, "Are we all not beggars?" (Mosiah 4:19).

"What about works?" someone may ask. "Don't ants work harder than grasshoppers?"

No. Grasshoppers work differently from ants.

I would like to rewrite the ending of "The Grasshopper and the Ants" like this: It is winter, and the grasshopper is walking in the snow, talking to herself and answering herself. She wears a yellow slicker over her sweater because she can't find her parka (which is buried in the debris under her bed). Because she was out of groceries this morning, she is eating a brownie with a carton of milk bought at the 7-Eleven which, thank heaven, is open 365 days a year. The door in the tree where the ants live swings open. The queen ant appears and says to the grasshopper, "We are bored to death. Won't you tell us a story or at least a good joke? Our teenagers are driving us crazy; maybe you could write them a play to per-form, or just a roadshow? Do you have any ideas for a daddy-daughter party?"

The grasshopper replies that she has ideas for all of them. So the ant invites her in and seats her at a spotless kitchen table with pencil and paper, and the grasshopper writes the roadshow.

The ant feeds her guest a slice of homemade bread, fresh from the oven, and a glass of freshly squeezed orange juice. "How do you get all of these ideas?" she asks the grasshopper.

"They come to me," says the grasshopper, "while I am taking long hot baths."

I am a grasshopper. I work hard at writing, at teaching, at singing and dancing, at mothering. I have taught my four boys some grasshopper ways. They all can make chocolate chip cookies and brownies without a recipe.

My mother used to say, "I don't know where you came from." This bothered me, because if she didn't know, I certainly didn't. But I found out where I came from years later when I went back to Holland for the first time since I was five years old. I stayed with my paternal grandmother—Oma—who lived in Utrecht. She set her alarm for nine o'clock in the morning. When I saw that, I knew where I came from. I came from Oma.

I came from you, too, Mother. Otherwise, I would never clean under my bed.

I came from God.

Notes

1. Flannery O'Connor, "Revelation," in *Everything That Rises Must Converge* (New York: Farrar, Straus and Giroux, 1965), 217.
2. Ibid., 238.

THE FAITHFUL HERITAGE OF A CONVERT

⌒∞⌒

Carolyn J. Rasmus

*F*ourteen years and four weeks ago this very hour, I was baptized at a stake center only four blocks from here. I could not have imagined and cannot now comprehend the life-changing effects of that act.

The first speaker on the first morning of this conference was Sister Camilla Eyring Kimball, our beloved "first lady" of the Church, a faithful sister, ninety years young and with ninety years of experience in the Church. She was followed by a panel that included the auxiliary general presidents—Dwan J. Young, Ardeth G. Kapp, and Barbara W. Winder. Two days later I am the first speaker of the morning—a convert of only fourteen years, a Mia Maid in the reckoning of Church life.

As I have focused on the difference of years of members in the Church, I began to realize that that was only one aspect of the diversity represented by the members of the Church—a diverse church made up of people with unique and different backgrounds. We represent a diversity in age, experiences, talents, family and personal situations, languages spoken and understood, education, marital status, and church callings. But more important than our diversity are the things that bind us together and unite us. For all of our diversity, we are united by our bond of faith in the Lord Jesus Christ and in our commitment to The Church of Jesus Christ of Latter-day Saints. We are people of faith. It is the thing which sets us apart from the world. It is what makes us brothers and sisters in the fullest sense of the word. Faith is the unifying factor that created a common bond between me and Sister Kimball, and Sisters Young, Kapp, and Winder. It is what unites us with people around the world, with our next-door neighbors or with the person seated beside or behind or in front of you. We are sisters and brothers of a common faith. It is our faith, I

Carolyn J. Rasmus is the administrative assistant to the Young Women General Presidency and has held numerous callings in ward and stake Young Women organizations. She received an Ed.D. in physical education with minors in child development and learning disabilities from Brigham Young University, where she is also a professor of physical education–sports. She was the executive assistant to the president of BYU and chaired the faculty advisory council.

believe, that not only brings us together but which will in the end be the only thing that really matters.

I began preparing for my talk by going to two of my favorite sources: the scriptures and the *Oxford English Dictionary*. What I have come to share today is not a neatly wrapped package but ideas that have come to me as I've thought and read and struggled with the title, "The Faithful Heritage of a Convert." These are offerings, given in the hope that they might trigger your own thoughts and ideas that will have personal meaning.

The dictionary tells us that *heritage* is something transmitted by or acquired from a predecessor. At that first conference session our hearts and spirits were touched as our faithful leader sisters shared with us that kind of a heritage as they related faith-promoting stories of their pioneer ancestors. I have no such direct heritage. Many others of you do not either, for now nearly half the total adult membership of the Church is composed of first-generation members.

But in an eternal sense, we all share a common heritage, which extends far beyond the days of handcarts and covered wagons. The scriptures tell us of our more important and common heritage, a heritage which comes from the fact that we are all sisters and brothers whose heavenly parents love us—we are literal offspring of God. George Q. Cannon tells us that as His children "there is not an attribute we ascribe to Him that we do not possess, though they may be dormant or in embryo."[1] We are also taught of our infinite worth and are told we have a divine and individual mission.

In the process of my conversion, knowledge of this heritage was reawakened in me. My spirit responded to what I believe I had known long ago when you and I were together in the presence of Heavenly Father. In addition to that eternal heritage, I—like many of you—inherited some other things in the process of conversion: among those things I include new scriptures and new knowledge and insights.

This triple combination, with my name imprinted on the cover, was given to me on the last day of class by a group of students who inscribed this message:

"Dear Miss Rasmus,

"You have shared with us things that are important and close to you. In return, we would like to give you something that means a great deal to us. And, we want you to know that we give it to you with a lot of love and respect.

"Sincerely,

"Your fans,

"BYU Summer School, Second Session, 1970."

It was to become a gift that made a difference. I was touched that a group of students cared enough about me that they wanted to give me a gift, though I could not begin to comprehend what it was they had really shared.

It is more difficult to identify specific new knowledge or insights gained as a result of the conversion process. Much of what I learned and am learning is, I believe, a literal reawakening of things known before, knowledge brought to this life from another. After I'd been at BYU for more than a year, several women who lived in Provo arranged an all-day hiking expedition on a beautiful fall day in October. I was eager to leave my studies and head for the mountains.

But as it neared 10:00 A.M., they began looking for a comfortable place to sit down. I didn't have any idea it was general conference. I didn't even know what general conference was. I certainly didn't know my fellow hikers were equipped with a transistor radio. I was without question a captive audience, and although I said nothing to any of the hiking group, when I returned home that evening I wrote on my daily calendar, "Everything sounds so right." It was, I believe now, a time of reawakening to truths learned long ago in a very different setting.

One of the things I became conscious of early was the reality of the still, small voice—a power that communicated to me thoughts and ideas I could not conceive in my finite mind. These stories illustrate what I mean. I made the decision to go to BYU because of my professional acquaintance with Dr. Leona Holbrook. We were kindred spirits from the moment we met and, quite frankly, I would have gone to study wherever she taught. When I first told her of my interest in enrolling at BYU, she suggested I visit the campus before making a final decision. She knew of my smoking habit and that I dearly loved wine. (I used to have a friend bring my favorite vintage by the case from her home in Minnesota.) Leona merely said to me, "BYU is a unique place. Visit before you make your decision." And so more than a year before I became a student, I visited BYU and recorded this after a two-day visit: "My stop at BYU only served to convince me that I made the right decision. Having been there made me realize I'll even be able to give up my much-loved wine for what I'll receive in return."

Other experiences followed that helped me become increasingly aware of what I now know was the light of Christ. Having decided to fast for the first time in my life, I was unsettled and unable to concentrate on studying for a statistics test. Finally, I knelt down to pray. I have no recollection of the prayer, but these thoughts came into my mind, and I felt impressed to record them. On a scrap piece of paper I wrote:

"October 12, 1970, 8:45 A.M. Go now, my child, for there is much work to be done. I send my Spirit to be with you to enable you to work and think clearly, to accomplish all that lies before you this day. Go and know that I am with you in all things, and later return to me, coming to me with real intent of prayer. Know that I am the Lord, that all things are possible to them who call upon my name. Take comfort in these words. Fill your heart with joy and gladness, not sorrow and despair. Lo, I am with you always, even unto the end of the world. Know me as Comforter and Savior."

I also had the impression, months before my baptism, that I should begin paying tithing. As members, we all know about the gray envelopes imprinted with the bishop's name. But, what do you do with tithing monies if you don't know the procedure? Each paycheck for three months, I took 10 percent of my meager student wages and put the cash in a white envelope, which I carefully hid in my underwear drawer. When Bishop Mayfield interviewed me relative to my worthiness to be baptized, I proudly produced evidence of my belief in the law of tithing.

Only two weeks before I joined the Church I sat in a sacrament meeting. As I passed the tray of bread from the person on one side of me to the other, these words came pounding into my head: "How much longer can you pass by the bread of life? Know, believe, do. Know that Joseph Smith was a prophet and that through him my church has been restored in these latter days. Know and believe, then do . . . be baptized into my church." Such thoughts are unsettling to say the least. I thought, and continue to think, about those words—"know, believe, do."

There is much knowledge in the world—both secular and spiritual. We are told of the importance of gaining knowledge, but that is only the first step. During this women's conference Sister Naomi Randall, author of the words to "I Am a Child of God," told us about President Kimball's contribution to the lyrics of that familiar song. He asked her to change the word *know* to *do*—"teach me all that I must *do* to live with him someday."

Her story triggered my thoughts back to the time those words came into my mind—"know, believe, do"—and I came to a new insight. In preparation for this women's conference, I read the book *The Teachings of Spencer W. Kimball*, a compilation of excerpts from President Kimball's many talks and addresses.[2] In the section on faith, he makes repeated reference to one scripture. "If any man will *do* [the Father's] will he shall *know* of the doctrine, whether it be of God, or whether I speak of myself" (John 7:17; italics added).

Initially, my interest in the Church came as a result of what I observed in the lives of others—how people interacted with each other and how they treated me. Quite frankly, I was not interested in what people knew. If anyone had asked me, "Do you want to know more?" I would have answered, "No." But I could not ignore what I saw people doing.

I will never forget going (I think "being taken" is probably more correct) to the ground-breaking service for the Provo Temple. It occurred less than a month after my arrival in Provo. I did not know the significance of that event, but what I saw and felt touched me deeply. I listened intently as a father quietly and patiently responded to the incessant questioning of his young family. He was kind and gentle as he held them and talked with them. And then that hillside of people began singing "The Spirit of God Like a Fire Is Burning." They all knew all the words without a hymnbook, and I felt the Spirit of God.

A woman I remember meeting only once left a homemade pie and a note on our doorstep. She wanted to welcome my mother who was coming to visit from Ohio. I knew nothing at that time about visiting teachers or that she was mine. But I remember well my feelings that she had done this for me, that she knew who I was and that she cared enough about me to take time to do something special.

Only after my baptism would I know that the Kocherhans family always made it a point to sit near me every sacrament meeting. "Because," said the father of the family and the priesthood bearer who baptized me, "we wanted you to feel our spirit and of our love for you." And, oh, how I did. I was not anxious to "know of the doctrine," but I could not ignore what people were doing. Likewise, I later became aware that many ward members had fasted and prayed in my behalf.

It is interesting to me that the first book of the New Testament, after the four Gospels, is entitled "The Acts of the Apostles." It is not the "lectures" or "sermons" of the apostles but the "acts." In the process of studying what the apostles did, we learn the doctrine—we come to know what they believed and why they did what they did.

We can read about how to ride a bicycle. We might even be able to explain it to others, but we really only know how to ride a bicycle after we have actually done it. I do not want to have surgery performed by physicians who know only what is written in the textbook. I want to make sure they have actually performed the surgery. Then I will believe they know what they are about.

And so it was with me. I am convinced that one of the major, and certainly the initial, factors in my conversion came as a result of what I saw people doing—their actions were evidence for me that they knew something I wanted to learn more about.

But John 7:17 tells us that we can *know* the doctrine if we will *do* His will. I believe I came to know the law of tithing by paying tithing—by doing it. The knowledge that scripture study and prayer and fasting can bring understanding and insight came to have meaning to me only after I did them.

We are inheritors of a gospel that is action oriented. There is nothing passive about phrases like "awake and arouse your faculties," "experiment upon my words," "exercise a particle of faith," or words such as "desired . . . , pondering, believing . . . " (Alma 32:27; 1 Nephi 11:1). This is a gospel of action, of doing. No wonder President Kimball had as his motto, "DO IT."

In a First Presidency message in 1975, President Kimball encouraged us to "read and understand and apply [or do] the principles and inspired counsel found in the [scriptures]." He promised us that if we did so, "we shall discover that our personal *acts* of righteousness will also bring *personal revelation* or *inspiration* . . . into our own lives."[3] It is he who also reminded us that "if [we] will do [God's] will, [we] shall know of the doctrine" (John 7:17).

Sometimes we know something but do nothing about it. In fact, there is often a discrepancy between what we say we know and what we do. I am convinced, from personal experience, that it is this discrepancy that creates inner strife and turmoil—a literal wrenching of our souls. Oh, that we might learn to act with integrity, having the moral courage to make our actions (our doing) consistent with our knowledge of right and wrong, to be able to say with Job, "Till I die I will not remove mine integrity from me" (Job 27:5).

I had another thought as I read the dictionary definition of *heritage*. It indicated that *heritage* may imply anything passed on to heirs or succeeding generations. I had always thought of heritage from the perspective of what I might receive from others. As I read that definition, I began to think about what I could pass on to others. We sometimes forget that our heritage is being created by us right now. Granted, we can build upon the past, but our heritage, that which we will someday give to others, is in process now—we are literally creating our heritage, whether we are twelve or eighteen, forty or eighty.

I began thinking about what I would pass on, what I would leave for others that might be meaningful—something others might build upon. I don't have a magic list. I don't think my list is even complete, but on this thirtieth day of March, 1985, I want to leave as a heritage to others four things: a message of hope and optimism, my commitment to The Church of Jesus Christ of Latter-day Saints, my faith in Jesus Christ as our Savior, and my belief in the principles of the restored gospel.

First, a message of hope and optimism. If we read only the daily news of the world, we would have our attention focused on crime, immorality, dishonesty, corruption, and abuse of every kind. If we focused only on the social ills of our day, we would be overcome with feelings of gloom and despair. But we know so much more. This is a glorious gospel and we, of all people, have cause to rejoice, for we have been given the knowledge to be able to view things in an eternal perspective. Without such perspective, it would be easy to lose our way in what Elder Maxwell calls this "secular dispensation of despair."[4] Elder Maxwell calls our attention to the young servant of Elisha who feared for the future until the Lord opened his eyes so that he could see what Elisha saw.

"And when the servant of the man of God was risen early, and gone forth, behold, an host compassed the city both with horses and chariots. And his servant said unto him, Alas, my master! how shall we do?

"And he answered, Fear not: for they that be with us are more than they that be with them.

"And Elisha prayed, and said, Lord, I pray thee, open his eyes, that he may see. And the Lord opened the eyes of the young man; and he saw: and, behold, the mountain was full of horses and chariots of fire round about Elisha" (2 Kings 6:15–17).

When we are feeling overwhelmed and we doubt that as individuals we could ever make any difference, we need to be reminded of Elisha and of the fact that we are not alone. We are told that we are agents, on the

Lord's errand; to "be not weary in well-doing, for [we] are laying the foundation of a great work. And out of small things proceedeth that which is great" (D&C 64:33). We learn from modern-day scripture that the Lord has "given the heavenly hosts and . . . angels charge concerning [us]" (D&C 84:42).

I also hope to share with others my commitment to building and defending the kingdom of God. I believe we learn what commitment is really about in the holy temple of God. We come to understand what it means to obey and sacrifice and consecrate our time and talents. In this day and in this land we are not presently called upon to make physical sacrifices—we are not driven from our homes, we have not been called to pull handcarts or to leave our homes and establish new communities. But ultimately to understand the principle of commitment, our knowledge of this principle will, like all others, need to be translated into action. In 1970, President Harold B. Lee said:

"We have some tight places to go before the Lord is through with this church and the world in this dispensation. . . . The gospel was restored to prepare a people ready to receive Him. . . . You may not like what comes from the authority of the Church. . . . It may contradict your social views. It may interfere with some of your social life. But if you listen to these things, as if from the mouth of the Lord himself, with patience and faith, the promise is that 'the gates of hell shall not prevail against you; yea, and the Lord God will disperse the powers of darkness from before you, and cause the heavens to shake for your good, and his name's glory.' (D&C 21:6.)"[5] I believe we will be "tossed to and fro, and carried about with every wind of doctrine" (Ephesians 4:14) unless we are covenanted and committed before we are confronted with difficult choices and hard times.

I want to commit to trying to live in such a way that others might know by what I do that when I raise my arm to the square to sustain the general authorities and officers of The Church of Jesus Christ of Latter-day Saints, I am anxious and ready to respond to their counsel and direction.

I want to commit to trying to live with my eye and mind single to his glory and purposes (see D&C 88:67–68). I find it easy to commit to such a thing in the quiet and solitude and aloneness of my room, but I want to learn to be able to have such focus in busy and rushed and difficult situations.

Finally, I leave for you and others a testimony of my faith in the Lord Jesus Christ. When we are feeling discouraged or put upon, left out or neglected, overwhelmed, unloved, ignored, or sorely tempted, we need to have brought to our minds that he "suffer[ed] pains and afflictions and temptations of every kind; and this that the word might be fulfilled which saith he will take upon him the pains and the sicknesses of his people. . . that he may know according to the flesh how to succor his people according to their infirmities" (Alma 7:11–12).

I believe we will come to know that truth as we try, as his agents and a covenanted people, to "bear one another's burdens . . . and are willing to mourn with those that mourn . . . and comfort those that stand in need of comfort" (Mosiah 18:8–9), as we strive to "lift up the hands which hang down, and strengthen the feeble knees" (D&C 81:5). I believe with President Kimball that "God does notice us, and he watches over us. But it is usually through another person that he meets our needs."[6]

I would leave my testimony of the boy prophet Joseph Smith and especially of the process that led to that great theophany. The boy had identified the problem (there were many sects and denominations), and he had searched the scriptures. Then he went to the Lord in humble prayer to inquire of Him. (Which church should I join?) And he modeled for us the attribute of patience as he spent the next ten years waiting and studying and preparing—all of which were necessary before the Church could be established and the work go forward.

I have great faith in the literal promises of him who is our exemplar of the perfect life. But lest we become discouraged in the pursuit of perfection, we should take comfort in President Kimball's encouragement that "working toward perfection is not a one-time decision, but a process to be pursued throughout one's lifetime."[7] In my own life I find I make periodic progress forward and then slip back into old habits and doubts. Sometimes I'm not pleased with what I do when compared with what I know. It takes courage to see ourselves as less than perfect.

Finally, I have faith that our Heavenly Father wants us to return to him. We agreed to come here so that we might be tried and tested and proven, but we came here with the full expectation that we could succeed, and with the help of the Savior we would, if we endured to the end.

> *And someday, when he's proven me,*
> *I'll see him face to face,*
> *But just for here and now I walk by faith.*[8]

Notes

1. George Q. Cannon, *Gospel Truth*, 2 vols. (Salt Lake City: Deseret Book, 1974), 1:1.
2. Salt Lake City: Bookcraft, 1982.
3. Spencer W. Kimball, "Always a Convert Church," *Ensign*, September 1975, 4; italics in original.
4. Neal A. Maxwell, *The Smallest Part* (Salt Lake City: Deseret Book, 1973), 16.
5. Harold B. Lee, "Uphold the Hands of the President of the Church," *Improvement Era*, December 1970, 126.
6. Spencer W. Kimball, "Small Acts of Service," *Ensign*, December 1974, 5.
7. Spencer W. Kimball, *Ensign*, November 1978, 6.
8. Janice Kapp Perry, "I Walk by Faith," 1985; used by permission.

"GET THEE BEHIND ME": THWARTING LATTER-DAY DECEITS

Tessa Meyer Santiago

The apostle Peter urged the early Christian Saints to "be sober, be vigilant; because your adversary the devil, as a roaring lion, walketh about, seeking whom he may devour" (1 Peter 5:8). Most of us recognize Satan's open warfare with good for what it is. In 2 Corinthians 11:13–14, however, Paul exhorts the Christians of Corinth to beware also of false prophets, "deceitful workers" who transform "themselves into the apostles of Christ. And no marvel; for Satan himself is transformed into an angel of light." Thus Satan, "the father of all lies" (Moses 4:4), can present himself as an angel, a counterfeit messenger of the Lord1 supposedly on a divine errand in which he seeks the immortality and eternal life of men and women, but he is really on an errand to make all of us "miserable like unto himself" (2 Nephi 2:27). And how does he mislead us? By persuading us that we are following God's ways when, in reality, we are following the enticings of Satan. If the adversary can induce us to misinterpret our Father's errand for us, then we will never become what we are meant to be. To that end, subtle twists of the truth are even more effective than monstrous lies. I would like to examine a few of the deceits—the "wind[s] of doctrine and cunning craftiness" (Ephesians 4:14)—by which Satan seeks to blind women's minds and distract their hearts, causing us to lose sight of our divine potential.

DECEIT 1: DIVINE DEMANDS ARE RESTRICTIVE

According to the Gospel of Luke, God sent the angel Gabriel "to a virgin espoused to a man whose name was Joseph . . . and the virgin's name was Mary" (Luke 1:27). In a few short moments, young Mary learned that she had "found favour with God" and would "bring forth a son, and shalt call his name Jesus . . . [who] shall reign over the house of Jacob for ever"

Tessa Meyer Santiago is a creative writer and a student at the J. Reuben Clark School of Law at Brigham Young University. She and her husband, Kevin Frank Santiago, are the parents of three children. She served a mission to Boston, Massachusetts, and teaches the Gospel Doctrine class in Sunday School.

(Luke 1:30–31, 33). Surely this was shocking news. She was a virgin and promised to Joseph. At that time, tradition demanded that an unmarried woman found pregnant be made a public example. Mary could have objected or responded in a myriad of other ways. Instead, she replies, "Behold the handmaid of the Lord; be it unto me according to thy word" (Luke 1:38). What faith, what commitment to the will of God can be heard in her simple consent.

Cynics may say she had no choice: If God wanted this of her, who was she to refuse? Brigham Young clarifies this idea with truth: "It is a mistaken idea that God has decreed all things whatsoever that come to pass, for the volition of the creature is as free as air."[2] Mary might have refused. Just as Christ might have. "When he came in the flesh he was left free to choose or refuse to obey his Father. Had he refused to obey his Father, he would have become a son of perdition. We also are free to choose or refuse the principles of eternal life," Brigham Young explains.

President Young also refutes the common notion that choosing to obey the will of God is choosing *not* to exercise our independent agency. "God rules and reigns, and has made all his children as free as himself, to choose the right or the wrong. . . . Does it follow that a man is deprived of his rights, because he lists in his heart to do the will of God? [For instance,] Must a man swear to prove he has an agency? . . . I can manifest to the heavens and to the inhabitants of the earth that I am freeborn, and have my liberty before God, angels and men, when I kneel down to pray, certainly as much as if I were to go out and swear. . . . [So] in rendering that strict obedience, are we made slaves? No, it is the only way on the face of the earth for you and me to become free. . . . All that the Lord requires of us is strict obedience to the laws of life."[3]

As Eliza R. Snow in hymn number 195 reminds us, "By strict obedience Jesus won the prize with glory rife: 'Thy will, O God, not mine be done,' adorned his mortal life."[4] Mary was great not only because she was chosen as the mother of Christ but because she positioned herself through her choices so that God could use her in his work. If we are to become women of Christ, we must learn to embrace the will of God. In return, Christ promises: "I [will] gather you as a hen gathereth her chickens under her wings" (3 Nephi 10:6).

DECEIT 2: THE WAY IS EASY

Alma teaches his son Corianton that it is "easy to give heed to the word of Christ, which will point to you a straight course to eternal bliss"

(Alma 37:44). The word *easy* here may mislead some readers. Nephi teaches that the Lord works in plainness: he "worketh not in darkness" (2 Nephi 26:23) but "doeth that which is good among the children of men; and he doeth nothing save it be plain" (2 Nephi 26:33). Our Father's definition of *easy*, then, is clearly communicated concepts and expectations, simple directions that are easy to follow, and an outcome that blesses his children. Our Father's definition of *easy* includes, however, a significant exercise of faith, diligence, and endurance—the heart-breaking spiritual work required to enter the kingdom.

Satan, the author of confusion, would have us believe that an "easy way" is one of quick, instant gratification. But pleasure is not the purpose and goal of our existence. Joy is (see 2 Nephi 2:25). Satan wants us to confuse the two: shortchanging ourselves by trading in joy for pleasure. Standing in the grocery store checkout line, I read the following magazine covers: one easy exercise to a washboard stomach; sparkling windows in just minutes; thirty days to a slimmer you. And I buy into the myth of instant, pleasurable change, completely ignoring the fact that it's taken years of absolute neglect for my body and windows to get into their current states. I forget that the only instantaneous change I know of comes in that luminous instant when we are washed clean of sins through the Savior's redeeming blood. Yet, even then we must choose to remain clean. Satan would dissuade us from believing that work or endurance is part of the gospel of change. He wants us to expect that change is instantaneous. And then to be disappointed when it is not. If in our disappointment at finding work part of the equation, we abandon our efforts to become better, his work is done.

If the adversary cannot get us to abandon hope, he will entice us to cheat. By appealing to our laziness, greed, or pride, he would have us arrive at a worthwhile goal in the wrong manner. I have learned that it is not so much the destination but the way in which I journey that God scrutinizes. As a child, I often played a party game called blindman's bluff. Blindfolded, walking slowly with my hands stretched out before me, I tried to catch the other children in the room. Somehow, I managed to maneuver an eyelid, or wrinkle a cheek, so that I could peek. Of course, if asked "Can you see?!" I would lie. Lying somewhat lessened the thrill of catching my friends so quickly. Plus, every time I cheated, I heard a voice that sounded remarkably like my mother's whispering: "But you cheated, my darling. You could see."

When Satan sought to tempt Christ in the desert, he challenged him to turn stones into bread. Elder Jeffrey R. Holland explains the significance of this temptation: "Here Jesus experiences the real and very understandable hunger for food by which he must sustain his mortal life. . . . Why not eat? . . . Why not simply turn the stones to bread and eat? The temptation is *not* in the eating. . . . The temptation . . . is to do it *this way*, to get his bread—his physical satisfaction, relief for his human appetite—the easy way, by abuse of power and without a willingness to wait for the right time and the right way. It is the temptation to be the convenient Messiah. Why do things the hard way? Why walk to the shop—or bakery? Why travel all the way home? Why deny yourself satisfaction when with ever such a slight compromise you might enjoy this much-needed nourishment? But Christ will not ask selfishly for unearned bread. He will postpone gratification, indefinitely if necessary, rather than appease appetite . . . with what is not his."[5]

It is not that eating is wrong, or that it is wrong to want a house with a second bathroom or to seek a Harvard education for an academically gifted child. These are not unrighteous desires. What is wrong are the ways we sometimes attempt to gain the good things of the world: We would have them now, because everybody else apparently has them, and we are sometimes willing to forgo ethics and to compromise morality to obtain them.[6]

DECEIT 3: THE WAY MUST BE GRAND

The children of Israel were three months out of Egypt, grumbling and moaning, when "the Lord sent fiery serpents among the people, and they bit the people; and much people of Israel died. . . . And Moses made a serpent of brass, and put it on a pole" (Numbers 21:6, 9), providing a way for those who had been bitten to be healed. Still many of the children of Israel refused to look. Nephi comments: "The labor which they had to perform was to look; and because of the simpleness of the way, or the easiness of it, there were many who perished" (1 Nephi 17:41).

This year my husband Kevin and I decided to run a ten-kilometer race together. In preparation we have begun an exercise program devised by an authority from *Runner's World*. Unlike other exercise programs begun and abandoned, we have actually stuck to this one for three weeks, and the future looks promising. Here is why: the program allows us to exercise only thirty minutes a day for only four days a week. At first, Kevin, who once played basketball for Brigham Young University, found himself playing challenge games in his mind: "Well, it says to walk four minutes and then run one, but I can probably run two. In fact, I could probably pull off three. . . . Or maybe I'll just run until I throw up." He caught himself, realizing that such grandiose schemes would sabotage his efforts.

Later on, Kevin and I discussed how we damage ourselves by imagining that we are somehow better than the norm, that we can or need to run faster, swim longer, jump higher than required. Jacob said of the Jews that "they despised the words of plainness. . . . Wherefore, because of their blindness, which blindness came by looking beyond the mark, they must needs fall" (Jacob 4:14). How many of us cannot have family home evening unless there is a lesson, a hymn, a snack, and a colorful, neatly laminated job chart on the fridge? How many of us, launching a new scripture reading program, say to ourselves, "Okay, I'll read thirty minutes a day, and then I'll write in my journal, and then I'll study the Sunday School readings and the Relief Society manual"? After the second day, finding ourselves hopelessly swamped in our grandiose scheme, we abandon ship for some desert island with no scripture study at all. What about the meals we cook, the lessons we teach, the children we raise and the clothes we buy for them: how have we fallen because of our pride and stubborn insistence on doing things our way? In many cases, I find I have looked way beyond the mark, making the way not easy but fraught with difficulty and complexity where there should be plainness. The Lord counsels us: "Do not run faster or labor more than you have strength and means . . . but be diligent unto the end" (D&C 10:4).

DECEIT 4: IF I AM AN AT-HOME MOM, MY HOME MUST BE PERFECT

Women who choose not to work outside their home sometimes labor under the misguided notion that the home itself reflects their mothering skills. They thus are bothered by the intrusion of children into the daily schedule of laundry, vacuuming, gardening, sorting, picking up, and putting away. Yes, a certain peace comes from living in an orderly, clean home. But I realize I have gone too far when I ban my son, Christian, from playing with his toys because his room is clean and I want it to stay that way.

My friend and visiting teacher, Gwen, has two beautiful daughters. This spring she also had a row of bright, cheerful tulips lining the front of her house. Maya, her four-year-old, one day brought her every single tulip bloom, leaving only headless stems to grace the front yard. Gwen said that just as she felt her body start to quiver with an imminent explosion, she thought, "What? Am I raising children or tulips?" President Ezra Taft Benson called the women of the Church home not to clean toilet bowls and wash dishes in immaculate houses but to teach children the gospel of Christ. If we think of ourselves only—or even primarily—as housekeepers, we neglect the next generation of souls.

Staying home also doesn't mean delaying the development of our God-given talents and abilities. Some husbands and wives believe—to the detriment of their own souls, the happiness of their families, and the health of their communities—that women who stay home have nothing else to offer the world. They mistakenly believe such women have no talents or that any talents they have must be used solely for the betterment of their families. They labor under the mistaken notion that "I have chosen to stay home to rear my children; therefore, I must delay the development of my skills and talents until I no longer have children at home." But a woman's circle of influence does not stop at the curb bordering her home. We must not underestimate the power and responsibility of our womanhood. We are equally under covenant both to rear and to teach our children and to recognize and develop our own considerable talents for the service of God.

DECEIT 5: WOMEN'S BODIES ARE TO BE ADMIRED FOR THEIR YOUTH AND BEAUTY

Perhaps one of the most discouraging struggles women endure is that never-ending battle with our own bodies. A woman's attitude toward her own body is fraught with misconceptions fueled by a world that celebrates an almost prepubescent female body as the ideal norm. Unfortunately for most of us, time moves on. We are no longer seventeen, a number of children have made their way through our birth canals, and gravity is exerting its inexorable pull. Whenever we look in the mirror, we are reminded of what we are not. Satan would have it just that way. He would have us think that because our bodies do not look a certain, supposedly desirable, way, they are not worth having at all. Thus, we enter into a war with our bodies, hating the very tabernacle our Father has given us, despising the flesh. If Satan can get us to fixate on our bodies, either in vanity or self-loathing, then he has caused us to misunderstand completely the role our bodies play in our salvation.

I was pregnant all one summer. I spent my time bobbing in the deep end of Deseret Towers' pool watching the women go by. I wondered why

the women who had contributed the most to our society seemed to feel
the least confident. Why did they cover their bodies as if in shame, dis-
robing only to plunge quickly down, their shoulders barely emerging
above the waterline as they stood watching their children swim? Why did
the freshman Deseret Towers' residents, young women who knew nothing
of what breasts and hips and wombs are meant to do, rule, queens of the
roost? In a better world, in a kinder, more saintly world, a mother's body
would be kindly regarded, with respect and honor for what she has given,
for what she has done. I am learning that a woman who mothers well
gives all she has: body parts, internal organs, limbs. Some parts are temporarily donated; others, irreparably altered; most effects are permanent.
And, if she lets this mothering sink into the marrow of her bones, if she
allows the job of nurturing to wrestle with her spirit, a woman's soul is
wrought in the image of God.

For me, having a woman's body has meant special tutoring in life and
death. I have been pregnant four times. Each pregnancy ended in a surgical procedure. Three times out of four, my stomach and uterus have
been cut open to retrieve, in all their bloody splendor, Julia, Christian,
and Seth. Each time, I have entered the mother's valley of death, bringing my body under the knife, to lie still as someone cut into my flesh to
release life from my womb. What should be a joyous moment is full of
fear for me. At the birth of Seth, our youngest, I lay on the operating
table trying so very hard to be brave. But I was petrified, and my body
knew it: my pulse raced, I hyperventilated and vomited in an allergic
reaction to the epidural. My eyes filled with tears. On one level, I desperately wanted to run from that certainty of pain and possibility of
death. Yet I had no other choice if I wanted the life within me to live.

As I lay on the table, my mind filled with the image of Annie Dillard's
tomcat, who would jump through her bedroom window at night covered
with the blood of his kill. When she awoke she would find herself "covered with paw prints in blood." "I looked as though I'd been painted with
roses," she recalled. Annie would ask herself, "What blood was this, and
what roses? It could have been the rose of union, the blood of murder, or
the rose of beauty bare and the blood of some unspeakable sacrifice or
birth."[7] She never knew exactly how to read "the midnight canvas." And
I never know when I am on that delivery table exactly what is happening
to me. Am I the site of some unspeakable horror or some unspeakable
joy? Paradoxically, I am both: An open womb, a uterus pulled out onto

my abdomen; an immense pressure, an indignant cry, and a wrinkled old man's face that looks at me from beneath the hospital beanie like a Sharpei puppy. Only after I place my swollen, reluctant body on the table can I hear those first sounds of life. And no, the recovery is never swift in return for my heroism. My stomach has been bisected, the severed nerves need to learn to stop screaming. My bowels remain sluggish from the epidural; my head pounds from the allergic reaction I have known was coming since my first pregnancy.

As I battle through the pains, my body begins to make milk for the child who needs to be fed. When I am barely coherent, unable to sit up, the nurses bring my newborn to me. "He's hungry," they say. "Put him to the breast." So I struggle upright, ignoring the burning incision, to cradle the little body that was so recently inside me. I turn his mouth to me and do for my son what he cannot do for himself. And I understand a little more now how the Savior would "take upon him death, that he may loose the bands of death which bind his people" (Alma 7:12). The demands and duties of life, of the soul, take precedence over the travails of the body.

The third of my four pregnancies ended in death. On a long November Monday morning, I labored for ten hours, knowing that the end would produce only the misshapen fetus that my body in its wisdom knew to expel. While my body tried to perform the labor which it knew was necessary, my spirit keened. Medicine calls it a spontaneous abortion. But I have no name for the desolate feeling that clouded my spirit as my body labored. I knew only my baby would not be born the same week my Emperor tulips were scheduled to appear. I knew I could reshelve the baby name books and stop doodling "Nicholas Kevin Santiago" on sacrament meeting programs. I knew my sister-in-law and I would not give my parents their twelfth and thirteenth grandchildren a mere three weeks apart after all. But most of all, I knew I wanted with all my heart to have this child, and I grieved for what was not to be.

But I did not grieve alone. In that valley of desolation brought on by physical travail, I believe the Savior sent angels to be with me, to succor me in my infirmity: My sister who rubbed my back, changed the bath water, and who, while I was at the hospital, cleaned my house, did my laundry, and fed my children; nurses who looked at me with compassion, calling me "dear, sweet Tess," their words a consolation, "how sorry I am you are here"; women, who knew and had also labored in vain, whose eyes looked at me with a special sweetness; a doctor who, sensitive to my pain, chose to shield me from a surgical procedure in the sterility of his office and instead administered a blissful ignorance through anesthesia as he cleaned my womb of what had been the promise of a child. Most comforting of all, the Lord gave me a husband who held my hand and stood by, waiting and watching, feeling helpless to stop my pain, wishing he could endure for me. I found him sobbing in his office three days later; he too had lost a child. In all my pain, no one had noticed his. Yet, I believe we both felt the arms of the Savior around us healing our hearts in the aftermath of that dreadful week. We felt our neighbors' tears, their hearts aching, sorrowing for our pain; we heard the faint whisperings of another child in time; we learned lessons in patience from Him who would gather us in his arms as a mother hen would gather her chicks.

Could I have broken my heart to the will of the Lord another way? Would I have come so heavy laden and willingly to the Savior's yoke? I don't know. I do know that the death of a small, misshapen body brought light to my soul that perhaps could not have entered any other way. I cannot help but think, as I remember those births, that this human body, also can make us most divine—that the peculiar pains of a woman's flesh teach her exquisitely, intimately. What they teach she cannot know beforehand or even know that she needs to know. But when the pain subsides or is grown accustomed to, she realizes that some time during the darkest of nights or mundanest of mornings, knowledge has descended like the dews from heaven and enlarged her soul.

Unfortunately, the experience has also enlarged her hips and thighs. If she's anything like me, she bears the physical scars of that battlefield: the burst blood vessel on my left cheek appeared during labor with Julia. It still spreads spidery-red fingers across my face. The root canal brought on by my pregnancy with Christian left me with a porcelain crown. A seven-inch, maroon scar bisects my lower abdomen. Just below it is another, faded to flesh. Stretch marks ornament my breasts and hips like silver ribbons. My hips are two sizes wider, my feet a size bigger than when I was married—my very bones have expanded in response to my mothering. Some of the effects are temporary, just for the moments of pregnancy: the bleeding gums, the weakened bladder, the hair that falls out in clumps, the intermittent back pain, and aching hips. These pass in their time, but the memory remains.

In that memory lies the glory of this earthly body: though we may be resurrected in a perfect frame, the lessons taught me by my mother-body will rise with me. The sacrifice, the pain, the fear and faith of my mothering will sink into my soul and remain with me in the eternities. My spirit and this woman's body inseparably connected constitute my fullness of joy. Time writes its messages on all of us. Our very bodies have become our book of life, "an account of our obedience or disobedience written in our bodies."[8] To what have we been obedient? To the purpose for which we were made: to provide a body and a safe haven for the spirits entrusted to our care. If we mother well, we wear out our lives bringing to pass the lives of others. Of the physical fruits—our wider hips, our sagging breasts, our flatter feet, and rounder buttocks—we need not be so ashamed.

DECEIT 6: YOUTH IS THE OPTIMAL PHYSICAL AND SPIRITUAL STATE

In the book *Tuesdays with Morrie*, the author observes as he drives to visit his dying university professor that nobody on a billboard is over the age of thirty-five.[9] A subtle adversary has devised a world fixated on youth. Magazine covers present the faces of women, airbrushed to erase any trace of aging or wisdom. Hair is lightened, eyelids tucked, cheeks acid peeled. I pale in comparison. I am left, if I allow myself to be so influenced, feeling worthless, insignificant, unattractive in a sagging, stretch-marked body. Even though Nephi tells us, quite beautifully, that "death hath passed upon all men [and women], to fulfil the merciful plan of the great Creator" (2 Nephi 9:6), many of us cling stubbornly to vestiges of youth. Satan would have it no other way, for with age normally comes wisdom and the ability to live your life according to God's plan. Experience, sweet or sad, is a grueling schoolmaster.

About twelve miles south of Provo, Rose Bleazard Castagno rests in her daughter's bedroom. Grandma Rose is dying: diabetes, a diseased spleen, a hole in her eighty-four-year-old heart. Her life has been a stalwart example of faith: homesteading with Stanley, her husband, and an icehouse near Stansbury Island in the Great Salt Lake, four children and two miscarriages, widowed at age forty, a mission to England in her fifties as a single sister. She can ride a horse like a rodeo queen. She got me hooked on parsnips in my pot roasts. She has much to tell this world of endurance, faith, sacrifice, and the love of the Savior. Can I not learn more from her than from the celebrity on Jay Leno's show last night, a twenty-two-year-old movie actor with large, white teeth holding court while America watched?

Our culture would have us learn nothing from our experience. The "truths" it espouses are those of an adolescent world: true love is the pitter-patter of hearts as that tenth grader walks by your locker; if I no longer feel *that* every time I look at Kevin, then I must not love him. True beauty is young, unblemished, rosy cheeked and golden haired; if I do not fit that criteria, I must not be beautiful. True worth is being able to eat with the cool kids in the cafeteria; if I take a sack lunch, I am a geek. Style is the latest clothes with brand names ablazing; if I trade off wearing the same two dresses to church, I must not be stylish. Flair comes from breaking the rules; if I am absolutely obedient, I am dull. The list continues. Adolescent theories about worth, popularity, beauty, wealth, and rules masquerade as truth in our adult worlds. We need to recognize them for what they are and root them out.

DECEIT 7: BETTER TO MAKE NO CHOICE THAN THE WRONG CHOICE

When Satan was cast out of the heavens, he "sought to destroy the agency of man" (Moses 4:3). This was and will ever be his primary purpose. At every turn he seeks to undermine, confuse, and paralyze our ability to choose. He often does this by introducing fear into the choice process.

When Kevin and I started the arduous task of car shopping, we approached this venture, new to both of us, with all the diligence of deciding what college to attend or what to name our child. Actually, our decision-making styles are considerably different: Kevin likes to deliberate painfully, considering every angle, determined to get it right. I just dive in with my eyes closed and hope I will be blessed for my courage, if not my intelligence.

Whatever our styles, our Heavenly Father's plan ably equips all of us to make choices; we are given opposition, agency, the gift of the Holy Ghost, time, and the Atonement to repent of any unwise decisions and their consequences. We have been taught that we are to make wise choices after prayer, deliberation, using our common sense; however, because most of us desire so strongly to make the right choice that the process is wrought with fear. Deciding what is right or wrong becomes very difficult for us. Deciding between two rights complicates matters even more.

Satan's strategy is to remove the Atonement from the decision-making process. He would have us believe that we have one and only one chance in which to get things right. Otherwise, we will be in his power. That unjustified but very powerful fear freezes many righteous women right in their tracks: should I marry this man, should I remarry, should I return to school, should I serve a mission, should I run for political office, should I leave this marriage, should I be raising my children this way, should I join this church? All crucial and significant questions to ask, all with large, sometimes eternal consequences. Because we desire to make the right choice, we make no choice until we know unequivocally that God has directed us. Unfortunately, most times God will not appear as a pillar of light to show us the way. He will speak to us through the gentle voice of his Spirit, perhaps best detected by a faithful, fearless heart. He has also promised that he will light the way through the darkness but only after we have taken the first steps. We must learn to act by faith to solve our earthly problems. Excessive fear of choice impedes our progress and nullifies the precious gift of agency.

To believe that a loving Father would give his children only one chance to choose wisely is the equivalent of asking my four-year-old son Christian to line up all the alphabet letters on our fridge in the correct order after showing him only once. Christian, in his eagerness to learn just like his older sister Julia, will do his earnest best, but I know he will make mistakes: after all, he still sings the song "lemon em o pee" and skips over fourteen, fifteen, and sixteen even though he has counted to twenty a hundred times in the last six months. He doesn't know or care that he is doing it wrong: he is delighted to be in the process of learning.

Adopting Christian's attitude is perhaps the greatest favor we may do ourselves regarding our agency. We must look at opportunities to choose as times for us to learn to use our agency wisely. If we continue to look at these choices as another chance to get it wrong, we will never progress beyond the fear of punishment into the gladness the gospel can bring. Many of us have progressed far enough in our spiritual lives, or at least in age, that the more obvious choices between right and wrong have already been made. We still, however, must learn to choose those things God would have us choose. In the decision-making process, the rejection of wrong and acceptance of right—meaning discovering the Lord's will for us—invests us with great personal spiritual momentum and confidence. We are then more fit to be used in our Father's kingdom. But we must learn first not to be afraid of our powerful responsibility to choose.

For some of us, the major decision to be made is whether to work or to remain home with our children. However we answer that question, once the decision has been made as prayerfully as possible, then that choice is over. What remains is the working out of that choice: how to mother or how to work and mother so that we can develop the qualities requisite for a woman of Christ. If every time we make a mistake on a project, or we spend hours sorting the toys into Ziploc freezer bags only to have the entire neighborhood descend en masse to unsort them, or we walk by our framed university diploma and wonder if we have chosen the wrong path—if every time something goes wrong, we run back to the site of our choice, wanting to dig it up and chew on it, like a dog to a buried bone, then we will find ourselves in constant motion but going nowhere. Perhaps we aren't going backwards, but we are at a standstill spiritually.

At times, we are so afraid to choose—because of the consequences—that we abdicate responsibility altogether for our agency. We would prefer not to choose. There are times that I wish Kevin would choose for me. Over the last few years, I have faced decisions about having another child, about whether to enter law school, about whether to return to teaching, about whether I should stop teaching. At each of these junctures, I have asked Kevin what he thinks I should do. Our conversation goes something like this:

"So, babe, do you think I should go to law school?"

"Oh, you would eat it up. You wouldn't even have to crack a book."

"No, I know I'll enjoy it, but do you think I should go?"

"Well, that's up to you to decide."

"But what will happen to the kids, and how will we do it as a family?" I ask.

"It's up to you. We'll manage if that's what you think we should do."

And there the conversation ends again: "It's up to you to decide." I hate that sentence. I wish sometimes Kevin would just tell me what to do: have another baby now, stop teaching now, write your book now—bring me my slippers now. But he doesn't. He leaves me to wallow in the marsh of my own choosing, turning options, listening to opinions, speaking to God in the car.

Why does he do this? Because when it's March, and the semester is three-quarters over, and I am two quarters behind, and students' papers litter the dining room table, I remember how I came to be there. Or when it's August, and one hundred degrees, and my hips are crumbling from the weight of the baby in my womb, in all my grumbling, I am brought back to the place of my decision. Revisiting that moment, I can say only, "Tessa, you chose this way. Now fulfill your responsibilities." Because my path has been of my own choosing, I must take full responsibility for the consequences. As I take the yoke of responsibility upon me, I am made able to bear the burdens of my choices. I come to understand that a loving Father will not desert his children in their time of need; that he will buoy us up as we work through this complicated maze of choice, agency, and personal responsibility.

I find it significant that our Father in Heaven rejected a plan by Satan that would have ensured the return of all his children. I envision a world under Satan's plan filled with Lamans and Lemuels: disgruntled because they had been told by somebody else what to do, even though that thing was good. When the hard times come, that world would fall to murmuring, rising up against the Lord's anointed because "they knew not the dealings of that God who had created them" (1 Nephi 2:12).

Some women, in a mistaken understanding of how the priesthood line of authority works, allow their husbands, or their bishops, or fathers to make their decisions for them. That is not a wise use of agency. Yes, we covenant to hearken unto the counsel of our husbands as they hearken unto the counsel of God. But we are entitled through our noble birthright as daughters of God to personal revelation and inspiration concerning our circles of influence. And we are duty-bound to work to obtain that inspiration, even at the peril of making a few unwise choices. At the judgment seat of God, our husbands will be called to give an account of their lives, not ours. Only we can stand before the bar of God to make an account of the earthly stewardships granted to us: our bodies, our children, our husbands, our intelligence, our talents, our time, our faith, testimonies and miracles, our communities, the sick and poor among us. These are our responsibilities, our chosen areas of stewardship. Some mistakenly believe that for a marriage to work, the woman must always acquiesce to her husband. Some remain silent, never challenging their husbands' ideas, believing they are being peacemakers.

If Satan can persuade a well-meaning woman to allow those around her to make her choices for her, then he effectively robs her of any spiritual progress. She remains essentially a child, not knowing good from evil, not able to distinguish between the two and thus not able to teach her children how to choose or to equip them with the very vital skills of deliberation and decision. And so, the sins of a well-meaning but misled mother are visited on the children.

The scriptures contain many examples of women who understood the principle of choosing and then working through whatever consequences followed. For one, Eve "saw that the tree was good for food, and that it became pleasant to the eyes, and a tree to be desired to make her wise, she took the fruit thereof, and did eat" (Moses 4:12). As a consequence, she and Adam were cast out of the garden of Eden, with commandments to "worship the Lord their God, . . . offer the firstlings of their flocks, for an offering unto the Lord" (Moses 5:5), and "be fruitful, and multiply, and replenish the earth" (Moses 2:28). Upon heading into the lone and dreary world, Eve could have cursed a God who would desert his children. Instead, she "did labor with [her husband]" (Moses 5:1), "bare unto him sons and daughters" (Moses 5:2), and "was glad, saying: Were it not for our transgression we never should have had seed, and never should have known good and evil, and the joy of our redemption, and the eternal life which God giveth unto all the obedient" (Moses 5:11).

Agency is the supreme gift. Even our poorest choices can lead us to God in humility and gratitude for the Atonement. When Satan's original plan to take away all choice was frustrated, his second plan was to have us enjoy the power of choice but rob us of the humility wrought from suffering consequences. If we are to progress as women of Christ, we must exercise choice and learn from consequences.

So what is the solution? How do we overcome the temptations to misunderstand our role, to abdicate our responsibilities to choose, to take the shortcuts, to fear and doubt our own capacities? The task seems almost overwhelming. The solution, however, is quite simple: We need to believe, as strongly as we know Joseph saw God the Father and Jesus Christ in the Sacred Grove, that we are women of strength and power. We need to recognize that fear and doubt come from the adversary, "for God hath not given us the spirit of fear; but of power, and of love, and of a sound mind" (2 Timothy 1:7). We need to rejoice in the privilege of our womanhood. Ultimately, we need to see ourselves as tools fit to build the kingdom of God. Julia Mavimbela, a black South African woman, wrote the following creed: "I give thanks to God that He has made me a woman. I give thanks to my creator that He has made me black; that he has fashioned me as I am, with hands, heart, head to serve my people. It can, it should be a glorious thing to be a woman."[10] Christ invites us in

Doctrine and Covenants 6: "Fear not, little flock; do good; let earth and hell combine against you, for if ye are built upon my rock, they cannot prevail. . . . Look unto me in every thought; doubt not, fear not. Behold the wounds which pierced my side, and also the prints of the nails in my hands and feet; be faithful, keep my commandments, and ye shall inherit the kingdom of heaven" (vv. 34, 36–37). It is my prayer that we will be able to move ahead boldly like Eve, to make wise, thoughtful choices like Mary, to root out disbelief, fear, and doubt, and believe that we are fit for this kingdom.

Notes

1. See LDS Bible Dictionary, s.v. "devil."
2. Brigham Young, *Discourses of Brigham Young*, sel. John A. Widtsoe (Salt Lake City: Deseret Book, 1941), 55.
3. Young, *Discourses of Brigham Young*, 55, 65, 225.
4. *Hymns of The Church of Jesus Christ of Latter-day Saints* (Salt Lake City: The Church of Jesus Christ of Latter-day Saints, 1985), no. 195; some capitals omitted for continuity of thought.
5. Jeffrey R. Holland, *Ensign*, February 1984, 69.
6. See Gordon B. Hinckley, *Ensign*, March 1990, 2.
7. Annie Dillard, "Heaven and Earth in Jest," from *Pilgrim at Tinker Creek* in *Readings for Intensive Writers*, comp. Susan T. Laing (Needham Heights, Mass.: Simon and Schuster Custom Publishing, 1997), 161.
8. Bruce R. McConkie, *Doctrinal New Testament Commentary*, 3 vols. (Salt Lake City: Deseret Book, 1965–73), 3:578.
9. Mitch Albom, *Tuesdays with Morrie* (New York: Doubleday, 1968), 117.
10. Carol Cornwall Madsen, introduction to Julia Mavimbela, "I Speak from My Heart," in *Women of Wisdom and Knowledge*, ed. Marie Cornwall and Susan Howe (Salt Lake City: Deseret Book, 1990), 63.

WHEN I WAS FIFTY-ONE

❦

Ione J. Simpson

When I was fifty, my husband Del and I lived in Idaho Falls. We had five children: one married, one on a mission, two at Brigham Young University, and one a senior in high school. We owned our own business and worked hard making it successful. We were a happy family. Del and I were nearing the time in our lives when the heavy responsibility of raising a family was easing. When we talked about what the future held for us, Del often said he wished he could serve the Lord full time. We looked forward to going on a mission together.

When I was fifty-one, Del and I, four other stake presidents and their wives, and a Church visitor from Salt Lake, went on an outing to Island Park in Idaho. We were boating down the Snake River when our canoe overturned in the swift current, and Del was drowned. In a matter of minutes, I was a widow. It is impossible to express my pain. Only one who has had the experience can know the anguish and sorrow of that time.

Wise friends counseled me to make no important decisions for at least a year, and I followed their counsel. It was a time of grieving, of adjustment, and of planning. The years ahead had seemed so safe and sure. This would be like starting over again. I knew I needed to do something where I could be with and help people. Counseling appealed to me, but that would mean going back to school. Before I married, I had completed two years of college and then had gone on a mission. The very thought of going back to school terrified me. Could I study? Could I take tests? Could I compete with younger students? It had been almost thirty years since I had been in the classroom.

When I was fifty-two, I went back to school. First, I took just one class at Ricks College. Then I enrolled at Idaho State University and commuted three days a week with other "older" women students, still wondering if I could make it. I studied constantly. I'll never forget my first

Ione J. Simpson received her master's degree in social work after the death of her husband and worked for LDS Social Services for ten years. She is the mother of six, grandmother of thirty-two, and a great-grandmother of six. She has served on the Relief Society General Board and teaches Gospel Doctrine in her ward.

test. I had stayed up most of the night studying. When I got to class the sociology teacher announced that it would be a computer test, and I panicked. I had studied for a sociology test. What was a computer test? I was too embarrassed to ask questions because it was obvious the other students knew what she was talking about. When I finally got the test and read the directions, I realized the teacher was talking about a *computer-graded* test. I recovered my bearings, took the test, and passed.

At the end of a successful semester, I decided to finish my degree at Brigham Young University. I closed my home and found an apartment in Provo. Every credit I had earned thirty years before was still good, and I was a junior. One of the greatest blessings of school was that I didn't have time to feel sorry for myself. My days and nights were filled with studying. Learning was immensely satisfying.

By now we had had two more weddings in our family, and all of us were at a university. At one time, three of my children and I were enrolled at BYU at the same time. The two married daughters seemed pleased to have me there, but the youngest, who was unmarried, was not at all sure she liked going to the university with Mother.

By Christmas of the second year at BYU, I needed only three credits to graduate. I arranged to take the three hours by correspondence and joined thirty-four young people and one other woman my age on a semester abroad in Israel for six exciting months. Upon my return to school, my three correspondence credits were accepted, and I marched with the other graduates to get my degree. Goal number one had been accomplished.

In the meantime, our home in Idaho Falls had stood empty for two years except for summers and holidays, when we gathered to be a family again. It looked as though I would not return to live in Idaho Falls, so I sold my home to my oldest son and bought a condominium in Salt Lake City.

When I was fifty-five, I began graduate school at the University of Utah. I had all kinds of experiences there: difficult ones, humorous ones, and challenging ones. But in two years, the day finally came that I could put on my cap and gown and graduate with a master's degree in social work. My first job after graduation was with LDS Social Services. I worked first with unwed mothers and then with adoptive parents. Helping deserving couples prepare for their families and then placing newborn infants in their arms was pure joy. I felt I had found my niche and spent nine fulfilling years there.

When I was sixty-six, I was invited to go to Washington, D.C., to act as director of policy for the National Committee for Adoption. It sounded like an exciting adventure, and even though I knew no one in Washington, I packed my clothes in my car and drove east with my son. We found an apartment for me close to my work, and he flew home.

At times my stay in Washington turned out to be more exciting than I had bargained for. That huge, beautiful city is without question the easiest place in the United States to get lost in. For someone directionally disabled, as I am, it was a challenge. On weekends, however, my sister who lived in Connecticut often came to Washington; together we visited the Smithsonian Institution, strolled down the Washington Mall (not a shopping center), boarded a bus and toured D.C., and traveled to fascinating historical spots in Washington, Virginia, and Maryland. My supervisor commented that I saw more of this part of the country in one year than he had seen in his nineteen years there.

When I was sixty-seven, while still in Washington, D.C., I was called to be a member of the Relief Society General Board. Upon my return to Salt Lake from Washington, I worked for a year part-time for LDS Social Services while also serving on the board. As I served, primarily with welfare services, I learned of the great strength and devotion of my sisters throughout the Church.

Not until I was seventy-two did I face retirement. How do you slow down after so many years of constant activity? For a short time it was hard, but I have found many exciting things to do. When you don't *have* to do anything, the opportunities are limitless. I've spent several years on family genealogy, I have written my husband's life story, and I have traveled to fascinating countries. Most rewarding has been my greater involvement with my children and grandchildren. My five children live in four different states—none of them Utah. My thirty-two grandchildren range from eight years old to married with small children.

Sometimes we feel that as grandmothers we are past the time when we can influence children and grandchildren. I'm finding that's not so. If being together in eternity is our goal, we need to practice now. We need to love each other and enjoy being together. I figure I have more time to make this happen than anyone else.

Every two years we have family reunions with a different family in charge each time. One year we rented a large bus with video screens, a table for games, and a microwave in the back. Thirty of us traveled from

Utah to the Palmyra pageant in New York, visiting Church and historical sites. We would have Captain Crunch and orange juice for breakfast in a park, sandwiches and soda pop for lunch in a parking lot, and often we stopped at Denny's or McDonalds for dinner. Parents occupied the front seats of the bus and laughed and reminisced about their growing-up years; teenagers were in the middle with their delightful and sometimes noisy entertainment; youngsters played games in the back. A time of rejoicing: I'm sure the only reunion that will top this one will be when we all meet again in the eternities.

Seven of the grandchildren are presently at Ricks College. Five married grandchildren attend BYU or the University of Utah. We hold family home evenings in my home once a month. Sometimes, such as at general conference, they all end up at my home. I make it as inviting as possible by keeping food on hand that they like but can't always afford, games they like to play, a bed or floor to sleep on, and a comfortable place to bring their friends. At every opportunity I let them know that I love them and remind them that our family goal is to share eternity together.

Now, at age seventy-eight, I will tell you what I feel has made my life rich after fifty.

First, I am firmly convinced that we came to this earth to succeed. Heavenly Father knows us better than we know ourselves. He knows our strengths and our weaknesses. He will help us build on our strengths and overcome our weaknesses, if we ask him. Every one of us will have challenges. We can let those challenges control us, or we can take charge. My greatest strength has come from my faith that this is true. I find direction and confirmation in the scriptures.

Second, don't be content to do the easy thing. Look for opportunities to stretch farther than you think you can. Going back to school was a frightening experience at first, but succeeding brought tremendous satisfaction. Also, I found that my practical experience as a wife, mother, and church worker gave me an edge over younger, less experienced students.

Third, several years before my husband died, he and I sat down together and talked about our finances. I knew what insurance policies we had and what they could do for me. I knew about Social Security, savings, and indebtedness; I had even gone to the safety deposit box in the bank and knew what it contained. Very few couples do that. Often a widow is left with no idea about her financial circumstances. Wise planning can make all the difference in whether or not you will have a good life after fifty.

Fourth, develop a good attitude. It is so easy to feel sorry for yourself. Don't. All you have to do to become unpleasant company is to talk about your ailments or about how you couldn't sleep last night. I learned through experience that no matter what your problem, someone else will top your story. Forget about yourself. One good way to do that is to do something for someone else. Volunteer regularly for a worthwhile cause, make a telephone call, visit someone who needs you.

Last and most important, many times you will feel alone, but you never are. Your Heavenly Father will always be there. He knows your potential better than you do and will help you through your trials and your joys.

Perhaps it sounds as though my life has been easy. It has not. Like everyone else, I have been depressed. I have felt, Why me? and have had times when I was so lonely I didn't want to get out of bed, times when I could have stayed home and cried—and sometimes I did. It got me nowhere.

One very important thing I know—I am responsible for my own happiness. Every once in a while I have to learn that over again, but I work at it. Life is good! These later years are the very best years of life when we have the time to really concentrate on what is most important—loving and caring about those around us.

BLUEPRINTS FOR LIVING

Barbara B. Smith

*R*ecently I have been made very much aware of what goes into the development of a blueprint. My daughter and her husband have just decided to build a home. They are in the process of selecting and planning—blueprinting, if you will. Let me review with you what I have observed in their exciting new venture.

First, they began by looking around for a lot, surveying all the available land in a location suitable for their needs. Then, when they finally found what to them was the perfect place for their house, they had it appraised and surveyed. Next, they purchased the property. Then came hours and hours of talking and intently planning together to identify the things they both wanted in their dream home. What style should it be: French, English Tudor, colonial, a ranch-type rambler? What general floor plan should they choose: one level or two? What kind of room requirements: a family room and dining room, and of course a kitchen and bedrooms, but how many, and where should they be located? And how many baths? With five children, a clothes chute into the laundry room was a must. What extras could they afford within their budget? A spiral staircase? built-in, rotating storage shelves? a fireplace?

What special needs does each member of the family have? What are their needs, individually and collectively: a stereo cabinet for one child, full-length mirrors for another, study areas?

They began to consider how they wanted the house finished. Of what material should it be made: brick, wood, stone? Or should they use some of the new and different sidings currently available? What colors? Earth tones and pastels are good now. And furnishings: period, modern, or Early American?

They spent hours putting down on paper their ideas, needs, and wants; then they sought the services of a good architect who could take their

Barbara B. Smith served as general president of the Relief Society from October 1974 to April 1984. She was also chairman of the Childhood and Family Committee of the National Council of Women and a member of the Brigham Young University Board of Trustees. She and her husband, Douglas H. Smith, are the parents of seven children.

roughly sketched ideas, refine them, and translate them into a blueprint. The blueprint is then to be professionally drawn with exact detail so that it can be given to a builder who will be able to estimate the cost, materials, and skilled craftsmen necessary to make that plan a reality.

My children are just in the beginning of this process, and I recognize that there are still so many fundamental and important decisions for them to make that it will be quite some time before they finally have a new home. But as I thought about them and the years ahead, and reviewed the process of building, I was forcibly struck by the parallel between the process of building a home, which they are in, and the process of building a life, which you are in.

Let us focus our attention on four similarities:

1. Selecting our lot in life.

2. Building our life's foundation.

3. Constructing a framework for all we do.

4. Finishing the structure by becoming what we want some day to be.

The first step I mentioned, selecting the lot, surveying the land, and making related choices, begins early in life; and as you approach adulthood, you have the responsibility of assuming the control and direction of your own life. In the decisions of adolescence, we begin to look around us and form impressions of the world in which we live. Often we experience terrible growing pains as we have certain experiences. Some we choose, and others are thrust upon us by our parents, our peers, or circumstances.

Regardless of circumstances, you must ultimately decide what kind of a human being you are going to be, upon what philosophies you are going to build your life, and what style of life you will live. Will your choices be based upon worldly or spiritual values?

What attitudes toward the experiences of mortality will you develop? Do you favor the cool, noncommittal way of breezing past events, or do you like a negative, pessimistic outlook, or, possibly, do you prefer a happy, optimistic attitude? I often think of a friend who smiled the moment she awoke. "I love to open my eyes to each new day," she confessed. There was optimism and enthusiasm in her approach—an attitude she *chose* to have.

What will you do with your life in your day-to-day living? How will you relate to the members of your family and your neighbors? Will you volunteer yourself to reach out to someone, or will you shut your eyes to everyone outside your own little circle?

What general scheme of planning will you adopt—a daily organized routine requiring self-discipline, or will you just let things come as they may?

Where will you stand in relationship to God? Will you have a program of daily prayer and meditation, will you become a scholar of the scriptures, or will you find yourself too busy to read? Will you choose to serve the Lord, or will you just wait and see what happens?

What kind of time are you willing to give, and what kind of planning for a lifetime of education, training, and continual growth do you want?

Experts who study human behavior point out that there is a great need for making a lifetime plan, realistically recognizing what each period of life is likely to bring. Alena H. Morris, president of Seattle's Individual Development Center, points out: "With some kind of a good design to life rather than a random existence which does not give security, one can lead a life that is potent and dynamic, one that provides all of the satisfaction of knowing that you are becoming what you are capable of being."[1]

Childhood is a special time. It is one of enormous growth and development. I remember my mother once said, "Spend all the time you possibly can with your children; they will grow up so fast and leave your home that you will hardly know it is happening." I thought, "Mother, you've forgotten how long the time is when you are so hard at work with and for them." Now I know she was right. Like it or not, believe it or not, children do grow up all too quickly; and, in large measure, they reach out and participate in the excitement of learning only when it is encouraged and nurtured in their home and in the larger environment in which those early years are spent.

Can there be any wonder at the vital importance of the home when we realize the profound effect these early years have upon the lives of children? It is in the home that the life of a child is primarily shaped. The home is also the significant factor in determining the existence, or the nonexistence, of the basic problems in society, such as divorce, crime, suicide, and all manner of social disorders.

After childhood comes the period of choice and preparation. That is where most of you are now, surveying the fields of interest, taking classes, and focusing attention on understanding and developing your personal interests and talents. I hope you realize that your potential for study and the opportunity to develop new educational skills will probably never again be quite as available to you as they are now. In this springtime of your life you should concentrate on learning and preparing yourself with professional skills, with a single-mindedness that may never be possible again.

I believe that one never gets too much education. In fact, one great principle of the gospel teaches us that we need to commit ourselves to a lifetime of continuous learning, and I think that learning needs to include ways of applying in practical ways newly acquired information.

This period of your life is the time to upgrade your marketable skills, for no one knows when or where a woman might be called upon to provide the money to support herself. Elder Howard W. Hunter stated it insightfully when he said: "There are impelling reasons for our sisters to plan toward employment also. We want them to obtain all the education and vocational training possible before marriage. If they become widowed or divorced and have to work, we want them to have dignified and rewarding employment. If a sister does not marry, she has every right to engage in a profession that allows her to magnify her talent and gifts."[2]

Your surveying should include selecting a mate, one with whom you can share the world's experiences and one with whom you will be able to build an eternal companionship. This selection is the single most important decision you will ever make. Upon this choice depends your mortal and eternal relationships. It will determine how you care for the children you bear and how they will increase in stature, in wisdom, and in favor with God and man. And it will determine your growth in these ways also.

Then, looking way down the road, what happens when your children are grown and off in pursuit of their own interests? Where will you spend your time so that you can make the most of that season of your life?

All of this is but a part of that important process of selecting your lot. Land is not always what it seems to be on the surface. A careful builder always has a contour map made before his work actually begins. He needs to know what kind of underground water is present. Are there huge boulders under the surface? What is the composition of the soil?

Remember that in living your life, you too must consider the lay of the land. The Lord has counseled: "Therefore whosoever heareth these sayings of mine, and doeth them, I will liken him unto a wise man, which built his house upon a rock: and the rain descended, and the floods came, and the winds blew, and beat upon that house; and it fell not: for it was founded upon a rock. And every one that heareth these sayings of mine, and doeth them not, shall be likened unto a foolish man, which built his house upon the sand: and the rain descended, and the floods came, and the winds blew, and beat upon that house; and it fell: and great was the fall of it" (Matthew 7:24–27).

No structure can stand long upon land that is faulty. Sandy soil will wash away, and no matter how strong the structure upon it, that building will be destroyed. So it is with all of us. If we choose to live in shaky, immoral environments, we have to recognize that the nature of the soil upon which we build will bring about our destruction.

After the lot is properly chosen and prepared, then the builder begins. He takes great care in preparing and pouring the foundation because he knows that a good, well-engineered foundation is critical.

Revelation from the Lord is the great foundation stone of all happy, productive living. He is the source of all truth and reliable knowledge. He has given us an open invitation to come to him for information, for direction, and for rest in times of trials and tribulations. A personal relationship to God is essential for a firm foundation.

You need to know how the mortal and the immortal fit together. You need to know how heaven and earth interrelate. You need to know that you can communicate individually with your Heavenly Father.

How do you come to such truth? The blueprints that the Lord has provided—the holy scriptures—tell you to use profoundly practical steps if you wish to know. You might think of it in scientific terms: formulate a hypothesis, act upon that hypothesis, evaluate the results of the experiment, and then reevaluate the hypothesis in the light of the new information.

How could that work with the gospel? Well, you make an informed observation, your hypothesis. For instance: God lives. Then you begin to live according to that hypothesis. Study the scriptures, and read as Joseph Smith did: "If any of you lack wisdom, let him ask of God, that giveth to all men liberally, and upbraideth not. . . . But let him ask in faith, nothing wavering" (James 1:5–6). And the truth will be manifest unto you.

In Matthew 7:7 we read: "Ask, and it shall be given you; seek, and ye shall find; knock, and it shall be opened unto you." This invitation to the most profoundly important information in the world is repeated over and over again in the scriptures. In fact, in the Topical Guide in the LDS edition of the Bible, "Knock, and it shall be opened unto you" is listed as appearing thirteen times in the Bible, the Book of Mormon, and the Doctrine and Covenants. It seems to be a very important detail in the blueprint for living. It is repeated carefully, simply, completely, and often. Listen to the way the Savior expresses it in Revelation 3:20: "Behold, I stand at the door, and knock: if any man hear my voice, and open the door, I will come in to him, and will sup with him, and he with me."

The fundamental unity of Latter-day Saint women comes from the one thing that each of us can have: a testimony of an eternal plan of life and salvation; the testimony that God lives; the testimony that we are his children and that we individually have access to the powers of heaven; and a testimony that we are led by his prophet here upon the earth today.

The journals of the early Mormon women of this dispensation tell us that they were seeking light and truth, and they could not find satisfaction in their souls that what they had was enough. Then they heard about Joseph Smith, or they heard about the golden plates, or an elder came knocking at their doors and told them the truth had been restored. They asked the Lord if what they were hearing was true, and light came into their lives. The witness of the Holy Spirit was like a light being turned on in their souls. They would not and could not be persuaded otherwise.

Sister Eliza R. Snow says that her father, in assisting widows and others, was detained until the very last day of grace allotted to the Mormons for leaving the county; the weather was very cold indeed, and the ground was covered with snow. She walked on to warm her aching feet until the teams would overtake her; meanwhile she met one of the so-called militia, who abruptly accosted her: "Well, I think this will cure you of your faith." The young heroine looked him steadily in the eye and replied: "It will take more than this to cure me of my faith." His countenance fell, and he responded, "I must confess you are a better soldier than I am."[3]

These sisters had a personal witness that the gospel was restored and that they could become part of building this kingdom of God on earth, which would then take that glad message throughout the world. I suppose the poet captured the feelings of their quest and the personal nature of this foundation when he declared:

> Back into the heart's small house I crept
> And fell upon my knees and wept,
> And lo, He came to me.[4]

If you remember nothing more of what I say today, I pray you will hear my own testimony and act upon this one truth. The strongest, firmest, most sure foundation for your life is a personal testimony of the truth that God lives, that he speaks again to us, and that he cares for each of us. This testimony will come to you if you will ask in faith, nothing wavering, and with sincere intent. My dear sisters, millions have a testimony, and it can be yours also if you will but ask the Lord in constant, secret prayer.

Regarding the third step, any good house blueprint calls for a strong framework upon which to build. And so it is with life. The individual needs to construct a strong framework upon which to build. In building a house, one selects good, firm timbers or strong, tempered steel that can bear the weight of the rest of the structure and withstand the ravages of weather and natural disaster.

In building a life, a person needs to choose good, strong tenets and assemble them into a design that gives stability and unity and yet allows for the constant addition of new information and further insights. This is the essence of gospel teaching.

The blueprint from the Lord suggests the need to build our lives using two fundamental principles.

The first is the personal quest for eternal perfection, achieved line upon line, precept upon precept, with each new insight giving us greater vision. When we seek to be constantly improving, overcoming faults and weaknesses, and searching for enriching, enlarging opportunities, life becomes full of meaningful experiences. Remember that perfection is a process, not a state we achieve. We are continually involved in learning today what will give us the information and experience we need for tomorrow.

The second fundamental principle is that we should give service to and perform acts of compassionate care for others throughout our lives, for doing so allows us to develop Godlike attributes.

Holding the framework securely together, and essential to every addition, is charity. According to the scriptures, without charity all else is as "sounding brass, or a tinkling cymbal" (1 Corinthians 13:1). Charity is the pure love of Christ—everlasting love—and unless we have charity, we cannot be saved. Further, we are shown in the Lord's blueprint that we should have charity for all, even those who despitefully use us, and that without charity, all that we do is of no value.

If you choose this sound, basic structure, you will have a life with end-less potential. You will be able to spend your lifetime finishing the structure—completing it, furnishing it, and enriching it. That is why it is important to have a good blueprint. Make your plans with such care that the structure will stand firm and unshakable. Then imaginatively and creatively go forward with the finish work of your house.

You can prioritize the items you want to add until the structure is complete. In your day-to-day living, that means beginning to develop within yourself the attributes that make you the kind of person you want to be. You might begin by developing your talents. You have special gifts, and the Lord expects you to develop them fully and then use them to build his kingdom here on earth. You might begin by increasing your knowl-edge, or you might choose to begin by giving service.

When you begin may not be nearly so important as that you do begin. The gospel provides a vision of your fulfillment as a woman, an under-standing of your future as an eternally oriented human being—a woman who is strong, competent, and filled with capabilities and commitment to a quest that will keep you constantly achieving.

I am sure you feel grateful, as I do, that you need not be fearful of life, for the Savior came to show the way and to conquer death. His atone-ment made possible your salvation and exaltation.

So if you are willing to accept the gospel blueprint and adapt the framework design to your own life, you can move forward, encouraged to finish your unique structure by developing all of your talents. You will look to the future with enthusiasm and hope, for the Lord has removed the pain of death and has taught that even errors are to be viewed as learning experiences.

Nothing that is for your good is forbidden, but cautionary signs do warn of those things that bring sorrow and unhappiness. Basically, this mortal experience is to give you a variety of situations in which you can test yourself and develop the qualities that will make you worthy to return again and dwell with him who made us.

Perhaps even more basic is the realization that you should be devel-oping the attitudes and character traits that will make you capable of eternal progression. Such is your birthright. The capabilities and powers are within you, and you must live to bring them forth.

When builders are working on a new structure, and the threat of bad weather comes or winter approaches, they quickly work to close things in. I've heard at least two reasons for this. First, good builders want to get the outer shell completed so that they can work throughout the storms to complete the inside of the building. Second, they want to protect the interior from the ravages of bad weather because usually the materials that are needed in finishing the structure are not designed to withstand the elements in the same way as those on the outside. The finishing work needed to complete a life is somewhat the same.

I do not offer these suggestions as a matter of preferential priority, but I do suggest that both exterior and interior finish work are necessary. In fact, the finishing work in building a life is never completed. It goes on throughout mortality and throughout eternity. Change from the outside will occur just as surely as the sun rises and sets. Change from the inside will likewise occur—for the worse if we just drift, for the better if we determine to work to achieve goals. Transferring general ideas onto a blueprint and then transforming the drawings into reality requires many carefully detailed tasks and countless thoughtful decisions. It is the work of a lifetime.

In looking to the exterior finishing, be aware of the great variety of exteriors available. No two women look exactly alike. It was never the intent of the Lord that they should, but he enjoins us to know and understand the workings of our bodies and thereby to comprehend what helps and what hurts their functions.

A healthy body is more pleasing to look at and its movements are more graceful, thus affording the benefits of both looking and feeling better. One of the Relief Society board members strives for a physically fit body by jogging in her room and memorizing scriptures at the same time, surely a pleasing combination.

The adornment of the human body is another point of exterior finish. It involves what you wear, your makeup, your jewelry, your grooming habits, your style preferences. Brigham Young told the people there was reason to believe that the angels of heaven were lovely to look upon. He encouraged the sisters to be neat and clean and beautiful. He also felt strongly that fashion excesses were to be avoided. That kind of balance should still concern us.

We should all keep ourselves neat and clean. Most of us can do this. Some time spent in making ourselves attractive is important, for it makes us feel better and helps other people feel better about us.

There is wisdom in developing one's sense of style. I once knew a young, attractive buyer in a large department store. She gave a talk to some blind women, at their request, about fashion and style. They had invited her to come to a meeting they held regularly for the purpose of helping them improve their looks.

She sat in that room as the preliminaries were being handled and looked at these well-dressed, sightless women. I don't know what thoughts went through her mind, for she was a woman trained in and sensitive to the visual line and color of ready-made dresses and coats. But when she stood up and talked, she explained to them the one thing that was the most useful for them to know. I have thought about this many times since, and I believe it is the most useful single thing for any of us to know about clothes.

"Fashion," she said, "has to do with fad and style. That which is high fashion is often faddish in nature. It will be good for a short season, and then it will be gone. Style, on the other hand, is the fashion line that is classic in nature. It will always be in good taste, with perhaps minor alterations now and then."

So a person can be well dressed by paying close attention to the purchase of a dress with a style that will have a long life and by paying only casual attention to the faddish elements of the new season.

This same effort to develop good taste in makeup, hair styling, grooming of any kind, shoes, dresses, coats, jackets, and clothing of all kinds will make it possible for us to be attractive on the outside.

I think it is important to be mindful of the cautions given in the past that we not become slaves to appearance and that we not put undue emphasis on externals. Nevertheless, how we look is important. Costume designers for dramatic productions spend their lives studying and trying to understand the language of external human appearances. And these appearances are very clever. They can create a mood; they can tell us something about a person's experiences in life; they can even tell us about a person's attitudes.

Sometimes on the stage, as in life, a costume will give insight into a person's character and feeling. A very dramatic example of this occurs in the play *The Prime of Miss Jean Brodie*. Miss Brodie is a flamboyant teacher of young girls who has dedicated her life to molding and shaping the minds and characters of her charges. She is very romantic and a little unrealistic. The colors and the fabrics used for Miss Brodie's costumes visually portray these facets of her character in the scene in which she comes into conflict with the headmistress. At the moment of dismissal from her position, she pulls on a gray coat, and as the top button is closed, the gray covers all of the vibrant, romantic color, and we see the transformation of Miss Brodie. The color and the line of the coat subtly reinforce the pathos of the play.

It is very unrealistic to assume that the clothes we wear and the appearance we are satisfied with have no effect upon the course of our lives. They do. We all respond to the visual appearance of people and to our own appearance. We must make personal decisions about our exterior finish.

Another aspect of this exterior finish is the matter of manners—our social behavior patterns, our attitudes, and the effect they have upon our relationships with others.

Think about the endless detail found in the variety of patterns that our associations generate. We live in a world of constant change. The most constant thing of all is the continuing change in human relationships. The world of people is like a giant kaleidoscope. A twist, a turn, or even a bump, and the relationships of human beings to each other change and move; another forward or reverse turn and the relationships change again. It's a very exciting, worrisome, satisfying, puzzling, challenging world in which we live.

I would not like to leave with you the impression that appearances and external relationships are so important as to justify spending all of your time with them. They are not, and you must use restraint and good judgment so that you do not waste precious time or become vain. What I do want to point out is that your exterior finish does influence your life. It invites people to you and to some extent governs their attitudes toward you. It is also true that what you wear, how you look, and how you think about yourself influence how you feel.

In the film *West Side Story*, Maria first discovers her feelings of love as she sings, "I feel pretty, oh so pretty." Of course, it is proverbial that a woman in love looks beautiful.

A stage designer I know once conducted a workshop for the Church. As he was teaching the volunteers how to make costumes, some wanted to use a shortcut and hem the period skirts by machine. Painstakingly, he explained that hand-stitched hems look better because they flow and move more easily. "That's important on the stage," he said, "because it helps the actress. If she feels that she looks graceful, she will perform better."

This is the reason I mention outward appearances and manners today. They are necessary to complete your life. The exterior finish of the house is what invites us in.

But of far greater significance is the finish on the inside. On the inside lies true beauty. On the inside lies the motivation for all that we do. You can select and polish those characteristics for which you wish to be known. Will you be honest? Will you be chaste? Will you be kind? Will you have integrity?

You and I alone determine the interior finish of our souls. The choices we make individually are the ones that ultimately set in place the furnishings.

Will you be part of the creative force that allows human life to continue on this earth? Only your personal decisions concerning the bearing of children, if you have a choice, can determine that. Will you be part of the rearing of children? Only your decisions and actions can determine that. Will you marry if a mutually satisfying opportunity comes your way? Only you can decide that.

Will you be lonely in this life? Probably. Everybody knows some loneliness. But will your loneliness engulf you and stop your progress? Only you can decide that. Single or married, you will have times of choice in your life. Will you seek out opportunities to give love or won't you? Only you can decide, but upon that decision so much else depends. One thing is certain, though: if you give love to all you encounter—and if you seek opportunities to give love to those who hunger and thirst and have great need—then love will flow back to you, and you will not be alone.

So it goes, down the whole catalog of human characteristics. Which ones do you wish to have? Which ones are you willing to cultivate and develop? The interior finish of your life depends upon such decisions.

One of the great teachings of the restored gospel is that each person has the right and the responsibility to determine the direction of his or her life. So it is with each of you. So it is with me.

The English writer Somerset Maugham, who was known as a great cynic, once wrote a book called *Summing Up*. In this volume he described each of the Christian virtues and put them down one by one as being full of fraud or hypocrisy. Then he came toward the end of the book, and he wrote that, despite his disillusionment with these so-called virtues, when he found himself in the presence of a truly good person, his heart knelt in reverence.

So finish your structure with the characteristics of faith, hope, and charity, remembering that the greatest of these is charity. Seek wisdom and give service freely. In these ways *you* will adorn your life with the beauties that radiate from within.

Circumstances and opportunities vary for each person. You have to seek out those opportunities that will allow *you* to develop, and you must be responsible for the choices you make as well as the consequences of those choices for yourself, for others, and for society in general.

The Lord requires only that you do the best you can to gain experience and that you continue your growth by participating with a willing heart and teachable spirit.

Think often:

> *The beauty of the house is order;*
> *The blessing of the house is contentment;*
> *The glory of the house is hospitality;*
> *The crown of the house is godliness.*

I testify that you will have order, contentment, hospitality, and godliness as you build your life according to an eternal blueprint.

Notes

1. Alena H. Morris, *Deseret News*, 10 April 1979.
2. Howard W. Hunter, *Ensign*, November 1975, 124.
3. Shirley Anderson Cazier, comp. and ed., "Eliza R. Snow, as Seen through the Woman's Exponent, 1872–87," unpublished manuscript.
4. Author unknown.

RELIEF SOCIETY, THE POSSIBLE DREAM

⟨✖⟩

Mary Ellen Smoot

*I*n 1605, Spanish novelist Cervantes wrote his masterpiece about an idealist named Don Quixote. You know the story. It later became the Broadway musical *Man of La Mancha*. Don Quixote believed in the power of vision, of seeing the good in every individual and lifting others to greater heights. He helped many to believe in themselves by teaching them to dream—to dream the impossible dream. I would like to visit with you instead about dreaming the possible dream. Good dreams, firmly grounded in the gospel of Jesus Christ, lift and inspire.

When I was a young mother, we were living in an apartment with two small children. My husband was finishing his schooling at the university, working full time, and serving in the bishopric. Because of two years' military service, we had already moved five times, both in and out of the state, and we had been married only three years. So, as you might imagine, I was thrilled at the idea of settling into a home of our own. It was an exciting day when we moved into that little home. I thought I was at the end of my troubles—but I did not realize which end.

For twenty-five years we lived in that home, and our family grew from two to seven children. From the beginning, the home presented great challenges. We had to dig a well for water, and the water we got from it was so full of iron that it often tasted as bad as it looked. Even though we purchased better pumps and found solutions to our continuing water problems, we had a steady stream of leaks, floods, and repairs while living there. If you turned on the cold water in the kitchen while the shower was in use, the person was drenched in hot water, causing a loud yelp. And when I turned on the water to wash a batch of clothes, I had to

---

Mary Ellen Wood Smoot began serving as Relief Society General President in April 1997. She loves family history and research and has written several histories of parents and grandparents and their local community. She served with her husband, Stanley M. Smoot, when he was called as a mission president in Ohio, and they later served together as directors of Church Hosting. They are the parents of seven children and the grandparents of forty-five.

506

watch closely to turn the fill cycle twice just to get enough water to wash the clothes. If I mastered that feat, I almost never could get enough water into the rinse cycle to wash out the soap.

This water system became the bane of my life. At times I felt trapped in what seemed an impossible situation. Do you think I dreamed about a better way? Of course I did. My father gave me some sage advice: "When you feel you have reached the end of your rope, tie a knot and hang on!" Sometimes I pleaded with my husband to move. But we both knew that was not the answer. For one thing, we couldn't afford it.

Once when my husband was out of town, my neighbor and I moved the washer and dryer to the garage, wallpapered the utility room, bought a love seat, rocker, lamp, and table, and made a sitting room. Then, for a period of time, I took all of our dirty clothes to the laundromat once a week. I would bring the clean and folded clothes home, place them in the children's drawers and closets, and feel better about my home.

We learned to live with our water problems, however annoying they became. Our children developed patience and long-suffering—and so did their mother. For the sake of my family, I determined to stop whining and make the best of our situation. And I did.

I came to the realization that the pluses were better than the minuses. We really had a happy life in that small home. Our children could work at their grandfather's dairy, ride horses, build forts, feed baby calves, and pick fruit from the orchard.

When we sold that home some twenty-five years later, I was thrilled with the new home we built: it had an excellent water system in it. My impossible dream had finally become a reality, but I now cherished the lessons learned. We had learned to live with some rather unfavorable circumstances that had actually helped us to achieve our more important dream of being a happy and united family.

As we work to realize our dreams, greater possibilities will unfold for us—and for those we love and serve. Throughout the scriptures, the Savior shares this truth in its full and most correct sense. He teaches us to do more than just dream. And he makes it clear that only "with God all things are possible" (Matthew 19:26). The Lord shows us the way; he is "the way" to make our dreams come true. With him, impossible dreams can become possible, even realities.

Let me illustrate with the story of Enoch. He built a city called Zion, in which the people were "of one heart and one mind, and dwelt in righteousness" (Moses 7:18). Building Zion must have seemed like an impossible dream even to Enoch at first. But as Enoch and his people worked toward their righteous goal, the Lord blessed them.

Establishing Zion not only is possible but is our charge as Latter-day Saints. It will not happen overnight, but each of us can be inspired by the way Enoch overcame challenges and became all that our Father in Heaven wanted him to be.

As members of Relief Society, we help each other. We unitedly seek for purity of heart. We strive to become all that our Heavenly Father wants us to be—individually and collectively.

The Prophet Joseph Smith reminded the first members of the Relief Society about our divine purpose: "This organization is not only for the purpose of administering to the sick and afflicted, the poor and the needy, but it is to save souls. If ye are pure in all things nothing on earth or heaven can hinder the angels from associating with you."[1]

As individuals and as a Society, we are here to save souls. As each of us does the Lord's work in our own sphere of influence, the Lord's great work of the latter day will be accomplished. We are here to usher this Society into the next century, to join hands with sisters across the globe, and to lead each other into life eternal.

In a recent general conference President Boyd K. Packer spoke of our essential role as Relief Society sisters: "However much priesthood power and authority the men may possess—however much wisdom and experience they may accumulate—the safety of the family, the integrity of the doctrine, the ordinances, the covenants, indeed the future of the Church, rests equally upon the women. The defenses of the home and family are greatly reinforced when the wife and mother and daughters belong to Relief Society."[2]

The time has come for the members of Relief Society to realize fully the magnitude of its mission and to represent the Lord and his leaders to the women of the world. The time has come to raise our heads and fly the banner of righteousness. Devote yourself to Relief Society. Or, as President Packer admonished, "Do not allow yourselves to be organized under another banner which cannot, in truth, fulfill your needs."[3] As a devoted Relief Society sister, you will see miracles happen in your own lives—and in the lives of those you serve. Under its banner, impossible dreams can come true.

Using Enoch's experience as a model, I'd like to suggest four steps toward realizing our righteous dreams as daughters of God—as wives, mothers, and Relief Society sisters.

LEARN THE WAYS OF GOD

In Moses 6:21 we read about Enoch's upbringing. His father, Jared, "taught [his sons and daughters] in all the ways of God."

We too must learn the ways of God. For Enoch and for each of us, learning gospel truths and living them is essential to all else. We begin with ourselves and then we strengthen our families. We always start in our own hearts and homes. By creating loving relationships with our husbands and children, they see and feel the difference from the ways of the world.

Prophets throughout the ages have counseled us to read, study, ponder, and pray—and to set the proper example of love and service to others. If we develop and then live our testimony, the kingdom of God will flourish and grow.

Every sister must find her Sacred Grove—whether it's a quiet place in the bedroom or a private spot in the yard. Go to the Lord with the desires of your heart and ask for strength and direction. If you feel you are short on faith and hope, start by asking for even the "desire to believe" (Alma 32:27). And then put to the test the process outlined in Alma 32. Plant a seed of faith in your heart. You will be blessed with answers. You will not be disappointed. For every principle you pray about and live, you will be assured of its truth, and your heart will swell with love, peace, and joy. The principle will become "delicious" unto you (Alma 32:28).

Being fully taught in the ways of God also means we must make and keep necessary ordinances and sacred covenants. Elder Boyd K. Packer has said: "Ordinances and covenants become our credentials for admission into [God's] presence. To worthily receive them is the quest of a lifetime. To keep them thereafter is the challenge of mortality."[4]

The completeness of the gospel of Jesus Christ is beautiful. It is a restoration rather than a reformation. You cannot find all that we have anywhere else because we have a fulness of truth. It will not fail us, if we live it. What makes the gospel of Jesus Christ unique? Through the teachings of the gospel of Jesus Christ, we learn the following:

1. We were spirit children of our Father in Heaven.

2. We lived with him before we came to this earth.

3. There was a Grand Council in Heaven, and we chose to follow his plan, which included receiving a mortal body and being sent to this earth

to be tested—to prove ourselves worthy to live with him throughout eternity.

4. The priesthood of God has been restored to the earth, and through the priesthood we may be baptized by immersion as planned by the Savior.

5. We can be together forever as a family if we live worthily and receive the saving ordinances.

6. We can also assist in the completion of the vicarious ordinance work for our ancestors through genealogy and temple work.

Let me share the story of one sister's conversion. About thirty-five years ago, a young girl of ten was introduced to the gospel when the missionaries started meeting with her family in Uruguay. She listened carefully and knew what she was hearing was true. She chose to be baptized, even though no one else in her family joined the Church.

That young girl prayed, studied the scriptures, and remained faithful through many years. Her faith in Jesus Christ carried her along. She weathered the challenges that come to someone so young and so alone in her beliefs because she continued to search the scriptures and to ponder and pray about them. She learned the ways of God, even though she had not been taught them by her parents. The Spirit of the Holy Ghost rested upon her and guided her. She received her education, filled a mission, and became a valiant instrument in the Lord's kingdom.

She eventually moved close to a temple and completed the temple work for thousands of her deceased family members. She will truly be a savior on Mount Zion and be praised throughout eternity for her strength, courage, and determination.

Neither this faithful sister nor I would say the way is easy. But as President Howard W. Hunter explains, the Lord would have us press forward with a perfect brightness of hope. President Hunter said: "This faith and hope of which I speak is not a Pollyanna-like approach to significant personal and public problems. I don't believe we can wake up in the morning and simply by drawing a big 'happy face' on the chalkboard believe that is going to take care of the world's difficulties. But if our faith and hope are anchored in Christ, in his teachings, commandments, and promises, then we are able to count on something truly remarkable, genuinely miraculous."[5]

For Enoch, and for each of us, the promise is sure: "Ask, and it shall be given you; seek, and ye shall find; knock, and it shall be opened unto you" (Matthew 7:7). It really will. The Lord told Enoch, and each of us in turn, how to achieve what some might consider the impossible. We begin by learning the ways of God and then teaching our children and those we love and serve. As we do, our dreams will take a more celestial shape. The Spirit of the Lord not only will help us design worthy dreams but will guide us in our efforts to realize them.

ASK, "WHY ME?"

Enoch's story begins in much the same way any of ours would. He was faced with a challenge, given him of the Lord, and—at first—he doubted his ability to meet it.

What challenges are you facing in your life? Now think of yourself in the place of Enoch. "[Enoch] heard a voice from heaven, saying: Enoch, my son, prophesy unto this people, and say unto them—Repent, for thus saith the Lord: I am angry with this people, and my fierce anger is kindled against them; for their hearts have waxed hard, and their ears are dull of hearing, and their eyes cannot see afar off" (Moses 6:27).

Much like the people in Enoch's time, our vision can so easily become clouded by worldly concerns and cares so that our "eyes cannot see afar off" (Moses 6:27). And when we are surrounded by hearts that "have waxed hard" (v. 27)—hearts that would tell us not to believe, not to dream—how do we keep our hearts soft and strong? How do we go forward with faith?

Even Enoch had a moment of asking, "Why me?" "And when Enoch had heard [the Lord's] words, he bowed himself to the earth, before the Lord, and spake . . . : Why is it that I have found favor in thy sight, and am but a lad, and all the people hate me; for I am slow of speech; wherefore am I thy servant?" (Moses 6:31–32). At first, Enoch could think only of his weaknesses. He was slow of speech, unpopular, and "but a lad" (Moses 6:31). But the Lord saw greatness in him.

President Gordon B. Hinckley wrote: "I believe that I am a child of God, endowed with a divine birthright. I believe that there is something of divinity within me and within each of you. I believe that we have a godly inheritance and that it is our responsibility, our obligation, and our opportunity to cultivate and nurture the very best of these qualities within us."[6]

When a reporter asked Helen Keller, who was blind and deaf from infancy, what could be worse than being blind, she responded, "Having eyes to see . . . and no vision."[7]

Like you and me, Enoch may not have caught in an instant the vision of what one person can do. We don't create a Zion society, people, or family overnight. But as we become pure in heart, as we not only dream the dream but also strive to live the reality, we will be blessed with strength and vision beyond our own.

Enoch lived in a very wicked world. He did not welcome the responsibility of calling the people to repentance. It must have seemed like an overwhelming challenge.

I will never forget when one challenge, in the form of a calling, was given to me. My husband and I had been serving as directors of Church Hosting for four years. We loved this calling and expected to remain in it for at least one more year.

On 25 March 1997, my husband and I left the First Presidency's office after introducing them to a dignitary from Russia whom we were hosting. This was not an unusual interaction. But receiving a call to return and meet with President Hinckley again, shortly after returning to our Public Affairs office, was unusual.

President Hinckley greeted us and visited warmly with my husband for a time. Then he sat back in his chair and said, "I would like to call Mary Ellen Smoot as the new general Relief Society president."

I could hardly breathe. I will never forget the first words out of my mouth. I said to a prophet of the Lord, "Are you sure?"

Much like Enoch, I was deeply humbled by this calling. I, too, felt slow of speech and inadequate. But I have taken great comfort in the fact that if we humble ourselves before the Lord and have faith in him, he will "make weak things become strong" (Ether 12:27). If we are willing to do our part, our Father in Heaven will make us equal to anything he calls us to do.

Have you ever wanted to ask, "Why me?" in your calling as a mother, a teacher, or a Relief Society leader? I suggest that you do ask, "Why me?" And this is the second step toward realizing impossible dreams. Yes, ask, "Why me?" Not with a quiver of doubt but, instead, with all the faith you can muster, humbly ask the Lord what he would have you do and why you are uniquely suited to serve. Ask yourself questions like these: "What can I contribute?" "Why was I chosen to be the mother of these children?" "What can I do to strengthen the sisters in my ward?" and so forth. We each have purpose and reason for being. Every sister has a thread to weave in the tapestry of time. Discover your thread and begin to weave.

We are living in a trying time, to be sure. We see evil all around us. But do you suppose the call that came to Enoch could be for each of us who knows the gospel of Jesus Christ and yet still wastes time complaining? Are we going to allow Satan to win? We can't afford to settle back in our easy chairs and say, "What can I do? I'm just one person."

Instead, we can say, "I am one person. And 'I can do all things through Christ which strengtheneth me'" (Philippians 4:13). How the faith of one person can make a difference if we forget ourselves and go to work!

One sister knelt in prayer and asked her Heavenly Father to help her have vision for her life. She wanted his help in defining a worthy dream, and so she humbly and fervently prayed, "How can I be of service? What would thou have me do?" And she received an answer in her heart. She felt that her calling on earth was to raise a righteous family.

This sister magnified her calling as a wife and mother and met the challenge of rearing a large family. Challenges do come our way as we teach our Father in Heaven's "Saturday's Warriors." In moments of frustration or doubt, she was able to recall the peace she felt for the direction she had taken. Because she knew that her calling came from the Lord, because she had sincerely and faithfully asked, "Why me?" she became equal to the task.

Upon such faith great families have been built. Upon such faith our Relief Society was established. At the celebration of the fortieth anniversary of the Relief Society, Sarah M. Kimball detailed how the organization came about. Eliza R. Snow wrote a constitution for the women to begin an organization to assist those who were building the temple. The Prophet Joseph Smith read her constitution and said that it was one of the best he had ever read. And then he declared: "This is not what the sisters want, there is something better for them. I have desired to organize the sisters in the order of the priesthood. I now have the key by which I can do it."[8]

The Prophet had vision for what this Society was to become. Not only would it be one of the largest organizations of women in the world but it would also be the only one organized "in the order of the priesthood." The purpose and mission of Relief Society extends beyond the year 2000 or the year 2002. Relief Society reaches into the eternities. What can you and I do to bring it out of obscurity? Why were we called to be Relief Society sisters in the latter day?

CHOOSE YE THIS DAY TO SERVE THE LORD GOD

Let's look back at the conditions in Enoch's time and see how similar they were to our own. The Lord said of the people of Enoch: "Ever since the day that I created them, have they gone astray, and have denied me, and have sought their own counsels in the dark; . . . and have not kept the commandments, which I gave unto their father, Adam" (Moses 6:28).

And yet, what did the Lord tell Enoch? "Go forth and do as I have commanded thee, and no man shall pierce thee. Open thy mouth, and it shall be filled, and I will give thee utterance, for all flesh is in my hands, and I will do as seemeth me good. Say unto this people: Choose ye this day, to serve the Lord God who made you" (Moses 6:32–33).

The third step I would suggest to you in realizing your dreams is just that: "Choose ye this day, to serve the Lord God who made you." Right now, renew your commitment. Choose this day to serve the Lord, and the windows of heaven will open for you.

Remember the new home my husband and I built after twenty-five years of living in that small home with water problems? Let me tell you the rest of the story. Shortly after we moved into our dream home, my husband and I were called to preside over the Ohio Columbus Mission.

The most difficult part about leaving home, however, had little to do with my leaving my lovely new home with its glorious water system. I was concerned about transplanting my thirteen-year-old son and leaving one of my married daughters who had just given birth to her fourth child, a son named Ben, who had been born with Crouzzons Syndrome, which created severe health problems.

I wanted to be there for her in her time of need. I wanted to be the attentive mother and grandmother I knew I should be, but I also wanted to serve the Lord.

And so I had to choose. I had to choose whether to answer a calling from the Lord or to stay at home and serve my family at a time when my help was really needed. At that point in my life, I knew that when the Lord calls, you go. But it still was not easy to say good-bye to my family.

What I came to realize, though, was that through my choosing to serve the Lord in the mission field, my family was truly blessed. The Relief Society rallied around my daughter. Our new ward in Ohio welcomed my teenage son. And with the perspective of many years, I can see how that single decision to serve the Lord blessed my family in ways that I would not have realized had I remained at home. But still, it took a leap of faith.

When we choose to serve the Lord, we choose to submit our will to his and to respond to the promptings of the Spirit. We start asking, "How can I be of service?" and "What would the Lord have me do?" By humbly and faithfully submitting our will to God, the once "impossible" dream ultimately becomes a living reality.

How could I have known that after arriving in Ohio our teenage son would find friends who were nationally ranked wrestling stars and coaches with an incredible wrestling program? He later became a state and national champion and then a coach of the junior high school that my daughter's son Ben would attend.

Ben, over the years, faced his health problems with faith and humility. Through obedience, he grew in testimony and confidence. Ben, under the skilled, experienced coaching of his uncle, won the regional championship as a seventh grader and was honored as outstanding wrestler of the tournament by all the coaches. My daughter and I stood and wept as the final buzzer of the championship match sounded, declaring Ben regional champion. I knew that the Lord had answered my prayers of many years ago.

Choice is essential to our Heavenly Father's plan for happiness. Happiness cannot be forced upon us; it comes as we make righteous choices. Joseph Smith explained: "I teach the people correct principles, and they govern themselves."[9] Using correct principles to govern ourselves is the challenge of mortality.

Think of all the good and important choices you have already made. You chose to come to this earth. That choice alone speaks of your faithfulness. At baptism, you chose to take the name of Christ upon you. In the temple, you chose to make sacred covenants. As your Relief Society leaders, we believe in your ability to make good choices. We trust you to make correct decisions that will bring you lasting joy and peace.

In our world today, we have more choices than ever before and a lot of tough decisions to make. It can be difficult to sort through it all—especially for those who must live with the unfavorable consequences of another's bad choice. But no matter what our status in life, no matter what choices were made in the past, we can choose to be on the Lord's side now. We may need to redesign some of our dreams, we may need to renew some of our covenants, but we can choose the Lord's plan for happiness today.

David Gelernter, the professor at Yale University whose life was nearly taken by the explosive package sent to him from the Unabomber, commends women such as you. Mr. Gelernter writes:

"Back in 1940 you could never tell why housewives did what they did, whether it was devotion or just momentum. But today you know exactly why homemakers do it: out of love. Some of their families can easily forgo the second income, some cannot; but every one of them could improve her standing in society by taking a job. So today you can see these stubborn women for what they are, the moral backbone of the country. A country with this kind of backbone can't be such a terrible place and is probably capable of weathering anything, in the end."[10] He goes on to say that nobody loves a child as does his or her own parent. And I wholeheartedly agree. Children are given to us as gifts from God; how we choose to rear them is our gift to him.

All of us who love, lead, and guide God's children know the depth of that commitment and the meaning of that gift. Mothers don't get sick days, time off, or overtime compensation. Their reward is of a heavenly kind. I salute you for your efforts to make righteous choices and to be where the Lord would have you be.

To "choose ye this day, to serve the Lord" (Moses 6:33) is to commit faithfully to be where the Lord would have you be, whether that is at home with your family, on a mission in a foreign land, in the temple serving your ancestors, or in the home of the afflicted.

WALK WITH ME

A great promise was given to Enoch, and to each of us in turn, if we will do as the Lord commands: "Behold my Spirit is upon you, wherefore all thy words will I justify; and the mountains shall flee before you, and the rivers shall turn from their course; and thou shalt abide in me, and I in you; therefore walk with me" (Moses 6:34).

What a magnificent blessing! What more could we dream of than abiding in the Lord and walking with him? And that is the fourth and final suggestion I offer for realizing your dreams: walk with the Lord.

Faithful people have walked with God all through the ages. King Benjamin taught his people what it is like to walk with Him: "And ye will not have a mind to injure one another, but to live peaceably, and to render to every man according to that which is his due" (Mosiah 4:13).

Zion is born of such purity of heart. Dreams are turned into realities with such peaceable and godly living. And that's what Relief Society is all about. As sisters in Zion, we help each other and our families to walk with God and return to our heavenly home.

As sisters we are united with the Brethren of the Church, and they have confidence in us. The Lord is allowing us to move the work forward in a rapid manner that will bless each of our lives. We must unite in

Relief Society as never before. Listen to the prophets and follow their words. Brigham Young explained that "a perfect oneness will save a people." And, he continued, "The religion of heaven unites the hearts of the people and makes them one."[11] We become one as we turn our backs on sin, selfishness, materialism, and self-indulgence. We become one as we look to God and give our lives to him.

In the early days of the Church, Relief Society president Bathsheba Smith taught how the greatness of the Relief Society is found in the pure hearts of its individual members. She encouraged the sisters to set aside petty grievances and unite in spirit and deed that they might bring to pass the great mission of this organization. On the occasion of the fiftieth birthday of Relief Society, she said, "Let us take renewed courage and be more united and earnest in this great work, and if anyone has ill feelings towards another, banish them and make this a Jubilee in very deed."[12]

Unity in our Relief Society, unity in our homes, unity in our hearts, is born of banishing ill feelings and taking renewed courage to be more earnest in our endeavors. As sisters in Zion, we can be nothing less than unified.

John Winthrop said of his band of Pilgrims in 1630, and we could say of ourselves and this Relief Society: "We shall be a city upon a hill. The eyes of all people are upon us, so that if we shall deal falsely with our God in this work we have undertaken, and so cause Him to withdraw His presence [and] help from us, we shall be made a story and a byword through the world."[13]

We will be a light to the world—but only to the degree that we are living the principles of the gospel of Jesus Christ and making them an integral part of our everyday lives. May we look to Christ to lift us up at a time when we truly can be a light to the world; when, in the coming years, we really will be "a city upon a hill."

Who will be prepared for the Lord's tremendous promises to those who hearken unto his words and receive his Spirit to guide and direct them? Who will dream what the world thinks is impossible but what the Lord, through his prophets, assures us is possible? Faithful women everywhere.

Does the Lord need each of us to walk with him? Does this world cry out for someone with a clear, clarion call to obedience, truth, and righteous living? Yes!

Everyone wants to find answers that will make the difference in this monumental time in history when we will soon enter the new millennial year. As Relief Society sisters, we can help all of God's children to see that answers are found where they always have been: in scriptures, in prophets' teachings, and in obedience to them.

Enoch was not especially looking forward to what the Lord called him to do. But as we read in Moses 7, Enoch was obedient. He taught and led the people in righteousness. The city of Zion was established, miracles occurred, and Enoch foresaw the coming of the Son of Man, his atoning sacrifice, and the return of Zion.

Ultimately, Enoch and his people did walk with God, and "he dwelt in the midst of Zion; and it came to pass that Zion was not, for God received it up into his own bosom; and from thence went forth the saying, ZION IS FLED" (Moses 7:69).

The people of Enoch walked with God because they walked together and bolstered one another. God did not ask them—or any of us—to walk only with him. He expects us to walk also with each other. Only as we are there to love and serve our family members, our ward members, and our neighbors can he work miracles in our lives. When the bishop calls us to serve, do we ask, "Are you sure?" When our children need extra love and attention, do we respond, "Not now"? Or do we offer a silent prayer and plead for strength, wisdom, and vision beyond our own?

At some time in our lives, each of us will go through a personal Garden of Gethsemane. And each day we have an opportunity to prepare ourselves to go through this period of life by strengthening ourselves spiritually and making righteous decisions.

Several years ago President Hinckley told about a divorced mother of seven children who felt that all of her dreams had been shattered. Not only was she afraid to dream anymore but she felt she faced a mountain of impossibilities. As she returned to her home late one night, she looked at her house and saw that all of the lights were still on. Her children, ages five through sixteen, were waiting for her. "I could hear echoes of my children as I walked out the door . . . : 'Mom, what are we going to have for dinner?' 'Can you take me to the library?' 'I have to get some poster paper tonight.' Tired and weary, I looked at that house and saw the light on in each of the rooms. I thought of all of those children who were home waiting for me to come and meet their needs. My burdens felt very heavy on my shoulders.

"I remember looking through tears toward the sky, and I said, 'Oh, my Father, I just can't do it tonight. I'm too tired. I can't face it. I can't go home and take care of all those children alone. Could I just come to You and stay with You for just one night? I'll come back in the morning.'"

And then she felt the peace of God. In her heart, she heard the answer: "No, little one, you can't come to me now. You would never wish to come back. But I can come to you."[14]

And he will. The promise is sure: "Draw near unto me and I will draw near unto you" (D&C 88:63).

No matter our circumstances, we can dream. And dreams can and will become possible for us as we learn the ways of the Lord, seek his guidance, and choose to serve him. He will walk with us. As individual sisters and as a Relief Society, let us have a vision of where we want to be and build inner strength to get there. Like Enoch, we can have the Spirit of the Lord with us each day as we strive to do his will and make impossible dreams come true.

Like the man of La Mancha and my grandson Ben, may we dream dreams and walk with God, who will assist us in making those dreams become realities as we look to the millennial year and beyond.

Notes

1. Minutes of Female Relief Society of Nauvoo, 9 June 1842, Archives of The Church of Jesus Christ of Latter-day Saints, Salt Lake City, Utah, 1:63.
2. Boyd K. Packer, *Ensign*, May 1998, 73.
3. Packer, *Ensign*, May 1998, 73.
4. Boyd K. Packer, *Ensign*, May 1987, 24.
5. Howard W. Hunter, *That We Might Have Joy* (Salt Lake City: Deseret Book, 1994), 95.
6. Gordon B. Hinckley, "I Believe," *Ensign*, August 1992, 2–7.
7. Helen Keller, as quoted in *May Peace Be with You: Messages from "The Spoken Word"* (Salt Lake City: Deseret Book, 1994), 5.
8. Minutes of Relief Society, 1:30.
9. Joseph Smith, as quoted by John Taylor, *Journal of Discourses*, 26 vols. (London: Latter-day Saints' Book Depot, 1854–86), 10:57–58.
10. David Gelernter, *Drawing Life: Surviving the Unabomber* (New York: Simon and Schuster, 1997), 115.
11. Brigham Young, *Discourses of Brigham Young*, sel. John A. Widtsoe (Salt Lake City: Deseret Book, 1954), 282, 285.
12. Bathsheba W. Smith, *Woman's Exponent* 20 (1 April 1892): 139.
13. John Winthrop, *A Model of Christian Charity* (1630).
14. Gordon B. Hinckley, *Ensign*, May 1991, 73.

"MY HANDS ARE MARTHA'S HANDS"

⟨∞⟩

Helen Candland Stark

My mind zeroes in on a small framed print, sitting for many years on my desk. It is a reproduction of Jan Vermeer's painting of Jesus in the house of Mary and Martha. It is one of only forty paintings the seventeenth-century Dutch artist produced in his short lifetime.

For me, it is an icon, a religious picture with symbolic meaning. For me, it represents two competing life forces in the lives of other women as well as in my own.

I was surprised to realize that Mary and Martha's story is told only in the book of Luke and that it comprises only four verses. Bible translations that I compared tell the story essentially in the same way:

"Now as they went on their way, he entered a village; and a woman named Martha received him into her house. And she had a sister called Mary, who sat at the Lord's feet and listened to his teaching. But Martha was distracted with much serving; and she went to him and said, 'Lord, do you not care that my sister has left me to serve alone? Tell her then to help me.' But the Lord answered her, 'Martha, Martha, you are anxious and troubled about many things; one thing is needful. Mary has chosen the good portion which shall not be taken away from her'" (Revised Standard Version Luke 10:38–42).

Does one consciously choose to be Mary or Martha? Are genes or the environment determining factors? I don't know.

I do know that for most of my eighty-eight years I have been Martha.

My life falls into three eras—life before marriage, married years, and postretirement years when we moved from Delaware back to Utah. For most of my life I bought the whole Mormon Martha package. I lived it,

Born 18 September 1901, Helen Candland Stark has lived through almost all of the twentieth century. Her experiences have been varied: pioneer, scholar (M. A., 1936), teacher of English and dramatics in high school and college, actress, wife (Henry M. Stark, DuPont chemist), mother, and writer. She is compiling a collection of her verse to be titled *Knots in the Grain*.

lock, stock, and barrel. But from earliest memory, I also knew a Mary tug. Here are some particulars:

Life on our ranch in Sanpete County was rugged pioneer stuff. I was the eldest of nine with my next sister ten years younger. Our menfolk came in late for supper, after which dishwater had to be heated on a coal range and the dishes washed under a kerosene lamp.

Once in a fit of adolescent self-pity, I wrote:

> The canyon breeze comes floating down
> A perfume-laden stream.
> The tired housewife only knows
> Its time to skim the cream.

Of course, someone quickly pointed out how lucky I was to have cream to skim.

Once, after a long, hard day at a treadle sewing machine, turning a bolt of outing flannel into winter pajamas for my five brothers, I was so tired I began to weep. My mother took me for a walk along the dusty country road. She said nothing, but her hand on my arm communicated, without words, "This is the way it is, Helen. This is the way it is."

I was an accepting participant in the way it was. And I did not, with conscious intent, dig in my heels for time of my own. But two limits I insisted upon. Sunday afternoons on the ranch were to be mine. I spent those hours putting together a newsletter, complete with columns, for two absent friends.

And I would not darn. If I managed, purposely, to complete an assigned task early, my mother was wont to say, "Good, Helen. Now you have time for a little darning." No way. The basket of hose for eleven people was bottomless.

But Martha chores were evidence of a good woman, so when I married belatedly and gratefully, I was determined to be the best wife known to man. That meant that I would never just open a can of beans. I would do tedious and intricate things to them.

My husband, a gardener at heart and raised in the same pioneer tradition, thought that was just fine. For his own part, he lavished loving attention on the vegetable patch and fruit trees. He was justifiably baffled, therefore, when one day I came up with a verse I titled "Green-eyed Dirge," with apologies to Joyce Kilmer:

Alas, that I can never be
As lovely as a garden pea.
The bulby beet, the carrot svelte,
Can both be tucked behind a belt.
The parsnip knows its proper place
Upon a plate beneath the face.
I was not even made to wear
A nest of parsley in my hair.
And I have cravings wild. I talk.
Not so, the docile celery stalk.
With bugs I am not overrun
To challenge sprayer and spray gun.
If I am nicked by careless prod
I do not meekly kiss the sod.
No charms, alack, my love will heed
Unless they have been grown from seed.

Still I wore my Martha role like a halo. If someone fell heir to a lug of kumquat plums, I was the expert to call. If our homeless branch in Delaware needed dinner space for eighty-five people, I could cope. In the struggle of our small LDS group to earn money for a chapel, our family raised and sold corn, raspberries, apples, and squash. I operated a bread route. With a laden basket, once a week one of the children delivered loaves to the neighbors. A student who brought his fiancee to call said, "I want you to meet the woman who bakes the best bread in Delaware."

But my specialty lay in salvaging borderline produce. Seventeen split cantaloupes in the morning became seventeen jars of cantaloupe butter by night. The celery crop that froze one night became quarts of puree for soup. A blender and assorted ingredients turned overripe corn into pudding. Eastern guests got the grand tour of the house and gawked at the row on row of bottled produce.

Perhaps I am carrying this too far, because my Mary side continued to ruffle the waters. What came out was verse. For others of you, it might well be music, painting, or dance, to name but a few Mary outlets.

At this juncture, I planned to share a few of those Ah-moments when I felt the Spirit break through. Instead, I now want to make a small end run. That series of words—*poetry, music, painting, dance*—prompts a new line of thought about the Martha role.

In the third period in my life, when after retiring we moved back to

Utah from Delaware, I inexplicably bought *new* bottles for canning. The culture prodded. My inner backlash was an essay for *Exponent II*, "The Good Woman Syndrome, or, When Is Enough, Enough?"[1] The *Era* had previously printed an article about cookies.[2] They were identified as a woman's "medals of honor." Apparently one whipped up a different recipe every day, for seven recipes were included.

My "Good Woman Syndrome" is almost a cliche statement about the role of females in my generation. My own rebellion in the 1970s I now explain as an early stirring of the women's movement, which prompted many of us to question our totally domestic script. Maybe, after all, we had been merely drudges doing chore work.

But the new enlightenment, while sorely needed, was not necessarily benign. Glad to abandon their aprons and even their children if urged, a new work force in tailored suits asserted itself into the market place. Before long, few households could function without two paychecks.

Implications for society have been widely explored. Are gender roles now more evenly divided? Do many of the new outside jobs offer restrictions similar to the old homebound ones? Are women less tired? And particularly, are they freer to touch life at many points?

This last question leads me back to Martha and Mary. Martha roles in *whatever guise* are essentially outer-oriented. Mary turns within for creative inspiration from feeling and from intuition. Hence, it seems to me, Mary is more truly feminine.

These ideas are all subject to argument. My thesis is that Mary-ness arises in the central core of the individual. It is not a persona that can be put on or taken off. It is a given.

Now please try to visualize with me some small Mary epiphanies. My poem called "Marriage Portion" tells of our pioneer heritage of hard work:

> *You muscle down defeat.*
> *By labor, deserts blossom as the rose;*
> *Weariness choked off yields shining wheat.*

The last couplet summarizes:

> *Roses from deserts are a brilliant yield*
> *If we prize, too, the lilies of the field.*

Here are three short nature poems. The first describes an experience with snow. The mother is an archetypal figure who speaks the one-line refrain of each quatrain. The daughter begins:

NIGHT SNOW
My mother and I will walk in the snow:
This is an hour to keep.
Drifts mount high on the tulip beds.
   "As snow, so falleth sleep."

Gone is the moon and gone are the stars.
The sky is foam tonight.
We tread on meadows of mother-of-pearl.
   "Snow filleth our hands with light."

The wire harshness of leafless bush
Is soft as a mourning dove.
Beautiful, gracious, transfigured world.
   "So sayeth all who love."

Quietly, patiently falls the snow,
Cool and sweet to the face.
We have not striven. The gift is given.
   "As snow so cometh Grace."

Next is a sonnet about autumn. My husband and I were visiting in the Vermont woods. He went off exploring, and I used my quiet time to write!

AUTUMN IN VERMONT
How shall I make myself one with this time?
Let go, let go, even your scarlet treasure,
Maple despoiled. Knee deep in gold. I measure
Leaves' profusion—know they melt to limn
With amber dust the fern's first leaf in spring.
In the cone's cup the blood-root makes its bed.
The bare fingers of birch so whitely dead,
Point to the pulse of each transmuted thing.

Now I am drunk with color, now at last
Submerged in peace. I turn for one more look
To hope the floating oak leaf on the brook
Returns, swirls into consciousness, to cast
In some dark hour its secret on my shore.
Oh, baby hemlock trees, be spirit's store.

Our house in Salem overlooked a little lake. Here is a Japanese haiku about a transient moment:

> COME!
> Over the dark water
> A soaring rainbow—
> Too late. It is gone.

Now I am eighty-eight years old. Jesus said, Mary has chosen that good portion *which shall not be taken from her.*

My Martha accomplishments have been taken from me. The prom dresses have vanished along with sumptuous dinner parties. Now I write a haiku about aging:

> HUSH!
> In the dark center
> DNA unravels
> Its intricate spirals.

All those years of domestic chores. Were they worth it? I was never consciously trying to influence my world. But yes, it did help my struggling branch in Delaware to have a home base. The woman with the kumquats happily managed. In our Wilmington Ward Cookbook, my Zuni bread is considered a minor classic.

And what do my children say who grew up within this framework? They say they are grateful. They say they may have kicked sometimes against a way of life that made finishing chores a condition for going out to play. But they learned responsibility to the family, to work efficiently so as to have private time, to develop skills especially useful for their marriages. We had two kinds of work: help work and money work. Raspberries had to be picked; that was help work. But polishing the silver could be money work. Order and efficiency are Martha gifts.

But I am just now gathering up my verses. Would a photocopy of them be a welcome present to my children? I see my son sharing an Ah-moment with his little daughter, and I hope so.

That brings me to my last poem. Martha is speaking.

> MARTHA AND THE WAY
> My sister, when our Lord was gone,
> Brought me a drink fresh from the well.
> I said, "O worthless one." I struck
> The cup of water so it fell.

She laid her fingers on my arm.
I threw them off. I would not stay.
The heavy house is quiet now.
She sought my Lord and went away.

My hands are Martha's hands, alert,
Skillful, strong, and swift to hurt;
But, ah, my soul, could I surprise
The look of Mary in my eyes!

Before I had compared the story in the various translations, I remembered—wrongly, as it turned out—that Jesus had said "Mary has chosen the *better* part." I thought, if there is a better part, then there must be a good part as well as a best part. And that is the way I still ponder that verse in my heart.

You notice that Jesus chided Martha with great tenderness. "Martha, Martha." The repetition of the name endears it. He loved Martha as well.

Not *either* good or better, not even *both* good *and* better, but something greater than both transcends toward wholeness. We enrich ourselves, and we bless each other. That is the reward of the creative blending of roles that I wish I could pass along, especially to you young women. All of us are "cumbered about much serving," as the King James Version so wisely puts it (Luke 10:40). It behooves us, therefore, to heed those quiet promptings to sit at the Lord's feet and listen.

Notes

1. Helen Candland Stark, "The Good Woman Syndrome, or, When Is Enough, Enough?" *Exponent II* (Winter 1976): 16; reprinted in *Dialogue* (Fall 1990): 34–38.
2. Florence B. Pinnock, "A Mother Ten Feet Tall," *Improvement Era*, May 1968, 68–69.

HEARING THE VOICE OF THE LORD

⟨≫⟩

Heidi S. Swinton

*T*wenty-two years ago, a tall, grave-faced doctor walked into my hospital room, sat down in the plastic bucket chair next to my bed, and took my hand. He looked at me for a few moments. We'd met just the day before when I came into the hospital at 2 A.M. pregnant with twins and in labor at seven months. My doctor had retired, and this high-risk specialist had taken over my case.

There I was, a young mother with one son who had just died and another son who was fighting for his life on a respirator. Two months premature, he couldn't breathe, and he had a hole in his heart and a litany of other problems. After miscarrying five babies, I had seen these twins as a blessing to make up for all the heartache and broken dreams. Now I was facing even deeper loss and disappointment.

I will never forget what the doctor said. "Heidi, I want you to know this. You have one son all the way home. That may be no comfort to you right now, but, believe me, in the years ahead, you will come to understand and know what it means. I have a teenage son, and I wonder if I will get him all the way home. Yours is already there." Over the days and weeks that followed, many friends called and came to see me and sent flowers and beautiful cards. But it was those words, "all the way home," that made the difference.

The doctor was speaking, but it was the Lord I was hearing. In Doctrine and Covenants 1:38 we are told, "Whether by mine own voice or by the voice of my servants, it is the same." The truth of eternal life borne to me that day was a spiritual witness from God. In the depths of my grief, the voice of the Lord sounded in my ears. "All the way home" spoke volumes to me then; it continues to speak to me today.

Heidi S. Swinton, a graduate of the University of Utah, has coauthored, compiled, and contributed to many books on Church subjects. She serves as a member of the Melchizedek Priesthood/Relief Society Curriculum writing committee. She and her husband, Jeffrey, are the parents of four sons.

I count much of my life from the experience of the death of my eldest son. It was then that I really began to understand personal revelation. The questions "Why?" and "How could this happen?" begged for answers, yet my soul searched for more than just resolution. Suddenly mortality took on a different dimension, became part of the plan but not all of it. Eternal glory and its promises now included a face and a name: Christian Horne Swinton. To be with him, I needed to get all the way home myself.

That focus didn't require a U-turn in my late twenties or even a sharp turn. He called for me to increase my willingness and my ability to have ears to hear, to listen. At one time, all of us knew the Lord's voice. We cheered in the premortal existence when Christ presented the Father's plan. We heard it there; we are living it here. I have no doubt that we are tied to the heavens by revelation. We sometimes call that spiritual tie "being in tune."

When the Savior spoke to the Nephites, his voice "did pierce them that did hear to the center . . . yea, it did pierce them to the very soul, and did cause their hearts to burn" (3 Nephi 11:3). I have felt that pure revelation. We have been guided, encouraged, shielded, and taught by the voice of the Lord. When we choose to have ears to hear, we step forward on the path that leads all the way home.

Revelation is a fundamental principle of the Church. Some revelations may open the heavens in a way that can't be ignored; others come as thoughts or ideas. Some promptings come when least expected, often when we're busy doing other things. Impressions may come in the car, in the kitchen, or on our knees. We may "hear" in a crowded room or in the middle of a cluttered day. Time and place are really only mortal terms. Revelation reaches through the veil, reminding us of who we are and where we want to go.

I'd like to share six truths I have learned about listening to the Lord. First, I don't need to see Jesus Christ to know he is there or to know of his love for me. I need only listen, for he has said, "My sheep hear my voice, and I know them, and they follow me" (John 10:27). We need to hear the voice of the Lord so that he can direct us all the way home. "Come unto Christ" is a phrase we all know well. Nephi, as he spoke of the way to eternal life, said, "After ye have gotten into this strait and narrow path, I would ask if all is done? Behold, I say unto you, Nay; for ye have not come thus far save it were by the word of Christ with unshaken faith in him, relying wholly upon the merits of him who is mighty to save" (2 Nephi 31:19). Following the word of Christ is another way of saying, I hear.

I see this truth in the experience of Peter in the New Testament. Jesus has been teaching the five thousand and feeding the multitude with a few fishes and loaves. He then sends his disciples ahead, out on the Sea of Galilee in their fishing vessel, while he goes up "into a mountain apart to pray." In Matthew we read: "And in the fourth watch of the night Jesus went unto them, walking on the sea. And when the disciples saw him walking on the sea, they were troubled, saying, It is a spirit; and they cried out for fear. But straightway Jesus spake unto them, saying, Be of good cheer; it is I; be not afraid. And Peter answered him and said, Lord, if it be thou, bid me come unto thee on the water. And he said, Come" (Matthew 14:23, 25–29).

I picture Peter scrambling over the side of the boat before walking on the water. Jesus has called to him: "Come." Water churns at Peter's feet, choppy waves surround him, the wind is blowing. His attention is drawn from the Savior to the dark, frothy water below. Distracted and losing focus, Peter begins to sink. Jesus reaches out and lifts him up.

The world calls it a miracle that Peter walked on water and stops there. But the scene says so much more about hearing the voice of the Lord. "Come," says our Savior. We've heard that call. "Come . . . that where I am, there ye may be also" (John 14:3).

Peter stepped out onto the water. Later, he became the valiant and dynamic leader of the Church and witness of the risen Lord. But he had to walk on unfamiliar territory to get there.

So do we.

When the Savior calls us to come, we sometimes need to turn, or change direction, and then press forward. "Follow me, and I will make you fishers of men," Jesus said to Peter and Andrew, James and John as he called them to leave their nets (Matthew 4:19). To Enoch he was even more pointed: "Prophesy unto this people, and say unto them— Repent . . . for their hearts have waxed hard, and their ears are dull of hearing, and their eyes cannot see afar off" (Moses 6:27). What was the result? A whole community heard that voice, "Come closer." "And the Lord called his people Zion . . . and lo, Zion, . . . was taken up into heaven" (Moses 7:18, 21).

And that is the second truth. Hearing the call to come has everything to do with how close we are to the Lord—close in distance and close in heart. If we can't hear his voice or feel his presence, we need to move closer.

Often the voice is so significant that the time, place, and setting are indelibly marked in our minds. I will always remember hearing the chair scrape across the floor in the hospital as my doctor sat down to try and help me put my life back together. At other times, His voice is a gentle prompting or a sweet spirit that whispers of peace. At these moments, we err in thinking we imagined our feelings, or that we simply feel better. The source of our strength is clear: "I the Lord am with you, and will stand by you" (D&C 68:6).

What does that mean in our everyday experience? President Brigham Young said: "If we would know the voice of the Good Shepherd, we must live so that the Spirit of the Lord can find its way to our hearts."[1] How we do that is clearly outlined: repent, live the commandments, live up to our covenants. Or, again as Brigham Young said: "Live so that [your] spirits are as pure and clean as a piece of blank paper that lies on the desk before the inditer, ready to receive any mark the writer may make upon it."[2]

President Joseph F. Smith, sixth president of the Church, said of his own experience receiving revelation: "I fervently believe that God has manifested to me in my present capacity, many glorious things, many principles and oftentimes much more wisdom than is inherent in myself; and I believe He will continue to do so as long as I am receptive, as long as I am in a position to hear when He speaks, to listen when He calls, and to receive when He gives to me that which He desires."[3] These important steps put revelation within the reach of each one of us: Be receptive; be in the right position to hear; listen; and receive when he speaks.

What stands in our way of receiving? In the Doctrine and Covenants 66:10, we are counseled: "Seek not to be cumbered." *Cumbered* is a good word to contrast with *Come*. *Cumbered* sounds weighted down with purses full of problems, programs, wants, needs, responsibilities, challenges. Every day we have long lists of things to do. Do this or that, come to this and drop off that, stop here, pick up there . . . you know the list. Fractured lives that live by the needs of the day have no peace. How can we hear the Good Shepherd's voice in our hearts when the Spirit has to take a number just to get on our day's list? *Come* means, "Lay aside the things of this world," as the Lord said to Emma Smith, "and seek for the things of a better" (D&C 25:10).

It's all about turning our lives over to God. If we yield our agency to Christ, he will, as President Ezra Taft Benson said, deepen our joy, expand our vision, quicken our minds, lift our spirits, comfort our souls, and pour out peace.[4] What a promise. "Pour out peace." Is there anyone who has enough peace in her life? Peace is the opposite of *cumbered*. He will lift our spirits if we will but listen. For centuries people have tried to find peace by sequestering themselves from the world, perhaps in a remote hamlet or other sanctuary. But peace is not a place; it is a state of mind. It is knowing that the Lord's promises are true and then living worthy to receive them. Such commitment is usually found over the side of the boat, out on the water.

The story of Naaman, captain of the host of the king of Syria, is a good example (see 2 Kings 5:1–14). When Naaman came to the prophet Elisha to be cured of leprosy, this mighty warrior was not invited in. Instead, "Elisha sent a messenger unto him, saying, Go and wash in Jordan seven times, and thy flesh shall come again to thee, and thou shalt be clean" (v. 10). A man of considerable wealth and power, Naaman, outside "with his horses and with his chariot," was angry that Elisha did not pay deference to him: "Behold, I thought, He will surely come out to me, and stand, and call on the name of the Lord his God." Besides, Naaman further objects, "Are not Abana and Pharpar, rivers of Damascus, better than all the waters of Israel? may I not wash in them, and be clean? So he turned and went away in a rage" (vv. 9, 11–12). Naaman's humble servant, knowing the Lord was speaking through his prophet, counseled him, saying, "If the prophet had bid thee do some great thing, wouldest thou not have done it? how much rather then, when he saith to thee, Wash, and be clean? Then went he down, and dipped himself seven times in Jordan, according to the saying of the man of God . . . and he was clean" (vv. 13–14).

Pride stands in the way of hearing the voice of the Lord. We so easily get caught up in what we think we need and what we think we want. We have a tendency to give a wish list to the Lord and expect our soft-spoken demands to be met. We want the water to be smoother, we want the wind more calm, and we want to be called to serve in a big name river. Listening suggests otherwise. Humility and meekness are manifest in "Thy will be done."

For the most part, it is a still, small voice that we hear. Elijah's experience in 1 Kings is our model: "And he said, Go forth, and stand upon the mount before the Lord. And, behold, the Lord passed by, and a great and strong wind rent the mountains, and brake in pieces the rocks before the Lord; but the Lord was not in the wind: and after the wind an earthquake; but the Lord was not in the earthquake: And after the earthquake a fire; but the Lord was not in the fire: and after the fire a still small voice" (1 Kings 19:11–12). The secret is to have ears to hear.

The still, small voice can be heard above the noise of the crowd or in the quiet of our silent prayers. It can catch our attention when we're thinking about something else or sound so loud that we will change direction and go another way. It is a miracle, really, one that reminds us who we are because of who is talking and who we will become if we will listen. The world may march on Washington crying loudly for attention, but the still, small voice speaking to the hearts of the Saints will have a far greater impact.

We usually associate Brigham Young with the call to come to Zion. His own call to the Restored Church came by the prompting of the Spirit. Samuel Smith, brother of the Prophet Joseph Smith, first introduced Brigham to the gospel, but the Lion of the Lord, as he would be known, wrestled two years for his own witness of the truth. How long do we keep on listening?

Brigham Young's answer and witness finally came through the simple testimony of a humble missionary, Eleazer Miller, a man whom Brigham described as being "without eloquence . . . who could only say, 'I know, by the power of the Holy Ghost, that the Book of Mormon is true, that Joseph Smith is a Prophet of the Lord.'" Said Brigham Young of that defining moment, "The Holy Ghost proceeding from that individual illuminated my understanding, and light, glory, and immortality were before me."[5]

President Gordon B. Hinckley, when being set apart as a stake president, was counseled by Elder Harold B. Lee to listen for the still, small voice. President Hinckley recalls, "I remember only one thing he said: 'Listen for the whisperings of the Spirit in the middle of the night, and respond to those whisperings.' I don't know why revelation comes sometimes in the night, but it does. It comes in the day as well, of course. But listen to the whisperings of the Spirit, the gift of revelation, to which you are entitled."[6]

And that leads us to the third truth: Hearing the voice, we must hearken.

Twenty-seven years ago, a fresh graduate from college, I was preparing to leave for a prestigious journalism program in the East. It seemed to be the next logical step in my life. I had been the editor of my college newspaper and an intern with the *Wall Street Journal*. Frankly, I was a news junkie, and I was on the cutting edge of opportunities opening for women in all professions, the media in particular.

So there I was, sitting in the living room of my home, reading a newsmagazine. I will always remember that day, 4 September 1971. In my journal I wrote: "Today I read an article about Gloria Steinem [a political columnist]. She was on the cover of *Newsweek*. . . . I read the whole article, becoming more and more convinced I want to be just like her. Respected, influential, famous. And rich. To top it all off, she's beautiful."

My entry then takes a turn. "While I was sitting on the couch thinking about Gloria Steinem, her picture staring up at me from the cover, a voice spoke to me, a voice through my thoughts that said, 'That's how the Devil gets to people like you; he leads them away from the work of the Lord.'"

That unexpected thought so startled me that I got up from my mother's cozy blue couch and left the room. Later, settled in a long, hot bath, I was back to reading *Newsweek* and planning a career worthy of a cover story. Again I heard in my mind the quiet voice, the same words, the same caution, "That's how the Devil gets to people like you; he leads them away from the work of the Lord."

What I had heard was a personal revelation from the Lord. *Heard* is the appropriate verb: I heard but did not hearken. The next day I got in the car and drove east. Alma's counsel to the people applied to me, "A shepherd hath called after you and is still calling after you, but ye will not hearken unto his voice!" (Alma 5:37). Three days later I knew I had done the wrong thing, but it took months to get the courage to hearken.

Peter jumped over the side of the boat and walked on water. I got in the car and drove the interstate to Washington, D.C., to attend graduate school in journalism. "My sheep hear my voice . . . and follow me" sometimes begins by first going the other way.

The fourth truth: What we often hear is how to help others.

We've had thoughts or impressions come to us—call, go visit, say this, write a note, bear testimony of Jesus Christ. There's no question where such promptings come from; there's no question how we feel when we respond. We are all busy; the question is, Busy doing what?

A *Christmas Carol* by Charles Dickens shows clearly the folly of thinking only of ourselves. As you remember, Jacob Morley comes back as a
ghost on Christmas Eve to warn his partner Scrooge of his misguided
ways. The ghost laments, "I cannot rest, I cannot stay, I cannot linger
anywhere . . . ; and weary journeys lie before me!"

"'But you were always a good man of business, Jacob,' faltered Scrooge.

"'Business!' cried the ghost, wringing his hands. . . . 'Mankind was my
business. The common welfare was my business; charity, mercy, forbear-
ance, and benevolence, were, all, my business. The dealings of my trade
were but a drop of water in the comprehensive ocean of my business.'"[7]

Last spring I rushed into Relief Society just before the meeting was to
begin. I sat down next to Eileen, new to the ward and the wife of our
home teacher. She smiled at me and asked, "How are you today?" It was a
stressful time at the Swinton home. Two or three deadlines behind, I was
heavily cumbered. I wondered momentarily how honest I could be with
Eileen. I smiled and said, "You know, I am at the point where I simply am
going to start buying socks because I don't have the time to wash them,
and I will never have time to match them."

She looked at me startled. She had on the tip of her tongue the usual,
"Oh, that's nice." But I hadn't answered, "Fine," so she just stammered
"Oh," and then the opening hymn began and we got caught up in the
meeting.

The next morning my husband got a phone call at his office. It was
Eileen. "I don't know what's going on at your house right now," she said,
"but I am going to bring dinner to you every night this week. Will six
o'clock be all right?"

Now I know Eileen is as busy as everybody else, but amazingly, that
night and every night for a week, dinner showed up at the Swintons. I
told the boys not to eat it all at once. We needed leftovers. And I needed
the message Eileen brought me—that the Lord was mindful of me. If we
are listening only for promptings about our own lives, we may miss a message sent to someone else by way of us. That kind of listening—Eileen's
kind—means attending to the second great commandment, "Love thy
neighbor as thyself."

Christ knows us. But he may not calm our troubled waters. He didn't
calm the seas for Peter. But he did reach out to him. Think about it.
When we respond to the voice of the Lord, do we only listen for those
things we want to hear? Those things that fit our needs as we see them,

that solve only our problems as we understand them? Do we ask, "Make things easier"? And when he doesn't, do we say, "He isn't there!"? Or worse, "He doesn't care"?

It's fair to say life is hard. Not long ago, the members of the Church celebrated the strength and fortitude of the pioneers who came west to build Zion. They gathered in Kirtland, hearing "Come." They gathered in Missouri and were forced to leave. They settled in Nauvoo and were driven again.

The Lord used those hardships to prepare a people, build them into a force, and teach them to hear his voice inviting, "Come." Their destination was not Salt Lake; it was celestial glory. The experience of Laleta Dickson, a member of the tragic Willie Handcart Company trapped in the early snows of winter, moves me deeply. "When morning came, Father's body, along with the others who had died during the night, was buried in a deep hole. Brush was thrown in and then dirt. A fire was built over the grave to kill the scent to keep the wolves from digging up the remains. I can see my mother's face as she sat looking at the partly conscious group. Her eyes looked so dead that I was afraid. She didn't sit long, however. . . . When it was time to move out, Mother had her family ready to go. She put her invalid son in the cart with her baby and we joined the train. Our mother was a strong woman, and she would see us through anything."[8]

I have stood on the harsh Wyoming hillside at Rock Creek where her father is buried and felt the chill of the wind as it whips across that rugged landscape. How did they press forward? The Lord speaks of these courageous women in latter-day revelations when he says, "For mine elect hear my voice and harden not their hearts" (D&C 29:7).

How do we do that? By turning to Christ, for he has promised us, "I will go before your face. I will be on your right hand and on your left, and my Spirit shall be in your hearts, and mine angels round about you, to bear you up" (D&C 84:88).

Another truth, the fifth: We are never alone. Not here, not now, not tomorrow. We've heard the promise, "Draw near unto me and I will draw near unto you" (D&C 88:63). There can be no greater sensitivity to our every need nor any greater succor.

In the center of Salt Lake City are nine stakes in what is called the Inner City, part of the Pioneer Welfare Region. It's an urban area filled with challenges. This past year, part-time missionaries from fifty-six surrounding stakes have been called as Inner City missionaries to provide help with home and visiting teaching and to teach welfare principles of self-reliance. Into this band of now more than two hundred missionaries was called a bank executive and his wife to help a bishop of a ward near the freeway in an industrial part of town.

Jump over the side of the boat. They heard the call.

The young bishop, with only ten active Melchizedek priesthood holders in his ward, gave the couple eight families to visit. The couple, a dignified man used to wearing a cashmere coat and his equally elegant wife, went to the first home. This family had a father in jail, sons in a detention center, and a mother struggling to find work and care for her small children. The missionary couple were at a loss how to help. In the next family, the story was similar. And so on through a handful on their list. They went back to the bishop, and the husband said, "We can't help these people. I'm a banker. I'm good at financial and estate planning. I can help with tax issues. These people don't need me. Don't you have someone I could really help?"

The bishop looked at them. I can imagine his silent plea, "Don't walk away from us. We can't make it without you." He said, "I prayed about your assignments and those were the names that came. Give it two more weeks. See if there isn't something you can do." Then, almost as an afterthought, he said, pointing to the list of names, "Have you been to see this sister?" The man shook his head. "She's in the hospital. Her leg was amputated. Would you go see her for me?"

The missionary couple went to the hospital and into the woman's room. She was asleep, so they sat down by her bed to wait. She eventually stirred and woke to see two strangers. "The bishop sent us," the banker said, trying to reassure her. She began to weep. After a moment, through tears she explained, "I went to sleep with a prayer in my heart. I am so alone. I feel so desperate. I told the Lord I couldn't go on— didn't want to. I said to him, 'If the bishop would just send someone . . .'" That couple left the hospital with new ears.

Hearing the voice of the Lord is a witness to us that he lives. This is the sixth and most important truth of all. To come to know Jesus Christ we must serve him with whole-souled devotion.

Mary, when visited by the angel, said, "Behold the handmaid of the Lord; be it unto me according to thy word." She went to Elizabeth who, filled with the Holy Ghost, "spake out with a loud voice, and said,

Blessed art thou among women, and blessed is the fruit of thy womb" (Luke 1:38, 42).

What of Mary Magdalene at the tomb where she said, "They have taken away my Lord, and I know not where they have laid him." And then later in the garden, "Jesus saith unto her, Woman, why weepest thou? whom seekest thou? She, supposing him to be the gardener, saith unto him, Sir, if thou have borne him hence, tell me where thou hast laid him, and I will take him away.

"Jesus saith unto her, Mary." I love that part. I can hear kindness and care in his voice. "She turned herself, and saith unto him, Rabboni; which is to say, Master" (John 20: 13, 15–16).

Joseph Smith was introduced to the Savior in the Sacred Grove. "This is My Beloved Son. Hear Him!" (Joseph Smith–History 1:17). Listen to him, said our Father in Heaven. Follow him. The magnitude of that moment is staggering. Our Father in Heaven visited this earth to intro-duce Jesus Christ to the world, to those who would listen. Think what that means. We focus keenly on Joseph Smith receiving that vision. But for what purpose? So that we, too, would listen and would know our Lord and Savior's voice.

His voice is often in scriptures. I use my scriptures, in part, as a journal of revelations to me. I write in the margin the date that a specific verse touched me or answered a longing to know. I will note a name or an experience so I can remember the context. Isaiah 43:2–3 has a host of dates by it: "When thou passest through the waters, I will be with thee; and through the rivers, they shall not overflow thee: when thou walkest through the fire, thou shalt not be burned; neither shall the flame kindle upon thee. For I am the Lord thy God, the Holy One of Israel, thy Saviour."

And this one: "Woe to them that go down to Egypt for help; and stay on horses and trust in chariots, because they are many; and in horsemen, because they are very strong; but they look not unto the Holy One of Israel, neither seek the Lord!" (Isaiah 31:1). There's no question what the Lord is saying: This is my beloved Son. Hear Him, not the choruses of the world. Listen to Jesus Christ. He will help us find peace and comfort. He will be our strength and our compass. Listening is an expression of our faith.

As I stood by the side of my son's grave in the cemetery, his tiny blue casket surrounded by flowers, I was aware of gathered family and friends, their sorrow so apparent. That day my husband and I were being asked to turn, to hearken, and most of all to believe. During the delivery, Christian had suffered from a brain hemorrhage, and tests had shown that the damage was severe. "He will never be able to run and walk like his twin brother may," the doctors had informed my husband at the hospital across town from mine where he held vigil over our newly born sons, "but we may be able to keep him alive." Jeff asked if there was somewhere he could go to be alone. They showed him to a small office. He was "out on the water." He knelt and poured out his feelings to his Father in Heaven. He spoke of our righteous hopes for a family and then he said, "But if Christian's work is done, we are ready to accept that." He walked out of the office and over to the isolette where Christian lay. The signal on the heart monitor flattened out. Christian had heard the voice as did Peter, "Come." Come all the way home.

Several days later in the cemetery, we heard the voice of the Lord in our hearts—a still, small voice spoke of peace and a promise found in John, "Peace I leave with you, my peace I give unto you: not as the world giveth, give I unto you. Let not your heart be troubled, neither let it be afraid" (John 14:27).

I bear testimony of this sixth and ultimate truth: Jesus Christ "the good shepherd giveth his life for the sheep" (John 10:11). He set forth his gospel; he took upon himself our sins. By him, through him, because of him and his atoning sacrifice, we may receive eternal life and exaltation. I believe with all my heart that my Redeemer lives. He is the Son of God, the Redeemer of the world, the Savior of all his Father's children. I have heard his voice and recognize his call to each one of us: Come. Come all the way home.

Notes

1. Brigham Young, *Discourses of Brigham Young*, sel. John A. Widtsoe (Salt Lake City: Deseret Book, 1941), 431.
2. Young, *Discourses*, 41.
3. Joseph F. Smith, as quoted in Joseph Fielding Smith, *Origins of the Reorganized Church* (pamphlet), (Salt Lake City: Deseret News Press, 1909).
4. See Ezra Taft Benson, *I Know That My Redeemer Lives* (Salt Lake City: Deseret Book, 1990), 203.
5. *Brigham Young*, Teachings of Presidents of the Church Series (Salt Lake City: The Church of Jesus Christ of Latter-day Saints, 1997), 315.
6. Gordon B. Hinckley, *Teachings of Gordon B. Hinckley* (Salt Lake City: Deseret Book, 1997), 556.

7. Charles Dickens, *A Christmas Carol* (New York: Stewart, Tabori & Chang, 1990), 33–34.
8. Laleta Dickson's History of William James of the Willie Handcart Company, Archives of The Church of Jesus Christ of Latter-day Saints, 1856, n.p.; spelling and grammar standardized.

LEARNING IS NURTURE

Emma Lou Thayne

$\mathcal{S}$omething every one of us will eventually deal with is the fear of aging. Even as one who is well into the delicate ruin, I would like to announce that I like *now*. Every day is a new awakening and a new chance at something I've never experienced. I'm convinced that life is indeed a stage and is made up of stages. Out of those stages comes learning.

Remember the wonderful Lily who says in a Maurice Chevalier movie of long ago, "You don't learn; you just get older, and you know." So true. In getting older you come to know a lot, most of it enriching, some of it not so. In the *Deseret News* recently there was a telling Small Society cartoon on the editorial page. Bill Yates's two little globby figures say, one to the other, "The only happiness I can seem to find anymore is finding my glasses soon enough to remember why I wanted them."[1] I had 20/20 eyesight till I was forty-five. Now I'm into trifocals—and seeing just fine.

Things happen along the way. Things just happen. And we're all having them happen to us, no matter what stage we're in. The secret is to learn from them. What is learning? education? What is it that attracts us to any learning? To me, it's *nurture*. I love the word *nurture*. Nurture is feeding; nurture is faith; nurture is learning, education. It can be what frees me from fear—at any stage.

Education turns my leaves green, brings my blossoms out, and allows me the full measure of my creation. I have to know a lot of things before I am free to do many things. My formal education freed me to receive nurturing from books. Now, at age sixty-four, I need my glasses to be free to receive that nurturing.

Still, beyond any aging and for all the credence I would give to formal education, it takes dealing with life to really teach us—the handling of the things that just happen to happen. In this nurturing, this discovering,

Emma Lou Thayne earned her B.A. and M.A. degrees from the University of Utah and taught part-time in the English department there for more than three decades. Her extensive publications include ten books as well as poetry and articles in many periodicals; her novel *Never Past the Gate* was a New York Book Club selection. She and her husband, Melvin E. Thayne, are the parents of five daughters.

this becoming familiar with, this never losing touch with what nurtures us, the constant growth ingredient has to be, "I want to know more." I need to *expect* in order to be educated, to be taught, to be filled. I have to have a prepared mind that says, "I wonder." What a gift, the ability to wonder. Not doubt, but wonder. Think what that persuades me to pursue—an education indeed.

About formal education. Yes, I did go back for a master's degree in creative writing, when our youngest daughter started school. I had been teaching part-time, one class a quarter, three hours a week, for most of thirty years. I had loved it! When we had five little girls under ten, teaching had given me a touch with the adult world, and I came back to my children better able to talk their language, having talked a grown-up tongue for even a little while.

During those hectic years we had unwed mothers from Relief Society Social Services live in our home. We were selected together as a match, our family and each of those young women, and they took creative care of things while I was gone. Since theirs had been a temptation I had not had to confront, I had been a moral snob, thinking, why didn't they just say no? But I found they were wonderful people, friends. And oh, did I learn from them—humility, understanding, graciousness, pain. They taught our children much about nurturing that I might never have known enough to teach.

Over the years, as I had had the fun of teaching those students—and oh, it was fun—I decided that when our youngest, Megan, started first grade, I would go back to school. I did—at age forty-five and scared to death. Talk about fear. I'd been colleagues with the people in the department, and all of a sudden I was going to be one of their students, writing in bluebooks and meeting all the terrifying demands that I'd been inflicting on other students all those years.

But I made a quite lovely discovery in going back. My fears were not grounded. I had learned in those twenty-five years out of school. I had learned a lot. As the poet Rilke says, all the things that I lavish myself on, grow rich and lavish me. I had lavished myself on my home, on my Church work, on the General Board, on whatever was happening in our neighborhood. On a tennis court, on friends, sometimes on people very unlike me, on my children, my family, my husband, I had lavished me and loved it. And it all came back to lavish me.

As I sat in my first class—Shakespeare—I listened to Dr. Harold

Folland talk about such things as Aristotelian unities and I thought, Did I ever know this? Petrified, I found that the bright young minds around me knew a lot more of some things than I did. But, oh, I knew some very important things, too, one of which was that I wanted to learn. As an undergraduate I had received a lot out of college that had much more to do with sociability than studying, and I'd bluffed my way through lots of tests. Now, as a graduate student, I was one of the "old alumni in tennis shoes" that we had moaned about when we were undergraduates—they were so intense!

Here I was, sitting in class, drinking it up, loving it. I remember my first trip to the library. I had all that space in a day—nobody coming home for lunch, nobody needing me. I had from nine to three—that's *six* hours to play. In that library I thought, hey, lady, you've got it all. I could go anywhere and pull any book off the shelf and read it and stay with it and talk about it and think about it. I was a rich woman.

I learned a lot in that formal education—my thesis, a collection of poems, was my first published book—at age forty-six. But along the way, in my anything but formal education, I had learned a lot from people, especially from the people I worked with in various capacities. Oh my, I had been fed! And it all came home when I took it to school.

I had learned a lot and I have learned more since about silence and solitude for nurturing. There were years when I felt totally accompanied with five little people. From room to room and wall to wall, even in the bathroom. What mother doesn't know the story? Silence and solitude were never mine. Unless I stayed up all night one night a week, which I did. Or I worked on my writing and projects between 11 P.M. and 3 A.M. when the rest of the house was quiet.

Stillness not only can give me acquaintance with where I am but lets me know what I have learned. I like to think what Neruda said when he accepted the Nobel Prize for his poetry: "I have always found somewhere the necessary affirmation, the formula which lay waiting for me, not to be petrified in my words, but to explain me to myself."[2]

Only in stillness did I find that affirmation and explaining, because then I could write. Write in a journal, at best. My friends, get it down, think about it, filter it out, all that keeps happening and happening. Let it appear on the page like invisible ink and tell you where you are and who you are and how you feel. Then feel cleansed and clarified for having found the stillness in yourself.

By that writing for school, I learned and was nurtured in my home, in my work. And most of all, I have learned and been nurtured by prayer and meditation to find the ultimate nourishment that has always come in the night. My mother's adage, "Pray at night; plan in the morning" has been as natural as breathing.

To be truly nourished, I must allow everything that happens to me to be assimilated—not only ingested but assimilated—if it is to be of value to me. If it is going to turn knowledge into wisdom, it has to work itself inside me and find a place. Theodore Roethke says it:

> I wake to sleep, and take my waking slow.
> I learn by going where I have to go.[3]

If I pay attention, I do learn by going where I have to go.

I had an accident two and a half years ago. Early on a Saturday morning, I was driving home on the freeway with a son-in-law. We had been camping with his family and my husband, and the two of us had to get back early, he to the hospital where he was a resident surgeon and I to help a friend who was having a party for her daughter.

We were driving up past Provo, almost to Murray. I was looking down, reading to him from the manual about how the car worked. We were driving my husband's new car that had multiple buttons on the dashboard, and we were laughing and trying them all out.

It was lucky that I was looking down. Without warning there was a crash, like a shot. I didn't see or know anything except that suddenly my hand was at my eye and was full of blood. I said, "Jim, I've been hit." I looked at the windshield, and there was a gaping hole. Glass was all over my lap. I said, "What hit me?"

Jim looked around and saw lodged in the back window a huge piece of metal, like an L-shaped crowbar. He said, "Grey, you'll never believe what hit you." It turned out to be the six-pound metal shaft that holds a mud flap on a big rig. It had fallen off and somehow gotten airborne and come through the windshield. We were going sixty-five miles per hour. It hit my face, missing my eye by a centimeter, then hit my temple and flew into the back window.

If you want to have an accident like that, you want to be riding with your plastic surgeon son-in-law. He got us to the hospital, to emergency, by going ninety miles per hour with his flashers on. Everybody—policemen, reporters, doctors—said, "Impossible. Nobody could have survived."

I never lost consciousness. I never was afraid. I never cried. Weeks later I began trying to understand what had happened to me in that time. It was a learning that I needed, and it was probably the most precious learning I've ever had. I had eight fractures in my face. Surgeons had to move my eyeball to operate, to screw my broken cheek and forehead to metal plates, most of the surgery done up through my mouth so the scars wouldn't show.

But scarring was the least of my worries. I wanted to be alive and able to read, to put my face down to do my work, to jiggle and run and hug. Reading had been my access my whole entire life. But for seven months I couldn't read; I couldn't bounce; I couldn't move fast. I couldn't lean my head down, so I couldn't write. I couldn't do any of the things I was used to doing.

But, oh, did I learn. I learned that the greatest learning of all comes from inside and is proffered always from a divine hand—if we pay attention. I remember Jack Adamson, one of my mentors at the university, saying as he confronted getting older, "You know, I'm reading less and thinking more." And I thought, I get to do that now, Jack. It wasn't that my recovery was not without peril or that I didn't have times of real concern. It's been only in the last little while that I've been able to understand that accident and to write about it. But now I know that I had a death experience. I went somewhere and knew a feeling way beyond joy, but by choice, I came back without fear. It was a remarkable privilege, both the going and the coming. Since then I have sensed a light that occupies me. And I see more of it in other people, even more than I knew was there before. I had to slow down, be slowed down, to find the stillness that allows it to be.

And that light is accessible if we simply let ourselves be lavished by it. I go to sleep to find out what I'm thinking, and without ever an exception, I find out in the morning what I'm thinking and where I am. The answers are there and very real.

Yes, I think formal education is important, that it's valuable. But I don't think it is all there is. The thing we do learn as we grow older and are nurtured is that we can abide in that place of no fear. Graciously it is given, that peace, to move us through this stage and these phases with at least some equanimity—if we simply stay in touch with the light that I know is so availably there.

Years ago in 1965, when I was a young mother with all those little girls, I wrote a frail poem to end my first collection, which I quiveringly entered in the Utah State Fine Arts contest so long ago. Such faltering beginnings, long before any formal education in the writing of a poem. But I dug that collection up last year and made copies for each of my daughters for Mother's Day because they're all now at the stage that I was in then—each a young wife and mother. And each expectant and wondering and sometimes afraid.

SO COME, TOMORROW
Security is not in knowing
what will come
nor if it will be
bad or good.

It is a faith drawn taut
with having learned
and seen and done
that says, Tomorrow, come.

The absence of fear, the presence of faith. It has to be a little like the prayer our seven-year-old granddaughter ended with, "Thanks so much. We've had a good ol' time."

Yes, thanks so much to learning, to being nurtured by all that comes along at any stage, in any time.

Notes

1. Bill Yates, *Deseret News*, 5–6 April 1989, A-7.
2. Pablo Neruda, *Toward the Splendid City: Nobel Lecture* (New York: Farrar, Strauss, and Giroux, 1972), 17.
3. Theodore Roethke, "The Waking," in *Collected Poems* (Garden City, N. J.: Doubleday, 1966), 108.

WHEN OUR REACHING REACHES HIS

❦

M. Catherine Thomas

I am an adult child of an alcoholic father. My father has since given up alcohol, but what I experienced in my childhood family seemed to color every aspect of my life. I came out of that home with many confused and uncomfortable emotions, but I didn't know until I was about forty how my childhood experience had affected—and was continuing to affect—the emotional and spiritual quality of my life.

When I was nineteen, I joined the Church. Much of my healing began at that time. But though my conversion was real, and I came to have real spiritual experiences, some of my emotions continued to be at odds with gospel teachings, and I didn't know what to do about them. As a young mother, I felt that I was only barely keeping my anger and overall distress from leaking out. I had to struggle too much to be cheerful at home. Inside I was unaccountably angry, I was guilty, I was driven, and I was afraid. On the outside I was tense with my children. I was irritable and controlling. Sometimes I was also loving and patient, felt the Spirit of the Lord, and did parenting things well, but not as consistently as I needed to.

I have observed that if we don't learn consistent and mature love in our childhood homes, we have to struggle to learn it when we become marriage partners and parents. We may spin our spiritual wheels trying to make up for childhood's personal losses, looking for compensation in the wrong places and finding it very elusive. But of course the significance of spiritual rebirth through Jesus Christ is that we can mature spiritually and make up for those deprivations, in perhaps unexpected ways, through our Savior.

In those days I carried the big three sick emotions: Fear, Guilt, Anger.

M. Catherine Thomas received her doctoral degree from Brigham Young University in early Christian history and is an assistant professor of ancient scripture in Religious Education at BYU. She and her husband, Gordon K. Thomas of the BYU English Department, are the parents of six children. She has served as Relief Society president of the BYU Second Stake.

After I'd spent some nineteen years in motherhood, my children seemed to me like enemies, I was a workaholic, I was exhausted, I thought I didn't love my husband or anybody, and I had no idea where to go for help or even what help I needed. I was functioning, but my emotions were very brittle. I felt deeply hungry.

About one o'clock one morning when I was waiting for my teenager to come in way past the agreed-upon hour, for the ninety-ninth time, I found myself in my upstairs study, sobbing. I cried out from the bottom of my soul for deliverance from my indefinable distress. I heard the words very clearly, "Go home." The next morning I made arrangements to fly back to Ohio, to my parents' home, where my father had just finished an intensive rehabilitation program for recovering alcoholics. That drying-out process had gone on before, but this time there was a new development. The program reached out to help all the members of the alcoholic's family, because all members of such a family are sick and need help until they know who they are, why they feel as they do, and what to do about it.

Thus began the second great healing period for me. My life started to come together in a new harmony after I attended an orientation program for children of alcoholics. I read books on being an alcoholic child, I talked to alcoholics and other adult children of alcoholics, and I didn't stop praying.

Something I have learned since is that many people who did not come out of alcoholic families nevertheless suffer from the same kinds of distress I did. Apparently it doesn't matter what the manifest problem is in the child's family, but in a home where a child is emotionally deprived for whatever reason, that child will take some emotional confusion into adult life.

Children from families with emotional problems are often addicted to stimulation. Steady living is difficult for them and perceived as boring. This adult-child is always looking for a high—if not a chemical or substance high, then an emotional high through seeking ego satisfactions, or even stirring up trouble among loved ones. Therefore, she is restless and always trying to change her life. She is very me-centered, finding it difficult to keep a steady commitment to others and to maintain real interest in their well-being. This adult-child is always taking her own emotional temperature, asking herself if she is happy and fulfilled. The answer is usually no, because she doesn't know what happiness is. When the Savior told us that we would find our lives if we would lose them for his sake, he meant that it would help us to deflect our consciousness from ourselves to him and to those the Lord has given us to love and nurture. That is not to say that we shouldn't seek to do fulfilling things but that preoccupation with our own needs is a dead end. The purpose of life, I have found, is not that everything and everyone (especially my children and my husband) should satisfy me but that I could grow. I could enlarge my patience and my tolerance, deepen my humility, and heighten my sensitivity to the Spirit of God. I could recognize and activate the divine power in me to nurture happiness and emotional security in those around me. My preoccupation with my own distress had actually created abuse for my family. I appreciate so much the way my family relationships improved as I got better.

In my early days my mental sonar seemed to operate relentlessly, searching out certain types of thoughts to dwell on, such as self-debasement, despair, anger, feeling unwell, self-pity. I did not then see the relationship between this mental sinning and my unsatisfying life. I was looking for a magic wand, even a priesthood wand, to solve everything right now. But there are no instant cure-alls. There is only the work that goes into repentance, the spiritual exertion that develops the new habits which soon bear the fruit of peace (see Alma 33:33; D&C 6:36).

I learned that I had to take responsibility for my own thought patterns: they were a key. I began to use what I found was a powerful agency to interrupt the thoughts that led me into emotional trouble. That is, I found new ways to deal briefly with bad thoughts or memories, to give to the Lord what hurt too much to carry around, to humble myself more deeply when I felt so below standard. I found I could interrupt critical thoughts about my children and my husband and replace them deliberately with mental images of oneness. I practiced a lot of forgiveness. I learned to let go of things that hurt me. I learned that the Lord would cause things that were important to come together right for me. I could quit manipulating events and stop trying to control people (see Romans 8:28; D&C 90:24).

Recovering alcoholics recognize what they call "stinking" thinking. If they want to get well and understand what the Lord's rest is, they have to repent of bad mental habits: fear, self-pity, self-condemnation, bad memories, unforgiveness, certain kinds of fantasizing. I found I did not have this power fully in myself to reshape and heal my mind, but Christ did.

I learned that my spiritual superficiality had been betraying me. On the outside I was going to church, teaching, paying tithing, and so on, but inside, I was allowing mental sinning. I learned that the real work of living the gospel begins in the microdots of the mind, in planting mental virtue deeply, in keeping my mind firm (see Alma 57:27; Jacob 3:1–2). What we sow in our minds and actions, we reap in our emotions. So, we cease searching for that elusive self-fulfillment and consciously, deliberately, give to others what we, ourselves, hunger for most. "For that which ye do send out shall return unto you again, and be restored" (Alma 41:15).

Essentially, I have described here my discovery of Jesus. Not one of my distresses has been outside his consciousness or power. When I have done as he has instructed, especially in keeping my mind firm, my reaching has reached his.

CHOICES AND
THE HOLY GHOST

⟨✳⟩

Shirley W. Thomas

*I*n a letter dated 5 December 1839, the Prophet Joseph Smith and Church historian Elias Higbee wrote to the high council in Nauvoo from Washington City, as it was then called, to report on their visit with the president of the United States, Martin Van Buren. They were seeking redress for wrongs suffered by the saints in Missouri. In part the letter read: "In the most honorable cause that ever graced the pages of human existence . . . we have taken up our cross. . . . Arrived . . . 28th November, and spent the most of that day in looking [for] . . . as cheap boarding as can be had in this city."[1] Reading that they had to spend time looking for the cheapest boarding in town makes me feel tender about them but not sorry for them. They were on the Lord's errand and filled with his Spirit; that's not a piteous state.

The letter continued: "On Friday morning, 29th, we proceeded to the house of the President . . . a very large and splendid palace . . . decorated with all the fineries and elegancies of this world. We went to the door and requested to see the President, when we were immediately introduced into an upper apartment, where we met the President." They next described the meeting, in which they showed remarkable poise at President Van Buren's prompt rebuff: "'What can I do? I can do nothing for you.'" They wrote, "We were not to be intimidated; and demanded a hearing [before the Congress], and constitutional rights."[2] The confidence of those two, lacking as they did training or experience in matters of politics or state, witnesses how decisive one can be when accompanied with the power of the Spirit.

Then, in a long postscript to the letter, Joseph Smith recorded an interesting statement about the Holy Ghost. Answering President

Shirley W. Thomas has served as second counselor to Barbara B. Smith in the Relief Society General Presidency and as a member of the Relief Society General Board. She and her husband, Robert K. Thomas, former academic vice-president at Brigham Young University, are the parents of three children.

550

Van Buren's question of how the Latter-day Saint religion differed from other churches of the day, Joseph said, "We differed in mode of baptism, and the gift of the Holy Ghost by the laying on of hands. We considered that all other considerations were contained in the gift of the Holy Ghost."[3] That is an unusual expression of breadth in the role of the Holy Ghost. Joseph understood that the Holy Ghost plays a crucial part in bringing to our finite world of decision making the infinite verities of truth and love. "Yea, by the unspeakable gift of the Holy Ghost," says the scripture, "God shall give unto you knowledge by his Holy Spirit" (D&C 121:26).

The Holy Ghost is also a means for the Father to stay close to us. As the Spirit touches our lives, the truth he conveys bears witness of the Father's love. Making the right decisions matters. God wants us to succeed. He wants us to return to him. And the Holy Ghost is our great ally. He sheds the light of truth on decisions we face, until right choices become clear.

We get an idea of the importance of this truth to us and how determined the Almighty is that we have it in his emphatic and reassuring statement to a discouraged Joseph Smith in Liberty Jail: "As well might man stretch forth his puny arm to stop the Missouri river in its decreed course, or to turn it up stream, as to hinder the Almighty from pouring down knowledge from heaven upon the heads of the Latter-day Saints" (D&C 121:33).

Elder Marion G. Romney counseled the women of the Relief Society: "Learn to recognize and follow the guidance of the Holy Spirit. Without such guidance, even a knowledge of the word of God is unfruitful. . . . Properly cultivated and developed, this gift is of inestimable value. . . . [It] will enlighten our minds, quicken our understandings, and increase our intelligence."[4]

I needed all these—light, understanding, and intelligence—when at age fifteen I was deciding whether to be baptized into the Church. I lacked the advantage of attending Primary to learn about the Holy Ghost and choosing the right. Also, because my association with the Church was through friendshipping efforts of members and at that time not every stake seemed to have missionaries, I missed receiving missionary discussions and did not have an acquaintance with the Book of Mormon, either. But I did, finally, have the permission of both my parents to become a member of the Church if I chose to. I wanted to know if the Church was true, but I did not hear a resounding *yes*. I received no impression or answer that I could call certain, but I had a good feeling about going to the church, a sense of being at home. I believed what I was learning there and liked the way I felt when I was with the members. I wanted to be one with them. So I chose to be baptized, and I didn't ever wonder again about the Church being true. I knew that it was. I have since learned that the Holy Ghost's quiet persuasion was what led me to baptism and witnessed to me the truth of the gospel.

I find important meaning in the scripture, "Rejoice, and cleave unto the covenants which thou hast made" (D&C 25:13). In the covenant of baptism, for example, we commit to following Christ, to being called by his name, and we are given a wondrous source of eternal truth, the Holy Ghost. In such covenants we can sense the heart of our Father in Heaven. He wants for his children all he can give, and so he grants them individual agency, despite the jeopardy that poses for them. Then, to bring about their safe passage through earth life, he establishes covenants. He wants us to return, and covenants, by defining the way of holiness and our commitment to it, form a protection against the power of evil.

I learned through the experience of coming to baptism that the Holy Ghost often manifests truth through good feelings. That may be the most common way—the response we usually call the feeling of peace, of accord. Moroni 7:16 states: "I show unto you the way to judge; for every thing which inviteth to do good, and to persuade to believe in Christ, is sent forth by the power and gift of Christ; wherefore ye may know with a perfect knowledge it is of God." The inviteth-to-do-good feeling is a useful guide.

After I had been a member of the Church nearly four years, I had a much different experience in making an important decision. At this time, I was a sophomore at Brigham Young University, sitting at my desk in Amanda Knight Hall writing a letter to a young lieutenant in the Air Force. I was telling him that I had approval from my parents to stay a day or two in California with my aunt en route home from school that spring. He was posted at nearby Santa Ana Air Base. He was a very nice Latter-day Saint young man whom I had met and dated the year before while I was home for Christmas. We had since been corresponding, a typical wartime friendship. As I was writing this letter, I received a message from the Spirit—in words. Often messages come to us in what we call strong feelings, but this message came in distinct, clearly defined words: "He is not the right one for you."

I had not known that could happen, and if I had, I certainly would not have expected it to happen to me. I dropped my pen, stopped writing, and never wrote to him again. (It would have been nice to have written something, but I didn't.) I was amazed. It was many years before I felt I could tell anyone about the experience. It was so personal, so singular, and so sacred. I have since heard of similar expressions of the Spirit, but it was new to me that day.

Although in the two instances I have shared with you the Holy Ghost manifested the truth differently, the truths in each case were equally valid. The decision made because of the quiet persuasion of a peaceful feeling following personal inquiry, weighing, "study[ing] it out in [my] mind" was as right as the one made because the Spirit intervened in what I was planning with a compelling, unmistakable direction that could not be misunderstood (D&C 9:8). Both reflected my need at the time; both were of eternal consequence. One decision was as right as the other. What's important is that we identify the Spirit, however it is manifest, and not only recognize it but act upon it. The marvel is that we can and do have the Spirit come to us. It is amazing to me that a member of the eternal Godhead can actually be a companion to me and to you. I don't even worry about the metaphysics of it. I have had experience enough to know that it is true, and as the hymn says, "I scarce can take it in."[5]

This same feeling of joyous surprise was shared with me by a dear sister many years ago after a sacrament meeting in the Hyde Park chapel in London. Her experience had to do with prayer. Deciding what to ask in our prayers is one of the important choices we have. Reading of the Nephite disciples of Jesus being given the words to pray suggests to us how the Holy Ghost has guided others (3 Nephi 19:24). That is sometimes called praying in the Spirit (D&C 46:28, 30).

That Sunday in London was in June 1978, the weekend of the announcement of the revelation on the priesthood. I happened to be in England on a Relief Society assignment. The lovely sister I spoke with was the mother of two boys of Aaronic Priesthood age. The

family was of African heritage. At the sacrament meeting, just finished, these two newly ordained priesthood holders had passed the
sacrament for the first time. The tearful mother was receiving expressions of love from the also-tearful ward members. They shared her joy.
Those two young men had faithfully attended priesthood meetings,
hoping for the day they could fully participate. I knew how faithfully
because one of our sons, participating in the BYU Semester Abroad in
London the year before, had taught the teachers quorum in the ward.
He had written from London to tell us about his class that each week
consisted of three boys, two of whom were the sons of this woman. He
had told us particularly of his admiration for the dedication and devotion of those two young men.

As the people in the foyer dispersed, the mother of the boys told
the small group remaining that only a few days before, as she was
praying, she had received the extraordinary invitation by the Spirit
that she might ask whatever she would like. With her eyes brimming,
she told us how overwhelmed she had been by the experience. She
had always tried to feel the direction of the Spirit in her prayers and
had never felt it appropriate to ask for the priesthood for her sons,
even though that had always been what she really wanted. Now, after
this experience was followed so soon by the announcement from
Church headquarters, she realized that while the revelation was for
the entire Church, the Lord acknowledged her individual hopes and
addressed them personally. The Holy Ghost had invited her to pray
for whatever she would like, knowing that this most important desire
could now be realized.

Although people have remarkable experiences with the Spirit,
most daily decisions we make are guided by peaceful feelings or by
promptings—the quiet workings of the Holy Ghost—still and small.
Many decisions must be made quickly, and for me, it is in these, with
the continual fine-tuning of my will to the Lord's that these require,
that I most often sense the companionship of the Holy Ghost. I have
learned to recognize the disruptive feeling that comes if I offend the
Spirit; I know quickly that something is wrong. As for the more
unusual manifestations, they are just that, unusual, and though we
cherish them, it may not be given us to ask for or even anticipate
them. President Spencer W. Kimball counseled that "expecting the
spectacular, one may not be fully alerted to the constant flow of

revealed communication."[6] Knowing the communication is constant prompts us to keep close to the Spirit, ready to receive. Elder Marion G. Romney said to the sisters, "Seek [the Holy Ghost] by faith and by prayer, by study, and by righteous living. Learn what the scriptures say about it, including, particularly, the teachings of the Prophet Joseph Smith."[7]

In the scriptures we learn of the breadth of the role of the Holy Ghost. Besides bringing wisdom, understanding, a sound mind, boldness, power, revelation, testimony, and healing, the Holy Ghost sanctifies (3 Nephi 27:20). When we are filled with the Spirit, we have no more disposition to choose anything contrary to the Lord's will; we purify our souls and yield our hearts unto God. That is not always easy.

Three years ago, one of our sons called to tell us they had just learned their oldest child, Sean, a handsome fourteen-year-old teacher in the Aaronic Priesthood, honor student, and Eagle Scout, had a brain tumor. I tried to finish vacuuming the floor I had been cleaning, but I kept stopping to plead with the Lord. My prayer went something like, "Surely, this can't be! There must be a mistake. Isn't there some other way? I know about thy Son, but that was such an important part of the plan, and there would seem to be nothing gained by this." After a long time there came the promised feeling of calm and a strong sense that it would be all right. I thought, Yes, Sean will be all right. I began to believe that it would just be a matter of time until he would be well again and shooting baskets on the driveway.

After the surgery and learning that the growth was actually larger than the image seemed to show and one grade more malignant than the doctors had at first believed, we had to realign our hopes. But maybe, I thought, they had been able to remove it all, and maybe the radiation would assure no tumor cell growth. For three years we watched and prayed. When each MRI (magnetic resonance imaging) gave a clear reading, we learned to hope that his would be one of the exceptional cases. I kept remembering the feeling I'd had.

Then in January the MRI was not clear. The tumor had returned. This time surgery was not possible, for the growth was too random. *Terminal* can be a terrifying word, but our son related this worst-case news, acknowledged our grief, and with an understanding born of faith and tried in pain, said, "Yes, it is hard," and then the words, *"but it's all right."*

What he and his wife had come to know, and what we all must, is that finally—and it may be in some of the most difficult of choices, the dearest of desires—our decision-making becomes acceptance. We come closer to Christ and, yielding our hearts, want only what is God's will. We may still hope for a "ram in the thicket"—I do—yet we know that, by choice, we must give our hearts to God. I have learned that in even trying to do this, we can feel peace, and in the love conveyed by the Holy Spirit, we can "cleave unto the covenants which [we have] made" and "lift up [our] heart[s]" (D&C 25:13). As Joseph Smith wrote that day in the city of Washington, all other considerations are caught up in this unspeakable gift, which testifies to us of the truth of God's love.

Notes

1. Joseph Smith, *History of The Church of Jesus Christ of Latter-day Saints,* 2d ed. rev., ed. B. H. Roberts, 7 vols. (Salt Lake City: Deseret Book, 1960), 4:40.
2. Ibid.
3. Ibid., 4:42.
4. Marion G. Romney, "The Guidance of the Holy Spirit," *Relief Society Magazine,* February 1965, 90–91.
5. *Hymns of The Church of Jesus Christ of Latter-day Saints* (Salt Lake City: The Church of Jesus Christ of Latter-day Saints, 1985), no. 86.
6. Spencer W. Kimball, *Teachings of Spencer W. Kimball,* ed. Edward L. Kimball (Salt Lake City: Bookcraft, 1982), 457.
7. Romney, "Guidance of the Holy Spirit," 91.

WAITING IN STILLNESS

⌒⌒

Anna Tueller

*E*leven years ago this week, I turned twenty-two and faced a crisis of such magnitude that even now I cower at the memory. I was graduating from Brigham Young University in two weeks, and I was unmarried. I notice that you laugh. I suppose that after eleven years, I can almost laugh with you, but it was with no sense of humor or perspective that I faced that particular unknown, and on fast Sunday in April 1978, I left my student apartment determined to find a secluded spot where I could plead, pound, batter at the doors of heaven until I received some guidance. I went to the Joseph Smith Building and wandered for a long time in its labyrinthian hallways. I read recently that the university will be replacing that building because its design is so confusing, but at least for me that day it served as a fitting symbol of my fear, perplexity, and uncertainty. I found an unoccupied room and for several hours pleaded, wept, and prayed, "Tell me what to do. Show me thy will. Make the fear go away. Please make it all better. Send me a man." Somehow, in spite of all my contradictory instructions, I felt the presence of the Spirit very clearly. In fact, its manifestation that day was very tangible. I was enfolded by strong, loving arms and heard or felt a voice that said, "It's going to be okay, Anna." I left that room comforted, energized, and motivated. I sailed through the last two weeks of my college career. In fact, I was notified within days of that bleak Sunday morning that I had received a fellowship for graduate school that would pay all my tuition and living expenses until I completed a Ph.D. During those two weeks, I was also asked to speak at the graduation convocation. The despair of that early Sunday morning disappeared easily and quickly in the midst of these laurels, and I was cocky and confident about my future.

In fact, I remember vividly the day after that graduation ceremony

---

Anna Tueller, a high school English teacher, received her bachelor of arts degree from Brigham Young University and her master of arts degree from the University of Virginia. She has taught English for five years in Morocco and Utah and is head of the Meridian School, a private school in Provo, Utah.

when I went to have all four of my wisdom teeth pulled. (It was what I had asked my parents to give me as a graduation gift.) I would like to attribute my delusions of grandeur that day to the laughing gas that the dentist administered—I couldn't possibly have been that naive—but as I sat in the chair, I confess that I saw the complete blueprint of my life: four years to a Ph.D., fame and fortune through my brilliant and scholarly research, tenure at a prestigious university, years of ease in the ivory tower, secure retirement. Indeed, I thought, it is going to be okay. Do I even need to rehearse the details of my well-deserved comeuppance, after describing the pride that went before the fall? Perhaps it is enough to say that my favorite poem during my graduate years at the University of Virginia was one by Robert Frost, the relevant lines of which are

> No memory of having starred
> Atones for later disregard
> Or keeps the end from being hard.[1]

The voice that whispered, "It's going to be okay," was not, as I had supposed, giving me a road map for my life. It comforted me, motivated me, energized me, and cleared the fog enough so that I could get on with the business of my life, but it was the business of my life, and it was for me to struggle and for me to decide and for me to wrestle with the decision to leave graduate school and to teach high school and to move to Washington, D.C., and then to move to Morocco and then to Boston and then back to Utah and now to . . . well, I keep on wrestling. And it is my salvation that I have to work out with fear and trembling. And during the passage of these eleven years, I have learned some things, I believe, about how the Spirit does not operate in our lives.

I have already suggested that the Spirit does not provide detailed instructions of paths to pursue. No matter how many times I read my patriarchal blessing, it does not contain directions to each and every destination, and, believe me, I have searched mine endlessly with all the expertise of an English teacher who can read something into nothing. Will you laugh at me when I confess my latest folly? The paragraph in my patriarchal blessing that promises me an eternal marriage with a righteous husband follows a paragraph that says that children will reach out to me and that I will teach and lead them. You can perhaps imagine how enthusiastically I accepted the calling to be Primary president two years ago; imagine, in turn, my chagrin when I was released from that same calling, only to discover that smooth, elegant transitions aren't any more sacred in patriarchal blessings than they are in my students' papers. Once again, I wanted a road map. I wanted the veil to be lifted, and I wanted to see my life set out before me, clearly defined, neatly arranged, and with no loose ends. How easily I forget that our corporeal existence includes separation from God, that the veil is an inherent part of the plan we joyously accepted, and that, in fact, without this veil to obscure the path back to him, we would be living a model of existence remarkably similar to one we deemed unacceptable and rejected. If we knew step by step, day by day, there would be no need for faith, no opportunity for growth, no chance for eternal life.

So the Spirit working in our lives is not a road map. Neither is it the host of *Let's Make a Deal*. We do not stand in front of three doors trying to second-guess a divine Master of Ceremonies. We will not be spending eternity with the gaggle of geese that we chose behind Door Number Three instead of with the dream vacation that we did not choose behind Door Number Two. Despite the outlandishness of that example, I think we often conceptualize the Spirit in this way. My younger sister Betsy, who has been home from her mission for about a year, recently repeated a conversation she had with several of her missionary companions. They were talking about marriage and their hopes and fears for the future. Betsy mentioned that she had two older, unmarried sisters, and one of her companions said, "Oh, but you don't need to worry about that; you went on a mission." Betsy is now engaged and will be married on May 12. Did I at some point stand in front of those three doors, choose the wrong one, and now live with my own, particular white elephant? I often feel that way about my life. I have many times microscopically examined my life, looking for that wrong turn that led to what too often appears to be a dead end. But I think I am wrong when I feel that way. In fact, I think it is destructive, dangerous, and damning. First, it ignores the spiritual confirmations that I have sought and received at each junction along the way. Second, it ignores the many promises that assure us that all things work together for good for those who love the Lord. Third, it negates the reality of repentance. I think, however, we are often tempted to try to make deals with the Spirit: "I will read my scriptures, do my genealogy, say my prayers, visit the sick, yea, even go to homemaking meeting and visit teach, and then, then, then I will get rich, get married, get well, get answers." The Spirit doesn't deal; it simply waits for us to be able to pray,

"Be it unto me according to thy will," not as I so often pray, "Be it unto me according to my will."

So how does the Spirit operate in our lives if it doesn't make deals or hand out road maps? (For I am convinced that we live in a world that is imbued with its power.) If it will not force us back to God, how do we feel its presence? I believe the Spirit cautions, confirms, cajoles, comforts, and cares. (And I am very proud of those alliterations.) How often I have felt the cautions. I call them "stupids of thought." For years I thought Doctrine and Covenants 9 really said "stupid" instead of "stupor," and recently I have decided that it should even if it doesn't. I feel those stupids of thought when the wrongness of a decision is demonstrated by my own lethargy and torpor, when my very inability to get out of my bed and throw away the junk food and the junk novel hints that perhaps movement in the direction I am considering would be wrong. Those moments are in direct contrast to those times when the Spirit confirms, when I have thought my path out in my own mind, earnestly sought for an answer, and reached a decision. On those occasions, lo and behold, I manage to arise from my bed, even make the bed, leave behind the chocolate chip cookie binge, and act. The miracle of that energy and renewal after the sloth, despair, and despondency, I have come to believe, is the Spirit confirming the rightness of the decision. And the Spirit cajoles, teasing our minds, bringing ideas, hints, nudges incessantly, unceasingly until we no longer ignore and begin to entertain the notion, when an idea just won't leave us alone until we take it seriously. And the Spirit comforts. In fact, above all else, I believe the Spirit is a Comforter. How often the Spirit is there healing the broken-hearted, giving rest to the weary, pushing us up one more mountain until we hit a valley, granting us a lull in the storm until we are ready to face it again with our usual gutsiness and tenacity, dispensing comfort and assurance that all is well, that it is going to be okay. And the Spirit cares, letting us know through a rain-washed spring day, through a speckled sunset, or through the gesture of a grateful student that we matter in this big, silent universe, that we are not alone, that if the journey seems long, it is not forever.

Often along this journey, the Spirit simply convinces us to wait, to be still. I teach a ninth-grade world literature class, and we often discuss journeys in that class. We trace archetypal journeys, those stories found so often in folktales and fairy-tales across the globe, stories of heroes who go out into the world and face dragons and temptations and trials, rescue princesses, descend into the depths of hell to get the silver chalice, and return to the world triumphantly to marry the princess and live happily ever after. I always start this class with *The Odyssey*, and I use Ulysses as the archetypal male hero who has all the exciting trials and adventures in his years of wandering and who then returns home to Ithaca victorious. When I began to teach this course five years ago, I also pointed out the inherent sexism of Western literature because while Ulysses is off adventuring, Penelope is home wasting time waiting until he returns. But my feelings about Penelope have undergone a radical change, and she is now a heroine of mine. Penelope is plagued with many suitors (poor, poor Penelope) who insist that Ulysses is dead and that she consider their proposals. They torment her so and become so rowdy and belligerent that she finally agrees to choose among them, but only after she has finished an elaborate tapestry. She diligently works on the tapestry all day, only to spend all night unraveling that same tapestry. I no longer believe that Penelope was wasting time; she was simply heeding the voice that whispered in the nighttime that her husband was alive and that she must wait. How often I make plans all day, only to unravel them in the silence of the night. How often I have plotted and planned, written resumes, filled out applications, made lists of people to contact, only to undo the plans because in the stillness of the night I have sensed that it is time to wait. Certainly, I believe that we will all have times in our life when we will be Ulysses, whom Tennyson describes as a man who seeks and strives and finds and never yields; we will have times when we flee the Lotus-eaters, combat Cyclops, and fight at the very gates of hell, and we will do all those things heroically, valiantly, strengthened by the Spirit. But there are other times when we are meant to wait, to be patient, to endure, to wonder, to question, to doubt. During those times, too, the Spirit is there, whispering peace, assuring us that it is going to be okay. I know this is true. I promise that it is going to be okay, that if we wait in stillness, we will hear the still, small voice.

Note

1. Robert Frost, "Provide, Provide," *The Poetry of Robert Frost*, ed. Edward Connery Lathem (New York: Holt, Rinehart, and Winston, 1969), 307.

WHY WE FORGIVE

༺∞༻

C. Terry Warner

*J*acob admonished his fellow Saints: "Look unto God with firmness of mind, and pray unto him with exceeding faith, and he will console you in your afflictions, and he will plead your cause" (Jacob 3:1). When the Lord came to earth, he fulfilled this promise in person: "And it came to pass that when he had thus spoken, all the multitude, with one accord, did go forth with their sick and their afflicted, and their lame, and with their blind, and with their dumb, and with all them that were *afflicted in any manner*; and he did heal them every one as they were brought forth unto him" (3 Nephi 17:9; italics added).

The world seems not to believe that he has such powers. In connection with one problem after another—depression, homosexuality, and abuse, to name only a few—I have, over the years, heard the solemn warning: This kind of challenge has nothing to do with spirituality or morality, righteousness or repentance. Only a scientific, professional approach has any hope of dealing with it. And yet when I have heard such talk, I have thought of the Source to whom we must look for healing and consolation in our afflictions. It is of him that I would like to speak.

I have read that Masai tribal doctors ask their patients not "Where do you hurt?" but "Whom have you wronged?" I do not know whether that is true, but it doesn't matter much if it isn't, for the same sentiment, pertaining to at least some afflictions, can be found in the scriptures. "My disciples, in days of old, sought occasion against one another and forgave not one another in their hearts; and for this evil they were afflicted and sorely chastened. Wherefore, I say unto you, that ye ought to forgive one another; for he that forgiveth not his brother his trespasses standeth condemned before the Lord; for there remaineth in him the greater sin. I,

C. Terry Warner received his doctorate in philosophy from Yale University. He has been a visiting senior member of Linacre College, Oxford, and has served as dean of the College of General Studies at Brigham Young University. He is bishop of a Provo, Utah, ward and is married to Susan Lillywhite Warner, a counselor in the Primary General Presidency. They are the parents of ten children.

the Lord, will forgive whom I will forgive, but of you it is required to forgive all men" (D&C 64:8–10).

This passage makes three amazing statements: First, when we refuse to forgive others, we do them wrong; we sin against them. Second, this refusal to forgive causes us, who do the wrong, affliction: we are sorely chastened for it. We suffer from doing wrong to others, as the Masai doctors are supposed to have said. Just how we suffer is an issue I will address later. Third, the Lord counts our refusal to forgive a greater sin than whatever trespass we are refusing to forgive. These truths can be restated in this simple maxim: "It is not the wrong that others do to us that harms us most, but the wrong we do to them."

We may resist these truths, especially if we have not yet fully forgiven those we believe have offended us. If I am unforgiving, I am certain my problems are the fault of those whom I refuse to forgive. "How false," I may argue in my heart, "to say *I'm* responsible for my unhappiness! And how unfair! For I just *know* that I'm the victim. I'm the one suffering. How can I be blamed if I'm the victim?" Many put forth this objection. Some push it to an extreme conclusion: "In effect, I am being told, If bad things have happened to you, it's your fault! What of those who suffered unspeakably in the Nazi death camps? What of children who undergo horrible abuse? What of any suffering at all? How can the victim be responsible?"

This argument distorts the passage quoted from Doctrine and Covenants 64. That scripture does not imply that we are responsible for the events that happen to us. It implies instead that we are responsible for how we respond to these events, for how we choose to let them affect us. Christ himself and Joseph sold into Egypt and Joseph Smith in Liberty Jail, great leaders eternally, suffered terribly without recrimination or resentment and so too have others less well known.[1] They sought no occasion in their hearts against their abusers but forgave, even in the very moment of their suffering. We have little to say about many of the events that befall us, but much to say about how we experience them, how we understand them, how they influence us.

This distinction miraculously opens up a bright window of opportunity, the opportunity of forgiveness. It permits us to remember wrongs done to us without believing they have damaged us irreparably, without feeling helpless or hopeless. We can remember those wrongs without retaliating in our hearts, without writhing in animosity and vengeance.

Forgiving, we avoid doing ourselves terrible harms. And repenting of our refusal to forgive, we put an end to such harms.

In a book subtitled *The Spiritual Advantages of a Painful Childhood*, Wayne Muller writes: "To let go of the ones who hurt us is to let go of our identity as the one who was hurt, the one who was violated, the one who was broken. It often feels like the bad guys are getting off scot-free while we are left holding the bag of pain. But forgiveness is not just for them. . . . Forgiveness . . . allows us to be set free from the endless cycle of pain, anger, and recrimination that keeps us imprisoned in our own suffering."[2]

Thus forgiveness transforms us in a marvelous way. It might be called an end of the worst, most damning kind of affliction, or, equally, the beginning of a journey that leads to the most exalted joy. The Savior's gift of himself makes this transformation possible. The price he paid for sin, including the greater sin of refusing to forgive, is infinite; and that means, among other things, that no suffering lies beyond his power to redeem, no sorrow cannot be turned into joy. That means—I put the case boldly—that even the worst horrors perpetrated by humankind, the death camp tortures, the abuse of innocent ones, scalding hatred toward the perpetrators—all can be redeemed on this simple condition: that the individual, *whether the one who has suffered or the one who has made others to suffer*, repents completely, which includes retaining in his or her heart no hardness toward any creature, no refusal to forgive.

Writes C. S. Lewis: "Not only [Heaven] but all this earthly past will have been Heaven to those who are saved. Not only [Hell], but all their life on earth too, will then be seen by the damned to have been Hell. That is what mortals misunderstand. They say of some temporal suffering, 'No future bliss can make up for it,' not knowing that Heaven, once attained, will work backwards and turn even that agony into a glory. [Others take pleasure in sin,] little dreaming how damnation will spread back and back into their past and contaminate the pleasure of the sin. . . . What happens to [the Saved] is best described as the opposite of a mirage. What seemed, when they entered it, to be the vale of misery turns out, when they look back, to have been a well; and where present experience saw only salt deserts memory truthfully records that the pools were full of water."[3]

Christ offers us spiritual advantages to be found in the afflictions through which we pass in this life, if we will accept them without resentment or hard feelings. Every experience can be redeemed in him: "*All things* work together for good to them that love God" (Romans 8:28; italics added).

Suffering without vengeance—does it not conform to the example of the Atoning One? Does it not overcome evil with good? Is it not the way of those who become saviors on Mount Zion? In choosing this way, and in no other, we can find a fulness of joy.

Speaking to the eleven apostles of his impending suffering and death and of the hatred and persecution and scattering and affliction and sorrow they would endure, the Savior promised: "Ye shall weep and lament, but the world shall rejoice: and ye shall be sorrowful, but your sorrow shall be turned into joy. A woman when she is in travail hath sorrow, because her hour is come: but as soon as she is delivered of the child, she remembereth no more the anguish, for joy that a man is born into the world. And ye now therefore have sorrow: but I will see you again, and your heart shall rejoice, and your joy no man taketh from you. . . . These things I have spoken unto you, that in me ye might have peace. In the world ye shall have tribulation: but be of good cheer; I have overcome the world" (John 16:20–22, 33).

However broad the offense or deep the sorrow, Christ bears away our sins, lifts from us their destructive effects, enables us to let go of our hardness. In ancient Israel the workings of this healing process were symbolized by a curious and wonderful element called the scapegoat, which was included in the sacrifice ritual of the Day of Atonement. The high priest offered both a sin offering and a burnt offering for himself and his house and the same offerings for the congregation of Israel. In addition, he also sent one goat, the scapegoat, alive into the wilderness, to bear away the sins of the people symbolically. Except by those without understanding, this animal was not thought actually to remove the congregation's sins but to call to remembrance and point the way to that pure and perfect Lamb of God who would, in the meridian of time, remove their sins. This he would do not just ritualistically but actually, once and for all (Hebrews 9:6–28). I believe it is through participating, by belief and act, in this real sacrifice that we live the one true religion, the one plan that actually relieves us of the pain, unfairness, and deep sorrow of life. We can call it "the religion of atonement."

From almost the beginning of time we have had a counterfeit of this religion. It also claims to rectify injustice and compensate for pain, though unlike the religion of atonement, it cannot deliver on its promises. This counterfeit religion, like the religion of atonement, features scapegoating, but not the kind of scapegoating that points toward Christ's sacrifice. Often this other scapegoating has been played out in community religious rituals. In these rituals, the uncleanness of the community is projected onto a particular creature or creatures, sometimes an animal, sometimes a human being. The scapegoat, a surrogate or substitute for all offenders, is sacrificed, or driven out from the community. It serves as a kind of sponge to absorb the guilt and uncleanness of the whole community.

In the most commonly cited examples, this rite of purification takes place in a formal ceremony, such as the mock warfare enacted among the Dinka people that gradually becomes a united frenzy as the participants actually strike a cow or calf tied to a stake.[4] In other cases, the community conducts this grim proceeding quite unaware of its ritualistic character, as in the Salem witch trials. It might be said of all such cases that accusers despise in the animal or person accused—the scapegoat—the evil they sense in themselves and cannot deal with directly. On the surface, they punish the offenders; on a deeper level, they desperately try to purify themselves.

Many of us practice the religion of scapegoating daily, when we find fault, condemn someone (even if we say it only to ourselves), or try to dig the mote out of another's eye. We may say we are only trying to help the other person "straighten up," or to teach that person an important lesson, or pay that person back for what he's done. But in the scapegoating pattern, the truth is that we want to make someone else pay for our miseries; we desire that because we do not feel clean ourselves, and without quite realizing why, we feel compelled to fixate on the sins or shortcomings of someone else. At least momentarily, finding another to blame relieves us, or at least distracts us, from the necessity of examining ourselves. We pin our hopes on establishing someone else's uncleanness so that we won't have to face up to it in ourselves.

Contrast this religion of scapegoating with the religion of atonement. In the religion of atonement, we don't feel compelled to scapegoat in order to find justice and bring relief from guilt; the Savior fulfilled the demands of justice by suffering the effects of sin. Because we believe he paid for every sin, we do not desire to exact payment for whatever we have suffered. Instead, we are able to forgive freely, seeing even those who have wronged us with compassion. We let go of enmity, much as one whose boat has capsized might let go of a satchel of belongings that is dragging him or her underwater, might let it simply float away as obviously the lesser of two losses. For us, what Christ endured on our behalf is enough, and therefore we want for nothing.

Dennis Rasmussen, author of the remarkable book *The Lord's Question*, has written: "To hallow my life [Christ] taught me to endure sorrow rather than cause it, to restrain anger rather than heed it, to bear injustice rather than inflict it. 'Resist not evil' he said in the Sermon on the Mount. (Matthew 5:39.) Evil multiplies by the response it seeks to provoke, and when I return evil for evil, I engender corruption myself. The chain of evil is broken for good when a pure and loving heart absorbs a hurt and forbears to hurt in return."[5]

Many, including people who have been wronged in the most severe ways, have come to this light. I spoke not long ago with a woman who six years earlier had recalled having been abused sexually by her father when she was a girl. She had worked with a psychiatrist for most of those six years. Despite her efforts, she had gained no fundamental relief, no healing. "I feel as if I am a set of pipes that are clogged. Life, the joy of life, does not flow through me." I asked whether she had forgiven her father. She said she had thought she had but wasn't sure, because still she had no peace.

Then I asked her, "Have you sought his forgiveness for your hard feelings, your resentment, toward him all these years?" She had not. It had never occurred to her to do so. I suggested that forgiveness consists not of forgetting what happened but of repenting of unforgiving feelings about what happened.

A light went on in her face. She pondered for a few moments and said, "I'm going to do that." The next day she told me she had written a letter to her father, asking his forgiveness. "I saw that by blaming him I was refusing to forgive, refusing to admit that he too had suffered in his life and needed my compassion," she said. "Now that I have done this, I feel free for the first time in my life. This morning, life is flowing through me, and it is sweet." Since then she has written me twice, letters filled with happiness. In one she said of her father, "Last week I even asked his advice, and he was shocked and pleased."

The two options I have described, scapegoating and forgiving, define the two available religions, the world's two fundamental conceptions of salvation. We continually choose between these two religions: either we accept Christ's payment for the losses we have suffered at others' hands, or we refuse it by demanding that they be made to pay for those losses. If we refuse it, we believe his suffering either does not apply to the offense we have suffered or is not sufficient. His sacrifice as the Lamb of God seems irrelevant to us. Inconsolably resentful, we want a scapegoat. Our offender, or at least someone on this earth, must pay the difference, make up for what we have lost.

That kind of talk suggests what the Lord might have meant when he said that scapegoaters—those who "sought occasion against one another and forgave not one another in their hearts"—are guilty of the greater sin (D&C 64:8). How can someone who refuses to forgive an injury be doing something worse than the person who perpetrated the injury? If we ask the question that way, we are unlikely to arrive at the answer. But if we ask what can make one sin greater than another, then we see that it is not how much blame it deserves (the Lord, after all, is scarcely interested in blame) but instead the degree of scapegoating in it, which is to say, the degree to which it rejects Christ's atonement. The rejection of the Atonement, it seems to me, is what makes an unforgiving heart so sinful. The sin of refusing to forgive involves us in the sin of refusing to accept Christ's forgiveness. As President Spencer W. Kimball wrote, "He who will not forgive others breaks down the bridge over which he himself must travel."[6]

Surely that is part of what the Lord meant when he said that his disciples who would not forgive one another were "for this evil . . . afflicted and sorely chastened" (D&C 64:8). What could be a heavier affliction, a sorer chastening, than the self-amplified misery of one who will not accept the relief the Savior offers from the corrosive emotion of resentment, the agony of a vindictive, hopeless heart?

Serious abuses seem not to be decreasing. Indeed, more and more of them are coming to light, of a kind that past generations often dared not name. They are perpetrated by the strong upon the weak. In too many instances the horror of the abuses has been so great that no adjectives at our disposal suffice to express it; it is unthinkable. They strike near the heart of everything most holy in life—everything critical for human wholeness. No one can seriously question whether exposing and trying to prevent such abuses is the right thing to do.

The issue I am concerned with is not whether we should oppose abuse; we must. I am concerned with how. Some, no doubt with good intentions, are resolutely unforgiving, contending that some abuses are simply too heinous to be forgiven. It would be wrong, they say, to let the offenders "off the hook." Or they say that the victims of such abuse cannot forgive, no matter how they might wish to, because the damage inflicted is too great.

This position assumes that forgiving someone requires that we pretend whatever they have done to us never happened. It assumes that our forgiveness of our abusers is designed to release them from bondage rather than to release ourselves—as if it had nothing to do with whether or not we accept the gift of the Atonement. The freedom that forgiveness brings is not, at least initially, for the forgiven; it is for the forgiver. It concerns not what the perpetrator did in the past but what the victim is doing now. Understood this way, forgiveness releases us from the thrall and anguish of the resentment that accompanies the belief that one has been irreparably damaged; it becomes an opportunity for sweet liberation. The horror happened, yes; but through forgiveness we find in Christ consolation, meaning, increased sensitivity, purification, and even feelings of pure love.

It may help to offer one example of the scapegoating mentality from among the many prevalent in our contemporary culture.[7] I refer to some adherents of the so-called "recovery" movement that has gained great popularity in recent years. (I do not speak of all of them by any means; there, as elsewhere, it is usually not the program or cause they support that makes particular individuals suspect but the motivation and attitude with which they support it.) These adherents describe, correctly, how the violated child suffers at the hand of abusive caretakers terrible feelings of humiliation and anger and is simultaneously taught by those same abusers to feel ashamed of having those feelings. The brilliant ethnologist Gregory Bateson called this contradictory set of expectations a "double bind": the expectations of the abusers both provoke and forbid the child's resentment. They coerce the child into hiding resentment behind outwardly "good" behavior that will please and pacify them.[8]

That makes the child an unwitting conspirator in the family's cover-up of the abuse. Many children in such a situation work doggedly to keep the family in equilibrium, despite constant tensions or outbursts from others; they deny even to themselves that anything might be wrong. But always these children harbor a deep sense of discomfort about their own worthiness and acceptability. They may become "addicted" to the counterfeit reassurance they get from pleasing others. In the vocabulary of the recovery movement, these children are said to avoid feeling the anger and resentment their abusers have aroused in them. They are said to be "in denial." They produce a false public self—or so the recovery movement says—to protect and to hide the private, angry, "real" self. The public self feels constantly driven to prove itself and win approval, as if trying to gain absolution for deep shame. This self seems to have no identity apart from others' opinions. But, of course, the shame and self-doubt abide, because the good opinion of other people never silences the haunting parental voices that say, "You can't," "It's your fault," "You aren't worthy."

The scapegoating mentality shows itself not so much in the foregoing diagnosis of the problem (though I think this diagnosis is deeply flawed) as in the remedy that some of the recovery movement adherents prescribe. According to them, to recover from the condition I have just described, the victim must acknowledge and fully feel long-suppressed anger. Only by so doing can the victim "come out of denial" and be liberated from the emptiness, fear, self-loathing, or other problems left in the wake of the abuse. Indeed, in many cases moving from this stifled condition to open anger temporarily brings with it a promise of relief, as if a new day were dawning. The freshly recollected or reconstructed abuse explains just about every personal difficulty or self-disappointment the individual has experienced; it feels like a repudiation, once and for all, of reliance on a damaging relationship; it goes a long way toward settling old scores. Is this not a pathway of escape from all that has gone wrong before? How could it not lead to something much better?

But the promise is illusory. Some victims, once embarked upon this journey that starts with anger, at last let their anger go and forgive their victimizers, often after long and difficult struggles; they abandon their initial path for a better one. In these cases, though certainly not in all, feeling angry may have served an important purpose temporarily. I have seen a few such instances but think they are in the minority. Those who indulge in anger without letting go of their identity as victims, and instead resolutely continue to accuse, grow increasingly miserable. You may have observed this yourself if you know an abuse victim who has taken the scapegoating "remedy" to heart. By attempting to put right the past wrongs, the individual who begins as scapegoat burns with increasing resentment and thereby takes up the role of scapegoater. He or she becomes a wrongdoer and bears the scapegoater's unwanted burden of conscience and desperate need to expend a continuing effort to justify a hard, retaliatory heart. Exchanging the role of scapegoat for that of scapegoater changes nothing fundamentally; it brings no end to retaliation and sorrow. Those who make this exchange must cling to their miseries as evidence of having been violated, and in some cases they "act out" their anger, becoming overt victimizers themselves. It is in this pattern that some abused children become abusers when they grow up.

Compare this counterfeit solution with forgiveness, as illustrated in the following true story. For most of his life, Samuel exhibited symptoms that would have led many therapists to assume childhood abuse even before talking to him about his history. Much of the time he was sunk in deep depression, a kind of utter darkness of spirit that often completely incapacitated him. He had been put up for adoption by his biological parents, and his adoptive parents were highly dysfunctional individuals who apparently could not relax their concern for their own agendas enough to nurture or to love him. Like many other victims, this was a child whose shocking introduction to this life was cold, systematic rejection and mistreatment. So harsh was his self-loathing that, though a believing member of the Church, he became involved in what he himself considered despicable sexual activities. Professionals labeled him an addict. He spent a great deal of time with psychiatrists who for years medicated him heavily with very limited success. One day he appeared at my door and asked me to help him. I told him I would stay by his side but wanted him also to consult with David Hamblin, a psychotherapist in private practice who believes in the religion of atonement as much as I do and who played an important role in what happened next.

The following week Samuel came to see me and recounted a significant event. That morning, he had been pondering a recurrent dream in which he found himself in an abandoned house—the furniture gone, the windows boarded up. The waning light of sunset filtered through the windows. He became aware of beings moving outside the house—vampires, scratching to gain entrance. As he continued in this reverie, he found himself reliving the dream, even though now he was awake. He realized this was the house of his grandparents, and in his mind he went out on the veranda, where he encountered his adoptive father, as a man in his early thirties, smiling.

The two men walked together onto the lawn and sat down to talk. Samuel felt a desperate yearning for his father to give him a blessing, to provide some of the care and love and emotional sustenance of which Samuel felt he had been deprived. As they sat there, his father put his head on Samuel's shoulder and then diminished in size, becoming smaller and more vulnerable than the adopted son sitting by his side. All of a sudden Samuel realized that his father was the one who needed a blessing. For the first time ever, he felt compassion for this man. Precisely with the advent of this feeling, the Savior appeared and silently held both father and son in his arms and, for the first time ever in his life, Samuel felt the Savior's love for him. He spent the hours before he came to see me that day walking in the mountains, weeping profusely, in a release, both painful and joyous, of pent-up feelings for which he did not even have a name.

"I anticipated that I would one day need to go through some sort of process of excusing my father for how he treated me," Samuel said. "But that is not at all what happened. Instead I came to the realization that he needed me even more than I needed him, and I had closed my heart toward him. This, I had to confess, I had always known in some deep and unadmitted way. I felt a tremendous sense of regret, not because I knew during my growing-up years what to do for him, but because I had not been able to help him. What left me in this moment was my conviction that my parents were to blame for my condition. Yes, in one sense they had misused me, but they could not have done better than they did. I remembered with great sorrow something I had once been told: that my father stuttered as he was growing up and his father took him to the basement and beat him to get him to stop.

"My problems have been rooted in a willful insistence on paying the price for all my troubles myself. By judging myself so ruthlessly, I kept myself from admitting that it was really my father I resented, and this I'm sure was a kind of cover-up. It allowed me to excuse myself for closing myself to my father and his needs. Being the mistreated and deprived one, I couldn't be expected to reach out to him. Opening myself to the Savior would have ruined that excuse. In long hours of introspection, I have figured out this much, at least—that my savage judgments upon myself are in some way connected with unwillingness to open myself to the people I blamed for my problems. That is why I am convinced that my refusal to let the Savior bear my burdens has in a certain way been willful—even though that would have seemed preposterous to me a year ago. I began to feel his love for me the moment I opened myself to love my father."

Samuel's story reinforces a profound truth about the unforgiving condition. It's a kind of trap. From inside it, the doctrine of forgiveness just doesn't make sense. Before letting his heart be touched by, and forgiving, the person he was blaming, Samuel could not see that blame was not the issue; he could not comprehend the meaning for him of the doctrine that the Lord has satisfied every debt we owe to one another. To him, blame *was* the issue—the only issue.

To be convinced, as scapegoating victims are, that someone is to blame is like living in Flatland, a country of only two dimensions where it is impossible to comprehend the possibility of a third dimension.[9] That is why, when I commend the therapy of forgiveness, those caught in a scapegoating outlook will tend to think that forgiving absolves the perpetrator of responsibility. As Wayne Muller suggests, saying that blame is not the issue sounds to them like saying the perpetrator should be let off the hook. And since in their minds blame *is* the issue, refraining from blaming the abuser must mean that the victim ought to be blamed for the abuse. "You are blaming the victim!" they often say.

We need to realize that they cannot, at least for the moment, see any other possibility—because it simply does not compute with them that the therapy of forgiveness blames no one. We would be wrong to find fault with them; we would be unforgiving. If we judge them, we ourselves will be caught in just such a box as they are, unable to see that we too are rejecting the therapy of forgiveness without realizing it.

Samuel's story also helps us appreciate a second truth—that forgiveness may not be easy to extend. No work is more demanding or, I believe, more significant. It heals individuals; it heals families; it heals generations united by blood or adoption. To forgive another might take years or become the work of a lifetime, and that is just as it ought to be.

Wendy Ulrich, a consultant with a background in psychology who says that "we deserve to forgive," writes that the process must not be cut short. As heart-wrenching as it may be, we need to pass through the difficult experiences that lead us to realize, by suffering them, the painful consequences of sin. This process, Ulrich says, "clarif[ies] our efforts not to repeat them" and enables us to "more fully appreciate what Christ endured during the Atonement."[10] Her work acknowledges the immense difficulty of coming to forgiveness without watering down the absolute need for it. She quotes President Gordon B. Hinckley approvingly: "If there be any who nurture in their hearts the poisonous brew of enmity toward another, I plead with you to ask the Lord for strength to forgive. . . . It may not be easy, and it may not come quickly. But if you seek it with sincerity and cultivate it, it *will* come."[11]

A terrible storm seems to be gathering on the horizon of our future. In increasing numbers, children are accusing their parents of rejecting, mistreating, or even violating them. Often the accusation comes after the children have reached adulthood. No doubt in many or most cases the recollections are true. But even when they are false, the mere accusation creates a presumption of guilt, just as it did in Puritan Salem. Today being accused of any kind of child abuse damns a person in the public mind.

It compounds this problem that the family takes sides, and hatred spreads like a contagion. Neighborhoods and even communities can become hideously divided. Perhaps the only thing as poignant as listening to a story of child abuse is listening to the story of parents completely broken and a family utterly shattered by allegations of abuse. A public accusation that is true shatters a family; a false one creates a tragedy at least as great. Although I don't want to deal here with the issue of false accusation (a number of responsible researchers have been writing with alarm on this subject[12]), I do want to point out what everyone who has ever exchanged accusations with another person knows: once we begin scapegoating, it becomes easier and easier to exaggerate and even contrive offenses.

What I have been addressing is whether scapegoating is constructive when the accusation is true. Many who encourage identifying the perpetrator and "feeling all their anger" typically insist that the victim avoid all contact with the perpetrator, even if the perpetrator is a parent. We must, of course, do everything necessary to prevent child abuse from recurring, but some think that means adult survivors of abuse must avoid all contact with their parents. They say this strategy is essential for the individual's healing. But following this advice virtually precludes forgiveness and reconciliation from the start. Is this not the same pattern as believing that a great cause justifies using oppressive methods—a kind of abusiveness in reverse?

What could be more demonically ingenious than to infect a noble cause—in this case, opposition to abuse of children—with ignoble motives? How could Satan strike a more telling blow than to enlist us in a counterfeit solution, one that in the end only increases the enmity among us? Unless we are vigilant, we not only will see but will ourselves foster division and sorrow within the human family and think we are doing God a favor.

To ensure that this never happens, we should always remember who established the scapegoating pattern: Satan, "which deceiveth the whole world," was "the accuser of our brethren" and "accused them before our God day and night" (Revelation 12:9–10). The religion of scapegoating will claim to end the cycle of enmity and suffering by setting things right once and for all. But we must not be deceived. We would do well to remember the Buddhist saying: "Hatred never ceases by hatred; but by love alone is healed. This is an ancient and eternal law."[13] "Therefore, renounce war and proclaim peace, and seek diligently to turn the hearts of the children to their fathers" (D&C 98:16). There is no real peace, ever, without forgiveness.

Whereas the religion of scapegoating seeks to turn many of us against our parents, the religion of atonement calls us all to turn our hearts towards them, even in their weakness and sins. Whereas scapegoating teaches us to refuse to reconcile, the Savior said that to come unto him we must be reconciled (3 Nephi 12:22–24). He commands us, if we would be his and enjoy the peace that passes understanding, to become of one heart, one with another (D&C 35:2; 38:27). He lives to help us do so.

True Christianity, the religion of atonement, is not merely one road to salvation among many others; it is the only road. The alternative, scape-goating, sets individuals against one another, giving each a sense of justi-fication in refusing to be reconciled. Though religions call certain scape-goating rituals "atonement," unless these rituals "[point] to that great and last sacrifice" of Christ (Alma 34:14), they provide at best only a tempo-rary and deceptive sense of purification; the cleansing they proffer is illu-sory—a psychological trick, a communal self-deception, an empty ritual. No real payment for sin underwrites the promissory note conveyed in these rituals.

On the other hand, Christ's willingness to allow himself to fully feel the effects of all the harms we have done to one another offers us the only actual, rather than merely ritualistic, atonement, the only actual payment for those harms. That entitles him and him alone to forgive us for inflicting such harms, to cleanse us from our guilt, and to convey to us, in an intimately individual and personal way, assurance of his having done so.

We have only to accept the payment and the forgiveness (which means renouncing all scapegoating claims against each other and repenting of the sins that make us want to make such claims) in order to be relieved of sorrow and discover peace. "For this is thankworthy, if a man for conscience toward God endure grief, suffering wrongfully. For what glory is it, if, when ye be buffeted for your faults, ye shall take it patiently? but if, when ye do well, and suffer for it, ye take it patiently, this is acceptable with God. For even hereunto were ye called: because Christ also suffered for us, leaving us an example, that ye should follow his steps: . . . Who, when he was reviled, reviled not again; when he suffered, he threatened not; but committed himself to him that judgeth righteously: Who his own self bare our sins in his own body on the tree, that we, being dead to sins, should live unto righteousness: by whose stripes ye were healed" (1 Peter 2:19–21, 23–24).

Only the real Atonement offers a truly cleansing power; only when forgiveness flows from acceptance of that atonement does the mercy in it respect the divine law of justice. As the scripture says, without a real atonement, "all mankind were lost; and behold, they would have been endlessly lost were it not that God redeemed his people from their lost and fallen state" (Mosiah 16:4). The religion of atonement and the unconditional forgiveness required to participate in it contain the only power to heal humankind.

Notes

1. Viktor E. Frankl, *Man's Search for Meaning* (Boston: Beacon Press, 1992); Corrie ten Boom with John and Elizabeth Sherrill, *The Hiding Place* (New York: Bantam Books, 1974); Jacques Lusseyran, *And There Was Light*, trans. Elizabeth R. Cameron (New York: Parabola Books, 1987).

2. Wayne Muller, *Legacy of the Heart: The Spiritual Advantages of a Painful Childhood* (New York: Simon & Schuster, 1992), 10.

3. C. S. Lewis, *The Great Divorce* (New York: Macmillan, 1946), 67–68.

4. See René Girard, *Violence and the Sacred*, trans. Patrick Gregory (Baltimore: Johns Hopkins University Press, 1977), 97–98.

5. Dennis Rasmussen, *The Lord's Question* (Provo, Utah: Keter Foundation, 1985), 63.

6. Spencer W. Kimball, *The Miracle of Forgiveness* (Salt Lake City: Bookcraft, 1969), 269.

7. See, for example, John Taylor, "Don't Blame Me!" *New York*, 3 June 1991, 26–34; Joseph Epstein, "The Joys of Victimhood," *New York Times Magazine*, 2 July 1989, 20–21, 39–41.

8. Gregory Bateson, "Toward a Theory of Schizophrenia," in *Steps to an Ecology of Mind* (New York: Ballantine Books, 1972), 201–21.

9. Dillon Inouye introduced me to this idea, found in Edwin A. Abbott, *Flatland* (New York: Dover Publications, 1952).

10. Wendy L. Ulrich, "When Forgiveness Flounders: For Victims of Serious Sin," in *Confronting Abuse*, ed. Anne L. Horton, B. Kent Harrison, and Barry L. Johnson (Salt Lake City: Deseret Book, 1993), 353.

11. Ibid., 347; italics added.

12. See, for example, Carol Tavris, "Beware the Incest-Survivor Machine," *The New York Times Book Review*, 3 Jan. 1993, 1, 16–17; David Rieff, "Victims, All?" *Harpers Magazine*, Oct. 1991, 49–56.

13. From the Dhammapada, quoted in Muller, *Legacy of the Heart*, 12.

SEARCHING DILIGENTLY
IN THE LIGHT OF CHRIST

Wendy L. Watson

When I was growing up, I read and studied in various places in our home. It didn't matter where I was—in the front room, at the kitchen table, or in my bed—my mother would always find me and say, "Would you like a little more light on the subject?" Actually, I usually wanted a lot more light on the subject. I needed increased illumination—of the pages, of my mind, and of the topic.

She would then turn on a light. Her consistent interest and comforting presence would tell me that even the seemingly impossible task before me was indeed possible, that with continuing effort on my part and the increased light she had provided, I would succeed.

Our theme for this women's conference volume is Moroni 7:19: "Wherefore, I beseech of you, . . . that ye should search diligently in the light of Christ that ye may know good from evil; and if ye will lay hold upon every good thing, and condemn it not, ye certainly will be a child of Christ."

Here Moroni is giving us the words of his father, Mormon, at a time when Moroni hadn't thought he himself would still be alive, let alone writing more on the plates. He begins his final addition to the record: "I had supposed not to have written more, but I have not as yet perished" (Moroni 1:1).

That puts a whole new spin on "publish or perish," doesn't it? These are some of the last recordings of a man who had thought he would be dead by then. Marilyn Arnold notes: "Not only did [Moroni] conclude and conceal the record, but he made of his very life a shield around it." I like that. "Preserving it became perhaps the primary purpose of his

Wendy L. Watson holds a Ph.D. in family therapy and gerontology from the University of Calgary in Calgary, Alberta, Canada. She is a professor in the Department of Family Sciences at Brigham Young University and serves as chair-elect for the 1998 BYU Women's Conference.

existence. We cannot begin to contemplate its preciousness to him who had lost everything but his life and his resolute faith."[1]

What words of great price does Moroni carefully select to conclude his record? Among them are these: "Search diligently in the light of Christ" and "lay hold upon every good thing" (Moroni 7:19). These two admonitions are, of course, related by their connection to Christ. In Moroni 7:24, Mormon tells us, "All things which are good cometh of Christ."

When Mormon admonishes us to search diligently in the light of Christ so that we can know good from evil, I hear his wisdom about these last days—our days—in which some people do indeed "call evil good, and good evil," and some "put darkness for light, and light for darkness," and some "put bitter for sweet, and sweet for bitter" (2 Nephi 15:20). Some call the prophets men without vision; and others call wickedness a right. Distinguishing good from evil, light from darkness, is critical in these latter days.

Many may say, "Good from evil? That's not a problem for me. I'm trying to figure out 'better from best' these days." We may need, however, to discern other subtle but significant distinctions that either invite more light into our life or dispel the light that is already there. Our spiritual wattage will often be increased or diminished, depending on the distinctions we make and hold to.

Sometimes we as Latter-day Saint women make distinctions about each other that are not useful. We distinguish between those women who do crafts, and those who don't; those who work outside the home, and those who don't; those who are married, and those who aren't; those who do their visiting teaching, and those who don't; those who are presently participating in Church activities, and those who are not. These deeply ingrained distinctions come complete with embedded assumptions, expectations, and permission to behave in certain ways toward the groups so distinguished. Should we go so far as to say that these distinctions—which subtly imply that some of us are "good Latter-day Saint" women and others are "bad Latter-day Saint" women—should we say that these very distinctions are in themselves bad—even evil? These distinctions certainly do not knit our hearts together nor make us His.

Mormon proposes that once we discern good from evil, we then commence to "lay hold upon every good thing" (Moroni 7:19). Before we can lay hold upon good things, however, I believe that we have to lay down some other things first. Let me offer you six beliefs that I find prevent women from laying hold upon every good thing:

1. *The belief that we have to lay hold upon every good thing all at once.* The grand smorgasbord of life is before us. It all looks so good. What do we choose? Can we have it all? More important, can we have it right now and all at once? Most women who appear to have it all, all at once, confess that they usually pay quite a high price with their own or their family members' physical, emotional, mental, or relationship health. One woman lamented, "I wish someone had told me I had to make a choice."

So what's a woman to do? The scriptures tell us, "To every thing there is a season" (Ecclesiastes 3:1). We all know that the season is in "the own due time of the Lord" (1 Nephi 10:3). There will be times that we need to "run with patience the race that is set before us" (Hebrews 12:1), and at the same time we are not supposed to run faster than we are able (see Mosiah 4:27). And there will be many times that we need to stand still (see D&C 5:34), to "be still and know that [he is] God" (D&C 101:16).

That leads us to the next constraining belief.

2. *The belief that we know how our life should be and will be and that we are the captain of our ship.* Being so certain about how our life will be, how our life will turn out, may constrain us from being open to continuing personal revelation from the Lord that can shift the direction of our life—even in a moment—moving us away from our destination and even away from our shipmates.

Made-to-measure ironies are part of each woman's compressed, personalized curriculum of life. The constraining belief that our plan for our life is the only one that counts causes problems when our life-ironies challenge our five-year plans—and some weeks, even our five-day plans. Diligently searching for more light and responding to these ironies with humility and resiliency allows us to live fully the perpetually unexpected life.

My mother loved the lights in the firmament. Each comet, each planet, each star—falling or not—each phase of the moon, was something to celebrate. She would phone from 150 miles away and excitedly invite me to "run out and look at the moon!" She wanted to share the good light she was seeing. One of my mother's life-ironies was that in the last months of her life, she lost her physical vision. She was blind. She, who had taught others to see more clearly, widely, and enthusiastically, now had her eyes veiled until she passed through the veil.

Her trial brought sorrow and anguish into my life. I needed extra light to understand and endure; however, enduring—rather than just persevering—often tutors us into remembering who we really are—perhaps even jogging loose a premortal memory of a commitment or two.

3. *The belief that we are more correct than others: the sin of certainty!* [2] Believing that there is one right way to look at something and we have it does not invite others or more light into our life. Wives have found that when they "know" the one right way to view everything and do everything, husbands are not invited to intertwine their lives, to really forge a marriage relationship.

When we hold to the belief that we are right and others are wrong, there is no room, let alone need, for further light. We already have it all—or so we believe. Our sin of certainty and subsequent actions allow no room for others to co-create with us even more good things.

What there is room for, however, and what is invited in, is unrighteous dominion. And as Elder H. Burke Peterson has pointed out, women can exercise unrighteous dominion just as well as men can.[3]

4. *The belief that words don't matter, that words can't hurt.* This belief is promoted by that old childhood rhyme: "Sticks and stones may break my bones, but words will never hurt me." What a terrible thing to teach a child in the name of building thick skins. Thick skins, yes; thin hearts, absolutely.

In 1 Peter 2:1, the apostle Peter speaks to the importance of words. He counsels us to "[lay] aside all malice, and all guile, and hypocrisies, . . . and all evil speakings."

Words do matter. They lodge in our cells and in our souls.

One woman told me: "My husband's words hit me, and they hurt me so much. I think the word *stupid* is the meanest word in the whole world because I've heard it so much. I'm not stupid. I know I'm not, but the word still hurts because this is the person I love, and when he calls me that, it makes me feel so bad. It hurts. It hurts my soul. My soul wants to run away and hide. But I can't because this is my marriage."

This young couple who came to me for marital counseling had been struggling with difficulties in their relationship from the beginning of their less-than-two-year marriage. They were successful in resolving their difficulties once they worked together on dissolving the barrier of words they had unwittingly co-created.

Over time, individual cutting words build into full conversations of accusation and recrimination.[4] These conversations are filled with complaints of unfulfilled expectations: "You never . . . "; "You didn't. . . . " Each person suffers emotionally and even physically, and the relationship disintegrates.

At the same time "building" words strengthen relationships, just words alone are not enough. In 1 Peter 1:22 we read about the need for unfeigned love. Feigned love occurs when the words of love are present but the behavior of love is not. I met with a young couple contemplating marriage whose relationship had drifted into trouble. In that anguishing interview, they repeatedly threw venomous words—*hate, trapped, violated, oppressed*—back and forth at each other, juxtaposing all those hateful words with the sacred word *love*.

Instead of "I love you," this couple should have added a few more words between *I love* and *you*. "*I love* oppressing *you*." "*I love* how you squirm when I berate *you*." "*I love* seeing *you* suffer." "*I love* being more right than *you* are—and showing you that!" These sentences would represent more accurately their experiences in the relationship. Using the word *love* is not enough. If the word *love* doesn't match your behavior or fit the experience of the one you claim so to "love," please use another word.

So, again, words do matter. They lodge in our cells and in our souls. Maya Angelou, past United States poet laureate, has written of words that lodge in the walls of our homes. If words lodge in our cells, souls, and walls, we need words—and tones that accompany those words—that build and maintain the temples of our bodies and the temples of our homes.

Elder Jeffrey R. Holland spoke of a hopeful, encouraging, peaceful word in a recent general conference. That word was *repentance*. He said: "The very beauty of the word *repentance* is the promise of escaping old problems and old habits and old sorrows and old sins. It is among the most hopeful and encouraging—and yes, most peaceful—words in the gospel vocabulary."[5]

His thoughts on repentance suggest a fifth constraining belief:

5. *The troublesome belief that sounds like this: "My past, which was filled with wrongdoing, predicts and determines my future. I am not worthy to lay hold upon any good thing, let alone every good thing, because I am bad, tainted, unclean, beyond hope!"* Does that sound familiar? For far too many women, it does.

This constraining belief needs to be laid on the altar of repentance. The guilt and grief we feel are a good sign, an indication of our continued goodness, in spite of our sins. We should congratulate ourselves on still being able to feel guilty! The light is still there. Guilt has had a lot of bad press in the past, yet for most of us, guilt—if used well—is exactly the help most of us need to stop sinning and start toward full repentance.

Let guilt start us on the path of the sincere, heartfelt, and therefore heart-changing process of laying down our sins, even giving away our sins to know the Lord (see Alma 22:18). And as we come to know him, and come unto him, we will also come to know our real selves, unshackled and free from the past. The Savior really did mean it when he said, "Though your sins be as scarlet, they shall be as white as snow; though they be red like crimson, they shall be as wool" (Isaiah 1:18).

The Savior and our ecclesiastical leaders will lead us along, helping us cast off constraining beliefs about repentance. My heart still aches for the woman who told me she believed that sin was like pounding nails into a beautifully smooth board and repentance was like pulling the nails out of that board. After repentance, the nails would be gone, but the board would still be left marred with holes from the nails, never to be as it had once been. She indicated she had learned this from a Primary teacher. (I say "learned" because I am not sure what the teacher believed or intended to teach.) But this woman, from her childhood on, had held that image of sin and repentance and as an adult saw herself as permanently unclean and unworthy. Oh, how we need to be careful about our metaphors when teaching children! The only board and nails that are important in teaching about repentance are the ones that formed the cross upon which the Savior was crucified for our sins.

This particular woman's belief that nothing she could do would ever make the board whole again is partially right. She can't do it, especially on her own. That's why she needs to take the board to the Savior. His grace is more than sufficient, not just to remove any nails but to remove the holes and make the board whole again, as though the nails had never been there. The Lord says he will remember our sins no more (see Hebrews 8:12), so why would he leave nail holes in the board to remind us of those sins? It is the prints of the nails in his hands and feet that he wants us to remember.

I love his words: "I, the Lord, forgive sins, and am merciful unto those who confess their sins with humble hearts" (D&C 61:2). *Please believe me*, I hear him saying, *I forgive sins. Come to me. Bring your humble heart. Confess your sins. I am full of mercy.*

As we take responsibility for our wrong choices, experience sincere remorse, and deeply desire to turn away from our sins (even our favorite ones)—choosing instead to keep the commandments and devote time to building up the kingdom—we each can experience the Savior saying, "Daughter, be of good comfort; thy faith hath made thee whole" (Matthew 9:22). He said it to the woman who touched the hem of his garment, and he will say it to me and to you as we come unto him.

6. *The constraining belief that involves unforgiveness and sounds something like this: "I don't have to forgive evil, cruel, or corrupt people."*

Many of us act as if forgiveness and repentance are only for the righteous: "Oh, she's a basically good person. I forgive her." What about those who have caused us physical, emotional, mental, or spiritual pain and suffering? What about those who have broken seemingly every commandment and who have profoundly affected our life through their choice to sin? What about hypocrites? What about the unrepentant? Do we have to forgive them?

Let's see what the Lord says. In Doctrine and Covenants 64:10 we read: "I, the Lord, will forgive whom I will forgive, but of you it is required to forgive all men." A lot of us act as if this scripture reads in the reverse: God will forgive all; we as mortals will pick and choose whom we will forgive, based on our own standard of forgiveability. And the ultimate criterion of what is or is not forgiveable seems to be that the sinner must first suffer more than those who have suffered at the sinner's hands.

And what happens if we don't forgive another who has wronged us? The Lord is very clear about the outcome: "For, if ye forgive men their trespasses your heavenly Father will also forgive you; but if ye forgive not men their trespasses neither will your Father forgive your trespasses" (3 Nephi 13:14–15). And "wherefore, I say unto you, that ye ought to forgive one another; for he that forgiveth not his brother his trespasses standeth condemned before the Lord; for there remaineth in him the greater sin" (D&C 64:9).

Could this possibly mean that if we do not forgive someone who has wronged and harmed us that we become more sinful than the initial sinner? I believe the Lord means what he says. He hasn't provided his words just to give us something to read at night. He has said that "the greater sin" is to remain unforgiving, and he means just that.

In my clinical practice I see almost daily the outcome and effects of unforgiveness. Unforgiveness increases suffering. Unforgiveness is lethal.

Bitterness, resentments, and malice, like dark words, lodge in our minds, hearts, cells, and souls and wreak havoc, causing more mental and emotional pain, more physical and spiritual agony, than even the initial sin brought about.

The Lord's plea that we quit hanging onto the sins of others in no way lessens the gravity of sin or the culpability of the sinner. As the 1995 proclamation to the world on the family states: "We warn that individuals who violate covenants of chastity, who abuse spouse or offspring, or who fail to fulfill family responsibilities will one day stand accountable before God."[6] But if we find ourselves drumming our fingers and saying to the sinner, either out loud or under our breath, "Your day will come," we just may have a little more soul work to do on forgiveness.

In Doctrine and Covenants 64:8, the Lord tells us that we are to forgive one another in our hearts—not in our mouths, not in our minds. This kind of forgiving is not easy, not something that happens overnight. To forgive in our hearts involves a deep spring-cleaning of our souls, even a change of heart so that all the acid constraints of unforgiveness are gone and can never come back. It may be a long process, but it is possible or the Lord would not have commanded us to do it. He will help us find the way if we ask him.

Now that we have laid aside six constraining beliefs, let's consider Mormon's words: "Lay hold upon every good thing" (Moroni 7:19). To "lay hold" upon something implies focusing and permanence. When we "lay hold" upon something, it becomes real to us. We embrace it and it becomes ours.

What happens if, instead of laying hold upon the good we find, we just touch it lightly?

What's the effect of superficial readings of the scriptures?

What's the effect of service that is done to be seen of women?

What happens when we join or belong to the Church in the same way that some of us join a gym, showing up only sporadically and without real commitment and sustained involvement?

What happens when year after year we do not lay hold upon the good things but continue to touch them only lightly?

After a while, we may find that we are not losing our life in His service and for His sake, but rather that we're just losing our life, losing our heart's former desires, losing our stamina, and sadly, even losing our interest in good things (see Matthew 10:39). Thinking we have "been there, done that" with good things, we may move from touching them lightly, to dabbling occasionally, to taking them for granted, and even sometimes to making fun of them.

As our spiritual life wanes, discouragement and despondency may set in, and we may wonder what is wrong when we are "doing everything right," albeit superficially. We're doing good things, aren't we? Yes, but without depth, without passion, without deep love, without vigor, without commitment, and without ever really laying hold upon the good things. And thus the joys that come from laying hold upon good things continually elude our wavering grasp.

Thus Mormon's words are rivetingly true: For our own happiness and salvation, we must "lay hold upon every good thing."

What are the good things that you need and want in your life? What are the good things that you already have in your life—that you do not want taken from you? In your deepest heart of hearts, what constitutes "good things" for you these days?

How about your family? We are all members of a family. Is yours a good thing? Are you laying hold upon every good thing in your family?

What good quality about your husband have you been noticing these days?

What good thing about your sister has been waiting for you to notice and lay hold upon?

When was the last time your child overheard you talking on the phone to a friend, saying, "I don't know what I ever did to merit having a daughter who . . . " or "I'm so blessed to have a son who . . . "

But what about family members with obstreperous behavior or borderline—perhaps even full-blown—prodigal-son ways? Now more than ever is the time to study them and lay hold upon every good thing about them. Secure their goodness. Make it real—for you and for them.

When we recognize and lay hold on the good things in our family, we actually increase the good; because in order to offer sincere commendations, honest compliments, and specific praise, we have to really study a subject. When we care enough to look closely, to get up close and notice, we will see our family members in a new light and be able to commend them on their goodness, their competence, their courage, their tenacity, perhaps even their patience with us. That means we need to be with them in a very different way, and that different way of being together will invite more light—and our ability to lay hold upon even more good things will increase.

One of the marvelous things about commendations, as opposed to condemnations, is that they increase the likelihood that our other words will be received with increased influence. Isn't that just what Joseph Smith told us? Listen to his words: "When persons manifest the least kindness and love to me, O what power it has over my mind."[7]

Is it any wonder that relationships start building naturally and securely in a commendation-saturated environment? The commendations build into conversations of affirmation and affection and confirm each family members' worth and value. These conversations assist in healing the mind, body, and spirit. When was the last time you had a heart-to-heart talk with a family member that in some way healed you?

Researchers have become very interested in what I am calling the commendation-versus-condemnation ratio. They have found that a certain ratio of positive to negative communication needs to be present in a marriage to keep it on a pathway to improvement and increased happiness.[8] I believe that their findings apply to all relationships within a family and to all relationships that feel like family.

The magic ratio the researchers found was 5:1. That is, as long as there are at least five times more affection, humor, smiling, complimenting, agreement, empathy, and active, nondefensive listening than there is criticism and disagreement, marriage and other relationships will prosper. So, what does the ratio in your home look like these days?

As we increase the number of conversations of affirmation and affection and decrease the conversations of accusation and recrimination and condemnation, every good thing about our family will become more palpable and therefore easier for us to lay hold upon. Not only that, but because there is such a connection between light and love, the increasing love in our family will invite more light, and the increased light will invite more love. Now, how's that for a virtuous cycle?

What other good things are you drawn toward? What other good things would you like to lay hold upon?

A greater understanding of the scriptures?

More peace in your life? More patience? More charity?

Mormon tells us, in the last verse of Moroni 7, to "pray unto the Father with all the energy of heart, that ye may be filled with this love [which is charity], which he hath bestowed upon all who are true followers of his Son, Jesus Christ; that ye may become the sons [and daughters] of God." Today is the day for us as Latter-day Saint women to search diligently in the light of Christ and to make choices that invite an increase of his light into our lives so that we can "lay hold upon every good thing." May we through our Lord's atoning power increasingly see as the Savior sees and love as he loves and become his own.

Notes

1. Marilyn Arnold, *Sweet Is the Word: Reflections on the Book of Mormon—Its Narrative, Teachings, and People* (American Fork, Utah: Covenant, 1996), 345.
2. Humberto Maturana, *Biology, Emotions, and Culture* (videocassette 6), November 1992 (Calgary, Alberta, Canada: Vanry and Associates).
3. H. Burke Peterson, "Unrighteous Dominion," *Ensign*, July 1989, 7.
4. See Lorraine M. Wright, Wendy L. Watson, and Janice M. Bell, *Beliefs: The Heart of Healing in Families and Illness* (New York: Basic Books, 1996).
5. Jeffrey R. Holland, *Ensign*, November 1996, 83.
6. "The Family: A Proclamation to the World," *Ensign*, November 1995, 102.
7. The Prophet Joseph Smith taught: "Nothing is so much calculated to lead people to forsake sin as to take them by the hand, and watch over them with tenderness. When persons manifest the least kindness and love to me, O what power it has over my mind, while the opposite course has a tendency to harrow up all the harsh feelings and depress the human mind." *Teachings of the Prophet Joseph Smith*, sel. Joseph Fielding Smith (Salt Lake City: Deseret Book, 1938), 240.
8. See John Gottman and Nan Silver, *Why Marriages Succeed or Fail* (New York: Simon and Schuster, 1994).

THE TEMPLE: TAKING AN ETERNAL VIEW

❧

S. Michael Wilcox

*H*ave you ever gotten excited at a sporting event? Have you ever gotten so excited at a sporting event that you actually shouted? Perhaps because your team scored a point or got a touchdown or made a big play? Have you ever been so excited that you not only shouted but actually rose from your seat to shout? Have you ever been so excited because you won or the victory was at hand that you rose and shouted and waved something? Your fists or a towel or a hat or a program? What is it about a sporting event that can elicit such exuberant exclamations of joy from us?

Whether or not you have had that experience, I hope that you have had the opportunity to rise, shout, and wave in an exclamation of joy and triumph that cannot be kept inside at an event of deep and eternal significance. I am referring, of course, to the dedication of the house of the Lord, the temple. The idea behind the hosanna shout is, in a reverent and very sacred way, the same idea behind our rising and shouting and waving at a basketball game. The joy is so great that we can't keep it inside, and we rise and shout and wave our excitement and joy. A temple dedication is the only time we do the hosanna shout in the Church, though we sing about it frequently:

> *The Spirit of God like a fire is burning!*
>
> . . . .
>
> *We'll sing and we'll shout with the armies of heaven,*
> *Hosanna, hosanna, to God and the Lamb!*[1]

If you have ever participated in that great hosanna shout, you will truly have sung and shouted with the armies of heaven, for the joy on the other side of the veil must be even greater than on this side.

A temple dedication is an occasion worthy of that one most significant

---

S. Michael Wilcox, a popular speaker and author, is an instructor at the institute of religion at the University of Utah. He received his Ph.D. at the University of Colorado. He and his wife, Laura L. Chipman, are the parents of five children. He serves as an ordinance worker in the Jordan River Temple.

exclamation of joy and happiness for many reasons. The temple is many houses all in one, like an accordion of houses folded together. The Doctrine and Covenants mentions many of those houses: a house of glory, a house of order, a house of fasting, a house of prayer, a house of thanksgiving, a house of learning, and a house of refuge and protection (see D&C 88:119, 137; 109:24–26). I would like to talk about one of those houses: a house of learning and instruction, where we are perfected in our understanding of theory, doctrine, and principle and also perfected in our understanding of our callings (see D&C 13–14).

I went to the temple to receive my endowments when I was eighteen years old and ready to go on a mission. I was unprepared for the temple experience, however. I don't know that anyone can ever be totally and completely prepared for that first visit to the temple, though we do a much better job preparing people now than we did thirty years ago. I was frightened and bewildered by the experience. To be absolutely honest, when I left the temple that day, I had to admit to myself that this did not seem like my church. The experience did not feel like anything I was used to, and I was a bit frightened by it. I have learned since that my first experience in the temple was not unique, that a number of people have some difficulty and bewilderment when they go. I felt that way because I did not know how to learn in the Lord's house. I did not know how to receive the instructions that he was giving me. If I had known how to learn, I would have still been as confused and bewildered, but I wouldn't have been frightened or doubtful or wondering how this could be my church.

The Lord chooses a unique and specific way of teaching in his house. If I could take a pair of glasses and put them on anybody who ever goes to the temple, whether for the first time or the hundredth, I would write in big red letters across those lenses the word *symbols*. Everything we see in the temple, we should see with that idea in mind. The Lord has chosen to teach his children in the temple primarily through symbols. But in our culture and in our world, we are not particularly symbol-oriented people. We like prose, well-measured sentences laid out so that we can't misunderstand them, sentences with only one very logical and easy-to-assimilate meaning. We are not particularly enthusiastic about poetry. Poetry uses fewer words, and so the words must mean more. The words don't have to be particularly logical. They may have multiple layers of meaning. They can be viewed with different eyes, can mean different things to different people. Many Church members prefer the Doctrine and Covenants because it lays out the doctrines so clearly, line upon line, that it is hard to misunderstand them. Many of us struggle with the Old Testament, which is a little more difficult. First of all, it is longer. But it also has strange rituals and historical events that we sometimes can't figure out, and at the end are all those prophets who don't speak like prophets speak today. We prefer Nephi, whose "soul delighteth in plainness" (2 Nephi 25:4). We don't like Isaiah, who is much more difficult and who paints word pictures. The temple, however, is more poetry than prose, more Old Testament than Doctrine and Covenants, and more Isaiah than Nephi. If we are to understand it, we have to train ourselves to learn through that unique way the Lord has chosen to teach us in his house.

Why does he choose to teach us this way? The primary reason may be that symbols can mean different things to different people at different stages of their life. In the temple we receive an *endow*ment, a particular kind of gift. If I gave an endowment of five million dollars to a university, the university couldn't spend the five million dollars. They could spend only the interest that that money generated. How long would my gift continue giving and blessing the university and the students who went there? Forever. The temple endowment is similar. The symbols— the ceremony, the ordinances, the narrative—are the original gift, and because they can suggest different things to the mind, they continue to generate interest.

The endowment is like the five barley loaves that Jesus used to feed the five thousand. This wonderful story can help us understand the power of the temple. When Jesus first asked for the five loaves, the apostles could not conceive of how he could feed so many with such a small amount of bread. But he had them sit down on the grass, and he blessed the bread, broke it into pieces, and began to distribute it. As the apostles distributed it, the scriptures say, everyone could eat as much as they wanted until they were filled. Afterward, twelve baskets of fragments were left over (see Mark 6:37–44). The endowment is like five barley loaves. We might not understand all that it can feed us the first time we see it, but we can eat as much as we will and be filled, and there will always be twelve baskets left over to feast on again and again. There will always be more to learn when you have finished feasting than you thought was there the first time you looked.

The Lord helps us to learn in his house. He prepares and guides us in a number of ways. Let me suggest four of those ways.

First, before we ever go to the temple, we are familiar with ordinances that have multiple layers of meaning—that are symbolic. The sacrament is a symbolic ordinance; baptism also is a symbolic ordinance—outward actions suggest inner truths. There really isn't a whole lot about a little piece of bread and a little cup of water that suggests to us a man's body or blood, but because the Savior told us what they should suggest to our minds and symbolize to our souls, we see past the everyday image, the symbol, to the reality that it represents. If you didn't know much about Christianity and you walked into a Latter-day Saint chapel and saw people sitting quietly, taking little pieces of bread and little drinks of water, you might think that is a strange way to feed people. When my daughter Megan was about four, she thought the sacrament bread was food. She was hungry, so she took a whole handful. We said, "No, Megan, just one piece," and she said, "Why?" And we answered, "Because there has to be enough for everybody." She accepted that until the deacons lined up, and they had bread left in the trays. Then she stood up on the bench, put her hands on her hips, and with great indignation declared, "They have lots left." She was too young to see past the symbol to the beauty and power of what it represents.

Baptism demonstrates in a wonderful way how an outward ordinance can suggest many different things. If I ask what baptism suggests to the mind, some might say, "A bath. It's a cleansing bath; our sins are washed away in the waters of baptism." Would we agree with that symbolism? We have to because it's in the scriptures (see, for example, D&C 39:10). Others might say, "To me baptism is a birth. The font is the womb, and the person being baptized is like a baby in its mother's womb in water. Just before the baby is born, the water breaks, and the baby comes out of the water, born into the newness of life, innocent. So, too, we arise out of the waters of baptism into newness of life." Would we agree with that symbolism? We have to; it's in the scriptures (see, for example, Moses 6:59). Somebody else might say, "Baptism suggests just the opposite to me. Baptism is a burial, and the font is the grave. We take the old man of sin, the natural man, and we put him off. As Paul says, we've crucified him. We bury him in the waters of baptism and resurrect a whole new being. So baptism is a burial and the font is the grave." Would we agree with that symbolism? We have to because that also is in the scriptures (see, for example, Romans 6:4; Colossians 2:12). What is baptism? Is it a bath, a birth, or a burial? It is all of them. In a similar way, the symbols in the temple may have many layers of meaning to suggest different and powerful truths to different people.

The second way the Lord prepares us to learn in his house is through the scriptures. Just as all three of those meanings of baptism are explained in the scriptures, so, for almost every symbol you encounter in the temple, verses of scripture will unlock some of its meanings. Sometimes as you sit in the temple being part of a session, a ceremony, or an ordinance, a verse of scripture will rise in your mind. The Holy Ghost will bring it into your thoughts, and you will say, "Ahh, now I know a meaning for that particular symbol."

The scriptures are full of symbolic language. Discussing scriptural meanings, we can practice learning the language of symbols. So even though I can't talk about the symbols or the narrative of the temple outside the temple, I can talk about Moses and the Exodus. The story of Moses leading the children of Israel out of Egypt into the promised land was designed by the Lord to be studied and applied exactly the same way the temple narrative is designed to be studied and applied. Everything that happened to the children of Israel I am to apply to my life. I must be led across the wilderness of life to the promised land of the celestial kingdom and cross the River Jordan, or the veil, to get there. In the wilderness I must feast daily on manna, the word of the Lord. I will be led across that wilderness by Moses, a prophet, and by the pillar of fire, the Holy Ghost, who will be there day and night to lead me always. I will go to Mount Sinai, the mountain of the Lord, there to receive his law and to meet with him. What's our Mount Sinai? The temple. In this way the scriptures, especially the Old Testament, give us the opportunity to practice with symbolic language and find deeper and deeper levels of meaning and application.

The Lord suggests that to us in the temple. In an ordinance room, what do you look at all through a session? The altar. And what sits on the altar? The scriptures. That's a hint. And do the ordinance workers hold them up occasionally? That's a bigger hint—that the meanings and the power behind so much of what we do in the temple will be found in the holy scriptures. It is also a suggestion, because an altar is a place of gift giving and offerings, that one of the greatest gifts God gives to us is the scriptures. His gift to us lies on the altars of the temple, and we also go to those same altars to give our gifts back to him.

There is a third way that the Lord helps us learn in the temple. Some of the symbols in the temple are very easy to understand. With a little thought, anybody can get them. Everybody wears white. What does that suggest? Purity. Can it also suggest equality in the sight of God? Can it also suggest that as white is a reflection of all the colors of the rainbow, all the beautiful spectrum, so too must my life, now that I have been to the Lord's house, reflect all the colors, all the spectrum, of God's gospel light? Mirrors in the temple face one another. What do they suggest? Eternity. For many years I went to the temple, looked down those mirrors in one direction, and thought, *This is my eternal past; I have always existed.* And I looked down the other way and thought, *This is my eternal future; I will always exist. This is eternity, and everything God does is eternal.* But it is dangerous to stop thinking about a symbol, or ever to think you know all of what it means. Symbols in the temple *mean,* and even the most simple symbols may have different, profound lessons at different times.

Let me give you an example. I was doing baptisms for the dead in the Jordan River Temple several years ago, and I was standing in the font with one of my children. I was waiting my turn. In the Jordan River Temple, mirrors surround the font. From the font I could look down those eternal mirrors and think about my ancestors who were being vicariously baptized. A verse of scripture came into my mind: "It is sufficient to know . . . that the earth will be smitten with a curse unless there is a welding link of some kind or other between the fathers and the children, upon some subject or other—and behold what is that subject? It is the baptism for the dead" (D&C 128:18). The words *welding link* reminded me of a chain. As I looked down those mirrors, the Spirit whispered, "You are looking at the chain." I thought about that. I looked down the mirrors again. You know, it does look like a chain. Each little box, each little reflection, is hooked to another. If I were looking at the chain between the fathers and the children, then who would be in the next link, the next box, the next reflection? My parents. And the next one, my grandparents, and then my great-grandparents, and so on. And each box would fan out too, in a sense. Who, then, is in the next link behind me? My children and then my grandchildren, and then my great-grandchildren, and so on. Then this thought hit me. I looked up the mirror at my ancestors, and who did I see inside of them, inside every link? I saw myself in my ancestors. And if they looked from their position up the chain down to my link, whom would they see in me? They would see themselves. If I were to look in my children, whom would I see in them? And if they were to look back into mine, who would they see in me? Themselves. When that thought hit, another verse of scripture came into mind: "I and my father are one. I am in my father and my father is in me" (see D&C 50:43). Why can I do work for my twelfth great-grandfather? I am in him and he is in me. That is why I can do the work for him—because we are one. And that is why Jesus speaks for the Father as though he were the Father. That is why I can do work for my ancestors as though I were my ancestors: I am in them and they are in me and we are one. Even the most simple symbols of the temple may hold beautifully profound truths personally for us. This personal truth made baptism for the dead a very wonderful thing for me.

A fourth way the Lord helps us learn is through levels of difficulty in the symbols of the temple. Because some symbols take more thought, more maturity, the Lord gives us at least one meaning for them as they are presented in the temple. In those cases, provided both a meaning and the symbol, we can see how the meaning arises naturally out of the symbol.

Other symbols in the temple are very difficult to understand, and the Lord doesn't tell us what they mean. We just see and experience them. But he says to us, in effect, "Before you came to the temple, I gave you symbolic ordinances with multiple layers of meaning. I've given you the scriptures, which contain symbolic language, verses, and ideas that will open up the symbols of the temple. I've given you some symbols that are very easy to understand. With a little thought, anybody can derive something from them. And I've given you some symbols that are more difficult, that require more maturity for understanding, but I've told you what they mean so you can compare the meaning with the symbol. In some cases I've given you more than one meaning for a symbol. Do you understand now how I teach in my house? You can spend the rest of your life on an adventure of discovery and revelation unveiling all the beautiful truths that lie behind the many and varied symbols of the temple."

We can be assured that everything in the temple is beautiful. If a symbol or anything in the house of the Lord has ever troubled you in any way, or if you have attached a meaning to any symbol in the temple that bothers you or makes you feel demeaned in any way, you will know you do not correctly understand the symbol. You did not get that meaning in the temple because everything in the temple is affirming and beautiful. When we come to understand the beauty and the power behind the symbols of the temple, we will always say, "Ahh, that is beautiful. Now I understand. That is beautiful and edifying and powerful." There is nothing that is not beautiful in any aspect of the Lord's ceremonies, and he wants us to understand what they mean.

Everything in the temple can teach us. Everything. The colors. Have you noticed how some temples get lighter and lighter as you move through? What can that teach? Think of the architecture, the clothing, the words, the actions, what we see, what we do, what we hear. Even the exterior can have symbolic significance. Next time you drive by the Salt Lake Temple, for instance, take off the spires in your mind. If you imagine the pointed parts gone, what remains seems to be a castle, a medieval fortress. The temple is also a house of refuge, protection, and safety. The very shape of the building suggests that to our minds, as it no doubt did to our pioneer ancestors who had fled persecution.

We can't talk outside the temple about many of the symbols of the temple and how they can teach. But a few architectural symbols are appropriate to talk about outside the temple. About every other year the *Ensign* prints pictures of the sealing rooms in various temples. When we go into a sealing room, we want to learn. The main teacher in the temple is the Spirit, but it is completely appropriate to sit down with our spouse, our parents, or our friends in the celestial room and in a reverent and a quiet tone share insights with one another or ask questions. The scriptural phrase, "He that hath ears to hear, let him hear" (Mark 4:9) does not mean that if you can figure it out all by yourself, go ahead. The expression means that those who have ears to hear—who *want* to hear—*may* hear. Every time Jesus was asked by his disciples what one of his parables meant, for instance, he told them what it meant. It is proper and appropriate to share and to want to know what is behind those symbols, remembering that the Spirit is the primary teacher.

When I look around a sealing room, I first notice the altar. What can the altar teach me? The Spirit begins to work with my mind. "What do you do at altars?"

"Well, I got married there."

"Good, I'm glad that you remember that. What else? In the scriptures, what did they do at altars?"

"They sacrificed, they gave gifts, they made offerings."

And the Spirit whispers, "Well, what gifts, what offerings, what sacrifice, what did you lay on the altar when you knelt with your spouse?"

I ponder and I reflect and I realize: I gave myself. I put myself on that altar, and my wife gave herself. We exchanged gifts with each other, and we accepted each other's gifts. And then we joined hands; we laid our hands on the altar. In that action we gave ourselves, as a couple, the two of us, to God and to his great work. Then we learned what that great work was, and we also learned what blessings and promises would be ours if we were faithful. Temple workers didn't tell us that. The altar told us that.

What's the second most prominent thing in a sealing room? Mirrors and a chandelier. I look at that chandelier and think, *What can that teach me?* It's almost too big for the room, isn't it? It hangs down low over the altar, over the couple that kneels. I begin to ponder, and the Spirit says, "What is associated with light in the scriptures?" Truth, the Spirit, the Savior. I stand up. I take my wife's hand. We look down the mirrors, and what do we notice going with us right down eternity? That chandelier. And the Spirit seems to say, "You must take me with you. You must walk always with the truth, with the Spirit, with the Savior. We will light your way to eternity. Never, never move out from under the chandelier."

I was standing in front of the mirrors once, bobbing and weaving to get a better look. It seemed an exercise in futility, and I thought, *I wish I could take myself right out of the mirrors and still stand in front of them. I could see eternity a lot better, but I keep getting in the way.* The Spirit whispered, "Truer words were never spoken." I was a bishop at the time, counseling couples with marriage problems, as most bishops do. When that thought hit me, I wanted to bring every couple from my ward that was struggling with a marriage—and those who weren't—into that room and stand them in front of the mirror, side by side, and say, "Can you see what the problem is? Do you understand? One of you or both of you are so focused on yourselves that you can no longer see eternity. The bigger you are in the mirrors, the less of eternity you can see. But if you look at a chandelier, or if you look at your wife, if you look away from yourself, you see much, much farther." No one teaches us that. The mirrors teach us that. Everything in the temple can teach us.

In 3 Nephi 17:2–3, we find a formula for temple worship. It isn't specifically designated as a formula for temple worship, but it serves wonderfully as one. Jesus has spent the day with the Nephites, and they are tired. They've listened a long time and heard a great deal, ending with

Isaiah and Micah. Now Isaiah and Micah in the morning are tough, but they are even more difficult when the mind is tired. So Christ is going to come back the next day, and he'll go over those same verses two more times to make sure the people understand. But as he looks around, he realizes that they're just not grasping everything, and so he says, "I perceive that ye are weak, that ye cannot understand all my words which I am commanded of the Father to speak unto you at this time."

Do you feel that way after attending the temple? I still feel that way. I say, "Father, I am weak. I don't understand it all."

And he says, "That's okay. You were never supposed to understand it all at once. This is supposed to feed you for a lifetime. There will always be twelve baskets left over. Don't feel guilty," he says. "Don't think, *I'm the dumbest person here. Everybody understands here but me.*" On the other hand, he also says, "Don't be apathetic. Don't stop going, or don't just go and sleep."

Instead, he instructs us to do five things. All five of them are in the third verse. "Therefore, go ye unto your homes." We say, "Lord, we can do that." The problem is that we do number one and that's it. We just go home. But the power is in two, three, four, and five.

So, what's the second thing? "And ponder upon the things which I have said." Ponder. If I want to ponder the scriptures, I can pull them out and read them again and again and go back and reread, look at individual words, and see how maybe one word in verse 5 matches a word in verse 20. I can really go over it. But I can't do that in the temple. I can't even take a little pencil to just write down a few thoughts. To effectively ponder the temple, I must have these things in my mind. The only way to do that is by consistent attendance. Some of us can get there quickly; others have to travel farther. But I believe the Lord will bless us according to our ability to go. Those who cannot go as frequently will have increased capacity to understand, if they go as often as they can. I ponder in my mind the phrases and actions and the things that I see and do.

The third thing the Savior tells us to do is this: "Ask of the Father, in my name, that ye may understand." I pray: "Father in Heaven, I'm going to the temple today. Why do we do this? What is the meaning and the significance of this thing?" When I first went to the temple, I thought some of the symbols were strange. That's the word I would have used then. Today I would use the words *unique* and *different*. It took me a while to realize that in God's great wisdom, he made the temple symbols unique and different. By their very nature they demand of us that we ask the questions the Lord wants us to ask. The first time I went to the temple, I thought, *Why do we do that? What is the meaning of this? Why is this significant?* These are the very questions the Lord wants us to ask. The danger is not that we will ask the questions; the danger is that we will become so familiar with the symbols that we will stop asking questions. We need to continue to ask the Father to help us learn.

The fourth thing to do is "prepare your minds for the morrow." How do we prepare our minds to receive revelation, remembering that the Spirit is the primary teacher in the temple and revelation is the primary mode of instruction? What prepares our mind to receive it? Let me give you a thought. I am a teacher by profession, but even if you're not a professional teacher, this Church is a church of teachers. You don't get out of the Church without teaching. What is irresistible to a teacher? Hungry students who sit at the edge of their chairs, looking, scriptures open, and saying, "Teach me." For those students you would open your soul. You want to give them everything you've ever thought or known. When Jesus came to the earth, what did he come as? A teacher. What is irresistible to him? Hungry students.

On the other hand, how do you feel as a teacher when you enter a classroom and the people are staring off in all directions, looking around, reading something else, or dozing? You want to get the lesson over with soon. You don't give as much of yourself. So, one of the best ways to prepare our minds to receive revelation is to go to the temple hungry to learn. Then we are irresistible to the teacher of the temple. Little by little he will open things to our minds. The Lord uses "teacher" words in the temple right at the beginning. He says "be alert"—that's a teacher word—and "attentive"—that's a teacher word—and "reverent." Those are teacher words, and if we're alert and attentive and reverent, we begin to learn.

The fifth and final part of our formula is "and I come unto you again." Go back to the temple. He will be there again. He will not cease to teach and instruct. That's the formula: "Go home, ponder, pray, prepare, return." So, the second time I'll understand it all? No. I'm still weak. "That's okay," the Spirit whispers. "Go home, ponder, pray, prepare, return." And as we do that time and again, to quote Ezekiel, the waters of understanding begin to rise.

My favorite scripture on the temple is in Ezekiel 47. Ezekiel sees in vision the temple that will one day be built in Jerusalem. When it's all finished, he is brought around to the east doors (because the temple faces the east). The first verse says, "He brought me again unto the door of the house; and, behold, waters issued out from under the threshold of the house eastward: for the forefront of the house stood toward the east, and the waters came down from under from the right side of the house, at the south side of the altar" (v. 1). A spring of water bubbles up right at the east doors of the temple. We have water in front of many of our temples—reflecting pools. Every time you see that water, please think of Ezekiel 47.

The water in Ezekiel's vision of the temple forms a river that flows down eastward into the Judean wilderness. Ezekiel returns to the bank of the river and finds "very many trees on the one side and on the other" (Ezekiel 47:7). The water goes into the Judean wilderness and then empties into the Dead Sea. Everywhere the water flows in the Judean wilderness, it cuts a swath of green through the desert. Everywhere water flows, life springs up. He says in verses 8 and 9: "These waters issue out toward the east country, and go down into the desert, and go into the sea: which being brought forth into the sea, the waters shall be healed. And it shall come to pass, that every thing that liveth, which moveth, whithersoever the rivers shall come, shall live: and there shall be a very great multitude of fish, because these waters shall come thither: for they shall be healed; and every thing shall live whither the river cometh."

When I read those words, the Spirit whispers this thought: "That which will one day be temporally true of my house in Jerusalem, is spiritually true now of all my temples." Out from the east doors of the Jordan River Temple, where I go most frequently, is a river of water. It is not a river you see with the eyes, but it is there nonetheless. It will do two things: give life and heal everything it touches—our families, our friendships, our bruised and broken hearts battered by the trials of life. Nephi tells us that the fountain of living water is the love of God (see 1 Nephi 11:25). The river that flows from the temple is a river of light, truth, and power, but primarily it is a river of love; it will heal and give life to everything.

How deep is the river? That depends on how often you wade into it. In Ezekiel 47:3, Ezekiel walks down the river a thousand cubits and wades into ankle-deep waters. That's not very deep. But on a hot summer day, even ankle-deep water is refreshing, healing, life-giving. Even ankle deep, the power of the temple is refreshing and life-giving. The message is,

Don't leave the river. Walk down another thousand cubits and wade in again. In verse 4, Ezekiel wades in, and this time it is to the knees. He says, in effect, "Don't leave the river. Walk down the bank farther, and wade in again." This time it is to the loins, the waist. And I love verse 5. He measures another thousand cubits down the river bank, and "it was a river that I could not pass over." The river was over his head now, "for the waters were risen, waters to swim in, a river that could not be passed over." He could now immerse himself in that wonderful, life-giving, healing river of light and love that flows from our Father's house. One day, the combined rivers from all the temples dedicated in all the lands will bathe this world in light and love and healing.

In your Martha-and-Mary life, in your careful, troubled, cumbered, and compassionate life of service that is so pleasing to God, occasionally take time to sit quietly at the feet of the Savior at rest and be taught. Remember it is needful, it is healing and life-giving, to sit quietly at the feet of the Lord in the temple and be taught by the Spirit. And when you attend a temple dedication and are invited to rise and shout and wave, may you rise and shout with all your soul that great expression of joy and triumph. Then another river begins to flow, and healing and learning and protection and order and prayer and fasting and all the other blessings of the temple are made available to more people. May you love the temple.

Note

1. *Hymns of The Church of Jesus Christ of Latter-day Saints* (Salt Lake City: The Church of Jesus Christ of Latter-day Saints, 1985), no. 2.

JOURNEYING TOWARD HOLINESS

⚬⚭⚬

Margaret Blair Young

*W*hen Deseret Book published my first novel, *House without Walls*, my loyal mother bought literally hundreds of copies and presented them to anyone who ventured to her home—including, I suspect, the Avon lady and the mailman. *House without Walls* didn't sell particularly well, despite my mother, but one copy went to a Russian woman—Nina—who, as a foreign language expert, spoke fluent English. As it happened, my novel touched somebody clear across the world and helped set in motion a series of God-directed conversions. That, to me, is a testimony of the power art can have—sometimes even holy power.

My father met Nina in Russia on a six-month teaching assignment. My mother had taken along a box of my novels to give away as thank-you gifts. Nina tells the story herself via e-mail: "I write to you about the special role of Dr. Blair in the life of my family. He was the first who told me about Joseph Smith and Mormons and the Church. He also gave me a book, and even though it was not one of the book of Scriptures, this book opened my eyes on the people who called themselves 'the Mormons.'

"Speaking about his family, Dr. Blair mentioned his daughter Margaret, who was a writer. In response I asked him if he could give me a book written by her. Thus it happened so that the Book of Mormon and the novel *House without Walls* by Margaret Blair Young got into my hands at the same time. I remember, I looked through the Book of Mormon and put it aside: it seemed too strange and foreign to me. Let me try something easier, I thought to myself. So I opened the *House without Walls*, read the introduction, and I could not stop till I turned over the last page of this book. The same world Dr. Blair told me about, which seemed so unusual and obscure, appeared real and alive. I saw the world of the real missionaries with their troubles and joys. I wanted to know more about their life

---

Margaret Blair Young is a part-time instructor on the creative writing faculty at Brigham Young University. She and her husband, Bruce Wilson Young, are the parents of four children. She has served in the Church as a stake cultural arts chair, choir director, and ward music chair.

and their religion. I desperately wanted to understand what made them sacrifice, leave their homes, and go to a foreign country to teach the Gospel. So I took the Book of Mormon again. This book led the missionaries over the world; it made them sacrifice their time and money. Evidently, there was something in this book which I missed. I had to understand the wisdom it contained, and I began to read it once again.

"It was the beginning of my way to the Gospel."[1]

Eventually Nina and her son joined the Church; a year later her husband was also baptized.[2]

President Spencer W. Kimball, speaking to the artists of the Church, encouraged them to raise their standards above the mediocre. "Our writers," he said, "our motion picture specialists, with the inspiration of heaven, . . . could put into [a work of art] life and heartbeats and emotions and love and pathos, drama, suffering, fear, courage."[3] His words encourage me not to gauge success by sales alone.

Several years ago, my daughter Kaila, now sixteen, got her teeth into some Sweet Valley High books. As you picture my darling little girl reading about the frenzied traumas of twin cheerleaders, remember that my husband, Bruce, is a professor of Renaissance literature, specializing in Shakespeare, and that I am an English teacher and a lover of great books. Where any number of parents would be pleased to see a child reading anything at all, we felt a need to raise our daughter's sights.

A few days later, Kaila and I chatted about the lives of the Sweet Valley High twins. I read some passages with her. And then I took another book—a fine young-adult novel by Utah author Margaret Rostkowski called *After the Dancing Days*. I suggested to Kaila that we compare the writing of the Sweet Valley High book with Margaret Rostkowski's. We read some of each book, comparing language and characters, after which I asked her which one she thought was better written. Of course, she knew my opinion. But whether she agreed with it or not, Kaila was able to provide the reasons why *After the Dancing Days* simply outclassed the other book—which was a lovely prelude to our reading *After the Dancing Days* together. For Kaila, our chat initiated a new era of "Great Expectations" for the literature she chooses to read. We were anxious for her not simply to read but also to appreciate good literature.

Should that matter? It is possible, and sadly easy, for writers to create simplistic work that provides stereotypes rather than distinctive characters;

shallow plots with easy resolutions; clichés rather than rich, original language; "tear-jerking" as a counterfeit for earned emotion.

Contrast such work with that of "Gentle Will" Shakespeare, so called by his peers, who was genuinely fascinated by his fellowmen and women and observed them so well that four hundred years later, we still love the characters he created: Cordelia and King Lear, Hamlet, and Beatrice and Benedick, to mention a few.

Surely the first hallmark of worthwhile literature, then, is its characterization, followed closely by the book's complexity, both in thought and in plot. Of course, there is a place for simplistic literature with easy problems, easy resolutions, and easy tears. But we want to move beyond such milk to the meat that great art can provide.

Next, we need a love of language. We can focus on the language of the scriptures, for example, as we try to raise our artistic standards and those of our children. We can inundate ourselves with the poetry of Isaiah and the allegories of Jacob and the symbols of Lehi. But inundating means pondering, not skimming.

It's easy to fall into quick interpretations of the scriptures without really paying attention to the language. Think of the metaphors in Lehi's vision, for instance. Think of the rod of iron. It's so simple to identify it as "the word of God" that we may not pay further attention to Lehi's figurative language. But where else is the same image used? Note Psalm 2:9: "Thou shalt break them with a rod of iron." Is Lehi suggesting that we cling to the "word of God" so we can be prepared for some hard-core Bible bashing? Not likely! Or how about Revelation 2:27: "He shall rule them with a rod of iron."

So what is a rod? For one thing, it's the insignia of authority—something a king (or even a shepherd guiding his sheep) might carry, and it's also something that might be used to whip someone into shape (see Proverbs 13:24). And why a rod of *iron*? What characteristics does iron have? How is God's word like iron? I'll leave the answer up to you and suggest only that rushing too quickly to the symbol's interpretation cheats us of the implications of the rich figurative language Lehi has given us. Much more is suggested by an iron rod than an easy, fill-in-the-blank answer. The iron rod is the word of God, but that word is conveyed with an image of sovereign power, even priesthood power.

Another characteristic of truly worthwhile literature is the author's sense of verisimilitude. We can guess the meaning of that word from its components: *veri-* (from *veritas*, "truth") and *similitude* ("similarity to"). We want literature that's like truth, like life. I get concerned over formula fiction that resolves difficult questions in a prayer and a paragraph. Such resolution is not only unfair to the reader but simply untrue—inconsistent with the plan of salvation. Novels that participate in this rather common deception, this lack of verisimilitude, suggest inadvertently that it is all right to answer somebody's pain with a cliché instead of with heartfelt empathy. The great writers, on the other hand, will always take us on wonderful, sometimes horrifying journeys, which we experience with their characters who are so well drawn that we can feel what they are feeling. Such journeys not only help us understand and empathize with our fellow beings but ultimately teach us about the plan of salvation. For the plan of salvation is not based upon quick answers and quick resolutions but upon hard journeys—which we thank God we are able to make. Remember, we shouted for joy when the opportunity to do so was presented to us in the premortal existence.

Let me return briefly to Lehi's vision—which, too, is full of journeys. Lehi is making his own journey across a wilderness when he has the dream and in the dream is likewise a wilderness, or (to use his own wonderful language) a "dark and dreary waste" (1 Nephi 8:7). When Nephi desires to know the interpretation of the vision, he simply asks, "What is the meaning of the tree?" (see 1 Nephi 11:11). The angel does not give him a list of all the symbols from Lehi's dream and a pencil to identify each symbol's meaning. He doesn't give Nephi a direct answer. No, the angel provides him a vision of the Savior's life—another journey, the greatest and hardest yet made, from his birth to his death and beyond the grave. When the vision closes, the angel asks, "Now do you know the meaning of the tree?" And Nephi answers, "Yea, it is the love of God" (1 Nephi 11:22). Though Nephi has not lived the Savior's life, he has seen and felt it. He has, in a way, accompanied Christ on his earthly mission and sensed the magnitude of the Atonement. He understands the meaning of the tree with his whole soul.

In the spirit of heeding President Kimball's admonition, I use these visions from the Book of Mormon as metaphors for what artists attempt and for what the best artists in "the best books" will accomplish (D&C 88:118). Just as Nephi learned the full meaning of the tree of life by experiencing the Lord's earthly sojourn in vision, so too can a reader learn something about guilt and grace by letting Dostoyevsky act as a sort of angel in opening up a vision—fictional, but true in the deepest senses—of Raskolnikov's sad pilgrimage in *Crime and Punishment*. Similarly, a reader can learn something about love and loyalty by accompanying Shakespeare's Lear as he rages into wilderness where the winds howl and "crack [their] cheeks."[4]

As I make my own way—often skinning my knees—in the mortal world and in the world of art, I come to understand the depth and beauty of the plan of salvation and the necessarily difficult journey each of us makes in mortality. I find that "the best books" let me follow others on their journeys and feel what they are feeling. The best artists—like the angel in Nephi's dream—open my mind to their visions as I open their books and let their characters open my heart and their language teach me something about myself, my own possibilities, and even about the love of God.

Notes

1. Personal communication with Dlora Dalton, 6 September 1996, in possession of the author.
2. At the time of this presentation, I was unaware that Nina had come to Provo for the 1996 BYU–Relief Society Women's Conference. After my presentation, LaRene Gaunt of the *Ensign* asked me if the woman I had referred to was the one who had addressed the women's conference earlier that day. I told her I didn't know. The more Sister Gaunt described Nina Bazarskaya to me, the clearer it became that she was indeed the woman my parents had met in Russia. I was able to meet Nina later that day. As soon as I introduced myself, she held open her arms and, weeping, said, "Your parents brought us light when all we had was darkness."
3. Spencer W. Kimball, "The Gospel Vision of the Arts," *Ensign*, July 1977, 5.
4. William Shakespeare, *King Lear*, act 3, scene 3, line 1.

INDEX